*ORGANIZATIONAL
BEHAVIOR AND
ADMINISTRATION*

Cases and Readings

The Irwin Series in Management and
The Behavioral Sciences

Consulting Editors
L. L. CUMMINGS and E. KIRBY WARREN

Advisory Editor
JOHN F. MEE

ORGANIZATIONAL BEHAVIOR AND ADMINISTRATION

Cases and Readings /

Edited by

PAUL R. LAWRENCE, M.B.A., D.C.S.
Wallace B. Donham, Professor of Organizational Behavior

LOUIS B. BARNES, M.B.A., D.B.A.
Professor of Organizational Behavior

JAY W. LORSCH, M.B.A., D.B.A.
Professor of Organizational Behavior

All of the Graduate School of Business Administration
Harvard University

Third Edition   1976

RICHARD D. IRWIN, INC.   Homewood, Illinois   60430
Irwin-Dorsey International   London, England   WC2H 9NJ
Irwin-Dorsey Limited   Georgetown, Ontario   L7G 4B3

Third Edition

First Printing, January 1976

Case material of the Harvard Graduate School of
Business Administration is made possible by the
cooperation of business firms who may wish to remain
anonymous by having names, quantities, and other
identifying details disguised while basic relationships
are maintained. Cases are prepared as the basis for
class discussion rather than to illustrate either effective
or ineffective handling of administrative situations.

ISBN 0-256-01760-3
Library of Congress Catalog Card No. 75–7276
Printed in the United States of America

*To the
Original Teachers of
Administrative Practices,
Professors Learned, Roethlisberger,
Hower, Lombard, and Glover*

Preface

This book, as were the two previous editions, is about the way people actually behave in business organizations. It is addressed to those who intend to assume positions of leadership in business organizations in line or staff, at top, bottom, or middle levels of management—all practitioners of the art and science of business management. The book is concerned with helping these people improve their own personal competence in understanding and dealing with the many human problems that arise in complex organizations.

How can we account for some of the stubborn human problems that prevail in many modern organizations? Why are some employees hostile, others apathetic? Why do some people restrict their output? Why are some groups enthused about their work experiences and others completely indifferent? Why are some supervisors so harassed? Why do some managers use their experiences to develop and enhance their capacities while others do not? What causes severe interpersonal conflict in organizations? Why do sales, production, engineering, and other groups often get into persistent costly feuds with each other? Why do superiors so often get "unintended consequences" from issuing seemingly "simple" directions. Why do misunderstandings so often develop between field forces and home office? Under what conditions are you more apt to find collaborative relations between different parts of an organization? In order to find better answers to questions of this kind, this book focuses on the *social* and *organizational* aspects of behavior, as well as the individual and interpersonal.

What kinds of material are in the book? In the first place the book presents a considerable number of case descriptions of the actual behavior of people in organizations. Many of these cases are new ones that have been prepared since the first revised edition was published. These cases were not written to demonstrate some point about how people are supposed to act. They were written instead, with careful attention to reproducing what was actually going on in the situation, no matter how confusing or contradictory some of the facts and events might seem. Of course, these cases do not and could not contain all the relevant facts. But the point is still valid that conscious care was taken to avoid writing them to "prove" some theory of human behavior.

On the other hand, these cases are not presented as if each one were a completely unique problem to be analyzed *de novo*, with no relation to other cases and the existing knowledge about human behavior. They have been grouped into clusters and given a particular ordering in this book, to help students accumulate and build the simulated experience that the discussion of cases can provide. One case can be used to build on another in a rough but effective kind of inductive learning.

Most of the sections in the book contain cases of several general types: cases that are richly *descriptive* of a pattern of behavior that is commonly seen in industrial organizations in our culture, cases that are designed for *drill* in the use of a conceptual scheme, cases that are fairly complete reports of systematic *research*, cases that present simply the fragmentary symptoms of a problem as it might initially come to the attention of an administrator responsible for taking *action*. Cases of all these types, if carefully analyzed, can provide means both for the accumulation of organizational knowledge and for the acquisition of increasing skill in diagnosing both the general and the unique about every case. The cases can also provide students with greater understanding of the process of decision making in organizations and the problems of implementation, as well as with a direct experiencing of decision making—the commitment to act under the burden of responsibility for multiple consequences.

In addition to cases, this book also contains readings selected to reflect widely accepted theories and relevant research. In this respect the volume has changed from the earlier edition that offered primarily summaries of discrete research studies. In the intervening ten years the field of organizational behavior has, in our judgment, matured sufficiently to now justify the survey approach used in most of the selected readings. The readings cannot, of course, in the limited space, cover all the current theories relevant to organizational behavior. We have presented a range of concepts that we have found to be particularly useful to managers. This was our primary selection criterion.

Finally, all the material in the book was selected to help develop students' faith that there is order in the human universe; that man's behavior is not a chaotic chance affair; that, within limits, it is predictable; that intelligence can usefully supplement intuition in the conduct of important human affairs; and that knowledge and skillful diagnosis of human behavior, our own as well as others', can help liberate us from slavish conformity and from narrow moralistic judgments, and can help us to become more realistic, more understanding, and, in the deepest sense of the word, more productive.

December 1975   PAUL R. LAWRENCE
                                                   LOUIS B. BARNES
                                                   JAY W. LORSCH

Acknowledgments

The authors wish to acknowledge their indebtedness to the following people who as staff members at the Harvard Business School played a major role in preparing some of the cases in this book: Jeanne Deschamps, Russell Johnston, Andre Ruedi, John D. Donnell, Peter B. Vaill, and Richard Harmer.

We are also indebted to many of our faculty colleagues, present and past, for various valuable direct contributions they have made to the materials in this book, and, even more importantly, the indirect contributions they have made over the years to the development of the basic ideas underlying the Human Behavior in Organizations and Organizational Problems courses here at the Graduate School of Business Administration, Harvard University. We are especially grateful to Joseph C. Bailey, Robert L. Katz, John A. Seiler, Larry E. Greiner, James V. Clark, Charles D. Orth, Arthur N. Turner, Gene W. Dalton, John J. Gabarro, Alan P. Sheldon, Richard E. Walton, Fred K. Foulkes, and Paul Thompson.

We thank the many publishers and authors who have granted us permission to quote the copyright material. The source of each of these quotations is indicated in the appropriate place. With only a few exceptions all cases in this book have been individually copyrighted by the President and Fellows of Harvard College. They are reprinted here by special permission and may not be reproduced in whole or part without written permission.

Finally, we wish very much to acknowledge the considerable help we have received in the preparation of the manuscript from Connie Bourke, Susan Christiansen, and Lisa Leask.

Even though we gladly acknowledge the many contributions of others to this book, we, the authors, are fully responsible for this book and accept any and all of its faults.

Boston, Massachusetts   P.R.L.
December 1975   L.B.B.
                                                           J.W.L.

Contents

Section IV
Intergroup Behavior

Section V
Organizational Design

Section VI
Organizational Change

Cases

Readings

Section I

Human Aspects of Management

Cases

1 | Dashman Company

The Dashman Company was a large concern making many types of equipment for the armed forces of the United States. It had over 20 plants, located in the central part of the country, whose purchasing procedures had never been completely coordinated. In fact, the head office of the company had encouraged the plant managers to operate with their staffs as separate, independent units in most matters. Late in 1940, when it began to appear that the company would face increasing difficulty in securing certain essential raw materials, Mr. Manson, the company's president, appointed an experienced purchasing executive, Mr. Post, as vice president in charge of purchasing, a position especially created for him. Manson gave Post wide latitude in organizing his job, and he assigned Mr. Larson as Post's assistant. Larson had served the company in a variety of capacities for many years, and knew most of the plant executives personally. Post's appointment was announced through the formal channels usual in the company, including a notice in the house organ which was published monthly by the Dashman Company.

One of Post's first decisions was to begin immediately to centralize the company's purchasing procedure. As a first step, he decided that he would require each of the executives who handled purchasing in the individual plants to clear with the head office all purchase contracts which they made in excess of $10,000. He felt that if the head office was to do any coordinating in a way that would be helpful to each plant and to the company as a whole, he must be notified that the contracts were being prepared at least a week before they were to be signed. He talked his proposal over with Manson, who presented it to the board of directors. They approved the plan.

Although the company made purchases throughout the year, the beginning of its peak buying season was only three weeks away at the time this new plan was adopted. Post prepared a letter to be sent to the 20 purchasing executives of the company. The letter follows:

> Dear ————:
>
> The board of directors of our company has recently authorized a change in our purchasing procedures. Hereafter, each of the purchasing executives in the several plants of the company will notify the vice president in charge of purchasing of all contracts in excess of $10,000 which they are negotiating, at least a week in advance of the date on which they are to be signed.
>
> I am sure you will understand that this step is necessary to coordinate the purchasing requirements of the company in these times when we are facing increasing difficulty in securing essential supplies. This procedure should give us in the central office the information we need to see that each plant secures the optimum supply of materials. In this way the interests of each plant and of the company as a whole will best be served.
>
> Yours very truly,

Post showed the letter to Larson and invited his comments. Larson thought the letter an excellent one, but suggested that since Post had not met more than a few of the purchasing executives, he might like to visit all of them and take the matter up with each of them personally. Post dismissed the idea at once because, as he said, he had so many things to do at the head office that he could not get away for a trip. Consequently, he had the letters sent out over his signature.

During the two following weeks, replies came in from all except a few plants. Although a few executives wrote at greater length, the following reply was typical:

> Dear Mr. Post:
>
> Your recent communication in regard to notifying the head office a week in advance of our intention to sign contracts has been received. This suggestion seems a most practical one. We want to assure you that you can count on our cooperation.
>
> Yours very truly,

During the next six weeks the head office received no notices from any plant that contracts were being negotiated. Executives in other departments, who made frequent trips to the plants, reported that the plants were busy, and the usual routines for that time of year were being followed.

2 | *The Road to Hell*...

John Baker, chief engineer of the Caribbean Bauxite Company of Barracania in the West Indies, was making his final preparations to leave the island. His promotion to production manager of Keso Mining Corporation near Winnipeg—one of Continental Ore's fast-expanding Canadian enterprises—had been announced a month before, and now everything had been tidied up except the last vital interview with his successor—the able young Barracanian, Matthew Rennalls. It was vital that this interview be a success and that Rennalls should leave his office uplifted and encouraged to face the challenge of his new job. A touch on the bell would have brought Rennalls walking into the room, but Baker delayed the moment and gazed thoughtfully through the window considering just exactly what he was going to say and, more particularly, how he was going to say it.

John Baker, an English expatriate, was 45 years old and had served his 23 years with Continental Ore in many different places: in the Far East; in several countries of Africa and Europe; and, for the last two years, in the West Indies. He hadn't cared much for his previous assignment in Hamburg and was delighted when the West Indian appointment came through. Climate was not the only attraction. Baker had always preferred working overseas (in what were termed the developing countries) because he felt he had an innate knack—better than most other expatriates working for Continental Ore—of knowing just how to get on with regional staff. Twenty-four hours in Barracania, however, soon made him realize that he would need all of this "innate knack" if he

---

* This case was prepared by Mr. Gareth Evans for use in an executive training program.

was to deal effectively with the problems in this field that now awaited him.

At his first interview with Hutchins, the production manager, the whole problem of Rennalls and his future was discussed. There and then it was made quite clear to Baker that one of his most important tasks would be the "grooming" of Rennalls as his successor. Hutchins had pointed out that not only was Rennalls one of the brightest Barracanian prospects on the staff of Caribbean Bauxite (at London University he had taken first-class honors in the B.S. engineering degree) but, being the son of the Minister of Finance and Economic Planning, he also had no small political pull.

The company has been particularly pleased when Rennalls decided to work for them rather than for the government in which his father had such a prominent post. They ascribed his action to the effect of their vigorous and liberal regionalisation program which since World War II had produced 18 Barracanians at mid-management level and had given Caribbean Bauxite a good lead in this respect over other international concerns operating in Barracania. The success of this timely regionalisation policy had led to excellent relations with the government—a relationship which had been given added importance when Barracania, three years later, became independent. This occasion had encouraged a critical and challenging attitude towards the role foreign interests would have to play in the new Barracania. Hutchins had therefore little difficulty in convincing Baker that the successful career development of Rennalls was of the first importance.

The interview with Hutchins was now two years old; and Baker, leaning back in his office chair, reviewed just how successful he had been in the "grooming" of Rennalls. What aspects of the latter's character had helped and what had hindered? What about his own personality? How had that helped or hindered? The first item to go on the credit side would, without question, be the ability of Rennalls to master the technical aspects of his job. From the start he had shown keenness and enthusiasm and had often impressed Baker with his ability in tackling new assignments and the constructive comments he invariably made in departmental discussions. He was popular with all ranks of Barracanian staff and had an ease of manner which stood him in good stead when dealing with his expatriate seniors. These were all assets, but what about the debit side?

First and foremost, there was his racial consciousness. His four years at London University had accentuated this feeling and made him sensitive to any sign of condescension on the part of expatriates. It may have been to give expression to this sentiment that as soon as he returned home from London he threw himself into politics on behalf of the United

Action Party who were later to win the preindependence elections and provide the country with its first Prime Minister.

The ambitions of Rennalls—and he certainly was ambitious—did not however, lie in politics for, staunch nationalist as he was, he saw that he could serve himself and his country best—for was not bauxite responsible for nearly half the value of Barracania's export trade?—by putting his engineering talent to the best use possible. On this account, Hutchins found that he had an unexpectedly easy task in persuading Rennalls to give up his political work before entering the production department as an assistant engineer.

It was, Baker knew, Rennalls's well-repressed sense of race consciousness which had prevented their relationship from being as close as it should have been. On the surface, nothing could have seemed more agreeable. Formality between the two men was at a minimum; Baker was delighted to find that his assistant shared his own peculiar "shaggy-dog" sense of humour so that jokes were continually being exchanged; they entertained each other at their houses and often played tennis together—and yet the barrier remained invisible, indefinable, but ever present. The existence of this "screen" between them was a constant source of frustration to Baker since it indicated a weakness which he was loath to accept. If successful with all other nationalities, why not with Rennalls?

But at least he had managed to "break through" to Rennalls more successfully than any other expatriate. In fact, it was the young Barracanian's attitude—sometimes overbearing, sometimes cynical—toward other company expatriates that had been one of the subjects Baker had raised last year when he discussed Rennalls's staff report with him. He knew too that he would have to raise the same subject again in the forthcoming interview because Jackson, the senior draughtsman, had complained only yesterday about the rudeness of Rennalls. With this thought in mind, Baker leaned forward and spoke into the intercom. "Would you come in Matt, please? I'd like a word with you," and later, "do sit down," proffering the box, "have a cigarette." He paused while he held out his lighter and then went on.

"As you know, Matt, I'll be off to Canada in a few days' time; and before I go, I thought it would be useful if we could have a final chat together. It is indeed with some deference that I suggest I can be of help. You will shortly be sitting in this chair doing the job I am now doing; but I, on the other hand, am ten years older, so perhaps you can accept the idea that I may be able to give you the benefit of my longer experience."

Baker saw Rennalls stiffen slightly in his chair as he made this point, so added in explanation, "You and I have attended enough company courses to remember those repeated requests by the personnel manager to tell people how they are getting on as often as the convenient moment arises, and not just the automatic 'once a year' when, by regulation, staff reports have to be discussed."

Rennalls nodded his agreement, so Baker went on, "I shall always remember the last job performance discussion I had with my previous boss back in Germany. He used what he called the "plus and minus" technique. His firm belief was that when a senior, by discussion, seeks to improve the work performance of his staff, his prime objective should be to make sure that the latter leaves the interview encouraged and inspired to improve. Any criticism must, therefore, be constructive and helpful. He said that one very good way to encourage a man—and I fully agree with him—is to tell him about his good points—the plus factors—as well as his weak ones—the minus factors—so I thought, Matt, it would be a good idea to run our discussion along these lines."

Rennalls offered no comment, so Baker continued: "Let me say, therefore, right away, that as far as your own work performance is concerned, the plus far outweighs the minus. I have, for instance, been most impressed with the way you have adapted your considerable theoretical knowledge to master the practical techniques of your job—that ingenious method you used to get air down to the fifth-shaft level is a sufficient case in point—and at departmental meetings I have invariably found your comments well taken and helpful. In fact, you will be interested to know that only last week I reported to Mr. Hutchins that from the technical point of view, he could not wish for a more able man to succeed to the position of chief engineer."

"That's very good indeed of you, John," cut in Rennalls with a smile of thanks. "My only worry now is how to live up to such a high recommendation."

"Of that I am quite sure," returned Baker, "especially if you can overcome the minus factor which I would like now to discuss with you. It is one which I have talked about before, so I'll come straight to the point. I have noticed that you are more friendly and get on better with your fellow Barracanians than you do with Europeans. In point of fact, I had a complaint only yesterday from Mr. Jackson, who said you had been rude to him—and not for the first time, either.

"There is, Matt, I am sure, no need for me to tell you how necessary it will be for you to get on well with expatriates, because until the company has trained up sufficient men of your calibre, Europeans are bound to occupy senior positions here in Barracania. All this is vital to your future interests, so can I help you in any way?"

While Baker was speaking on this theme, Rennalls had sat tensed in his chair, and it was some seconds before he replied. "It is quite extraordinary, isn't it, how one can convey an impression to others so at variance with what one intends? I can only assure you once again that my disputes with Jackson—and you may remember also Godson—have had nothing at all to do with the colour of their skins. I promise you that if a Barracanian had behaved in an equally peremptory manner I would have reacted in precisely the same way. And again, if I may say it within these four walls, I am sure I am not the only one who has found Jackson and Godson difficult. I could mention the names of several expatriates who have felt the same. However, I am really sorry to have created this impression of not being able to get on with Europeans—it is an entirely false one—and I quite realise that I must do all I can to correct it as quickly as possible. On your last point, regarding Europeans holding senior positions in the company for some time to come, I quite accept the situation. I know that Caribbean Bauxite—as they have been doing for many years now—will promote Barracanians as soon as their experience warrants it. And, finally, I would like to assure you, John—and my father thinks the same too—that I am very happy in my work here and hope to stay with the company for many years to come."

Rennalls had spoken earnestly and, although not convinced by what he had heard, Baker did not think he could pursue the matter further except to say, "All right, Matt, my impression *may* be wrong, but I would like to remind you about the truth of that old saying, 'What is important is not what is true but what is believed.' Let it rest at that."

But suddenly Baker knew that he didn't want to "let it rest at that." He was disappointed once again at not being able to "break through" to Rennalls and having yet again to listen to his bland denial that there was any racial prejudice in his makeup. Baker, who had intended ending the interview at this point, decided to try another tack.

"To return for a moment to the 'plus and minus technique' I was telling you about just now, there is another plus factor I forgot to mention. I would like to congratulate you not only on the calibre of your work, but also on the ability you have shown in overcoming a challenge which I, as a European, have never had to meet.

"Continental Ore is, as you know, a typical commercial enterprise—admittedly a big one—which is a product of the economic and social environment of the United States and Western Europe. My ancestors have all been brought up in this environment for the past two or three hundred years, and I have, therefore, been able to live in a world in which commerce (as we know it today) has been part and parcel of my being. It has not been something revolutionary and new which has suddenly entered my life. In your case," went on Baker, "the situation is different because you and your forebears have only had some 50 or 60 years' experience in this commerical environment. You have had to face the challenge of bridging the gap between 50 and 200 or 300 years. Again, Matt, let me congratulate you—and people like you—once again on having so successfully overcome this particular hurdle. It is for this very reason that I think the outlook for Barracania—and particularly Caribbean Bauxite—is so bright."

Rennalls had listened intently, and when Baker finished, replied, "Well, once again, John, I have to thank you for what you have said, and, for my part, I can only say that it is gratifying to know that my own personal effort has been so much appreciated. I hope that more people will soon come to think as you do."

There was a pause, and for a moment Baker thought hopefully that he was about to achieve his long-awated "breakthrough," but Rennalls merely smiled back. The barrier remained unbreached. There remained some fives minutes' cheerful conversation about the contrast between the Caribbean and Canadian climate and whether the West Indies had any hope of beating England in the Fifth Test before Baker drew the interview to a close. Although he was as far as ever from knowing the real Rennalls, he was nevertheless glad that the interview had run along in this friendly manner and, particularly, that it had ended on such a cheerful note.

This feeling, however, lasted only until the following morning. Baker had some farewells to make, so he arrived at the office considerably later than usual. He had no sooner sat down at his desk than his secretary walked into the room with a worried frown on her face. Her words came fast. "When I arrived this morning I found Mr. Rennalls already waiting at my door. He seeemd very angry and told me in quite a peremptory manner that he had a vital letter to dictate which must be sent off without any delay. He was so worked up that he couldn't keep still and kept pacing about the room, which is most unlike him. He wouldn't even wait to read what he had dictated. Just signed the page where he thought the letter would end. It has been distributed, and your copy is in your 'in tray.'"

Puzzled and feeling vaguely uneasy, Baker opened the "Confidential" envelope and read the following letter:

FROM: Assistant Engineer
To: The Chief Engineer, Caribbean Bauxite Limited

14th August, 196–

ASSESSMENT OF INTERVIEW BETWEEN MESSRS. BAKER AND RENNALLS

It has always been my practice to respect the advice given me by seniors; so after our interview, I decided to give careful thought once again to its main points and so make sure that I had understood all that had been said. As I promised you at the time, I had every intention of putting your advice to the best effect.

It was not, therefore, until I had sat down quietly in my home yesterday evening to consider the interview objectively that its main purport became clear. Only then did the full enormity of what you said dawn on me. The more I thought about it, the more convinced I was that I had hit upon the real truth—and the more furious I became. With a facility in the English language which I—a poor Barracanian—cannot hope to match, you had the audacity to insult me (and through me every Barracanian worth his salt) by claiming that our knowledge of modern living is only a paltry 50 years old whilst yours goes back 200 to 300 years. As if your materialistic commercial environment could possibly be compared with the spiritual values of our culture. I'll have you know that if much of what I saw in London is representative of your most boasted culture, I hope fervently that it will never come to Barracania. By what right do you have the effrontery to condescend to us? At heart, all you Europeans think us barbarians, or, as you say amongst yourselves, we are "just down from the trees."

Far into the night I discussed this matter with my father, and he is as disgusted as I. He agrees with me that any company whose senior staff think as you do is no place for any Barracanian proud of his culture and race—so much for all the company "clap-trap" and specious propaganda about regionalisation and Barracania for the Barracanians.

I feel ashamed and betrayed. Please accept this letter as my resignation which I wish to become effective immediately.

c.c. Production manager
Managing director

Readings

1 | On the Balance between Skill and Knowledge

Joseph C. Bailey

"Education is the acquisition of the utilization of knowledge. This is an art very difficult to impart."
—*Aims of Education*
ALFRED NORTH WHITEHEAD

It may not be readily apparent from Professor Whitehead's concise language that his aphorism applies with especial force to training for the professions. Yet consider, for example, its applicability to law and medicine. One point, in schools devoted to the latter subject, on which agreement is nearly universal among medical educators is that: "The most we can hope to do while we have a student is to get him to think like a doctor." An equal unanimity of view exists, I undestand, in the better law schools just as it does with us, where we desire students to take a professional attitude toward their careers in business. Clearly, it is impossible to teach them all there is to know about the extravagantly diverse world of business; yet if we can help them to acquire the art of the utilization of knowledge someday to be needed, we have been helpful in a way that should last a lifetime.

A teaching goal that aspires to such an aim may inspire great efforts and sustained dedication. It leads, however, into repeated failures, unforeseeable frustration, and to never-ending change and experimentation with all the materials and methods we use in trying to impart the art that is the key to the education Whitehead writes of. Out of our collective experience, we consider nothing more important or more useful than to try to point out, as quickly and as clearly as possible to colleagues

13

who may pursue kindred aims, the nature of the recurrent failures and the reasons behind the frustrations we have encountered. Our hope is that if we do so we can reduce for others the failures and frustrations that may be inherent or, if not that, then at least forewarn, and thereby forearm.

Basically what we have learned is the necessity of teaching administration as a skill (i.e., "art") linked inseparably to knowledge. Knowledge, without the skill to use it, is inert and surplus baggage to the practitioner. Skill without the continual infusion of new knowledge leaves its possessor practicing in the grip of unmodified routines, subject to boredom, and, in the end, certain of seeing the skill he uses outmoded by men able to alter, elaborate, and extend their skill with new knowledge. Therefore, in imparting this art, we have learned the hard way that our most difficult task is the struggle to keep skill linked to knowledge in delicate balance, so that they will reinforce, and not nullify, each other. They must be acquired hand in hand or in linked sequence, otherwise the art of the utilization of knowledge has not been gained.

Our courses have illustrated, in the phases of their development at Harvard, both the difficulty and the necessity of maintaining the balance between skill AND knowledge. The history of these courses is an account of getting-out-of-balance followed by the effort to gain a new equilibrium. Sometimes skill was given overemphasis at the expense of knowledge. Then, in subsequent reaction, skill became subordinated to knowledge. An effort to reestablish balance, in every instance thus far, has asserted itself. It does so because annually, in our student product, it becomes painfully clear to us that overemphasis on either skill or knowledge fails equally to impart to students the art we know they need.

Men overdosed with knowledge discourse with prolix glibness on what is wrong in the cases before them and what is needed to set matters straight again. They are then generally unable to exhibit any of the practitioners' skill as to how to resolve the problems they had analyzed verbally, and, what is equally discouraging, they clearly feel no responsibility for doing so—no responsibility, in short, for utilizing their knowledge. Indeed, many such students show disdain for trying to practice in an elementary way what is the unavoidable daily skill of an operating executive. Such students climb high into an untroubled ivory tower where they cannot, and do not, feel any challenge in trying to exercise the fascinating art of utilizing their knowledge.

Men are as easily, and as dangerously, misled by an overemphasis on skill. When this occurs, which is understandably less frequent in an academic setting where most tendencies favor knowledge, theory, erudition, students may acquire a surprising deftness for untangling separate problems, but the distressing result is their inability to discern any uniformities from case to case, and they are reluctant to pry out recurrent phenomena. They feel it is unfair, "longhaired," to require them to seek a few limited generalities, to articulate a simple, useful way of thinking about all the phenomena in front of them. No ivory tower for them. They're "operators," "pratical men"—period! This overemphasis on skill prevents their acquiring some simple scheme wherewith to organize and to conceptualize their learning so that they can articulate and transmit their experience to others. Such men cannot cumulate and contribute to the stream of conscious knowledge. They are not prepared to pass on the torch of increasing skill and knowledge from hand to hand.

Partisans for stressing either skill *or* knowledge have to experience these results of lack of balance before they "believe" in the necessity of linking both. Both must be achieved if the teacher is to realize his golden opportunity of multiplying his efforts endlessly through others. He is quite without comfort in learning that overemphasis on skill leads directly to the same cul-de-sac as overemphasis on knowledge.

Why have we been plagued with these pendulum swings from side to side? Why is one overemphasis succeeded by another? Is it we, or is it something inherent in the task we've set ourselves? The causes for these oscillations are more numerous than we can cover here. There are probably some we fail to see, but we shall point out a few that are important.

It is primarily in professional graduate schools that instructors feel a continual pressure to "make men think like doctors" (lawyers, administrators, etc.). Gifted teachers in nongraduate schools often do this in their subjects brilliantly, yet for their students it comes as a windfall, a memorable extra. In professional schools it is a must. As a consequence, the problem of balanced training is a pressing one only in the smallest fraction of our educational system.

A further reason why emphasis oscillates between skill and knowledge arises from the constant circulation of personnel within a teaching group. New members bring with them new interests and personal insights—sufficient reasons in themselves to plan for circulation. The new interests customarily spring from newly accomplished research work which, for young men, realistically represents the main highway to academic advancement. Furthermore, as men with intellectual gifts they are keenly alert to all the news and rumors about similar work by their colleagues and competitors everywhere. From the ferment generated by this enthusiasm for research (i.e., knowledge) it is easy for them to suppose students will be equally excited, and if an instructor's enthusiasm is contagious, they are. And, off they all march, even deeper in minutiae, up into an ivory tower! Earliest it dawns on the instructor where they all have come to rest, and his surprise is paralleled by a genuine dismay, because he usually shares the conviction of the teaching group as to the inutility of skill without knowledge, and vice versa. What had happened to him was simply his first personal experience with how unintentionally, imperceptibly, insensibly, the required balance between skill and knowledge is lost. This is a lesson that must be learned at first hand, for it cannot be grasped—believed—from the experience of others at second hand. While he, and others, too, are learning thus how delicate is the balance sought, the course emphasis, perforce, has shifted and, when acknowledged, must be again redressed. Nonetheless, the healthy and inevitable fact of circulation of personnel accounts for some of the oscillation.

A factor related to the foregoing two plays a part of indeterminable importance. This factor relates to erudition, or what Whitehead terms inert knowledge, which to outward appearances can be transferred in large doses daily. Impressive amounts can be recalled for testing at the close of each semester. This is familiar academic terrain. The skill required to do this is less taxing than the one Whitehead had in mind. The standards are conventionalized; they are understandable to students, teachers, and deans, all habituated to them. It is a measurable input-output operation far less trying on the nervous system than to be reaching for intangibles which need to be put in doubtful phrases such as a frame of mind, an attitude, an outlook, or "getting a man to think like a doctor."

When such intangibles are sought, even when some small, observable accomplishment seems attained, the instructor unavoidably feels less sure of *his* accomplishment, of the value of his contribution. Years must pass, not semesters, before the gains will be clear to either student or instructor. And, in the best cases, when either student or instructor, or both, do have a conviction of accomplishment, it often seems to the latter a frail and untrustworthy outcome for so much effort. It can require years for a teacher not merely to have faith, but to truly *know*, that even a small difference in a man's way of thinking and perceiving can make a very large difference in all he does thereafter. Instructors who adopt our aim must have time to discover for themselves the lifelong chain reaction which is set off, once skill-plus-knowledge are linked together indissolubly in a student's mind. Until this truth is validated for each instructor, their continuing uncertainties also will contribute to the oscillations of the course.

The reasons given so far for the difficulties we have encountered in trying to transmit skill and knowledge in a balanced relationship, and which we believe to be essential to the art of the utilization of knowledge, all stem from the problems of the teacher and his teaching group. There are still other reasons, and serious ones, too, that make impartation of Whitehead's art difficult. These will be ignored here, because it is about those given that teachers can do the most—if they choose.

The reasons given, in substance, amount to saying that teachers, too, must learn their art—an art, by Whitehead's definition, that takes at least as long to learn as to learn to do recognized, first-rate research. The rewards of teaching are as uncertain and as remote as those of research work; and they are accompanied by equally long periods of frustration and doubt. These facts generally come as a shock to brilliant young men who have won advanced degrees with distinction yet have had no warning that success in pedagogy may easily require of them an effort as strenuous and protracted as the one they have so recently completed.

So still another force bears on the oscillations experienced. The actual time and effort required, from men who are *willing* to shoulder the risks inherent in making skill AND knowledge, linked and balanced, their goal in teaching, is quite considerable. For each new man, or each group of new men, must be allowed to explore what the limitations on his efforts are, must be encouraged to probe for shortcuts, to question existing practices and their premises, while he learns how he, as an individual, can make his most effective contribution to the goal of teaching men "to think like administrators." This is a lonely task to which others can contribute little beyond support and encouragement.

Taking a wider view, the art of the utilization of knowledge strikes us as the inner key to most of the momentous issues confronting the people and the nations of the world today. Knowledge, especially scientific and technical knowledge (and belatedly, social and psychological knowledge), is accumulating at geometric rates while the art of its utilization falls further and further behind. Sufficient evidence of this widening gap appears daily in the news from underdeveloped countries, where political instability and technological helplessness underscore a simple proposition: knowledge without the skill to utilize it is no better than no knowledge at all. Skill to utilize knowledge must coexist in balance with knowledge, or the results are frustration and futility.

The most critical problem that lurks behind the looming crises of our century is how to break the bottleneck between the current accumulations of knowledge AND the skill to utilize them. This art must now reach vastly greater numbers of people than ever before. Until it does, our complex, interdependent, industrially based culture has not become adaptive to the environment it has created and may not survive.

Historically, the pedagogical tool upon which we have put our principal reliance in facing the challenging dilemmas and difficulties outlined here has been the case method. That method is surely not the only pedagogy that fosters the welding of skill and knowledge. Out of the present ferment about education we pray that others will emerge to equal or surpass it, for the need of pedagogical creation and invention is acute. Yet, it is one that we know invites the welding of skill and knowledge and, when rightly used, compels it. Since the problems of its use and misuse have been presented elsewhere[1] no more need be said here than to point out that some implements do exist for attacking the key problems of our day.

To those then, who embark with this course book on the endless adventure of teaching organization and administration, we fervently hope that at times of discouragement their spirits will be renewed by remembering that they are playing for stakes that involve the destiny of a civilization. They are battling to breach the massive walls that everywhere retard mankind's ability to utilize knowledge, already available and able to deliver our species from illiteracy, hunger, and perhaps even from the self-destructive compulsions that erupt periodically in war. Such a goal is distant, but is attainable and must be striven for. There is no longer any evasion of the problem of learning how to transmit skill-plus-knowledge to the generation that faces us. Even now we are runners in that race H. G. Wells foresaw for our century—"the race between education and catastrophe." May awareness of the issues at stake be a tonic to us—to all of us, students and learners, still striving for the never-ending education Whitehead summoned us to seek.

An administrator confronted with discouragingly complex human and social situations is repeatedly tempted to single out one piece of behavior as responsible for the desirable or undesirable consequences he must cope with. To guard him against this fallible but fatal human tendency to "find the villain." the emphasis in this book will be to examine each element of behavior, whether of an individual, a small group, or a large organization, as a responsive part of a system of *interrelated* and *interdependent* parts. Every element performs a function in relation to the whole. This is "the functional point of view" (that opposes and displaces the "find-the-villain" point of view), which is a key concept for this book and for the course it offers. The excerpt from Alexander Leighton's book, *Human Relations in a Changing World,* presents this important concept. We urge you to read the excerpt and thereafter apply the concept to every case we take up and study for discussion, for it is central to the understanding of a system.

---

[1] Kenneth R. Andrews, ed., *The Case Method of Teaching Human Relations and Administration* (Cambridge, Mass.: Harvard University Press, 1953); and F. J. Roethlisberger et al., *Training for Human Relations, An Interim Report of a Program for Advanced Training and Research in Human Relations, 1951–1954* (Boston: Division of Research, Harvard Business School, 1954).

2 | *The Functional Point of View**

Alexander H. Leighton

The concept of function has been borrowed by certain social scientists from physiology. In the latter field it has to do with asking such questions as, What is the role (function) of the heart or a gland in relation to the whole body? As applied to anthropology, Radcliffe-Brown puts it this way:

> The concept of function . . . involves the notion of a *structure* consisting of a *set of relations* among *unit entities,* the *continuity* of the structure being maintained by a *life-process* made up of the *activities* of the constituent units.

If, with these concepts in mind, we set out on a systematic investigation of the nature of human society and of social life, we find presented to us three sets of problems. First, the problems of social morphology—what kinds of social structures are there, what are their similarities and differences, how are they to be classified? Second, the problems of social physiology—how do social structures function? Third, the problems of development—how do new types of social structure come into existence?

By the definition here offered "function" is the contribution which a partial activity makes to the total activity of which it is a part. The function of a particular social usage is the contribution it makes to the total social life as the functioning of the total social system. Such a view implies that a social system (the total social structure of a society together with the totality of social usages in which that structure appears and on which it depends for its continued existence) has a certain kind of unity, which we may speak of as a functional unity. We may

* Alexander H. Leighton, *Human Relations in a Changing World* (New York: E. P. Dutton & Co., Inc., 1949), pp. 156–61.

define it as a condition in which all parts of the social system work together with a sufficient degree of harmony or internal consistency, i.e., without producing persistent conflicts which can neither be resolved nor regulated.

Opposition, i.e., organized and regulated antagonism is, of course, an essential feature of every social system.[1]

Bronislaw Malinowski says: "The primary concern of functional anthropology is the function of institutions, customs, implements and ideas. It holds that the cultural process is subject to laws and that the laws are to be found in the function of the real elements of culture."[2]

Since this matter is difficult to realize on the basis of abstract terms alone, three illustrations are offered: the first is from animal ecology, the second from entomology and the third from medicine. Although drawn from non-social science fields because less entangled, they are nevertheless relevant.

Suppose that a naturalist is studying a wilderness area for purposes of conservation. He finds that the various plants and animals as they go through their life cycles of growth and reproduction exist in a state of complex interdependence. His attention is directed toward mountain sheep that are diminishing in number and also to the presence of wolves. Were he a sportsman or rancher, he would be likely to assume that the wolves were *the cause* of the reduction in sheep and to maintain this view with no little heat. The naturalist, however, does not stop with such a single idea. He observes, theorizes and tests his theories with further observations. He finds that the wolves kill the sheep but that they also kill numbers of other animals that are in competition with the sheep for the same food. He discovers that the sheep suffer from scarcity of food, from the washing out of certain chemicals from the soil due to erosion, from diseases and from the winter killing of lambs. In the end, the naturalist may find that the wolves are one of a number of serious threats to the sheep and that their reduction would help the sheep population. Or, he may find that the balance of nature is such in this particular case that the wolves aid the sheep more than harming them, by keeping down the number of animals that eat the same food. In either event, the naturalist sees multiple forces at work in a state of interdependence, rather than a single cause that fits like a key into a lock. Moreover, he does not take sides with sheep, wolves

---

[1] A. R. Radcliffe-Brown, "Concept of Function in Social Science," *American Anthropologist,* vol. 37 (July–September 1935).

[2] "Culture," in *Encyclopedia of the Social Sciences,* vol. 4 (New York: Macmillan Co., 1931).

A mathematically oriented discussion of functional dependence may be found in Eliot Dismore Chapple and Carleton Stevens Coon, *Principles of Anthropology* (New York: Henry Holt & Co., 1942).

or other animals in such a way as to blind his understanding of how they are interdependent.

Suppose another naturalist is studying insects purely from an interest in advancing knowledge. If he turns his attention to bees he will find that complex interrelationship of individuals to make a hive that has often been described. There are the workers, the drones, and the queen, each with patterns of behavior that aid the continued existence of the colony with a striking disregard for the well-being of any one individual. The drones are starved, mutilated and thrown out when their functions have been performed. Workers that arrive home with frayed wings or begin to fail in their productive capacity receive the same treatment. Even the queen, ordinarily surrounded by attendants who minister to her needs, is destroyed when infirmities begin to creep upon her. The naturalist will observe further that all this behavior does function with considerable efficiency to perpetuate individual hives and bees as a whole. He will make these discoveries in a spirit of finding out how it all works and without pronouncing judgments on the bees, without calling the drones "useless" or the destruction of damaged workers "wicked."

For the third picture, suppose a doctor is carrying out research on the cause of tuberculosis. His first goal is to understand the process, and he finds before long that he cannot regard the tubercle bacillus as *the cause* of the disease. It becomes evident that millions of people harbor the germ without developing any signs or symptoms of tuberculosis. The research physician must, therefore, study the reactions and interactions of glands, nerves, blood vessels, lymphatic system, and other organs and functions of the body in relation to the whole, to the tubercle bacillus and to other germs that might have a predisposing or immunizing effect. Nor is the list exhausted here, for it is also necessary to look into such matters as diet, light, nature of work, and the possible presence of hereditary and psychological factors. The germ, it turns out, is only one of a number of conditions that must be present before tuberculosis occurs. At no time does the doctor get wound up in hating the germ and in weaving patterns of revenge into his research. He keeps his mind on the central aim of finding out what is going on so that remedial change can be introduced.

In these illustrations at least two common elements are evident. The first is an attempt to understand any item as part of a larger whole, as the product of multiple interacting forces, rather than the result of a single cause that can be ferreted out like a detective uncovering a murderer. The second is that the forces are regarded as natural rather than good or bad. One's own hopes, fears, and ideas of what *should be* are set aside in favor of discovering what *is*. Whether the naturalist likes or dislikes wolves is not relevant to understanding their relationship to the sheep. The man who studies the bees may be himself a believer in democracy, fascism, or communism, but this must not be allowed to intrude itself into his reports about their social life and how it works for them. The physician does not permit belief in the wickedness of the tubercle bacillus to lead him into underestimating or overestimating its power, nor to neglecting all the other matters that are equally important in understanding and controlling tuberculosis.

Few people will quarrel with all this as long as it is confined to the natural sciences, but many difficulties arise as soon as these few and simple points are transferred to the study of human behavior and an effort is made to view society as the naturalist looks at the animal kingdom, the physician the functions of the body and the astronomer the stars. In place of such a view the policy maker, like most other people, has it ingrained in him from his early years to measure human affairs in terms of good and evil. Starkly simple explanations are sought to the neglect of deeper understanding and hence opportunity for control.

This kind of thinking recurs continuously in all sorts of contexts. If war is threatened, if an economic depression descends, if unemployment appears, if Congress fails to pass the Fair Employment Practice Bill, if a strike takes place, if patients in a mental hospital are mistreated, if a child is found neglected, we always give far more attention to discussing the rights and the wrongs of the situation, in deciding who is to blame and in taking sides, than to understanding the forces that have brought it about and deciding what can be done to control them. If we can make somebody suffer for it, we are likely to go away satisfied, leaving the situation no better than before.

We are always looking for the villain instead of human beings going through the business of living as best they can, some helpfully and some destructively in their actions toward the welfare of others. Preoccupation with the search for the villain blinds us to the constellation of events past and present that gave rise to him. From the functional point of view, "what gives rise" is the question. Can we, through understanding the forces that produce villains, alter situations so that there will be less ground on which they can flourish?

Must we be forever content with trapping rats? Cannot we also stop up their holes and rid ourselves of the places that breed them? The world is getting too small for the luxury of villains and there is a widespread need for the physician's obsession with getting at causes and not tinkering with symptoms only.

These, then, are the implications of the functional view. By and large, they enter only a little into most of the thinking that gives rise to policy.

Section II

II

Individuals and Their Relationships

Cases

1 | James Short

Early in 1953, David C. Davis, a management consultant, received a phone call from his friend, James A. Short, executive vice president of the Hudson Corporation, requesting a personal conference at the close of business that day. Although Mr. Davis had some social engagements for the evening that would need adjustment, he was glad to meet Mr. Short's request because he had been on the point of arranging a meeting for himself with Mr. Short.

Mr. Davis felt that he could guess what Mr. Short had on his mind. About seven years earlier, when his close acquaintance with Mr. Short began, Mr. Davis had assisted Mr. Short in locating a new job, after he had resigned abruptly from the Hudson Corporation. Mr. Short had been persuaded to return to the Hudson Corporation about two years later. The new job in his old company was a marked improvement for him in terms of remuneration, explicit definition of responsibilities and authority, and a title designation that clearly indicated his post as number two man in the company hierarchy. Mr. Davis knew that matters had gone much more satisfactorily, from Mr. Short's point of view, during the years since his return, although Mr. Davis recently had heard indirectly that some of the earlier difficulties between Mr. Short and the president of Hudson Corporation had arisen once more.

The meeting between the two men began in Mr. Davis's club not long after five o'clock and continued through dinner and into the evening. The information that follows, together with the gist of the conversations reproduced, were written out by Mr. Davis, at the request of a casewriter from the Harvard Business School, soon after the conference occurred. The case was cleared for accuracy and disguise with Mr. Short by Mr. Davis.

Mr. Short opened the conversation immediately upon his appearance with the remark, "I expect you know what's up—J. G. [Connell, president of Hudson Corporation] can't keep his hands off any longer; and this time if I quit it'll be for good, and I want to plan ahead for it a bit more than I did last time."

Mr. Davis smiled. "How long can you hold onto yourself? You act teed off."

"I am," Short replied, "but I managed to finish the day and get up here without calling for a showdown. And tonight is Friday night, so there's the weekend ahead of me. Furthermore, I've had two good offers recently that still stand open waiting for my answer."

"That ought to help," Davis said. "Added to which, I have a third offer that was specifically drawn up to appeal to you and about which I was planning to see you next week. Shall we move over to the dining room and get into all this over dinner?"

Settled at their table Mr. Davis urged Mr. Short to bring him up to date on what had been happening in Hudson Corporation since their last meeting about six months earlier. "I thought you had your troubles pretty well cleared up. At least you made no complaints at that time."

SHORT: That's the devil of it. They were cleared up until somewhere around 12 or 15 months ago. Beginning then J. G. has made my job increasingly difficult by postponing decisions I put up to him—ones that require his approval, and quickly too, to be worth acting on, by questioning a lot of my smaller decisions—ones I've been making for years without his objection, and really aren't important by themselves but only as a symptom of his intentional meddling, by making more and more suggestions about how I ought to handle my personnel—suggestions he knows damn well I won't accept. They concern the way he treats people and are the ways I never have and never will use.

Well, that's the way it's been going for more than a year. This morning when I went in to go over the next budget for my divisions he said he'd been studying it and thought I ought to cut the figure for promotion and advertising one million dollars. I said, "Not unless I cut the figure for projected sales several times more." He didn't like that, but he wouldn't argue with me about it. We've gone to the mat on that one too often. So he went back to the million dollars he said I could save. I wouldn't take it without a proportionate cutback in sales. Finally he said, "You aren't the president around here yet." I wanted to say, "Damn lucky for you I'm not." But I held onto it, and merely said, "That's right." He said, "I think you ought to cut one million out of that one figure. Think it over." I said, "I will," and walked out. And here I am.

DAVIS: What's he want?

SHORT (*slowly, after a long pause*): I hate to say this because it ought not to be true, but I think he's afraid of me. He ought not to be. He's the biggest figure in the industry, one of the old-timers too, out of the rough and tumble era. He owns a lot of the stock, he controls a solid majority of the company directors, he's a very wealthy man and has been for years. It's taken a long time for me to admit this to myself, but it's the only explanation that fits the pattern of his recent behavior.

The figures for my divisions are coming out the way I predicted them to him almost two years ago—I have lifted two of our perennial money losers out of the red. They're in the black now, and next year they'll both be solid money makers. I think he's afraid to allow the company stockholders and directors, the bankers, and the employees to see the transformation from perpetual red to dependable black as a result of the work I have been doing for the last four years. He fears they might figure he wasn't needed, and he's becoming more touchy every day about that since he passed the 70-year mark some time ago.

DAVIS: He can't last forever, and you're the only possible successor he's got in the whole organization. Everyone in the company knows that, from top to bottom, and a good many are praying for the day. You've put in 25 years all over the company, abroad and at home, getting ready for a take-over when the old man retires—the last 10 years as the heir apparent, chosen and trained by himself. You think you can't take the punishment any longer?

SHORT: It isn't that simple, Dave. I've never taken any "punishment" from him, except lots of hard work and tough assignments—and I asked for those. It's most of the other executives in the company who have taken the punishment—that is, the ones who stayed on for the sake of the high salaries he pays. The ones who wouldn't, left. I guess I'm the only one who wouldn't put up with his galley-slave tactics who stayed with him.

DAVIS: Maybe that's the reason you're the only one he has groomed as his successor.

SHORT: He groomed me as his successor because I always studied my problems until I was certain what the trouble was. Once that was done, a promising solution or two were never hard to find. When I went in to him I always took along my recommendations, and then fought for them. Usually I won, because I double-checked and triple-checked on everything. I never minded those combats and I don't think he did either. The other guys generally took only the problems to him and then asked him what to do about them. That's where they got in trouble. He'd tell them, and at the same time call them stupid or dumb or incompetent. Right in front of their own people, too. It used to make me sick at times, but I'd tell them afterwards, when they came to see me, that they'd asked for it by going in that way. I'd try to get them to see the only way to avoid a public horsewhipping was to go in with their own plan and battle for it.

You know he lives for nothing but his business. He lives in a hotel in the center of town so as to be close to the office. He and his wife don't own a home anywhere. They have no children. She's been a confirmed neurasthenic for decades, going from doctor to doctor. She shifted some time ago to cults and fads and healers.

Any time of night, or on weekends, or on vacations, he'll phone any officer in the company he wants to and either order them in for an afternoon or evening of work while the office is closed, or else keep them on the phone as long as he wants to bat a problem around. He tried that on me not long after I got back from that foreign assignment. I was expecting it, because some of the other men had complained about it to me—or rather, their wives had to my wife. I told our maid to tell him I was busy entertaining our guests and that I would be in to see him first thing in the morning. He never mentioned it and never tried it again.

No, I'm not the one who's had to take that sort of punishment—it's the other men, the whole executive structure in fact.

DAVIS: We've gone over some of this before, but I'm still a little puzzled. Between bonus and salary you went well over the $100,000 bracket two years ago. You don't put up with the bullyragging old Connell has been notorious for; on the contrary, you're almost indispensable to him. You've worked hard a long time for what you've almost got in your hand. It can't be so far off now. Why can't you go along until the ship is yours?

SHORT (*after another long pause*):   Age is one angle—his and mine. I've just touched 50 and if I'm going to accomplish anything particularly noteworthy in an organization as big as ours I've got to get a really free hand soon. Ten years is hardly enough. Fifteen may be. At least I'm still ready to try hard. I may not feel that same way when the time gets shorter.

He is over 70, but all his close relatives—uncles, cousins, parents—were long-lived, many into their 90s. I believe he's going to hold on as long as he can. I may be wrong on this. He often talked with me about his retirement, and I think he meant it. But not during the past two or three years has he mentioned it again. I don't know whether it was his 70th birthday or my breaking into the black with the losers he could never rescue that made him clam up.

He still works like a horse, though he is slowing down and won't admit it. He may keel over one of these days—but I just don't know. It's a question mark, Dave—his retirement. I've speculated over that ever since he got over 65 and stayed on to 70. Now I'm 50, and I've concluded that I'm the fellow who's got to make the decision.

DAVIS: Jim, what if a taxi ran him down this evening. What would you like to try for most with Hudson Corporation? Why would you stay there rather than go to any of the three openings we are going to look over later on? What's Hudson got that I can't top on behalf of Casper?

SHORT (*startled*):   Have you got an offer from Casper?

DAVIS: I've got the executive vice presidency for you. Not at once, but explicitly inside one year, to give Gene Darnell a decent interval in which to move back to the chairmanship. With it goes a salary, bonus, deferred payments, and pension tentatively proposed to meet your wishes, and with full authorization to me to meet any offer you get from any firm in the industry on each of the points I mentioned—salary, bonus, and so on.

Short sat silent. He was not prepared for such an offer from the chief rival in his field. His thoughts had been so much preoccupied with the tangled difficulties of his own situation at Hudson that he found it hard to grasp Davis's statements. Finally he asked, "Is that true?"

Davis gestured toward his briefcase, "I have the papers in there when you're ready to look them over. Now how about my question: 'What's Hudson got for you that I can't top for Casper?'"

SHORT: Well, for one thing I know Hudson like the inside of my own house. I know every move I want to make, who I want to make the moves, and when, and how. I know what our weaknesses are and many remedies I am sure will help correct them. I know also where we have unrealized sources of strength which I am confident could be developed to such a degree that before I am through, we could attain a commanding lead in the industry. And that means (he said with a glance at Davis) that we could overtake Casper's present 10 percent lead in sales and go 20 percent to 25 percent ahead of them.

That's one thing Hudson's got for me.

Another is—and I should have put it first—I think I could release the energies and capabilities of a lot of good men that J. G. has used as chore boys. I think I could attract and hold a lot of good men who would never enter our doors so long as Connell's practices are followed. And this is something I've wanted to do in Hudson longer than anything else. I sort of feel I owe it to a lot of men who never got a decent chance to show what they could do in an encouraging atmosphere. I owe it to some friends of mine whose spirits or whose health were broken, and to some whose lives were shortened because they worked in Hudson.

That is a serious thing to say, but I mean it. And the funny thing is that I owe more to J. G. than I owe to any man alive. He gave me my chance in sales when I asked to transfer out of the accounting department 20 years ago. He sent me abroad in charge of sales when our subsidary in Austria looked weak. He put me in full charge in less than one year when they had to replace their general manager there. He gave me a free hand over the whole outfit for nearly a decade before the war ended that operation. He asked for results, sure, but I would do exactly the same thing. During his two visits per year we took our operations apart down to the last penny and I learned as much about running my own show during his inspections as I did during the rest of the year.

He's a rough and often ruthless man, but you've got to remember the period when he was growing up. He was at work selling at the time of the Spanish-American War! I've told him a good many times that he is a holdover from the old robber barons who built our railroads and steel mills.

DAVIS: Quite a compliment to pay your boss. How did he take it?

SHORT: Sometimes he'd frown, sometimes he'd grin. Don't forget he is perhaps the greatest promoter and one of the greatest salesmen our industry has produced. Nobody could touch him ten years ago. Remember he merged the first truly national organization in our field, just as he was the first to move aggressively into the foreign field in a really big way—at least from an American base. And he carried competition to every market that could be made to pay. In our field there's no personality like him left on the scene.

DAVIS: Sounds like hero worship to me.

SHORT: Why, yes, I guess it does. I guess I've felt that way about him for years. But I don't any longer. At least not much. Not since I've been continually at headquarters where I've seen him in action every day with the personnel of the organization. I was in Europe nearly ten years, you know, and after I came back he sent me out again to put the southern subsidiary on its feet. I didn't really get to know him, or the situation in the home office, until the war was over, scarcely eight years ago.

I think maybe he's changed too. I'm pretty sure he has in the last two or three years. He lies to me now. He goes behind my back and then denies it. He never used to do that. I've lost my respect for him.

DAVIS: Well are you ready to look over the material I've got on Casper?

SHORT: Not yet, Dave. I can't swing around that fast. Nor that far.

What I mean is I never expected that kind of an offer from that source. Except for two years I've worked all my life for Hudson. I can't get up out of the trenches and walk straight across to the principal enemy I've spent most of my business years fighting all over the globe. It sort of makes me feel like a deserter.

It would be a whale of a kick in the pants to the old man, though. Maybe it would jar some perspective back into him. Still he treated me awfully well that first time I resigned. I just walked out. You remember?

Well, he said I had to keep my title and my office until I made a connection. He wanted to pay my salary too, but I wouldn't take that. Furthermore, he met my terms when I was willing to go back and he kept them, until these past months.

No, Dave, I've got to think out a lot more of the angles on Casper first. Casper does need rebuilding though, doesn't it? I think it's gotten into much worse shape since the war than anyone seems to realize. Still it's a backbreaking chore to get such a scattered and loose-jointed giant trained into fighting shape, isn't it?

DAVIS: Well, what about the two offers you mentioned earlier. What have they got?

SHORT: You'll laugh when I tell you about the first one. Annual sales are barely over $10 million a year. Isn't that something, when both Hudson and Casper's sales run over $300 million a year?

Still they made it awfully attractive for me personally. And for my family, too. It's the M. B. Madison Company. You know the wonderful country club location they have built for themselves well out in one of the nicest unspoiled suburbs in the whole metropolitan area? I could live a country life—and you know I like the country—and not have more than a pleasant 20-minute drive to and from the office. I could live with my family once more, which I haven't been doing these past 4 or 5 years while I've put in about 12 hours a day trying to pull those divisions out of the red. My boy and girl are in college now, but if my wife and I don't make every opportunity to see as much of them as possible while we can it will soon be too late.

I owe something to my wife in all this. We were close together in Europe and nearly as much so when we went South. But since this last deal got underway she must think I'm beginning to resemble J. G. She hasn't said much, but I know how she looks at the way those two have lived their lives. Our years in Europe gave us a lot of interests that I've had to neglect recently. There really isn't much point in working yourself like J. G. does, especially since they tax it away nearly as fast as you can make it.

I'll never get her to make the choice, and I wouldn't want her to, but the M. B. Madison setup is closer to what we both feel makes all-around sense than anything I've got in sight. Let me tell you a bit more about it.

The presidency is opening soon and that is what they're offering me. The salary is $40,000 with a profit sharing arrangement which I figure could make me an additional $30,000 after the two or three years we would need in which to substantially increase their sales. There is a capital gains opportunity through an option on 5 percent of their total stock which is attractive. The stock is low currently but has a growth potential that I believe could triple its prices before I needed to sell—all in all, I see almost a quarter million dollar gain between the buying and selling price. The pension possibility for me is limited, and I'll have to build my own estate along the other lines.

The salary drop is severe, especially over the next five years, so moneywise I have to balance the near-term versus the long-run considerations in this offer against the immediate gains in the other openings.

Probably I'd have a freer hand in that organization because of its size, for one thing. In a year I'd know its people as well—maybe better—than I do my own now. Its officers are decent people; the company has an excellent reputation for its business standards. It's one of the oldest in our line, and I'm confident there is a fine base for doubling its share of the market. Most of all, right now, I'd be on my own again; and the directors who have talked with me are ready to accept any reasonable conditions I want to set in regard to running my own show.

It's a temptation all right: the country, my wife and family once more, a sure chance to make a good record, and a dependable nest egg—all without killing myself as I have been doing.

DAVIS: What about the other offer?

SHORT: It's another presidency, after a year. I'll go in as executive vice president at $60,000, which will go up somewhere around $80,000 when I take over the president's office. There is a bonus which runs around 10 percent of the salary each year. The pension would enable me to retire with $30,000 annually from that source alone. The stock option proposal is a complicated formula but it works out so that I can buy stock on a basis which virtually assures me of doubling my money, and if the stock increases further in value I would secure that additional increment.

From a financial angle it would be hard to beat from my point of view. The salary and bonus are a reduction from what I'm getting now, but about three years ago I found that the huge bonus I got that year melted down to just a few thousand dollars after the treasury took its bite. As a matter of fact, I bought tax anticipation warrants with what was left simply to remind myself that a big bonus often doesn't mean a thing.

It's the Martin Brachall Company. A fine old reputable concern with a name for honesty and integrity—a factor that appeals to me more and more as time passes. All the officers are gentlemen. I've known many of them for years, and I've admired the atmosphere of goodwill and cooperation they work in. They know what teamwork means, and it is an asset I am definitely counting on when I estimate what I can do for the company.

They have a line of staple products, some of them virtual monopolies, not only because of worldwide consumer preference and brand prestige, but also because of entrenched marketing arrangements. As an old marketeer, I have a deep hunch that there is a tremendous potential, both in the company's position as well as in its products, that is ready for a long-pull expansion. The stock is closely held and hasn't missed a dividend in over two generations. The financial standing is gilt-edge. Actually all that is needed is a period of concentration on promotion and sales—the very kind of assignments I've handled successfully three times straight at Hudson. Sales are running close to $30 million annually, and I can see a dozen ways to begin lifting that figure nearly 10 percent a year.

DAVIS: I can't tell whether the Madison Company or the Brachall Company excites you the most. Aren't there any catches in the last one?

SHORT: That's the question, Dave, I asked myself after my confidential talk with Mr. McKee [president of Brachall Company]. I'm sure there is, but I haven't found it yet; and I've gone over it a dozen times. All I've found, in fact, are some more plusses. Their offices occupy part of their own building, which leaves room for a convenient expansion. It is in the part of town I like best. It's very handy for me to reach from where we live now—and where we're really taking roots in the community at last. Even the president's office has exactly the view I like best in all the city, and it combines with an executive office layout that creates a mood in which I feel good and do good work. Maybe I'm oversensitive to such things just now, and perhaps it's silly to mention it, but I'll bet there are a lot of similar hidden considerations that lie deep in these kinds of decisions. I'm only trying to look at mine, and to me the building location and the offices I'll occupy are a clear plus.

DAVIS: Is it any use to look over the draft proposals I've got from Casper for you?

SHORT: I don't see why. At least not this evening, Dave. It's getting late, and I've got a lot of thinking and deciding to do this weekend. I know the gist of the proposition: they will write me a better ticket financially than I can get anywhere else.

DAVIS: They'll go further than that. They're ready to . . .

SHORT (*interrupting*):   I know it's a big organization, Dave. I know what they can and can't deliver. Money they can—the rest is only a chance to try to turn a whale around. Maybe I'll want to; it's the kind of animal I'm most familiar with. Maybe these smaller organizations are simply "greener pastures" to me right now. I'm grateful to Casper—perhaps I ought to say, to you, because you're probably the prime mover here—but it's good for my morale, coming from my friends the enemy.

Short arose. "Thanks for the evening, Dave. I did all the talking, but I've found that helps clear up my thinking a lot if I find someone who is able to listen. Somebody beside my wife, that is. I didn't want to pour all this out to her without a preliminary run-through on you you see, because this time she's more thoroughly involved than in any other single decision in my whole business career. This time her opinion isn't what I need. I want her to say frankly what kind of life she would like a part of for the next 15 years—from there on it's up to me to make the choice that meets her wishes, and mine too. Doesn't that make sense to you?"

Davis smiled, "It makes sense to me all right, but I'm not the one you have to make sense to from here on. Good luck, and call me up any time I can be of use again."

James A. Short was born in Minnesota in 1903; worked part of his expenses off in going through college and graduated from the University of Iowa in 1924 with Phi Beta Kappa honors. He majored in business administration and specialized in accounting. He married in 1925. In 1933, after it was clear that children of their own would not be forthcoming, he and his wife adopted two babies, a boy and a girl, born eight days apart.

Mr. Short began work in 1924 as a cost accountant for a firm in Chicago that was merged with several others in 1927 to create the Hudson Corporation. His work with company figures soon disclosed to him that progress upward in the ranks of management was slow in his department and was most rapid then in foreign sales. He requested a transfer to that department which was effected in 1931. The years 1926–31 were spent in domestic sales to prepare for entrance into foreign sales.

From 1931 into 1939 he was briefly sales manager for, and then general manager of, the Austrian subsidiary of Hudson Corporation. During his managership, sales increased from approximately $100,000 a year to more than $5 million. The outbreak of war terminated operations in Austria; and Mr. Short returned to the American headquarters of Hudson Corporation, now substantially larger, and located in the New York metropolitan area. Shortly thereafter he was sent South to liquidate an old-line subsidiary of Hudson that had defied years of effort to make profitable. Close attention to its accounts suggested ways in which money could be saved. These were instituted by Mr. Short and together with increased sales produced results that led the president of Hudson to encourage Mr. Short to continue his efforts. Between 1940 and 1943 sales rose from $5 million to $7.5 million, though net profits rose much more steeply.

Mr. Short was called back to headquarters in 1943 and made assistant to the president with the title of vice president. He was given trouble-shooting assignments throughout the whole corporation—a position he quickly grew to dislike. He requested, on several occasions, some definite responsibilities on which he could make his own record, pointing out that if he found trouble when dispatched on such missions it made other vice presidents look bad, whereas if he did not, it made him look bad. Once or twice he was dissuaded from pushing his request; thereafter it was agreed to, but fulfillment was frequently postponed. Mr. Short, at this point, resigned abruptly and worked for the two years, 1945–46, with a smaller concern in the same industry which was only obliquely a competitor of Hudson.

Upon his return to Hudson in 1946, which was negotiated with Mr. J. G. Connell, Mr. Short was made vice president of the whole company and soon thereafter executive vice president and, in addition, was given direct responsibility in 1948 for the two most difficult divisions in the corporation. Mr. Short began his conversation with Mr. Davis over events that derived from that assignment.

2 | *E. J. Weiver*

Columbia Products Corporation, where E. J. Weiver works as a product manager, is situated 40 miles from New York City in a pleasant suburban community. The casewriter visited E. J., who is single and a transplanted New York advertising executive, to discuss the job demands of being a product manager for two nationally known shampoos in the Toiletries Division of Columbia Products.[1]

Before meeting with E. J., the casewriter talked to E. J.'s boss, Tom Bird, a product group supervisor, who supervises E. J. and several other product managers.

CASEWRITER: If I understand you correctly, you don't really have a specific problem with E. J., but you do wonder what's going to happen to E. J.'s career and how to help in planning it?

TOM BIRD: That's right. E. J.'s a hard charger and that's been just great. We had two new products to get out on the market in a short time, and how they got there wasn't important—E. J. got them out. But now, as the pressure is easing off, I'm trying to see how to give E. J. new challenges as a product manager and beyond that how to help him develop into a good *general* manager. It's a question of style, in part.

CASEWRITER: At the risk of sounding partisan, I could suggest you ship E. J. off to the Harvard PMD [Program for Management Development].

BIRD: I can't spare the loss. E. J.'s products are out on the market, but they have to be monitored for at least another year. I have to figure out something to do right here. You see, E. J. has a very responsible position in charge of two new toiletries products. Now E. J.'s just beginning work to pep up another set of older products. The toiletries products are grouped

---

[1] An organization chart for the division is shown in Exhibit 1.

35

together with each product being managed by a product manager. Some, like E. J., manage several products. People in my job work with the product managers seeing not only that the products are produced and marketed but also that the product managers themselves get a chance to develop.

CASEWRITER: Tell me about E. J.; how long have you two worked together?

BIRD: For four years, not all of them here. E. J. was at our ad agency as our account executive, and then came here. We've had no problem in going from the agency relationship to the company one.

E. J. is proving to be one of the most effective people in moving this business ahead—in cutting through lethargy and shaking people up a little bit—and with lots of management support for it. E. J.'s assignment was to get some products out fast. If it took some waves to do it—we took them. But E. J.'s maturing now—still making waves, but you might say the surf is not as violent as it used to be.

E. J. has a very definite style, and I have to figure out how to effectively utilize it. Talk to E. J. You'll see what I mean.

E. J. was talking on the phone when the casewriter appeared at the door; a hand was waved toward one of the three leather chairs in the office. While waiting for E. J. to finish the phone call, which was accentuated by desk pounding and arm wavings, the casewriter had time to read the motto on the wall. Written in gothic script was: "I will walk through the valley of the shadow of death and fear no evil, for I am the meanest son-of-a-bitch in the valley." On the desk was a wooden nutcracker, a gift from some sales promotion employees. It is inscribed: "1971 Nutcracker Award. E. J., for outstanding performance, from the sales promotion group."

E. J. plunked down the phone, leaned across the desk to shake hands, and said, "So you want to see how a product manager operates! Stick around. I'll try to fill you in on what I do."

CASEWRITER: How did you get started in all this?

E. J.: After graduating from the Harvard Business School in 1964, I accepted a job with an ad agency in New York.[2] I was in a two-year training program, which sounds unappealing to most new graduates, but we were in each department long enough as a functioning member so that we really got to know it well.

At the end of the training period, I asked one of my friends what could be a good account to get onto. My friend suggested an airlines account, saying, "If you live through that, you'll live through anything." And he was right. I guess I lived through it.

I worked on consumer products after that and did public service accounts, too. Then, I had an offer from Columbia Products, and I took it. One difficulty I'd had with advertising was that, as an account executive, I never felt as if I created the end product. The account executive represents the agency

---

[2] E. J.'s résumé of work experience is included as Exhibit 2.

EXHIBIT 1
Company Organization Chart

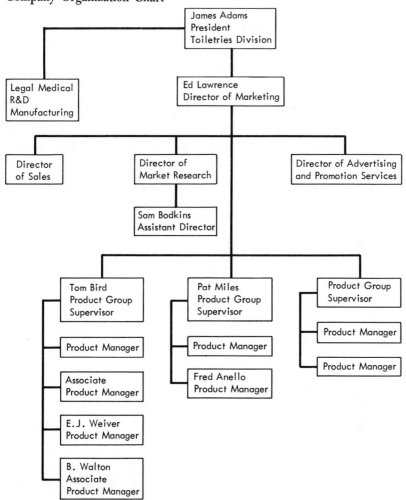

to the client and presents someone else's copy, art, etc. You never represent your own thing, and I wanted involvement with the actual end product. Here I have that.

We do as much R&D as we can afford but we have seat-of-the-pants type thinking, too. I can actually point to my brands and say that I invented them.

Initially, my job here was unusual since I was given new products. You develop a rationale for marketing the products in the first place, talking to R&D, then working with market research to see if there is a viable concept that will motivate people to buy it. Then you work with advertising. You

EXHIBIT 2
Résumé of E. J. Weiver

Experience:

Columbia Products Corp., Toiletries Division—March 1970 to present:

Product manager. Responsible for the conceptual development and market introduction of two new toiletries products in 1971, and for assorted current brands.

Advertising Agency—July 1964 to March 1970:

June 1968—March 1970. Senior account executive—for toiletries, clothing, and
public service accounts, including Columbia Products. Responsible for planning and executing plans in marketing, advertising, promotion, and collateral
areas.

August 1966 to June 1968. Account executive—airline account. Responsible for
the planning and executing of all sales promotion materials, also for development of their segmented approach to the special travel markets (ethnic, sports,
honeymoon, youth).

July 1964 to August 1966. Executive trainee. Trained in research, traffic, media,
and marketing departments. Program included six months of sales experience
with client. Accounts included magazines, toiletries, automotive, food, clothing,
furnishings, and public service.

Summer, Part-Time Positions:

Trainee positions at department store in Washington, D.C., and bank in Boston,
Massachusetts.

work with everybody to get all the elements together into a cohesive piece
or program. You have to see that the product is good, that it fits a need,
that its ability to fill the need can be communicated to people. Then you
have to make the product right and get it to the people. There are a lot
of details that have to be covered. For example, ordering the change parts
on the assembly line for bottles takes six months lead time.

Now, with the new products essentially launched, my role is shifting to
that of planning a total ongoing program for the brands. We plan from
a profit point of view, and a brand is judged on its profit program. I have
ongoing profit and market responsibility for the brands that are out now.

I enjoy strategy most of all in this job. For example, last October we
found out another major toiletries company was bringing a competitive product
out at exactly the same time as ours. We had to react to this—it's fascinating.
You'd try to guess what they were doing. You do a lot of figuring out of
the most profitable positioning for your brand, that is, do you be first with
a new product on the market, or what are the implications of being second.

Because of Tom's style, I've made more decisions than usual. I attribute
a lot of this to Tom—he knew he could trust me, and he let me have more
responsibility. Some other product managers don't feel they have as much,
but they're not working for Tom either.

You have to spark the things that *are* done. There is a difference between
just doing the things that have to be done and making the spark. You have
to motivate people. Now I'd like to get into the broader planning areas,
thinking of broader implications for the division. I'm trying to make my
job into more. I'm finding out more. About knowing how our products are

formulated, and building on that knowledge to get a broader sense of our division's place in the total toiletries market. What are our limitations on sales since we don't have many salesmen? Are there other ways of selling? It's a broader investigation. I try to think of a future strategy for our division. Understand that none of this is my responsibility, but I want to help Tom who in turn can help his boss. It's not my job directly, but I enjoy thinking about it. We have not traditionally had innovative products, but we may decide for once to be the first ones out with a product. These are the types of questions that interest me.

CASEWRITER: How would you describe your style?

E. J.:   Halfway between a bulldozer and a Mack truck. It depends on what I perceive other people to be in their attitude toward their job. There are some people I trust with their jobs, and others I constantly tend to push. If I feel that the man in question agrees with something I've given him, then I'll just go down later and say how's it coming—can we help? If he doesn't agree, or I sense that he's hesitant, then I'll push him to find out what he's thinking.

I came here not knowing anything about packaging, manufacturing, sales promotion. I had to jump in and make a lot of decisions in these areas, and I found that my judgment is pretty good. Looking back, I can see one poor strategy decision, but on the whole it's been pretty good. So now if I believe I'm right, the chances are I probably am. And if being extremely forceful and directive is the only way to get it done—to get two new products out in one year—then I feel the ends justify the means. There's so much to be done, I often sacrifice personal relationships in order to get the job done. Like with sales promotion—there I give directions down to crossing the T's. I may sacrifice some people's feelings to get the job done as completely and thoroughly as possible. I was brought here to do a job, though.

But now I have to train people who report to me. It's a different task. Now that we've got the basic job done, my assistant, Bill Walton, can get training. Now more time will have to be spent helping him become a complete product manager. My role will begin to be that of backup or consultant to him, helping him when he needs help, but he'll have to tell me. He used to come in and say, "I have a problem." I'd say, "I'll solve it." That has to stop. It will be interesting to see if I can be as good a leader as I was an activist, because as far as supervising is concerned, I still get uneasy in delegating authority.

CASEWRITER: How do you find supervising Bill?

E. J.:   I'm judging him on how much he can pick up with these new products. I can't do everything. I want someone who will say "no" to me. It's not been a good training period for him though because of the rush we're in. However, I am now forcing him to write our reports and to take a more active part in policy decisions. It bothers me when I realize there are things that haven't been done, but I will have to get used to delegating. It's tough when you're used to doing everything yourself.

CASEWRITER: Has Bill worked for someone like you before?

E. J.:   Oh, no. He said to me that he'd worked for someone with whom he could work for a month and the guy would make one decision and you'd know how he made it. Bill said to me, "You make 30 decisions and I don't know how you got there." He's a really nice guy, and I haven't leaned on him too much and I've tried not to be too directive. It's tough, since you have to be up on every detail of every other department. Like market research—you have to know how it's done so you can evaluate it. Advertising, production, etc., I can recognize what is reasonable and what isn't. You have to know so much about so many things, and I'm convinced that you just have to wade in and do it.

CASEWRITER: You feel he's been wading.

E. J.:   Yes. But he has a different motor. It runs at a slower speed than mine.

Bill Walton came in, and E. J. mentioned that a meeting was going to be canceled. Bill said, "Pending further notification?" E. J. said, "Yes, let's try on Monday. Then why don't you talk to Mr. X? There are too many dates floating around—I don't know. Double-check with Linda and apologize for this. Cancel the room so Time-Life doesn't expect us. Double-check his schedule. See if Mr. Y can come."

CASEWRITER: What priorities do you put between your job and the rest of your life?

E. J.:   My free time is limited to one or two nights a week, but I often have last minute delays. I have a tough time making the transition from a "work" personality to a "social" personality. I have a bad temper. Poor performance irritates me, and in my performance reviews I've had it said that I am "intolerant of people less smart than I." I'm really very intolerant of dummies, I guess. I can explain something one or two times, that's OK. The third time I get curt, and the fourth time is a bad time. I have no patience. I tend to lose my temper. If you *know* someone isn't bright—then you're tolerant. But if someone's been 15 years on the job and he comes in from 9 to 5 and has the dullard mentality with no pride in his work—that's what really irritates me. I get to be a table pounder—I curse and shout. My losing my temper, when I *really* do it, unfortunately is really effective. There are types here who after I do it will really produce for at least two weeks. I use it as a little management tool. It's theory X. Normally we like to be theory Y. But sometimes it's X time.

CASEWRITER: What lies ahead do you think?

E. J.:   Having achieved some success, it gives you confidence. The divisions go through cycles of where executives come from. Our division is currently experiencing accelerated growth and profitability. So, we can see unlimited possibilities for us and our bosses moving up. Also, Columbia just bought a related company. So the opportunities will be there, too.

I know how to get things done across—horizontally. I need to learn how to develop people, how to convince people, how to work vertically. My career path coming up appears to have two forks. Either I'll stay in a corporation like this, having people work for me, and having management responsibilities to develop them to function well within the organization. Or, I could go to a small company where I'd have ownership interest. And there I'd be an activist, particularly if it was my money. I've gotten self-confidence this year in my marketing ability. I'd get to know it all—whatever business I was in. I'd devote 15 hours a day and be totally absorbed.[3]

The casewriter then talked with E. J.'s assistant, a young man named Bill Walton.

WALTON: Before coming here, I spent two and a half years in training at a major cosmetic marketer. I wanted to go into international marketing, but there weren't any jobs, so I accepted one with the marketing group here. I moved here because I liked the idea of coming into a smaller, less structured situation where you could do it yourself. Here there are only eight to ten product managers. Basically, I'm in a training period. I've always felt like an interloper on the two new brands because they were already in process when I came, but I have a chance now for creativity with the third new product we're developing.

E. J. has a fairly important job, with about 30 percent of all the division advertising dollars. This means there is horrendous detail and a lot of opportunities for panic. Before, I worked on a couple of old brands; but here, working on new brands we're constantly putting out fires. This job makes you capable of holding 360 balls in the air at the same time. At my other company, I spent 90 percent of my time on advertising and promotion duties. This job is filling in my experience in a lot of areas—financial, production, working through the manufacturing department.

Implicit in the system here is a strong brand product manager system. The other departments don't resent us because they know we're supposed to be involved. The thread of continuity comes from brand management people. The brand managers set the key dates for each element of the program, for example.

E. J. goes at such a pace the list never quits. At first, I was bothered by it, trying to juggle all the things, trying to select which thing to do. It was very frustrating. Now I'm not frustrated by it. I try to select the important things and do them.

E. J. is very thorough—never satisfied until he knows that things are being done his way. This may be going overboard. E. J. tends to get into such detail that people who'd normally do a job on their own end up waiting to be told exactly what to do, or exactly what E. J. wants, because they know it will have to be done that way in the end. For example, suppose we were to do a merchandising piece for a magazine. Ordinarily, the product manager would call in someone from the sales promotion area and outline the whole thing briefly and say, "You coordinate it and draft up a merchandising piece and let me see it." Generally, what they draft up would be OK. But with E. J. it's not that way. If it's not precisely what E. J. would have written, it's changed. So pretty soon these guys stop trying. They're tired

---
[3] The casewriter's observations of a typical morning for E. J. are outlined in Exhibit 3.

EXHIBIT 3

Casewriter Observations of E. J.'s Morning Routine

8:30 1. Sales department employee visits E. J. for social purposes.

      2. Market researcher, Sam, comes in to discuss note he left that morning.

      3. E. J. calls New York City ad agency.

      4. Bill comes in to discuss what E. J. told Sam earlier.

      5. Manufacturing man comes in to discuss labels for box. Says memo is coming down about the cost, the making, and the applying of labels.

      6. Sales planning man comes in to get information.

      7. Call from agency to E. J. re marketing. E. J. discusses conversation held with agency member yesterday. Raises the fact of feeling strongly on an issue that should be discussed seriously.

      8. Bill comes back. E. J. tells him how to cut the paper to have it fit the Xerox machine.

      9. E. J. calls back agency to continue conversation. Tone of conversation is reasonable and friendly. E. J. acknowledges personel feelings, says, "But I can be overruled, this is my own feeling, but I want to know your feelings and also how to use the test scores." Reviews a production schedule for TV shooting.

9:30   In the subsequent half hour, E. J. read three memos, and then wrote a one-page reply very quickly, with a quick phone call to check some data. Then E. J. called Bill in and gave him some directions to pick up samples from manufacturing, to check on the status of some concepts from the medical division, and made two more phone calls.

10:00 1. Call from a salesman for *Good Housekeeping*. E. J. searches files for information.

      2. Agency employee calls and long detailed discussion follows on market test results, the amount of time needed to make a film, and methods needed to get the film done on time.

11:45 1. Four more telephone calls and a meeting, initiated by E. J., for sales promotion.

      2. E. J. goes to comptroller's office for some financial data and is back just before noon to drive to New York City for meeting with the ad agency.

E. J. paces a lot, reads everything that comes onto the desk, and scribbles a note, discards the item or puts it off with a notation into the out basket. Nothing sits on the desk very long.

of doing something and having it rejected, and so they come to think, "Why put myself out?"

CASEWRITER: What would you do differently in that instance?

WALTON: If I were doing it, the merchandising piece, I'd be a little more charitable. I'd accept their work from them more readily. I wouldn't agonize over one or two words if the piece basically said what I wanted it to. Because you'll never find anyone who is exactly like yourself.

CASEWRITER: What would you borrow from E. J's style?

WALTON: E. J. has made me much, much more aware of details. I'll be aware of details when I'm on my own, but I'll stop short of caring that much. To die over one or two words is not my style. After all, how much time is there to devote to the job? Generally, you try to minimize the small things so you have more time to devote to the important. However, if you're willing to work from 7 to 7 every day like E. J. does, you can give time to the minutia. Not many people can work that way.

The job of being a product manager best utilizes the talents of an entrepreneurial-type person. E. J. is this type. But if you're truly an entrepreneur, you can't be happy in a corporation. The product manager job seems to attract the entrepreneurs, but it can't keep them satisfied forever. Product managers are always looking for a better situation. Because it's not truly entrepreneurial, they tend to get frustrated. If you're an entrepreneur, you want to do it yourself. You can't do it in a larger corporation, because you have to work through groups, and things are beyond your control. A person like E. J. is much more used to the corporation than the corporation is to E. J.

I think ultimately E. J. would be happier as an entrepreneur—with a finger in every pie. The mistakes would be E. J.'s own making. On the other hand, in a corporation, other people do make mistakes for you. There are things that you have no control over. For example, you have no real control over the assembly line in a plant, but if things go wrong, it affects you.

To gain impressions from other people who worked with E. J., the casewriter talked with Sam Bodkins, assistant director of market research, and Pat Miles, who like Tom Bird is a product group supervisor.

BODKINS: E. J., in particular, is much more inquisitive than most product managers—very demanding and very bright. E. J. understands research, always asking "What about this or that?" More often than not, E. J. is right, which is sort of annoying. All product managers suffer from wanting answers to come out the way they want them to. Product managers, including E. J., are interested in research only in the short run, for short-run solutions and justifications—on the grounds that (a) they may not be here next year, (b) they may forget about it by next year, and (c) there are so many things mucking up a situation that you can't blame anybody. If something goes wrong, is it advertising, distribution, etc.—whose fault is it? A product manager is judged by how well a product does. You can be a hero this year and a bum the next.

CASEWRITER: What makes a good product manager?

BODKINS: It's hard to say. Essentially a product manager has to be a tremendously diversified person with a diversified background. A lot of it is gut feel. Knowing when to do things. You have to rely on the ad agency and on a sales force—and you have to nudge them. You're a traffic cop. You're a monitor with a lot of curiosity and sensitivity. They usually tend to be strong-willed and egocentric, but I'm not sure that's a necessity. E. J. is. I wonder sometimes if it doesn't work against them. Working with E. J. can develop into a pain in the ass. It's nice to work for someone who isn't always after you. What's more amazing about E. J. is being right most of the time. Usually you get a tough time from the product managers and they don't know what they're talking about. But E. J. is usually right, along with being tough, bright, strong-willed—everybody admits E. J. is bright, but every once in a while you have to get slapped down.

PAT MILES: E. J.'s style is successful and effective. The majority of the people around here are financial marketing types rather than merchants. They don't have a feel for products; they feel the balance sheets and the charts. So they need someone who is constantly whipping and nudging, who has a sense of the product. E. J. wears everybody down—it doesn't make for great friendships, but it gets the job done.

E. J.'s one of the few who has the capacity to learn all aspects of one job. But as promotions come, E. J.'s going to have to temper that pushy style.

E. J. would be fantastic as an entrepreneur. But I don't see E. J. putting up with a corporate structure or a political structure—E. J. is a person with too much to do.

3 | *Charles Bullard (A)*

For Charles Bullard the weekend at home was the only break in the management training course to which the company had sent him at a distant university. Nevertheless, Bullard and his wife spent a part of that weekend visiting with Bullard's boss, Jim Winship.

The Winship home, in Kansas City's finest residential area, was a comfortable one. Bullard and his wife listened with real interest as Jim Winship told anecdotes about the old days with the company. Winship, now in his early 50s and regional manager for Kansas and six surrounding states, had begun working for the company nearly 30 years ago in this same territory. His stories reflected his fondness for the independent distributors and retailers in the territory, his loyalty to the company, and above all his almost religious commitment to the company's principal product—the carefully milled, clean bakers' flour which had been the beginning of the company reputation.

Bullard would have appreciated a drink. Somehow social occasions with his boss seemed smoother when lubricated with alcohol. But the Winships, gracious hosts though they were, did not tolerate smoking or drinking in their home.

Seated comfortably, listening to Winship's pleasant drawl, Bullard mused about the paradox of their relationship—he admired Winship, admired his logic and clarity, but there was always a powerful element of tension and stress present when they were together.

Perhaps, he thought, it stemmed from the differences in their aims. Winship had been offered the big job in Chicago which entailed management of the company's activities for the entire central United States and included the post of chairman of the board of the large bakery supply firm which the company owned in Chicago.

And he had turned it down, as he refused any promotion which would require his move from Kansas City. Winship's marriage had brought him position in local society, and probably money as well. He enjoyed his road trips through the territory—the independent distributors and commercial bakers in cities like Emporia, Dubuque, Grand Island, and Joplin were old friends. He was on the board of his church and participated actively in its work. He was at home, and at ease.

While he himself, Bullard thought, was still pushing. He had joined the company 15 years ago in the marketing services group, covering a number of states from his home base in Hutchinson, Kansas, where he lived with his mother. His job then had been to aid the independent distributors in their promotions of flour to bakers and grocery chains, actually using the flour in demonstration work in the bakeries and setting up displays and taking inventories in grocery stores. Although his territory was within the region under Winship's management—and Winship had been of great help to him in using his good relationships in the region to introduce Bullard—he reported formally through a different channel (see Exhibit 1—"old" organization chart) to a manager of marketing services whose responsibilities spanned the entire country.

EXHIBIT 1
"Old" Organization
(partial chart)

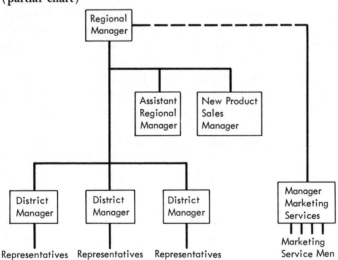

I traveled all over hell's half acre. I traveled all the way to Miami, to New Orleans . . . the company didn't hesitate to call me off my regular work and send me anywhere. . . . I'd go home on weekends if I was in driving distance, and if I wasn't I stayed out.

And I was put into marketing and sent to Iowa, which was a cesspool; they moved me in there because with my promotional background and Winship's introductions, I could talk to the distributors there where we were losing market share every year. I was able to do some things with these people . . . local advertising campaigns, baking demonstrations, in order to get them broader distribution. If they couldn't afford to hire the work done I had to be on the go, roll up my sleeves, and spend weekends working. A lot of that was not my job, but I did it.

One of Bullard's successes in Iowa, which had brought him to the attention of the company's top management, had been his "conventionette." He had decided, when he took over the Iowa territory, that one of the chief problems which the company faced in maintaining its market share lay in the low morale of the salesmen who worked for the independent distributors. Accepting full responsibility for sales in Iowa, he felt no need to consult with Winship; he took the format of a major convention which the company had recently run for its own organization, scaled down the original quarter of a million dollar show, and organized a "conventionette" for the distributor salesmen in Iowa.

We got tapes and a lot of slide material and I hired some college kids and we did, with a few kids and these tapes, an approximation of the show. As word leaked out that this was going to be a pretty hot item, officers of the company wanted to get on the program. And they did, and they sent in a professional director to take it off my hands and really brush it up . . . and we put on a show that was really out of this world.

And Winship didn't even come. He was the regional manager, and he had some excuse to be somewhere else. The distributors in Nebraska heard about it, and it was repeated there, and they embellished it because now they had the professional who had taken it over. Then they moved it to Missouri. And though the general manager of our department and other officers of the company had been highly complimentary to me, the next time I was with Winship he read me out for the time that I had spent.

I had put it on for less than $3,000. . . . In Nebraska it cost them $13,000, and $16,000 in Missouri to do no more than we had done . . . and my salary at the time was $700 per month.

During this period the company was moving into new product areas, mainly in consumer convenience frozen foods, primarily through acquisitions. Winship made no secret of his disdain for these new products; like "conventionette," he felt that products like Toast-n-Taste (a line of frozen breads and rolls) were beneath the stature of his company . . . they were passing fads which could not replace well-milled flour. Nevertheless, management personnel from the acquired firms were moving into important positions in the company, and Bullard was expected to persuade—and did persuade—his distributors in Iowa to take on and sell the new lines, often requiring that they cease selling competitive merchandise. He took action and generated acceptance of the new products, often before consulting Winship or his immediate superior, the district manager, because he understood that company policy now required new product distribution.

Actually, the district manager, who at that time had occupied the organizational position between Bullard and Winship, was not deeply involved. He was an elderly man, the nephew of a founder of the company, who had once said: "Look, you're Winship's boy . . . you're getting things done, and you keep me informed—which is more than a lot of people do. As long as you keep me informed, that's all I want."

And it had been true that Bullard was "Winship's boy." He had been living then in Iowa, and Winship would telephone him at home and chat for hours with advice, instruction, and company gossip. Winship took pride in the many compliments which the distributors paid to Bullard's capacity for hard work and long hours; he seemed to feel that the training and guidance which he had provided had been largely responsible for Bullard's success.

Winship's region was a part of the Central States Division, whose top-management group was heavily comprised of men who had come to the company in the recent series of acquisitions. The general manager of the division was William Tuck, who had been president and major stockholder of Friar Tuck Frozen Foods—he had no special commitment to the flour product which was the company's mainstay; his real interest was in the development and promotion of new products.

Bullard's vigorous promotion of new products came to the attention of division management people. With their backing Bullard was promoted from his Iowa sales job and named new products sales manager, reporting directly to Winship. Looking back, Bullard stated:

> I had known about that job for three months and knew that I was going to be promoted. And Winship called me into his office and said he had a job like this and there were five or six people around the region who could really do a good job on the thing . . . he didn't mention me. One of them was a kid out of the training program who had been with us for 15 months. I never understood why he discussed them with me. At that time I had had more than ten years with the company.
>
> And when I came to Kansas City and got started on the new job, Winship started trying to change my method of operation and he wanted to get me back on the old product. He repeatedly tried to get me off the new products that I was responsible for . . . responsible to him for.

Bullard thought back to the experience with Toast-n-Taste, one of the new products for which he had been responsible:

> The pressure was on to get broader distribution of Toast-n-Taste. . . . We were selling Toast-n-Taste to only about 50 percent of our distributors . . . and everytime I'd want to go to some big distributor to make a Toast-n-Taste presentation Winship would block me; he'd say: "No, it's not the time, there are other things that are more important." And finally, Winship left town one Friday for a month's vacation and the division manager called me in and said, "Go," and by the time Winship got back from vacation we were up to 90 percent distribution.

Bullard had learned later that his actions with Toast-n-Taste became a source of difficulty for Winship, although Winship never discussed the matter with him. Division management had understood the episode to mean that Winship was hindering new product sales and that Bullard was able to accomplish more only in Winship's absence.

Shortly thereafter a new job—the number two job in each region—was created throughout the company with the title of marketing planner for the region (see Exhibit 2). Winship announced Bullard as the man

EXHIBIT 2
"New" Organization
(partial chart)

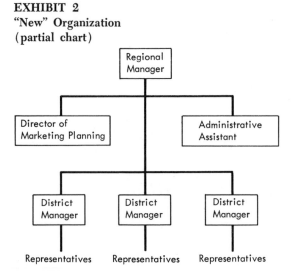

for this job in his region and indicated to the people in his organization that this meant that Bullard would be a sort of promotion man.

> That man put me in that job and never told me it was a promotion. I found out later that this was a real promotion. Tuck had me in his office one day telling me what a great promotion I had and I said, "What

promotion?" He blew his top and asked if I hadn't gotten a raise, and when I said, "No, sir," he said, "Well, you'll have one . . . back to the first day."

Musing over the past in the comfort of Winship's home, Bullard suddenly realized that he was being addressed directly.

At the conclusion of the management training course, Winship was saying, Bullard need not necessarily come back to his position as marketing planner in Kansas City. Division management was interested in having him in Chicago as part of the division headquarters staff in an assignment which would constitute a significant promotion. Winship seemed awkward as he expressed this good news.

Bullard was uncomfortable. He would have preferred to learn about this potential promotion and relocation without his wife present. He realized, too, that what really made him uneasy was that after 15 years in the region under Winship, he did not like the idea of leaving.

4 | *Charles Bullard (B)*

When Charles Bullard returned to the management training course after his weekend at home, he was distracted and unable to keep pace with his classwork. Whether to take the promotion to division headquarters staff or to continue in the region as marketing planner plagued him. He approached one of his instructors at the school explaining that his preoccupation was keeping him from participating in class. The instructor suggested that Bullard might be able to clarify his dilemma by talking it out. In the ensuing discussion Bullard made the following comments:

> I walk that room back there a hell of a lot and I've gone down to the ocean and sat on the rocks down there by myself a good bit and I hear the pigeons every morning when they start up about 5:00 A.M. This thing is bugging me. . . .
>
> I don't know whether it's frustration over my problem with Winship. . . . I wonder if I'm upset about progress or lack of progress in the job. Although in the last three or four years, I've moved farther and faster than almost anyone in the company. . . . I don't put all the blame on Winship; I'm inclined to think that probably 60 to 70 percent is my fault. . . . I really think that most of my problems are self-induced.
>
> I'd really rather not go back [to Kansas City] because frankly Jim Winship has surrounded himself with people I don't want to work with. One of them is a liar, a thief, and I mean this. Another guy there is hated by everyone in the whole place—I don't want to be around him. He's got another one that's incompetent. The man seems to surround himself with incompetents. . . . I don't want to be around them.

51

But if I don't go back I see it as a kind of failure, that I couldn't sell this man on what I could do for him, and I couldn't sell him off of some horrible mistakes he made on personnel selection.

I have had in my life two real failures: I got kicked out of West Point, with a medical discharge, and that has always concerned me. After that, I went to Tech and I really screwed up at Tech. The first year I was there I carried about 40 semester hours and they kicked me out of school and they should have. And those two failures came at a time when my family was not too well-heeled financially.

My father was 56 when I was born, my mother was 44. Both of them had been married before. I had five half brothers and three half sisters . . . there are only two of them still alive. My oldest brother was an officer in World War I, and he had been married long enough for me to be his child. My father thought he was almost God reincarnated, really. He was a hero. He had the DSC, Silver Star, Purple Heart. . . . He went to the military prep school at home and he was the senior cadet officer. . . . He was sort of a God to me. . . . My father died when I was 14 years old. My mother put me in the dorm over there [at the military prep school] and she had to go back to work after the old man died. But I was living in the school. . . . My half brother had been senior cadet captain for one year. Well, I beat him. I was it for two years.

My father's children for some reason at that point didn't speak to me. It had to do with some mess with my mother about money. They quit speaking to my mother and me, and this was ridiculous because we lived in the same town. So I set out to show them, and I had the drive to do that. . . . It was the biggest disappointment in my life when that guy [his oldest brother] quit speaking to me. And I was all of 14 years old.

Anyway, after getting kicked out of Tech I went to the West Coast and worked for six months. I got hepatitis, and they had to ship me home. When I got better I went back to Tech, and from that point on I did it all right at school. . . . I ended up with an A.B. in math.

I've always been regarded, frankly, as an oddball. I've been to gatherings and stand up and tell management that this program, and this and this, is wrong. And I've infuriated people doing this. . . . Winship has several times saved my neck when I was pushing for something.

I like the man. I get horribly mad with him, angry when I perceive what he has possibly done to me and the positions he has put me in. On the other hand, I realize that the brass of our company have used me to beat the devil out of him.

I perhaps have allowed myself to be used this way. . . . I haven't consciously gone after the guy. I think I can say what my problem is: I tend to put on my armor and charge right out.

I can give you one other thing: I have more diplomas from armed forces correspondence schools than anyone. I'm a major, and never have been on active duty.

5 | Arthur Walton

Art Walton left the meeting in something of a daze. It was hard to believe that he was going to lose control of the key engineering group around which he had so painstakingly built his department. He'd have nothing left but a scattering of service groups, now. It wasn't that this loss would hurt him financially or damage his chances for promotion. It had nothing to do with him, really. He knew he had a well-established reputation for running the best department of its kind in the company. It was just one of the battles in the war between R&D and production, just part of the struggle for survival that Art's latest boss was going through. As much as Art could understand that his production engineering group had to be transferred to the production department during this period of crisis when development contracts for the division were dwindling away, it still left him with no real job. Now, Art couldn't continue ignoring that conscience of his which had been nagging him for some months, insisting that he leave the Ribble Company and get back on the track of the career he had always wanted for himself.

ART WALTON—THE EARLY YEARS

Art Walton was a Vermonter by birth and upbringing. His father had represented a large company in the northern New England region until the early stages of the Depression, when he was asked to return to New York City for assignment. He refused the offer, preferring to resign, in spite of the scarcity of jobs, rather than leave the small-town Vermont life which he and his family had come to love. The Waltons were forced to live quite simply thenceforward, but Art never felt they were "poor." In fact, he recalled his childhood with great enjoyment. His family was a close unit, sharing together—mother, father, and two sons—household and athletic activities, particularly ice skating. Art's father found more time than most fathers to be with his family.

Art had to admit, when his friends kidded him about it, that the stereotypical image of the Vermonter, the "Green Mountain Boy," was one he cherished. He wanted to be resourceful and independent as his father had been and as, it seemed to Art, most of the important adults in his childhood were. Too, he wanted to feel that he was being true to the basic, even earthy, values which were so often associated with Vermont.

Art considered himself an adequate student in high school. He got B's most of the time. He enjoyed school as an integral part of an enjoyable growing up, though he never considered himself a prime student. More important to his life were extracurricular school activities, social functions and athletics, most particularly skating. In his senior year of high school, he won membership on the Olympic hockey team. During the year after high school, he worked in a small industrial plant to get money for college, trained for the Olympics, and won hockey scholarships at several northeastern colleges. Then, just before he was to leave for the Olympics, he had a serious skating accident which resulted in a permanently disabling spine injury.

For a year he recuperated. As he thought back on the incidents of this period, he could not recall undergoing serious shock,

> . . . a breast-beating type of thing that you see in the movies. There were temporary unsettling thoughts and reflections, but I never felt a terrible loss. I guess I simply took it as a fact that I wouldn't be able to do all the things I had always done. I got pretty good at living in a brace. I don't skate nearly so well as I used to, but I can get around. I did a fair amount of traveling around for a while, helping other people get used to orthopedic difficulties.

HIGHER EDUCATION

Even before his personal association with the profession, Art had wanted to be an orthopedic surgeon.

> Then some teacher told me I was so punk in Latin I would not make premed requirements. I've since found that is no longer true and it makes me mad. Anyway, I decided on engineering.

Several of his college scholarships were honored, despite Art's inability to skate competitively.

Being a year older than my classmates and still not too ambulatory, I ground away and got straight A's, each term getting more boring than the one before. Then I heard about a program at another university, a joint affair between the business and engineering schools leading to a Masters in engineering and management. This seemed to me to be just what I wanted, and I was accepted. I wanted to be more technical than business people I'd known in Vermont, but even more I wanted to do things on my own, to manage something. I guess that was why I was so attracted to surgery; you were on your own but with good technical training behind you. Shortly before I was to start this combined program, it was discontinued, so I went through with the regular engineering program and got my M.S.

After graduation, Art married a Vermont girl and immediately matriculated in the M.B.A. degree program in the same university in which he had taken his M.S. In his application Art described his ambition

. . . to be the largest frog in a small, well-run puddle. I hope to work for a larger firm or firms for a few years, in positions of liaison between businessmen and scientists. There is a real need for more mutuality of knowledge and sympathy between the two.

He went on to declare that he planned, after gaining this experience, to manage the affairs of a small company, preferably one in a rural setting with substantial opportunity for outdoor activity.

Art's business education experience was both intensive and just what he had been aiming for.

I loved the small-business course; did well in production, which was a natural with my background; had a great deal of trouble in finance; enjoyed the course for sales managers and did well in it; the course in human behavior was interesting and I did so-so in it. I was pretty much a slightly above-average student.

ART'S JOB HISTORY

When graduation from business school came, along with the Waltons' first child (they were to have three more over the next few years), Art decided to short-cut his original job plans and go right into a small business.

In seven years I had taken only two summers off from studying. I'd gotten pretty sick of it and the late hours. I wanted autonomy and the good life of Vermont, or some place like it. Small business was my main drive; getting away from the hard-driving, cosmopolitan life was second.

Before school ended, Art heard of a small food-processing company which was looking for a manager.

I spent a month looking at that opportunity but turned it down. Instead I went back to Vermont and joined a small-business consulting company which had just been formed. The consulting was kind of interesting as an interim thing, but I think all of us in the company were trying to find the perfect opening in the perfect little company. The job was satisfying in many ways. It was frustrating in one respect. You never saw anything through to completion. Your best-laid plans were lodged in someone else's hands, and they too often misfired.

Through a friend, Art learned of a small machine tool company in New Hampshire.

A fellow a little older than I had just bought it and wanted a second in command. I came in as vice president, and while he acted as salesman, I stayed home and ran the place. For a while we did quite well, building up from 15 to 40 employees. We sold a limited line of tools to textile companies. Then came the Australian wool embargo, and our regular business just disappeared. We staved off failure for a while by getting small subcontracts. Every Friday afternoon, pay time, we'd meet the mail train, hoping customers we had phoned the day before, begging for our money, would have put their checks in the mail. Sometimes we made the payroll, sometimes we didn't. This was a wearing experience, but in many ways it was very gratifying.

Eventually the banks foreclosed us. Maybe if both of us had had five years' more experience we'd have seen farther ahead, used our imagination more, and developed some market possibilities. It would have taken real genius with what we had to work with—practically no capital and rundown machinery, but maybe somehow we could have gotten around our problems. But we were blinded by our optimism.

Art's next opportunity brought him back to the city, where he was offered a business manager's post in a small, new, manufacturing subsidiary established by an engineering consulting firm to carry on a government contract. He and a design engineer

. . . set up the facility in a small industrial town near the city, built our own buildings, a half-dozen or so, hired and trained some of our own people, and did all our own development and manufacturing work. I guess I just plain react to power. I enjoyed having a certain amount of power over the destinies of our several work groups. We lost the contract, I think, because we kept ourselves too insular technically. We tried to do it all ourselves without getting any development consultation. I didn't really understand that for a long time, neither did my partner. He has remained one of my closest friends, by the way.

For a time Art thought of going into the consulting part of the company's business.

With them behind me I thought I could get farther into the doing of things without having to bid adieu to my ideas once I'd thought of them. But, then a golden opportunity, at a 70 percent salary increase, came along to manage a young company, a specialty sheet metal forming outfit.

Art's new firm was owned by a few retired executives who turned operations over to Art. The major stockholder,

. . . an elderly gentleman, took a good look over my shoulder, but he was always a great help, never an impediment. He died, and none of the other stockholders took such constructive interest in what I was doing. I didn't realize what a loss this was until later. When I stepped in, it was a roaring business. Volume varied tremendously from month to month; but on three-fourths of a million dollars annual sales, we usually netted between ten and fifteen thousand dollars a month. The profit was fantastic. Then sales went to pot when two prime contractors of ours lost their contracts. Each week I had to lay off more people. I got to the point of staying full time on sales trips myself, doing anything to buttress our reps and drum up business when I should have been home some of the time, at least, looking after operations.

That was when I began to miss the old man. He would have made me cut back sooner, held back my youthful optimism and that of the other directors, and kept us from needlessly spending money holding onto people. It bothered the devil out of me laying off people who'd been there ten years and I'd only been there a year and a half.

Then I got into a disagreement with another senior stockholder. He wanted us to get into things I felt and feel were ridiculous, and which would simply have eaten away what few assets we had left. And he wouldn't back us in a joint venture with a complementing firm which I and the other directors felt held promise. It was a tough industry. We had a few unique production tricks, but there were others who could do much the same as we could. We did drive most of our local competitors to the wall before we went there. It does my ego good to know that the people who are running it now, under a recapitalization, aren't doing any better, and I am still credited, I hear, with having developed the only two profitable lines the company has.

It was the biggest shock of my life when I got kicked out. I should have seen it coming. I was the highest salaried person in the place, so my leaving would make the biggest saving. And this old stockholder kept asking me if one of my subordinates was ready for more responsibility. I just didn't pay any attention. I felt I was putting my all into it and, no matter what, in spite of all the layoffs, I wouldn't be let go. If we went under, we'd go under; but they wouldn't can the manager, as they do in baseball. I *was* the company. But, I was canned. It set me back for a while.

I think my trouble, my failure on that job, was I just wasn't such a hot salesman. I hated to go in and approach some pipsqueak buyer.

I used to stew about it. And I hated to go through those evenings out in Cleveland or someplace with some buyer and his wife whom I was obviously doing my best to bribe nicely. I despised it and didn't do it well. I was just too young to be hard-nosed and flint-hearted about it.

As I look back on it, I like to think now that I'd have sense enough not to break my back over every single buyer but say the hell with it, so-and-so just isn't worth this or send someone else to take him out on the town or send him a bottle next Christmas. Or, if I just had to do it, do it without all the zeal and yet repugnance behind the zeal. I think I could discriminate better now. I think if I had really decided one buyer was critical, I could have been more comfortable with the uncomfortable part of it. I'm afraid I just let fires come at me, and I fought them all as though they were all alike.

At this point I joined one of those so-called miracle electronic outfits, Solon Electronics. I went into Solon saying, "The hell with it, I will not try another small company." I'm ashamed to think how long I just existed in that job, not putting anything in or getting anything out. I just didn't really give a damn.

Solon was run by a charming guy. He welcomed me as the white-haired lad he'd been waiting for to be his number two man. It took me a month to discover that that's what he'd told three others. Each, like me, lasted as the golden boy for six months, and then we got shunted off and just hung around. Toward the end I picked up a bit. I became co-director of engineering, and then I started up a production engineering function. I was looking around for opportunities in other companies when Solon closed its doors.

THE RIBBLE COMPANY

During the year and a half at Solon, while he "convalesced" from so unceremoniously being fired, Art slightly modified his career aspirations. He still wanted a small-business management opportunity. But he hoped to find it within a larger, more stable institution, looking for an opportunity not vastly different from the management of the consulting firm subsidiary which he had so greatly enjoyed.

About the time I was thinking of getting on my feet and moving out of Solon, there was a lot of talk about the Ribble Company acquiring small firms and leaving them in at least a semiautonomous state. Ribble figured they could beat competition by buying up a small outfit with a unique idea, pour in a heavy investment from a central research group but in all other ways leave it pretty much autonomous. I figured what I needed to do was get into a job at Ribble that would give me the kind of background they would want for a manager of one of these small companies. I thought production engineering would do just that. I wanted a job that would be the bridge between research and manufacturing so I could say that I knew the big-company system, and that I knew how to manage this tension-member between the developers and the producers. Then I'd be the logical choice to run a smaller part of the company.

Art was hired as manager of the engineering section in one of Ribble's more advanced development divisions. The Ribble Company's annual sales were in the several hundred million dollar range. Art's division dealt almost exclusively in government contracts, each of which amounted to several millions of dollars revenue. As the division developed, so did the extent of Art's jurisdiction, until, by 1962, he had built what he considered to be an integrated production engineering liaison unit effectively operating between basic research and manufacturing.

A lot of graduates from the business school I'd gone to were in it at that time. They were trying to get more people with such training to bolster their technical people. One of them helped me get the job. A lot of them have left since. I think lack of direction in the company has driven them to find some company which seemed to have a straighter aim. But, at the time, the company seemed to me to have the stability I was looking for. A lot has happened in the past four years to convince me otherwise, at least partly. Direction is terribly quixotic. Divisions come and go, and so do presidents. The people are handled kindly. It's kind of a welfare state. A man loses his job overnight, but they always find another spot for him where he can't do any harm, and without a loss in pay. It makes people think it really doesn't matter what they do, they'll always be taken care of somehow. Not a very healthy situation for the company.

I started out with two production engineering supervisors reporting to me. Then when my superior, the development department head, left, I applied for and got his job and that added several more sections: components and material engineers, publications prototype shops and procurement. Then our outfit merged with another lab, and I got several more sections, which gave me all of engineering for our division, except for purely design groups. My lack of electronic system engineering training keeps me from wanting or getting the latter.

There were a lot of political shenanigans going on during all of this. In each case, at least two departments could logically have made a case for getting hold of the sections I got. We each would sell various parties on what we had to offer. The Machiavellis in this process tended to lose out. The winning tactic, at least the one I always used, was to put up the logic as I saw it and let the logic do my fighting for me. It always worked for me.

In some other places this idea has gotten me in trouble. I tend to my knitting, do the job, and let that pull me through. It has worked for me at Ribble in spite of the fact that I have been somewhat insensitive to some of the political maneuverings which have gone on around me. I'm just one level below where all the chaotic shifts tend to take place—I've had seven bosses since I came here.

I guess I've been rather single-minded about running my own operation and letting the rest of the corporate world go into all kinds of gyrations around me without it getting to me. I get my kicks out of meeting and wrestling with the day-to-day things. As I've added groups to my jurisdiction, each has presented problems. My attention has focused on each of them successively until they became integrated and were working well. When that job is over, I step back two or three steps and look for another trouble spot. Of course, we spend a lot of time on long-range planning meetings. In fact, it is those plans that have been so shaken by the recent loss of our most central unit, production engineering.

The last trouble spot left in the department was the publications group. I guess I'm pretty paternalistic. Unless someone who works for me has his affairs running pretty smoothly, I tend to get pretty much into his business, mostly by sweet talk. I worked with the publications head for a long time on this basis. I tried to find a way we could help each other. I wanted him to let me get him some people to help get some facts together that would help make sense of his problem. In this case he just wouldn't accept my help. I felt he needed to replace two of his people or reorganize their units and get them some help. He flatly refused. It was only then that I had to agree with the rest of my staff people that nothing more could be done. Finally, I backed off and simply told him that if those two people failed, it would be his neck which was out, not theirs. They failed and I had to replace him. This has been my usual way of operating. So long as we can work out a way to help each other, I'll stick with him. But if he refuses the help, then that is his decision and he's got to live by it. If his decision is wrong and he can't keep up, then he is going to forfeit something and maybe it's his job.

Now I just don't have any fires left to fight. We've won the respect of the design engineers. I have a group of men who are very loyal to me and to the way the department is being run, who work extremely well together—they seem to sense what needs to be done before anyone brings it up overtly. And my last real trouble section has been getting straightened out in the last few months.

Art had been singled out by divisional and corporate management on a number of occasions for managing the most effective product support engineering department in the Ribble Company. His salary level reflected the confidence of his superiors. However, the Ribble Company, shortly after Art joined it, abandoned its policy of purchasing and maintaining the autonomy of small manufacturers. Art's expectation to head one of these subsidiaries, thus, disappeared. Still, while there were production engineering fires to be fought, he thought little of moving on to a situation which would provide the small-company satisfactions he still so deeply desired.

> To some extent the short run obscures the long. The fires come up, you deal with them and move on to the next. It's like surgery, a kind of sport, a challenge from the immediate environment. Either you win or you lose, but then the game is over and you go on to the next game, next week.
>
> I have never really understood myself well enough to know whether I was being cowardly in not going back into the small-business fray, or whether I was misguided in thinking that that's where I should be just because it was across the brow of the hill. I think I've gotten too much of a kick out of doing a good job totally within my limited responsibility. I've got very much fun out of that, and I have paid too little attention to the world around me, just hoping that this kind of record will open up other vistas if the larger environment fails around me. Which is a kind of naive hope.

THE LOSS OF PRODUCTION ENGINEERING

The sudden news that the production engineering section was to be withdrawn from his department brought Art up short as he was driving home from the meeting that night.

> That production engineering section is the core of my department. I created it. My 300 people revolve around that section. Without it I will have a lot of people reporting to me, a great variety of functions, but I won't and the department won't have the real driving interest. With our contracts slipping away, overhead has to be cut, and we and production have been duplicating a lot of functions. We can't continue to exist separately. I had hoped we could take over the two smaller groups in production which do our kind of work. More of that infighting I've been trying to steer clear of. This isn't important to a lot of people but it's major to me. If it goes through, as I guess it will, I'll get so frustrated I don't see how I can avoid making a major job change for myself.
>
> I can't kid myself any longer that I've really got anything here—I know I'm doing wrong by myself to stay on—it's just been so much fun. I can't see anything at Ribble for me once I set aside those day-to-day challenges. And now that I've been able to get the pieces of the department working well together, I can't say I haven't fulfilled my responsibility for developing my department. Of course, even with the loss of the production engineering group there will still be day-to-day challenges but not a long-term challenge to be worked through and solved. Is it enough to say at my age [39] that I have a smoothly running department filled with people who are loyal to me and to the concepts we've developed? Wouldn't I rather be able to say I've run an organization of some size, some scope, and done it competently, imaginatively, with drive?

Am I just kidding myself and that's why I've been holding back and haven't done anything? Am I just temporarily frustrated with large business and the politics? But, in a smaller outfit, at least you deal directly with everyone who influences you and what you're doing. It's more than just reporting to a different level. Is that what I want then, another chance in a smaller business? Then again, maybe after the shock of this disappointment wears off in a few days, I'll see it just a little differently.

6 | *Betty Johnson*

In 1971, Betty Johnson was a product manager in the Toiletries Division of Acme Products Corporation. She was single, in her early 30s, and faced the career choices confronting an entrepreneurially oriented product manager in a large corporation.

The casewriter discussed with Betty and others how, if at all, the fact of her being a woman affected her business life.

CASEWRITER: How did you happen to choose business?

BETTY JOHNSON: I got kicked out of college for "underachieving" in my sophomore year. My parents couldn't believe it! The dean said, "Take a year off." So I worked during the day as a receptionist, and went to college at night; and then second semester I went to school full time. I realized how limited my future was without more education. My original school took me back for my senior year. During that year, I visited both law school and business school classes and realized, purely and simply, I enjoyed making profits, making money.

I had a marketing concentration at Harvard and I wrote to the top ten advertising agencies, came to New York for interviews, and kept hearing the fact that none of the clients had women as product managers. They said things like, "As a woman, you can't eat with men, you can't travel with men, you can't talk to men about a million dollar budget."

I had one interview with the agency I eventually went with and heard this jazz about women again. But by this time, I was getting annoyed so I replied, "I can do one thing with your clients that you can't or else you'd be fired." The man interviewing me thought that was funny; then he asked, "What if you got pregnant?" I said, "Well, I'm from the South and my mother's old-fashioned, so I'd probably get married." He thought that was funny too, so he hired me. What I didn't know at the time was that he was the chairman of the board.

I see myself for the next three or four years in business. My critical middle-age identity crisis will come around age 35. At that point I would have to decide what should take what proportion of time. This is excluding the possibility of meeting a man I wanted to marry. If that happened, I'd probably decide to get into my own business. With the security of a husband, I could take risks and have fun—not spend 16 hours on the job, because he'd be a major interest in my life. So far, I really haven't had to make the decision of what is the job, how big is that? And what is home, how big is that?

I have a laissez-faire attitude toward the future. I haven't plotted my next step here in the company. I've seriously thought of getting field sales experience, because I lack that. As long as I have a degree of success in my job, I'm not worried about whether I'm going to go up or sideways. I've never worried about promotions because I've always gotten them.

In terms of money, I guess I've always made the same amount of money or more than any man I've worked with. I expect it and I demand it. I think the money's important, but primarily because it's a measure of how you're doing.

I'd like a strong man to come along, but if he didn't it would not bother me all that much. Now, it's often a nuisance though, not to be married. You need an escort. A lot of people give you grief about it. It would be an asset, but if I never get married, I'd learn to live without it. I've dated three guys long term and could have gotten married. But in those relationships we found we never grew at the same rate, and I don't ever want to be in the situation where four years out you're not together anymore.

In social situations, I'm a little more relaxed—I'm not as driving as I am at work. I find I'm not flexible. Everything is fine as long as it's done my way.

I was adopted at birth, and my total home environment was completely different from the way I am. My parents are not drivers. My father enjoys small business, and my mother enjoys being a nursing instructor. I can remember asking them, "What do you want me to be?" And they said, "Anything you want to be is fine." They've never consciously pushed me in one direction or another. I'd be curious to see one of my natural parents—just to see what there might be of me there.

I've seen many of my friends getting married and grow apart. It's made me worry. Perhaps in breaking up three long-term relationships I have made that decision—home versus career—and chosen career. If I'm not married in four years, I intend to have a family, maybe by adoption, maybe not. You know I have two new products on the market. Big deal. I guess everybody wants to do something great and meaningful, and I'm convinced one of the most meaningful things you can do is to have children. It's an ego thing. To have something of you in someone else. But I would continue to work, too.

Other people in the company had opinions on Betty Johnson's managerial style and her role as a woman in business, including Fred Anello, a product manager; Ed Lawrence, director of marketing; and James Adams, president of the Toiletries Division.

FRED ANELLO: Betty has her own style. It's very animated and excitable. She's very vocal about positive and negative things, and her effectiveness is good. Could a man have done a better job? Probably not. It's a question of style.

In the beginning, I was annoyed because she could do things I never could as a man. She could be so vocal and never be shot down—because she's a woman. I've known three women professionally who've had jobs either ahead or equal to me. All three have been extremely vocal. Even their language may be overcompensating—profanity, swearing.

ED LAWRENCE: Betty's very fast afoot. She has very positive ideas. We hired her because we decided we needed a woman's point of view. In fact, we hired two women with that in mind. We wanted bright people with marketing experience and with a feminine orientation, so we wooed her away from the agency.

I have found that both women are apt to be more critical of our sales force than a man who's been out there would be. I found I had to get adjusted to them. They both have very definite and strong views. But I like them—they're bright. They have a warped point of view, preconceived ideas about distribution. And women get impatient—they think it should be done in 24 hours. I attribute this to their lack of experience as salespeople. With "belly-up" selling in your early days, you really get a feel for what's out there and what's possible.

Betty makes waves, but that's the price you pay for having a smart girl. Sometimes the price seems awfully high. But we hired her knowing she'd make waves—and she never wears out. God, that girl can work.

PAT MILES: Now is the time women should be going into larger corporations. They're more open-minded. Women are better trained and doing better jobs. The only problem here is that they have two women who are respected. They may not like us, but they respect us. They know they can't hold us back. If they could just figure out where we'd fit in—they'd be happy. They would like to find the *best* spot for us. Before, management types used to say, "She's good, so we'll try and keep her by giving her more dollars and a phoney title."

I cannot juggle a career and a marriage. I was married, and I chose a career—I divorced early. My husband insisted that the career be second, and I said it wouldn't be. It's a mistake for some women to try to juggle both. Certain people can do only one thing well. I'm very happy at what I'm doing.

CASEWRITER: How did you feel initially about being assigned to work for a woman, Bill?

BILL WALTON: Fine. I knew Betty. She wasn't a stranger, so it didn't bother me. I've never worked for a woman before; so if when I first came to the company I'd been told I was to work for a woman, I'd have been uncomfortable.

CASEWRITER: Would you work for a woman again voluntarily?

WALTON: It would depend on the woman. Betty's unusual. She's more male in her approach than most women. She tends to be more objective. Most of her decisions are based on logic rather than emotion, in contrast to women I've dealt with, not worked for, in the past.

CASEWRITER: In general, how would you characterize women in business?

WALTON: Most tend to be petty. Their feelings are hurt easily. Basically they're emotional.

CASEWRITER: Are there any positive things about women in business?

WALTON: Yes. Just because they are women, they can be charming and attractive. They provide a different point of view—they tend to look at things differently. They tend to be charitable.

CASEWRITER: How would you characterize men in business?

WALTON: They tend to be more logical, objective. Their feelings, at least overtly, get hurt less easily. They don't read deeper meanings into well-intentioned remarks. There are advantages to having women in business, single or married. They, like the bachelor males, feel no blow to their ego if they're fired. They have no responsibilities.

JAMES ADAMS: I can see women coming into the company in two ways—coming in on the board of directors, since about 15 to 20 percent of Acme Product's business is consumer oriented. And I can see them coming up through the ranks. The problem is with the women themselves. They've selected relatively definite areas. And the problem is that at the corporate level you try to get executives with more than one skill, even though one is predominant. Among the women here now, I haven't seen any inclination to get that other broad exposure. Furthermore, I think Betty would be lonely if she transferred over to manufacturing, for example. The work environment here seems to be more important for women.

I think women have a definite advantage in business if they are single. A single woman is really comparable to the 35-year-old bachelor who can afford to be more cavalier about things. A man with a family and who has 80 percent of his income going to fixed expenses is apt to say, "Oh, New York City isn't so bad," when you criticize it to him; whereas a person without those commitments is apt to be much more critical of things.

7 | *Glenn Taylor*

Glenn Taylor, age 50, held the position of vice president for finance and controller of the Sage Electronics Company.

Sage was a large and profitable electronics company which manufactured and marketed its products on a worldwide basis; its stock was listed on a major stock exchange. Mr. Taylor had joined the company ten years earlier as an assistant treasurer. Prior to joining Sage he had had a very successful career in the field of public accounting. Sage in fact used to be one of his clients when he worked for a large public accounting firm.

Taylor's work at Sage was impressive, and James Johnson, Sage's president, considered him one of the strongest men in top management. On several occasions James Johnson had credited Taylor for playing a valuable role in the rapid growth and success of the company. In recent years Sage had made a number of acquisitions, and Taylor had played a key role in negotiating the purchase terms. In addition, and almost single-handedly, Taylor had introduced most of the planning and control systems which guided the company. These systems included a management-by-objectives program and both long- and short-term profit planning systems involving budgeting of sales and expenses which were used for control purposes. They had been introduced as part of a major reorganization of Sage which took place several years ago. Taylor had designed the systems for use by line managers at the request of James Johnson who had hired him originally.

Glenn Taylor was born and raised in the Presbyterian faith. He considered himself a religious person, and tried to practice his religious principles in business. Business associates respected his high moral and ethical standards and his sense of fair play. Discussing his job, Glenn stated: "Central to the idea of controllership, it seems to me, are the ideas of responsibility, controls, and defining the rules of the game. The rules have to be administered fairly."

In the spring of 1970, Mr. Taylor hired Philip Hawkins as a special staff assistant. Hawkins started work on July 1, just three weeks after he had received his M.B.A. degree from a well-known eastern school of business administration. Hawkins had been in the top third of his graduating class; and although he had concentrated in finance and accounting, he had taken several courses in the organizational behavior area as part of his second-year program. During his second year Hawkins had written a research report on the behavioral aspects of control systems which Taylor considered "quite interesting." Though Hawkins viewed his staff assignment with excitement, he considered it as a stepping stone to a line position within 12 to 15 months in one of Sage's divisions. When Hawkins accepted the job in early May, Taylor said that he would have a real HBO problem for him when he started work, and he would appreciate hearing his views on it then. "In fact," Taylor said, "I'll write it out in case form on a confidential basis and give it to you on your first day of work." Without inquiring about the nature of the problem, Hawkins replied that he would look forward to tackling Taylor's case problem when he returned to Sage.

Glenn Taylor had been thinking long and hard about the problem he would write out for Philip Hawkins, for it had been bothering him for a considerable length of time. While he had talked about the problem with his wife and with Kenneth Johnson, who was both vice president for domestic operations of Sage and a close friend, he had never talked about it to anyone else inside or outside of the company. He did say, however, that he had informed the president, James Johnson, "in

EXHIBIT 1

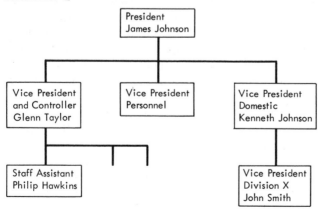

general" about the situation. James Johnson and Kenneth Johnson were brothers and major stockholders of the company. (See Exhibit 1 for an abbreviated organization chart.)

Before giving his written case to Philip after they had lunched together on July 1, Glenn emphasized the confidential nature of this problem. "Confidentially," said Glenn, "the biggest damn problem I have is John Smith. Sometimes I think I should say the hell with it and forget it, but I'm afraid if I do that it will hurt the company too much." He suggested that Philip read the case that evening and that they get together to discuss it the following day. Philip thought this approach made sense, and was flattered that Taylor was willing to confide in him. Before departing for a meeting Glenn said, "John Smith is the problem, and if you can solve this problem you will go a long way in Sage." The written case which Glenn gave to Philip appears below:

John Smith is one of the key executives in charge of operations for a significant geographical area of my company. He has been an employee for over 15 years, first in the role of a production supervisor, then division production manager; there were other position changes until his present position as a divisional domestic vice president.

He has enjoyed a succession of promotions and is highly regarded by all those who have worked for him. In part, this is a reflection of his personality as the other side of the coin is being reflected in difficulties I am encountering with him.

First, John is a law unto himself and gives favorite treatment to those working for him. He freely disregards company personnel practices and procedures and administers to his people as he chooses. His secretary gets the highest salary of any secretary in the company, works on a time schedule ignoring regular office hours, etc. This situation is widely recognized and resented by many others, but he has always gotten away with it and as a result he considers this his prerogative.

As he has progressed, this disregard for policy has become more noticeable on a higher level, even to the point of disregarding presidential requests or responding to them in such a way that they have been disregarded for all practical purposes. For example, he has never chosen to completely comply with annual profit-plan requests. He will present location plans without review and personal commitment, or at times he will submit data sufficiently different from standard forms to make collation and comparison difficult.

This has been accompanied by attempts to impose an iron curtain over the flow of information. This occurs with him personally and with operations under his supervision. When I request a meeting to discuss mutual problems, it rarely takes place unless forced by me.

Communications with others working under him become most troublesome, and strong measures are sometimes required to keep avenues of communication open to operations. Relationships with an operating location become noticeably different when he is in charge of it or his responsibility no longer covers it.

This can be very unfortunate since many of our mutual areas of responsibility frequently overlap into areas with which he has no knowledge. To date we have been fortunate in preventing any serious losses, but solely by accident.

He works hard—long hours—travels a large part of his time—is unstinting as to his time on company affairs. He has a keen, analytical mind, but tends to let small things prevent his deciding on major things.

Personally, away from the office we get along fine. He is affable, good company, and there is a free, open conversation without strain.

These relationships also appear to apply to others at his level and above.

When Philip entered Glenn's office late in the afternoon on July 2, Glenn offered him a seat and then closed his office door. He told his secretary they were not to be disturbed.

TAYLOR (*laughing*): Well, Phil, I bet you didn't run into any cases like my case in your business school studies. Believe me, Phil, this guy is getting away with *murder* over there. I sure would like to know what to do about it next. . . .

HAWKINS: Glenn, I don't know whether I can be of any help, but I would like to try. I wonder, though, if. . . .

TAYLOR (*excitedly*): The whole trouble is this guy thinks he's a law unto himself . . . he runs his damned division the way *he* wants to and says to *hell* with everybody else! I don't know, maybe the best thing for me to do is. . . .

HAWKINS: Excuse me, Glenn, but frankly I'm still not clear just on some of the facts here. For example, just what is the background history on this problem?

TAYLOR: Ever since John was promoted to the vice presidency several years ago the relations between our people have become more and more difficult. It's gotten to the point now where my people come to me and say they can't get any information out of that division, and they're supposed to get reports as a matter of course. . . . They're spending so much time trying to pry things loose there that other divisions and problems are suffering. When we finally do get stuff from him it's likely to be scratched on the back of an envelope or something—absolutely no thought has gone into it, obviously. I tell you, he has no regard for the problems we're trying to deal with here.

HAWKINS: Glenn, do you think a part of this problem may be explained by the image of your office? We had a lot of case studies about that at the B School, and I found that to be the case in my research report.

TAYLOR: You have put your finger on something there. There can be no doubt about it. We're known as the checkers, the probers, and the spies. The office of the controller does not have a good image, and it is part of the problem. But we have a job to do, too, and I am responsible for developing full reports that go to the board of directors.

HAWKINS: I wonder what it's like working for a guy like Smith. . . .

TAYLOR: Oh, I can tell you he gets tremendous loyalty—his people just love him. He goes to bat for them, too . . . his secretary is the highest paid in the entire company. And this is pretty well true of many of his people—they get more pay and benefits and sometimes even faster promotions than any other division—I tell you, after John's been in a slot for a while it begins to close up to any kind of corporate-wide control. . . . The guy is really getting away with murder. . . .

HAWKINS: What do you think Smith himself thinks about all this?

TAYLOR: Well, he's convinced he's doing what he should. He's a real seat-of-the-pants manager—he just doesn't take any time for the systems we've introduced. He's been around a long time—he's 46 now—and he knows this business inside out. It's like pulling eye teeth to get any information out of him. He doesn't pay any attention to routine requests of mine for meetings—and he certainly never takes the initiative to arrange one or ever try to find out what our procedures are. The only time we get together is when I *force* a meeting.

HAWKINS: He must be difficult to deal with.

TAYLOR: That's for sure. But it's funny, you know, he's not an angry type. Off the job, as I wrote in the case, we get together occasionally at a party at Jim or Ken Johnson's club and everything's fine—we get along fine. . . . I've only seen him mad about something once. That was when he was trying to protect another secretary of his after she had caused all kinds of trouble over in another division getting information she had no business getting—those people wanted Smith's head! Well, the personnel director and I put our foot down. Smith got mad, I got mad and I held firm. I said, "That girl has to go, and that's the way it's going to be!" He backed down at that point.

HAWKINS: What does Smith's boss—Kenneth Johnson—know about all this?

TAYLOR: Oh, Ken is very aware of all this. He knows the whole story, but he says he has the same trouble with John as I do. He can't get any information either. He's wringing his hands over this guy running his division like it was his own company.

HAWKINS: Well, what about the president? Does he know about it? Can't he get action?

TAYLOR: Yeah, he knows about it too . . . we've *had* to tell him why there are gaps in our reports or where the unlikely estimates come from.

HAWKINS: Why doesn't he crack down?

TAYLOR: Well, the trouble is, Smith does turn in the results—he gets the profits. Last year he turned in the most profits of any division in the company. It's been like that just about every job he has. He's always gotten the promotions, all along the line since he came to Sage 15 years ago.

HAWKINS: Oh, I see. . . .

TAYLOR: I'll tell you, though, something has got to be done. I think Jim is beginning to see more and more the problems Smith is causing—and *could* cause. He told me last week he was going to look into this whole thing again.

HAWKINS: You mentioned there were problems he *could* cause. What kinds of things?

TAYLOR: Why, my God, he's writing contracts with suppliers and making sales agreements all the time with nobody around here knowing about it! A year ago he was about to sign a licensing agreement with another manufacturer that would have put us smack into a lot of trouble because of a new product being developed by another division! He just charges ahead, thinking only for himself. The key point is that Smith could hurt the long-run profitability of the company in the area of trademarks, patents, and taxes. He almost gave away the company's patents in one horror case, and if he changed one licensing agreement the way he wanted to it would have cost the company $25,000 in taxes. There is a need for close cooperation between Smith and me, otherwise there will be lost profits.

HAWKINS: Who runs his division while he's away? You say he travels a great deal and he's away now on a long business trip.

TAYLOR: Ken Johnson is trying to run it, and he's asked me for help. As a matter of fact, I have a meeting with him tomorrow to see what we can do. Apparently, Smith's people are tighter than ever since he's been away—Ken says they won't tell him any more now than they ever did.

HAWKINS: What kinds of things have you thought of doing?

TAYLOR: I've beat my head on this one so much with so little results to show for it that I've just about decided to say "to hell with it." I don't know. . . . I suppose if I didn't care what happened to the company I would just sit back and do my job and let the chips fall where they may, but I'm not like that; I couldn't do that after all the effort that's gone into building up the new organization.

Continuing, Taylor stated:

> Smith and I have never competed. He always gets promoted, yet he is a complete nonconformist who gets away with murder. He causes serious morale problems with his peers who try and follow our team management concepts. Here is a good question for you: What do you do when a guy rejects management concepts (management by objectives, long-range planning, and budgets, for example) and still makes better than average profits? Top management has worked hard to develop what it considers the best available management and control techniques. To be honest, Phil, it may be that the best thing for me to do is to say "the hell with it," but I find it hard to accept defeat and admit that "seat-of-the-pants" management is best after all.

As Taylor talked about his case, Philip noted that he got red in the face on several occasions and appeared quite nervous. Philip knew that this was a serious matter for Glenn Taylor, and he truly wanted to help him with his problem.

Readings

1 | The Four Possible Life Positions:

1. *I'm Not O.K.—You're O.K.*
2. *I'm Not O.K.—You're Not O.K.*
3. *I'm O.K.—You're Not O.K.*
4. *I'm O.K.—You're O.K.*

Kenneth Lamott*

On a recent weekend, I sat in a circle of two dozen people in a room belonging to a hillside estate whose windows look out on Monterey Bay and Carmel and watched a pretty, dark-haired young woman beat a large red cushion to death. Her long hair streamed down over her flushed, tear-wet cheeks and her slender fists went *thump, thump, thump, thump, thump* as she pounded the cushion and sobbed. Then she hurled the cushion to the floor, picked it up and threw it violently down again. After some final thumps, she leaned back in her chair, mouth open and panting, her whole body transmitting the message that she had been through an absolutely consuming experience.

Robert L. Goulding, the psychiatrist who, with his wife, Mary, was directing this week-long workshop in Transactional Analysis, asked the

* *The New York Times Magazine*, November 19, 1972. Reprinted by permission of the New York Times Company.

girl, "Why are you breathing so hard? You're going *puff, puff, puff.* Are you trying to blow your mother away?"

"Oh, God," the girl said. "I wish I could."

"How do you feel now?" Dr. Goulding asked.

"I feel a lot better," she said, mopping her cheeks with Kleenex. "I feel great."

During a break in the group session at the Gouldings', I sat with them on a garden wall in their 30-acre spread. Bob Goulding, a large, untidy man with a bloodhound face and shaggy gray hair, explained to me that the symbolic murder we had witnessed—for the dark-haired girl had, in thumping the pillow, been killing her mother—was less important for its immediate emotional relief than for the insight it had given her into the processes of her own mind and the support it had given her in working her way to making a Redecision (Initial capitals are common in the vocabulary of Transactional Analysis, or T.A.) In the Gouldings' version of T.A., the Redecision is the milestone event, the point at which the sufferer breaks through a self-created impasse and consciously opts for a happiness, creativity and fulfillment rather than continuing to waste vital energies in frustration, anger, game-playing, and symbolic or literal suicide. "In psychoanalysis you don't make a decision for five years," Goulding told me. "In T.A., you're encouraged to make a decision right away."

Transactional Analysis is not synonymous with group therapy, which can be based on a variety of other theoretical underpinnings, from classical Freudianism to the Gestalt therapy of the late Frederick Perls. Yet, the group situation is particularly congenial to Transactional Analysis, which, compared to psychoanalysis, puts less emphasis on probing the dark places of the psyche and more emphasis on understanding the personality as it reveals itself in social situations, or transactions. The language of Transactional Analysis is colloquial and its therapeutic approach is direct and pragmatic. Its flavor was summed up by its founder, the late Eric Berne, when he described himself as a "cowboy therapist" who preaches the dictum: "Get well first and analyze later."

This simplicity and directness has surely contributed to T.A.'s recent accelerated growth. During the past couple of years T.A. has broken out of California, where it began in the late nineteen-fifties, and has been moving in great leaps along the East Coast and even through the Middle West. A bored T.A.-er, imprisoned in an airplane recently, calculated that at its present rate of growth the International Transactional Analysis Association would by 1900 include the entire English-speaking population of the world. (In fact, the I.T.A.A.'s current membership is a modest 2,500, most of whom are psychiatrists, psychologists or social workers.)

Goulding was one of the early disciples of Eric Berne, whose book,

Games People Play, published in 1964, was the first about T.A. to crack the best-seller lists and still contributes to the gaiety of cocktail parties from San Diego to Bangor, Me. The sharp observations and mordant humor of that book served, however, to obscure what T.A. really is, for this theory of games is only an incidental part of T.A.'s message.

Although T.A. has, as we shall see, developed in a number of different directions, its basic theory is still based on Berne's belief that each of us is capable of displaying three ego states—Parent, Adult and Child (or P-A-C)—in our dealings with other people as well as in our internal dialogues. When Dr. Thomas A. Harris, the psychiatrist author of the currently best-selling *I'm O.K.—You're O.K.,* was recently asked if Parent, Adult and Child corresponded to Freud's Superego, Ego and Id, he answered, "Hell, no! The Parent, Adult and Child are real things that can be validated." (Dr. Harris, it might be noted, went through five years of orthodox psychoanalysis.) In terms of P-A-C, the healthy personality is one in which the rational Adult is in control, but is indulgent toward the Child (who likes fun and sex) and resistant toward the Parent (who keeps trying to enforce ancient injunctions that tend to get in the way as the personality develops).

The three ego-states of T.A. do, of course, parallel the Freudian description of the psychic apparatus, but whereas the emphasis in classical psychoanalysis is on the sexual experience of the growing child, the emphasis in T.A. is on the growing child's sense of his or her own worth or lack of worth. Although T.A. often delves into the past ("What was the worst thing your mother ever said to you?"), its focus is on the here and now. The operative terms are "P-A-C" and "transaction."

When we converse with or communicate with another person in nonverbal ways, we are engaging in a transaction. The analysis of transactions in terms of P-A-C is what the theory of T.A. is all about. There is no doubt in the minds of its advocates that T.A. works better than other methods. As Dr. Harris once wrote: "If only one hour were available to help someone, the method of choice would be a concise teaching of the meaning of P-A-C and the phenomenon of the transaction."

A troubled person who goes to a T.A. analyst for help is likely to find himself quickly referred to a group, which may be one that meets at regular intervals or one that crams a concentrated T.A. experience into several days. Getting results may take anywhere from a week to a year or longer. Many transactional analysts make a "contract" with the patient to achieve some particular change. T.A.-ers are, above all, pragmatists, and when the desired behavior change comes about, treatment can either stop or a new contract can be negotiated.

The most frequently used tool of T.A. represents two interacting people as three circles each, thus:

Steps of the transaction are shown by drawing arrows from one circle to another. Let us imagine a married couple, John and Barbara. These two adults (but not at the moment, in T.A. vocabulary, Adults) are having fun at a party. The transaction of having fun together involves the Child ego-state on both sides, like this:

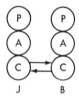

If, however, when John suggests they have another drink, Barbara should answer, "You always drink too much at parties," she has moved into her Parent state. John can respond in either of two ways. If he remains "in his Child" (using the T.A. phrase), saying, "Aw, come on, sweetie, let's have fun," the transaction looks like this:

This is an example of a complementary transaction, and so long as Barbara stays in her Parent, and John stays in his Child, it isn't likely to lead to real trouble. John may, however, elect to respond by saying, "You know very well that I don't *always* drink too much at parties, and furthermore you said you'd drive us home, and furthermore if I'm hung over tomorrow it's my hangover and not yours, and anyway it's Sunday," he has shifted into his Adult, or the data-gathering, rational, problem-solving state, and his remarks are addressed to Barbara's Adult, although it is fair to guess that Barbara's Adult isn't listening. This transaction looks like this:

This is an example of a crossed transaction, which Berne once described as "probably the most frequent cause of misunderstandings in marriage and work situations as well as in social life." The potentialities for disaster in John and Barbara's case are clear. The next step may be a memorable public game of—in Berne terminology—Uproar, or, if John really does get plowed, of Now I've Got You, You Son of a Bitch.

But game-playing is incidental to the main point, which is that the basic tool of T.A. is so easy to understand and so esthetically satisfying that it is practically impossible to resist using it. After my initiation into T.A. I became all too ready to offer my insight to friends complaining of their daily vicissitudes. To Max, who had suffered through a maddeningly inconclusive discussion with the head of the firm, I offered the opinion that his boss had been speaking as a Parent admonishing an ungrateful Child, while Max himself had been trying manfully to respond as Adult to Adult.

Looking at the circles I'd drawn with my finger on the damp bar-top, Max said with an air of enlightenment that the situation seemed much clearer to him now. Of course it isn't this simple—or, at least, not *quite* this simple. To begin with, we really aren't three different people, a Parent, an Adult and a Child, although beginners in T.A. often talk as if they thought they were. In the Gouldings' barn, where their group meetings take place and where the walls are covered with sheets from large newsprint pads, almost all of which bear variations of the three- or six-circle diagrams, one fellow told us, in the course of reporting how he felt, that "My kid [i.e., Child] sure had a good time at the party last night." Goulding leaped to his feet and drew the familiar three circles with a flow-pen on the newsprint pad, saying, "Look here. I'm not a Parent, an Adult and a Child—I'm a 55-year-old guy named Bob Goulding, and everything's contained inside my skin, like this":

This leads directly to an even more important qualification, which is that the psychic troubles from which most of us suffer don't come from crossed transactions with other people—our spouses, our bosses, our bridge partners—but from a malfunctioning of the P-A-C states within our own skins. The pretty girl who was using the cushion to beat her mother to death was working out, while in her own Child state, her feelings about the Parent inside herself. In the Gouldings' formulation of T.A., it is the function of the Parent to enforce an Injunction delivered long ago (along with reinforcing "strokes") by the real parent. They have catalogued a number of these Injunctions: *Don't Be, Don't Be You, Don't Be a Child, Don't Be Grown Up, Don't Be Close, Don't Make It, Don't Be Sane, Don't Be Important, Don't Belong*—and just *Don't.*

The child (the real child, not the Child) reacts to the Injunction by making a Decision. A familiar and not severely pathological example suggested by Bob Goulding is the child "who decides to obey the Injunction *Don't Be a Child* [and who] often works hard from the time he is 6 years old to accomplish things, and is amply rewarded for his efforts but isn't really enjoying life. In fact, this Injunction frequently underlies the life script of the professional . . . who does not permit himself to enjoy childlike pleasures. Even when he is relaxing, he may be pushed by his internal Parent to get off his rear end and get something done."

A more serious case was that of Tony, a tall, bearded professional man of about 40, who, sitting in the therapeutic circle in the Gouldings' barn, told us of suicidal behavior that had been troubling him. (On the wall behind him was a hand-lettered poster that said, in part: "WHAT'S THE RACKET? WHAT GAMES ARE PLAYED TO SUPPORT THE RACKET? WHAT EARLY DECISIONS DID PATIENT MAKE? IS THERE ANY GALLOWS LAUGHTER?")

It was almost by accident that Tony got into discussing his trouble, which was that he recognized he was risking his life every time he got behind the wheel of a car. When a woman told us about her tree-climbing girlhood, Tony remarked, "My mother once told me, *If I catch you doing anything like that again, I'll kill you.*"

A little later, Mary Goulding, who, like her husband, is large and casual about clothes, said to Tony, "You said your mother said she'd kill you if she caught you climbing trees again. Was that the worst thing she ever said to you?"

Tony looked puzzled and said he didn't remember saying quite those words. Bob Goulding punched the rewind button on the tape deck that was recording the session, and in a moment Tony's voice was repeating, "If I catch you doing anything like that again, I'll kill you."

"I guess that's right," Tony said. "That was the worst thing she ever said to me." He laughed as he spoke—"gallows laughter."

"What about this fast driving?" Mary asked

"I get a kick out of it. It makes me feel good," Tony said. He laughed again.

"Why don't you have a conversation with your mother?" Bob suggested. Somebody put a chair in front of Tony so that he was facing the empty chair and he began to talk, first in his own voice as he sat in his own chair and then taking the part of his mother as he sat in the other chair. Boiled down, the conversation went like this:

Mother: "I want you to be a good boy. I want you to do things that will make me proud of you, but you keep disappointing me. You keep doing bad things that upset me. You mustn't upset me and disappoint me anymore."

Tony: "I keep trying, Mom, but whatever I do isn't good enough for you. You want me to be a good boy and I am a good boy. You want me to get good grades in school and I get good grades in school. I try to do things that will make you proud of me. But whatever I do, Mom, nothing seems to be enough."

As the dialogue continued, Tony began to cry. The Kleenex box, which is a necessary fixture of all group-therapy sessions, traveled around the circle to Tony. He blew his nose and wiped his eyes. When he was calmer, Tony told us he was beginning to understand what was behind his fast driving. Every time he got behind the wheel of his E-type Jaguar he was playing with death, doing something for which he should be punished, betting his life, not letting his mother kill him but taking a chance on killing himself. His Child was defying his Parent in a way that his Adult recognized to be self-destructive.

Tony suddenly straightened up and, with determination in his voice, said, "I'm going to make a decision. I'm not going to drive fast anymore. It's just dumb. I have too much going for me to take a stupid chance on smashing myself up." Everybody around the circle told Tony how proud they were of him for making this Decision (really a Redecision). The woman sitting next to him put her arm around him and nuzzled his shoulder and cried happily ("stroking").

Afterward, I asked Goulding how he could be sure that Tony's Redecision would stick and that, the next time he was driving, his Jaguar, his Child wouldn't take over and cause his foot to bear down on the accelerator in the familiar fashion. "Tony was really with it," Goulding said. "You'll remember he was crying when he got into his Child state during the dialogue with his mother. Our experience has been that you get into the Child ego-state when you're really making a decision in your guts. His whole body and his whole being was in that decision."

If Eric Berne was the Martin Luther of the Transactional Analysis movement in its relation to classical psychotherapy, then the Calvins,

Knoxes, Zwinglis, and Servetuses were such therapists as Goulding, Claude Steiner, Stephan Karpman, and Thomas A. Harris. And, as was the case after the Reformation, the reformed sects have gone in directions that are as distinctive as Presbyterianism and Unitarianism—the emphases varying along a spectrum that includes as its central points the Redecision, the Life Script, the Life Position and the Dynamics of Strokes. As Goulding describes his own moving away from Berne, "We recognized . . . that the treatment method developed by Berne and his followers, although beautifully clear and crisp insofar as they made the patient aware of his life patterns, were not really getting the patient out of his bag."

Therapeutic methods—getting patients out of their bags—differ as much as do the emphases on theoretical underpinnings. One T.A. therapist, who shall remain nameless here, was reported to end each group session by having the participants hold hands as they danced in a circle and sang, "Ding, Dong, the Witch Is Dead." Goulding has referred without admiration to another therapist who "shouts, 'You're O.K.!'" at his patients, thinking that this will change them."

Practitioners of T.A. are qualified under regulations set up by the International Transactional Analysis Association, whose headquarters are in a converted gray-shingled residence at 3155 College Avenue, Berkeley. To become a clinical member requires course work, training as a member of a group, leadership of groups under supervision, and written and oral examinations. It takes at least three years to become a teaching member, the highest category.

Currently, the best known, most widely read and possibly the richest practitioner of T.A. is Tom Harris, the leader of the Sacramento group, whose book, *I'm O.K.—You're O.K.*, has been on *The Times's* best-seller list for seven months. *I'm O.K.* is the classic example of a sleeper. Published in 1969, it sold moderately but not extraordinarily well until about a year ago, when it simply took off. Dr. Harris told me that it has now sold about 700,000 copies and that his editor at Harper & Row predicts it will sell a million copies before the paperback edition comes out next spring.

The success of his book has made Harris much in demand as a speaker and as a leader of workshops for people in the "helping professions." In the course of six weeks during which I tried to get in touch with him, Harris conducted workshops in Hawaii; returned to Sacramento just long enough to turn around and go to Canada for more workshops; came home and turned around for Des Moines, where of course he "workshopped"; came home and turned around for Las Vegas, where he told a convention of internists how to cope with their own stresses; and then came home and then left to speak at a junior college near

San Francisco—where I at last caught up with him having a cup of coffee in a restaurant with his wife, Amy, while they planned the evening's speaking engagement (fee, $400) as well as a flight to Washington, D.C., the next day.

In person, Tom Harris is not many people's picture of a psychiatrist. A rather short, stout man in his mid-50's with a bullfrog face, he talks in a slow, rich, gravelly South Texas drawl and sounds and looks rather like a garage owner on his day off—seer-sucker suit, clip-on tie, a white shoe on his left foot and a walking-cast on the right, for he'd done something disastrous to his ankle by slipping in the shower while "work-shopping" at Banff.

A one-time chief of the psychiatric branch of the Navy's Bureau of Medicine and Surgery, Harris (who took his M.D. at Temple) was an orthodox analytically oriented psychiatrist until he came under Eric Berne's influence in the days when Berne was conducting the San Francisco Social Psychiatry Seminars, which historically were the fountainhead of T.A. As Harris recalls the occasion of his conversion, it was at a professional meeting in Los Angeles in November, 1957, that he heard Berne read a paper on T.A. that convinced him "this was not just 'another paper,' but indeed a blueprint of the mind, which no one had constructed before, along with a precision vocabulary, which anybody could understand, to identify the parts of the blueprint."

Both as a theorist and a practitioner of T.A., Harris differs from Berne, Goulding and the others, in the importance he sees in the "four life positions." This was an idea suggested by Berne in a paper he published in 1962, but which Harris has carried much farther (like Goulding, Harris discovered Berne in the late nineteen-fifties). The four possible life positions are:

(1) I'M NOT O.K.—YOU'RE O.K.
(2) I'M NOT O.K.—YOU'RE NOT O.K.
(3) I'M O.K.—YOU'RE NOT O.K.
(4) I'M O.K.—YOU'RE O.K.

The first position, Harris maintains in the face of much criticism, is the universal position occupied by the child, who is small, dirty and clumsy in a world controlled by tall, clean and deft adults. (Or so it seems to the child.) Here lies a critical theoretical difference between Harris and Eric Berne, for as Harris described it to me, Berne believed that "we're born princes and the civilizing process turns us into frogs" while he himself believes that we're all born frogs.

The second life position is the severely pathological one of the autistic child. The third position is shared by criminals and psychiatrists, among others. The fourth, of course, is the position enjoyed by you and me, for we are sane, humane, successful and civilized. (When Harper &

Row complained to Harris that *I'm O.K.—You're O.K.* didn't strike them as a title that would move many books, Harris countered with the suggestion of "Love in the Fourth Position." The publisher backed off rapidly.)

Like the theological state of grace, the fourth position does not descend on us unbidden but is, as Harris has put it, based on "thought, faith and the wager of action." It is not an easy position to reach or to maintain—"an eyeball-to-eyeball commitment with nothing held back, a dangerous, a risky, a rarely seen relationship contract. Yet, it is one of hope, and it *is* attainable."

Harris's popularity as an author and a speaker is enhanced by at least three other powerful factors that work in his favor. The first is his wife Amy, an attractive, friendly, brown-haired woman with a brilliant smile whom I judge to be in her 40's. Amy Harris is a writer by profession, and for six years was press secretary to the Governor of Washington. (When I suggested to Mrs. Harris, while her husband was away from the table, that perhaps she was the real author of the best-seller, she merely protested mildly and flashed that all-conquering smile. She will appear as co-author of Harris's next book, *Staying O.K.*)

The second factor is that Harris, like T.A.-ers generally, tends to be direct and colloquial, while psychoanalysts in general seem to be circumlocutionary and ponderous. When I invited him to compare T.A. with P.A. (psychoanalysis), Harris snorted and said, "After about five years in psychoanalysis you get about a ton of garbage and an ounce of usable material. In T.A. we go after that usable material right away."

The third factor working toward Harris's success is that, in some real sense, he is Middle America's psychiatrist. Psychiatry generally, and psychoanalysis in particular, has been from the beginning, to the point of stereotype, the territory of cosmopolitan agnostic Jewish practitioners, with or without Viennese accents. (Even Berne was born Eric Lennard Bernstein—although in Montreal.) Tom and Amy Harris not only look and sound Middle American, but they are also active in the work of their church (Fremont Presbyterian in Sacramento) and count many clergymen as their friends and as contributors to their ideas. (Prominent among these are the late Episcopalian Bishop James A. Pike and the Quaker philosopher Elton Trueblood.)

Harris is by no means solemn about his church upbringing. He regaled the audience at the junior college with a favorite story of how his mother, after going through the appropriate parental stage-setting for a momentous announcement, once advised him that whatever else happened, he must remember to hew to the central principle that "Wherever you go and whatever you do, son, the best people will be Methodists." Harris added a kicker to the story by drawling, "And ever since then, I can't walk by a Methodist church without breaking out in a rash." (He was in fact reared as a Methodist but baptized a high-church Episcopalian before taking up his present affiliation.)

In spite of this talent for irreverence, Harris's churchmanship and the respectful references to God and His works are a central part of Harris's message. As he has written, "I believe the Adult's function in the religious experience is to block out the Parent in order that the Natural Child may reawaken to its own worth and beauty as part of God's creation." Or, as Amy put it, "The way we see it, the way we say it to people, is that inside each of us there is an infinitely precious Child." (There is not necessarily a contradiction here with Harris's notion that we are all born frogs. If the Child is convinced that he really is a frog rather than something infinitely precious, that is indeed the problem.)

As a therapist—or, more precisely, as a teacher of therapists, for he sees few private patients nowadays—Dr. Harris's main strategy is to help the "patient" (a word he doesn't like) move from one of the first three positions to the fourth position: "I'M O.K.—YOU'RE O.K." Or, in somewhat more words, "the goal of treatment is to *cure* the presenting symptoms, and the method of treatment is the freeing up of the past." Like the Gouldings', the Harrises' version of T.A. operates mainly through group sessions, although, unlike the Gouldings, the Harrises finish their weeklong workshops with a 24-hour marathon.

In the course of therapy, Harris will sometimes engage in such unorthodox practices as writing out for one of his patients a "prescription" on a regular prescription pad, such as "I want you, John, to smile and greet 10 new people every day, by name if possible, and report back." He says that very often the patient calls back in a day or two and asks with wonder, "Hey, what's going on? I was convinced most people saw me as a nonperson."

In T.A.'s own terms, success comes with a blocking out of the Parent which allows the rational Adult and the fun-loving Child to take charge of the personality. (The importance of the Child should not be neglected. To a rambling question by a young man at the college who wound up by asking what he'd be like if he achieved 100 percent Adulthood, Dr. Harris shot back, "You'd be a godawful bore.")

When I wondered aloud how one could measure the success claimed by those who practice T.A. Harris answered, "We have thousands of letters—these are all validating. I take these letters at face value, and when an individual in Missouri pours out his soul to me and tells me what happened to him while he was reading the book, why I sense that something really *did* happen."

Responses like this, with the flavor of conversion and the revival meeting, have not recommended Harris to the generality of psychiatrists, some of whom (in Harris's words) have attacked him as a faddist and a crusader. One of the more powerful assaults on the entire world of Transactional Analysis was delivered recently when Dr. James S. Gordon, a psychiatrist with the National Institutes of Mental Health, reviewed Berne's posthumous book, *What Do You Say after You Say Hello?* in *The New York Times Book Review.* After commenting on Berne's "glibness [which] figures forth a deep and dangerous moral and social complacency that he cloaks in the guise of therapeutic neutrality," Dr. Gordon went on to describe Transactional Analysis as "a way of looking at some forms of social action, and a potential adjunct to psychotherapeutic practice [that] has been transformed . . . into a world-view—a theory of personality, of social transmission and social action, and of healing. And that world-view, insulated by material comfort, is a moral and spiritual vacuum."

Dr. Harris has of course introduced (or reintroduced) moral values, as he sees them, into Transactional Analysis. Yet he has not been immune to attack, both from scientific colleagues who believe he has no business messing about with moral and religious values and from those to whom T.A., with or without moral values, simply does not seem adequate to the complex problems to which it addresses itself.

In search of enlightenment, I visited a friend, Dr. Donald A. Shaskan, an analytically oriented psychiatrist who practices group therapy in and around San Francisco, and who knew Eric Berne. Don Shaskan described T.A. as "an attempt to popularize psychoanalysis," and added, "In many respects I think it's failed because it's reductionistic and simplistic in explaining such a complicated thing as the human mind. Both Harris and Goulding set a goal by working out a contract with the patient. They ask, 'What do you want to get over?' And the patient says, for example, 'Drinking.' And so you work out a reduction of the drinking and the problem seems to be over. But human beings are a little more complex than that. Drinking may be just a symptom of something else; you get over the drinking and then you have to get over an even more destructive urge—perhaps a suicidal tendency."

I told Shaskan that Goulding had described to me a follow-up study of 734 people who, while in T.A. therapy, had made the decision not to kill themselves. At the time of the study, none had. Shaskan observed cautiously, "I have my doubts about that, and I have my doubts about its being able to be repeated. I'd like some verification because I just don't think that there's this much conscious control of destructive impulses. Goulding and Harris have tried to popularize—in the best sense of the word—psychotherapy. They've made it too simple, and that's where they've failed. Maybe everybody has to fail in popularization. I don't know."

It seems unlikely to me that criticism such as this will have much effect in slowing down the T.A. movement. It is a powerful thing that Bob and Mary Goulding and Tom and Amy Harris and the other people who are carrying the message have to offer their listeners, perhaps the most powerful thing in the world, the promise of personal liberation and change. As Amy Harris described it to me, "Whatever you've done, to date, whatever games you've played, whatever scripts you've had, whatever it is, it's O.K. because it's been your attempt as best you know how to do two things for this little kid in you. One is to protect him and the other is to get 'strokes' to keep him alive. You've gotten your 'strokes' by turning over tables or playing Uproar.

What we say is, *That's O.K.* What we're going to do *now* is to show you a different way."

2 | The Natural Triad in Kinship and Complex Systems*

Morris Freilich

The structural form containing the roles "High-Status Authority," "High-Status Friend," and "Low-Status Subordinate" is analyzed as a "natural triad." The occurrence of this form in systems otherwise very different suggests that it solves a number of basic system problems. The work of Heider and Homans is used to illustrate the utility of further study of the natural triad. Propositions concerning tension, power and sentiment in natural triads are offered, with the conclusion that this form is most frequently in a state of imbalance.

Many scholars have been intrigued by social systems containing three units—three people playing a game, three friends, three nations in a power conflict and so forth. Game theorists have studied the triad as part of a general interest in two-, three-, and n-person games. Historians and journalists have vividly described coalition formation in triads, and sociologists have studied the three-person group.[1] The sociological literature primarily stems from the provocative writings of Simmel.[2] Triadic relationships have been explored in experimental studies and theoretical papers. This work is so promising that Caplow has described it as "one of the most interesting and satisfactory areas

---

* Reprinted by permission of *American Sociological Review*, vol. 29, no. 4 (August 1964).

[1] For a short summary of these three approaches see William A. Gamson, "A Theory of Coalition Formation," *American Sociological Review*, vol. 26 (June 1961), pp. 373–82.

[2] Georg Simmel, *The Sociology of Georg Simmel*, trans. and ed. by Kurt Wolff (Glencoe, Ill.: The Free Press, 1950). See particularly pp. 358–76.

of current research activity."[3] Anthropologists who study kinship systems can also contribute to triad theory; with a small change in orientation, these studies can help isolate the triadic forms which frequently appear in kinship systems and which seem to have structural-functional counterparts in the sub-systems of many complex societies. I shall develop this point further, starting with an analysis of the structural characteristics of certain patrilineal and matrilineal systems.

Many writers have noted that three roles are often intimately interlinked in patrilineal societies: ego (son, sister's son), his father, and his mother's brother.[4] The father has jural authority over ego: he has the right to give orders and ego has the obligation to obey them. This relation, between a superior and an inferior, is often marked by formality and considerable restraint, while relations between ego and his mother's brother are characterized by ease and freedom. The mother's brother, though superior in status to ego, frequently plays the role of intimate friend, adviser and helper. The role triad of father (authority over ego), mother's brother (ego's friend) and ego exists in many societies including Batak, Gilyak, Karadjeri, Lakher, Lhota, Lovedu, Mbundu, Mende, Murngin, Sema, Venda, Wik-Munkan and Tikopia. In matrilineal societies the same three roles are also interlinked, but here the behavioral aspects of the roles father and mother's brother are reversed: The mother's brother often has jural authority over ego, while the father plays the part of friend, confidant and helper. This situation occurs among the Trobriand Islanders, the Haida, the Tlinget and the Pende.[5]

Comparing the patrilineal Tikopia with the matrilineal Trobriand Islanders, Homans concluded: if we forget about biological kinship and look to the *working group*, the systems are the *same*.[6] Homans' insightful inductive leap points to structural similarities between patrilineal and matrilineal systems and suggests that underlying similarities are being obscured by kinship terminology. Thus, the biological terms, *father*,

---

[3] Theodore Caplow, "A Theory of Coalitions in the Triad," *American Sociological Review*, vol. 21 (August 1956), p. 489. See also Caplow's "Further Developments of a Theory of Coalitions in the Triad," *American Journal of Sociology*, vol. 64 (March 1959), pp. 488–93. Caplow's claim for this area of research is supported by the many interesting studies that have been done recently with triads. See, for example, Richard H. Willis, "Coalitions in the Tetrad," *Sociometry*, vol. 25 (December 1962), pp. 358–76, for an attempt to extend triad theory to the tetrad, and Sheldon Stryker and George Psathas, "Research on Coalitions in the Triad: Findings, Problems and Strategy," *Sociometry*, vol. 23 (September 1960), pp. 217–30, for an attempt to provide more adequate experimental designs to test various aspects of triad theory.

[4] For example, see George Homans, *Sentiments and Activities* (New York: The Free Press of Glencoe, 1962), pp. 218–19.

[5] This analysis follows Homans, ibid., pp. 213–42.

[6] George Homans, *The Human Group* (New York: Harcourt Brace & World, 1950), pp. 248–61.

mother's brother, son and *sister's son* may usefully be replaced by structural-functional terms emphasizing positions and activities. The basic elements of the system discussed are the status-roles: *High-Status Authority, High-Status Friend,* and *Low-Status Subordinate.*

Once the biological terms are discarded it becomes obvious that this triad of status-roles—hereafter designated as HSA, HSF, and LSS, respectively—is not limited to situations where the actors are, biologically, the father, the mother's brother, the son and sister's son. An HSA-HSF-LSS triad found in many patrilineal systems—including the BaThonga of Portuguese East Africa, the Nama Hottentots of South Africa and the Tonga of the Friendly Islands—is that of father's sister (HSA), mother and mother's sister (HSF) and ego (LSS). Father's sister is treated in much the same way as father, and mother and mother's sister are treated in much the same way as mother's brother.[7] In many societies where authority over household members lies in the hands of the father's side of the family (patrilineal kin are HSA), friendly equality exists between children (LSS) and their maternal grandparents (HSF). This situation exists among the Lemba, the Venda, the Thonga, the Dahomey, the Nankanese, the Bena, the Swazi, the Lenge, the Comanche, the Zulus, the Tswana, The Hehe, the Hera, the Tonga, the Kurtatchi, the Murngin and the Eastern Cherokee. Conversely, in many societies where the mother's kin have authority in the household (matrilineal kin are HSA), friendly equality exists between children and their paternal grandparents (HSF). This is the case among the Haida, the Hopi, the Navaho, the Truk, the Marshallese and the Manus.[8]

In societies more complex than these kin-based systems, the same triad is common to various subsystems. In a prison it includes the warden (HSA), the chaplain or social worker (HSF) and the prisoner (LSS). In a mental hospital, it includes the ward psychiatrist (HSA), the social worker (HSF) and the patient (LSS). In the armed services there are the noncommissioned officers and field officers (HSA), the chaplains (HSF) and the G.I.s (LSS). In universities, some professors play the role "buddy prof" (HSF), others the role "authoritarian director of studies" (HSA) to the students (LSS). In many field work situations anthropologists (and at times sociologists) are the HSF to their informant (LSS), whose activities are directed by various people (HSA).

The frequent occurrence of the role triad HSA-HSF-LSS under natural conditions—in real life, rather than in the experimental laboratory—suggests the name *natural triad* for this form. Its appearance in systems that otherwise show marked differences in ecology, complexity, social

---

[7] This matter is fully discussed by A. R. Radcliffe-Brown, in *Structure and Function in Primitive Society* (Glencoe, Ill.: The Free Press, 1952), especially pp. 15–31.

[8] See Dorrian Apple, "The Social Structure of Grandparenthood," *American Anthropologist,* vol. 58 (August 1956), pp. 565–63.

structure, culture and history, suggests that it is a structural unit of some importance and deserves considerable study. As a prelude to such study I shall describe the basic elements of this form.

The natural triad exists where all of the following conditions obtain: First, *three status-roles* are present in a subsystem containing at least two status positions. Second, one status-role (LSS) has lower status than the other two status-roles (HSA and HSF respectively). Third, LSS is a common alter to both HSA and HSF. Fourth, the dyadic relationship HSA-LSS is that between a superordinate and a subordinate such that (a) the position of HSA is that of a jural or legitimate authority, based on "rational," "traditional," or "charismatic" grounds, or on a combination of these;[9] (b) HSA initiates activities for LSS and not vice versa; and (c) the dominant type of sentiment in the relationship HSA-LSS could be described as *negative*, ranging from formality and considerable restraint to dislike and hate. Fifth, in the relationship HSF-LSS, status differences are "played down," so that (a) the relationship can be described as based on "friendly equality" and intimacy; (b) the intimate content of the relationship tends to be initiated by the LSS: LSS confides in, "takes liberties with," cries on the shoulder of HSF and not vice versa; and (c) the dominant type of sentiment in the relationship could be described as *positive*, ranging from strong regard and admiration to liking and loving,

The natural triad may occur within a *group* such as the nuclear family or in social situations where there are only three people, but *group* and *people* are not intrinsic to the concept of the natural triad. The basic elements of the natural triad are *three status-roles* interlinked in the manner described above. One or more actors may play each of the roles described, and at times one actor may play more than one role.

FUNCTIONS OF THE NATURAL TRIAD

Why is this form found so often, frequently under very different socio-cultural conditions? I suggest that the answer lies in its multifunctional nature, for the natural triad serves a number of functions on at least two levels of analysis, the sociological and the psychological. On the sociological level, all socio-cultural systems have goals, the

---

[9] Following Max Weber, the three types of legitimate authority are: *legal authority*, which is based on "rational grounds," *traditional authority*, which is based on "an established belief in the sanctity of immemorial traditions," and *charismatic authority*, "resting on devotion to the specific and exceptional sanctity, heroism or exemplary character of an individual person." I am suggesting that a role player whose status is higher than LSS's and who gives orders to LSS is an HSA if his right to direct is based on any of these types of legitimate authority. See Max Weber, *The Theory of Social and Economic Organization*, trans. by A. M. Henderson and Talcott Parsons, ed. by Talcott Parsons (Glencoe, Ill.: The Free Press, 1947), pp. 324–36.

achievement of which requires the direction and coordination of the action of various role players in the system. And, as Weber tells us:

> . . . the imperative coordination of the action of a considerable number of men requires control of a staff of persons. It is necessary, that is, that there should be a relatively high probability that the action of a definite . . . group of persons (LSS) will be primarily oriented to the execution of the supreme authority's (HSA) general policy and specific commands. . . . It is an induction from experience that no system of authority voluntarily limits itself to the appeal to material or affectual or ideal motives for guaranteeing its continuance. In addition every system attempts to establish and to cultivate the belief in its own 'legitimacy'. . . .[10]

In short, an efficient way of achieving group goals is to institute the dichotomy of "legitimate authorities" and followers. It should be added that Weber's experience is supported by the "ethnographic record" in which societies without legitimate authorities are rarely described.

The status-roles HSA and LSS are now understandable; but why the HSF? Lord Acton's frequently quoted statement, "Power corrupts and absolute power tends to corrupt absolutely," is helpful here. The HSF seems to function as a check on the power of HSA. For, should the latter become corrupt, social and cultural goals might be downgraded in favor of HSA's personal goals. Homans' analysis of Tikopia social structure supports the proposition that HSF is a power balancer in the system. Grandfathers (HSF), who have retired from active management of family affairs by the time their children grow up, form close ties with their grandchildren (LSS) in contrast to more formal relations with their sons (HSA) who now rule the family. Homans adds, "In these circumstances, grandfather and grandson are, so to speak, *allied in opposition* to the man in the middle."[11]

Recent experimental work with triads also supports my proposition that a power alliance exists between HSF and LSS. These studies demonstrate a strong tendency for coalitions to form where three people interact. Further, where power is unevenly distributed in the triad—as in the natural triad—the weakest member is always part of a coalition.[12] Thus the natural triad illustrates the form of power balance that is predictable from the results of experimental studies with triads. The friendship between LSS and a higher-status alter is understandable in that their status roles are so structured that they do not compete for

---

[10] Weber, pp. 324–25.

[11] Homans, *The Human Group,* p. 251.

[12] See Theodore M. Mills, "The Coalition Pattern in Three Person Groups," *American Sociological Review,* vol. 19 (December 1954), pp. 657–67; and W. Edgar Vinacke and Abe Arkoff, "An Experimental Study of Coalitions in the Triad," *American Sociological Review,* vol. 22 (August 1957), pp. 406–11.

any of the resources and benefits of the system: this alliance is unlikely to be broken due to competitive endeavors between the allies.

A second explanation for the frequent occurrence of the natural triad is a psychological one involving tension states in sociocultural systems. The status-role HSA not only initiates and coordinates action in a given sub-system but also creates tension therein, while the status-role HSF acts as a tension reducer as well as a power balancer.[13] Differently put, as HSA gives orders, he also "feeds" tension into the system, and as HSF balances the power relationships, he also "feeds" positive affectivity into the system, reducing the tension therein. It seems logical to assume that the tension created by HSA is mainly picked up by the LSS, for whom HSF functions as a tension reducer, and that HSA himself absorbs some of the tension he created and is forced to find some release for it.

The writings of Homans, Radcliffe-Brown and others support the proposition that HSF reduces the tension created by HSA. Homans states that men tend to fear, avoid and feel some constraint in the presence of persons placed in authority over them.[14] Radcliffe-Brown suggests that in many societies friendly equality exists between grandparents (HSF) and grandchildren (LSS) as a relieving reaction to the tension created between parents (HSA) and children (LSS) by parental authority.[15] The tension reduction function of the HSF is vividly described by Homans in his discussion of the mother's brother role in Tikopia:

> In all the great occasions of life . . . the mother's brother . . . helps him [ego] over the rough places . . . It should be clear by now that the mother's brother is a practical and *emotional necessity* to a Tikopia man.[16]

If it is true that HSA picks up some of the tension that he has "fed into" the system and therefore is forced to find some release for it, and as a corollary proposition, that HSF picks up some of the positive affectivity that he feeds into the system, then the status-roles HSA and

---

[13] In this context, the role HSA should not be viewed simply as a "harmful" tension creator. The HSA has rather the positive function of creating "normal" tension, without which humans would be in a state of boredom. Normal tension, however, can develop into disruptive "abnormal" tension. This analysis follows Lewin's view of tension states: "Although the popular view may place a negative value on tension per se, Levin treats tension states in a relatively value-free manner. Thus the person does not strive to eliminate tension: a tensionless life-space would be lifeless. Instead, there is a tendency toward the equalization of tensions in various neighboring regions of activity." See George Levinger, "Kurt Lewin's Approach to Conflict and Its Resolution," in Warren G. Bennis, et al., eds., *The Planning of Change: Readings in the Applied Behavioral Sciences* (New York: Holt, Rinehart and Winston, Inc., 1961), pp. 244–49.

[14] Homans, *Sentiments and Activities*, p. 252.

[15] Radcliffe-Brown, *Structure and Function*, pp. 96–97.

[16] Homans, *The Human Group*, p. 218, italics added.

HSF are complementary to each other; one creates tension in the actor, the other reduces it. To ensure a tension balance within a given actor over a given period of time, socio-cultural systems might well "force" actors to play both these roles in sequence. This seems to be exactly what occurs in many patrilineal systems, where every father (HSA) in one subsystem is also a mother's brother (HSF) in another. Similarly, in many matrilineal systems, every mother's brother (HSF) in one sub-system, is also a father (HSF) in another. In short, an actor who plays the role HSA creates tension for both LSS and himself. The LSS is "forced" to interact with an HSF to reduce his own tension. The HSA can play the role HSF in another subsystem, thus reducing his own tension and helping the system "make certain" that an HSF exists for each LSS.[17] The necessity for socio-cultural systems to manage tension has been discussed by many theorists; Goffman has recently made a strong case for the proposition that the management of tension is a *central problem* for socio-cultural systems.[18] I suggest that this problem is often solved through the status-role HSF.

If indeed the natural triad has the various important functions attributed to it, it is reasonable to expect any socio-cultural subsystem to develop status-roles approximating HSA, HSF, and LSS. Although it is beyond the scope of this paper to test this hypothesis adequately, it is possible to approach a test by examining data on two extremely different types of subsystems: small groups in experimental settings and nuclear families.

TASKS AND EMOTIONAL SPECIALISTS IN SMALL GROUPS

Students of small groups bring various actors from natural systems into contrived social situations and get them to play roles relevant to the hypotheses of the experimenters. No matter what roles these actors are expected to play, however, I suggest that some will also play HSA, others HSF and yet others LSS.

---

[17] It follows that a given HSA could reduce his own tension by finding a friend whose status is higher than his own. This may be difficult to do, particularly in kinship-based societies, where the number of status positions is frequently limited, so that a given ego with very high status may have no higher-status friends. He can, however, reduce his tension by playing the role HSF himself. Even in complex systems some individuals have such high status that they have no HSF. These people, too, are "pushed" to play HSF, as, for example, in the role implied by the term *noblesse oblige.*

[18] The views of Howard Becker, Kingsley Davis, Robert Merton and Talcott Parsons (and others) on the problem of tension management are summarized in Charles P. Loomis and Zona K. Loomis, *Modern Social Theories* (Princeton, N.J.: D. Van Nostrand Co., 1961). See also Erving Goffman, *Encounters: Two Studies in the Sociology of Interaction* (Indianapolis, Ind.: The Bobbs-Merrill Co., Inc., 1961).

Summarizing the findings of a number of small group studies, Carter categorized descriptions of the behavior of individuals working in groups into three dimensions: as behaviors of the individual related to his efforts (1) to stand out from the others and individually achieve various personal goals, (2) to assist the group in achieving its goals, and (3) to establish and maintain cordial and socially satisfying relations with other group members. Carter also states that the first two factors are combined in the trait "leadership." In terms of my analysis, Carter has isolated the three roles of the natural triad: the leader (HSA), the establisher of cordial relations (HSF) and other group members (LSS). Further, implicit in Carter's statement that personal goals can be combined in the leadership role is the notion that *some* personal goals may run counter to group goals, giving rise to the need to balance power in the system.[19]

Bales and his students often analyze group activity in terms of the behavior of an "idea man" and the behavior of a "best liked man."[20] Slater refers to these actors respectively as "task specialists and social-emotional specialists." He suggests that the "most fundamental type of role differentiation in small groups is the divorcing of the task functions from the social emotional functions," and further, that while the social-emotional specialist is well liked, the task specialist tends to arouse negative feelings.[21] Task specialists may be equated with HSA, social-emotional specialists with HSF, and other group members with LSS.

It might be argued that by equating task specialist with HSA and social-emotional specialist with HSF, I disregard some important differences between the small group situation and the natural triad. That is (the argument could continue), in some small group studies the task specialist and the social-emotional specialist are *not* obviously accorded status for the roles they play. My answer would be that it takes time to obtain status from a group for the performance of necessary group functions, and that small group experiments of long duration will more clearly show the higher status of the roles task specialist and social-emotional specialist. Further, I would argue that if the group is to have the continued contributions of these two role players, the group must "give" these actors higher status. Differently put, since it is generally accepted that reciprocity is basic to social life, what occurs here is an "exchange" of status for the performance of critically important

[19] See Launor F. Carter, "Evaluating the Performance of Individuals as Members of Small Groups," *Personnel Psychology*, vol. 7 (1954), pp. 477–84.

[20] For summaries of the work of this group see Michael S. Olmstead, *The Small Group* (New York: Random House, Inc., 1959); and W. J. H. Sprott, *Human Groups* (London: Penguin Books, Inc., 1962).

[21] Philip E. Slater, "Role Differentiation in Small Groups," in A. P. Hare, E. F. Borgatta, and R. F. Bales, eds., *Small Groups: Studies in Social Interaction* (New York: Alfred A. Knopf, Inc., 1955), pp. 498–515.

roles.[22] In his summary of what occurs in small groups, Bales draws a similar conclusion:

> As particular functional problems (instrumental, adaptive integrative, or expressive) become more acute, pressing, *or continuous* . . . strains are created toward the definition of specific social roles, differentiated in terms of particular persons, who are given . . . responsibility of meeting and solving the specific functional problems as they arise in the group. Furthermore: As the felt importance of the specific function performed by a particular person increases, *strains are created toward an increase in his generalized social status.*[23]

Bales' and Slater's analyses together provide a rationale for the frequent appearance of the task and social-emotional specialists which is similar to my explanation of the frequent appearance of the HSA and HSF roles. A small group has two basic types of problem to solve: problems involving goal achievement and adaptation to external demands, and problems involving internal integration and the expression of emotional tension. The solution of the former problems demands activity in the "task area," often guided by the occupant of the role "task specialist" (HSA). The solution of the latter problems demands activity in the "social-emotional" area and requires that someone fill the role "social-emotional specialist" (HSF).

THE NATURAL TRIAD AND THE NUCLEAR FAMILY

Zelditch[24] has provided important data for my hypothesis that the natural triad frequently occurs in the nuclear family. Starting from a different vantage point—considering the nuclear family as a special case of the small group—and using the terminology of small group studies, Zelditch proposed, first, "If the nuclear family constitutes a social system stable over time, it will differentiate roles such that instrumental leadership and expressive leadership are discriminated." Second, "If the nuclear family consists in a defined 'normal' complement of the male adult, female adult and their immediate children, the male adult will play the role of instrumental leader, and the female adult will play the role of expressive leader." To use Zelditch's data I shall equate instrumental leader with HSA, expressive leader with HSF and the children with

[22] See Alvin W. Gouldner, "The Norm of Reciprocity: A Preliminary Statement," *American Sociological Review*, vol. 25 (April 1960), pp. 161–78.

[23] Robert F. Bales, "Adaptive and Integrative Changes as Sources of Strain in Social Systems," in Hare, Borgatta, and Bales, *Small Groups*, p. 128, italics added.

[24] Morris Zelditch, Jr., "Role Differentiation in the Nuclear Family: A Comparative Study," in Matilda White Riley, ed., *Sociological Research: A Case Approach* (New York: Harcourt Brace & World, 1963), pp. 212–23.

LSS. Zelditch found that among 56 societies of his sample, differentiation of instrumental and expressive leadership roles occurs in 46 cases, thus supporting my proposition that the natural triad occurs frequently in nuclear families. Moreover, Zelditch was testing for the discrimination of the leadership and expressive roles in the system, while I am interested in the presence or absence of these roles in the system. All of his positive cases thus support my proposition, while his negative cases do not necessarily deny it. The natural triad may still be present where these roles are not discriminated, as long as the roles HSA, HSF, and LSS are part of the system, and one actor plays more than one role.

Students of the American nuclear family provide a variety of data and some contradictory conclusions about the structure of this form. To take two extreme points of view: Parsons sees sharp differentiation in the parental roles, with the father usually playing the instrumental role and the mother the expressive role.[25] Bernard assigns both the instrumental and expressive roles to the mother and describes the father as having little importance to or authority over the children; she adds that in "many homes the mother's wishes control family policies even when these are in opposition to the father's."[26] Bott helps to resolve conflicting views of the American family by suggesting that the family form is related to the social matrix in which the marital couple finds itself. Bott distinguishes between "loose-knit networks," in which relatives, friends and neighbors of the couple tend *not* to know each other, and "close-knit networks," in which relatives, friends and neighbors of the couple know and frequently interact with each other. Bott suggests that families with close-knit networks are likely to be of the working class, while families with loose-knit networks are likely to be in the professional classes. She finds that "Couples in close-knit networks expect husband and wives to have a rigid division of labor. . . . In contrast, families in loose-knit networks have a less rigid division of labor."[27] In short, following Bott, we would expect lower-class families with close-knit networks to clearly differentiate instrumental and expressive roles, while middle class families with loose-knit networks should not show such role differentiation.

The work of Bronfenbrenner and Slater and others supports Bott's analysis. Bronfenbrenner found that in American families with adolescent children, particularly in the lower class, each parent tends "to punish the children of the same sex and to indulge and intercede for the child

[25] Talcott Parsons and Robert F. Bales, *Family: Socialization and Interaction Process* (Glencoe, Ill.: The Free Press, 1955), pp. 45, 80.

[26] See Jessie Bernard, *American Family Behavior* (New York: Harper & Bros., 1942), p. 269.

[27] Elizabeth Bott, *Family and Social Network* (London: Tavistock Publications, 1957), pp. 111–13.

of the opposite sex."[28] Slater describes the middle-class family as existing in an informal setting, where parents tend to agree on what is good for the child and where both parents play both instrumental and expressive roles for children of either sex. Slater's description of the middle-class family is consistent with the writings of many social scientists, and it is also supported by his argument that in our society high value is placed on the ability to alternate instrumental and expressive role performance.[29]

In the terminology of this paper, lower-class families with adolescent children contain two triads: father (HSA), son (LSS) and mother (HSF); mother (HSA), daughter (LSS) and father (HSF). In the middle-class family, both father and mother play both HSA and HSF, depending on the demands of the situation. In both classes adults play the complementary roles of tension creator and tension reducer: HSA and HSF. Although this is similar to the situation in primitive kinship systems where father (HSA) is also mother's brother (HSF), an important difference is that in primitive societies the actors who play both HSA and HSF do so in different subsystems. In the American family, not only are these roles played in the same subsystem, but in the middle class, the very different roles HSA and HSF are played to the same alter.[30]

SENTIMENTAL CONGRUENCE, INTERACTION AND THE NATURAL TRIAD

The frequent occurrence of the roles HSA, HSF and LSS in primitive kinship systems, in experimental small groups and in many nuclear families, suggests that the natural triad is a basic structural form which functions on various levels to solve a number of universal system problems. To illustrate the value of studying this form in depth, I shall now consider the work of Heider and Homans relative to the natural triad.

Heider and his students are concerned with the problem of *sentimental congruence* within a given group or subsystem. They postulate: (1)

---

[28] Urie Bronfenbrenner, "Toward a Theoretical Model for the Analysis of Parent-Child Relationships in a Social Context," in John C. Glidewell, eds., *Parental Attitudes and Child Behavior* (Springfield, Ill.: Charles C Thomas, Publisher, 1961), pp. 90–109.

[29] See Philip E. Slater, "Parental Role Differentiation," *American Journal of Sociology*, vol. 67 (November 1961), pp. 296–308.

[30] A clear and well documented statement of differences in family life between the American middle and lower classes is provided in Lee Rainwater, *Family Design: Marital Sexuality, Family Planning and Family Limitation* (Chicago: Aldine, 1964). Rainwater's book supports the analysis here presented.

that sentimental ties in a system tend toward balanced states; (2) that balanced states are achieved when all relationships in the system are *positive* (hiking, helping, admiring, etc.) or when each *negative* relationship (hating, hindering, admonishing, etc.) is balanced by another negative relationship, or when there are unrelated roles (called a case of vacuous balance); (3) that sentimental relationships tend to be transitive: if A has positive ties with B, and B has positive ties with C, there is a "psychological tendency" for positive relations to develop between A and C; (4) that in an unbalanced system, tensions will be produced and forces will arise pushing toward balance.[31] If Heider is correct—and experimental studies have thus far born out his theory—then certain relations must exist between HSA and HSF. The relationship HSA-LSS has been described as a negative one: the authority forces the subordinate to do things and the subordinate reacts with coolness, fear, etc. The relationship HSF-LSS has been described as a positive one based on "friendly equality." To balance the system the relationship HSA-HSF should be *negative;* or, to achieve vacuous balance, there should be no relations between HSA and HSF.

Let us assume a natural triad situation in which relations between HSA and HSF can be described as *positive.* According to Heider, this system would be in imbalance and strains would be created toward balance. The forces set in motion by such strains could take, via the process of sentimental transitivity, either of two directions: (1) if the relationship HSF-LSS remains positive, pressure would be exerted to change the relationship HSA-LSS from negative to positive, creating a sentimental congruence in which all relationships are positive; (2) if the relationship HSA-LSS remains negative, pressure would be exerted to change the relationshp HSF-LSS from positive to negative, creating a sentimental congruence in which one negative relationship (HSA-LSS) is balanced by another (HSF-LSS). If either one of these changes occurs, however, the natural triad becomes a basically different form, and the multiple functions ascribed to it are lost to the system. We may therefore expect the system to set up "barriers to change."

Homans, too, is concerned with sentimental states in given systems, and he has stipulated relations between interaction rates and sentiments: other things being equal, "If the frequency of interaction between two or more persons increases, the degree of their liking for one another will increase, and vice versa."[32] This implies that *interaction rates among HSA, HSF, and LSS must be kept constant.* Should the rate of interaction between HSA and LSS *increase,* greater familiarity may change their

[31] Heider's theory and some of the relevant experimental work are summarized in J. Berger, B. P. Cohen, J. L. Snell, and Morris Zelditch, Jr., *Types of Formalization in Small Group Research* (Boston: Houghton Mifflin Co., 1962).

[32] Homans, *The Human Group,* p. 112.

relationship from a negative one to a positive one. Should the rate of interaction between HSF and LSS *decrease,* coolness and formality may develop between them, changing their relationship from a positive one to a negative one. According to Heider, change in either one of these relationships starts a chain reaction to alter the other relationships in the triad, thus depriving the system of the functions attributed to the natural triad. Again it is logical to assume that the system will set up "barriers to change."

Not only is it logically possible that barriers to change will be created in social systems, but, I suggest, such barriers actually *do* exist in the form of *role protectors.* First, *formality systems* include signals that warn role players when they must pay special attention to their role requirements. For example, military salutes, or addressing various role players by such titles as "Sir," "Father's sister," "Your honor," "Professor," etc., reduce the probability that familiarity will develop between a superior with legitimate authority (HSA) and a subordinate (LSS). In effect, they protect the HSA role, even in situations where interaction with the subordinate is increasing. Second, certain phenomena, which could be called *interaction controllers,* tend either to inhibit interaction or to increase or maintain it. Such phenomena as uniforms, officer's clubs, faculty dining rooms, the "speaking chief" (protecting the role tribal chief) and the mother-in-law tabu, come immediately to mind as interaction inhibiters. Post-marital locality rules, and "social equalizers" such as institutionalized joking relationships, exemplify phenomena conducive to increased interaction.[33]

The American middle-class family illustrates a number of concepts introduced in this section. Father and mother each play both the HSA role and the HSF role, establishing, in sequences, both positive and negative relationships with the children. The absence of formality systems—in some situations even the status terms "father" and "mother" are dropped in favor of "pop," "dad," "ma," "mamma"—and the value of "togetherness" (functioning here as an "interaction conducer") imply that minimal protection exists for authority roles. Little wonder that children often react with the equivalent of *et tu Brute* when forced to take orders!

The dyadic relationship husband-wife lies at the core of this structure: it must be maintained as "generally positive" or divorce proceedings will break up the family. Yet strong strains are present which periodically change the husband-wife relationship to a negative one. For example,

---

[33] Although interaction inhibitors, such as officers' clubs and faculty dining rooms, reduce interaction between role players of different status, they increase interaction between role players of similar status. Interaction with others of similar status reinforces role behavior, thus protecting such status-roles as HSA. Robert K. Merton has made a similar point about the function of interaction between actors who have similar status-roles in "The Role-Set: Problems in Sociological Theory," *British Journal of Sociology,* vol. 8 (June 1957), pp. 106–20.

if one parent plays an instrumental role (HSA, tension creator) in the presence of his mate, the latter will tend to react in the role HSF (tension reducer). In this situation, pressure to put the triad into sentimental congruency will tend to develop negative feelings between the parents: the negative feelings between HSA and LSS will be balanced by negative feelings between HSA and HSF. Negative feelings between HSA and HSF, however, strike at the base of this system, so that situations leading to them tend, I suggest, to be avoided. Two alternatives open here are, first, one parent does not play HSA in the presence of the other; second, one parent does not play HSF when the other plays HSA. But the first alternative creates serious problems when situations demanding instrumental action within the family arise, particularly since spatial segregation in the household is not sufficient to permit one parent to play HSA unobserved. If the second alternative is taken, then tensions created by HSA cannot be resolved within the household, leaving the family in a tension state not conducive to "good family living." The middle-class American family, with its loose-knit network and lack of institutionalized support for instrumental leadership roles, would seem to require the complementary role HSF to reduce this internal tension. Depending on the financial situation of a given family and its religious convictions, role players ranging from clergymen to psychiatrists are available to satisfy its tension-reducing needs.

AN INDEX OF SYSTEM BALANCE

Homans' analysis of Tikopian social structure raises an additional question about natural triads. Homans described the mother's brother as an *emotional necessity* to a Tikopian man. In terms of natural triad analysis, the mother's brother is important in Tikopia as *one* of the actors who plays HSF and reduces tension created by HSA. But a given ego may turn to alternative players of the HSF role: his mother, his mother's sister, and his grandfather. What then makes the mother's brother an emotional necessity to his sister's son? There are two ways of considering this problem: first, Homans has misread the ethnographic data and the mother's brother does not play the critical role he suggests. Second, this is a real problem requiring modification of the previously stated propositions concerning the natural triad. Since Homans' analysis of the mother's brother role in Tikopia is consistent with other scholars' statements about the importance of this role in many socio-cultural systems, the second alternative seems the more reasonable one.

Thus far, I have assumed that all actors who play HSF fulfill the same functions for the system. But Homans' analysis of the mother's brother's role makes it necessary and logical to propose that the HSF's contribution to the system is related to his status. More specifically, the higher the general status of HSF, the more he is able to reduce tension for a given LSS in the system. That is, I now stipulate that various HSF role players reduce tension *differentially* and that *the amount of tension reduced by a given HSF is directly proportional to the difference in status between HSF and LSS.* The critical importance of the mother's brother role becomes clearer if it is further stipulated that *the amount of tension produced by a given HSA is directly proportional to the difference in status between HSA and LSS.* In kinship systems of the type I have discussed, the general status of the mother's brother is higher than that of the mother, mother's sister, or grandfather. Thus, the mother's brother can reduce tension more effectively than these other HSF actors. Further, the general status of mother's brother (HSF) is roughly equal to the general status of father (HSA), so that the amount of tension reduced by the former is roughly equal to the amount of tension produced by the latter. Hence the critical importance of the status-role mother's brother in kinship systems such as the Tikopia.

The proposition that the tension-production and tension-reducing functions of HSA and HSF, respectively, are directly related to the general status of these role players makes it possible to develop indices of various tension states in natural triads. Ranking the statuses of any given system from one to s, and assigning status numbers to HSA, HSF, and LSS respectively on the basis of this ranking, we can arrive at the ratio $\frac{a}{f} \times 100$, where a is the difference between the statuses of HSA and LSS, and f is the difference between the statuses of HSF and LSS.

When HSA's status is equal to HSF's status, the tension index is 100, representing a state of balance. Indices greater than 100 represent triads "overweighted" toward authority; these could be called *instrumental structures*. Indices less than 100 represent triads "overweighted" toward friendship; these could be called *expressive structures*.[34] Any given triad can be simply described by three numbers representing the general statuses of HSA, HSF, and LSS, respectively. Thus 451 implies a tension index of

$$75 \left(\frac{4-1}{5-1} \times 100 \right)$$

which represents an expressive structure.

---

[34] I have distinguished instrumental from expressive structures to help solve the following type of problem: If three people or groups of people are working together on a given project, what type of triad will lead to optimum performance? Evidence exists indicating that in instrumental activities, such as those performed by bombing crews, very satisfactory social relationships (i.e., where sentimental ties overbalance instrumental ones) are correlated with *poor performance.* See Homans, *Sentiments and Activities,* p. 101. But in projects concerned with changing sentiments—for example, an attempt to integrate "white" schools in the South, or an attempt to settle a labor-management dispute—expressive structures should be more effective.

If general status is assumed to be correlated with power in a socio-cultural system, then the tension index also provides information on power relationships. In instrumental structures, the authority (HSA) has more "net" power than in expressive structures. Structures in tension balance—e.g., the situation of the father, mother's brother and son-sister's son in Tikopia—are also, roughly, in states of power balance.

Balance and imbalance in natural triads can be described more completely by combining the tension index with Heider's sentimental congruency. States of sentimental congruency or balance can be denoted by a plus sign ($+$), and states of sentimental imbalance by the minus sign ($-$). A state of tension balance and sentimental balance is now described by the signed index $+100$, and various states of imbalance by minus signs with indices greater than or less than 100.

Future studies of the natural triad will indicate the utility of these indices. For the present, they provide a simple way of describing various states of balance and imbalance, and they permit mathematical descriptions of the various properties of a given system. For example, in a system of statuses ranked from one to s, HSA and HSF can assume any status higher than one, as long as this status is higher than that of LSS. If we assume that every combination is equally possible, then this system has:

(1) $\sum_{n=1}^{s-1}(s-n)^2$ possible natural triads, where n = the status of LSS.

(2) $\sum_{n=1}^{s-1}(s-n)$ natural triads in tension balance.

(3) $\sum_{n=1}^{s-1}(s-n)(s-n-1)$ natural triads in tension imbalance.[35]

CONCLUSION

The evidence presented from kinship systems, studies of small experimental groups, and from various sub-systems of complex societies tends to support the proposition that the natural triad is a basic structural form capable of solving problems common to all socio-cultural systems. Two general conclusions are, first, that statements appearing in the social

---

[35] In a system with s status positions LSS can move from status level n = 1 through n = s — 1. When LSS is at any given status level there are always $(s-n)$ number of possible triads that can occur for each one of the $(s-n)$ HSA levels and for each one of the $(s-n)$ HSF levels. Thus as LSS moves from n = 1 to n = s — 1 there are $\sum_{n=1}^{s-n}(s-n)^2$ *possible triads* in this system. Let us call this equation A. When LSS is at any level of the system, a total of $(s-n)$ triads can be in balance (i.e., where status HSA = status HSF). As LSS moves from status level n = 1 to n = s — 1 the total number of *balanced* triads is $\sum_{n=1}^{s-1}(s-n)$. Let us call this equation B. The number of *imbalanced* triads is thus A — B = $\sum_{n=1}^{s-1}(s-n)^2 - \sum_{n=1}^{s-1}(s-n) = \sum_{n=1}^{s-1}(s-n)^2 - (s-n) = \sum_{n=1}^{s-1}(s-n)(s-n-1)$.

science literature on systems in states of balance, equilibrium, harmony, etc., have minimal utility unless they specify what phenomena are in these balanced states. The state of such phenomena as power, tension and sentiments in a given system should be considered before general statements are made about the condition of the system as a whole.

A second conclusion is that *socio-cultural systems are most frequently in states of imbalance*. Given a small structure like the natural triad, and given, for example, a five-status system, there are but ten types of natural triad in tension balance as against 20 in tension imbalance. Since there are also a few possible states of sentimental incongruence the probability that a given natural triad is in a state of sentimental and tension balance is small indeed. It is then even less probable that a structure with more than three roles will be in a balanced state.

The conclusion that socio-cultural systems are most frequently in states of imbalance, though unexpected, is not contradictory to the proposition central to this paper; namely, that socio-cultural systems *tend toward states of balance*. My conclusion describes the probable state of a given system at any given time, while the central proposition describes its goal, or the direction in which it is moving. This distinction, between the probable state of a system at a given time and its direction, is of fundamental importance to modern functional analysis. Cognizance of this distinction would help to solve the current dilemma of explaining why systems in a "stable, integrated and harmonious equilibrium"[36] ever change.

---

[36] See Wayne Hield, "The Study of Change in Social Science," *British Journal of Sociology*, vol. 5 (March 1954), pp. 1–11. My second conclusion supports Dahrendorf's assertion that it is more realistic to consider societies in differential states of disequilibrium than in states of equilibrium. See Ralf Dehrendorf, "Out of Utopia: Toward a Reorientation of Sociological Analysis," *American Journal of Sociology*, vol. 64 (September 1958), pp. 115–27.

3 | Giving and Receiving Feedback[*]

John Anderson

The purpose of this article is to discuss a few considerations involved in telling another person how you feel about him—"how to do it" considerations that are apt to be important, if your objective is to help him become a more effective person, and also to arrive at a more effective working relationship between him and yourself.

BACKGROUND

One of the central purposes of group experience in a managerial grid or sensitivity training lab is to help the participant become more clearly aware of the impact he has on others. That is, during the laboratory experience, the participant has an opportunity to talk with others, solve problems with others, and in general interact with others in ways that are characteristic for him. The image he projects, then—the impression that others have of his behavior—is communicated back to him by other group members. And this sort of exchange is usually a good deal more open than what is common in everyday life. The intent, at least so far as the objectives of the program are concerned, is that this feedback will be helpful to the recipient—that he may see, for example, some discrepancies between the effect he wished to create (and, in fact thought he was creating), and what actually took place, with the hope that he will be able to use this information in making a more intelligent choice of behavior with which to deal with similar situations in the future.

---

[*] Internal company document. Reproduced by permission of Procter & Gamble Co.

Unfortunately, such feedback (for reasons of content, timing, and the way it is given) does not always turn out to be useful to the recipient. And, although the very large majority of managers who participate in public sensitivity or grid training labs return saying that overall the experience was a very helpful one for them personally, still, many have felt that "This is a kind of thing you sure couldn't do with people you work next to all the time!" The fear is that if the members of a work team did attempt to enter into an experience of this kind together, either:

1. They would not dare to be open and candid with one another, and the result, therefore, would be a superficial and useless experience, or
2. They would dare to be open with one another, and the result would be one of disruption in team working relationships, escalation of bad feelings carried over from old grievances, etc.

Several companies have now experimented with some sort of team lab. In my own, Procter & Gamble, the design we have used has varied considerably depending on the needs of the particular group. But in no instance have the two fears mentioned above (organized slumber or total destruction) materialized. Each has turned out to be, in the judgment of the large majority of participants, a very useful and very worthwhile experience from the standpoint of building more effective working relationships on the job. In general, people seem to be both concerned enough for one another, and trusting enough of one another that they are able to be *appropriately* open in exchanging feedback during a team lab situation. It's my belief that instances in which people have only hurt or confused one another in exchanges of this kind have been the result not so much of motivational problems, as problems of skill in giving feedback—that is, knowing *how* to do it well, and what kinds of pitfalls to watch out for. So, so much for background. What follows, then, is a summary of what I feel are some of the more important considerations drawn from fairly limited and scattered literature on the subject, and from my own personal observation of some of the holes people seem to dig themselves into, in experiences like this. I think it is particularly important that these thoughts be given some attention in groups that are to be conducted without the benefit of outside help— that is, where a trained, skilled, experienced, outside observer will not be available to get things back on track if they should begin to wander off in useless directions. I'm thinking of managerial grid, or other instrumented, trainerless lab designs. No doubt the following considerations also have some application to the conduct of "performance appraisal" discussions as well as other informal exchanges that often take place between people in or out of the workplace.

THE FIRST GENERAL TEST

I think the first, most general, and most significant criterion that "helpful feedback" must meet is simply that it be *intended* to be helpful to the recipient. That is, the sender of the message should ask himself beforehand, "Do I really feel that what I am about to say *is likely to be helpful to the other person?*" I need to examine my own motivation, that is, and be sure that I am not simply about to unload a burden of hostility from my own breast and for my own personal benefit, quite regardless of the expected effect on the receiver. Otherwise, I may convince myself that my only obligation is to be open and honest—that the name of the game is "candor"—and that so long as I truly and completely "level," I have fulfilled the only necessary obligation. If my objective is to *help* the recipient of the feedback, then, three things are necessary:

1. The other person must *understand* what I am saying.
2. He must be willing and able to *accept* it.
3. He must be *able to do* something about it if he chooses to.

GETTING UNDERSTANDING

Two most important considerations in getting understanding of the message sent are:

1. Feedback should be specific rather than general. If I can give the man I am talking to specific examples of instances in which he has behaved in the way I am describing, it will be much easier for him to understand what I am talking about than it will if I speak only in terms of generalizations about "what he is like." For example, if I tell him that I think he talks too much, or doesn't express his thoughts very clearly, this is likely to be *less* helpful to him than if I am able to cite a particular situation, tied to time and place, where I thought he exhibited this behavior. If I can recall vividly to his mind a particular instance in which he rambled on long after I had gotten the idea of what he was trying to say, or when he had gone on and on and on without ever getting across clearly the idea of what he was trying to say to me or to a group, he is more likely to be able to get a handle on what it is I am trying to tell him. Or at least I will have opened up an area for him that we can then explore further to try to understand what was going on in the situation, so that he can come out of it with a clearer idea of some specific things he might consider doing differently in the future. The key here is, don't just generalize about what kind of a person he is. Give examples.

2. Another important factor in getting understanding is this: Other things equal, recent examples of behavior are better than old ones. To understand what was happening in the situation, a person obviously has to be able to recall the situation somewhat vividly. What happened two minutes ago will be more vividly recallable than what happened an hour ago, which will in turn be more easily remembered than what happened yesterday, last week, last year, five years ago, etc.

GETTING ACCEPTANCE

There are circumstances in which anyone will find it most difficult to accept critical, negative, feedback—times at which it will be very difficult for anyone to face what is being said to him in an open, objective frame of mind. I think five things are most important in getting this acceptance:

1. There needs to be a minimum foundation of trust among members of the group before this sort of experience is entered into. If A is to accept critical feedback from B, A must be somewhat convinced from his previous associations with B, that B's motivations where A is concerned aren't entirely self-serving—that is, that B *does care* for A and can be trusted to be saying what he is saying because he really feels that it will benefit A to do so. Where B has a deep distrust of A going into this situation, there is probably very little that A can do to get B's voluntary acceptance of what he is telling him.

2. How A addresses himself to B in this specific situation, however, can also be an important factor. If A's tone of voice, the expression on his face, his choice of words, and everything about him communicates directly to B the impression that, "I value you, and I really would like to help you, and that is the only reason I am telling you this," then B is more likely to attend to the message with an open mind than if A simply rattles off a list of intellectual observations about B's behavior, perhaps without even looking directly at him while he does so.

3. In sending negative feedback to another person, he will also be more likely to receive it in an accepting frame of mind if I am descriptive rather than evaluative in what I say to him—that is, if I simply describe what happened as I saw it in a particular situation and tell him of the effect it had on me, as opposed to evaluating in more general terms the goodness or badness, rightness or wrongness, of what he did. If I tell you, for example, that "This may not be your problem; it may be mine. However, I want you to

know that when you act toward me the way you do sometimes (describe a situation, in time and place) it is very difficult for me to (think straight, keep from getting mad, keep my mind on what we are talking about, keep from going to sleep, etc.—whatever fits the situation that I am trying to describe)," you are much more likely to be able to accept this message in an open frame of mind than if I tell you, "I think it is just terrible when you act toward people that way, I think you ought not to be that way, that's a completely senseless way to act, why don't you grow up, etc. . . ."

4. Before giving a person negative feedback of any kind, I ought to ask myself whether *now* is a good time to do it—whether he *appears* to be in a condition of readiness to receive information of this kind. If he appears, for example, to be angry, confused, upset, highly distraught, defensive, etc., the answer is probably no. I ought not to load any more on him right now.

Perhaps in a way it is for this reason that feedback which is solicited by the recipient is somewhat more likely to be received in an open state of mind than feedback which is simply sent at him whether he has asked for it or not. And the more specific the area in which feedback is solicited, the more likely it is to be expected and received in an open frame of mind. For example, suppose the leader of a group says to his people, "How about the X decision I made last Friday? Do you feel that that was one I arrived at in an appropriate way, or do you feel that I should have involved you all more before arriving at a conclusion?" As a member of the group, I would feel that this solicitation of feedback was more genuine and could be responded to more openly and with more confidence that it would be received in an open frame of mind, than I would feel when the leader of the group, perhaps a bit too intensely or with a laugh that is a little too loud, says something like, "O.K. men, this is my turn in the barrel! Really level with me now! I want to hear everything you don't like about me!" He may or he may not. All I am suggesting is that if overt solicitation is indicative of probable acceptance, the former sort is apt to be more meaningful than the latter, all by itself.

5. There is always the problem that feedback sent one man by another will be accepted as valid when in fact it ought *not* to be. For example, if I tell you that there is a particular thing you do in our relationship that I find most upsetting, it may be that the problem isn't yours at all, but rather that it's mine. One of the values of entering into this sort of exchange in a group, as opposed to doing so only in a one-to-one relationship, is that the feedback that each man gives another can be checked around the group to see whether anyone else has common experience of this kind which would support

or clarify the meaning of what is being said. This should always be done, both as a check on the validity of the observation, and to be sure that the recipient gets as many examples as are available to help him understand what is being said.

ASSESSING THE RECEIVER'S ABILITY TO USE PARTICULAR FEEDBACK

The third criterion I mentioned that "useful" feedback should meet is that the recipient be able to do something with it.

1. Suppose I feel that a man does not present his ideas as forcefully and persuasively as he ought to, to get the attention he deserves from the group; and I decide I want to tell him about this. This is still a pretty general feeling, and before saying anything, therefore, I should consider what specifically there is about his delivery that makes me feel that way. Now if I think, for example, that he doesn't organize his thoughts as well under some circumstances as I know he is capable of (from other experiences I've had with him), this is an example of something I might assume he could do something about, and so I probably should tell him I feel that way, especially if I can give him specific examples of instances in which he has done this. Or suppose I feel that he gets his ideas out all right, but that as soon as he receives any static from anyone about them, he withdraws, either from indifference, lack of confidence in his own ideas, or whatever. This too I might choose to tell him about, because I could expect that he might be able to do something about it.

    On the other hand, suppose I feel that one of the key things that interferes with his ability to persuade, to carry his ideas over to a group forcefully, is that he is physically a very little fellow, and with a high squeaky voice, or possibly an even more pronounced speech impediment. If I am really trying to be helpful to him there obviously is no point in calling these to his attention.

    So, by this criterion, you might or might not decide it would be helpful to tell the other person you felt he did not project his ideas in the group as forcefully or persuasively as he might. Whether you chose to do so or not would depend on your best estimate of his ability to do something about the particular barriers you saw to his effectiveness in this particular area.

2. During a group session in which members are exchanging their views of and feelings about one another in this way, there may be a tendency to feel that you haven't really done a man justice unless you have told him "everything that bothers you" about him. It is not

at all necessarily desirable, however, to be "complete" in the negative feedback you might give a person. It may be quite a large enough task, for example, for me to understand, accept, and consider doing something about my characteristic ways of behaving in two or three key areas. To give me more than this to think about may be simply spreading my attention beyond what I am capable of dealing with at this particular time. Also, other things equal, the more you unload on me, the more threatening the experience is liable to be, and the more difficulty I am likely to have accepting any of it in an open frame of mind.

SUMMARY

So, to be maximally useful to the recipient, feedback should meet the following criteria. It should be:

1. Intended to help the recipient.
2. Given directly and with real feeling, and based on a foundation of trust between the giver and receiver.
3. Descriptive rather than evaluative.
4. Specific rather than general, with good, clear, and preferably recent, examples.
5. Given at a time when the receiver appears to be in a condition of readiness to accept it.
6. Checked with others in the group to be sure they support its validity.
7. It should also include only those things that the receiver might be expected to be able to do something about.
8. And he should not be told more than he can handle at any particular time.

RISK OF EXCESSIVE CAUTIOUSNESS

Finally, the question might be asked, "Isn't there some risk that if all these cautions are followed, people might be induced to be overly cautious, and decline to take any risks (and what would probably be desirable risks) in being open with one another?" This is a reasonable question, and I think the answer is yes—this is a risk in itself. Many of us have a tendency to feel that we couldn't possibly share with other people the negative feelings we have about them. They would be crushed if we did so. Or they would never forgive us. All of the criteria listed above are simply considerations that should be given some attention by the sender of feedback. But it will no doubt be impossible to meet all of them, all of the time, and still have something to say. And so, I think in such cases it is appropriate to take prudent risks—to be open more than closed, experimentally, and see what happens. If you at least really *intend* to help—and there is no doubt that you intend to help by the manner in which you say what you say—then a good deal of clumsiness is almost certain to be overlooked by the receiver. Even if he doesn't understand or agree with what you are saying, he at least will probably not hold it against you. And if his defenses stay down, together you may be able to clarify meanings, draw out essentials, and in general compensate for your initial clumsiness in trying to help.

RECEIVING FEEDBACK

I think there is less to say to the recipient of feedback about ways in which he might approach this opportunity:

1. First of all, he should make a sincere effort not to be defensive. This has as much to say about what he allows to go on inside him, as about what he allows himself to say overtly to those who are giving him feedback. He should try to look at what is being said with an open mind, trying to understand it, and not all the while explaining to himself and others "They simply don't understand; it isn't what I meant at all."

2. If the recipient of feedback is having difficulty understanding what people are trying to tell him, and they are unable to come up with examples that clarify things for him, he should begin to seek and speculate on possible examples himself with the group—to say, for example, "Remember the time we met last Friday, and I did such and so. Is that the kind of thing you are talking about?"

3. To be sure he understands, I think it is a good idea for the recipient of feedback to try to summarize briefly for the group what he understands them to be saying. This gives them a final opportunity to check misunderstandings that might have taken place.

4. I think it can be very helpful to an individual and to a group if the recipient of feedback from others is allowed, and encouraged, to share his feelings with the group about the kind of thing they have been discussing—that is, his behavior in certain situations. The risk of defensiveness is one that all should be alert to. However, if a man can explore openly some of his feelings about why he tends sometimes to behave in "that" way, two things can happen. First, he may arrive at a better understanding himself of why he behaves in the way he does, simply in talking it through, and thereby be in a better position to consider what he might do about it. Secondly, if he does find it difficult or impossible to do anything about the behavior that has been negatively described to him by the group, even though he tries, if he has genuinely shared with them some

of his concerns and some of the internal struggles he had in these situations, they may at least find it a little easier to understand and accept that behavior from him in the future.

5. As a final point, I believe some people react negatively to the very idea of doing this sort of thing—that is, meeting as a work team and exchanging in a quite open fashion our views of how we see one another, positively and negatively. The feeling may be that, "I am what I am, and I have a right to be that. And no group of people has a right to dictate to me what I should be like." My feeling is that this is exactly right. It remains, and should remain the right of each individual to evaluate what he hears, decide what he believes of it, and decide in what respects, if any, he feels it is personally worth his while to make the effort to change. The purpose of a team lab of the kind described here, and of the kind of information that is exchanged in it, is simply to give a man better and clearer information than he ordinarily receives and on which to make his own judgment of his personal effectiveness in working with others, and of how or whether he wishes to further develop that effectivness.

4 | Douglas McGregor's Theory of Motivation

Louis B. Barnes

In an attempt to understand and account for human behavior, a number of theories of motivation have been advanced. A common approach has been to list the various "drives," wants, or needs which apparently motivate men. These attempts have often been criticized because the lists were long and unmanageable, because they failed sufficiently to take into account the nonphysiological needs, and because the needs often appeared to be contradictory.

A somewhat different way of thinking about man's needs has been suggested by Maslow.[1] He views man's needs in terms of a hierarchy, certain needs becoming operative only when other needs have been relatively satisfied. In an excellent summary of Maslow's scheme (originally prepared for a group of business executives). Professor Douglas McGregor of Massachusetts Institute of Technology describes the need hierarchy as follows.[2]

PHYSIOLOGICAL NEEDS

Man is a wanting animal—as soon as one of his needs is satisfied, another appears in its place. This process is unending. It continues from birth to death. Man continuously puts forth effort—works, if you please—to satisfy his needs.

Human needs are organized in a series of levels—a hierarchy of importance. At the lowest level, but pre-eminent in importance when

---

[1] A. H. Maslow, *Motivation and Personality* (New York: Harper & Bros., 1954).

[2] Douglas McGregor, *The Human Side of Enterprise* (New York: McGraw-Hill Book Co., Inc., 1960), pp. 36–39.

they are thwarted, are his physiological needs. Man lives by bread alone, when there is no bread. Unless the circumstances are unusual, his needs for love, for status, for recognition are inoperative when his stomach has been empty for a while. But when he eats regularly and adequately, hunger ceases to be an important need. The sated man has hunger only in the sense that a full bottle has emptiness. The same is true of the other physiological needs of man—for rest, exercise, shelter, protection from the elements.

A satisfied need is not a motivator of behavior! This is a fact which is . . . ignored in the conventional approach to the management of people. I shall return to it later. For the moment, an example will make the point. Consider your own need for air. Except as you are deprived of it, it has no appreciable motivating effect upon your behavior.

SAFETY NEEDS

When the physiological needs are reasonably satisfied, needs at the next higher level begin to dominate man's behavior—to motivate him. These are the safety needs, for protection against danger, threat, deprivation. Some people mistakenly refer to these as needs for security. However, unless man is in a dependent relationship where he fears arbitrary deprivation, he does not demand security. The need is for the "fairest possible break." When he is confident of this, he is more than willing to take risks. But when he feels threatened or dependent, his greatest need is for protection, for security.

The fact needs little emphasis that since every industrial employee is in at least a partially dependent relationship, safety needs may assume considerable importance. Arbitrary management actions, behavior which arouses uncertainty with respect to continued employment or which reflects favoritism or discrimination, unpredictable administration of policy—these can be powerful motivators of the safety needs in the employment relationship at *every level*, from worker to vice president. In addition, the safety needs of managers are often aroused by their dependence downward or laterally. This is a major reason for emphasis on management prerogatives and clear assignments of authority.

SOCIAL NEEDS

When man's physiological needs are satisfied and he is no longer fearful about his physical welfare, his social needs become important motivators of his behavior. These are such needs as those for belonging, for association, for acceptance by one's fellows, for giving and receiving friendship and love.

Management knows today of the existence of these needs, but it is often assumed quite wrongly that they represent a threat to the organization. Many studies have demonstrated that the tightly knit, cohesive work group may, under proper conditions, be far more effective than an equal number of separate individuals in achieving organizational goals. Yet management, fearing group hostility to its own objectives, often goes to considerable lengths to control and direct human efforts in ways that are inimical to the natural "groupiness" of human beings. When man's social needs—and perhaps his safety needs, too—are thus thwarted, he behaves in ways which tend to defeat organizational objectives. He becomes resistant, antagonistic, uncooperative. But this behavior is a consequence, not a cause.

EGO NEEDS

Above the social needs—in the sense that they do not become motivators until lower needs are reasonably satisfied—are the needs of greater significance to management and to man himself. They are the egoistic needs, and they are of two kinds:
1. Those needs that relate to one's self-esteem: needs for self-respect and self-confidence, for autonomy, for achievement, for competance, for knowledge.
2. Those needs that relate to one's reputation: needs for status, for recognition, for appreciation, for the deserved respect of one's fellows.

Unlike the lower needs, these are rarely satisfied; man seeks indefinitely for more satisfaction of these needs once they have become important to him. However, they do not usually appear in any significant way until physiological, safety, and social needs are reasonably satisfied. Exceptions to this generalization are to be observed, particularly under circumstances where, in addition to severe deprivation of physiological needs, human dignity is trampled upon. Political revolutions often grow out of thwarted social and ego, as well as physiological, needs.

The typical industrial organization offers only limited opportunities for the satisfaction of egoistic needs to people at lower levels in the hierachy. The conventional methods of organizing work, particularly in mass production industries, give little heed to these aspects of human motivation. If the practices of "scientific management" were deliberately calculated to thwart these needs—which, of course, they are not—they could hardly accomplish this purpose better than they do.

SELF-FULFILLMENT NEEDS

Finally—a capstone, as it were, on the hierarchy—there are the needs for self-fulfillment. These are the needs for realizing one's own potentialities, for continued self-development, for being creative in the broadest sense of that term.

The conditions of modern industrial life give only limited opportunity for these relatively dormant human needs to find expression. The deprivation most people experience with respect to other lower-level needs diverts their energies into the struggle to satisfy *those* needs, and the needs for self-fulfillment remain below the level of consciousness.

For purposes of initial explanation and simplicity, McGregor speaks in terms of separate steps or levels. Actually, Maslow suggests that these levels are interdependent and overlapping, each higher need level emerging before the lower needs have been satisfied completely. In our society, most people tend to be partially satisfied in each need area and partially unsatisfied. However, individuals tend to have higher satisfaction at the lower need levels than at higher need levels. Maslow helps to explain this by picturing the average citizen as (for illustrative purposes) 85 percent satisfied in his physiological needs, 70 percent satisfied in his safety needs, 50 percent in his belonging needs, 40 percent in his egoistic needs, and 10 percent in his self-fulfillment needs.

Some writers have added to this original concept of hierarchy the idea of "elaboration at one level." They suggest that when the individual is blocked in his progression up the hierarchy ladder, he may begin endlessly to elaborate at one level of need satisfaction—for example, the endless pursuit of groups and friends for the emotional support they provide or the endless pursuit of more and more status symbols and the needs for recognition they satisfy.

A MODIFICATION OF MASLOW'S NEED HIERARCHY THEORY

In a study of engineering groups, Barnes implicitly assumed a modification of Maslow's need hierarchy theory.[3] Now, let us explicitly state this modification, since it has both teaching and research implications. Whereas Maslow arranged human needs in a hierarchy arrangement from low (physiological) to high (self-actualization) needs, Barnes proposed a more equal, but related, arrangement of man's higher need categories. Maslow postulated a hierarchy or ladder of four successive need categories following the physiological, that is, safety, belonging, ego (self-esteem and other esteem), and self-actualization, each of which he believed must be relatively satisfied before the next need was really activated. Some observers question the hierarchy concept, however, and see difficulties in making concepts like self-actualization (i.e., to become everything that one is capable of becoming) operational.

Consequently, in his study of two engineering groups, Barnes set aside the category of self-actualization and viewed man's safety needs as overlapping the other higher needs. Whenever one of these was threatened, so was man's safety. This left a base of physiological needs and

---

[3] Louis B. Barnes, *Organizational Systems and Engineering Groups: A Comparative Study of Two Technical Groups in Industry* (Boston: Division of Research, Harvard Business School, 1960), pp. 167–69.

a higher need level consisting of self-esteem, esteem of others, and belonging, each in mutual relationship to the other. Barnes also related these needs to the three dimensions (autonomy, opportunity for interaction, and influence) which defined an organizational system in his study. Consequently, an individual's self-esteem needs were met to the extent he had autonomy and freedom on the job. Other esteem needs related to the ways in which influence relationships were structured. Belonging needs were satisfied or frustrated according to the opportunities for interaction provided beyond those required by the job. Autonomy, interaction opportunity, and influence are not only crucial dimensions for a concept of organizational system, claims Barnes, they also relate to an individual's pluralistic needs, described by Maslow and other psychologists. The difference is that needs are now seen as interdependent variables, not as hierarchically dependent upon lower level satisfactions. From this point of view, whenever the safety of one need is threatened by external system structuring, all are threatened.

The reader can fit these relationships into this course book's earlier conceptual scheme on small groups by noting that autonomy, interaction opportunities, and influence are respectively related to the activities, interactions, and sentiment categories of George Homans's external system concepts. (See Exhibit 1.)

EXHIBIT 1

A Possible Relationship between the Concepts of Organizational Systems and an Individual's Needs

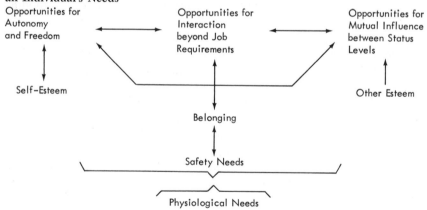

Section III

III

Group Behavior

Cases

1 | Excelsior Bakeries, Inc.[*]

Upon completing my junior year in college in early June, I returned to my hometown, Pottersville, New York. The next day I went to see Roger Farnum, the plant superintendent of the local branch of Excelsior Bakeries, Inc., to find out when I should report for work. I had worked at the Excelsior plant the previous summer as a general helper on the slicing and wrapping crew for hamburger and hot dog rolls. Since I was a union member and had spoken to Farnum during spring vacation about a job for this summer, I was positive of being rehired.

When I walked into the office, Farnum said jokingly: "Hi, George! Ready to go to work for a change after all that book learning?" I was rather surprised to see Farnum so jovial and cordial. I remembered him as always having a long face and never saying more than two words at a time. I finally answered: "Yes, sir, any time you say and as soon as possible."

"Well, on the recommendation of Murphy, you're going to run the hamburger and hot dog machine this summer. Murphy wants to work on the ovens; and since we don't want to change a regular worker over to the wrapper just for a couple of months, we figured you would accept the added responsibility and could handle the job."

Phil Murphy, a regular employee of the plant, had run the wrapping machine last summer and had been leader of a crew of three other summer workers and me. I had visited Murphy at the plant during

[*] During the winter following the events described in this case, the writer submitted it as a report for a course in administration he was taking in a graduate school of business.

spring vacation, and he had told me he was going to work on the ovens this year because it was daywork and paid more. I had casually mentioned to him at that time to try to get me the wrapping machine job, but I hadn't thought of it again, since it had always been assigned to a regular worker.

I was extremely pleased to accept the job, for I knew it meant 6 cents more an hour, and it would entail some leadership responsibility. I thought to myself: "Now I will be part of management and not just another worker."

Farnum told me to report for work that following Sunday, a week earlier than I had expected, so I could familiarize myself with the machine before the "rush season" started.

Excelsior Bakeries, Inc., was a large firm with many plants spread across the entire United States. The Pottersville branch produced mainly white, rye, whole wheat, and French bread, but supplemented these major lines with hamburger and hot dog rolls, dinner rolls, doughnuts, and other bakery products. It also distributed, in its area of operation, pies, cakes, crackers, and other specialities produced in the Boston plant.

Pottersville was located in a region noted for its many summer resorts, camps, and hotels, which are open from June until September. During the summer season, production and sales of the local Excelsior plant increased tremendously as the summer population swelled the normal demand. This seasonal rise was especially significant in hot dog and hamburger rolls, whose sales increased over the winter months by approximately 100–150 percent in June, 150–250 percent in July, and 250–300 percent in August. Because of this great seasonal increase, the company had to hire about 15 employees just for the 3 summer months. Five of the "extra help" were needed on the wrapping crew for hot dog and hamburger rolls. These workers were usually drawn from college students on vacation, employment agencies, and transients. In the past several years the extra help had been predominantly college students, because they were more dependable and willing to remain on the job right up to Labor Day.

After I reported to work, I spent the first week with the regular employees. Ed Dugan, a past operator of the wrapping machine, worked with me, teaching me all the techniques of operating the machine efficiently. The machine was rather old and had to be tended carefully at all times so that the cellophane wrapping paper would not jump off the rollers. The wrapping paper was expensive, and Joe McGuire, the night foreman, "blew his top" whenever a lot of paper was wasted.

Exhibit 1 shows the working area and the positions of each operator on the slicing and wrapping crew. Worker No. 1 took the pans of rolls from the racks and fed the rolls out on a conveyor, which carried them

EXHIBIT 1
Wrapping Machine Layout

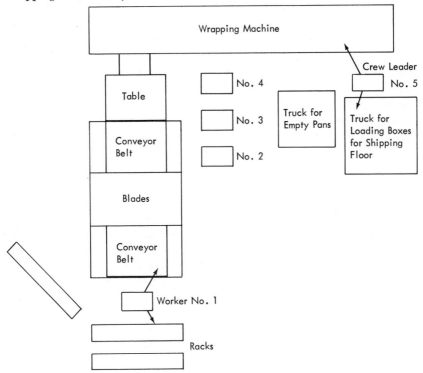

into the slicing machine. Worker No. 2 stacked the sliced rolls into two rows, one on top of the other, making groups of eight or one dozen. Worker No. 3 slid the groups of rolls down the table to worker No. 4, who fed them into the wrapping machine. Worker No. 5, the wrapping machine operator and crew leader, placed the wrapped packages in a box, keeping count of the actual number packaged. The work was rather routine and extremely monotonous and boring. Workers No. 1 through No. 4 continually exchanged positions in order to break the monotony.

The plant employees worked on a five-day week—working on Sunday and Monday; off on Tuesday; working Wednesday, Thursday, and Friday; and off again on Saturday. Production was on daily orders from the various sales routes. The salesmen left the plant early in the morning with their loaded trucks and, after making their deliveries, returned in the afternoon with the orders for the next day. The volume varied from day to day, and the rolls were ready for wrapping at varying times. Therefore, the wrappers generally reported for work at a different time each day, being notified by the plant superintendent. Usually, the crew began about 6:00 to 8:00 P.M. and worked until all the orders were filled for that night. The number of hours worked ranged from 7 to 15 or even more. All time over eight hours was overtime and paid for as time and a half. If a worker was a union member, the company had to guarantee him seven hours' pay for any night on which it called him in. If there were not seven hours of slicing and wrapping, the foreman found something else for the men to do, such as thoroughly cleaning the machines, greasing the pans, or doing other odd jobs. If a man wished, though, he could ask to punch out before seven hours were up, thereby forfeiting the guaranteed seven hours' pay for that night and receiving pay only for the hours he had worked.

Four different types of packages were wrapped on the machine: hamburger and hot dog dozen-roll packages, and hamburger and hot dog packages of eight rolls. A different size and type of paper was used for each package. Different-sized plates had to be used in the machine also. On an average night a complete changeover of the machine had to be made about six times, each alteration taking about ten minutes. In addition, it took about five minutes to replace a roll of paper when it ran out, and two to three minutes to replace the labels and seals. During these changeovers and replacements, which were made by the machine operator, the rest of the crew smoked cigarettes out on the shipping dock or else folded boxes for the operator if he needed them. I never asked anyone to make boxes if he wanted to have a cigarette or wanted to get a drink of water. But if a man was just sitting around or "goofing off," I would ask him to fold boxes, as the crew is supposed to do during these breaks. McGuire hated to see anyone sit around, but he never begrudged anyone a cigarette.

With the start of my second week, orders rose, and the rest of the summer help was called in. I was very pleased when three of my close friends were assigned to my crew. Art Dunn, a student at Williams, had worked on the wrapping crew with me the previous summer, as had Jack Dorsey, a student at the University of Vermont. Bill Regan, a Fordham student, had not worked for Excelsior the previous summer; but he had lived next door to me, and we had grown up together. The four of us had been close friends during high school days and since graduation, even though we went to different colleges. Harry Hart, the fourth man, was also new to the wrapping crew. Hart had graduated from high school a year before the rest of us and was attending the University of Massachusetts. We old-timers were already union members. The new men joined soon after they began work.

With the help of Dunn and Dorsey, I was able to train Regan and Hart quickly; and within a couple of nights, they were thoroughly proficient in all four positions. During these first two nights, Dunn and

Dorsey thoroughly indoctrinated Regan and Hart into the "code" of the wrapping crew.

Excelsior Bakeries offered college students an excellent opportunity to make a considerable amount of money during the summer, paying an hourly rate of $1.63 and providing plenty of overtime. The code of the wrapping crew was a concerted group action to set the number of hours to be worked on a certain night. At the beginning of the night's work, the crew could fairly well estimate from the production orders just how long it should take to put the work out. If it was estimated to take about eight hours, the crew would purposely slow down to stretch it to nine or nine and a half hours, so they could get overtime pay. On almost any night the work could be stretched out by an hour or so. Only on big nights of 12 or more hours did the crew work at normal speed. As an indication of the effectiveness of this slowdown, there were several occasions when a seven- or eight-hour night was estimated, but the crew "pushed the stuff through" and finished in six hours in order to have a few beers before the local bar closed at 3:00 A.M.

As a member of this crew the previous summer, I was one of the strong advocates of this code. If a new worker or a temporary replacement from somewhere else in the plant appeared on the crew, he had to conform, or the group gave him much verbal abuse or the even worse "silent treatment." These were unbearable conditions, and the new man always accepted the code.

Murphy, the previous year's leader, although a regular employee of the plant, had cooperated with the group and never complained. He used to say: "After all, I want the overtime, too!"

After the first few nights of work, I noticed the code had begun to operate. I had never stopped to think of the effects this slowdown had on management and the operations of the plant. It raised labor production costs, delayed the salesmen in leaving for their routes, and raised other problems as well. At first, I was rather confused as to whether I should allow this practice to continue or, as "part of management," put my foot down and take action to stop it. Because I could not think of any satisfactory course of action which would satisfy everyone, I allowed the code to operate I rationalized myself into believing: "Well, if management isn't going to do anything about it, why the hell should I worry about it?"

The first couple of weeks went smoothly. The only problems I had to face were minor arguments among the crew and the usual horseplay and "goofing off" in the middle hours of the morning.

McGuire, the night foreman, occasionally would say to me, smiling: "Took you guys a pretty long time to get those rolls out tonight, didn't it?" or, on a really short night: "You can really shove those rolls through when you feel like having a few brews!" McGuire could not see us working from his office, as the line of racks blocked his view, but he regularly walked over to check on us. When he appeared, the man feeding the slicing machine would place the rolls on the conveyor belt "back to back" with no space in between, the maximum rate at which the crew could operate. When he was in his office or "up front," a space of about 6 to 12 inches was allowed between rolls, thereby reducing the speed of production by 10 to 15 percent.

Occasionally, a "little war" would break out between the wrapping crew and two doughnut men across the aisle from the wrapping machine; the members of each group would throw doughnuts or hot dog and hamburger rolls at the others. One night, one of these battles was beginning to get out of hand to the point where the boys had stopped work. I reprimanded them and told them to "knock it off" and get back to work. Regan called me a "company man," and Dunn said something about the "lieutenant with the gold-plated bars."

I was trying to ignore the comments when suddenly I heard the paper snap. I stopped the machine and adjusted it; but even after the machine had been adjusted, package after package kept coming through unwrapped or "crippled." I tried everything I knew to find the cause of the trouble; but just when I thought I had the machine running properly, something else would go wrong. By this time, I was ready to give up and call McGuire for his advice.

Then I noticed the four crewmen having a good laugh for themselves. I had been so concerned about trying to change the adjustments on the machine that I had not noticed Regan tinkering with the machine at the other end. He was also feeding the hot dog rolls improperly, breaking them before putting them in the machine so they would slide off and get caught, thereby drawing unevenly on the paper. I lost my temper completely and was in the process of a real argument with Regan and the rest of the crew when McGuire came down to see why the machine was shut down. When he asked, I stuttered: "Hell, Joe, these— ah—this damn machine isn't drawing right. I've tried everything, but I think I've finally found the real reason. Let's try it now, fellas!"

That night, when I was making my final count with McGuire and the shipping foreman, I was considerably short on hot dog rolls, because of the many losses caused by Regan's tampering with the machine. McGuire gave me quite a reprimand and said I'd better "watch it."

The next night, when I came to work, Farnum stopped me and asked why I had lost so much paper the night before. I told him it was a breakdown in the machine. He gave me orders to weigh each roll of paper before we started wrapping each night and to weigh it again when we finished. I was to record the weights on tabulation control sheets kept in his office.

That night, before starting work, I told the crew what had happened and what McGuire and Farnum had said to me. I told them that I was being held responsible for paper and production control, and that I would tolerate no more "horsing around," especially tampering with the machine. I emphasized that I would not go "on the carpet" again for *anyone.*

Relations between me and the crew, with the exception of Hart, were rather strained for a couple of nights. None of them said very much to me. Also, I did not go swimming or play golf with them for a couple of days, as we usually did every afternoon. However, I had no more incidents of this sort, and the crew continued to meet the output schedule as they had previously. Gradually, the incident was forgotten, and relations among us became what they had been before.

During the latter part of August, the annual Excelsior clambake was held. In the late afternoon, McGuire called me over to the bar to have a drink: Mr. Farnum and Mr. Sommers, the plant general manager, were with him. McGuire threw his arm around me and said to Farnum: "George did a great job this summer on the wrapper, didn't he, Rog?"

"Best season we've had so far, Joe."

2 | *The Slade Company*

Ralph Porter, production manager of the Slade Company, was concerned by reports of dishonesty among some employees in the plating department. From reliable sources, he had learned that a few men were punching the timecards of a number of their workmates who had left early. Porter had only recently joined the Slade organization. He judged from conversations with the previous production manager and other fellow managers that they were, in general, pleased with the overall performance of the plating department.

The Slade Company was a prosperous manufacturer of metal products designed for industrial application. Its manufacturing plant, located in central Michigan, employed nearly five hundred workers, who were engaged in producing a large variety of clamps, inserts, knobs, and similar items. Orders for these products were usually large and on a recurrent basis. The volume of orders fluctuated in response to business conditions in the primary industries which the company served. At the time of this case, sales volume had been high for over a year. The bases upon which the Slade Company secured orders, in rank of importance, were quality, delivery, and reasonable price.

The organization of manufacturing operations at the Slade plant is shown in Exhibit 1. The departments listed there are, from left to right, approximately in the order in which material flowed through the plant. The diemaking and setup operations required the greatest degree of skill, supplied by highly paid, long-service craftsmen. The finishing departments, divided operationally and geographically between plating and painting, attracted less highly trained but relatively skilled workers, some of whom had been employed by the company for many years.

EXHIBIT 1
Manufacturing Organization

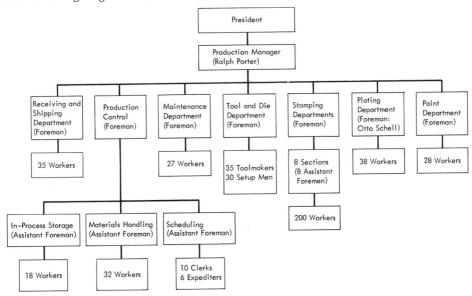

The remaining operations were largely unskilled in nature and were characterized by relatively low pay and high rate of turnover of personnel.

The plating room was the sole occupant of the top floor of the plant. Exhibit 2 shows the floor plan, the disposition of workers, and the flow of work throughout the department. Thirty-eight men and women worked in the department, plating or oxidizing the metal parts or preparing parts for the application of paint at another location in the plant. The department's work occurred in response to orders communicated by production schedules, which were revised daily. Schedule revisions, caused by last-minute order increases or rush requests from customers, resulted in short-term volume fluctuations, particularly in the plating, painting, and shipping departments. Exhibit 3 outlines the activities of the various jobs, their interrelationships, and the type of work in which each specialized. Exhibit 4 rates the various types of jobs in terms of the technical skill, physical effort, discomfort, and training time associated with their performance.

The activities which took place in the plating room were of three main types:

1. Acid dipping, in which parts were etched by being placed in baskets which were manually immersed and agitated in an acid solution.

EXHIBIT 2
Plating Room Layout

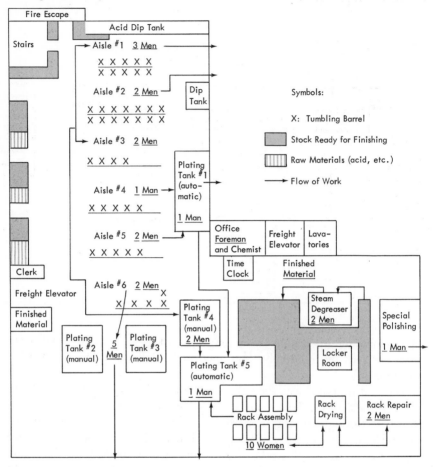

2. Barrel tumbling, in which parts were roughened or smoothed by being loaded into machine-powered revolving drums containing abrasive, caustic, or corrosive solutions.

3. Plating, either manual, in which parts were loaded on racks and were immersed by hand through the plating sequence, or automatic, in which racks or baskets were manually loaded with parts which were then carried by a conveyor system through the plating sequence.

Within these main divisions, there were a number of variables, such as cycle times, chemical formulas, abrasive mixtures, and so forth, which distinguished particular jobs as they have been categorized in Exhibit 3.

EXHIBIT 3
Outline of Work Flow, Plating Room

AISLE 1:	Worked closely with Aisle 3 in preparation of parts by barrel tumbling and acid dipping for high-quality* plating in Tanks 4 and 5. Also did a considerable quantity of highly specialized, high-quality acid-etching work not requiring further processing.
AISLE 2:	Tumbled items of regular quality and design in preparation for painting. Less frequently, did oxidation dipping work of regular quality, but sometimes of special design, not requiring further processing.
AISLE 3:	Worked closely with Aisle 1 on high-quality tumbling work for Tanks 4 and 5.
AISLES 4 AND 5:	Produced regular tumbling work for Tank 1.
AISLE 6:	Did high-quality tumbling work for special products plated in Tanks 2 and 3.
TANK 1:	Worked on standard, automated plating of regular quality not further processed in plating room, and regular work further processed in Tank 5.
TANKS 2 AND 3:	Produced special, high-quality plating work not requiring further processing.
TANK 4:	Did special, high-quality plating work further plated in Tank 5.
TANK 5:	Automated production of high- and regular-quality, special- and regular-design plated parts sent directly to shipping.
RACK ASSEMBLY:	Placed parts to be plated in Tank 5 on racks.
RACK REPAIR:	Performed routine replacement and repair of racks used in Tank 5.
POLISHING:	Processed, by manual or semimanual methods, odd-lot special orders which were sent directly to shipping. Also, sorted and reclaimed parts rejected by inspectors in the shipping department.
DEGREASING:	Took incoming raw stock, processed it through caustic solution, and placed clean stock in storage ready for processing elsewhere in the plating room.

---

* Definition of terms: *High or regular quality:* The quality of finishes could broadly be distinguished by the thickness of plate and/or care in preparation. *Regular or special work:* The complexity of work depended on the routine or special character of design and finish specifications.

The work of the plating room was received in batch lots whose size averaged a thousand pieces. The clerk moved each batch, which was accompanied by a routing slip, to its first operation. This routing slip indicated the operations to be performed and when each major operation on the batch was scheduled to be completed, so that the finished product could be shipped on time. From the accumulation of orders before him, each man was to organize his own work schedule so as to make optimal use of equipment, materials, and time. Upon completion of an order, each man moved the lot to its next work position or to the finished material location near the freight elevator.

The plating room was under the direct supervision of the foreman, Otto Schell, who worked a regular 8:00-to-5:00 day, five days a week.

EXHIBIT 4
Skill Indices by Job Group°

Jobs	Technical Skill Required	Physical Effort Required	Degree of Discomfort Involved	Degree of Training Required†
Aisle 1	1	1	1	1
Tanks 2–4	3	2	1	2
Aisles 2–6	5	1	1	5
Tank 5	1	5	7	2
Tank 1	8	5	5	7
Degreasing	9	3	7	10
Polishing	6	9	9	7
Rack assembly and repair	10	10	10	10

* Rated on scales of 1 (the greatest) to 10 (the least) in each category.
† The amount of experience required to assume complete responsibility for the job.

The foreman spent a good deal of his working time attending to maintenance and repair of equipment, procuring supplies, handling late schedule changes, and seeing that his people were at their proper work locations.

Working conditions in the plating room varied considerably. That part of the department containing the tumbling barrels and the plating machines was constantly awash, alternately with cold water, steaming acid, or caustic soda. Men working in this part of the room wore knee boots, long rubber aprons, and high-gauntlet rubber gloves. This uniform, consistent with the general atmosphere of the "wet" part of the room, was hot in summer, cold in winter. In contrast, the remainder of the room was dry, was relatively odor-free, and provided reasonably stable temperature and humidity conditions for those who worked there.

The men and women employed in the plating room are listed in Exhibit 5. This exhibit provides certain personal data on each department member, including a productivity-skill rating (based on subjective and objective appraisals of potential performance), as reported by the members of the department.

The pay scale implied by Exhibit 5 was low for the central Michigan area. The average starting wage for factory work in the community was about $1.25. However, working hours for the plating room were long (from 60 hours to a possible and frequently available 76 hours per week). The first 60 hours (the normal five-day week) were paid for on straight-time rates. Saturday work was paid for at time and one half; Sunday pay was calculated on a double-time basis.

As Exhibit 5 indicates, Philip Kirk, a worker in Aisle 2, provided the data for this case. After he had been a member of the department for several months, Kirk noted that certain members of the department

EXHIBIT 5
Plating Room Personnel

Location	Name	Age	Marital Status	Company Seniority	Department Seniority	Pay	Education	Familial Relationships	Productivity-Skill Rating*
Aisle 1	Tony Sarto	30	M	13 yrs.	13 yrs.	$1.50	High school	Louis Patrici, uncle; Pete Facelli, cousin	1
	Pete Facelli	26	M	8 yrs.	8 yrs.	1.30	High school	Louis Patrici, uncle; Tony Sarto, cousin	2
	Joe Iambi	31	M	5 yrs.	5 yrs.	1.20	2 yrs. high school		2
Aisle 2	Herman Schell	48	S	26 yrs.	26 yrs.	1.45	Grade school	Otto Schell, brother	8
Aisle 3	Philip Kirk	23	M	1 yr.	1 yr.	0.90	College		.†
	Dom Pantaleoni	31	M	10 yrs.	10 yrs.	1.30	1 yr. high school		2
	Sal Maletta	32	M	12 yrs.	12 yrs.	1.30	3 yrs. high school		3
Aisle 4	Bob Pearson	22	S	4 yrs.	4 yrs.	1.15	High school	Father in tool and die dept.	1
Aisle 5	Charlie Malone	44	M	22 yrs.	8 yrs.	1.25	Grade school	Brother in paint dept.	7
	John Lacey	41	S	9 yrs.	5 yrs.	1.20	1 yr. high school		7
Aisle 6	Jim Martin	30	S	7 yrs.	7 yrs.	1.25	High school		4
	Bill Mensch	41	M	6 yrs.	2 yrs.	1.10	Grade school		4

* On a potential scale of 1 (top) to 10 (bottom), as evaluated by the men in the department.
† Kirk was the source of data for this case and, as such, was in a biased position to report accurately perceptions about himself.

EXHIBIT 5 (*continued*)

Location	Name	Age	Marital Status	Company Seniority	Department Seniority	Pay	Education	Familial Relationships	Productivity-Skill Rating*
Tank 1	Henry La Forte	38	M	14 yrs.	6 yrs.	$1.25	High school		6
Tanks 2–3	Ralph Parker	25	S	7 yrs.	7 yrs.	1.20	High school		4
	Ed Harding	27	S	8 yrs.	8 yrs.	1.20	High school		4
	George Flood	22	S	5 yrs.	5 yrs.	1.15	High school		5
	Harry Clark	29	M	8 yrs.	8 yrs.	1.20	High school		3
	Tom Bond	25	S	6 yrs.	6 yrs.	1.20	High school		4
Tank 4	Frank Bonzani	27	M	9 yrs.	9 yrs.	1.25	High school		2
	Al Bartolo	24	M	6 yrs.	6 yrs.	1.25	High school		3
Tank 5	Louis Patrici	47	S	14 yrs.	14 yrs.	1.45	2 yrs. college	Tony Sarto, nephew Pete Facelli, nephew	1
Rack Assembly. . . .	10 women	30–40	9M, 1S	10 yrs. (av.)	10 yrs. (av.)	1.05	Grade school (av.)	6 with husbands in company	4 (av.)
Rack Maintenance. .	Will Partridge	57	M	14 yrs.	2 yrs.	1.20	Grade school		7
	Lloyd Swan	62	M	3 yrs.	3 yrs.	1.10	Grade school		7
Degreasing	Dave Susi	45	S	1 yr.	1 yr.	1.05	High school		5
	Mike Maher	41	M	4 yrs.	4 yrs.	1.05	Grade school		6
Polishing	Russ Perkins	49	M	12 yrs.	2 yrs.	1.20	High school		4
Foreman	Otto Schell	56	M	35 yrs.	35 yrs.	(not available)	High school	Herman Schell, brother	3
Clerk	Bill Pierce	32	M	10 yrs.	4 yrs.	1.15	High school		4
Chemist	Frank Rutlage	24	S	2 yrs.	2 yrs.	(not available)	2 yrs. college		6

* On a potential scale of 1 (top) to 10 (bottom), as evaluated by the men in the department.

tended to seek each other out during free time on and off the job. He then observed that these informal associations were enduring, built upon common activities and shared ideas about what was and what was not legitimate behavior in the deparment. His estimate of the pattern of these associations is diagrammed in Exhibit 6.

EXHIBIT 6
Informal Groupings in the Plating Room

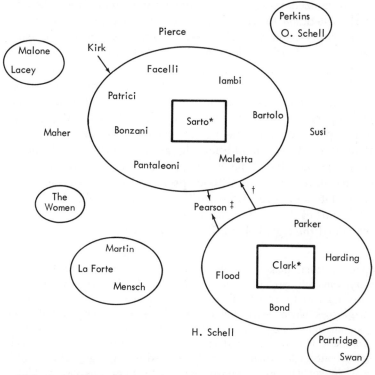

* The boxes indicate those men who clearly demonstrated leadership behavior (most closely personified the values shared by their groups, were often sought for help arbitration, and so forth).

† While the two- and three-man groupings had little informal contact outside their own boundaries, the five-man group did seek to join the largest group in extraplant social affairs. These were relatively infrequent.

‡ Though not an active member of any group, Bob Pearson was regarded with affection by the two large groups.

The Sarto group, so named because Tony Sarto was its most respected member and the one who acted as arbiter between the other members, was the largest in the department. The group, except for Louis Patrici, Al Bartolo, and Frank Bonzani (who spelled each other during break periods), invariably ate lunch together on the fire escape near Aisle 1.

On those Saturdays and Sundays when overtime work was required, the Sarto group operated as a team, regardless of weekday work assignments, to get overtime work completed as quickly as possible. (Few department members not affiliated with either the Sarto or the Clark groups worked on weekends.) Off the job, Sarto group members often joined in parties or weekend trips. Sarto's summer camp was a frequent rendezvous.

Sarto's group was also the most cohesive one in the department in terms of its organized punch-in and punch-out system. Since the men wre regularly scheduled to work from 7:00 A.M. to 7:00 P.M. weekdays, and since all supervision was removed at 5:00 P.M., it was possible almost every day to finish a "day's work" by 5:30 and leave the plant. What is more, if one man were to stay until 7:00 P.M., he could punch the timecards of a number of men and help them gain free time without pay loss. (This system operated on weekends, also, at which times members of supervision were present, if at all, only for short periods.) In Sarto's group the duty of staying late rotated, so that no man did so more than once a week. In addition, the group members would punch a man in in the morning if he were unavoidably delayed. However, such a practice never occurred without prior notice from the man who expected to be late and never if the tardiness was expected to lay beyond 8:00 A.M., the start of the day for the foreman.

Sarto explained the logic behind the system to Kirk:

> You know that our hourly pay rate is quite low, compared to other companies. What makes this the best place to work is the feeling of security you get. No one ever gets laid off in this department. With all the hours in the week, all the company ever has to do is shorten the workweek when orders fall off. We have to tighten our belts, but we can all get along. When things are going well, as they are now, the company is only interested in getting out the work. It doesn't help to get it out faster than it's really needed—so we go home a little early whenever we can. Of course, some guys abuse this sort of thing—like Herman—but others work even harder, and it averages out.
>
> Whenever an extra order has to be pushed through, naturally I work until 7:00. So do a lot of the others. I believe that if I stay until my work is caught up and my equipment is in good shape, that's all the company wants of me. They leave us alone and expect us to produce—and we do.

When Kirk asked Sarto if he would not rather work shorter hours at higher pay in a union shop (Slade employees were not organized), he just laughed and said: "It wouldn't come close to an even trade."

The members of Sarto's group were explicit about what constituted a fair day's work. Customarily, they cited Herman Schell, Kirk's work partner and the foreman's brother, as a man who consistently produced below that level. Kirk received an informal orientation from Herman during his first days on the job. As Herman put it:

> I've worked at this job for a good many years, and I expect to stay here a good many more. You're just starting out, and you don't know which end is up yet. We spend a lot of time in here; and no matter how hard we work, the pile of work never goes down. There's always more to take its place. And I think you've found out by now that this isn't light work. You can wear yourself out fast if you're not smart. Look at Pearson up in Aisle 4. There's a kid who's just going to burn himself out. He won't last long. If he thinks he's going to get somewhere working like that, he's nuts. They'll give him all the work he can take. He makes it tough on everybody else and on himself, too.

Kirk reported further on his observations of the department:

> As nearly as I could tell, two things seemed to determine whether or not Sarto's group or any others came in for weekend work on Saturday or Sunday. It seemed usually to be caused by rush orders that were received late in the week, although I suspect it was sometimes caused by the men having spent insufficient time on the job during the previous week.
>
> Tony and his group couldn't understand Herman. While Herman arrived late, Tony was always half an hour early. If there was a push to get out an extra amount of work, almost everyone but Herman would work that much harder. Herman never worked overtime on weekends, while Tony's group and the men on the manual tanks almost always did. When the first, exploratory time study of the department was made, no one in the aisles slowed down, except Herman, with the possible exception, to a lesser degree, of Charlie Malone. I did hear that the men in the dry end of the room slowed down so much you could hardly see them move; but we had little to do with them, anyway. While the men I knew best seemed to find a rather full life in their work, Herman never really got involved. No wonder they couldn't understand each other.
>
> There was quite a different feeling about Bobby Pearson. Without the slightest doubt, Bob worked harder than anyone else in the room. Because of the tremendous variety of work produced, it was hard to make output comparisons, but I'm sure I wouldn't be far wrong in saying that Bob put out twice as much as Herman and 50 percent more than almost anyone else in the aisles. No one but Herman and a few old-timers at the dry end ever criticized Bobby for his efforts. Tony and his group seemed to feel a distant affection for Bob, but the only contact they or anyone else had with him consisted of brief greetings.
>
> To the men in Tony's group the most severe penalty that could be inflicted on a man was exclusion. This they did to both Pearson and Herman. Pearson, however, was tolerated; Herman was not. Evi-

dently, Herman felt his exclusion keenly, though he answered it with derision and aggression. Herman kept up a steady stream of stories concerning his attempts to gain acceptance outside the company. He wrote popular music which was always rejected by publishers. He attempted to join several social and athletic clubs, mostly without success. His favorite pasttime was fishing. He told me that fishermen were friendly, and he enjoyed meeting new people whenever he went fishing. But he was particularly quick to explain that he preferred to keep his distance from the men in the department.

Tony's group emphasized more than just quantity in judging a man's work. Among them had grown a confidence that they could master and even improve upon any known finishing technique. Tony himself symbolized this skill. Before him, Tony's father had operated Aisle 1 and had trained Tony to take his place. Tony in his turn was training his cousin Pete. When a new finishing problem arose from a change in customer specifications, the foreman, the department chemist, or any of the men directly involved would come to Tony for help, and Tony would give it willingly. For example, when a part with a special plastic embossing was designed, Tony was the only one who could discover how to treat the metal without damaging the plastic. To a lesser degree, the other members of the group were also inventive about the problems which arose in their own sections.

Herman, for his part, talked incessantly about his feats in design and finish creations. As far as I could tell during the year I worked in the department, the objects of these stories were obsolete or of minor importance. What's more, I never saw any department member seek Herman's help.

Willingness to be of help was a trait Sarto's group prized. The most valued help of all was of a personal kind, though work help was also important. The members of Sarto's group were constantly lending and borrowing money, cars, clothing, and tools among themselves and, less frequently, with other members of the department. Their daily lunch bag procedure typified the "common property" feeling among them. Everyone's lunch was opened and added to a common pile, from which each member of the group chose his meal.

On the other hand, Herman refused to help others in any way. He never left his aisle to aid those near him who were in the midst of a rush of work or a machine failure, though this was customary throughout most of the department. I can distinctly recall the picture of Herman leaning on the hot and cold water faucets which were located directly above each tumbling barrel. He would stand gazing into the tumbling pieces for hours. To the passing, casual visitor, he looked busy; and as he told me, that's just what he wanted. He, of course, expected me to act this same way, and it was this enforced boredom that I found virtually intolerable.

More than this, Herman took no responsibility for breaking in his assigned helpers as they first entered the department, or thereafter. He had had four helpers in the space of little more than a year. Each had asked for a transfer to another department, publicly citing the work as cause, privately blaming Herman. Tony was the one who taught me the ropes when I first entered the department.

The men who congregated around Harry Clark tended to talk like and copy the behavior of the Sarto group, though they never approached the degree of inventive skill or the amount of helping activities that Tony's group did. They sought outside social contact with the Sarto group; and several times a year, the two groups went "on the town" together. Clark's group did maintain a high level of performance in the volume of work they turned out.

The remainder of the people in the department stayed pretty much to themselves or associated in pairs or triplets. None of these people were as inventive, as helpful, or as productive as Sarto's or Clark's groups, but most of them gave verbal support to the same values as those groups held.

The distinction between the two organized groups and the rest of the department was clearest in the punching-out routine. The women could not work past 3:00 P.M., so they were not involved. Malone and Lacey, Partridge and Swan, and Martin, La Forte, and Mensch arranged within their small groups for punch-outs, or they remained beyond 5:00 and slept or read when they finished their work. Perkins and Pierce went home when the foreman did. Herman Schell, Susi, and Maher had no punch-out organization to rely upon. Susi and Maher invariably stayed in the department until 7:00 P.M. Herman was reported to have established an arrangement with Partridge whereby the latter punched Herman out for a fee. Such a practice was unthinkable from the point of view of Sarto's group. It evidently did not occur often because Herman usually went to sleep behind piles of work when his brother left or, particularly during the fishing season, punched himself out early. He constantly railed against the dishonesty of other men in the department, yet urged me to punch him out on several "emergency occasions."

Just before I left the Slade Company to return to school after 14 months on the job, I had a casual conversation with Mr. Porter, the production manager, in which he asked me how I had enjoyed my experience with the organization. During the conversation, I learned that he knew of the punch-out system in the plating department. What's more, he told me, he was wondering if he ought to "blow the lid off the whole mess."

3 | *Work Group Ownership of an Improved Tool**

The Whirlwind Aircraft Corporation was a leader in its field and especially noted for its development of the modern supercharger. Work in connection with the latter mechanism called for special skill and ability. Every detail of the supercharger had to be perfect to satisfy the exacting requirements of the aircraft industry.

In 1941 (before Pearl Harbor), Lathe Department 15–D was turning out three types of impeller, each contoured to within 0.002 inch and machined to a mirrorlike finish. The impellers were made from an aluminum alloy and finished on a cam-back lathe.

The work was carried on in four shifts, two men on each. The personnel in the finishing section were as follows:

1. *First Shift*—7 A.M. to 3 P.M.   Sunday and Monday off.
   a.   Jean Latour, master mechanic, French Canadian, forty-five years of age. Latour had set up the job and trained the men who worked with him on the first shift.
   b.   Pierre DuFresne, master mechanic, French Canadian, thirty-six years of age. Both these men had trained the workers needed for the other shifts.
2. *Second Shift*—3 P.M. to 11 P.M.   Friday and Saturday off.
   a.   Albert Durand, master mechanic, French Canadian, thirty-two years of age; trained by Latour and using his lathe.
   b.   Robert Benet, master mechanic, French Canadian, thirty-one years of age; trained by DuFresne and using his lathe.

---

* The following case is reprinted with permission from Paul Pigors and Charles A. Myers, *Personnel Administration: A Point of View and a Method* (New York: McGraw-Hill Book Co., Inc., 1956).

3. *Third Shift*—11 P.M. to 7 A.M. Tuesday and Wednesday off.
    a. Philippe Doret, master mechanic, French Canadian, thirty-one years of age; trained by Latour and using his lathe.
    b. Henri Barbet, master mechanic, French Canadian, thirty years of age; trained by DuFresne and using his lathe.
4. *Stagger Shift*—Monday, 7 A.M. to 3 P.M.; Tuesday, 11 P.M. to 7 A.M.; Wednesday, 11 P.M. to 7 A.M.; Thursday, off; Friday, 3 P.M. to 11 P.M.; Saturday, 3 P.M. to 11 P.M.; Sunday, off.
    a. George MacNair, master mechanic, Scotch, thirty-two years of age; trained by Latour and using his lathe.
    b. William Reader, master mechanic, English, thirty years of age; trained by DuFresne and using his lathe.

Owing to various factors (such as the small number of workers involved, the preponderance of one nationality, and the fact that Latour and DuFresne had trained the other workers), these eight men considered themselves as members of one work group. Such a feeling of solidarity is unusual among workers on different shifts, despite the fact that they use the same machines.

The men received a base rate of $1.03 an hour and worked on incentive. Each man usually turned out 22 units a shift, thus earning an average of $1.19 an hour. Management supplied Rex 95 High-Speed Tool-Bits, which workers ground to suit themselves. Two tools were used: one square bit with a slight radius for recess cutting, the other bit with a 45-degree angle for chamfering and smooth finish. When used, both tools were set close together, the worker adjusting the lathe from one operation to the other. The difficulty with this setup was that during the rotation of the lathe, the aluminum waste would melt and fuse between the two toolbits. Periodically the lathe had to be stopped so that the toolbits could be freed from the welded aluminum and reground.

At the request of the supervisor of Lathe Department 15–D, the methods department had been working on his tool problem. Up to the time of this case, no solution had been found. To make a firsthand study of the difficulty, the methods department had recently assigned one of its staff, Mr. MacBride, to investigate the problem in the lathe department itself. Mr. MacBride's working hours covered parts of both the first and second shifts. MacBride was a young man, twenty-six years of age, and a newcomer to the methods department. For the three months prior to this assignment, he had held the post of "suggestion man," a position which enabled newcomers to the methods department to familiarize themselves with the plant setup. The job consisted in collecting, from boxes in departments throughout the plant, suggestions submitted by employees and making a preliminary evaluation of these ideas. The current assignment of studying the tool situation in Lathe

Department 15–D, with a view to cutting costs, was his first special task. He devoted himself to this problem with great zeal but did not succeed in winning the confidence of the workers. In pursuance of their usual philosophy: "Keep your mouth shut if you see anyone with a suit on," they volunteered no information and took the stand that, since the methods man had been given this assignment, it was up to him to carry it out.

While MacBride was working on this problem, Pierre DuFresne hit upon a solution. One day he successfully contrived a tool which combined the two bits into one. This eliminated the space between the two toolbits which in the past had caught the molten aluminum waste and allowed it to become welded to the cutting edges. The new toolbit had two advantages: it eliminated the frequent machine stoppage for cleaning and regrinding the old-type tools; and it enabled the operator to run the lathe at a higher speed. These advantages made it possible for the operator to increase his efficiency 50%.

DuFresne tried to make copies of the new tool, but was unable to do so. Apparently the new development had been a "lucky accident" during grinding which he could not duplicate. After several unsuccessful attempts, he took the new tool to his former teacher, Jean Latour. The latter succeeded in making a drawing and turning out duplicate toolbits on a small grinding wheel in the shop. At first the two men decided to keep the new tool to themselves. Later, however, they shared the improvement with their fellow workers on the second shift. Similarly it was passed on to the other shifts. But all these men kept the new development a closely guarded secret as far as "outsiders" were concerned. At the end of the shift, each locked the improved toolbit securely in his toolchest.

Both Dufresne, the originator of the new tool, and Latour, its draftsman and designer, decided not to submit the idea as a suggestion but to keep it as the property of their group. Why was this decision made? The answer lies partly in the suggestion system and partly in the attitude of Latour and DuFresne toward other features of company work life and toward their group.

According to an information bulletin issued by the company, the purpose of the suggestion system was to "provide an orderly method of submitting and considering ideas and recommendations of employees to management; to provide a means for recognizing and rewarding individual ingenuity; and to promote cooperation." Awards for accepted suggestions were made in the following manner: "After checking the savings and expense involved in an adopted suggestion [the suggestion committee] determined the amount of the award to be paid, based upon the savings predicted upon a year's use of the suggestion." "It is the intention of the committee . . . to be liberal in the awards, which are expected to adequately compensate for the interest shown in present-ing suggestions." In pursuance of this policy, it was customary to grant the suggestor an award equivalent to the savings of an entire month.

As a monetary return, both DuFresne and Latour considered an award based on one month's saving as inadequate. They also argued that such awards were really taken out of the worker's pockets. Their reasoning was as follows: All awards for adopted suggestions were paid out of undistributed profits. Since the company also had a profit-sharing plan, the money was taken from a fund that would be given to the workers anyway, which merely meant robbing Peter to pay Paul. In any case, the payment was not likely to be large and probably would be less than they could accumulate if increased incentive payments could be maintained over an extended period without discovery. Thus there was little in favor of submitting the new tool as a suggestion.

Latour and DuFresne also felt that there were definite hazards to the group if their secret were disclosed. They feared that once the tool became company property, its efficiency might lead to layoff of some members in their group, or at least make work less tolerable by leading to an increased quota at a lower price per unit. They also feared that there might be a change in scheduled work assignments. For instance, the lathe department worked on three different types of impeller. One type was a routine job and aside from the difficulty caused by the old-type tool, presented no problem. For certain technical reasons, the other two types were more difficult to make. Even Latour, an exception-ally skilled craftsman, had sometimes found it hard to make the expected quota before the new tool was developed. Unless the work load was carefully balanced by scheduling easier and more difficult types, some of the operators were unable to make standard time.

The decision to keep the tool for their own group was in keeping with Latour's work philosophy. He had a strong feeling of loyalty to his own group and had demonstrated this in the past by offering for their use several improvements of his own. For example, he made avail-able to all workers in his group a set of special gauge blocks which were used in aligning work on lathes. To protect himself in case mistakes were traced to these gauges, he wrote on them: "Personnel (*sic*) Prop-erty–Do not use. Jean Latour."

Through informal agreement with their fellow workers, Latour and DuFresne "pegged production" at an efficiency rate that in their opinion would not arouse management's suspicion or lead to a restudy of the job, with possible cutting of the rate. This enabled them to earn an extra 10% incentive earnings. The other 40% in additional efficiency was used as follows: The operators established a reputation for a high degree of accuracy and finish. They set a record for no spoilage and were able to apply the time gained on the easier type of impeller to work on the other types which required greater care and more expert workmanship.

The foreman of the lathe department learned about the new tool soon after it was put into use but was satisfied to let the men handle the situation in their own way. He reasoned that at little expense he was able to get out production of high quality. There was no defective work, and the men were contented.

Mr. MacBride was left in a very unsatisfactory position. He had not succeeded in working out a solution of his own. Like the foreman, he got wind of the fact that the men had devised a new tool. He urged them to submit a drawing of it through the suggestion system, but this advice was not taken, and the men made it plain that they did not care to discuss with him the reasons for this position.

Having no success in his direct contact with the workers, Mr. MacBride appealed to the foreman, asking him to secure a copy of the new tool. The foreman replied that the men would certainly decline to give him a copy and would resent as an injustice any effort on his part to force them to submit a drawing. Instead he suggested that MacBride should persuade DuFresne to show him the tool. This MacBride attempted to do, but met with no success in his efforts to ingratiate himself with DuFresne. When he persisted in his attempts, DuFresne decided to throw him off the track. He left in his lathe a toolbit which was an unsuccessful copy of the original discovery. At shift change, MacBride was delighted to find what he supposed to be the improved tool. He hastily copied it and submitted a drawing to the tool department. When a tool was made up according to these specifications it naturally failed to do what was expected of it. The workers, when they heard of this through the "grapevine," were delighted. DuFresne did not hesitate to crow over MacBride, pointing out that his underhanded methods had met with their just reward.

The foreman did not take any official notice of the conflict between DuFresne and MacBride. Then MacBride complained to the foreman that DuFresne was openly boasting of his trick and ridiculing him before other workers. Thereupon, the foreman talked to DuFresne, but the latter insisted that his ruse had been justified as a means of self-protection.

When he was rebuffed by DuFresne, the foreman felt that he had lost control of the situation. He could no longer conceal from himself that he was confronted by a more complex situation than what initially he had defined as a "tool problem." His attention was drawn to the fact that the state of affairs in his department was a tangle of several interrelated problems. Each problem urgently called for a decision that involved understanding and practical judgment. But having for so long failed to see the situation as a whole, he now found himself in a dilemma.

He wished to keep the goodwill of the work group, but he could not countenance the continued friction between DuFresne and Mac-Bride. Certainly, he could not openly abet his operators in obstructing the work of a methods man. His superintendent would now certainly hear of it and would be displeased to learn that a foreman had failed to tell him of such an important technical improvement. Furthermore, he knew that the aircraft industry was expanding at this time and that the demand for impellers had increased to such an extent that management was planning to set up an entire new plant unit devoted to this product.

4 | *Tubident, S.A.*[*]

"Yes, we have a serious organizational problem around here. My supervisors don't know how to supervise, and I just can't control production the way we must in this business. Until about a year ago, I used male foremen to supervise the female workers on our production lines, but we had a lot of playing around that hurt both morale and production. I think I have that problem solved. But I still have discipline problems, and high quality and volume standards are always in danger. My supervisors just aren't aggressive enough."

Sr. Lopez, a founding stockholder and the general manager of Tubident, S.A., was explaining his supervision problem to a casewriter from the Harvard Business School who visited the plant in the summer of 1966. "I can't explain this problem sitting in this office. Let's go out to the plant floor so I can show you how the production lines operate. Then I can explain what's wrong with my supervisors."

COMPANY BACKGROUND

The Tubident plant was located near a poor residential area in the outskirts of the capital city of Cozuela. Cozuela was a member of a recently established protected trade area composed of a number of neighboring nations in Latin America. The company was founded in 1962 by Sr. Lopez and two investors well known in the country with the hope of obtaining the contract to supply metal tubes for the recently

---

established local plant of a large international toothpaste manufacturer. Although importing tubes from abroad, the management of the company had refused to encourage the initiation of Tubident, despite the promise of substantial cost savings. Packaging was considered to be of primary sales importance, and the firm maintained rigorous quality standards which it doubted that Tubident could meet. Reliable delivery was also considered essential, and it was noted that local firms with limited mechanical experience and an untrained workforce sometimes suffered unexpected delays. Although discouraged by their failure to achieve a supplier contract and by the resulting uncertainty of their market prospects, Tubident organizers decided to initiate the enterprise anyway, and success had gradually followed. After four years, the firm had become the exclusive metal tube supplier to its initial customer and to a number of other toothpaste, cosmetic, and detergent firms in the area, increasing many times both its volume and the types of tubes it produced. Recently, a line of plastic extruding machines had been added and a second expansion of plant facilities was contemplated.

Investors gave much credit for the success of the enterprise to Sr. Lopez. Trained in a technical institute in Europe, he had several years of production experience with local firms, frequently working in process design and equipment installation. At Tubident, Sr. Lopez had designed and set up the plant, and served as sales executive, purchasing agent, and financial officer, as well as general manager. (See Exhibit 1 for Tubident's organization chart.)

PRODUCTION

All production facilities were located in the central factory area. A small volume of plastic bottles and other extruded plastic containers was produced in this area, but the principal product was toothpaste tubes of a variety of types and sizes. Crude types were produced from small aluminum washers on the company's extrusion machine, which was equipped with a synchronized screw machine to thread the neck and carve the collar design. Crude tubes were stored in large wire baskets until they were needed for finished processing on the two tube production lines. At the first four stations on the production lines, tubes were passed on a conveyer through an oven for heat treating to create the proper degree of flexibility—soft enough to be squeezed easily yet hard enough to withstand further processing. Then tubes were given their exterior color base on the lacquering machine, which contained three revolving cylinders on which the tubes were rolled through a lacquer base. An overhead conveyor then passed the tubes through a drying oven and to the printing machine station. The mechanical operation of the printing machine was similar to that of the lacquerer, except

EXHIBIT 1
Organization Chart, 1966

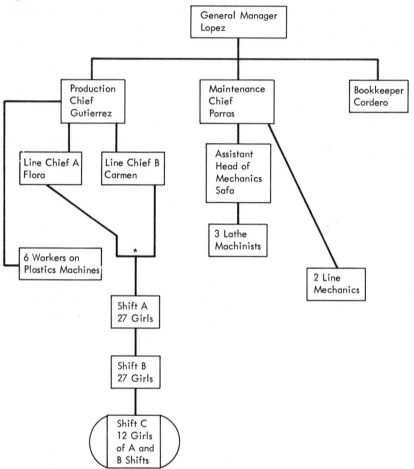

* The dual responsibility of the two line chiefs represents the fact that each chief supervised each of the two shifts for different parts of each day.

that the tubes were rolled against a mat which applied a design and written message. The work of the unloaders at the lacquering and printing machines required manual speed, dexterity, and good vision. The machines were preset to discharge roughly a tube per second. The unloader had to remove the tube by the neck, inspect it for various kinds of defects, place it precisely on a hook on the conveyor, and wipe excess lacquer from the cylinder before the machine moved through its next cycle. Next, the tubes were conveyed through a second drying oven to the packing table where packers removed them from the hooks, inspected them, screwed on plastic caps, removed excess ink from the interiors, and boxed them for shipment. Above every machine was a sign indicating the cost to the plant of each hour of downtime. Exhibit 2 is a floor plan of the factory area.

The tube production lines were operated on a two-shift basis six

EXHIBIT 2
Factory Floor Plan, 1966

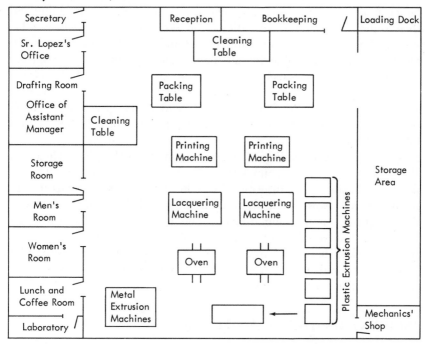

days a week. Two complete shifts, composed entirely of women, worked on the line. Because of a government regulation requiring a half-hour lunch break for straight eight-hour shifts, the two shifts' crews worked alternate four-hour periods, 6 to 10 A.M.—2 to 6 P.M. and 10 A.M. to 2 P.M.—6 to 10 P.M. Work crews exchanged shifts every week. Approximately eight months out of the year, a third shift was added. It operated one of the two production lines between 10 P.M. and 6 A.M. Permission to work women after 10 P.M. had to be renewed periodically by the Ministry of Labor and sometimes required weeks of negotiation, during which period the late shift had to be discontinued. To man the night operations, workers were selected from the two permanent day crews and were replaced on the day shifts by permanently employed extras who otherwise performed service jobs in the plant. Night workers were paid one and one half times the day rate.

Each day shift employed approximately 27 women. Women at the oven and the lacquering and printing machines worked in teams of two, while four to five women worked at each packing table. Exhibit 2 also shows the distribution of workers across the floor. The forelady and her mechanic worked straight eight-hour shifts and thus supervised each of the two shift crews for four hours a day. When a night shift was operated, each forelady and mechanic team worked 12 consecutive hours a day. The forelady was officially responsible for assigning girls their duties, maintaining discipline, and doing odd jobs such as filling the ink buckets and making simple adjustments to the machinery. The mechanic was responsible for all maintenance, setups, and satisfactory operations of all machinery on the lines. Although one of the girls at the packing table was designated as the inspector and held responsible for quality control, Sr. Lopez said, "I hold every girl responsible for quality production." A production manager was responsible for the overall operation.

Several physical conditions affected the work in the plant. Heat from the ovens made the area unusually hot, especially at midday. The lacquering machines gave off a pungent odor, which was nauseous to some of the women. Noise from the machines, particularly from the extruders, made normal conversation difficult. The factory floor was surrounded by offices and supplementary rooms, all opening onto it. People constantly walked back and forth across the floor, inventories were piled in free spots, and women worked at two or three cleaning tables, giving the impression of crowding and great activity.

INCIDENT ON THE PLANT FLOOR

As he guided the casewriter past the machines during his explanation of the operation, Sr. Lopez indicated a lacquering machine which had been brought to a halt, its two operators standing idly beside it. "That is exactly the problem I was telling you about in the office. That machine is down. The chain is slack. In another two minutes the printing machine will be idled for lack of tubes coming out of the drying oven. Five minutes from now, the packers will have no tubes. The minute a machine goes down like that, the mechanic ought to be on it. Gutierrez (the production manager) should never let this kind of thing happen, but it constantly does. Will you excuse me a minute? I've got to get this thing under control."

Sr. Lopez walked over to the girls and spoke with them for a moment. Then he left and went towards the laboratory, emerging a few minutes later with a mustached man in a white shirt and slacks. They spoke for a few minutes with the girls and then bent over the machine, which the white-shirted man began to tinker with. A man in levis appeared with a wrench and screwdriver, spoke with the two other men, and then also bent over and began to make adjustments. After about five minutes, the machine was back in operation.

As Sr. Lopez was returning to the casewriter with the white-shirted man, a secretary ran up saying that Sr. Lopez had a phone call. Sr. Lopez said, "This is Sr. Gutierrez, our production manager here. Perhaps he can help you clear up any technical questions you have while I take this call." He again excused himself and followed the secretary off the floor.

Sr. Gutierrez began to talk about the technical problems of the machinery and the job of keeping the lines running. The casewriter, however, had noticed a number of things about which he had questions and began by asking Gutierrez why he had seen a few girls sitting alone on packing boxes cleaning tubes while others worked in groups.

GUTIERREZ: It disturbs Sr. Lopez to see the girls talking too much. On the lines, it's hard enough keeping the talking down so that they can check the printing and lacquering on each tube. When they get into groups to clean defectives, sometimes one of them really begins to act up, and the rest of the girls become silly and really loud. This distracts the girls in the group and also others working on the line. So we sometimes have to put the troublemakers to work by themselves.

CASEWRITER: Why do the girls have to be quiet on the lines?

GUTIERREZ: It's not that they really have to be quiet. It's just that they have to concentrate to spot defectives caused by their machine and by previous operations. Each of the machines can produce its own type of defective. For example, the extrusion machine could produce defects in shape or design; improper oven temperature or conveyor speed can make the tube too hard or too soft. Lacquer might be too thick and smudge or crack. And the most difficult one, of course, is the printing machine, which might produce a few flawed letters of tiny type. Because of the speed of the machines, the checking we require is tough and requires great concentration.

The casewriter asked Sr. Gutierrez what his biggest problem was in supervising the girls on the line. He said: "Sometimes the girls get the mechanics to fuss with the machines when it isn't necessary, or they stop them every half hour for cleaning. Now, you can't say anything about this because it's hard to judge whether the tubes are right. Sr. Lopez is a real stickler for quality, and if you've told the girls to get the machine going and he comes in and spots a tube he doesn't like, you're not doing your job."

CASEWRITER: What does Sr. Lopez have to do with supervising the plant operation?

GUTIERREZ: Unfortunately (*smiling broadly*), everything. When he gets to the plant in the morning, the first thing he does after hanging up his coat is to come out here. He looks at the quality of the printing and the lacquering, the tube shape and its feel, the oven temperatures and the conveyer speeds, or a machine we're repairing, and he always has suggestions. He picks a tube off the line (*Sr. Gutierrez picked up an imaginary tube, raised it to within a couple of inches from his face, and scrutinized it with his head cocked and one eye closed*) and says to me, "Gutierrez, don't you believe this tube could use a little more ink?" It's a very good question.

CASEWRITER: Does this bother you?

GUTIERREZ: No, not really. I've been with this plant since the beginning. And by now, I'm used to it. Besides, if there's a mistake out here, it is my responsibility. Sr. Lopez knows this machinery and he knows the quality that our customers want better than any of us. So he's helping, not hurting me, when he points out errors . . . (*Sr. Gutierrez thought a moment*). No, I'm very appreciative of Sr. Lopez's help. But Porras, who was production manager before me and who is now chief mechanic, used to blow up whenever Cordero, the bookkeeper, came out here. Cordero doesn't know anything about machines, yet he'd come running out here all the time, waving his papers about wastage or defectives or production rates. And he didn't care who he talked to. I guess he's learned better, though, because he doesn't do it now except when Sr. Lopez is out of the country. Since he owns a few shares of stock, I guess he feels responsible for filling in for Sr. Lopez.

THE PROBLEM OF SUPERVISION

At this point, Sr. Lopez returned and accompanied the writer to the office saying, "You've seen the operation and understand how it works. Let's have some coffee and I'll explain my supervisor problem. Let me start from the beginning. When we began to produce here, we decided to use women for a variety of reasons. Most important, female labor is less expensive than male labor, and the work on the line requires no special knowledge or technical skill and is not heavy. We took only young women, and, as is natural, women who weren't ugly, in order to give the plant a more attractive appearance. We thought that young women wouldn't have children and thus would be able to work more freely in a factory. We also felt they would be more energetic and thus able to boost production. We used male line chiefs, who supervised the girls and also served as mechanics.

"But having males supervise all-women crews led to nothing but trouble. Almost immediately, some of the girls began to complain that the line chiefs were showing preference towards certain other girls. The girls said that the sweethearts were given the best jobs so that they could make the best pay and were treated far more leniently than the others. You can imagine the kind of thing: A favorite says she feels badly or wants to be excused for the day, so naturally the man has a soft heart and gives her time off or sends her to rest in the coffee room. Naturally, the less attractive girls must have resented being denied these privileges. I suppose that sometimes the line chief lost interest in an old favorite and to make the point, he perhaps treated her a little harder than the others. Maybe the discarded girl felt resentful and wanted to get even with him.

"Two things worried me about this: one, I want good morale, and, two, I could imagine what was going on at night. None of the administrators are here at night and the shift chief would really have a chance to fool around. Fooling around, he would lose everyone's respect and be unable to maintain discipline. And if he were fooling around, he would have to give a chance to the mechanics, too. You can imagine the kind of problem that I could have on my hands.

"Of course, had I had proof of any of this, someone would have gotten fired on the spot, but everytime I brought it up, it was staunchly denied.

"What was I to do? I liked the idea of replacing outright the young girls with older, uglier women who would be more responsible, less chatty, and less attractive to line chiefs. But that would have meant loss of the training time I'd already invested and possible labor problems which might have jeopardized the night shift. Furthermore, all that severance pay would have been expensive. And anyway, I don't believe in treating workers that way.

"My other idea was to replace the male shift foremen with women. We heard that women were working when they didn't feel well because they were embarrassed to tell their supervisors. Also, women are emotional and get easily upset when men are gruff, which often happened because the foremen were in a hurry or angry at something. With a forelady, the workers would feel more comfortable and would be able to communicate better. But I didn't want to do this because I didn't want to lose my men, who were by this time good mechanics, and I also feared that the foreladies would be unable to maintain discipline, especially at night when there were no administrators around. I just couldn't picture a woman obeying another woman. I also wondered if a woman would be able to get the mechanics to cooperate.

"There was my original problem. What would you have done?"

CASEWRITER: It sounds very complicated. How did you handle it?

LOPEZ: It proved easier than I had thought, and I made both moves. I replaced the young girls gradually as they left the plant of their own accord. We still have a lot of the earlier workers with us, but you can see the older ones scattered through the lines, and they are much more satisfactory. As for the shift chiefs, I got rid of those who had been causing the trouble. We picked our two best women and assigned them as foreladies. We got rid of all the men who had been causing the trouble. The good men, who liked learning about machines, were made mechanics of the new plastics line which we were opening. At the same time, I created a separate mechanics staff with Porras, our old production chief and best mechanic, as head. Then I assigned a mechanic from that staff to work with each of the foreladies. Gutierrez, one of our old line foremen, was made production manager.

CASEWRITER: And what were the results?

LOPEZ: Well, I have no more complaints of favoritism, and my production jumped considerably. But the basic problems of quality and volume are always with us, and I have to be constantly on top of them, or they will get out of hand.

CASEWRITER: Could you explain these problems?

LOPEZ: I guess the simplest way is to explain a little more about the people I've got. The girls don't always pay attention and aren't the most intelligent of workers. For example, lots of times they miss the defectives as they pass through. That's why I try to get everyone to watch for defectives. And girls aren't mechanical, and I don't want them fooling around with the machines. Lots of times they aren't even able to judge whether something is really wrong. That's why the mechanics must jump right in whenever the girls think there is a problem, and often when they don't see anything, too. The trouble with mechanics is that they are often more interested in exploring interesting technical problems than they are in getting a machine fixed and the line back in operation. That's why the production manager must always be on top of them. But you saw out there what happens all the time. People don't move when problems occur.

Basically the biggest problem facing most businesses in this country is that no one knows what supervision means—we just don't have well-qualified supervisors. Most chiefs are accustomed to working with the government. There, they have no pressure to produce, nor do they learn to put pressure on others. When there is no pressure, people get sloppy. It's not just that my supervisors don't know how to do their job; they get frustrated with it and want to quit. One of my foreladies now wants to go back to the lines. And the one before her smashed her thumb and had to be given other work. That's why I have to be on top of things all the time.

CASEWRITER: Could you explain how you do keep on top of thing?

LOPEZ: The biggest thing is to be on the floor as much as possible. Whenever I find a defective or see a machine down, I point it out to the workers and supervisors. It's been a tremendous educational job explaining to everyone what a quality tube is and persuading the foremen and mechanics to move when something goes wrong. I used to hold weekly assemblies with the whole crew at which I'd explain problems I'd discovered and the need to improve. I just don't have time for that anymore, but I think that the large signs you saw above each machine helped the personnel to understand the importance of keeping the machines running.

CASEWRITER: What kind of production records do you keep?

LOPEZ: I only really have daily and weekly totals and they aren't that helpful. I had thought that the girls might take an interest in these and perhaps the groups would work to see who could produce more. But the production of the two groups always seems to be about equal, and the inspector who keeps the records tells me that nobody ever looks at them.

One interesting thing, though, that puzzles all of us is that when we run our night shift, we sometimes get on one line three quarters of what we produce on two lines in the daytime. Even taking into account the fact that we do most of our setups in the daytime, we still get proportionately more production at night. We can't understand this because the forelady and mechanic are there alone and don't have any backup from the administration.

CASEWRITER: Is there any explanation?

LOPEZ: I don't know. One reason might be that the machines are all prepared in the daytime, so that they run throughout the night without breaking down. But this doesn't seem valid because our worst time for breakdowns is the four hours around midday, and the machines generally run pretty well in the later afternoon and early evening, when they should be wearing down from their morning tuneups. The most satisfactory explanation I can think of is that the cool temperature at night is a factor. When it is very hot, as it is around noontime, the ink flow is uneven and the machines require constant minor adjustments. The nights are much fresher, and perhaps the ink flow is smoother. To be truthful, I can't figure out the answer, but it's got me curious.

The casewriter expressed an interest in spending a few days in the plant in order to gain an insight into the problems of supervision. He also hoped to learn more about the night shift.

LOPEZ: Yes, that's a good idea, though I think the night thing's a fluke caused by the more favorable temperature. I doubt whether there is anything in the night conditions which could be reproduced in the daytime, though I'd be mighty interested to know if there were.

The casewriter visited the plant for a number of days, observing the operations and conversing with the workers to learn more about supervision and the night shift at Tubident. One day, he encountered one of the foreladies, Flora, appearing very upset. (Flora had been supervising the line for about two months, having previously worked on the lacquering machine. Sr. Gutierrez had told the casewriter that he had selected Flora as supervisor because "she is one of our most serious workers. She always stays alone and never gets into trouble.") The casewriter asked her what was the matter. "The girls are rude and spoiled. Whenever you reprimand one for a mistake, she talks back to you. I get in trouble when the girls talk too much. I used to get along with them when I was their work partner, but now they won't respect me or do what I tell them. The trouble is that Sr. Gutierrez didn't send around a note authorizing me as chief and explaining how the girls would have to treat me. I get very upset when things aren't done well. The girls say I'm bad-tempered. It isn't that; it's just that Sr. Lopez told me very strictly how I was supposed to do this job, and I'm trying to do it. Sr. Lopez hates to see defectives on the floor.

This morning the girls have been throwing them all over the place. I said very pleasantly, 'Couldn't you pick those up and keep your places clean?' They just gave me dirty looks and didn't do anything about the mess. I know I must be doing something wrong, and I told Sr. Lopez I didn't want the job any more. He just told me to reprimand the girls sternly or suspend them for a few days. I can't suspend them because they are as poor as I am. Now I'm going to go tell Sr. Gutierrez to ask the girls himself to pick up the things instead of telling me to do it. I'm also going to ask him to write me a note authorizing me to be chief."

A short time later, the casewriter spoke with some of the girls about Flora. One of them said, "She bawled me out yesterday for not having asked permission to go to the restroom. I'd like to say something to her but I guess I'd better not. She forgets that when she was a worker, she did the same thing when none of the bosses was around."

Later in the day, the casewriter encountered Flora leaving the floor. She said tearfully, "I don't know what to do. I can't go to Sr. Gutierrez everytime something happens. I just asked them nicely not to talk too loudly. They said, 'Why can't we talk? We're working with our hands, not with our mouths.' " She excused herself and hurried away.

Later that day the casewriter was discussing the work of the foreladies with Sr. Gutierrez. Mariela, the former forelady, had seriously injured her hand and had been assigned to work in the warehouse. The casewriter asked Gutierrez how the injury had occurred.

GUTIERREZ: Well, I'm not really sure. She wasn't very clear about it. She said that she was cleaning the printing machine and stepped on the start lever. (*Pause.*) But I can't see how she could have done that. (*Pause.*) Maybe one of the girls did it.

CASEWRITER: Do you mean intentionally?

SR. GUTIERREZ: No, of course not.

CASEWRITER: Then, why wouldn't she have mentioned it?

SR. GUTIERREZ (*pause*): Maybe she didn't want to get anyone else involved. She probably would have wanted to keep it quiet if it happened that way.

The casewriter tried to observe the relationships among the workers and to discover their feelings about each other and their jobs. He noticed that some of the younger looking girls, who comprised about two thirds of the line workers and manned the faster operations, often came into the plant laughing in small groups and gathered to converse in the coffee room or around the machines before taking their places on the lines. Older women and a few of the younger girls came and left by themselves. The girls made a number of comments about one another to the writer. Josefina, a sweet-looking girl, appeared to be very popular.

She said, "We are all good friends around here. We tease each other a lot and talk about our boyfriends." Another girl said, "This was my first job. I'd heard stories of how badly some of my friends were treated where they worked, but everyone here is very nice. Even the bosses are friendly." Many of the women were the sole support of their children, and those without children usually gave money to their parents. While some of the younger ones said they enjoyed working where there were friends instead of staying at home where there was just housework, other young ones seemed to share the attitude of the older women, that work meant only earning money for their families.

The casewriter noticed one very pretty girl named Sara, who always entered and left the plant alone and barely talked to anybody. She always came dressed up and appeared bored and sullen. When the casewriter asked Sr. Gutierrez about her, he said that she had been part of a group of the original workers. They had learned their jobs fairly well but had become more and more talkative, noisy, and playful and had distracted the other workers and upset everyone. Gutierrez said he had finally felt obliged to talk to Sara about her boisterousness and had urged her to become independent of the "troublemakers." She had accepted his scolding and now worked alone, bothering no one.

He now considered her one of his best workers.

The casewriter asked her how she felt about her work and the other workers. "I used to have many friends; Maria, Roxana, Teresa, Josefina, Julieta, and I were the first workers and used to have a lot of fun. Most of them are still here, but they gossip and start rumors and it's better not to get mixed up with them. Now I work my four hours thinking about what I'll do when I leave, and I don't have to pay so much attention when the girls feel like working and keep pushing me to hurry. I used to go to the inspector's table to see how much we had produced when the machines were good and we felt like working. Our shift used to be better than A. But I don't know who's better now, because I don't bother to look."

One day, when the machines were stopped and Gutierrez and the mechanics were conferring on what was to be done, the casewriter struck up a conversation with Maria, one of the popular workers, about supervision on the day shift. She said, "Do you know how many chiefs we have around here?—everyone from the manager to that mechanic over there. They all give us orders. One tells you the tubes are OK. Another says they aren't and wants to adjust the machine. It's good, though. They do our work for us." The writer turned to Julieta. She told him, "The job is boring. We like to talk and sing, but it's hard to know when they [the management] will get mad at us for talking, so we always try to talk just loudly enough to hear one another over the noise of the machines."

Another girl, discussing the desire of the workers to talk and sing, mentioned that they had previously had a radio. "We used to have music on the radio, but the bosses liked formal music. Finally they decided we weren't paying enough attention to our work. We weren't sorry because we didn't like that kind of music anyway."

Carmen, the other shift chief, was a short, slim woman, striking in her dignified demeanor. One afternoon, she and Neddy, her mechanic, had just come on duty with the two o'clock shift (composed of the women who had already worked from 6 to 10 A.M.). None of the bosses was in the plant that afternoon. The changeover was effected with much joviality. Before the girls took their places at the machines, Carmen ran around cleaning up defectives and joking with everyone. One worker commented to the casewriter that this was "going to be a good afternoon." Soon the lines were going full steam. Carmen began to run around the machines, filling ink wells at one, picking up stray defectives at another, with a pleasant word to each of the girls as she passed.

Occasionally, someone would shut a machine down, clean the roller for about 30 seconds, and get it going again. Suddenly, Josefina, at one of the lacquering machines, said to the loader at the machine, "Tell Carmen to get over here quickly. I'm running out of ink." The word was passed down the line to Carmen, who was helping the packers because they'd fallen behind. Carmen grabbed an ink bucket, filled it from a barrel, and ran over to fill Josefina's well. Immediately after that, as Neddy strolled in from the mechanics room, the two girls at the printer on the other line shouted, "Carmen, Carmen!" A chorus of laughing voices rose, "Carmen, Carmen! Neddy, Neddy!" Carmen and Neddy started towards the printing machine, then looked around and laughed with the others. Everyone kept working. As Carmen passed the casewriter, she said, "We're way ahead today." At one point, Julieta's machine was stopped. Carmen immediately ran over. One of the extras, who was sweeping the floor, dropped her broom and ran to look for Neddy in the machine shop. Soon Neddy, Carmen, and Julieta were working on the machine and got it started rapidly.

As the afternoon wore on, various girls quickly asked extras to take their places and went out for coffee. The casewriter asked Carmen why she wasn't insisting that they ask for permission. "Whenever the bosses aren't around I don't insist. But when it gets out of hand, I go up to one of them and say (she frowns sternly and wags her finger), 'You know you're supposed to ask permission.'" The casewriter said, "You mean when the bosses are around?" She just laughed and ran over to help the packers again. Watching her work at the packing table, the casewriter remembered what Carmen had told him about her job: "My job is to help the girls do their work. My other job is to please everybody. For example, when the bosses are around, I tell the girls to keep the talking down, and if there are defectives lying on the floor, I clean them up fast."

A little later, the casewriter saw Julieta in the coffee room and asked her why things were going so well today. "Today we all just feel good and want to see how much we can turn out. We had a terrible time this morning because Flora was mad at us for talking and Sr. Lopez kept coming around. It's really fun when Carmen and Neddy are here alone. I want to learn about mechanics, and Carmen and Neddy let me help. You know, the chiefs don't like us to work on the machines, and we can't do it when they're around. Also, Carmen helps us, and she never bosses us around unless there's a reason."

The production of that day was unusually high. On the following day, it was very hot in the plant. No one seemed animated, and a few girls commented that they didn't feel much like working. At almost any moment, at least one machine could be seen stopped with its operator spending a long time cleaning it. Carmen commented to the casewriter, "It's too hot in here, and the girls are tired and don't feel like working fast. You can't blame them, and you can't keep them from stopping the machines because one of the bosses usually agrees that the machine needs adjustment."

Gutierrez, shaking his head over the slow progress of the work, said, "One problem today is that a part on one of the printing machines is causing trouble because it's worn out. The mechanics are building me a new part and once we get it in, the machine will stay in adjustment much longer. They've been working on the part since eight this morning. Come into the machine shop and I'll show it to you." In the machine shop, they saw the mechanics gathered in a group in one corner. On the bench lay the new printing part apparently untouched. Sr. Gutierrez looked at the part, then at the mechanics, cursed to himself, and walked out.

Though there was no night shift during the casewriter's visit at Tubident, he tried to discover why night production was higher by questioning the workers. Carmen's reply was:

> I like working the night shift best. I need the extra income for my child and I'm grateful to be able to earn time and a half for the extra work. The work at night is much simpler, because you don't have to worry about anything except the machines and the girls. We only run one line, and the mechanic and I can easily attend to this. The girls take care of their machines and keep them running. When they call you over at night, you know they really need your help.
>
> There's a good spirit at night. I think the girls realize that all the management is interested in the next morning is the number of boxes of tubes we produced the night before. We say to them, "Let's really turn it on so they can see how much we've done." We want them

to see we've been working hard and not sleeping or playing games. If we have a breakdown, need more mechanics, or don't produce enough tubes, it might not be worth the management's while to keep the night shift going. And all of us want the extra money.

The casewriter asked other girls how they felt about night work and following are some of the answers:

Sure we get tired. Lots of times one of the girls will get so tired she almost goes to sleep at the machine. But we do everything we can to keep her awake; we turn on the radio real loud, or we'll sing special songs, or her companion will tell jokes and laugh or tell her everything she can think of about her boyfriend. Pretty soon she gets over it and feels fine again.

We have a good time. Even Flora gets along.

The reason we produce more is that we're a well-selected group. Some girls get sick or fall asleep at night. They aren't selected for the shift. It's kind of an honor to be chosen for night work.

At night, you are really responsible for your machine. You have to decide whether it is running properly and whether the tubes are properly soft and have the right amount of lacquer on them. You only stop the machine if something is seriously wrong. If you see one tiny bad line or speck on the print, you know it's not important and keep going. When you *do* stop the machine, you get to fix it. You may talk things over with the chief, but you really feel responsible to keep things under control yourself, because nobody's going to do it for you.

We get all greasy but change everything around with the pliers until the ink is coming out just right. Of course, we've got to hurry, because we want to produce a lot for the morning. I can fix and adjust the machine in lots of little ways. You're not supposed to do that in the daytime.

One day the casewriter noticed that Flora was back on the line and that Carmen was working as forelady for both day shifts. When he asked what had happened, Sr. Gutierrez replied, "She finally just refused to be chief anymore. She'd been getting more and more moody lately. When the girls called her for help, she'd get upset that they weren't doing their work. She thought the girls were just trying to bother her. She came to me finally complaining about a group of girls who were ignoring her orders, she said, and insulting her, too. She asked me to do something. I felt it was my obligation to call the three girls together to ask for their cooperation. I explained to them what Sra. Flora had said and that she was new and didn't know any better. They said they hadn't done anything and that Sra. Flora must be making it up.

"Sra. Flora had gone to see Sr. Lopez, wanting to switch back to the line and after my meeting with the girls, Sr. Lopez decided that it was important enough to call another meeting of the three girls, him, and me, this time inviting Sra. Flora. Flora explained what disturbed her but the girls couldn't understand it. They denied it all. We decided that it wasn't right for her to be upset and that it would be better to get another line chief. Carmen's working 16 hours temporarily until we choose a replacement."

POSTSCRIPT

When the casewriter had completed his observations, he returned with a rough draft of the case to check with Sr. Lopez on the accuracy of statements attributed to him, and to obtain approval for clearance use of the case. When he arrived, Sr. Lopez welcomed him with a smile. "Here's the man who really understands what I'm up against. Now you can tell me how I can train these supervisors of mine better."

Sipping coffee, the casewriter learned that Sr. Lopez was considering replacing Flora with Mariela, depending upon the latter's recovering the use of her thumb, "since she's one of our most experienced girls. She really knows what I want and it will be easier to work with her than breaking in a new girl. I know what we need out there, and it's very hard breaking a new person in. I don't have the time for it I used to have. Well, enough of that. Let's see what you've got."

Sr. Lopez took the case and began reading. When he reached the section early in the case commenting on his success in achieving high quality standards, he stopped, looked in his desk, and handed the casewriter a recent letter from a principal customer, congratulating Lopez on the consistent good quality of the Tubident products and commending Sr. Lopez personally for his achievement.

For the next hour Sr. Lopez continued to read, making occasional corrections or comments and frequently chuckling. As he finished, he looked up at the casewriter, smiled, and said: "Well, I think you've got it all down here. We've had a real job on our hands and still do. It will make an interesting case for your students. Now if you'll wait a minute while I make my rounds, I'll drive you into town for lunch."

The casewriter followed Sr. Lopez into the plant, watched him remove the tubes from the line to check them carefully, occasionally stopping to point out a problem to the girls. Once Sr. Lopez looked over at the casewriter, grinning, and said, "Just like in your case, eh?" Then he took the casewriter's arm and they left for lunch.

5 | Claremont Instrument Company

One of the problems facing the supervisory staff of the Claremont Instrument Company in the summer of 1948 was that of "horseplay" among employees in the glass department. For some time this question had troubled the management of the company. Efforts had been made to discourage employees from throwing water-soaked waste at each other and from engaging in water fights with buckets or fire hoses. Efforts to tighten up shop discipline had also resulted in orders to cut down on "visiting" with other employees. These efforts were made on the grounds that whatever took an employee away from his regular job would interfere with production or might cause injury to the employees or the plant machinery.

Production was a matter of some concern to the officials of the company, particularly since the war. In spite of a large backlog of unfilled orders, there were indications that domestic and foreign competition in the relatively near future might begin to cut into the company's business. Anything which could help to increase the salable output of the company was welcomed by the officers; at the same time, anything which might cut down overhead operating expenses, or improve the quality of the product, or cut down on manufacturing wastage was equally encouraged.

The Claremont Instrument Company had been located for many years in a community in western Massachusetts with a population of approximately 18,000. The company employed approximately 500 people. None of these people were organized in a union for collective bargaining purposes. The company produced a varied line of laboratory equipment and supplies. Many of its products were fabricated principally from

160

glass, and over the years the company had built up a reputation for producing products of the highest quality. To a considerable extent this reputation for quality rested upon the company's ability to produce very delicate glass components to exacting quality standard. These glass components were produced from molten glass in the glass department. Exhibit 1 presents a partial organization chart of the company.

The entire glass department was located in one wing of the company's main factory. In this department the glass components such as tubes, bottles, decanters, and glass-measuring devices were made from molten

EXHIBIT 1
Partial Organization Chart

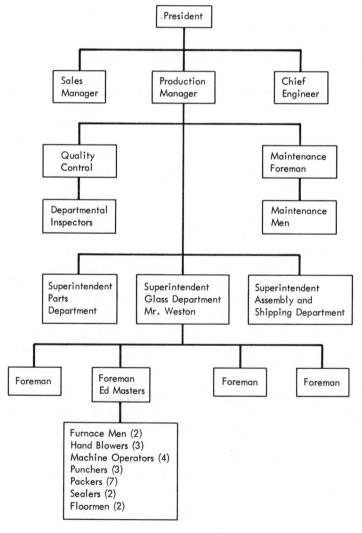

glass. Some of these glass parts were produced by hand-blowing operations, but most of them were produced on bottle-making machinery which in effect blew the molten glass into a mold. This operation of blowing the glass by hand or by machine was the most critical operation in the department and required a high degree of skill. Immediately following the bowling operation some of the parts were "punched." The "puncher" was a mechanical apparatus into which the glass components were placed; as the machine revolved, a small gas flame melted the glass in a small area and blew a hole in the glass component. Next the parts were placed on a mechanical conveyor where they were annealed by an air-cooling process. Then the parts were picked off the conveyor by women known as packers, whose duty was to inspect them for defects of many kinds and to give them temporary packaging in cardboard cartons for transit to other parts of the factory. The final operation in the department was performed by sealers, whose job it was to seal these cardboard cartons and place them in stacks for temporary storage. Exhibit 2 is a floor plan of the glass department.

The glass department was operated on a continuous, 24-hour, 7-day-a-week basis, because of the necessity of keeping the tanks of molten glass hot and operating all the time. Four complete shifts worked in the department. The different shifts rotated as to the hours of the day they worked. Roughly, each shift spent two weeks at a time on the day shift, on the evening shift, and on the night shift. Each shift worked on the average five days a week, but their days off came at varying times throughout the week. The glass department was located in a separate wing of the plant, and the employees of the department used a special entrance and a special time clock.

Each of the four shifts employed about 23 people. Each shift had its own foreman and assistant foreman and hourly workers as indicated in Exhibit 1. All these workers were men, with the exception of the packers. The foreman was a full-time supervisor, but the assistant foreman usually operated a glass machine and only substituted for the foreman in his absence. The furnace men prepared the molten glass for the glass blowers while the floormen cleaned up broken glass and other waste and filled in on odd jobs.

An inspector from the quality-control department and a maintenance man from the maintenance department were assigned on a full-time basis to each of the four shifts. The inspector worked with the packers and was responsible for the quality of all glass components. The maintenance man was responsible for the maintenance and satisfactory operation of all machinery in the department.

Several physical conditions made work in the glass department unique in the plant. The fact that the glass furnaces were located in this department meant that the department was always unusually hot. The glass-

EXHIBIT 2
Floor Plan of Glass Department

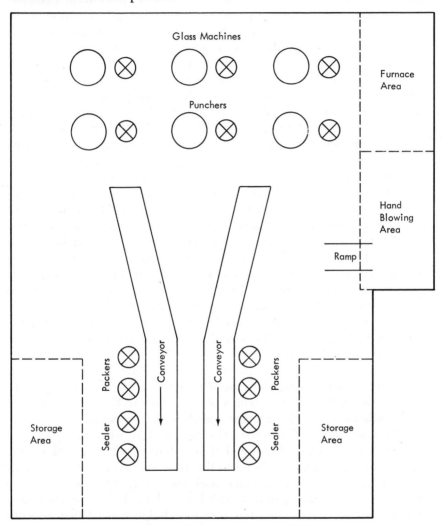

blowing machines were run principally by compressed air, and each movement of a machine part was accompanied by the hiss of escaping air. This noise combined with the occasional sound of breaking glass made it impossible for the members of the department to converse in a normal tone. An oil vapor was used to coat the inside of the molds on the glass machines, and when the hot glass poured into the mold, a smoke was given off that circulated throughout the department.

In the summer of 1948, Ralph Boynton, a student at the Harvard Business School, took a summer job as one of the floormen on one of the shifts working in the glass department. While on this job, he made the above observations about the Claremont Instrument Company in general and the glass department in particular. In the course of the summer, Ralph became particularly interested in the practice of engaging in horseplay, and the description that follows is based on his observations.

The foreman of Boynton's shift, Ed Masters, had worked a number of years in the glass department and had been promoted to foreman from the position of operator of one of the glass machines. In Ralph's opinion the foreman was generally liked by the shift employees. One of them commented to Ralph, "If everything is going okay, you don't see Ed around. If anything goes wrong, he's right there to try and fix it up." Another one of them commented, "He pitches right in—gives us a hand—but he never says much." Frequently when a glass machine was producing glass components of unacceptable quality, Ralph noticed the foreman and the maintenance man working with a machine operator to get the machine in proper adjustment. On one occasion Ralph was assigned the job of substituting for one of the sealers. Shortly after Ralph had started work, Ed Casters came around and asked how he was doing. Ralph replied that he was doing fine and that it was quite a trick to toss the cartons into the proper positions on the stack. Ed replied, "You keep at it, and it won't be long before you get the hang of it. You'll be tired for a while, but you'll get used to it. I found I could do it and I am a '97-pound weakling.'"

Ralph also picked up a variety of comments from the employees about one another. The shift maintenance man, Bert, referred to the men on the shift as "a good bunch of guys." One of the packers referred with pride to one of the machine operators, "that guy can get out more good bottles than anybody else." On one occasion, when the glass components were coming off the end of the conveyor at a very slow rate, one of the packers went around to the glass machines to find out what the trouble was. When she came back she reported to the rest of the packers, "Ollie is having trouble with his machine. It's out of adjustment but he will get it fixed in a few minutes." Ralph noticed that a record was kept of the total daily output of each shift of packers. These women seemed anxious to reach a certain minimum output on each shift. When the components were coming through slowly, he heard such comments as, "This is a bad night." If the work had been coming slowly, the packers regularly started "robbing the conveyor" toward the end of the shift. This was the practice of reaching up along the conveyor and picking off components for packaging before they reached the packer's usual work position.

A short time after Ralph started to work, the company employed another new floorman for the shift. This new man quickly picked up the nickname of "Windy." The following were some of Windy's typical comments: "My objective is the paycheck and quitting time." "I love work so much I could lay down and go to sleep right beside it." "These guys are all dopes. If we had a union in here, we would get more money." "I hate this night work. I am quitting as soon as I get another job." Most of the other employees paid little attention to Windy. One of the sealers commented about him, "If bull were snow, Windy would be a blizzard." One night Windy commented to three of the men, "This is a lousy place. They wouldn't get away with this stuff if we had a union. Why don't the four of us start one right here?" None of the group replied to this comment.

Ralph had a number of opportunities to witness the horseplay that concerned the management. At least one horseplay episode seemed to occur on every eight-hour shift. For example, one night while Ralph stood watching Ollie, one of the machine operators, at his work, Ollie called Ralph's attention to the fact that Sam, the operator of the adjacent machine, was about to get soaked.

"Watch him now," Ollie said with a grin, "last night he got Bert and now Bert is laying for him. You watch now." Ralph caught sight of Bert warily circling behind the machines with an oil can in his hand. Sam had been sitting and quietly watching the bottles come off his machine. Suddenly Bert sprang out and fired six or seven shots of water at Sam. When the water hit him, Sam immediately jumped up and fired a ball of wet waste which he had concealed for this occasion. He threw it at Bert and hit him in the chest with it. It left a large wet patch on his shirt. Bert stood his ground squirting his can until Sam started to chase him. Then he ran off. Sam wiped his face and sat down again. Then he got up and came over to Ollie and Ralph. Sam shouted, "By Jesus, I am going to give him a good soaking." Ollie and Ralph nodded in agreement. Later Ollie commented to Ralph, "It may take as long as three hours for Sam to work up a good plan to get even, but Bert is going to get it good."

Sam was ready to get back at Bert as soon as he could be lured close enough to the machine. Sam pretended to watch his machine but kept his eye out for Bert. In a little while Bert walked jauntily by Sam's machine. They grinned at each other and shouted insults and challenges. Bert went over to a bench to fix something and Sam slipped around behind his machine, pulled down the fire hose and let Bert have a full blast chasing him up along the conveyor as Bert retreated. Sam then turned off the hose, reeled it back up, and went back to his machine.

All the other employees on the scene had stopped to watch this episode and seemed to enjoy it. They commented that it was a good soaking. Bert came back to the machines after a while, grinning, and hurling insults while he stood by Sam's machine to dry off from the heat of the machine. The other operators kidded him some, and then everyone went back to work seriously.

A little later the foreman came through the department and noticed the large puddle of water on the floor. He instructed Bert to put some sawdust on the puddle to soak up the water. Ralph was told later that Ed Masters had told Bert, "I want more work and less of this horsing around." A few minutes later Ed Masters and Bert were discussing a small repair job that had to be done that evening.

On another occasion Ralph asked Ollie what he thought of the horseplay. Ollie commented, "It's something each guy has to make up his own mind about. Personally, I don't go in for it. I have got all the raises and merit increases that have come along, and I know Bert hasn't had a raise in over a year. Whenever something starts, I always look back at my machine so that I can be sure that nothing goes wrong while I am looking away. Personally, I just don't care—you have to have some fun, but personally, I don't go in for it."

Just at this point Al, one of the punchers, came down from the men's lavatory ready to take his turn on one of the punch machines. He was a moment or two early and stood talking to Sam. Ollie got up from where he had been talking to Ralph and started to holler, "Hey, Al—hey, Al." The other operators took up the chant, and all of them picked up pieces of wood or pipe and started drumming on the waste barrels near their machines. Al took up a long piece of pipe and joined in. After a minute or two, one of the operators stopped, and the drumming ended quickly. Al lit a cigarette and stepped up to take the machine for his turn.

Ralph later had an opportunity to ask Bert what he thought of the horseplay. Bert said, "You have to have some horseplay or you get rusty. You have to keep your hand in." Ralph noted that Bert's work kept him busy less than anyone else, since his duties were primarily to act as an emergency repairman and maintenance man. Ralph asked, "Why doesn't Ollie get into the horseplay?" Bert replied, "Ollie can't take it. He likes to get other people, but he can't take it when he gets it. You have got to be fair about this. If you get some guy, you are surer than hell you will get it back yourself. Now you take Sam and me. We've been playing like that for a long time. He don't lose his temper, and I don't lose mine. I knew I was going to get that hose the other night; that was why I was baiting him with a squirt gun." Ralph asked, "Does Ed Masters mind it very much?" Bert answered, "Hell, he's just like the rest of us. He knows you're got to have some of that stuff, only he gets bawled out by the superintendent if they see anything going on like that. That's why we don't play around much on the day shift. But the night shift, that's when we have fun. The only reason we don't squirt the foreman is because he's the foreman. As far as we're concerned, he is no different from us. Besides he ain't my boss anyway. I'm maintenance. I don't care what he says."

About the middle of the summer, the superintendent of the glass department returned from his vacation and immediately thereafter an effort was made by him through the foremen to "tighten up" on shop discipline. The men on the machines and the punchers were forbidden to walk up to the other end of the conveyor to talk to the packers and sealers and vice versa. The foreman starting making occasional comments like "keep moving" when he saw a small group together in conversation. On one occasion a small group stood watching some activity outside the plant. Ed came by and quite curtly said, "Break it up." Everyone seemed quite shocked at how abrupt he was.

About this same time, the word was passed around among the employees that a big push was on to step up the output of a certain product in order to make a tight delivery schedule. Everyone seemed to be putting a little extra effort into getting his job done. Ralph thought he noticed that the foreman was getting more and more "jumpy" at this time. On one occasion Ed commented to some of the employees, "I am bitter today." One of the machine operators asked him what the trouble was, and Ed made some comment about a foremen's meeting where the superintendent was telling them that the playing around and visiting would have to stop.

One night a short time later, Ralph saw that preparations were being made for an unusually elaborate trap for soaking Jim, one of the sealers who had recently begun to take part in the water fights. A full bucket of water was tied to the ceiling with a trip rope at the bottom in such a way that the entire contents would be emptied on Jim when he least suspected it. Many of the employees made a point of being on hand when the trap was sprung. It worked perfectly, and Jim was given a complete soaking. Ralph thought Jim took it in good spirit since he turned quickly to counterattack the people who had soaked him. Shortly after all the crew had gone back to work, Ruth, one of the packers, was coming down the ramp from the area where the hand-blowing operations were performed. She was carrying some of the glass components. Ruth slipped on some of the water that had been spilled during the recent fight and fell down. She was slightly burned by some of the hot glass she was carrying. Those who saw this happen rushed to help her. The burn, while not serious, required first-aid attention and the assistant foreman went with Ruth to the company dispensary for treatment. Ralph thought that the employees all felt rather sheepish about the accident. Ruth was one of the more popular girls in the department. The word went around among the employees that a report on the nature and cause of the accident would have to be made out and sent to higher management. Everyone was wondering what would happen.

6 | Textile Corporation of America

In 1963 the Textile Corporation of America (TEXCORP) was formed from three family-owned companies: (1) Smith-Abbott Mills, centered in Fitchburg, Massachusetts, and directed by William Abbott; (2) North Carolina Mills, owned by the Ford family and headed by Robert Ford; (3) Carolina Cotton Company, a single large mill located in South Carolina and owned by John Rand. The three family companies had not been direct competitors. Smith-Abbott Mills produced high-grade spun rayon and wool blended fabric, North Carolina Mills specialized in fine cotton fabrics and staple synthetic fabrics, and the Carolina Cotton Company made high-quality print cloth. By combining their firms' resources, Abbott, Ford, and Rand became owners of a major firm in the fine textiles industry, with sales in 1963 of $45 million.

Due to family loyalties and the strength of long-standing reporting relationships, TEXCORP existed as a single company in name only. Few functions were integrated, although accounting for all three firms was done at the corporate office in New York City. Because his North Carolina Mills represented the largest portion of the TEXCORP (1963 sales of $25 million), Robert Ford and his management team were able to dominate the company through 1966. William Abbott, the wealthy owner of Smith-Abbott Mills, avoided direct participation in TEXCORP management. He kept an office in the New York headquarters, attended board meetings, and watched the Fitchburg operations, but much of his time was spent vacationing in Europe or playing golf. In 1967, Mr. Abbott decided to spend more time in New York City.

By 1967 it was clear that the fine cotton fabric market was declining in importance in the United States. In June of 1967, representatives of the National Chemical Company were approached by TEXCORP management at the suggestion of William Abbott. National Chemical was a multinational corporation with 1967 sales of over $2 billion. They had recently begun to diversify into nonchemical markets, and several TEXCORP executives were personal friends of National executives. These informal relationships led to official discussions, and National Chemical purchased TEXCORP in early 1968.

In the exchange of TEXCORP stock for National Chemical stock, all of the directors of TEXCORP became wealthy men. TEXCORP's directors controlled 68 percent of the voting stock of the company when it was purchased by National Chemical. William Abbott became one of the largest individual shareholders of the National Chemical common stock. Robert Ford, then 65 years old, agreed to step down as president of TEXCORP, and William Abbott became the chief executive. Mr. Ford, although not entirely happy with the management arrangements, had considerable financial security in that his family's trust fund now owned over $10 million of National Chemical stock. Richard Hicks, the National Chemical vice president responsible for TEXCORP, felt that Mr. Abbott would make a better chief executive than Ford, and encouraged the management transition. Abbott made several organizational changes himself at this time. Andrew Thompson, who had been the star salesman for Smith-Abbott Mills, was promoted to vice president of sales for Smith-Abbott Mills. Walter Hogan, a former plant manager for Smith-Abbott Mills, became vice president of manufacturing.

TEXCORP's sales in 1967 had risen to $65 million. Profits had grown from 1963 through 1966, but had dipped somewhat in 1967 to $2 million. Exhibit 1 outlines the TEXCORP organization in February of 1968, and Exhibit 2 presents the background of key personnel.

JOHN MITCHELL, MBA

John Mitchell, 27, was married and had one child. He grew up in Darien, Connecticut, and graduated from Harvard College in 1963. Mitchell had chosen Harvard because it was supposed to be a very liberal school. For the first two years he remained conservative, but during his junior and senior years he committed himself as a political liberal. He took courses in religion and psychology and briefly considered being a minister. After graduation he thought about entering law school or medical school, but his father wanted him to go to HBS. After receiving his MBA in 1965, he joined a Peace Corp project in the Far East, where he taught industrial psychology.

John Mitchell liked to think of himself as good at the "gamesmanship" of life. His interest in psychology led to a certain degree of introspection, and he prided himself on his ability to describe the games people played.

EXHIBIT 1
February 1968: TEXCORP Organization

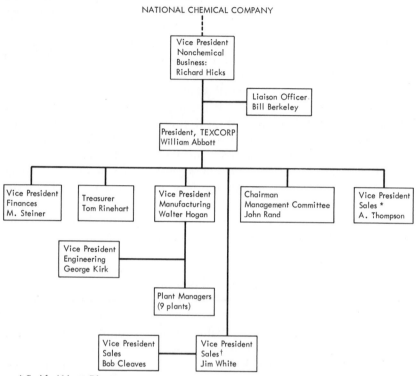

NATIONAL CHEMICAL COMPANY

Vice President
Nonchemical
Business:
Richard Hicks

Liaison Officer.
Bill Berkeley

President, TEXCORP
William Abbott

Vice President
Finances
M. Steiner

Treasurer
Tom Rinehart

Vice President
Manufacturing
Walter Hogan

Chairman
Management Committee
John Rand

Vice President
Sales *
A. Thompson

Vice President
Engineering
George Kirk

Plant Managers
(9 plants)

Vice President
Sales
Bob Cleaves

Vice President
Sales †
Jim White

* Smith-Abbott Plant.
† North Carolina Mills.

In high school, for example, Mitchell was often called an "apple polisher" because his school work seemed to follow the particular concerns of his various teachers. He was a straight-A student. In college, he hardly ever cut classes and was a Dean's List student for four years. He was active in athletics and was a starting fullback for the Harvard team. John Mitchell even considered football a "psychological game." Commenting on his football experiences, he said:

> If the coach was in a mean mood, you growl and hit somebody . . . if not, you joke and try and have fun. Hell, the guys that were on the field to make the big plays not only *did* the right thing in practice, but *thought* and *said* the right thing too. . . . It's all a fantastically complicated game.

Mitchell earned a varsity letter each year in college.

Mitchell's experiences overseas strengthened his political "liberalism" (labeled "radicalism" by his mother). While at the Business School,

EXHIBIT 2
Personal Background of TEXCORP Personnel

Name	Age	Background
William Abbott*	55	Former president of Smith-Abbott Mills, ex All-American football player from Princeton, independently wealthy.
Andrew Thompson	41	Former salesman for Smith-Abbott Mills, former professional golfer, long-time friend of William Abbott.
Walter Hogan*	62	Former plant manager of Smith-Abbott Mills, former football coach, long-time friend of William Abbott and Mr. Abbott's father. (Founder of Smith-Abbott Mills.)
John Rand*	66	Former president of Carolina Cotton, Harvard College '25, independently wealthy.
Martin Steiner	42	Former chief financial officer for North Carolina Mills.
George Kirk	45	Hired in 1964, chief engineer for four TEXCORP engineers, offices located in North Carolina.
Sam Jarvis*	54	Plant manager of Carolina Cotton Plant, brother-in-law of John Rand.
Bob Hogan	36	Plant manager of Smith-Abbott Mills, son of Walter Hogan.
Jim White	55	Former sales manager of North Carolina Mills.
Bob Cleaves*	42	Former president of a small textile company bought out by TEXCORP in 1964, independently wealthy, a bachelor.
Tom Rinehart*	63	Treasurer of TEXCORP, former treasurer of North Carolina Mills.
Bill Davis	50	Plant manager of largest North Carolina Mills plant, appointed in 1965, son-in-law of John Rand.
Bill Berkeley	29	MBA from Berkeley, hired by National Chemical in 1967, worked for Hicks since December 1967.
Richard Hicks	50	Vice president of National Chemical, HBS class of '49, known as a "real professional" to other National Chemical executives.

* Indicates that an employment contract was in effect. (These contracts lasted through 1971 and guaranteed the men salaries ranging from $40,000 to $70,000 per year.)

he had participated in many lengthy discussions about the businessman's social responsibilities. John Mitchell was sometimes shocked by what he considered to be the narrow-mindedness of some of his classmates, and he often wondered if the business world could offer him the satisfactions he believed he needed in life.

His interest in psychology eventually led Mitchell to a one-year research project while at the Harvard Business School, and the co-authorship of a book on psychological aspects of motivation.

In 1968, Mitchell decided to return to the United States. He did not think he had the patience to be an effective teacher, although he had been very successful as a teacher in the Peace Corps. The business world in the United States in 1968 further challenged him because of the new emphasis being placed on social responsibility. Mitchell hoped he could find a job that offered an outlet for his growing social conscience. Also, he was anxious to test himself in a real business organization:

> I wanted to see if I could compete with my classmates from HBS. But at the same time I love travel, love other cultures. But I kept wondering, if I were back in the States, would I be such a hot shot?

NATIONAL CHEMICAL COMPANY

Richard Hicks, the vice president of National Chemical and responsible for TEXCORP, heard about Mitchell through family friends. Hicks was in charge of National's nonchemical operations, and he wrote Mitchell and asked him to come to National Chemical's offices in New York to talk about the company's operations overseas. When they met, Mitchell told Hicks that the chemical industry didn't really interest him because it was dominated by large corporations; however, after many meetings and several offers, Mitchell agreed to go to work as assistant to the president of TEXCORP, William Abbott. Mitchell would be trained for a year in the textile business and then go to a textile mill that National was planning to buy overseas. The job sounded ideal to Mitchell. He could test himself in the world of big business and also indulge his interest in travel and living abroad. The Mitchells rented a small house in Darien.

In July of 1968, Mitchell went to work at TEXCORP, which was located in an office building about ten blocks from the National Chemical headquarters in New York. William Abbott had been told very little about his new assistant, except that he was to train him for a year. Since Mitchell knew nothing about the textile business, he asked to spend two months in the mills—part of this time as a loom operator, which he did, even though this was theoretically against union regulations.

Mitchell's initial impressions about TEXCORP and TEXCORP management were very favorable. Andrew Thompson, the VP in charge of textile products and the number two man at TEXCORP, was a very outgoing and personable man, and Mr. Abbott told Mitchell to see Thompson if there were any "problem" with his training. John Mitchell spent most of his time at the large Smith-Abbott Mill in Fitchburg. Although the workers believed him to be a "spy from the chemical company" at first, they soon relaxed and Mitchell developed several strong friendships. Since he was living in a motel in Fitchburg without his family, he spent 12 to 14 hours a day at the mill and got to know the personnel on both the day and the night shifts.

When he returned to New York in September, Mitchell found that there was nothing planned for him to do. Although Abbott spoke to him every day in his office for about 20 minutes in order to find out how he was getting along, Mitchell felt that no one was really interested in what he did. Consequently, he willingly accepted responsibility for helping to collect and organize the financial figures for the first TEXCORP five-year plan. (Systematic planning was one of the most well-developed management techniques at National Chemical.)

Mitchell was beginning to learn more about headquarters personnel at TEXCORP. He observed that four offices, which he called "Executive Row," were large, spacious, and thickly carpeted, while the rest of the TEXCORP offices were relatively modest. The four offices were occupied by William Abbott, Walter Hogan, John Rand, and Tom Rinehart. Mitchell was surprised to discover that Rand and Rinehart were rarely involved in the regular management meetings, and Hogan was not highly respected by many of the headquarters personnel.

Although he got along well with all the TEXCORP executives, Mitchell found that he had too little in common with them to spend much time socializing:

> I was too young and unimportant. Also, I didn't play golf and I didn't drink. I had tomato juice at lunch while they were boozing it up.

Bill Berkeley, who was the "liaison man" assigned to TEXCORP by Richard Hicks, became Mitchell's closest friend, since they were the same age approximately, and the only men at TEXCORP under 40. Also, both Mitchell and Berkeley reported to Hicks:

> Bill Berkeley and I got along very well. . . . Berkeley spent half of every day over at TEXCORP talking to Abbott or one of the financial VPs about liaison work. You know, fill this form in, the appropriations meeting is next month, etc.

Mitchell was distressed at the unsophisticated level of management he found at TEXCORP, and he developed the habit of having long, one-sided conversations with his wife when he arrived home each evening:

> What a day! Discovered that I was the only—get this!—the only guy who could use a slide rule in TEXCORP, except for Kirk . . . but he's an engineer . . . I don't know. It sure seems like some of those men waste a lot of time and stuff trying to butter-up Bill Abbott, and there's so little real *analysis*. Hell, no!! I'm not "buttering him up"

with my slide rule! You ever tried doing 20 discounted cash flows without one!?!

As October wore on, John Mitchell began to feel frustrated and bored. One day he went around the TEXCORP office asking executives if they had any jobs or projects he might help them with. He spent a day filing expense reports and three days drawing graphs and charts showing loom utilization for the first half of 1968. He later told his wife:

> It's kind of dull right now. I didn't think it would be like this. What? Sure, I've talked to Andy. He doesn't know what to do with me. Let's face it . . . none of them really know what to do with me. First I was a "spy," you know. Now I'm a "bright kid with a lot of potential." I don't want to be underfoot all the time. You can only ask a guy for work so many times, then you just have to try and make work. What a drag.

And, in early November:

> Well, I finally talked to Andy today. Told him I was really going out of my mind. And I talked to Bob Cleaves. Anyway, they both told me I should lay it on the line to Abbott. "Talk to him at Oscar's," they said. [Oscar's was a large bar and restaurant often frequented by TEXCORP executives.] I'm going to ask him for more responsibility. Hell, I've got absolutely zero now. He must know how I feel . . . but he's so damn silent. No one ever knows what's on his mind. . . . Except Andy, of course. Those two are like father and son.

Because William Abbott seemed constantly preoccupied and was often out of the office, Mitchell was reluctant to speak to him about his job. ("If I catch him wrong, he'll just see me as a complainer, or, worse, an overly ambitious 'whiz kid,'" he explained to his wife.) Abbott ran TEXCORP with the help of the two executives who had come with him from Smith-Abbott Mills in Fitchburg, Andrew Thompson and Walter Hogan. Thompson and Abbott were particularly close, and virtually all company decisions were made by these two men. Abbott had also continued to direct Smith-Abbott Mills personally, and he and Thompson spent five to eight days a month in Fitchburg. Finally, in mid-December, Mitchell followed Thompson's advice and asked William Abbott if he could speak to him at Oscar's after work.

Mitchell discovered that his boss was much easier to talk to at Oscar's. Abbott liked to drink, and Mitchell found it relatively easy to ask his boss for a line position with specific responsibilities. Abbott replied that he would like to have a boy like Mitchell on his "team" and would give him a position if he would pledge to stay "with him" for three years. As the evening progressed, Mitchell observed that Abbott spoke more and more about "loyalty" and the value of a man who would "stick it out." Mitchell was reluctant to commit himself to any time period; and at 10:30, when the two left Oscar's, he remarked that he would "certainly stick it out if things went well."

During the second week of November, Mitchell had spoken to Richard Hicks. It was their first meeting since July, and Mitchell had requested it because he had heard that the National Chemical Company's plans to purchase an overseas textile firm had "fallen through." Richard Hicks's dynamic personality had been a large part of Mitchell's decision to work at TEXCORP, and he enjoyed the 30-minute meeting with the National Chemical vice president. However, he learned that plans for expansion into overseas textiles had been delayed indefinitely. That night he warned his wife:

> Don't pack those bags for Europe, Baby; probably will never need them. Yeah, the deal fell through . . . looks like it's TEXCORP or nothing. . . . Anyway, the glamour has worn off a little; how about you? Good, if things go well, maybe we can rent a little bigger house next year.

This change in Mitchell's original career goals forced him to examine his present situation at TEXCORP even more closely.

TEXCORP PERFORMANCE

For the next month, Mitchell continued to make work for himself. In order to keep completely busy, he fulfilled a long-time desire and signed on as a volunteer consultant for the New York Urban Coalition. Beginning in December, Mitchell spent at least two nights a week working late in New York City. He found the excitement and satisfaction of volunteer work made his late arrival home almost worthwhile. (Mitchell often skipped dinner and arrived home at midnight.) But in December, the November financial statements were released and the usual good humor in the TEXCORP offices became strained. Sales had dropped sharply, and most of the plants were losing money:

> They're all waiting for some kind of axe to fall from Hicks. Man, were the figures rotten. One of our plants was showing a 22 percent loss before taxes! I don't know what National is going to do, but I hope they do it fast. What do you mean, *I* should do something?! Who am I! Anyway, I think there is a project I could do.

The disappointing financial statements brought no immediate response from the Chemical company. TEXCORP managers, however, began to express their concern to Mitchell. Andrew Thompson and Walter Hogan pointed to the relatively stable performance of the Smith-Abbott plants, and at management meetings they emphasized the need to upgrade the plant efficiency at Carolina Cotton. Sam Jarvis, Carolina's plant manager, complained openly to Mitchell and other TEXCORP executives that his product mix was unprofitable because several North Carolina Mills plants were now producing what he used to produce and he was never given the money he needed to buy needed new equipment. Bill Berkeley spent two or three days each week at the TEXCORP executive offices. Berkeley and Mitchell often spoke about TEXCORP organizational problems and the need for reform. Berkeley was often asked what, if anything, the Chemical company was going to do about TEXCORP in light of the poor operating statistics, and his usual reply was one of assurance. "Calm down, fellas," Mitchell heard him say. "Just get out there and sell a little, and we'll do all right." Privately Berkeley admitted to Mitchell that he knew Hicks was concerned about the poor performance, but he didn't know if major policy changes were planned.

By the end of December, it was obvious that the year-end financial statements would also show sharp declines in sales and profitability. Although Andrew Thompson was beginning a two-week vacation in California and William Abbott was on a week's vacation in Florida, John Mitchell decided to put together a marketing research study of TEXCORP'S two biggest plants. Rather than "clear" this study with the two absent executives, he approached the two plant managers involved and they responded enthusiastically to his proposed studies. For the next several weeks, Mitchell spent most of his time in Fitchburg and South Carolina (the location of the two plants he decided to study).

The poor performance reflected in the late 1968 financial reports prompted a minor TEXCORP reorganization in December. Mr. Hicks moved to create operating divisions and attempted to formally alter the old family reporting and communications channels. After close consultation with William Abbott, he announced the formation of temporary committees to run three operating divisions. Each committee would have a chairman, and the chairmanship would rotate every quarter. It was understood that this was a short-term and temporary arrangement, and that permanent division managers would be appointed as soon as possible. Andrew Thompson was made chairman of the Consumer Products Division (primarily high-grade spun rayon and wool blends), Jim White (former VP of sales for the South Carolina Mills) was made chairman of the Industrial Products Division (fine cottons and synthetic fabrics), and the chairmanship of the Specialty Products Division was left vacant. Exhibit 3 illustrates the new organization. This chart was drawn up by Bill Berkeley, but was never identified as "official." The presence of the "unofficial reorganization chart," however, was known and accepted by TEXCORP executives.

Mitchell completed his first marketing study in mid-January. The study included an analysis of profitability by product line and by major customer, and was enthusiastically accepted by the plant manager.

EXHIBIT 3
"Unofficial" Organization of TEXCORP in December 1968

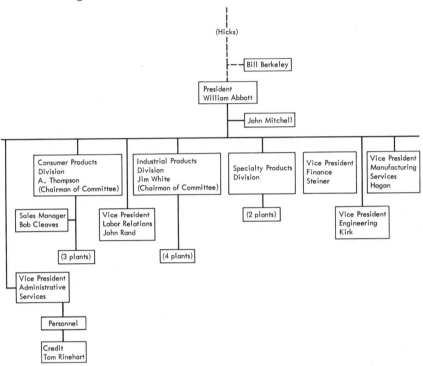

Mitchell sent a copy of his study to William Abbott, but Mr. Abbott did not comment on it.

A REQUEST FOR PROMOTION

John Mitchell was growing increasingly impatient. He had developed a close relationship with Mary Fagan, the president's secretary, and the two often had coffee together in the cafeteria in the basement of the TEXCORP office building. Mitchell found Mary a perceptive and intelligent girl, and soon he was discussing a wide range of company problems with her:

> You know, if it weren't for Mary, I think I'd got nuts in the office. Today we talked about Kirk. She agreed with me that he's a brilliant engineer . . . but really out of sight when it comes to company politics. You know, he calls Mary from his engineering offices [located in North Carolina] just to find out what kind of a mood Abbott is in before calling him. And today he called me and asked who was meeting in

the board room. He'd heard there was this big meeting and he wondered why he hadn't been invited.

The reorganization of TEXCORP into divisions had not, in Mitchell's opinion, straightened out the most serious company problems. Lines of authority were still unclear. Old, informal relationships still prevailed over the new (and as yet "unofficial") lines of communication. Abbott and Thompson continued to make most of the decisions. And overall marketing and sales objectives were left undefined. Mitchell became more and more disgusted with his situation:

> I've decided that TEXCORP reminds me of a country club. Abbott and Thompson are both top golfers. They must spend $300 a month taking customers, friends, etc., golfing. And when it comes time to make a few decisions, they do it like they might select an iron. You know, squint down the fairway, laugh a little, say "What the hell," and blast away. I'm convinced there are three or four of our top executives who ought to be retired . . . permanently . . . but Abbott could no more do that than he could give up his booze or his golf . . . Yeah, I am depressed. . . .

Prompted by his continued frustration and the company reorganization Mitchell decided to write Andrew Thompson a letter asking for a new job. He anticipated that Thompson would show the letter to William Abbott. It is reproduced as Exhibit 4.

EXHIBIT 4
John Mitchell's Letter to Andrew Thompson, dated January 13, 1969
Dear Andy:

I hope this note will help you understand my as yet unresolved anxieties concerning my future here in TEXCORP. I am putting this in writing to save your time and to facilitate any further discussions. Let me try and describe my perspective.

First, I see a lot of work to be done at all levels of the organization. Much of this work is a matter of analysis (data collection, organization, setting priorities, etc.). Systems must be set up, studies made, programs established and monitored, etc.

Second, I see a limited number of people with the background and training to accomplish all of the analytical work that has to be done.

Third, I see myself and my own selfish goals. I have spent all of my lengthy (four-year) business career doing analytical staff work. I have developed a certain facility for this kind of work. But it no longer offers the challenge I desire. I want to assume more complete responsibilities. I want to be a boss. I want to be able to look back and say, "Look, I did that . . . that's my success." When I spoke to you earlier, I hoped you might have a line position for me in your division. I have been told—and I am forced to agree—that I lack the experience to be a line manager in sales or in manufacturing. Those are the only two lines at the divisional level.

Given what I see around me, I conclude that from the organization's point of view, I should be in a position where I could move freely about, conduct market

EXHIBIT 4 (*Continued*)

studies in the divisions, assist engineering in plant relocation studies, help establish systems and procedures, etc. (As William would say, "For Chrissake, John, we have so much to do, let's just do it!") I would need some source and position of authority that everyone saw as "legitimate" so that cooperation would be maximized. I guess my present status and title of "assistant to the president" seems best suited to these organizational needs.

From a personal point of view, however, this role is less than ideal. William, I suspect, has never quite known what to do with me. I am always a little "in the way" or "under foot." My duties too often dissolve into those of a clerk-secretary-adding machine. I bear much responsibility for this, I will admit. I haven't tried to be "pushy" and I have avoided playing too many games with too many people. And I have paid a personal price: boredom. The frustration I can handle; the boredom slowly destroys me. All of this has been changing, but the deeper I get into the problems and the personalities, the less secure any "assistant to" position becomes. As your assistant, for example, a careful (and probably not very convincing) explanation would have to go out if I were to involve myself in the Industrial Products or Specialty Divisions. I guess it comes down to the fact that I don't think being anyone's assistant will offer me the kind of challenges I desire. (Man, this is sounding more and more presumptuous and egotistical every minute.) Anyway—from my own standpoint, I would like to be in the position of vice president of administrative services. Here I would have the challenge of line responsibility and the opportunity to test myself (although I still wouldn't have the kind of "line" challenge and satisfaction you have when you sell a good fabric order, or a plant manager has when he reads the bottom line of his P&L statement). In charge of administration I would still have both the time and the authority to conduct the needed analytical studies and services. I would be available to all departments—both informally and formally. In this position I would also be able to involve myself in those kinds of administrative tasks that do not require 20 years of experience in the textile business.

Before you laugh at my conceit, let me explain why I think it's a reasonable gamble from the organization's point of view. We all agreed some time ago that the job should be created. We knew that systems were needed and that a man was needed to supervise these tasks as well as purchasing and credit (neither of which involves close or imaginative supervision). Bill Berkeley can handle the job, and I've heard his name mentioned. But he has said "No" to both of us privately, and I doubt anyone will change his mind.

"NOW WAIT A MINUTE!! You really want me to say you can be VP of administrative services?!?!" Yes, I'm only 27 (But, just think! I'll be 28 in June!) Yes, I just started shaving last year. Yes, only six months in textiles . . . only six months in this company. I realize William is the man to talk to in the end. It's his ball game. But with your understanding and support, my feelings, expectations, and anxieties can be more carefully presented to him. Anyway, I've got enough guts to think I can do a better job there than anyone else we've got. And I don't think it's the kind of position that a new man would be able to take over. I'd be the lowest paid VP in the city, and that'll help our budgets.

I'd like to speak with you about this note and try to cover the 100 other questions that arise from my cocky, impertinent ambition before approaching William.

If and when you show this to William, remind him he once told me to stick around because "the way we are, there are plenty of opportunities to learn." Remind him he said that, and then ask him how he learned to catch a football.

John

Mitchell continued to work on his final marketing study. It was completed in February and focused on the declining profitability of the large Smith-Abbott Mill in Fitchburg. Using it as an excuse to talk to William Abbott, he tried to broach the subject of the unfilled position of administrative vice president. Mr. Abbott ignored Mitchell's casual inquiries, and at the end of February Mitchell's letter of January 11 still remained unanswered.

> Well, scratch one effort. I guess they couldn't have made me any vice president. Who did I think I was. . . . Oh well, it sounded good at the time. Here I am. A guy's who's supposed to be an expert in human relations. And I'm tied up in knots by a bunch of dumb playboys! I can't figure it out. One day I think I know why Hicks hasn't done anything. I see a little spark of hope for Abbott. And the next day I hear that Abbott has gone and wasted more money on a project that has no chance of success. You should hear the other executives talk about him. They're all losing confidence. And, you know, he hasn't called me into his office in almost three weeks now. Hell, he used to give me little odd jobs every day.

On February 1, 1969, Bill Berkeley resigned from the National Chemical Company. The day he left, he and John Mitchell had a long luncheon and Berkeley talked about National Chemical and Richard Hicks:

> John, I've worked for that man longer than any of his previous assistants . . . I still don't really know him. The "infighting" at National is intense as hell nowadays. The president resigned last year, and they still haven't filled the position. Hicks knows he's in line. I'm sure the lousy 1968 TEXCORP figures shook him up. Abbott keeps telling him "things will improve, things will improve," and I think he believes it! He won't listen to me. I've heard a lot of talk around the Chemical company about Hicks and some of the other vice presidents. There's the "pro-Hicks" and the "anti-Hicks" factions. . . .

Mitchell expressed his surprise at the extent of the office politics at National Chemical, but admitted that he knew Hicks must be under considerable pressure. Mitchell refrained from telling Berkeley that he believed that Berkeley could have prevented the "communications gap" between National Chemical and TEXCORP by being more frank with his boss.

TEXCORP MANAGEMENT

Mitchell was also beginning to believe that everyone in TEXCORP and National Chemical was guilty of "playing politics." TEXCORP's plant managers operated with considerable independence. Martin

Steiner, the VP of finance, was the only home office executive who dealt with plant personnel on a continuing basis; yet, by January of 1969, he had been unable to implement a company-wide cost accounting system. The controller of Smith-Abbott Mills, for example, was very "secretive" with his cost information, and Steiner received only token cooperation from him. On several occasions Steiner remarked to John Mitchell that "things were sure different when old Bob Ford was running the company."

In spite of Richard Hicks's attempts to restructure the TEXCORP organization, the old company loyalties and factions continued to function. William Abbott, Walter Hogan, and Andrew Thompson directed the Smith-Abbott plants; Jim White and Martin Steiner spent most of their time dealing with the North Carolina Mills plants; and John Rand and Sam Jarvis concerned themselves with the Carolina Cotton plant. As the profitability of this latter plant declined, both Rand and Jarvis tried to "mind their own business" and avoided discussions with TEXCORP executives of overall policies and problems.

Management meetings were held once a month in the TEXCORP boardroom. The members of the management committee were: William Abbott, Andrew Thompson, Walter Hogan, John Rand, Martin Steiner, George Kirk, Sam Jarvis, Bob Cleaves, and Richard Hicks. John Mitchell was invited to attend many of the meetings. His increasing concern over the company's viability and his interest in psychology prompted him to reflect upon the "patterns of communication" that emerged among the TEXCORP executives.

When Hicks attended the meetings, a business-like atmosphere prevailed. The management meeting was almost formal, and the men seemed "on their toes." Many even took notes as the National Chemical vice president asked his pointed questions. However, Hicks was unable to attend all of the meetings. In his absence William Abbott would usually begin by smiling and saying, "Well, what'll we talk about today?" Mitchell noticed that these meetings often degenerated into rambling discussions of the performance of the three family companies. Members of the management committee were constantly being called to the phone to "put out a fire," and little seemed to get accomplished. Mitchell soon realized that it was an "unwritten rule" that nobody paid much attention to management committee meetings or decisions made there, for William Abbott consulted afterwards with Thompson or Hogan and decided upon the actions to be taken.

To John Mitchell, the most confusing aspect of the TEXCORP management and communications system was the lack of objectivity. No matter what subject was raised—be it a question of buying a new loom or expanding a product line—everyone seemed to have a known and fixed position. TEXCORP executives *expected* Andrew Thompson to fight for increased expenditures for blended wool fabric capacity, and everyone *expected* Sam Jarvis to say that cotton prints were the best long-term investment for the company, and Mitchell observed that they were never disappointed. Since the members of the management committee were already "on record" as holding certain opinions, discussions were usually routine and (Mitchell thought) uninteresting. New facts were seldom presented. The voluminous industry-wide marketing statistics published by the Textile Trade Association were never cited. TEXCORP executives seemed to rely on their intuition and "gut feel" for the situation. The engineering studies of George Kirk were privately referred to a "worthless." Bob Cleaves and Martin Steiner confided to John Mitchell that on several occasions Kirk had changed his facts and figures to make the studies "come out the way Abbott wanted."

Mitchell tried to remain neutral as far as office politics were concerned, but this was often difficult:

> With a climate so politically sticky—I never pulled punches or played politics. This got me into trouble. When someone said, "How's it going?" I said, "Lousy." I was everyone's friend, and they [the execs] all wanted me for their assistant. All the division managers lacked management expertise.

Mitchell had tried to figure out why NCC was so reluctant to examine the situation at TEXCORP. He thought one reason might be the fact that the presidency of NCC had been unfilled for several months and a successor had not yet been chosen:

> Hicks may be mixed up in the hassle over who gets to be president of NCC. He wants to sweep TEXCORP under the rug because it's a bomb. They have lost at least five million in profits because of TEXCORP, and part of this is company politics. Bill Abbott is one of the largest single stockholders in NCC, and he also knows Bill Scott [board chairman of NCC]. So Abbott is formidable.
>
> What really shocked Mitchell, however, were the day-to-day politics at TEXCORP:
>
> The number-one priority here is personalities. The prime commodity people fight for is Abbott's time. I'm shocked at the amount of time spent on personalities. Eighty to 85 percent of people's time is spent warming up somebody or cooling off somebody or on other nontask conversation.
>
> Another related commodity is information—facts about what's going on, who's talking to who, etc. But you can't get any data from the responsible people—the secretaries are the people to talk to if you want information. Everyone relies on rumor, and people here ask the secretaries to relate casual conversations they've overheard so they can figure out which way the wind is blowing. Mary Fagan even says that Abbott has asked her to spy on me!

Many people at TEXCORP used Mitchell as a confidant, and Mitchell felt he had to keep a delicate balance of discretion and candor. For instance, Martin Steiner would complain to Mitchell that he desperately needed a new accountant, and this complaint would serve as a smoke-screen if Steiner's department got behind in its work. Mitchell felt that George Kirk, the head engineer, was almost paranoid about authority. If Abbott requested that Kirk see him in his office, Kirk would call Mitchell first to find out what Abbott wanted.

In February an incident occurred that John Mitchell found to be almost humorous. Three new looms had been installed in Bill Davis's (North Carolina Mills) plant, and William Abbott sent Walter Hogan south to "supervise the breaking-in period" at the plant. Bill Davis was not informed and was upset when Hogan walked into his plant and began asking questions. Davis placed quick calls to Jim White and John Rand protesting Hogan's presence, and finally called William Abbott. The irate plant manager said he could handle any "breaking in." Abbott explained that Hogan was just "inspecting" the new looms and said that George Kirk had suggested that Hogan be present when they started operations.

John Mitchell became involved in the controversy when he had lunch with Kirk the day following Hogan's arrival at Bill Davis's plant. Kirk was furious. He did not respect Walter Hogan and said he "didn't par-ticularly care for Bill Davis" either. But he stated that he had never suggested that Hogan be sent to Davis's plant; "Now Jim and Marty Steiner won't speak to me. They think I sicked Hogan on Davis. You should talk to them, John, and tell them what really happened. . . ." Mitchell discovered from Mary Fagan that Kirk had, in fact, written a memo about the looms to Abbott. When questioned by Abbott, the chief engineer had evidently agreed that Hogan might "supervise the looms for a few weeks." A few days later, Mitchell mentioned the matter to Bill Berkeley. The young National Chemical representative pointed out that George Kirk seldom disagreed with anything William Abbott suggested. The entire incident seemed ridiculous to John Mitchell, but Berkeley pointed out that such "misunderstandings" were common at TEXCORP.

A FINAL CONFRONTATION

Mitchell was becoming increasingly aware of his unique position in the TEXCORP organization. More and more often he was asked to listen to the problems of various company executives. Bob Cleaves con-fided in him almost daily. Cleaves's responsibilities had been reduced when TEXCORP was reorganized, and he constantly spoke of "retiring" or quitting. Walter Hogan was also expressing personal opinions to

Mitchell. Hogan's new position as "manufacturing services manager" was a clear demotion. Hogan was 62 years old and admitted to Mitchell that he knew "his days were numbered." Martin Steiner and Jim White spoke to Mitchell in January about the financial and sales deficiencies they had observed at TEXCORP. They encouraged Mitchell to "speak to someone at National Chemical" to see if Abbott could be replaced and new talent recruited. Mitchell responded by speaking to Bill Berkeley, but advised both Steiner and White that they should be the ones to approach Hicks:

> I don't know, the atmosphere is getting thick as glue around TEXCORP nowadays. The company's going downhill. Abbott's spending more time on the links. Everyone comes to me with their problems. What am I supposed to do? Except Andy. . . . He and Abbott don't talk to me any more. I guess they know I think they're both doing a lousy job. But, hell, they're in charge. All guys like Cleaves and Jarvis and Steiner seem to be doing is bitching. . . .

During the months of February and March, Richard Hicks was out of New York City. This only added to John Mitchell's feelings of helplessness. He was now convinced, beyond doubt, that TEXCORP was being badly mismanaged. His personal future seemed to depend on the National Chemical Company: when and if it would step in and replace Abbott and his management "cronies." On March 2 he spoke with William Abbott and told him he was "thinking of quitting." Mr. Abbott reacted very calmly and remarked that it was "too bad," but that it was his (Mitchell's) own decision:

> Hell, he just sat there. The bastard. Didn't even bat an eye. I gave him the chance to try and talk me out of it. It was half a bluff anyway. Man, now I have to find another job! Wait 'till Hicks hears this. He's going to wonder what's been going on while he was away.

The following day, Mitchell told Bob Cleaves what he had done. Cleaves reacted emotionally and told Mitchell he was a fool. "The future of TEXCORP will rest with guys like you," he exclaimed. "You're throwing away a great opportunity. You know National Chemical will have to move in soon. And when they do, you will be the one who comes out on top!" Later on that day, William Abbott called Mitchell into his office and asked if he would "reconsider" his resignation. He said he could only reconsider if "major changes" were implemented at TEXCORP, but Mitchell agreed to spell them out in writing. Abbott said he would read what Mitchell wrote and "we can talk when I get back from Augusta."

Mitchell proceeded to write a three-page description of what he saw wrong with TEXCORP and what changes might be made. Excerpts from this letter to William Abbott are reproduced as Exhibit 5. When

EXHIBIT 5
Excerpts from Mitchell's Letter to William Abbott, Dated March 3, 1969

Mr. William A. Abbott
Augusta National Golf Club
Washington Road
Augusta, Georgia
William—

I am sorry to bother your golf, but all of this is important to me and I wanted you to have time to think about it. I have not gone into personal requests. If this letter makes sense to you, we can speak about my future when you return to New York.

I. Prerequisites for Success in Textiles
   1. Must have market specialization with a well-focused sales effort. This is the only way to avoid competition based on price alone.
   2. Must develop those services our key customer groups want (and will pay for).
   3. Must carefully control costs. Because of the competitive situation and the large capital investments involved, incremental profits derived from cost control are often the key to success.
II. Obstacles to TEXCORP success in the Market

   We lack almost all of the above prerequisites.
   We are trying to serve too many markets. . . .
   We are being forced to compete more and more on price alone . . . (cf. my Smith-Abbott study). Major product lines are declining in value and suffering heavy losses (cf. North Carolina Mills study).
   We are unable or unwilling to specialize . . . our sales efforts are poorly directed . . . our cost controls are inadequate . . . Where are our budgets?
III. Organizing to Meet the Market
   . . . must begin with the New York office.
   Planning is critical . . . real planning and risk taking depend on some very simple things; rapid, clear communication, getting the right people together to make the right decisions, collecting the right kind of data in the fastest amount of time, getting quick and decisive answers to questions that can be answered quickly.
   The office of the president can set the whole "organization" in motion . . . By demanding prompt decisions, by demanding facts (rather than feelings or opinions), and by demanding that standards be met, the office of the president can begin to make TEXCORP one company.
   And this is impossible unless the example at the top is consistent with what is being asked of the rest of the organization . . . There are many decisions that I think can be made today . . .
   While doing this housecleaning and planning, talent must be recruited . . .
IV. Some Specific Examples
   Bring talent into central office.
   Redefine head office responsibilities. Much housecleaning is needed . . . Have you reviewed Andy Thompson's budgets? His plans? If the office of the president can't answer yes to these questions . . . then why not?
   Reorganize the Engineering Group. . . . Create budgets for all vital functions . . . change the layout of the head office. . . . Establish a uniform cost accounting system for all of the plants . . . create a system of sales man-

EXHIBIT 5 (*Continued*)

agement . . . without reports and communication, how can we expect focus and direction?

If you were to consult others in TEXCORP, and if you could get honest responses, I am absolutely positive many other specific examples could be cited— examples of things that should *and can* be decided and implemented immediately. Your organization, William, will withhold information from you because they do not have confidence that the information will be used wisely.

In all honesty I must say that I really don't know if my leaving the company is a very good thing for TEXCORP or a very bad thing. Because, in the clutch, I guess none of the fancy degrees, and none of Harvard's "principles" count for much. And I've never been there in the clutch.

He was really upset. I mean, he had the letter with him. And he would read for a while then say, "You're right." Then he'd read on. He said he agreed with everything I said. He didn't even argue!! He didn't question anything I said. I know now it was a mistake. I've hurt him . . . he can't even read the words I wrote. If he *were* reading them, I know he would have disagreed with some of what I said.

Abbott returned to New York, he asked Mitchell to have lunch with him at the Union League Club. During the lunch, it became clear to Mitchell that writing the letter was a mistake. After the lunch Abbott said he wanted to show the letter to Andrew Thompson. He said he would talk to Mitchell later that week.

John Mitchell was very discouraged. Word of his letter had spread around the TEXCORP offices, and he spent the next several days answering questions about what he had said. His efforts to evade questions only added to the tension in the office and gave the entire incident "mysterious" overtones. Without exception, TEXCORP managers told Mitchell he was making a personal mistake to leave the company at this point in time, but they admired his "guts" and hoped his confrontation would force National Chemical into taking some action with respect to Abbott.

On March 11, Mitchell decided to speak to Hicks about TEXCORP and what he had done. Hicks was in Washington, D.C., and Mitchell flew to the capital city and spoke with Hicks for two hours. Hicks was disturbed that Mitchell had acted so precipitously and rebuked him for not having come sooner. Mitchell showed him a copy of the letter he had written Abbott and told him that it was "impossible" for him to have come to Hicks before. "I felt I should quit first . . . before telling you all of what I know about what's going on at TEXCORP. I guess it sounds hollow and self-righteous now, but it's how I feel." After Mitchell talked for a while about TEXCORP's problems, Hicks asked him to write a more detailed analysis of the textile company's prospects for success. The National Chemical Company vice president cautioned Mitchell to be "cool" and reasonable in this report: "Tell me what my alternatives are; tell me how much it will cost to make the changes you think should be made; and tell me what the risks are."

For the next month Mitchell worked on his report for Richard Hicks. William Abbott did not ask to see him, and Mitchell decided not to renew their Union League Club luncheon discussion. On April 10 the 1969 first quarter results were published. They showed that TEXCORP had lost over one million dollars after taxes during the first three months. TEXCORP executives now spoke openly of "moving to greener pastures," and the offices on Executive Row were usually empty. William Abbott took three- and four-day weekends; Walter Hogan, at Abbott's suggestion, spent all of his time at one of the large North Carolina Mills's plants in the South; Tom Rinehart seldom came into the office; and John Rand took a month's vacation.

John Mitchell, while researching and writing his report, was also actively searching for another job. He talked to his wife:

> This time I can forget about overseas work. How would you like to work in Denver? I've got a contact out there. No, I don't know if I'd stay at TEXCORP no matter what Hicks does. You never know when action might be taken. A couple of other National vice presidents have been calling Steiner and asking for some financial data, so I guess the word is finally out that all is not well with their new acquisition. But I've waited too long already. The way I see it, it'll be a year before that company's alive again. Just not worth waiting around for. . . . What do you think?

On April 17, as Mitchell was putting the finishing touches on his report, Jim White stopped in his office. White announced that he had just spoken to Hicks and that he had tried to communicate to the National vice president some of the facts concerning "how bad things were at TEXCORP." White smiled and said, "John, you just can't leave now. From what Hicks told me today, I'm sure we'll see big changes very soon. Really, this time I know it will happen. You've got to stay. We'll all be better off if you do!"

7 | *Markham Instrument Company*

In the spring of 1959, the management of the Markham Instrument Company was confronted with an impasse in pricing the latest addition to its line of scientific measuring instruments. Markham had two basic product groups, instruments for use in scientific laboratories (Laboratory Products), and industrial instruments for use in manufacturing processes (Industrial Products). The present problem centered around the Dual Sensitivity Level Instrument (DSL) which was intended for the more specialized scientific laboratory market.

HISTORY OF DEVELOPMENT OF THE LABORATORY PRODUCT LINE

The line of scientific measuring devices which the Markham company introduced in 1924 was adversely affected by the business decline of the 1930s. In 1935, however, the potential for reversing this trend appeared in the form of a major product innovation. A company salesman discovered a young inventor who had developed an electronically controlled measuring device. Markham officials found from comparative tests with their own instrument that the "shoe box" (a name derived from the new instrument's dramatically reduced size) was superior in performance, and they purchased the rights to develop it.

No one at Markham understood the new machine sufficiently to complete its development. Just at this time, however, Alfred Reece (Markham's director of research in 1959) approached the company seeking part-time employment to support his doctoral studies. When he demonstrated a thorough understanding of vacuum tube technology, he was immediately hired. Working with Roger Finlay (representing sales and engineering) and Caleb Webster (mechanical engineering), he redesigned the shoe box until it met scientific and commercial standards.

Several competitors had already introduced comparable electronic devices to the scientific market, but they met considerable customer resistance. Dr. Markham pointed out in retrospect, "The change from electrical controls to a vacuum tube amplifier was a big one for Markham. Scientists and technicians were against it. We had advertised the electrically controlled version as the only reliable standard regulator, and this had become the general consensus among our customers. Radio types on the market had been widely criticized, and we needed strong evidence to justify our change in attitude."

While Markham management believed their shoe box to be superior to competitors' electronic machines, they did not rely on this to overcome customer resistance. Instead they appealed to the customers' conservatism, which had been the major factor in blocking acceptance of competitors' machines. The new machine was designed to look and operate as much like the old machine as possible, even to the extent of compromising a few of the advantages of the electronic design. As Finlay said later, "Our customers distrusted the electronic devices which were already on the market, so there was nothing else to do but make ours look and act like the electrical one they were familiar with."

This strategy was successful. Dollar sales volume in 1936 doubled that of 1935, while the number of units actually tripled. Consistent with its past success, however, Markham continued to rely heavily on conscientious customer service to enhance its position in the scientific measurement field. Field sales offices and branch service agencies were set up throughout the country. Company salesmen, continuing their traditional practices, carried customer service to the extremes of repairing competitors' equipment, extending liberal credit and trade-in terms, and offering rapid emergency replacement service.

The next major change in these products occurred in 1946 when the company developed a chemical-sensitive paper, which among other improvements, eliminated the inconvenient use of recording inks. This development gave Markham a competitive advantage and simultaneously, due to sole control of the paper supply, provided an increase in profit margins. During this period a portable measuring device, long sought by scientific field workers, was also developed. Although these innovations gave Markham a technical lead, the company still depended on customer service for the basic maintenance of its market position.

During the early 1950s competitors began work on a machine which gave the scientist the option of measuring either of two sensitivity levels simply by throwing a switch. In 1957 the competitors' development work reached fruition, and these Dual Sensitivity Level (DSL) machines were introduced commercially. Markham was not disturbed by this new feature on competitive instruments, since potential applications for the additional sensitivity level were extremely limited. Furthermore, management's attention was diverted from this development by the addition to its own line of a transistorized portable, 40 percent lighter than any then available. This machine's compactness was expected to attract scientists engaged in field experiments, while its price, flexibility, and reliability were expected to make it also a replacement for most applications of the standard model.

Markham elected to push the transistorized model at the expense of the older, larger instrument, basing its decision on a prediction that customers would prefer the smaller machine. In adopting this strategy, management was confident that its ability to take the customers' viewpoint, a company strength over the years, still enabled it to judge what the scientists wanted. Markham had historically been able to lag in technological innovation with little risk, because when their new products were finally introduced, they surpassed competition in meeting customer needs. Markham managers believed that this intimate relationship with the market was as strong as ever.

Company executives were quite pleased when sales of the transistorized model surpassed expectations. They were surprised, however, by two trends. First, sales of the older machine did not decline as had been expected. Secondly, Markham salesmen began asking for DSL instruments such as competition was offering.

To determine the feasibility of producing a DSL while maintaining the basic strategy of promoting the transistorized instrument, exploration was begun on the redesign of the transistorized model. By the end of 1957, a tentative DSL design was developed, although two stubborn technical problems peculiar to a transistorized DSL remained unresolved. Before devoting more time to the solution of these difficulties, top management decided to review the entire issue of producing a DSL machine. After some deliberation the DSL was dropped as being a short-lived fad rather than a long-term trend. It was felt that the difficulties in overcoming the remaining technical problems would not be worth the effort, in view of the limited applications the customers had for the DSL feature.

During 1958, requests from the field for a DSL became more frequent, and Herb Olson (vice president, sales) began pressing for a reversal of a decision not to produce such a device. He pointed out that salesmen were becoming increasingly embarrassed by customer insistence on DSL features. In view of these increasing requests, Roger Finlay (president) became convinced in the fall of 1958 that Markham should add a DSL to its line, if only to satisfy the "gadget" appeal of such an innovation.

Since the older standard machines were continuing to sell, and since the development of a transistorized DSL was still problematical, it was decided to proceed with a DSL redesign of the older machine.

Shortly after making the decision to go ahead with a DSL, Roger Finlay met with Herb Olson (vice president, sales), Alfred "Doc" Reece (director of R&D), Caleb Webster (in charge of mechanical design of the DSL), and Bill Reynolds (responsible for electronic design of the DSL). Finlay told the three R&D men that while he was anxious to get the new machine into production as quickly as possible, the company's reputation was also involved, so that it would be necessary to do the usual careful job. Reece asked if all the same features that were in the standard would be included in the DSL. Finlay replied that while the DSL was to be patterned after the standard model, he wanted all the latest features included. Herb Olson explained that although the DSL was to be offered at approximately the same price as the standard model, they would still have to maintain the traditional external appearance and features on the DSL. In response to a question from Doc Reece, Olson pointed out that they were not too concerned with the weight of the DSL, since it was not to be a portable. As the meeting ended, Reece indicated that they would have to do some careful planning to keep costs down, but he was sure it could be done. Webster and Reynolds agreed, stating that they thought the design could be completed by the end of the year.

In spite of this optimistic appraisal the members of the research and development department did not greet the decision to redesign the older machine with unrestrained enthusiasm. In the first place, they felt that completing the redesign of the transistorized machine would be ultimately feasible and would be more stimulating technically. Secondly, they had several other challenging ideas which they believed would place the company in the growing space and missile field. The redesign of the standard machine would cause them to put aside these more exciting projects for several months.

In spite of these reservations, design work went ahead on the DSL. Meanwhile, inquiries and complaints from the field about the delay in offering a DSL continued to come into the home office. While many sales personnel blamed R&D for the delay, Herb Olson explained the problem differently. "All these problems that the laboratory salesmen are having aren't just the fault of engineering. Top management simply didn't think the DSL was important. Well, this was a mistake. Of course, when this happens the people out in the field get to feeling sore and they come ask us why we don't have the equipment."

Ed Greene expressed a similar view: "Sollie (a formerly influential but now deceased member of R&D) was screaming four years ago for a DSL, but top management could see no need for it. Now all the machines on the market have this feature and we are breaking our neck trying to catch up."

PRICING MEETING, MARCH 6, 1959

The development work on the DSL machine was completed by the end of 1958; and late in January 1959, production received the information it needed to establish production methods and estimate costs. By early March, cost estimates had been completed by the production department; and a meeting was arranged for the morning of March 6 to discuss the DSL selling price. The ten executives named in the seating chart, Exhibit 1, were all present when the meeting started, except Mr. Webster, who arrived later.

EXHIBIT 1
Seating Arrangement—Pricing Meeting, March 6, 1959

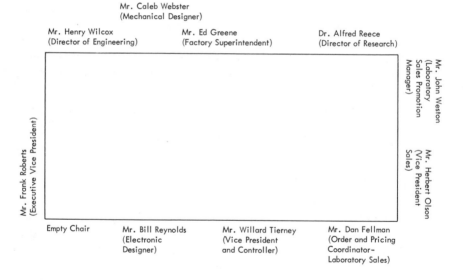

Willard Tierney, acting as chairman, opened the meeting by asking Ed Greene to present his cost estimates. Greene's initial position (which he maintained throughout the meeting) was that the DSL was more expensive than had been expected. He concluded his presentation by saying, "You are going to have to sell this machine for a lot more than you thought. I think these figures are sound. If anything, we have been too loose in our estimates and the figures are too low. We can't lower them any more."

Herb Olson took a different position, maintaining that something had to be done to lower costs so the new machine could be sold at a realistic price. Representative of his remarks is the following statement: "The fact that the figures are sound isn't going to help us meet competition. The way you [others at the meeting] are talking we would have to sell this machine for $1,000. If we did that our volume would go to hell in a hand basket."

Olson was not alone in finding the costs higher than expected. Caleb Webster remarked, "I am really surprised at these estimates. I didn't think they would be that high." Doc Reece also felt the estimates were higher than he had thought they would be. Bill Reynolds, on the other hand, found the estimates realistic as far as the electronic parts were concerned: "I'm not at all surprised at Ed's figures, because I knew what they would be from my design work."

Confronted with this impasse, Tierney summarized the situation at the end of the meeting: "I didn't think we could arrive at a decision today, and it doesn't look like we will, so why don't we adjourn and meet again next week? In the meanwhile Ed (Greene), Dan (Fellman), and Doc (Reece) can check over these costs to see if we can reduce them."

As the meeting broke up, Olson remarked, "If we can't do something about these costs, you guys can take it (the DSL) out in the field and give it to the salesmen yourselves. I won't do it."

PRICING MEETING, MARCH 13, 1959

During the next week, Reece, Greene, and Fellman reviewed the cost estimates; and on March 13 a second meeting was held. The participants arranged themselves around the conference table as shown in Exhibit 2. Willard Tierney again served as chairman, opening the meeting by explaining that Doc Reece, Ed Greene, and Dan Fellman had agreed to certain minor changes in the DSL and that they now felt that it could be produced at $110 more than the standard. (This figure represented a decrease of $35 from the highest figure quoted at the previous meeting.) On this basis Tierney proposed that the DSL be priced at $875, $90 more than the standard. After he completed his remarks there was a full minute of silence which Caleb Webster interrupted.

MR. WEBSTER: I still don't understand it. I'd like to know where the big differences lie, because I didn't think it would be that much.

MR. TIERNEY: Doc [Reece], can you itemize these so we will all know what they are in detail?

Reece and Greene then spent several minutes explaining the costs of various components, as well as the basis for their estimate of assembly cost. Webster, however, remained unconvinced. Tierney suggested that

EXHIBIT 2

Seating Arrangement—Pricing Meeting, March 13, 1959

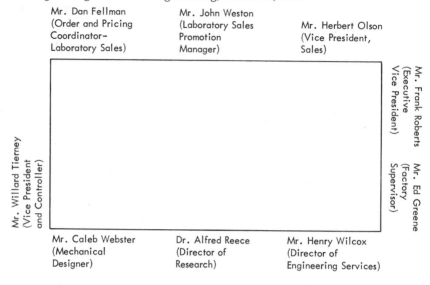

Mr. Dan Fellman
(Order and Pricing
Coordinator–
Laboratory Sales)

Mr. John Weston
(Laboratory Sales
Promotion
Manager)

Mr. Herbert Olson
(Vice President,
Sales)

Mr. Frank Roberts
(Executive
Vice President)

Mr. Ed Greene
(Factory
Supervisor)

Mr. Willard Tierney
(Vice President
and Controller)

Mr. Caleb Webster
(Mechanical
Designer)

Dr. Alfred Reece
(Director of
Research)

Mr. Henry Wilcox
(Director of
Engineering Services)

Absent: Mr. Bill Reynolds (Electronic Designer)

he and Greene work together to discover if further cost savings were possible. Greene replied.

MR. GREENE: I don't think there are many big changes we can make. It has been cut to the bone already.

MR. OLSON: Well, for example, look at that little trap door. It costs a lot of money.

Several minutes were devoted to the costs of the door which Roger Finlay had suggested to improve appearance and operating access. No one suggested changing the door, and the discussion then centered on the differences between the two models. Doc Reece concluded his explanation of the major causes for the difference.

DR. REECE: Look, there is twice as much shop time for parts on the DSL as there is on the old one. That is a big part of the difference. (*Pause*) Sitting around the table here we aren't going to remove Caleb's [Webster] doubts about the reasons for this big difference. He thought it would be less than $25, and it turns out to be between $90 and $120.

The meeting then divided into several conversations. Herb Olson and Frank Roberts talked together with John Weston listening; Doc Reece and Ed Greene carried on a conversation with Henry Wilcox listening.

The others waited. After several minutes Roberts addressed the entire group.

Mr. Roberts: It appears to me that you aren't going to change the spots on the leopard. We have to fix a realistic price. You have all the estimates you can get.

In spite of this statement, discussion about cost differences continued with Reece and Greene furnishing more details about the costs of subassemblies to Webster. Roberts interrupted this discussion.

Mr. Roberts: We haven't heard from Herb [Olson]. He's probably got a lot to say.

Mr. Olson joked with the group, and then began to discuss the competitive aspects of the situation.

Mr. Olson: We have to consider the selling price of this machine in comparison to competition. Competitors are selling their machines at between $440 and $460 to the dealers, which means they are about $800 at retail. Measuretech [a competitor] retails at $785, and their machine does everything ours does. Of course, they, like everyone else, offer discounts. Whatever we do, we have to be in the ball park on the initial list price. Perhaps controlling trade-ins will help some.
Mr. Roberts: What do you think this price should be?
Mr. Olson: Oh, I suppose about $795, that's only $10 above the Standard Model.

Roberts, Wilcox, and Tierney then discussed the minimum DSL selling price. They agreed that using estimated costs, it would be necessary to price it at $875 to obtain the normal margin. Wilcox proposed that they set a target for cutting costs through redesigning the machine, because he thought cabinet and purchase part costs could be reduced in this manner. Olson supported this proposal, but Tierney disagreed.

Mr. Tierney: I don't know what we can find. Ed [Greene] has made a careful estimate, and there is still a $110 difference.
Mr. Roberts: Well, maybe it is just being hopeful, but I think we should do what Henry [Wilcox] suggests.
Dr. Reece: All Ed can control is the shop costs, shop time, and assembly time. I don't think there is much fat in any of these figures.
Mr. Webster: I still can't see why the machine should be that high. The mechanical costs should be much less.
Mr. Greene: Let him [Webster] go somewhere to figure and add them up. Then he'll see. Damned if I'll give him any of my figures.
Mr. Tierney: You know, I still would feel more comfortable pricing it at $875. Otherwise I think we might be cutting it too close.
Mr. Olson: Competition is rough in this line, Will; $850 sounds much better than $875. Even at $850 we will have to work like hell to beat Asprey and some of the others.

MR. GREENE: I'll tell you this, I'd still rather build that Asprey machine than ours.

The relative merits of competitors' machines were then discussed. The consensus was that competition was making the same machine, selling it at about $75 less than the $875 figure which had been suggested for the DSL. Olson suggested that Webster be allowed to restudy the design to see if he could reduce the cost so that the DSL could be priced at $850. Tierney replied.

MR. TIERNEY: All right, maybe we should call this meeting off, and give Caleb [Webster] a chance to satisfy himself.

MR. ROBERTS: That's just a waste of time. Let's get this settled.

Greene and Wilcox also objected to further study, and Tierney withdrew his proposal.

MR. TIERNEY: You're right. After all, we have never priced any instrument with as much information as we have on this one.

MR. OLSON: That really doesn't make any difference. We still have to get the price down where we can sell it.

Tierney then continued the discussion of competitors' machines and prices. There was general agreement that the Simpson Company had, at $785, the best DSL presently on the market. Olson expressed particular concern about the advantage competitors had because of the light weight of their machines.

MR. OLSON: Look at these competitors' weights. Simpson's only weighs 20 pounds, while ours will be 34. Even Asprey's is 10 pounds less than ours. This is an important selling point, and we can't ignore it.

DR. REECE: Damn it, don't start talking weights at this point. We were told from the start that they weren't important.

MR. TIERNEY: Herb [Olson], what do you think the end user pays for an Asprey?

MR. OLSON: Anywhere from $650 up. It depends entirely upon the deal and the trade-in. I was just wondering, though, if maybe we haven't got too many features on this machine. After all it is supposed to be sold as a general-purpose machine.

DR. REECE: We designed it according to what sales wanted. We have to go by what you fellows need. The trouble is that around here everybody wants everything with frosting on it.

MR. OLSON: Right, and then we price ourselves out of the market.

MR. TIERNEY: It seems to me that we had better change our whole official attitude if this is the way our market and our competition are acting.

MR. GREENE: OK. Then we ought to start with an estimate of the market and the price and then design within that.

MR. OLSON: That's exactly what got us into this mess. The district managers are really going to be unhappy about this one. Finlay told them the

EXHIBIT 3
Organization Chart—1959

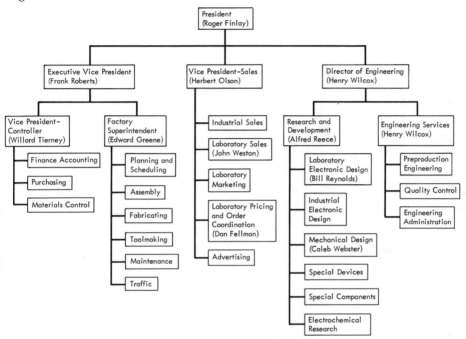

Note: Names are furnished only for persons mentioned in this case.

DSL would be available at $800, and now you are talking about a minimum of $50 or $75 more than this. They aren't going to be happy about pushing this one. I still would like to see Caleb [Webster] take another crack at cutting the cost.

MR. ROBERTS: Doc, can you and the mechanic [Webster] take another shot at redesign after we get it into production? Maybe we can reduce costs then.

MR. TIERNEY: I think that is wishful thinking. We have to resolve this on the basis of the information we have.

Readings

1 | The Comparative Effectiveness of Groups and Individuals in Solving Problems

Douglas R. Bunker
Gene W. Dalton

For a number of years various researchers have been studying the problem-solving effectiveness of groups as compared with individuals working by themselves. A review of this literature suggests the carefully qualified conclusion that certain kind of groups can be more effective than individuals in solving certain kinds of problems. This quibbling statement is derived from both the variety of substantive findings reported and a recognition of some of the methodological limitations of these studies in providing generalizable conclusions which apply to natural groups dealing with "real" problems.

THE TASK AS A VARIABLE

It is characteristic of research on group-versus-individual problem solving for the experimenter to impose a task with clearly defined work rules and a standard, quantifiable criterion of success. The nature of the task is critical to the type of research results obtained. If its performance requires merely the pooling of additive bits of information until some fixed quantity is achieved, then groups will routinely do "better" than individuals. If, conversely, the task requires a division of labor in which the performances of all group members are linked in series, then the group can do no better than the performance of its poorest member—the weak-link phenomenon. Both types of studies are reported in the literature, but neither directly represents the work of a group *qua* group.

One early experiment reported by Thorndike[1] illustrates both the methods and typical results from research focusing on task differences. The principal hypothesis tested in this study was that greater group superiority will be associated with tasks which require greater range of responses. This tended to be confirmed across a series of different tests in which it was indicated that the superiority of groups increased as you moved from a task involving the choice of a response from among several given alternatives to a task requiring production of a free response to fit fixed criteria. One of Thorndike's tasks which did not directly fit with his other results confirming the hypothesis is independently illuminating. He found that groups were superior to individuals in *solving* a crossword puzzle, but that individuals were more efficient in *constructing* a crossword puzzle. In solving a puzzle, success is facilitated by the production of a profusion of alternative responses, for they can be immediately and objectively tested for fit, and while incorrect responses are sifted out, correct responses accumulate toward a complete solution. In constructing a puzzle, however, clear-cut, simple criteria of success are not available. Responses cannot simply accumulate toward a successful solution by a process of gradual confirmation. The task is more complex, requiring that many things be kept simultaneously in mind and developed as an integrated whole. The group product, Thorndike reports, "frequently amounted to nothing but the best individual performance of a member of the group, turned in for the group."

In making the point that the efficiency of groups for problem solving depends somewhat on the task, let us keep in mind that the types of tasks for which individual and group performance differences have been explored cover only a limited range of the types of work requirements which groups must meet in organizational settings. In experimental studies the group goal is generally given, while in real-life situations goal formation is an important and demanding aspect of group work. Continuing work groups also frame policy, develop strategies, solve technical problems, and devise tactics for the implementation of group decisions. Such work is qualitatively different from the purely intellectual process involved in solving or constructing crossword puzzles.

GROUP SUPERIORITY—MAJORITY RULE OR DISCUSSION

In a more recent experimental study Barnlund[2] not only compared the problem-solving abilities of individuals compared within groups,

---

[1] R. L. Thorndike, "On What Type of Task Will a Group Do Well?" *Journal of Abnormal and Social Psychology*, vol. 33 (1938), pp. 409–13.

[2] Dean C. Barnlund, "A Comparative Study of Individual, Majority, and Group Judgment," *Journal of Abnormal and Social Psychology*, vol. 58, no. 1 (January 1959).

but also developed a number of clues as to what tends to enable experimental groups to secure superior results. Is it because the superior individual supplies the correct answer to the group, because the simple majority of the answers of individuals working alone provides a superior answer, or is it because of the problem-solving qualities of an open discussion within the group? To explore these questions, Barnlund used a complex intellectual task involving the ability to draw logical conclusions from given arguments. Individuals receiving similar scores when working alone on the first half of the test were assigned to the same experimental groups so that the factor on individual differences in ability would be reduced to a minimum. The experimental group then, using discussion, worked out the second half of the test in the same amount of time allowed for the first half. This procedure allowed comparisons between three problem-solving methods: (1) individual work, (2) "group" results determined by mathematically tallying the majority decision of each experimental group's members working alone, and (3) group results under discussion conditions. The results indicated that:

1. Majority decisions, when deadlocks are evenly divided between right and wrong answers, are not significantly different from those made by the average individual and are inferior to those of the best member of the group working alone.
2. Group decisions, reached through cooperative deliberation, are significantly superior to decisions made by individual members working alone and to majority rule.

In order to throw additional light on these findings some of the group discussion sessions were recorded and analyzed for clues to the psychological factors affecting the high level of group performance. Barnlund reported that the following factors were contributing to group success:

> *Membership in the experimental groups produced a higher level of interest in the successful completion of the task.* Members concentrated more intently on the assigned problems after being appointed to a group than they did when solving the problems individually. Group members found themselves more and more deeply involved as they proposed, and were forced to defend, their ideas. Participants identified with their own groups to such a degree that when some members became fatigued, others urged them to continue working.
> *Membership in the experimental groups had an inhibiting as well as facilitating effect.* Knowledge that one's opinions were to be shared publicly made group members more cautious and deliberate in their own thinking. The necessity of explaining a conclusion forced many students to be more self-critical. Errors that might have been committed privately were checked before they were communicated to others.
> *Groups had greater critical resources than did individuals working alone.* In spite of the uniform level of ability, group members saw

different issues and a larger number of issues than did a single person working alone. A greater number of viewpoints increased the group's chances of selecting a valid one. Even the poorest members contributed significantly to the quality of the group product. Remarks that went no deeper than "I don't understand" or "That's absurd" often saved the group from error by forcing others to justify their opinions and in so doing disprove their own conclusions.

A more objective view of the problem resulted from competition between the private prejudices of group members. The test arguments were stated in loaded terms designed to make the choices between conclusions as difficult as possible. Each individual, however, brought a different set of values to his group. When arguments were stated so they appealed to persons of one persuasion, those in opposition were anxious to detect their error. In this way, liberals counteracted conservatives, Republicans offset Democrats, and "independents" guarded against critical lapses on the part of fraternity members. Groups were forced to become more objective, and this, of course, increased their chances of drawing valid conclusions. The significance of this one factor alone would be hard to overestimate.

Discussion of the test items also prevented other incidental mistakes from occurring. Some groups had to check their instructions several times because members had different interpretations of them. Discussion often led to a clarification of terms used in the test, and, where logical fallacies spring from ambiguous terms, this may account for some of the gains. A number of groups formulated general principles as they went along to help them avoid repeating errors in later problems.

What, then, prevented experimental groups from attaining even higher scores than they did? Analysis of the transcripts revealed two factors that together accounted for a majority of the group errors. The first was that group members agreed immediately and unanimously upon the wrong answer to a problem. Further study of the issue was then considered unnecessary and wasteful. . . . The virtue of disagreement and the possible function of a "No-Man" in group deliberations needs further testing.

The second factor was that groups, when they reached a deadlock, were unable to use their differences of opinion for their own advantage. When conflicts became intense they were resolved by surrender of the less aggressive members or by compromising on a third solution which was almost always incorrect but served to protect the egos of the parties to the controversy. Apparently disagreement stimulates thought up to a point; beyond that point, groups may lack the patience and skill to exploit it.

EFFECTIVE GROUPS—EXPERIMENTAL VERSUS NATURAL

The generalized issue of groups versus individuals as problem solvers must also include the point that groups differ in their capacity to deal effectively with problems. One important factor, of course, is the "life-span" of the group.[3] Experimental groups are usually contrived, short-lived collectivities in stark contrast to working groups, which have continuity and meaningful identity as a group. While the experimental group does have the advantage of several disparate points of view, it does not have the necessary accompaniment of a set of relationships and mutually understood decision-making mechanisms to enable the members to utilize efficiently their varied resources.

But long-lived groups also vary greatly in their effectiveness. Shared experience, alone, is no guarantee of high performance. From the various studies of long-lived experimental groups and natural work groups, a number of attempts have been made to formulate those features which are characteristic of effective problem-solving groups.[4] Although the orientations of the investigators have varied, there are a few features which tend to be common to these formulations.

> Central among these is the idea that effective problem-solving groups have worked out some mechanisms for (*a*) sharing and building on another's information and ideas, and (*b*) examining and resolving differences.
>
> They are conscious of their own operations. For example, at some point there is an open discussion of the objective or task of the group until it is formulated in such a way that it is well understood and accepted by the members. Likewise, a balance is maintained between the task and emotional needs of the members of the group.
>
> There is an open confrontation of differences. Disagreements are not suppressed or smoothed over before they are examined and understood. Criticism and attempts to influence are both overt and legitimate.
>
> Decisions are made in some way which facilitates the examination and comparison of differences and alternatives. Some kind of consensus is reached which goes beyond simple majority voting or steam-rollering.
>
> Finally, supportive relationships are established which provide a context in which differences can be confronted and new ideas tested. The members listen to one another. Divergent ideas are given a hearing. Ridicule is not utilized to suppress extreme ideas. Respect is shown for the point of view of others both in the way contributions are made and received.

---

[3] R. F. Bales and F. L. Strodtbeck, "Phases in Group Problem-Solving," in D. Cartwright and A. Zander, *Group Dynamics, Research and Theory* (Evanston, Ill.: Row Peterson, 1960).

[4] For examples, see Rensis Likert, *New Patterns of Management* (New York: McGraw-Hill Book Co., 1961); and D. Kretch, R. Crutchfield, and E. L. Ballachey, *Individual in Society* (New York: McGraw-Hill Book Co., 1962).

2 | The Individual in the Organization: A Systems View

Jay W. Lorsch
Alan Sheldon

INTRODUCTION

Our purpose is to develop a set of concepts which can aid the reader in thinking about and dealing with issues which arise in managing relatively small work groups in an organizational setting. Underlying the entire discussion will be the notion that the individual and the group of which he is a member can both be thought of as a system of interrelated parts. For example, in both a biological and psychological sense, the individual can be regarded as a system. Biologically, the individual is a complex hierarchy of systems ranging from the cells upward through tissues, organs, organ systems (e.g., nervous systems) to the whole. Psychologically, the individual is a system of thoughts, motives, and values which interact with external stimuli to produce the behavior we observe.

Socially the individual is a system and is, as well, a subsystem of larger social systems. The individual participates in many activities and many areas in his life. The most important of these are probably the family, work, and the group of activities called "social life." In each of these areas or systems, the individual has a part to play, his role. This role is in part determined by his own preferences and personality, and in part by the system in which he is an actor. Thus a man plays a part as father, manager, community leader, etc. His behavior may differ to varying degrees as he assumes different roles, but nevertheless the underlying consistency of his personality is present.

The demands that the various roles make upon the individual may be harmonious and consonant with each other, or may be in conflict. A conflict may be apparent and external; for example, a man may be a foreman on shift work which involves his being at work when his children are at home. Here his role in the family system as a father and his role as a manager are clearly in conflict. But such conflicts may be much more subtle. His role as manager may require him to be aggressive, determined, and exacting; while his family role as father requires him to be gentle, patient, and tolerant.

The manifestations of such conflict may be obvious to others or barely evident even to oneself. Furthermore, such conflict may turn up in unexpected places. And frequently conflict within a particular system which cannot be dealt with there can appear in other systems. Thus as a psychological defense, a man who for very good reasons finds it difficult to speak up to his boss may displace his resentments into his family life.

Up to this point we have dealt with the way that various systems interact upon the individual. But there may be more direct interaction between the systems to which a person belongs. In a small company town, it is difficult to avoid the group of people socially that one knows at work. Families often know as much or more about company gossip as the employees themselves know. Or, some types of interaction that may occur are attempts by the company to monitor and even influence areas of a man's life beyond his job.[1] A particular company might feel that the demands of the job are such that the man has to have an appropriate wife and family life, and therefore company management might not only make inquiries about these but also attempt to influence them. While it is important to recognize that the demands of membership in various systems can interact, our focus will be on how the work organization as a system, and particularly its smaller units (subsystems), affect the behavior of its members.

THE ORGANIZATION AS A SYSTEM

Any work organization is an open system consisting of the patterned activities of a number of individuals and engaging in transactions with the surrounding environment. The system has a boundary which separates it from its environment, and most organizations having several subunits also have a number of internal boundaries. The organization takes in inputs from the environment and executes transformation processes which turn these inputs into outputs. Thus, a manufacturing company imports raw materials, converts them into products, and acquires a profit from selling the product. It also recruits employees, trains them, assigns them to jobs, and sooner or later exports them by resignation, retirement, or dismissal. It imports and consumes supplies and power.

---

[1] William Whyte, *The Organization Man* (London: Jonathan Cape, 1957).

It also collects intelligence about its market and its competitors; analyzes this information; makes decisions about the quality, quantity, and price of the product; and issues communications of different kinds as a result of the decision made.[2]

The *environment* of the system is important in a number of ways. In the first place it is the source of the inputs and the market for the outputs. Second, other organizations also exist in this environment which may well be competing with the organization under consideration. Furthermore, the environment in general may influence the organization directly or indirectly, and in a way not connected with the major operating task of the organization. For example, in the last few years concern with the rights of black citizens has put pressure on organizations to hire more blacks.

In order to perform its task of converting inputs to outputs, an organization essentially engages in two types of processes: maintenance and task performing.[3] The *maintenance process* is essentially those activities which the organization engages in to remain viable. It must build and maintain staff, plant, etc., in order to perform any task at all. The second set of processes, *task performing*, are the actual activities by which raw materials are transformed into finished products. Finally, there are import and export processes across the organization boundary, as organization members gather resources and distribute products or services.

As an organization grows, efficacy requires that many activities which have to take place become divided, and the organization therefore develops subsystems. This process is called the division of labor, specialization, or task differentiation. Thus personnel departments, purchasing departments, service departments, etc., evolve, while production departments attend to the process itself, and advertising and sales departments distribute the product to the customer. Although such specialization is efficient, as this specialization increases it causes problems of coordination or integration. Control of the various components in the system and the subsystem, as well as their linking together, become a major issue. A traditional method of control and coordination is that of the formal organization, with specific regulations and routines, and use of a management hierarchy. This formalized control is essentially a form of feedback. Feedback is the monitoring of output so that inputs can be changed to maintain a steady state in the system. Thus, if the performance of the task starts to deviate from acceptable limits, the supervisor may instruct the employee accordingly and rules may be enforced. More complex forms of feedback control include the development of special-

---

[2] Kenneth F. Berrien, *General and Social Systems* (New Brunswick, N.J.: Rutgers University Press, 1968).

[3] Eric Miller and A. K. Rice, *Systems of Organizations* (London: Tavistock Publications, 1967).

ized subsystems (e.g., quality control, production control) to perform a similar function.

We have thus far talked about the individual, specialized units, and the organization as systems in their own right as well as parts of a larger system. Our major emphasis in the balance of this reading will be on subsystems which so far have been described essentially as specialized task units. However, usually an individual has face-to-face contact only with a portion of the work force engaged in such a subsystem and the term *work group* is usually reserved for this group. Since our concern is with the individual as an actor in the organization, we therefore want to focus here on such work groups as subsystems.

SUBSYSTEMS IN OPERATION

How do such subsystems (work groups) operate? What produces the behavior we observe in a particular work group? Why are some work groups more productive than others? Why do some groups resist innovations in technology or organization while others welcome them? The answer to these and related questions are important for any manager. They not only enhance his understanding of his own behavior but also that of peers, superiors, and subordinates.

To answer these questions we need to focus on the factors which determine the behavior of the members of a work group.[4] One reason people behave as they do in a work group is because of the functioning of their personality systems. We shall refer to this as *individual inputs*, since it is an input to the subsystem from the individual members of the unit. But this is only one of several forces which affect members' behavior. Two other clusters of factors which affect behavior in a subsystem are imposed from the larger organizational system. The first is the nature of the work assigned to the unit—what we shall call *task inputs*. The second is the formal organizational practices (supervisory arrangements, control systems, procedures, rules, etc.) which are usually defined by the management of the larger system. These we shall term *organizational inputs*. While we shall discuss each of these inputs in more detail below, two points about them require emphasis now.

First, these three factors are interdependent. They interact with each other. For example, an organizational input (personal selection procedures) may affect the kinds of individual inputs in the system. Similarly, the character of organizational inputs may be affected by the task inputs. When a highly routine task is to be performed, management may find it feasible and efficient to rely heavily on formal rules and procedures

---

[4] The ideas which follow are derivations and modifications of those contained in John A. Seiler, *Systems Analysis in Organizational Behavior* (Homewood, Ill.: Richard D. Irwin, Inc., and The Dorsey Press, 1967).

to regulate the work, but when a more uncertain or problem-solving task is to be performed, it may be impossible to rely on such predetermined procedures. Recognizing the interdependence of the inputs is crucial, because it means that when a manager thinks about altering one of them he should be aware of the effects on the other inputs if he is to keep the system operating effectively.

Inputs not only interact, but this interaction creates a fourth determinant of behavior in the work group—*the emergent social controls and structure*—which in turn interacts with the inputs to produce the behavior which emerges in the subsystem. By social controls we mean the traditional ground rules or *norms* about how members should behave which develop in a work group and which guide behavior, and the methods which develop within the group to enforce these norms through feedback. Social structure includes such factors as the status hierarchy which develops informally in any group, the established power relationship in the group, and the stable pattern of friendships which supports this pecking order.

Although social controls and structure are treated more fully below, it is helpful to illustrate the interdependence of this set of variables with the task, organizational, and individual inputs. One obvious example of this interdependence is provided by the degree of physical proximity of group members required by the task. If they must work in a confined space together, this is likely to result in more stringent norms about behavior, such as one should not talk loudly if it will disturb others. Organizational inputs, such as compensation schemes and measurement methods, can also affect the extent to which a group develops into a tightly knit subsystem with strong social controls and a well-defined social structure. In those situations where measurements and financial compensation emphasize group accomplishment, instead of individual output, stronger social controls are apt to develop. The interaction of individual inputs with social controls and structure is even more obvious. As an illustration, the needs, interests, and skills a member brings into the group and the way he is perceived by others will have a great deal to do with the position he ends up with in the group status hierarchy.

These examples are brief and oversimplified and are intended only to demonstrate what is meant by the interdependence of social controls and structures with the three sets of inputs. This interdependence is illustrated in Exhibit 1. Note that the relationship between behavior and these inputs and subsystem social controls and structure is diagrammed as a two-way relationship. We shall explain these feedback loops from behavior to the other variables shortly, but we first need to examine further the interdependence of these variables. As we do this, we shall define each set of variables more precisely and shall de-

EXHIBIT 1
Interdependent Determinants of Behavior

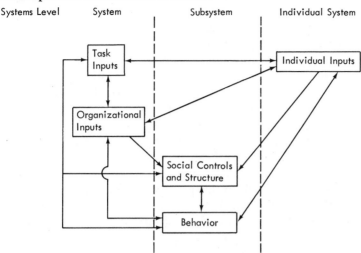

scribe briefly some of the research which suggests a relationship among them and their impact on behavior. In this discussion we use the term "behavior" loosely to refer to both task and subsystem maintenance activities. When we discuss social controls and structure more fully we will clarify this distinction.

Organizational Inputs

Organizational inputs, as we shall use the term, consists of two sets of variables—the formal organizational practices imposed from the system level and the management style of managers supervising the subsystem. By formal organizational variables we mean such factors as the following:[5]

Division of Work. This means the way work is divided among units and people within the unit. The work may be divided by product, by process, by time, or by geographic territory. Obviously, such organizational choices are closely related to the nature of the task inputs for the subsystem. For example, they define whether persons will work on a small portion of the total task or the whole task. The psychological

---

[5] William Evan, "Indices of Hierarchical Structure of Industrial Organizations," *Management Sciences*, September 1963; Joan Woodward, *Management and Technology* (London: Her Majesty's Printing Office, 1958); Tom Burns and G. M. Stalker, *The Management of Innovation* (London: Tavistock Publications, 1961); R. H. Hall, "Intraorganizational Structural Variables," *Administrative Science Quarterly*, December 1962; and Paul R. Lawrence and Jay W. Lorsch, *Organization and Environment: Managing Differentiation and Integration* (Homewood, Ill.: Richard D. Irwin, Inc., 1967).

consequences of such choices may be important also. Usually people working on a whole task get more satisfaction.[6] Similarly, these organizational choices can determine whether people will work relatively independently or will have frequent contact with others.

Span of Control. This is the number of subordinates reporting to a common boss. In some subsystems the span of control may be very narrow, with few subordinates reporting to each supervisor, while in others the span of control may be wider, with many subordinates reporting to each supervisor.

Hierarchy. This means the number of levels in the management hierarchy. As suggested above, the principal function of the hierarchy is to provide a mechanism for coordinating the work of organization members. Through a network of common superiors the work of individual members can be coordinated. In this process information can move both up and down the chain of command.

Rules and Procedures. This aspect of formal organization is concerned with the extent to which explicit rules and procedures about conduct (such as safety procedures) are imposed by higher management. In some situations rules and procedures can be so prolific and detailed as to cover every possible contingency. In others, formalized rules and procedures are nonexistent. The only rules are those norms which emerge within the subsystem itself.

Measurement and Evaluation Practices. These formal practices are concerned with the measurement and evaluation of performance—both for the subsystem as an entity and for individual members. Such practices can vary from those which have many detailed criteria for performance evaluation to those which have only a few general criteria. Similarly, measurement and evaluation of performance can take place at frequent intervals or only infrequently. We should emphasize that these practices provide feedback to the individual, to the subsystem, and to upper management.

Compensation. Financial remuneration has several parameters which can impact on behavior. First is the relative amount of compensation members are getting relative to other opportunities available to them. While recent research has indicated that high pay alone does not motivate people to work harder, it also suggests that people can become disenchanted with their situation if they feel their pay is inequitable, given their level of self-esteem and their view of other opportunities.[7] A second parameter is the basis upon which payment is made. As we

---

[6] A. K. Rice, *The Enterprise and Its Environment* (London: Tavistock Publications, 1963).

[7] M. Scott Meyers, "Who Are Your Motivated Workers?" *Harvard Business Review,* January–February 1964; and Elliott Jaques, *Measurement of Responsibility* (London: Tavistock Publications, 1956).

have already suggested, a group incentive plan can have one impact on people, while payment based on time or individual effort can have others. The third dimension of compensation which is important to consider is the range of payments within the subsystem. The distribution of pay can be one important determinant of status in the subsystem social structure.

Selection Criteria. Here we are concerned with the formally established criteria used to select new members for the subsystem. Characteristics such as skill, experience, age, psychological attributes (from tests) are frequently used to make selection decisions. While such criteria obviously will be affected by task requirements, if they are rigidly adhered to, they can have a significant effect on the individual inputs to the group. If these criteria are specific and many, they will create a group with members who are homogeneous in many characteristics. If the criteria are few and more general, they may lead to a more heterogenous collection of members.

With the exception of division of labor and the type and amount of compensation, these organizational inputs can be arranged on a continuum from high formality to low. (See Exhibit 2.) By formality we

EXHIBIT 2
Formality of Organizational Inputs

	High Formality	*Low Formality*
Span of control	Narrow	Wide
Hierarchical levels	Many	Few
Rules and procedures	Many and specific	Few and general
Measurement and evaluation	Frequent and specific	General
Range of compensation in the subsystem	Wide	Narrow
Selection criteria	Specific and many	Broad and few

mean the extent to which the formal organization is intended to control behavior tightly. Recent research suggests that within many subsystems these variables tend to move in the same direction.[8] Thus, we can think of a subsystem as falling at some point along a continuum of formality of organizational inputs. As we shall see shortly, the formality of these organizational inputs can affect the attitudes of subsystem members about the organization, and partially determine the degree of autonomy they feel. These inputs are also closely related to the task inputs of the subsystem. But before we turn to task inputs, we want to touch on the second major type of organizational input—management style.

[8] Lawrence and Lorsch, *Organization and Environment;* and Jay W. Lorsch and John J. Morse, *Organizations and Their Members: A Contingency Approach* (New York: Harper & Row, Publishers, 1974).

By style of management we mean the behavior pattern which is characteristic of the managers in the larger systems of which the subsystems are a part, as well as in the subsystem itself. Such behavior patterns have been characterized by different labels by a variety of theorists and researchers, but in essence most seem to be concerned with the extent to which managers are concerned with exercising unilateral control over subordinates versus the extent to which they foster a mutual influence process.[9] Since issues of leadership are dealt with in other readings in this book, the important points to be made here can be summarized briefly. First, management style obviously does interact with the other determinants of behavior to influence how a subsystem operates. Second, no one management style is appropriate for all situations. What style of management will facilitate subsystem performance depends on the other inputs to the system as well as its social controls and social structure.[10] Thus, as you consider your own management style you must be concerned not only with what is comfortable, given the dynamics of your personality, but also what fits the other variables in the subsystem to which you belong.

Task Inputs

Our purpose now is to delineate certain characteristics of tasks, which research has shown are related to individual and organizational inputs and behavior. In discussing these task characteristics, it is useful to remember that in many work groups efficiency dictates that members perform similar tasks (e.g., all are purchasing agents).

The first task characteristic which is important is the relative certainty or uncertainty of the work. Several recent studies have amassed considerable evidence that there is a relationship between the certainty of a subsystem's task, its organizational inputs, and the effectiveness of the subsystem.[11] When the task is highly certain and predictable (e.g., an assembly line, turning out a standard product), the subsystem, if it is effective, will tend to have a highly formalized organization. Subsystems with more uncertain tasks (and again effective outputs) tend to have less formalized organizational inputs. An example of the latter

---

[9] Fred E. Fiedler, *A Theory of Leadership Effectiveness* (New York: McGraw-Hill Book Co., 1967); Rensis Likert, *The Human Organization: Its Management and Value* (New York: McGraw-Hill Book Co., 1967); and Robert R. Blake and Jane S. Mouton, *The Managerial Grid* (Houston: Gulf Publishing Co., 1964).

[10] This point is supported by the work of Fiedler, *A Theory;* and Tannenbaum and Schmidt, "How to Choose a Leadership Pattern," *Harvard Business Review,* March–April 1958.

[11] Edward Harvey, "Technology and the Structure of Organizations," *American Sociological Review,* April 1968; Lawrence and Lorsch, *Organization and Environment;* and Woodward, *Management.*

situation might be found in a product management unit or a research laboratory.

The behavior of subsystem members also can vary with the task.[12] For example, in an effective research laboratory there is more autonomy of action among members, and each member has more influence over his own work. In a manufacturing plant there is often less freedom of action for individual members, and the amount of influence over activities tends to correspond closely to the formal hierarchical level of the member. The reasons for this interdependence between this task characteristic, organizational inputs and behavior, and outputs are still being explored, but a promising explanation has to do with the fit between tasks and organizational variables. A good fit seems to have a motivational effect on subsystems members—providing them with a sense of competence in and mastery over their work.[13]

One problem with the concept of task certainty is that it is very broad and often difficult to apply to a specific task within a subsystem. A study by Turner and Lawrence, which is closely connected to those referred to above, suggests six more specific task attributes which were also found to be linked to formality of organization in a number of manufacturing plants. These are: (1) the amount of variety in prescribed activities; (2) the amount of discretion in job activities permitted and required of the job incumbent; (3) the frequency and diversity of interaction with others required by the job; (4) the amount of optional interaction possible; (5) the learning time required for job proficiency; and (6) the amount of responsibility assumed by incumbents as measured by the likelihood of serious error, the uncertainty about appropriate corrective action, and the length of time before feedback is received about the results of the work.[14] When jobs were rated low on these dimensions (e.g., little variety, limited discretion, little required interaction, etc.), it was found that the organizational inputs in the plant were more formalized. The organizations were less formalized in those situations where tasks scored higher on these dimensions. While there has been no empirical attempt to link these findings to those on certainty, it seems clear that jobs which score low on these dimensions are more likely to be highly certain.[15] We can therefore use these dimensions as more specific tools for analyzing and understanding the operation of subsystems.

That such task variables are related to behavior is demonstrated not

---

[12] Lorsch and Morse, *Organizations and Their Members.*

[13] Ibid.

[14] Arthur N. Turner and Paul R. Lawrence, *Industrial Jobs and the Worker* (Boston: Division of Research, Harvard Business School, 1965).

[15] That there can be exceptions to this conclusion is suggested, for example, by a task that is highly certain and still permits a high rate of interaction with others.

only by the Turner and Lawrence study, but also by Robert Blauner in his study of workers in the automobile, printing, and textile industries.[16] Blauner found that workers had varying attitudes toward work, depending on the technology. Specifically, Blauner was interested in the extent to which workers felt alienated from their work. In the automobile industry (which would be very certain and score low on the task attributes discussed above) workers were alientated from the company and its goals by an inability to influence the work situation, a loss of meaning in the work, a sense of being isolated, and a lack of self-involvement in the task. Textile workers, who had similar tasks to the automobile workers, did not feel the same way about their company. One reason was that they came from families in communities in which they were taught not to expect meaning in their work. These individual inputs plus organizational inputs, which were consistent with the values of the small communities in which the plants were located, caused these workers to be reasonably satisfied in spite of tasks which, in other circumstances, might lead to alienation. At the other extreme of task characteristics were the printing workers who engaged in a task which would score high on our job attributes, and did not feel alienated from their work. The chemical workers, with a continuous process technology (but one which was changing and complex), felt responsible for controlling the process, had considerable autonomy, and felt they were members of cohesive teams. As a result, these workers felt integrated into the subsystem of their plant. Blauner's study, as this brief discussion implies, suggests not only that task attributes do have an impact on behavior but also that this impact cannot be fully understood without also considering individual and organization inputs.

In addition to task certainty and the task attributes identified by Turner and Lawrence, there are other task characteristics which can have an important impact on subsystem operations. One of these is the physical conditions in the workplace. In manufacturing operations particularly, such factors as heat, odors, noise, and cleanliness can have an effect on the operation of the subsystem. For example, high noise levels can block oral communication and lead to feelings of isolation unless group members can find some way to communicate in spite of this constraint. Poor working conditions such as extreme heat, odors, etc., can often contribute to subsystem members drawing together in a more cohesive group. By banding together they gain a sense of support in the face of this hostile environment. While we tend to think of such factors as being relevant only in production settings and having a negative impact, it is worth noting that these factors are present in settings other than factories and can have a positive impact. Evidence of this

---

[16] Robert Blauner, *Alienation and Freedom* (Chicago: University of Chicago Press, 1964).

is the time and money devoted to planning office environments so that they offer physical surroundings conducive to contemplative and problem-solving behavior.

Another important task variable is the spatial arrangement of the workplace. As suggested above, whether subsystems members are close together or apart can have an important bearing on the amount of contact they have and how the group functions. Recent research by Allen suggests, for example, that the spatial layout of research laboratories can be an important determinant in getting scientists to interact with certain colleagues who had a particular capacity to bring new technical information into the laboratory.[17] Such interaction was important to the successful accomplishment of the laboratory's mission.

There is a final way in which task inputs affect subsystem operation, and it is perhaps the most obvious one. Since different tasks require different skills and interests, they are likely to attract personnel who have particular individual characteristics even if formal selection criteria are minimal. The reasons individuals select particular jobs are complex, and our knowledge in this area is far from complete. Yet there is mounting evidence that persons with particular needs are attracted to different job opportunities.[18] That this interaction of individual and task inputs can affect behavior is documented by Blauner's example of the textile workers mentioned above. Since these workers placed low value on the meaning of work, they adapted to the routine textile technology without the sense of alienation workers with other personality characteristics might feel. We will return to the issue of individual inputs in general shortly, but first want to make one final point about tasks.

In this discussion we have outlined a few of the task characteristics which affect behavior in subsystems. As with the other variables discussed in this paper, this cannot be a comprehensive discussion of the topic both because of space limitations and the fact that our knowledge about these matters is growing rapidly. Rather, we have suggested some of the important task characteristics and their relationship to other subsystem variables. As you apply the conceptual scheme outlined here, you will come to understand these and other relationships more fully. The essential points at this juncture are to recognize that these and other task characteristics can and do vary among subsystems; that these task inputs are interdependent with the other inputs and social control and structure; and that together these variables produce the behavior which you will be trying to understand and manage.

---

[17] Thomas J. Allen and Stephen I. Cohen, "Information Flow in Research and Development Laboratories," *Administrative Science Quarterly*, March 1969.

[18] Gene W. Dalton, Louis B. Barnes, and Abraham Zaleznik, *The Distribution of Authority in Formal Organizations* (Boston: Division of Research, Harvard Business School, 1968); and Anne Roe, *The Psychology of Occupation* (New York: John Wiley & Sons, Inc., 1956).

Individual Inputs

Where organizational and task factors are inputs from the larger organizational system, the individual characteristics with which we are concerned are largely inputs from the personality system. Since personality issues are discussed in another volume in this series and because we will deal with individual inputs at length in considering social controls and structure, our discussion here will be limited to a few essential points.

Individuals bring to the subsystem a complex but balanced internal system of their own. In their role as subsystem members, they will behave in ways which are consistent with this internal balance. While the nature of the task and organization may attract people with somewhat similar characteristics, there will still be differences among members in terms of their particular internal balance and the factors which motivate them to work. This has an important impact upon the type of membership roles individuals seek in the subsystem.

But the way people behave in a group is not only a function of their internal needs in relation to task and organizational inputs, but also in relation to the ongoing social controls and structure present. One important implication of this fact is that one's role in a group is to a certain extent also a function of how other members perceive him in relation to their expectations of what a good group member shall be. These perceptions of a person are not only a function of how he behaves, given his personality, but also of certain *external characteristics* which a member brings to the subsystem. By *external* characteristics we mean such relatively visible factors as age, seniority, sex, ethnicity, skill level, and so on. As a very simple example, take the case of a young MBA who, as his first job in a company, joins a top-level planning group whose other members are all long-service employees and older managers. He will certainly be treated differently than an older, more experienced manager joining the same group. We shall elaborate on this point in discussing social controls and structure.

Social Controls and Structure

As pointed out earlier, social controls and structure are different from the other factors discussed above in that they develop within the subsystem out of the interaction of task, organizational, and individual inputs. Social controls refers to the norms about appropriate behavior for subsystems members which develop in a group and the mechanisms employed to gain compliance to these norms. Social structure is the hierarchy of membership positions which actually emerges in the subsystem.

The relationship between these social forces and behavior is highly interdependent, and the distinction between them is very subtle. In fact the only way we can really track the social controls and structure which exist in a subsystem is by observing the behavior—interaction and activity patterns, feelings and attitudes expressed—over a period of time. This is so because social controls and structure represent relatively enduring subsystem-wide expectations about how members should behave collectively and individually. Actual behavior can and does deviate from these expectations, but in general the social controls constrain behavior so that it supports and reinforces structure. The connection between behavior and social controls and structure becomes clearer if we examine why and how the latter develop in a subsystem.

To do so, we need to answer the question, why do people become actively involved in work groups? After all, just because one is formally assigned or working in a subsystem is not sufficient reason to become involved in a process of social control. The answer to this question is simple enough—whether the subsystem we are talking about is defined on the organization chart or whether it just grows up in the organization without formal sanction. People become involved in work group activity because it meets certain of their needs. First, by joining a group, persons are often able to accomplish task objectives they cannot achieve alone. For formally established groups, this may be the solution of a complex problem one person could not solve alone or the manufacture of a complicated product. In such cases, the member is satisfying important ego needs for mastery or competence as well as meeting the task requirements of the larger system. Put another way, the needs of individuals and the primary task of the subsystem are consistent with the requirements of the larger system.[19]

But in other situations the group's primary task is not the same as the task inputs defined by management. For example, a group of workers who have developed a healthy distrust for management may implicitly define as their primary task protecting themselves from management pressure for higher productivity. By banding together, they can resist attempts to get them to work harder. Alone they could not accomplish this, but by coordinated activity, they can protect themselves from what they perceive to be a hostile environment.

Both these examples suggest the same essential fact—by joining into subsystem activity, members get things done which could not be accomplished alone. At the same time, they are also meeting important internal needs. By joining together to accomplish work, they can manage their drives for affection and aggression, can get reinforcement for their values, gain a sense of self-esteem from the acceptance by others, and so on.

[19] Rice, *The Enterprise.*

As members work together on a task and satisfy their needs, the group as a whole develops certain expectations about what is appropriate behavior. In the second example above, for instance, the group might expect that members should not produce more than a certain number of units of output per day. Such shared expectations about behavior are what we mean by group norms. Variations in individual behavior from such work group norms can have major negative consequences for the group and the individual. First, it can prevent accomplishment of the task. Eventually, if a group ceased to fill such a major purpose, this could lead to its breakdown. Second, since people have needs which are being satisfied by group membership itself, as well as task accomplishment, they are reluctant to see this happen and they become involved in maintenance behavior aimed at controlling norm-breakers. This often painful sanction is what we mean by the process of social control.

Attempts at social control are a form of feedback about an individual's behavior and often consist of verbal sanctions—such as sarcasm, invectives, jokes, and the like. If these types of punishment don't work, the ultimate weapon is disregard or ostracism. Whether or not these controls will work on individual members depends upon the extent to which they value subsystem membership. If the group is an important source of need satisfaction for them, they will comply. If the group is not important to a member, he can safely disregard these sanctions. This point is closely connected to the formation of social structure; but before we discuss this, we want to make one other point about norms and social control.

In the discussion above of norms aimed at restricting productivity, we were, in effect, suggesting that the social controls of the subsystem would be operating in opposition to the organization and task inputs defined by the larger system. While this is often the case, social controls also often support organization objectives. An example of this is reported by Blau in his study of a government agency.[20] In this agency the group of investigating agents had developed a norm stipulating that the more competent agents should help the less competent ones when the latter were having difficulty. While this norm was contrary to a formal rule that agents should only confer with supervisors, Blau concluded that this interagent consultation improved the quality of agent decisions and contributed to the overall effectiveness of the agency. Obviously, the negative consequence of this norm was that it tended to weaken the authority of supervisors. However, the problem in this situation was not so much the norm but the rigid rules which seemed inconsistent with task requirements and social controls.

---

[20] Peter M. Blau, *The Dynamics of Bureaucracy* (Chicago: University of Chicago Press, 1955).

Turning now to the issue of social structure, we have already seen that different members may value subsystem membership to differing degrees. Similarly, certain individuals are more or less important to the group. This importance can take the form of contribution to task accomplishment or to their role in the maintenance of the group. For example, in Blau's group of agents the competent agent was an important member because of his ability to help others in task accomplishment. Simultaneously, the group was important to him because it fed his sense of self-esteem. These competent agents were high in the social structure of their group. In another situation a person might become a central member of a group because of his capacities to help maintain group cohesion at times of stress. For example, in a task force of managers working on a complex problem, one of their number who was skillful at reducing tension through humor might become a valued member with high status. Also, as suggested in the discussion of human inputs, one's status in a social structure can also be determined by characteristics like age, skill, and the like. Which ones will be important depend on how task, organizational, and individual inputs interact with group norms to shape the attributes that group members value. What is essential to remember is that such hierarchies do develop and people's positions in them are related to their contribution to the group. At a minimum, such a contribution means adherence to group norms.

One way to illustrate these points is to describe four categories of group membership identified by Zaleznik, Christensen, and Roethlisberger.[21] The lowest of these on the totem pole is the *isolate,* a person who has been isolated from the group. This can happen because he has so little to offer the group that they isolate him and because the group is so unimportant to him that he chooses to stay out. In essence, he has signaled that group membership either is not important to him or he is not capable of meeting group expectations, and the group, through its rejection, has indicated that he is not important to them. Next in lowest standing is the so-called *deviant.* He deviates from the expected patterns of behavior but is still tolerated by others. This tolerance may be because he is making some important contribution to the group in spite of his deviance or because other group members feel that there is still hope that he will conform to group behavior standards. In either case, a deviant can be identified because, instead of being ignored like the isolate, he will be the focus of much interaction directed at bringing his behavior back into line.

Next in line up the social structure is what these authors called the *regular.* As the name implies, such members are squarely in the group.

---

[21] Abraham Zaleznik, C. R. Christensen, and F. J. Roethlisberger, *The Motivation, Productivity, and Satisfaction of Workers* (Boston: Division of Research, Harvard Business School, 1958).

They adhere to most, if not all, group expectations about behavior, so they are making the contributions expected of a good member. In exchange for this contribution they are rewarded by being included in the group. Finally, at the top of the pecking order are the *leaders*. These are the subsystem members who are seen by others as making the greatest contribution to the group. This may be the leader as defined by the formal organization, but they may also be another person. As a minimum contribution these members adhere to group norms. But beyond this, they make some special contribution which others value. It may be the contribution of helping others, as in the case of the agents in Blau's study, or it may be a tension-reducing role, like the task force example above. Whatever their contributions, the leaders can be identified because they will be at the center of the group in the receipt of interactions and in terms of influence. In fact, this relationship between interaction and positions in the group can be seen throughout this discussion of membership roles. The more central a person is to the group in terms of his contribution, the more he is apt to be involved in positive interactions with others. This is another example of what we mean by the interdependence of behavior and social controls and structure.

Two other points need to be made about leadership in subsystems. First, throughout this discussion we have intentionally used the plural term leaders. The reason for this is that most subsystems often have a number of leaders playing slightly different roles. One very visible example of this point is in the top-management subsystem of larger firms where two or three executives play different leadership roles based on their unique competences. Such an arrangement has been formalized in the office of the president in many companies. One executive may deal with external problems such as finance or marketing, while another devotes his efforts to internal issues of management development, organization, and so on. Such division of leadership is frequently agreed upon among the top group and is not necessarily officially recognized in titles or job descriptions. This is an example of the fact that in human organization of any size leadership must handle both task and maintenance functions. We should note in passing that for one individual to do both is often difficult.

The final point we wish to make about leadership has to do with the concept of authority. Too often we think of authority as coming from a formal position. This certainly is one basis of authority. But, as this discussion suggests, authority in organizations is also derived from the special contribution a leader makes to the subsystem of which he is a member. Often in management it is the particular competence a man demonstrates which makes him a valued group member whom others respect and are willing to follow. While this view of leadership and authority is more complicated than conventional ones, it is also more accurate. As a student of organizational phenomena who will be concerned with the use of power in organizations, it is important for the reader to recognize this complexity, and it is hoped that this discussion of subsystems in operation will help him to understand it. For leadership behavior like the behavior of any other subsystem member can only be understood in terms of the inputs and the issues of social control and structure.

To conclude this discussion, we want to consider one other facet of subsystems—their capacity to adapt and change. This is important because for many years students of organizations in general and groups in particular have thought of organization systems and subsystems as being more or less unchanging.[22] Such a view is contrary to the experience of many managers who live in changing organizations and who cause them to change. It is also contrary to more recent sociological theory which views organization systems as having the capacity to change.[23] We now want to examine briefly just how and why subsystems do adapt and change.

ADAPTATION AND CHANGE IN SUBSYSTEMS

At the outset it is necessary to distinguish between the important processes of adaptation and change. The distinction between these is somewhat fuzzy; essentially change is an alteration in the state or level of some subsystem variable. For example, at one time it may be very easy to get unskilled labor as a human input to the organization, and because of economic changes, at another time very difficult. This represents a change in the level of the human input to the system. Adaptation is the adjustment which the organization subsequently makes in order to accommodate the change in the level of such a variable. Thus, when the availability of unskilled labor drops, the organization has to do something about it. If it does this "something" effectively, this is called adaptation. If it fails to do this effectively, this is failure to adapt. In summary, adaptation is a second order change which enables the subsystem to maintain its balance in the new situation.

There is a tendency to think of change in organizations as being only such dramatic alterations as the introduction of automation or the formal reorganization of a company. But there are several kinds of change which we should at least touch upon that appear all the time

---

[22] George C. Homans, *The Human Group* (New York: Harcourt, Brace & Co., 1950).

[23] Walter Buckley, *Sociology and Modern Systems Theory* (Englewood Cliffs, N.J.: Prentice-Hall, Inc., 1967).

in less evident ways. Most organizations are growing in size, just like the human organism, and this continual growth necessitates continual readjustments. For example, as an organization expands in size, it is apt to develop more subsystems which somehow must be linked. As subsystems grow in size they may be divided into separate units. A further "natural" and continuing change is the movement of people through an organization. People leave and are replaced by others. As new people join, they and the organization have to undergo adaptive processes so that the newcomers can become effective replacements for their predecessors. This process of socialization is part of the social control mechanisms described earlier. As the new member is socialized he learns the norms and expectations of the subsystem, and the subsystem learns what it can expect from the individual. For a while during this period, deviant behavior on the part of the newcomer is tolerated as part of the learning process. This period may be as long as six months, but shortly thereafter organization members feel the newcomer has had time enough to learn and meet their norms and expectations.[24]

It is also useful to make a distinction between change which originates outside the subsystem, and to which the subsystem must then adapt, and change which originates within the subsystem. As suggested above, most subsystems have a capacity to initiate change in themselves as well as in others.

Change may occur in any aspect of the system. For the organization as a whole, there may be changes in inputs so that the availability of raw materials, of financial support, or of appropriate personnel may vary; there may be changes in outputs so that the organization's position in the market changes; there may be changes in processes so that a new technology is developed (as, for example, the introduction of automation); lastly, there may be a change in the political environment —for example, the federal government may decide not to tolerate mergers. The changes of most concern to subsystem members are those which have to do with the nature of the task, the means by which the task is performed, or the way in which people are formally organized. A *task* may be changed, so that a work group will be asked to make book paper instead of writing paper; *technology* may change, so that instead of having machines to make paper, which are run largely by hand, automated processes make the paper and fewer workers are involved in simpler tasks; or there may be the *reorganization* of a department, and two groups which have hitherto worked separately may now be required to work together. In practice, because of the interdependence of subsystem variables, such changes rarely occur singly.

---

[24] Robert S. Weiss, *Processes of Organization* (Ann Arbor: Institute for Social Research, University of Michigan, 1956).

Feedback

Before describing the dynamics of change and resistance to it, let us first relate change processes to the concept of feedback. By feedback we mean information received within the system or subsystem comparing actual events with expectations. Essentially, feedback describes the comparison of actual output with expected output, and the linking of information back to modify the input-output process. In the strict cybernetic sense, negative feedback reduces discrepancies between actual and expected outputs, or variations from a norm, while positive feedback increases such discrepancies or variations. In popular usage, positive feedback describes information which supports a given direction or output, while negative feedback is critical of it. If the comparison is unfavorable in relation to the desired state of affairs, it is called negative feedback; if it is favorable it is defined as positive. The channels through which this information moves are feedback loops. One obvious example of feedback is the attempt by subsystem members to influence deviants to conform to group expectations. The feedback loop is between the subsystem and the deviant, with information moving in both directions. The deviant is receiving information about the consequences of his behavior; the rest of the system is learning whether or not their sanction is having an effect. Most changes in organizations or in subsystems occur because of information going through such feedback loops. Thus, if the environment changes, producing a market which is more competitive and therefore requires a change in outputs, feedback loops conduct this intelligence through the marketing department to the production department. Here a series of decisions might be made depending on the situation: technology might require altering, people might require reorganizing, or costs may have to be reduced. As these internal adaptive changes are made the effects on output will be measured by the organization's capacity to compete in the market. Some feedback loops prompt alterations in the internal organization to improve its task performance and ability to compete in the external environment, while other feedback loops may stimulate organizational changes which are not related to such outputs. For example, an organization may be performing effectively, but its members may still feel that feedback from the internal environment demands change. Employees may be dissatisfied or alienated and so managers decide that an internal reorganization would increase their feelings of satisfaction with employment.

Resistance to Change

When changes are made in any aspect of an organization, whether in technology, task, or the arrangement of people, such changes frequently are met by the people they affect with concern, if not active resistance. People have become very accustomed to doing certain things in certain ways and even if new ways are suggested which are in fact improvements, they will still be resisted. There are many reasons for this. A few examples are:

1. Any change involves the introduction of some uncertainty. What is affected and how is never entirely clear until it happens. Therefore, some individuals tend to prefer what is familiar.
2. Change usually involves the introduction of new things and the dropping of old things. As a result, a psychological sense of loss may be experienced, and this is uncomfortable.
3. Very often people's sense of competence at work is closely related to their having mastered a particular way of doing a task. When asked to change this, they may feel a lessened sense of competence.
4. Changes often also entail an alteration in valued interpersonal relationships. People may no longer have the same intensity of contacts with former associates or may be required to interact more intensively with strangers.
5. Finally, people may react to the way the change is introduced. If the change is imposed upon them unilaterally, persons who are accustomed to having a voice in decisions may resist the change to counteract their feelings of powerlessness.

It should be stressed that these factors are not mutually exclusive, nor is this list exhaustive. Furthermore, in any given situation one particular reason for resisting change may be more important than others. This means that an important task for a manager engaged in making changes is to determine why his subordinates and associates are resisting a change. It is inevitable that people involved in a change will experience feelings such as those described above, but an effective manager can minimize the effects of these feelings.

The forms this resistance takes are many. Sometimes there is an explicit rejection of the new proposal. Sometimes indirect manifestations of behavior will indicate resistance, such as an increase in people reporting sick or mistakes being made. After a period of initial resistance, there is usually a period of waiting and seeing. At this time people are often convinced that the change is going to be made but are not prepared to support it in case the effort fails. They do nothing to undermine it but also they will probably do nothing to help it. Finally, if the change persists, people will usually incorporate it as part of their everyday life and accept it.

Managing Change

There are several important implications about change which stem from this systems view. First, the manager must recognize the interdependency of all subsystem variables in producing behavior. Managers who rely on an overly simplistic view of human behavior instead of a systems view such as that presented here run great risks of selecting an inappropriate course of action. Understanding the functioning of a system cannot only guide the manager in working out his own behavior, given the constraints of the social forces and inputs facing him, but also can be crucial in determining which of the various inputs to alter. Such understanding may be the difference between the successful introduction of action in general and of change in particular.

A second major point for the manager to recognize is that an important element of the behavior which occurs in subsystems is the feelings of the members. As we have seen, the interaction of subsystem inputs and social mechanisms produces feelings among the people involved. It is these feelings which lead to the manifest behavior we call resistance to change. In thinking about action taking and change, managers must recognize and deal in some way with these feelings because they are as real as the mechanical hardware on a factory floor.

The manager must also recognize that in groups, members work together to control their environment and to satisfy their own needs. A unilateral introduction of change can upset the members of the subsystem and can create negative feelings about a management action. It is therefore important to educate group members to the rationale and details of change and wherever feasible to foster their active participation in the planning and implementation of change. While a manager has the responsibility to make certain decisions, it is clear that the quality of these decisions and their implementation will be greatly enhanced if the manager is open to feedback from others in his subsystem. In fact, as a manager makes a diagnosis of the problems facing him, he is engaged in the process of collecting feedback about the current state of his subsystem. The more open he is to this feedback, the more adequate will be his diagnosis.

CONCLUSIONS

This issue of an adequate diagnosis provides a useful way to close this reading because the set of concepts described is basically a set of diagnostic tools. With them a manager should be able to increase his understanding of the multiple factors which lead to the results he gets from his particular subsystem. However, even with a thorough understanding of these concepts, it is no simple matter to make an accurate analysis of the causes of behavior in an organization. The number of factors involved is large, and they are related in complex ways. For the student using these concepts for the first time, they may seem too complicated and awkward. He may be inclined to revert to his own intuitions to explain what is happening in a particular situation. While such intuitive insights are often accurate, our experience indicates that the student who struggles to apply these concepts to case situations will soon find that he is achieving a more accurate understanding of human problems in organizations than he can from his own intuitive feel. This does not mean we should ignore intuitive hunches, but rather that they should be tested against the facts of the situation and organized with a systemic perspective.

Section IV

Intergroup Behavior

Cases

1 | Belmont-White Company

Two months ago, at an operating committee meeting, the president of the Belmont-White Company[1] asked Thornton Peet, the general sales manager, and Paul Robb, manager of the organization planning and procedures department, to get together and determine if better forecasts of sales and of inventory requirements could be made available in order to improve factory schedules, financial planning, and so on. Bert Kent and Charles Stevens, both of whom worked for Robb, and Robert Henry, Edwin Merrill, and David Spitz of the sales department were assigned by Robb and Peet, respectively, to work on the problem. Stevens and Henry, being older and more experienced, and being regarded as rather senior men, immediately became the informal leaders of the work group. The five men worked out the technical problems to the satisfaction of both Stevens and Henry. The group attempted to consult with its immediate superiors as the work progressed.

After the study had been under way for some time, Henry told Stevens that he, Merrill, and Spitz seemed to be blocked by the opposition of the product division managers. Henry also told Stevens that he felt "he could not go over the division managers' heads" to Peet; and he asked Stevens to have his boss, Robb, inquire of the sales manager whether a conference might not be held to appraise the progress of the work. Stevens told Robb of Henry's request and the reason for it. Accordingly, Robb talked to Peet about the matter. Peet acquiesced, as he believed the problem ought to be solved as rapidly as possible. Peet invited the four product division managers, Robb, and the five-man working group to the conference and set the time for it. Peet told Henry

---

[1] A partial organization chart of the company is shown in Exhibit 1.

229

EXHIBIT 1
Partial Organization Chart

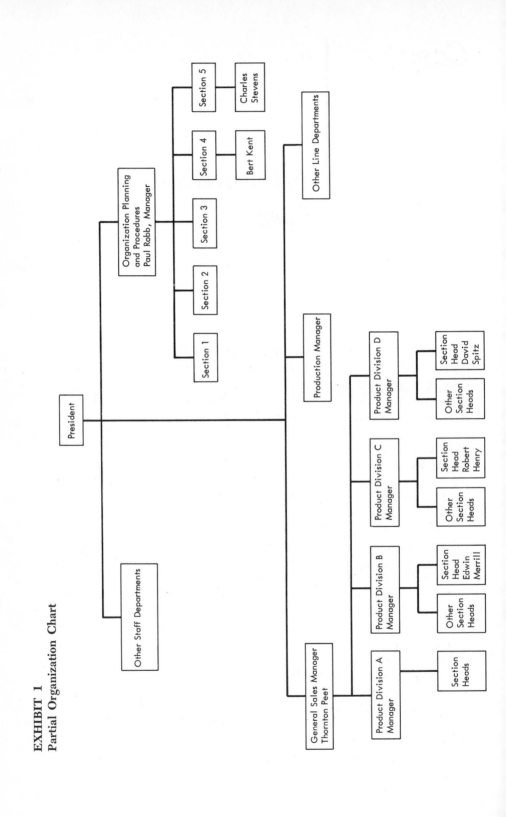

to go ahead with Stevens and set up the presentation to be made at the conference.

As Henry and Stevens planned the conference, they decided that the group from the sales department—Henry, Merrill, and Spitz—were really on the spot. The three men all agreed that in order not to embarrass themselves or their bosses, the presentation of the joint conclusions of the working group ought to be made by Stevens.

At the meeting, Peet, the four product division managers, and the three men from sales who worked on the study were present, as were Robb of the organization planning and procedures department and his two assistants, Stevens and Kent. When Peet asked who was going to report progress, Henry suggested that Stevens was the best man to present their findings. Peet asked Robb if that was OK. When the latter agreed, Stevens used half an hour to outline the concept of their work; he stated that both groups had agreed upon details and believed their recommendations would work; they were prepared to take personal responsibility for them. Both Merrill and Spitz asked Henry to amplify certain points during the presentation. It seemed to Robb that they had in mind clarifying matters for their own bosses who might be opposed or might not understand.

Following Stevens's statement, the sales manager called upon his product division managers to give their reactions to the proposals. One of them gave the plan lukewarm support; the three others said it could not be accomplished. There was much discussion among the three who were opposed. Occasionally, Henry, Merrill, and Spitz tried to "get a word in edgewise," without much success. Once, Kent asked the Division B manager a question; the effect seemed to be mild anger at being interrupted.

Robb watched the whole proceeding with interest. He recalled that it had seemed to him that for the past two years, this same group of four product managers had opposed every step involving changes in methods or procedures. In his opinion, their "delaying tactics" had been costly to the company. Robb knew that the president expected him to break some of these bottlenecks. Robb was only a staff adviser, but he knew he "had the president's ear" whenever he needed it. He considered the sales manager to be progressive and thought Peet could not tolerate these conditions much longer. It seemed to Robb that Peet had line responsibility to get something done in this area. Robb liked these "old-line" product managers and did not want to hurt them if he could avoid it.

While Robb was in the midst of these musings, and after two hours of apparently fruitless discussion, Peet turned to him and said: "Robb, you have heard this whole discussion; what do you think we ought to do next?"

2 | *Stuart Aircraft*

"I've become quite concerned about the losses in the managerial ranks at our newly acquired CANCOVER [Canadian Coverings Limited] operations," Jim McGregor told the casewriter. McGregor was vice president for manufacturing of Stuart Aircraft, a large West Coast producer of commercial and business jets.

First we lost several Americans that we transferred up there after the acquisition. Now we're losing Fred Colby, sales and purchasing manager at CANCOVER and the top Canadian that we retained, and I'm afraid that after he goes, others will follow. Fred has accepted an offer to head Canadian operations for one of our subcontractors, Banks Tool, at a sizable salary increase. I sure hate to lose him, and I'm going to try to talk him out of leaving. I guess Fred really didn't get much salary advance after taxes in the takeover when you consider that the old CANCOVER management paid his country club membership and made arrangements for gas and an automobile. I can remedy that some when I talk to him. But I have a hunch that the only thing that would have interested Fred when we took over was the job at the top, and I was afraid to take that kind of risk with a man I didn't know. Seat covers and interior trim for aircraft may not seem like a big item, and as a percentage of production costs, it's not; but there are a lot of combinations of materials and colors. There are rapid changes in requirements and short lead times. And a couple of commercial jets sitting on the apron waiting for interior trim is a very disconcerting sight to a production man. I'm also mad about our profit performance in the six months since we took over, and I'm pushing them on that. We're still in the red, and when we shut down our Boise plant and

232

bought CANCOVER, we expected a $500,000 annual profit using the Boise cost as a transfer price.

THE ACQUISITION

In July 1968, Stuart Aircraft sold their Airfit Division located in Boise, Idaho, to Consul Products, a conglomerate. About 20 percent of Airfit's sales were aircraft parts, and about half of this amount was parts for interior trim (seat covers, curtains, partitions, rugs, etc.). Because the workers in the aircraft segment of the business were paid higher wages, Consul had no desire to retain the aircraft operations (which amounted to about $8 million in annual sales). Stuart Aircraft therefore had to find another source of supply for these items.

The alternatives considered initially were:

1. Relocate in Boise, Idaho. This had advantages in terms of work force retention but would result in high labor costs.
2. Move to a site in Salem, Oregon. This would result in lower labor costs but it would take some time to build a plant and an effective organization.
3. Consolidate all interior trim production in Omaha, Nebraska, where 35 percent of Stuart's requirements were produced at the time. However, the Omaha facility was already crowded.
4. Buy the necessary trim from Canadian Covering Limited (CANCOVER), an existing and independent supplier.

In the early fall of 1968, Stuart management discovered the possibility of purchasing the CANCOVER operations in Banff, Alberta. The owners of CANCOVER were all over 60 and anxious to end their responsibilities at CANCOVER; if they sold the company, Canadian tax treatment of capital gains would permit them to retain a large portion of the sale price. To Stuart management this new alternative presented certain advantages: low labor costs in an established organization, tight control over operations, and increased Canadian-produced content of Stuart's jets (a strong tax factor in export sales to Canada). These advantages more than compensated for the additional day of delivery time for parts coming from CANCOVER to the United States due to customs procedures.

After CANCOVER negotiated a three-year union contract with the Canadian local (reaching $3 per hour in the third year), Stuart was able to arrange for a favorable purchase price. The sale was announced on January 5, 1969. One of the former owners immediately flew to Trinidad and bought a beach club, and the other two owners retired to their homes near Banff.

CANCOVER

Before Acquisition

Prior to the acquisition by Stuart Aircraft, Canadian Coverings Limited was a small, privately owned firm located in Banff, Alberta. Of the three owners, two had been inactive and the third, Mel Bruce, had become somewhat restless. Fred Colby, sales and purchasing manager, reported directly to Bruce, but in recent years he had acquired considerable latitude in running CANCOVER operations. These operations were characterized by informal organization, control systems, and decision-making procedures. CANCOVER had a reputation as a dependable, high-quality producer of seat covers and other interior trim.

At the time of the purchase by Stuart Aircraft, CANCOVER was producing about 15 percent of Stuart's requirements for trim. These sales represented about 80 percent of CANCOVER's current business; the remaining sales included seats for snowmobiles, interior trim for a small producer of private aircraft, and a subcontract for interior trim for military "spotter" aircraft. Once the news of the sales of the Airfit Division broke, management of the Canadian firm moved quickly to seek additional business from Stuart. CANCOVER had been experiencing declining sales for several years. All other major aircraft producers had acquired a captive source of supply for trim. Zarren Aircraft's move to a captive source several years previously had meant the loss of a substantial portion of CANCOVER's business. Employment had fallen from 200 to 65. During the period after the loss of the Zarren contract, management had made a desperate effort to find new sales opportunities, but results had been meager and the prospects looked grim.

Post-Acquisition Developments

The original post-acquisition plan called for continued production of all trim for the Stuart 800 at present locations (15 percent at CANCOVER, 50 percent at Boise in a facility retained by Stuart, 35 percent at Omaha). Upon phase-out of production on the 800 in May 1969, the Boise facility would be closed; and during a one-month lull before production began on the Stuart 1107, all necessary equipment, material, and staff would be moved to CANCOVER. Prior to that key personnel would travel to Banff occasionally to help CANCOVER "gear up" for their new role. The long-range plan called for building a new plant in Banff to consolidate all of Stuart's trim production at one location.

The first hitch in the plans occurred when Stuart employees at Boise began to leave for other jobs sooner than expected. The final terms of the Airfit sale had included arrangements for 150 hourly workers and 20 supervisors to be retained by Stuart to complete production on the 800 trim prior to closing down in Boise. Charles Bartlett, who had been assistant plant manager in charge of production for Airfit, was retained by Stuart and placed in charge of the Boise trim operations. Bartlett was directed to inform the Stuart personnel in Boise of all alternatives for trim sources, except the negotiations for purchase of CANCOVER. They were also told by Jim McGregor, vice president of manufacturing for Stuart Aircraft, "Stuart will have a job for you," regardless of the outcome of the location decision. The first news of the negotiations for CANCOVER reached some union members at Boise through the international union offices.

Shortly after official announcement of the CANCOVER purchase, Consul products began a drastic reduction in work force at the former Airfit plant. The hourly payroll was reduced from 3,500 to 1,200, and 300 salaried employees were terminated. Stuart employees in Boise, seeing the possibility of a return to the Airfit operations eliminated, became concerned about their future. Bartlett, who was to become production manager at CANCOVER, relayed the employees' concern to McGregor. He was told that Stuart would pay most relocation costs for all staff members and that the company management particularly wanted five or six key Boise employees to transfer to Banff. Despite these assurances, personnel losses accelerated, forcing a shift of some trim work for the 800 from Boise to Banff.

Stuart was unsuccessful in gaining employee commitments for the move to Canada. Eight or nine key people had been sent to Canada to appraise the prospects; but all found the wages, fringe benefits, tax situation, cost of living, and the idea of moving to Canada unappealing. As Tom Anderson, quality control manager at Boise, told the casewriter, "Banff is a beautiful, active town of 25,000 in the summer, but the Americans were seeing it with over 4 feet of snow. I've never seen a place that looked so dead. I thought, 'Maybe spring doesn't even come here.'" Jim McGregor, Charles Bartlett, and Bert Parsons, who was selected as new plant manager for CANCOVER, met on April 30 individually with those key men who were left in Boise. Some of the offers originally made to these men were improved, involving salary increases, even though doing this meant salary inequity problems with some employees of the prior CANCOVER organization. Several American managers received offers of $300 to 400 per month more than Canadians were receiving at the same level. Still there were no decisions to transfer to Canada, even though continuing personnel losses caused further transfer of 800 trimworkers to Banff. The work transfer forced some staff members to spend 2–3 days per week in Banff even though they would not move permanently. Stuart managers reassured people that they would be given a job within the company, and interviews at other plants were arranged. However, no Boise personnel accepted offers at other plants. Stuart then offered "extra benefits" to people who would remain at Boise until final closedown. Production at Boise dwindled. Prior to closing, four men, including Charles Bartlett, agreed to transfer to Banff. (See Exhibit 1.)

Meanwhile, back at Banff the Canadians were having some problems. The shift of work from Boise meant not only an increase in volume but an increase in the combinations of colors and styles, making production more complex. This shift placed a strain on a limited production control system already stretched by the changeover to Stuart's mode of operation. Much of the CANCOVER equipment and inventory was outdated and was therefore removed to make room for equipment brought in from Boise. A new production layout had to be developed in an antiquated four-story building with inadequate space and numerous materials handling problems. New products and methods had to be taught simultaneously with a buildup in work force (from 65 hourly employees to over 200 in less than eight months). The push to expand production forced considerable interaction and joint decision making among department managers to resolve problems such as space allocation, quality of materials, delivery schedules, rescheduling of production in response to changed requirements from the home office, shifting personnel, and so on. These problems were further complicated by the fact that the managers' offices were spread over three floors of the building. Some antipathy arose between members of the old CANCOVER management and the Americans, particularly those from Boise. As Bob Trimble, industrial engineering manager and an American who had been with Stuart in the United States, put it:

> The CANCOVER people are good people. They know their jobs but they have a different approach and different intensity about things. I guess it comes from the diversity of background and ideas. We need to tell them what is expected, but as it is I think they have a feeling of being pushed. We have a pretty headstrong crew here. The people from Boise tend to be argumentative—maybe you got things done there by shouting and really raising sand, but the Canadians are sensitive about it. There's a tendency for the Boise managers to say that the CANCOVER equipment is junk and their methods are backward and the Boise equipment and methods are better. I just find the Boise people tougher and pushier than the Canadians. They're aggressive and tend to grab the show while the Canadians are more reserved. Frankly, I prefer dealing with CANCOVER people. But I think they're a little bit afraid—afraid to talk up—to buck Stuart people.

EXHIBIT 1 Canadian Covering Ltd., June 10, 1969

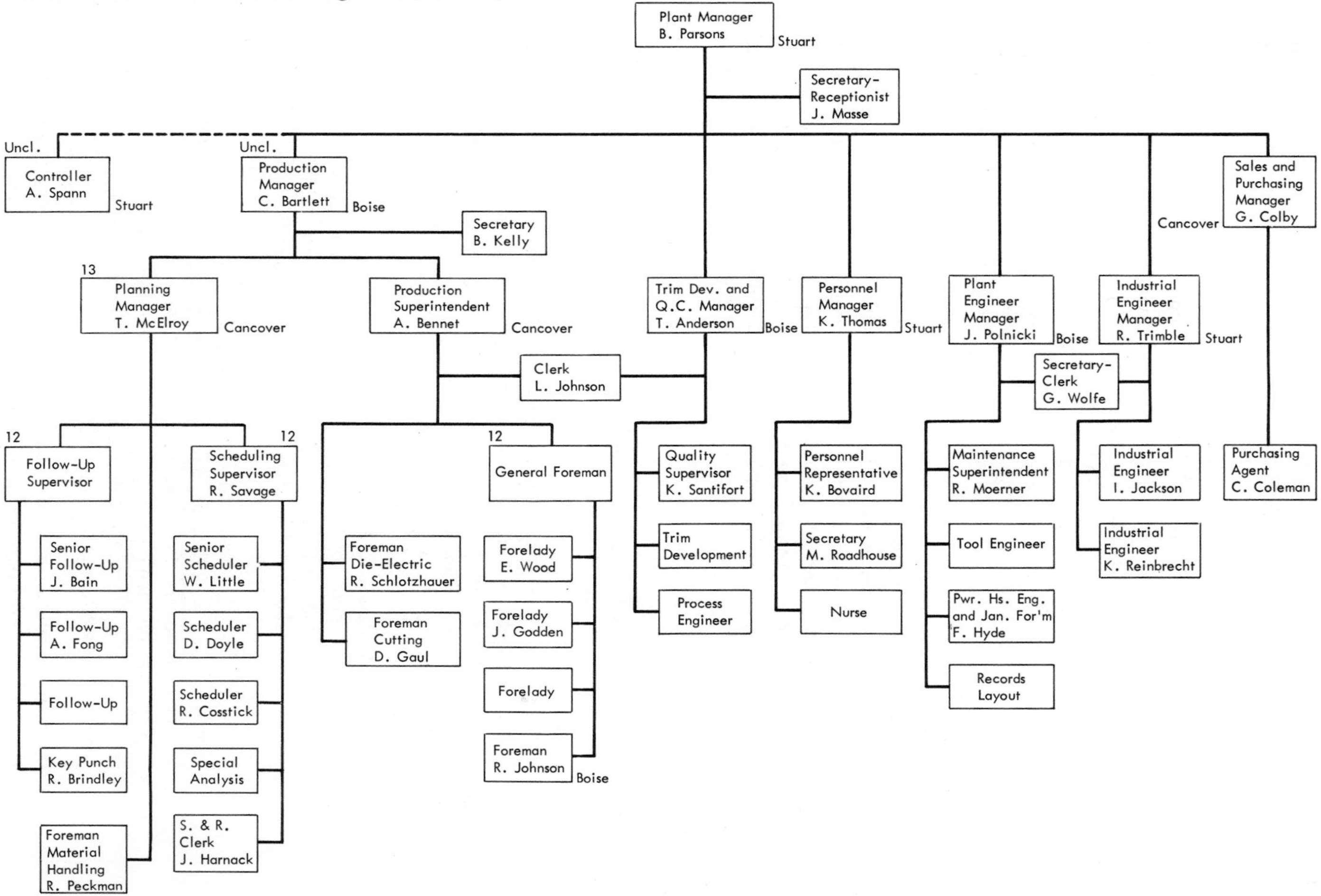

Plant Manager
B. Parsons — Stuart

Secretary-Receptionist
J. Masse

Uncl.

Controller
A. Spann — Stuart

Uncl.

Production Manager
C. Bartlett — Boise

Sales and Purchasing Manager
G. Colby — Cancover

Purchasing Agent
C. Coleman

Industrial Engineer Manager
R. Trimble — Stuart

Secretary-Clerk
G. Wolfe — Boise

Industrial Engineer
I. Jackson

Industrial Engineer
K. Reinbrecht

Plant Engineer Manager
J. Polnicki — Stuart

Maintenance Superintendent
R. Moerner

Tool Engineer

Pwr. Hs. Eng. and Jan. For'm
F. Hyde

Records Layout

Personnel Manager
K. Thomas — Boise

Personnel Representative
K. Bovaird

Secretary
M. Roadhouse

Nurse

Trim Dev. and Q.C. Manager
T. Anderson

Quality Supervisor
K. Santifort

Trim Development

Process Engineer

Secretary
B. Kelly

Production Superintendent
A. Bennet — Cancover

Clerk
L. Johnson

12 General Foreman

Forelady E. Wood

Forelady J. Godden

Forelady

Foreman R. Johnson — Boise

Foreman Die-Electric
R. Schlotzhauer

Foreman Cutting
D. Gaul

Planning Manager
T. McElroy — Cancover

13

12 Scheduling Supervisor
R. Savage

Senior Scheduler
W. Little

Scheduler D. Doyle

Scheduler R. Costick

Special Analysis

S. & R. Clerk
J. Harnack

12 Follow-Up Supervisor

Senior Follow-Up
J. Bain

Follow-Up A. Fong

Follow-Up

Key Punch R. Brindley

Foreman Material Handling
R. Peckman

THE CANCOVER VIEWPOINT

Tim McElroy, planning manager, a Scot who had been with CAN-COVER prior to the takeover, described some of the problems he faced:

> Our people have been kind of scared at what might happen—kind of defensive. I talked to Jim McGregor in January and I was pretty well reassured, but I still didn't know what my job would be for a while—I was apprehensive. Economically I got a good deal out of it. Professionally I'm not any worse off and I'm learning to enjoy it. For a while I wasn't sure it was going to go. It's taking some submerging of personalities. I had a pretty free rein all over the production area. Now I've had to learn to keep my nose out of some parts of it and get used to taking orders again.
>
> The Boise plant was a trim facility and a very good one. They had built their own methods and organizations. We operated on a shoe-string here and didn't spend money unless we had to since it was a proprietor's place—not like a corporation. We got used to making decisions on the spot and pretty informally—we didn't have to inform a home office and wait around for them to make up their mind. And paper work—boy!—I wish I could recover half of the cost of paper around here now.
>
> We had enough vanity to think we were doing things the right way and so did they. There's been a tendency to try to overshout people. There's been a lot of overtime and hustle and bustle, and people have gotten tired. You see, the switchover to 1107 production started in April, and we didn't get the one-month shutdown to get ready because of the extra work from Boise. About that time the flow of information from other plants and the home office was way worse than perfect. It created a lot of problems. Some of those people didn't even know where we were—somewhere north of Seattle.
>
> The one big plus we've had here is that the union is desperate for this to go. It was a case of business coming into Canada from the United States, and it's been going the other way a lot in the last few years. People took it as a challenge, and their pride was on the line. Stuart was putting their bets on a Canadian outfit, and people wanted to make it work. Remember, too, that our business had really declined—we had gone from 200 down to 65 people in the last several years. So Stuart coming in here was like a shot of adrenalin. We're already back to 200 and will add even more. The pay for women is good—probably the best in the area—and we're probably in the top quarter on men's pay. So the hourly people are behind us. Developing trust is the key to the thing and developing some friendships—getting almost to a family sort of arrangement.

Fred Colby, sales and purchasing manager, had been with CAN-COVER for over 30 years prior to the Stuart takeover. He was leaving to become manager of an aircraft parts supplier in a nearby town:

I've never worked for anyone else since I was a kid. Before the takeover I worked for a family company directly for the owner. I want to see if I can take over and do the whole job as boss . . . and of course there's money involved, too. It's a desire on my part to see just what my capabilities are. Even before Stuart I was interested but I just couldn't leave them. I had a pretty free rein before and a lot of responsibility, but now with Bert [the plant manager] and Charles [Bartlett] here I've gotten frustrated, I guess. I guess I just feel like they don't need me. Really deep down that's it. This other company has been after me for a while, and finally I talked to them. The job is managing director of Canadian operations, and the salary is far more than my needs. Well, after a couple of visits and some sleepless nights I said, "OK."

You know, Charles [Bartlett] ran the show at Boise and he has the same problems as I have. I was into everything, and all of a sudden you don't have the authority. The American personnel naturally did things differently, but I must say we did a few things right here. I've told Charles Bartlett and his men, "Just because you did it that way in Boise doesn't make it right."

It's kind of hard to wait on decisions from a home office after so many years of making them all on the spot. It must be rough on Tim [McElroy] because his job of production planning is one of the roughest jobs in Stuart. A mistake there can stop the entire delivery schedule. He's had a lot of information problems . . . who to contact for this or that. I notice he goes ahead and does something and then—boom— "What have I done?"

THE VIEWPOINT OF STUART MANAGERS

Charles Bartlett, the new production manager at CANCOVER, had lunch with the casewriter, during which he talked with pride about the educational accomplishments of his children, who were in graduate school in the United States. He talked also about his and his wife's activities in scouts, church, and other community activities with "the kids." They had not formed many new relationships since coming to Banff. Bartlett was described by other Stuart managers as hard driving, powerful, and very loyal to his Boise people. He talked at length about the problems these men had faced during the phase-out and how he regretted that most of them had left Stuart. Bartlett's regret suggested a feeling of responsibility for their rights:

I wish I could have done more for them. I tried to help them as much as possible. I still get calls from companies asking about them. I thought all the people who came here were treated well on economics, but they are all leaving. Tom Anderson's [development and quality control manager] wife just wouldn't make the move. He came up hoping she would relent. He gave it a try but she had a job making about

$5,000 a year working a couple of days a week as a tool designer. Another fellow, a young foreman named Johnson, had some problems with his love life and left. This is kind of an isolated place for a bachelor.

Just recently John Polnicki [plant engineering manager from Boise] accepted an offer from another company in the States. He had just bought a house here the week before but the offer was too good to turn down. So now I'm the only one from Boise who'll be left when Tom and John leave this month. I came because the other interesting jobs required relocation and also to maintain service with the company. I've been with them about 30 years. I lost money on the transfer after taxes, which are a lot higher here, but I was hoping for a bit slower pace on the job. It's been hectic traveling back and forth between plants and kind of hard to adapt to the new organization. We've had to be careful not to say, "This is the way we did it in Boise." I'm not completely relaxed in my job now, and it's very disappointing to me to see Tom and John leave. I'll be all alone then and I feel trapped and caged in. I'll miss having someone I can talk to. Usually when a manager goes to a new place he takes along someone he can depend on—someone who talks the same language. It helps a lot. Those things are choking me, but maybe I'll get over it. I can't help wondering if I've made the right decisions, but I feel morally committed to the company.

The plant controller, Art Spann, was a Canadian who had been with Stuart since receiving his Master's degree in management from MIT in the early 1960s. Spann reported directly to the corporate controller rather than to the plant manager. He strongly felt his responsibility for installing adequate control and reporting systems at Banff. He talked about the problems he had experienced at CANCOVER:

Records were in bad shape. Even the payroll was sloppy. Fringes were a mess. Hall [the bookkeeper] had been here for 40–45 years, and it was hard to get him to change because of his age . . . and he's a little stubborn. It's not easy for him to change and understand the new systems.

They never had a standard cost system, so we started trying to get some labor distributions from the floor, and it has been a real hassle. There's still resistance . . . they look on it as a waste of time. The main resistance is that they don't know the reasons for it, and the second is the pressure for production. The girl foremen are worse than the men because the men are from other companies where they got used to it. Basically production comes first and finance is a poor second, but we're going to make it work. There's no choice about it.

MANAGERIAL CONFRONTATION

A meeting of the managers in plant manager Bert Parson's office produced several heated exchanges between Art Spann and Charles Bartlett over foreman training and reporting procedures, and between Bartlett and Fred Colby over vendor and material quality problems. Bartlett appeared to win both arguments by forcefully burying both opponents under a long recitation of the problems which they were causing him in his efforts to increase production.

Bert Parsons, plant manager, discussed his views of the situation after the meeting:

> I'm happy about the apparent attitude of the hourly worker. They have been very cooperative and have worked hard to get this thing going. This pleases me no end. I just hope we don't ruin it. But this management thing . . . I've never worked with such a hard-headed group. We'd do a better job if these guys didn't fight all the time. Art Spann is very, very critical of poor bookkeeping in the time sheets and so on. He's got reason to be concerned. But I'm concerned about the problem, and we're doing our best and we're working on this thing. But this fighting business is tough, and I'm fed up. And I've gotten tough with Art a couple of times. I've had the most trouble with the Boise people. I've often said, "What are we fighting about? We're just discussing this thing." But Charles is a great one for "the sky is falling" stuff. He has a tendency to grab the show. At Boise the way to get things done was to shout and make things sound as rough as possible. That may sound strange but that's the way the atmosphere was there. It's been rough enough here as it is. There's been a lot of pressure on people to get production up to our planned levels, and now we're losing key people. Fred Colby is going to the home office next week to talk to Jim McGregor, and I'm still hopeful that we can change his mind. I've tried using him as an unofficial troubleshooter, but he has been frustrated by a loss of responsibility. Fred is also pretty involved in local society, and we've got a mismatch in titles with the other companies here. For example, I'm just a plant manager, whereas most of the other plants around are run by VPs. This can be a big thing in small-town social circles.

3 | *Product Management at United Brands (A)*

They are the chosen few . . . the MBA Club. They've got the fastest timetables in the company.

They're a bunch of young, bright, and terribly egotistical guys.

They're very smart . . . shrewd is a better word.

It's the Momma's-chicken-soup syndrome. These guys assume they know how to do it best.

What they call creative thinking would be called B.S. any other place.

They're bringing people in from the outside all the time; because they don't know their own business. They can't develop their own people; they promote them instead.

They have charisma. They are always great personalities . . . a bunch of actors . . . a superior race. They're the prestigious group, the comers.

All these statements are about product managers. They were made by people in the various departments of the Butternut Division of United Brands, Inc.* Only the last statement was made by a product manager.

THE DEVELOPMENT OF PRODUCT MANAGEMENT AT UNITED BRANDS

Established in the late 1920s through the merger and acquisition of a number of independent packaged foods producers, United Brands was one of the United States' first multiproduct packaged food marketers.

---

* Disguised name, and has no connection with the real company of the same name.

United Brands was also a pioneer in the use of the product management form of organization.

Originally, at United Brands, as in most companies, each function— production, research, marketing, and financial services—played a specialized role in the total operation of the company. The general manager of a division coordinated the work of the functions in implementing the corporate strategy. However, as the number of products each division produced and sold increased, the job of coordination became increasingly complex. The product management type of organization was United Brands' response to this complexity in coordinating the functional departments in the development, production, and marketing of a large number of products.

The product management organization was superimposed over the traditional functional organization, cutting across functional lines, as shown in the matrix below:

	Market Research	Sales	Production	Accounting and Control	Product Research
Product Group A					
Product Group B					
Product Group C					
Product Group D					
Product Group E					

Each product manager played a role similar to that of the division general manager, coordinating the work of people in the functional departments, in implementing the strategy for the product (or products) for which he was responsible. An important difference, however, was that he had little structural authority over the people whose work he coordinated, as did the general manager. In fact, a product manager had to sometimes compete with other product managers for the services of the functional departments. For example, in the Butternut Division of United Brands, the same sales force handled all the products of all five product groups. In other departments, such as financial services and, to some extent, market research, employees were assigned to work with particular product groups, while at the same time working for their superiors within the function.

In 1970, United Brands marketed a wide range of packaged food products in the United States through four operating divisions, each of which was treated as a relatively autonomous unit.

THE BUTTERNUT DIVISION

The Butternut Division of United Brands maintained its own production facilities, sales organization, product management section, marketing research group, research and development organization, raw foodstuffs purchasing group, and personnel and controllership functions. (See organization chart and division headquarters floor plan, Exhibits 1 and 2.) Its products included peanut butter, jams and jellies, honey and maple syrup.

According to Mr. Lee Edwards, Butternut's marketing manager, the Butternut Division had traditionally been United Brands' largest division and the backbone of the company in terms of sales and contribution. In 1970 the Butternut Division accounted for 37 percent of domestic sales.

However, although Butternut sales had continued to steadily increase over the past five years, their share of United Brands' total and domestic sales had decreased over the same period, due to a leveling off of the market for their group of products, United Brands' renewed acquisition program, and United Brands' increased activity in the institutional and international markets.

According to United Brands' 1970 annual report, the business of the Butternut Division would "remain a dependable and profitable business, but will account for a relatively smaller share of overall sales and earnings as other areas of the company grow more rapidly."

PRODUCT MANAGEMENT IN THE BUTTERNUT DIVISION

According to Mr. Edwards, Butternut's marketing manager, the product manager's was a key role in the operations of the division. Characterizing them as "little general managers," he described how the product managers are central to the planning and execution of marketing strategies:

> The product groups, with the advice of the various functional departments, formulate the marketing strategies and then pass them up the line of management for modification and/or concurrence. When agreement on the strategy is finally achieved, responsibility for the execution of the strategy rests with the product manager. This approach keeps senior management in control of policy and strategy, but it puts the burden of "managing" on the product manager. It also serves as a built-in manpower development program, as the product manager must constantly think up solutions to business problems and accomplish their successful execution.

The casewriter discovered that product management in the Butternut Division had traditionally been the route to top-management positions

EXHIBIT 1 Butternut Division Organization Chart

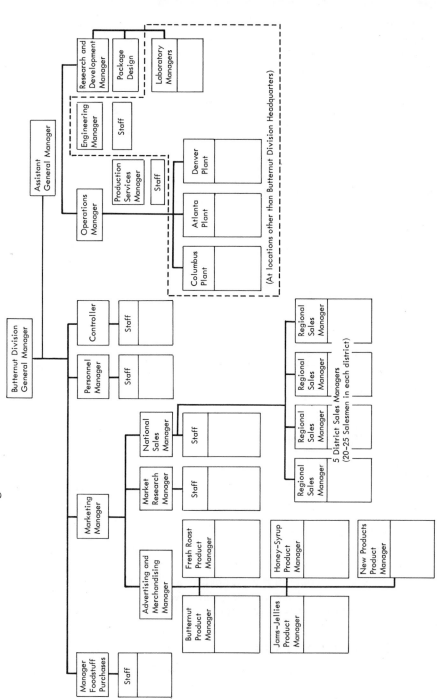

* Each product group was made up of a product manager and, usually, two associate product managers and two assistant product managers.

EXHIBIT 2
Floor Plan of Butternut Division Headquarters*

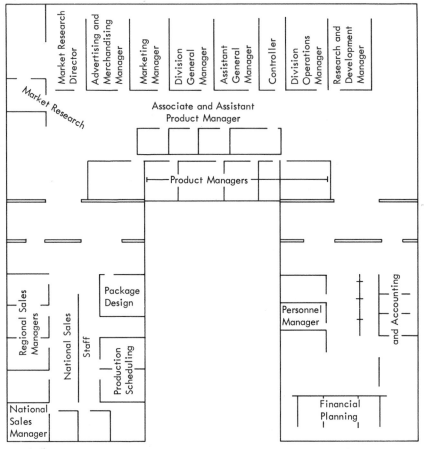

* The production plants and research laboratory were at separate facilities.

in the company. The chairman and the president of United Brands and 12 of the corporation's 16 top nonproduction operating officers[1] were once product managers in the Butternut Division.

On the whole, people in the product management group were younger and more highly paid than their counterparts in other departments of the division. Most of them had MBAs.

WHAT THE JOB ENTAILED

The product manager's work in implementing the product strategy could be divided into two broad categories:

---

[1] Division managers, marketing managers, national sales managers, advertising and merchandising managers.

1. The Administration of Trade Discounts on Current Products. But-ternut management considered most of their products to be commodities in the packaged food business. Therefore, in terms of marketing expendi-tures, the division's marketing emphasis was on price competition. Three fourths of the division's marketing expenditures were spent on trade deals.[2] Trade deals were administered on a district by district basis over the 20 sales districts. (The four regional sales managers each had five district sales managers working for them, who in turn each had 20–25 salesmen.) Managing trade deals required negotiating the types and amounts of the trade deals for each district with the regional sales managers and coordinating the volume requirements with production. In the negotiations with the regional sales manager, the product manager had the final say as to how and where the marketing money would be spent; he controlled the purse strings.

2. Managing Advertising and Product Changes. This could entail introducing a new product, changing a current product, or changing its advertising. These activities required working together with the prod-uct research group, the market researchers, the product group's advertis-ing agency, sales, and production. An extremely simplified example of the process follows: Product management and market research deter-mined what could sell. This had to be reconciled with what product research could create and what production could produce within cost limits. Production was then established on a limited basis. Product man-agement, market research, and the advertising agency then developed selling concepts and introduced them through the sales force to test market the product. Test market data were evaluated, and decisions were then made on a final strategy. The controller was involved in financial analysis throughout the complete process.

While this example was sequential, in actuality all the different func-tional departments were involved in the process at all points along the way to some degree. A large number of unforeseen problems would come up in coordinating the work of the functional departments; and much of the product manager's job involved getting these cross-func-tional conflicts resolved and getting decisions made, so that schedules and objectives could be met. The product group served as the focal point of most coordination and decision making.

When the casewriter asked Mr. Edwards, the division marketing man-

---

[2] Trade deals were promotional expenditures aimed at distributors and retailers, rather than directly at the customer. They included discounts off regular trade prices and allowances to retailers for running special newspaper advertising and retail coupon offers. These expenditures were often made with the intent that price reduc-tions be passed on to the consumer. Sometimes trade discounts or dealer promotions required action by the retailer before the money was turned over; sometimes they did not. Trade deals did not include consumer promotions, such as sweepstakes con-tests, merchandise send-ins, and the like.

ager, the basis on which product managers were evaluated, he answered, "On how well they did their job." He was reluctant to be more specific, explaining that even though a product manager had met all the financial and market objectives of his product strategy, he could still be judged as performing poorly because of other circumstances, such as momentum in the product before his arrival, or his ineffectiveness in dealing with others.

A successful product manager, he pointed out, must be able to not only coordinate the work of others, but must also be able to get good ideas from them and motivate them to carry out the decisions he ultimately makes, following the timetable he establishes.

PRODUCT MANAGEMENT AS SEEN BY THE OTHER DEPARTMENTS

The casewriter arranged to talk with people in each of the functional departments and with representatives of the advertising agency, with whom the product managers came in contact. His intent was to find out what constituted "effective dealings" with each of the groups. The casewriter asked these people two questions: (1) What are the basic conflicts between your department and product management? (2) In terms of helping you do your own job more effectively, what constitutes a good product manager and what constitutes a poor product manager?

Representative answers to the two questions appear below:

QUESTION No. 1: *What are the basic conflicts between your department and product management?*

Advertising Agency

The thing that has always bothered me about Butternut is, where their businesses are so huge and the funds are there, they don't try new approaches to advertising enough. They spend too much time on the day-to-day operations, making sure the deals are effective, making sure they meet their monthly share objectives. Product management simply does not experiment enough.

Production

Plants are basically big, thick machines. Product management is constantly thinking of ways to market the product that don't fit those big machines, that require a significant amount of change. These big machines don't like to get changed. So this basic plant wish—in an ideal world, to run everything in a one-pound jar—is basically at odds with product management, who are trying to make up exotic things to sell, exotic ways to make products, and exotic ways to package them.

The product management people seem to continually come up with new ideas that the plant cannot do.

One conflict is the speed with which product management would like to react. Once they have an idea, our cycling times to get that idea from a drawing board into a package is usually far too long for product management; and they try their damndest to get us somehow to commit to a date that's unrealistic.

Market Research

What keeps competent people in the department is the opportunity to be personally creative, the opportunity to develop new market research techniques. Too often product management gets in the way of that. They're constantly sending us out to put out brush fires—little projects, the same kinds of things all the time. What's worse is when they ignore your results because they don't fit the product manager's preconceived conclusions.

Controllership

Our main job is helping them project the results of their programs and then tracking what they've done and determining how successful it's been. They've got so many programs going at the same time—and these programs overlap—that it makes our job very difficult. And there's always something new and different that doesn't fit our ways of doing it. It's really a can of worms. But, then, that's what we're paid for. I shouldn't really complain about that.

Product management has traditionally not paid close enough attention to profits and has emphasized market share. They have rationalized that they were buying future profits; but until recently they haven't tried to cash in on their past investment. That's beginning to change now. Mr. Parkes, the new division manager, is putting increasing emphasis on the profitability of brand strategy; and the product managers are catching on. But it is still something of a problem.

Sales

Some of the product managers are inexperienced. They don't know what the hell they're talking about. For the most part, they're trained to think profits and how to increase profits and spend the least amount of money. Or maybe it's the reverse—spend the least amount of money and, therefore, get more profits. Unfortunately, it doesn't work out that way.

Product management's job is to make sure the consumer wants our product. Sales' job is to make sure the product is there. That means sales has to know what is the best way to present it to the trade, which is the key execution in getting the product to the shelf.

Every market is different. But our salesmen are in each and every market. So we know our customers' needs; we have accumulated knowledge of those markets. Given our intimate knowledge of each of these markets, we can recommend to the product management people how they should spend their promotion money. Sometimes they follow our recommendation; sometimes they won't. When they don't, then there's conflict.

The major complaint in sales is that we don't handle the money. Product management has complete control of the purse strings. We try to get X amount of dollars from the product group for a program we feel will be beneficial to the division. They may not give it to us. And they have the final say.

Product Research

The overriding basic conflict is we can't make what they want as cheaply as they want it. And they don't want what we can make. Of course that's an exaggeration. But the conflict is there.

There's a tendency on the part of the product management people to theorize and postulate, etc. They see themselves as being very creative. They'd much rather argue than go out and try to get the information, to run the experiment. They shouldn't be creative to the point that they neglect facts. There's too great a tendency, I think, to fly by the seat of their pants, and not to get the facts.

QUESTION No. 2: *In terms of helping you do your own job more effectively, what constitutes a good product manager and what constitutes a poor product manager?*

Advertising Agency

A good product manager doesn't use me just for working up copy. He includes me in on the full range of marketing strategy formulation. That makes it very satisfying for me personally. It also insures that what we're thinking at the agency is in sync with what's brewing here. And, occasionally, I'm able to contribute something valuable that may have been overlooked by the product management people.

Production

A good product manager is a guy who understands the production function. So when we are unable to meet some of his timetables, he better understands the situation. He should be a guy who's quite open-minded, quite willing to listen, and perhaps give some part of his day, or some importance, to production.

Some product management people are honest and aboveboard. They tell you what they want, their reasons, and the impact on the company if they get it and if they don't get it. Others, you feel they're not really being honest with you. Their objective is to make short-term heroes out of themselves at the expense of long-term gains. They are in such competition with each other. There's a lot of backbiting.

A manufacturing guy will bust his rear end to get something for a product guy if he knows it's in the interests of the division or the corporation. But if they think it's just to make the guy look like a hero, they're not going to.

A good product manager is willing to make a decision and stand by it.

Marketing Research

He will ask the staff to make recommendations on how best to solve a problem. He will *not* tell them what test to use, what kind of sample, and so on. Instead, he will allow the market researcher to do his job and make recommendations. Of course, he has the right to question the program—you know . . . "Is this question really answered?" But he won't tell you what to do; he will define the problem and then await your recommendations.

A good product manager gives us the opportunity to be directly involved in the formulation of marketing strategy, the chance to make and defend our own recommendations.

What I don't like in a product manager is indecisiveness. If I work out a program with a product manager, and he likes it and has bought it, I think he should support me in his recommendations to senior management. If there are points of conflict, he should be willing to let the market researcher into the discussion, where senior management is present, and let him defend it, too.

Controllership

The man who fails as a product manager is the one who is not able to meet schedules and timetables.

The good product manager is not only good at dictating, he's also a good listener.

Sales

A good product manager has to have a good personality—almost a sales-type personality. He has to be able to come down like he has just stepped out of the shower, and give an amusing, enlightened presentation to the sales force. He has got to be an extrovert, to be able to project a good image.

I have never seen a negative, or introverted, or nasty dispositioned product manager make it.

A good product manager will come right out and tell it like it is. "Here's how much I have. I'm sorry I can't give you more," rather than, "We feel this strategy would be better for you."

My bag is tell me what your story is and, if you don't have the funds, I can sit down with my guys and explain that to them. But I can't tell my guys we didn't get X promotion dollars because product management didn't think we were right. Because we know we were right!

You've got to have people to deal with who will act, who will make decisions, not the ones who think, "If I don't do anything, it will go away."

A good product manager can develop a strong point of view, articulate it correctly, and stand up to his superior with it.

Product Research

The poor product managers tend to look down on people in the other departments—like "you're my lackey."

A product manager must be able to speak the languages of the people he deals with, which is quite different from those of technical research, operations, or financial people.

He must have a basic desire to communicate with the different functions and be sympathetic to their needs as they relate to the total business. Not to their gripes, but to really try to understand and appreciate the problems a guy is trying to explain. He must be willing to give up valuable time to communicate to these people what he is trying to do and the reasons why.

PRODUCT MANAGEMENT AS SEEN BY SUBORDINATES OF THE PRODUCT MANAGERS

Another group each product manager dealt with was his own subordinates. The casewriter asked several junior members of the product management group what kind of product manager they preferred working for. Some of their answers appear below:

> A good product manager will give his subordinates new chances to develop their skills and new types of things to work on. I don't want to stay on one thing for too long after I've learned it. Then I'm just wasting time. I want to move on and up in the business. To do that I've got to learn all aspects of the business. A good product manager won't hold me back.

> A good boss will always be ready to help you out with a problem; but he won't hover so closely over you that you can't grow through overcoming the difficulties of the problem yourself. He'll be there when you want him.

> He'll include me in on what's happening in the product group, beyond the particular project I'm working on, so I know where my work fits in.

PRODUCT MANAGEMENT AS SEEN
BY PRODUCT MANAGERS

The casewriter also asked two product managers to describe what they thought differentiated the successful product manager from his less successful counterpart:

Product Manager No. 1

> The most difficult part of the job is to get the uninvolved, the not-interested people to be involved and interested in the business, like the production and packaging guys, the nine-to-fives, the people who have no future in their jobs. A good product manager can do that.
>
> You have to understand what the guy needs—a kick in the ass or a pat on the back. Some fellows like to be loved. So you ask, "How's your dog today? Did your wife sleep well last night?" He'll think, "Hey, there's a nice guy. I'm going to take care of him next time." If you're sending pen and pencil sets to retailers as a promotion gimmick, you send him one. So he feels he's part of the brand. Others you have to lean on, get tough with, threaten. It depends on the guy.
>
> Let me give you an example—the purchaser in the production department. If you don't get his attention, and you miss your target date, you may have the best program, but without glass to pack the product in, you don't have *any* program. And he is the guy who orders glass. He is the guy who can make supply work extra hard for you. But he works for 5 product groups, 7 brands, and 30 different sizes. If he doesn't like you, you're in trouble.
>
> So it's a function of how you show your respect for him, and how you communicate with him, how you build up this rapport.

If you need to get something done in three weeks, and the book says it takes four to six weeks to get it done, but you know if he wants to help you he can do it in three weeks, then it's that critical area of whether he's going to help you that makes or breaks you, makes you look good or bad.

That's why it's important to know how to deal with each of these guys.

There are other things too, of course. If a guy can't handle the complexity of many things going at the same time, he'll never make it.

Also, there are some guys who have great ideas, but can't sell them. They're just poor salesmen. They will yield right away when the boss gives them the pressure treatment, even if it's just to test them. They don't last.

There's another type that is extremely competent, but won't succeed because they can't live within the system; they won't observe all the protocols, they won't follow the procedures. If you want to succeed, you can step out of bounds only once in a while to show you're a tiger. You can be sort of a bastard; but not much, just sort of. You step on people's toes only once in a while to show you're a tiger.

The organization demands that its people be good Christian soldiers. That also means that you may stay in a position longer than you should, or take a job that you don't want; but you don't say no, you say, "yes, but." You have to strike the right balance between independence and compliance.

Product Manager No. 2

To become a product manager, you have to be smart, aggressive, and creative. The smarter you are, the better. By aggressive, I'm referring to a people-oriented aggressiveness. To get ahead and succeed as a product manager, that aggressiveness must be attached to a commitment to get things done. Creativity is very important; but it's not necessary that the guy be creative himself with new and appropriate ideas. It's more important that he be able to recognize appropriate creativity in others when he sees it. He should continually be running across things others do with the reaction, "Gee, I wish I'd thought of that." The important thing is that the fact that he didn't come up with it doesn't bother him—that he is delighted to accept an idea someone else has.

To get ahead as a product manager, a fellow has to have a commitment to the results rather than to a particular technique or to a personality or to the source of the ideas. He has to show aggressiveness and a toughness, a tenacity that doesn't stop when somebody says "No, you can't do it." He'll try to figure out another way to do it.

Another thing a fellow needs to get ahead in product management is the broadest scope view of the job possible—that means he goes beyond the requirements of his own job. There are three kinds of people who start off in product management: (1) Those who look upon the job as a crappy job; that go through the motions, not wanting to do it. The job suffers. (2) Those who manage to do the job adequately; that are committed to it; that want to do it well, so they can move on to something else more fun and exciting. (3) Those who do the job adequately and have the time—no, make the time—to do other things as well, that they think are important. They are the ones who go beyond their jobs. They are the ones who will succeed in product management.

Another important factor is what I call public relations (the cynic would probably call it politics). The fact that someone is using a great new idea in his work doesn't do any good unless the right people know about it. That is the job of the product manager. I am continually sending things up just to keep them posted as to what guys in my product group are doing that is good.

Finally, a little humility goes a long way. That's trying to know as much as you possibly can without flaunting it. The guy who says "I've been in this business 20 years, so I ought to know more about it than you do"—that's categorically wrong. He knows more about his job; but I know more about how his job is related to what I'm trying to do—which is what we're sitting down to talk about.

So his attitude is wrong, if that's his attitude. But making him see that does not move the ball ahead. Playing got-cha is sometimes satisfying; but it doesn't help much.

4 | *Product Management at United Brands (B)*

David Alpert was the product manager for Butternut Peanut Butter in the Butternut Division of United Brands, Inc.* (See organization chart, Exhibit 1, Product Management at United Brands (A).) A year ago—five years after receiving his MBA degree—he had assumed responsibility for Butternut Peanut Butter, one of United Brands's top selling products. (Over the previous five years, Butternut sales and profits had been 9.1 percent and 15.4 percent of corporate sales and profits, respectively.)

EVALUATION OF DAVID ALPERT AS A PRODUCT MANAGER

As far as the casewriter could tell, David Alpert was doing well in his work as product manager. Lee Edwards, Butternut Division marketing manager, had referred Alpert to the casewriter as a good example of a strong, effective product manager. Other people from the various functional areas in the division described Mr. Alpert in the following terms: ". . . Flexible . . . prompt . . . decisive . . . a decision maker (sales); receptive to different ways of looking at the business (control); sympathetic to problems we might have in accomplishing our task . . . tries to understand . . . a good communicator (product research); very fair-minded person . . . generally given to listening to all sides of a thing, given to letting people express their opinions . . . parochial in terms of pushing for his brand's priorities, but easy to work with (market

---

* Disguised name, and has no connection with the real company of the same name.

EXHIBIT 1 Butternut Division Organization Chart

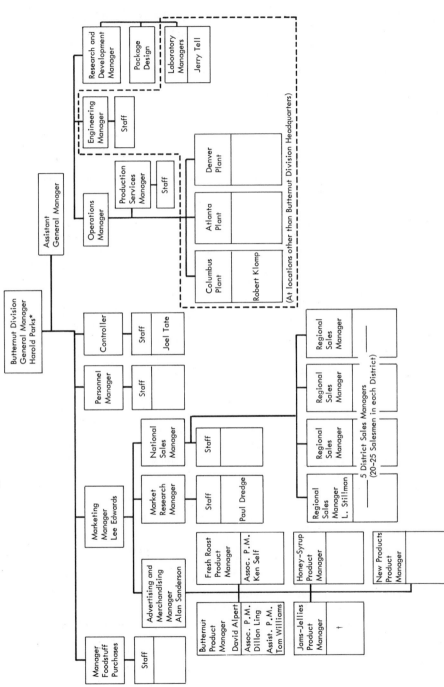

* Only names mentioned in the case are given.

† Each product group was made up of a product manager and, usually, two associate product managers and two assistant product managers.

research); excellent . . . a good listener . . . keeps us informed as to
how we fit into the overall picture (production)."

DAVID ALPERT'S EVALUATION OF THE JOB

David Alpert told the casewriter he liked his job. He listed a number
of reasons why:

> First, I like the responsibility the job entails and I like the fact
> that I can measure my accomplishments. There are measures like market
> share targets and return on investment. There is also a certain measure-
> ment in the sense that we deal with programs that can be completed.
> We've just completed a successful program that involved spending an
> awful lot of money. It had a lot of little pieces to it. It was a real
> executional nightmare. It was satisfying to fit all these pieces together.
>
> Second, I find a lot of personal satisfaction in being responsible for
> the expenditure of a lot of money and spending it well. I guess beneath
> that is the fact that I like to be looked upon as a guy who has things
> under control. It means something to me to have that reputation in
> the company.
>
> Another thing about project work that is fairly appealing to me is
> the fact that on no given Tuesday do I have the same thing to do
> from week to week. There are no routines in the work.
>
> Then I guess that I would have to say that there are people that
> I like to work with. First, there are those outside the product group.
> I find a great deal of satisfaction in cranking these people up to get
> a job done. Secondly, within the product group I have four people
> working for me, and I think I'm relatively good at getting them to
> progress—getting them to feel they are progressing.
>
> There are two aspects to this. The first one is the training aspect.
> I enjoy working with my people and helping them to develop along
> the lines that I think are important for product manager types to have.

David then paused for a moment before he went on.

> The second aspect you might call the public relations job. I like
> to insure that my people will have their day in court and be exposed
> in the way that will help them to get promoted. I think I'm pretty
> good at that.
>
> Finally, the material rewards—the money—are, of course, very impor-
> tant. It's strange how you are consistently able to live just beyond
> your income; so that you're looking forward to each raise as it comes.
> I guess that's very much the American way of life. In any case, my
> salary progression has been fairly dramatic. My salary has increased
> fourfold since coming to United Brands. I am making in the high 30s
> now; and that's pretty damned important. Especially when it comes
> by doing something I like—that I'm making progress by doing things
> I enjoy doing.
>
> Of course, he added, it's not all a bed of roses.

It's aggravating to any product manager who wants to get the job done to sit and listen to somebody else tell you about their problems. If they didn't have problems they wouldn't have a job; and because they've got problems, they become one of your problems. On the other hand, if reciting their problems to you helps to solve their problems through some ego satisfaction or whatever, and your job is to solve their problems, then you are doing your job by listening to them talk about it.

But that's really not the most important part of our job—listening to somebody create a problem before your very eyes, which he will then proceed to solve and be a great big hero. When they do that, it's a fairly obvious ploy.

DAVID ALPERT'S DEALINGS WITH OTHERS IN THE BUTTERNUT DIVISION

The casewriter spent three days with David Alpert, recording his dealings with others in the Butternut Division. Later he asked David to comment on these exchanges.

Monday—Task Force Meeting

David Alpert headed a task force, formed to make up the five-year plan for the two peanut butter brands sold by the Butternut Division. Alpert represented butternut peanut butter, United Brands' popularly priced line. Representing fresh roast peanut butter, United Brands' premium brand, was Ken Self, an associate product manager in the fresh roast product group. Other members of the task force representing other groups in the division were:

> Robert Klomp, production
> Joel Tate, control
> Larry Stillman, sales
> Paul Dredge, market research
> Jerry Tell, product research
> Ned Ashby, advertising agency representative

Below are excerpts from one of the task force meetings (the control and sales representatives were absent):

The meeting began at 9:00 A.M. Jerry Tell (product research) summarized to the group the results of a meeting with higher management on task force objectives. He had attended the meeting representing David Alpert, who had been on vacation. Fifteen minutes into the presentation, Ned Ashby, the advertising agency representative, walked into the meeting late. He made a short apology and excuse and took a seat.

David Alpert answered his apology:

ALPERT: I told the secretaries there were two things we were missing—Ned Ashby and the coffee—and I wasn't sure which we were missing most.

ASHBY: You're being polite. (*Everybody laughed.*)

The meeting then continued. Jerry Tell (product research) finished his summary with a comment on the use of market research in the division:

TELL: The next issue was that in a business as consumer oriented as ours is, we are not spending really enough time, money, effort on trying to improve our ability to communicate with and to the consumer in the way of basic marketing research. The comment was generally made that there should be a great deal more effort in this area.

ALPERT: Did you make the comment or did higher management?

TELL: I did. That's a personal thing I've been carrying around for quite a while. . . .

ALPERT (*joking tone*): You got that off your chest?

TELL: Yes, I felt a lot better. I slept very well that night.

Later, the discussion turned to looking into areas of peanut products other than peanut butter, such as peanut candy bars, peanut cake frosting mixes. Several possibilities got batted around by the group in an animated discussion for about ten minutes. During that time, David Alpert remained silent. He then cut the discussion off, saying that what they were discussing were areas for the division to look into, but they were probably more appropriate for the new products group—that the peanut butter group would not have to worry about them.

Alpert then went through the five-year plan point by point with the group. All members of the task force participated freely in the discussion.

Robert Klomp (production) raised the question of whether changes in taste preferences were going to come about in the next ten years, or whether it had been assumed that tastes would stay the same. Klomp suggested that it should be possible to project future changes in taste preferences on the basis of changes over the past ten years. Alpert answered him in a roundabout way:

ALPERT: Well, you've gotta have some givens—you've got to establish some base objectives. And the easiest ones to establish are markets and margins. You just can't cope with all the variables. You have no control or relatively no control over what the market's gonna be. We hope we can expand it, but we made the best guess we can.

Jerry Tell (product research) joined in the discussion.

TELL: With our share of market, we have more control than I think we tend to exercise.

ALPERT: Well, we don't know how to exercise it.

TELL: But with margins. . . .

ALPERT: Yes, we've gotten some control over margins. But if the cost of peanuts is 70 percent of cost of goods sold, a . . . Fred [the raw foodstuffs buyer] doesn't know what the cost of peanuts is one day to the next, let alone one week or month to the next.

ALPERT: All you can do is assume you will take active pricing action and adjust it as you go along.

The casewriter noticed that during the meeting, Ken Self, the associate product manager from the fresh roast group, challenged David Alpert a number of times on points such as use of merchandising methods, perceptions of the consumer, and advertisability of the brands. Each time, when Alpert answered his challenge with a milder response, Self backed off.

The meeting concluded at 12:15 P.M.

After the task force meeting was over, the casewriter asked David Alpert about aspects of the meeting that intrigued him:

Rivalry and Competition among Product Managers

CASEWRITER: I thought what I saw going on between you and Ken Self was friendly rivalry. Was it?

ALPERT: No, it wasn't. I haven't been in a position to develop a lot of respect for his talent. The guys he works with think he's pretty good. I just haven't seen it. He hasn't really been any help on the task force. I thought it was nit-picking.

CASEWRITER: How did you try to handle it?

ALPERT: Just as briefly as possible without being rude. Because, obviously, any obvious dissension between product manager and associate product manager in a group like that would be picked up by the other functions. Probably with some relish, even though they are pretty mature people. There was nothing there to call for his being put down. In meetings like that, when somebody like Ken brings up something, I just tend to lose interest in the conversation. I let it wander around for a while, then pick it up again after a few minutes.

CASEWRITER: But, still, it looked like rivalry. Is there much competition among the product management people?

ALPERT: Not really. I can't think of any. There is no reason to be. United Brands needs all the good product managers it can get.

Use of Humor

CASEWRITER: Let's turn to something else in the meeting. I noticed you used humor a number of times.

ALPERT: Humor goes a long way.

CASEWRITER: Like when you asked Jerry Tell if it felt good to have it off his chest, after his analysis of the marketing situation. It seemed to me he wanted to get involved in marketing decisions.

Dealings with Product Research

ALPERT: Nearly everyone does. That's where they think the action is. It's where the status is.

Jerry Tell is very easy to work with. He is far and away the most competent man at the laboratory from my standpoint. He thinks more like a manager than a technician. He evaluates a proposal on rational return on investment criteria rather than on whether it would be technically fun. He is a delight to talk to, a real breath of fresh air in the organization. But there are others who don't act that way. Really, he is the exception.

CASEWRITER: How do you deal with others in product research?

ALPERT: Those are the kind of guys you coddle. They have just as much education as you do. But they need experience on the job before they become effective. We spring full blown from business school as "marketing experts." They don't; so our counterparts there are generally older than we are. Therefore, we tend to exclaim loudly and make a terribly big fuss over their accomplishments.

For example, I'll call a guy down in the bowels of the laboratory someplace and congratulate him, and make it very clear that a product improvement was his accomplishment. Which it was.

Dealings with Production

CASEWRITER: How about the production man, Robert Klomp? His major contribution was some speculations on the probability of taste preferences changing. It seemed he wanted to play marketer too, perhaps.

ALPERT: Could be. He was really here primarily so the production people would feel included, although there could be some things where I could use his knowledge.

I've simply learned that bridges built to the plant will pay innumerable dividends. Primarily the junior product managers deal with them; but I try to keep in touch because they can screw us up so bad.

And those are the kinds of people that, if they want to, will ruin an entire plan just to prove that they're right and you're wrong. And they can do it.

I have no idea what goes on down there in the plants. And most of it, I suspect, would horrify me if I did. But that's not really important, so long as I can get them to do what needs doing for us. And change is by definition bad at the plants. So it's very important that I win them over to my side. It is important that they feel that they can come into my office and tell me that they are not able to do what I want them to do. If they don't come, but shove the problem under the rug, we can't work things out before it's too late. So the key there is communications—direct and easy communication and access. When they come to me with a problem, we sit down and try to figure out what we can do to overcome the problem.

Dealings with Market Research

CASEWRITER: What about Paul Dredge, the market researcher?

ALPERT: He is a bit parochial, but that's what he's paid to be. When he says he'll go away and think about ways we can incorporate research into our presentation and make it a little more research oriented, he'll probably be back in here first thing Tuesday morning with a bunch of ideas about how to do it. He's a good man. I've got few worries in that department. I was the market research director for four months before I got this position. Now they're convinced true or false that I know enough of what's going on down there that they can't fool me. The key there is to keep them informed about the business so that they can keep their research program up to date. They don't need a lot of guidance.

CASEWRITER: Your sales and control people were not at the meeting.

ALPERT: They are both out of town. I'll be meeting with Joel Tate, the accounting guy, tomorrow morning to discuss ROI calculations. I have to find out how United Brands does it before the next task force meeting. Our sales representative is a very good man for this job. He worked in product management for a while and has a broader view of things than most of those guys.

Dealings with Sales

CASEWRITER: Tell me about your dealings.

ALPERT: The day-to-day dealings are handled almost exclusively by our junior people in product management. I usually get involved when they can't get a problem worked out.

The sales people resent us. And yet maybe they are the most crucial people we have to work with. That whole relationship is a difficult one from their point of view. The regional sales manager sees you as younger and less experienced than he (which we are). And yet as his volume and sales promotion planners, his success depends on our ability to get him his share of the total dollars for promotion and spending. So I can certainly understand the resentment—particularly against the people who don't do well at it.

We treat them with a combination of deference—because they are a little older, and particularly when we are junior—and candor. Candor is the key to the thing. They like to deal with decision makers. It's good for their own self image, plus it saves time—which is an important commodity for any guy.

When they make a request for a program that they think is necessary, they would far prefer they be told that we don't have enough money to do it. Whether it's a good idea or a bad idea, it's wasting time to debate it when you don't have the funds.

But if *you* don't think it is a good idea and you can convince the sales manager yourself, that can take you miles. If you can disagree and give him your reasons and really communicate, so that you end up working out something that you agree to, or at least he can understand your position, then that's very good. There's a lot of respect built in that kind of relationship. Say, "I can't afford it" when you can't afford it, and say, "I don't agree" when you don't agree.

Tuesday—Meeting with Control

The next morning, Alpert had a short meeting with Joel Tate, the control representative to the task force, to talk about ROI calculations for the five-year plan. Alpert needed the material for a meeting with his superiors, Alan Sanderson, the advertising and merchandising manager, and Lee Edwards, the marketing manager.

ALPERT: Where are your ROI calculations for the five-year plan? I've got to get some by Thursday. I need at least one, and perhaps several exhibits on the subject. Because that's probably the most important number—at least the second most important after share—that we'll talk about. And I can't just go say to Edwards it ought to be approximately 35 percent.

TATE: I'll have to do some work on it. I'm not too sure I can have all the data and all the . . . a . . . things together by Thursday.

ALPERT: I mean we've got something, haven't we, we've got . . .

TATE: (*cuts in*):   Oh, I have the actual of how we came up with fiscal '70—the 35 percent.

ALPERT (*acts impatient*):   Well. . . .

TATE: And, and I just got pieces for the other years.

ALPERT (*speaking firmly*):   I'd like to see what those pieces are.

TATE: OK. . . . as far as projections. We can maintain, I'm sure we can. . . . We should say that minimum is 35 percent.

ALPERT (*more impatient*):   I mean over the last three years, can I see the calculations?

TATE: Sure . . . I'll bring them in. (*Tate leaves.*)

After Tate had left, Alpert turned to the casewriter and volunteered:

ALPERT: You needn't worry about stifling creative ideas that the elves down in accounting may have; because they don't have any. I think the secret with those guys is that you not deal with them at the middle management level; that is Tate's level. Because I think that the truth of that department is that they occasionally get lucky and hire somebody that's good. But they can't keep them long enough to promote them through the ranks to get them to Tate's position. It's only the relative dullards, like Joel, that stay. I suppose he is a capable guy in his own right. He is not really stupid. He's not awfully smart; he can add a column of figures. But he is not going to become treasurer of the corporation or controller of the division or anything else.

The best way to get real performance there is to latch on to a young guy who's aggressive and good and very junior in the organization and just have him working his ass off for you.

We've got a financial analyst under Joel who's assigned directly to Butternut. He is very good. He's the guy through whom we get things done. He is practically a member of the product group. A very, very junior member; because he doesn't create anything, he just does what he is told. But he is a tremendous help.

Tuesday—Meeting with Subordinates

Later that same day, Alpert met with Dillon Ling and Tom Williams, associate and assistant product managers on Butternut, about a test market they were proposing in Atlanta. Ling was Chinese; Williams was a black. Alpert listened quietly to the presentation, now and then probing their assumptions, asking extra questions to see how well they had thought things out. After Williams finished his last points, Albert spoke.

ALPERT: That's a very thorough way to go about analyzing what it ought to be. . . . The only question I have. . . . We've traditionally gone from a Northeastern test market like Albany south and west without any compunctions. If it tested well in Albany, Syracuse, or Indianapolis, we'd take it South. We haven't got any experience with anything testing it in the South and taking it North.

LING: We don't?

ALPERT: I don't see any radical differences. But we don't want to get ourselves into situations where we've selected test markets that rationally people would think okay, but when it comes right down to it, they won't accept it emotionally—

They discussed that issue. Ling pushed for Atlanta, citing advantages with media and outlet control.

ALPERT: OK, let's assume it will be Atlanta. In the meantime, I'll do a little spade work across the hall with the advertising and merchandising manager and the marketing manager and see if that makes people uncomfortable. Because I think it clearly is the best market. But I think we ought to be pragmatic about it. We want it, not because it's Atlanta, but because it's the best way we can think of to test our product.

WILLIAMS: We had a couple minor positives and negatives to going into Atlanta.

ALPERT: OK, I'm convinced.

WILLIAMS: I think you want to hear these, though. One thing, a positive, is I'd go to the Hyatt House; I've never seen it.

Another, a negative one, it's not a great area for minority groups to take their field trips. (*Williams laughs cautiously.*)

ALPERT: Well, Atlanta's all right; but I'm not so sure about eastern Tennessee. (*Everyone laughs.*)

LING: Johnny Cash is the spokesman for Nashville.

ALPERT: Yes. For eastern Tennessee, you want to send your white Anglo-Saxon Protestants; and we ain't got any of those kind of people.

WILLIAMS: Buy somebody some cutoff Levi's and get him a rope to tie 'em up and a T-shirt, and send him to eastern Tennessee. (*Everyone laughs.*)

LING: The introductory promotion in March could be a shotgun; then for 50 cents you can get the shot and shoot the revenuer. (*Laughter.*)

ALPERT: Make the ammunition the continuity. (*Laughter.*)

After the meeting, the casewriter asked Alpert about his dealings with the subordinates in his product group.

CASEWRITER: How do you train your people?

ALPERT: A lot of the training is in your expectations. Junior product managers are, in their individual ways, terribly anxious to please. You don't have to give them orders, you just have to make known simply what you want and be clear about what it is you want done, and then stay out of their way. Because they will go to great lengths and work terribly hard to get it done just the way they think you would want it done. That's a characteristic of the good product manager. The thing that separates the good ones from the excellent ones is that the good ones get it done just the way they think you want it done, and the excellent ones will get it done that way, unless they think there might be a better way—and they'll stop and think about it. I think my people know about the distinction, because we've discussed it and will continue to discuss it. The key is initiative. You tell them something and they do it—that's awfully important. There are not a whole lot of people that can do exactly what they are told effectively. On the other hand, if you tell them something, and they come back to you and say, "I heard you, but this is a better idea," that's sort of a step beyond.

The most important thing is getting the job done, achieving the objectives. I don't have a lot of pride of authorship. I'm not really creative in bringing up new ideas of my own. I'm better at being able to take other people's ideas and adapt things that have been done before to problems that we have now.

Wednesday—Meeting with Superiors

On the morning of the third day, Alpert met with his two immediate superiors, Alan Sanderson (advertising and merchandising manager) and Lee Edwards (marketing manager), to discuss the final stages of the five-year plan. Alpert was concise in his remarks and candid in his presentation. Several times the marketing manager disagreed with market assumptions he had made. Alpert defended his ideas, saying that he thought the issues were more complicated than the marketing manager perceived them. He suggested that they look into them further.

After the meeting, the casewriter commented on Alpert's skill in making a persuasive, concise presentation. Alpert replied.

ALPERT: I've learned most of that from Alan [the advertising and merchandising manager]. He's a very good businessman and he's hard-nosed. And he doesn't like to beat around the bush. If you start to give him something in a roundabout sort of fashion, he's very good at cutting right through to the meat of it. And, he will do it disapprovingly, because he doesn't like you to be wasting his time telling him something in five sentences when you should be able to tell him in one. He doesn't like you to take five minutes on justification when one minute will do. He's a terribly busy guy. He has an incredibly time-consuming job. He can't afford the luxury of people who can't afford to talk straight, and his style is blunt enough; he'll tell you if you're wasting his time.

CASEWRITER: You were pretty candid in the meeting yourself.

ALPERT: Ed and Alan encourage that. They encourage opposition. They're open enough so that if they don't agree with you, and you tell them you think they're wrong, they'll very quickly admit it if they agree with you. Alan, in particular. He'll sometimes test you to see whether you've thought things out. He'll ask for five reasons you feel the way you do, and very often, he will cut you off after reason No. 2 and say, "OK."

That starts, of course, with the general manager—to tell people what you think. That's Harold Parks's style.

5 | Interview with Tom Craig

Prior to starting his second year of M.B.A. training, Tom Craig dropped by the office of one of his first-year professors to talk with him about his summer job experience. After listening to Craig for about five minutes, the professor asked if he could record the discussion on a tape recorder. Craig agreed, and the conversation proceeded without notes or preparation. A major segment of the interview is transcribed below.

Tom Craig completed his first M.B.A. year in June 1966. Before that he had worked for four and one-half years as a general foreman, production foreman, and plant engineering supervisor in two plants of a chemical company in Massachusetts. He also served three and one-half years in the Navy as an engineering officer on two destroyers. Craig majored in philosophy at Amherst. At the time of the interview, he was 30 years old, married, and had two children. According to Craig, his decision to attend a business school was part of an "overall plan which hopefully would lead to a rapid rise in general management."

The first five minutes of the interview (not included below) were devoted to a brief description of how Craig obtained his job and the company where he worked. He was hired, along with five other M.B.A. candidates, to work at the Beverly, Massachusetts, plant of the United Shoe Machinery Company. Prior to arriving at the plant, he was assigned to the company's Harmonic Drive Division and given four projects to work on; Craig indicated that his primary interest was in a "computer project designed to speed up the processing of sales orders," because it sounded like an area to become "better informed about" and which "sounded important to the company's future." He reported to the controller of the Harmonic Drive Division, Charles F. Terrell.

Craig explained that the Harmonic Drive Division had been in existence for only one year but that it had already experienced a rapid growth in sales. It specialized in servomechanism devices, such as gear reducers, which were in heavy demand by the aerospace industry. In Craig's opinion, the division was a "self-contained," though "marketing-oriented," organization that lacked only in manufacturing facilities. All production operations were performed by the United Shoe's main plant, which was located a short distance from the division's offices. Craig described the main plant as a "huge job shop designed primarily to produce large machines for manufacturing shoes." The plant manufactured products for other United Shoe Divisions, such as Harmonic Drive, as a way of making up for a slackening demand in shoe machines.

PROFESSOR: Could you tell me something about your first few days there and what struck you and made an impression on you, and so on?

CRAIG: Well, I walked into the office and everybody was very nice, and they were all interested in telling me that they had a lot of problems, and I thought that this was kind of unusual that they should want to open up their . . . let me know what all their problems are at the beginning. But it turned out that the problems that they were opening up weren't their problems, they were problems of the factory. I described the factory as separate from this division, which is principally a marketing division as it sits right now. It receives orders and it places them with the factory, and then it deals with the customer and then the factory ships out the order. Now, it also has pricing problems and it has a few inventory problems, but it doesn't carry its own inventory, it doesn't determine how much inventory to carry. Then, in a second area, in the area of government contracts and special products, they have a great deal to do with an engineering department that tries to design these products. And then once the factory has built the parts, or the components that are required, they assemble the products. This is only in special areas. In the standard product line the factory does all this . . . the engineering, the inventory of parts, the assembly, everything is . . . ordering of raw materials . . . everything is done by the factory.

PROFESSOR: You said you were surprised that people were telling you about their troubles. You just walked in and . . . did they ask you to go around and see people . . . to find out about? . . .

CRAIG: Yes, what I did was I started out by getting involved in the sales order system and I went around trying to follow an order through the system. And I got to see a lot of people and to get a pretty good knowledge of how the company worked in a mechanical sense of the term.

PROFESSOR: Did you decide to do this yourself—to follow something around?

CRAIG: Well, yes, I had the choice of four projects. I looked at this one and thought it would be a good place to start because it would get me out and get me to know a lot of people. As I started around asking embarrassing questions, I was surprised at the answers. Most of the answers were in terms of: "Well, the factory can't do this for us, and we don't get any of that from the factory and we never know when the factory is going to ship the product." And what looked to be problems from their side . . . then I went over to the factory and got almost the opposite view from the factory. They were all talking about: "The problem is the people over in Harmonic Drive never tell us anything. We never know what to do and we're always three weeks late before we get started with an order" . . . Well, I was able somehow to keep an open mind through this a little bit and also I think. . . .

PROFESSOR: You don't think the factory people saw you as a spy?

CRAIG: No, and I think this was one of the important things that I . . . I'm not quite sure how I did this but I managed to make everybody think that I was a little bit on their side. I wasn't deceitful about it, I didn't go around with two faces. But I was very careful not to criticize either side too much and to try and understand the problems of people I was talking to. If I was talking to the manufacturing people, I would try to see their view and try to understand what troubles they were having, rather than try to say: "Well, the marketing people can't live with this." I wasn't criticizing either side, I was trying to take the positive view of "What's your problem and how can it be done." And in a lot of cases I think . . . just in the beginning . . . they began to see from the questions that I was asking that they had problems that didn't . . . that they hadn't thought about it, because they were blaming them . . . it was very easy to pass the buck to the other side.

PROFESSOR: What kinds of questions were you asking them?

CRAIG: Well, I was asking sort of . . . I was just trying to get deeper and deeper into the system as it worked. I tried to find out how the particulars that they were talking about . . . an order that was placed too soon . . . I was trying to find out how they thought the order got placed and what they did with it after they got the order and then just try and, I suppose, follow it through as logically as I could to what would happen. And I tried also, I think, tried specifically to avoid drawing conclusions but tried to let them draw the conclusions.

PROFESSOR: What did these people know about you, you know, in terms of what they heard ahead of time . . . Had there been any announcement, was it word of mouth . . . ?

CRAIG: There was a letter sent around to the department heads in the Harmonic Drive Division explaining the four projects, that I was a summer project student from the Harvard Business School, and the four projects that I was to work on. That was all, none of the people under them knew and most of the people I was dealing with were under them, at least in the beginning, were under the department head level, and none of them knew who I was until I arrived on the scene and I was introduced as a summer student who was working on the sales order system. Over in the factory they knew even less. They hadn't been told . . . the department heads . . . no one had been told of my existence, and I arrived on the scene with the same spiel about being a summer student and tried to put across the fact that I wasn't there to tell them how to run their organization, which would have been silly, but to try and find out what the organization was, and then see if there was anything I could see from an outsider's point of view that might be different.

PROFESSOR: Did they know you had access to anyone who might be able to do anything about their problems?

CRAIG: There were perhaps only two ways . . . they knew I worked for Charlie Terrell and he's the controller of the company and he's a pretty influential guy in the division that he works for. The second thing was that, . . . the first day that I arrived and every Monday thereafter, except well it wasn't always Monday but it was supposed to be Monday, there was a department heads meeting and I went to most of those meetings. I'm sure that people noticed this and that may have been some indication, but those were the only things that I can think of that would have indicated really where I stood in the organization. It didn't show, except . . . well, I had an office and not everybody had an office. I suppose there was a little status there. But that was . . . the people in the factory didn't know that much.

PROFESSOR: So one of the impressions that you got from going around was this blaming between the factory and Harmonic Drive. . . .

CRAIG: There was tremendous buck-passing involved.

PROFESSOR: What were some of your other initial impressions of the place?

CRAIG: Some of my other impressions were that the company was behind the times in terms of . . . well they used a full cost system that sort of hid a lot of what I thought were the relevant costs in the projects. They didn't do very much planning, advanced thinking. They were talking about the computer, but nowhere in the company did they seem to have a computer really operating, except to pay people. Production control was very loose; inventory control, however, was very good. And then, just the very fact that they had these two organizations there caused quite a bit of repetition. It was production . . . in Harmonic Drive it was called production coordination, in the factory it was called production control, production scheduling. But these people were doing the same job twice, and any planning that was done was done twice because nobody in the factory got any benefit from the planning that was done in the Harmonic Drive Division and vice versa. So that I had the feeling that they were pretty far behind in terms of an organization that's ready to move out on a new product. This was a new product, it was only about 18 months old and really it only had about a year of sales on it, a few samples were out for the first six months, but it was just barely beginning to build a volume and . . .

PROFESSOR: Did you get the impression that people there were concerned about the same things you were, or did people seem pretty self-satisfied?

CRAIG: No, I got the impression that the one thing that really made the organization click was that they knew who they were, that they had some work to do to catch up, or maybe catch up isn't the right term, but to get moving. And they were all very anxious to do it. They didn't all have the same ideas of what had to be done; and because they didn't get together, they were perhaps all going in different directions. I think one of my biggest values for the summer was the fact that I served as a link between a lot of different groups, between the group at the factory and the group in the Harmonic Drive Division. I think that's the biggest and most obvious one. But I also served as a link between marketing and engineering, production coordination and marketing. Just by being or appearing to be a neutral, people would come to me and say: "Gee, you know, I wish we could get those guys over there to understand this." And these weren't solicitations. I hadn't said: "Well, come to me with your problems," because I didn't really feel that was my job.

PROFESSOR: How did you feel about being in this sort of neutral role, or trying to be in it . . . is this something you had been in before and were accustomed to?

CRAIG: No, it was certainly not something I had been in before. I had always been, I think just by my nature I tend to be a . . . very partisan. I tend to side or associate myself with a group that I'm involved with very strongly and any challenge that comes to the group I take personally. So this was certainly not the situation . . . before, for instance, when I worked for Dewey and Almy in manufacturing, probably some of these same problems existed, but I'm sure that my blinders were on just as much as the blinders were on some of these fellows. I wasn't about to take criticism about the manufacturing area as opposed to the engineering area or some other area. On the other hand, I was, I think, a little more open about my thoughts in the manufacturing area. In other words, I wouldn't hesitate to criticize myself or someone else in the manufacturing area among, so to speak, among the group. If the challenge came from some other group, then I was the first one to toot the horn. But if the challenge came within the group, then I might have been a little more objective. But the idea of being a sort of a neutral with no home was unusual for me, that's for sure.

PROFESSOR: Did it bother you, or did you enjoy it?

CRAIG: It bothered me at first, but I think perhaps I got to enjoy it more and more as I found that it worked. When a guy came to me with a problem and I'd listen . . . I think that one thing that is in my nature is that I tend to listen, perhaps too much. When someone comes to me with a problem I get interested in it, and sometimes this means that I just don't have time to do what I was doing before they came in. But getting interested in it and doing something about it in terms of just passing this information on to somebody else and seeing that, by golly, you know, the other guy listened as well. And I knew that he, in some cases, I knew that he was listening when he wouldn't have listened to the guy who was first bringing it up because there were lots of closed minds in this organization. And if somebody from marketing came in to tell the production coordination group what to do, or the production control group, or even the engineering group, it was automatically wrong because it was thought of by marketing. I didn't mean to single out marketing, this was true of a lot of the groups. So my position of being a neutral was very important, I think, in getting the information across the lines. I'd like to think that later on in the summer, as a result of some of the things that I had passed back and forth, these guys understood a little bit more about what the other half was doing and were a little more willing to talk about it, but at the beginning it was very surprising to have a guy come up to me and . . . you know, he's been working in this business for a while. . . . In fact, most of the guys that were involved had been out in business for 15 years or so at least, and they would come into me and without any real reason, they just sort of appeared at the door and would want to talk and they'd sit down and talk. I'm afraid that this idea sort of snowballed because they found it . . . that this was a tool that they could use because it did get results sometimes. So more and more there'd be people appearing at the door with. . . . And I was surprised . . . you know, sitting down working with the sales order systems. It was very interesting but it was unusual to me.

PROFESSOR: What happened as you began to get this information? . . . I noticed from some of your materials that you began to put together some reports.

CRAIG: Yes, I started working on the sales order system and probably being very analytical in trying to create a flow chart, and I was reading a book on the side about computers and there was a guy in the factory that had some computer experience and I'd done some talking with him. So that I was really looking at this as a computer problem, very analytical, very dry . . . probably to me at least it was getting very boring. And it did, however, provide me with a lot of information to start out with and as I . . . I guess I had one other thing that really helped and that was a set of financial statements or financial reports that come out every month. And I spent a few hours in the first week trying to play with this as if it were a case and see what kind of things I could make out of it in terms of finance, in terms of marketing . . . I was just playing around because I really didn't know where to go or what problems were really important and what problems weren't. After playing around with this information for awhile, I have a pretty . . . I found later, although I didn't really know at the time, I had a pretty good picture of what was really going on in the company. One of the : . . . I guess it was the second department head meeting that I was in, it struck me particularly that the manufacturing manager and the marketing manager were talking about two different things. One of them was saying that, "Gee, he was just getting out all the sales that he could think of getting and it was too bad we weren't making money," and the other guy was saying, "Gee, they were selling all they could, it's too bad they weren't producing enough so that they could make money." And I sort of sat quietly in the meeting and thought about this and then when I got out of the meeting I talked to my boss about it, and I tried to point out a couple of things that I had seen in the numbers that I had, and he got very interested in it and asked me to follow it up a little bit. The result was that we made several different tries at trying to explain this problem in terms of numbers because. . . .

PROFESSOR: What was the problem?

CRAIG: The problem was that they just, the factory, was unable to produce the products that marketing required. The reason behind this was probably that marketing hadn't asked for them long enough in advance so that the factory could plan and get the equipment ready, get the capacity ready. I don't think that the company now has the capacity to meet its sales requirements and that its sales are growing very fast. It's getting worse and worse, and it was hard to show this to a general manager who had been looking at sales figures going down every month. They were going down because the backlog of orders was building up behind them and they were trying, . . . they were shuffling around, instead of building a hundred units all one size, they'd build five units of that size and then have to shift to another size because another customer needed it badly, and they were just locked into a situation where sales were bound to level off or even in fact go down. And I was trying to pinpoint this and nobody in the organization had made, really made the distinction to themselves. . . . The difference between a product shipped out the door and a product sold in terms of the customer calling up and placing an order. So I started talking about shipments and orders as if they were different things, and it didn't, just didn't make much sense to them but it gradually began to sink in.

PROFESSOR: You got the interest of your boss?

CRAIG: Yes, I got that right away and there were several times during the first few weeks when I was worried because we weren't involved at all in the projects that we said we were going to be working on. But I guess three different times during that period I went back to him and said: "Now look, we're not doing what we said we were going to be doing, I think what we're doing is important but I want to be sure that you understand that we're not working on the sales order system, any of these projects, this is something different." And in my reports which I was making at the beginning of the year, or the summer. Every week I tried to make some report . . . I don't know whether it was for me to collect my thoughts or to pass on to him, or what. It just seemed like a good idea. And in my reports I tried to make it obvious that I had shifted my emphasis and I was working on something that was entirely different from what we started out with.

PROFESSOR: How did he respond to this?

CRAIG: Well he responded . . . he was worried he said, that I wouldn't have something concrete to hang my hat on at the end of the summer. He wanted me to be able to say, "Well, I went to work for United Shoe and I did this, and here it is." And he was worried that there might not be something like this at the end of the summer. But he was, I guess he was willing to take the chance for a while in order to get something that he thought was worthwhile. And as it grew, it became obvious that this was something that you could hang your hat on very easily; in fact, to me it seemed a great deal more important than the sales order system or any of the other projects.

PROFESSOR: Now the "this" that you could hang your hat on, is trying to . . . around the sales order shipment?

CRAIG: The shipments and orders, yes. Well, the first problem was to make this distinction so that people could understand that there was a difference. And the second problem seemed to be, from both sides, to determine how much we could ship in a month, or whatever period, and the second problem was to try to determine how much we were selling. And it sort of . . . so we could say: "All right, we're not getting what we need." Then from that we went on to produce a forecast which would show what we, what the people in the organization thought could be sold in the future, and from that, once again to follow it up, we tried to make a schedule of what equipment we needed, what size factory we needed, did we have enough plant? We didn't know the answer when we started out. Now do we need three. . . . So we tried to determine the kind of equipment that we needed, and all the implications that we could think of along the way. And this kind of helped me a little bit in my neutral plan, too, because I became an oracle of information from both sides, so that lots of times people found that they didn't have . . . I wasn't just a middle man . . . I had the answer. Perhaps they were better answers than had been around before. None of the stuff that I had was original, though; I didn't go out and do marketing research, and I didn't go out in the plant and study how, make a time study on how much time it took to do any operations. I took information that was already there in some form and changed it into another form that looked usable, and then tried to point out to people how it could be used, and this was the result. One of the final results was that we came to the conclusion that we didn't really have enough information . . . enough capacity to meet our forecasts for this year. And for next year it was going to be worse and for the year after that it was going to be worse. We actually set up a plan where we were going to try to make several steps of it and move to a new plant eventually. We worked with the facilities, the equipment, the people that we'd need. We took a really whole broad range of what we would do, to set up when we got through a new company or a new separate, autonomous division.

PROFESSOR: Now, who is the "we" here? How were you working . . . ?

CRAIG: Well, as I told you before that I rapidly associated with the people I worked with. The *we*, I guess, is the Harmonic Drive Division, but it's not the Harmonic Drive Division that exists now. It includes the manufacturing manager who works for the factory, it includes the production scheduling clerk who works in the factory, it included the foreman, the manufacturing engineer, as well as my boss, the marketing department. . . .

PROFESSOR: Were you meeting with these people as a group or were you going around to each individually and sort of gradually bringing them to some consensus around what needs to be done or . . . ?

CRAIG: Well, mostly, we took it step by step. In other words, we . . . I started out with the marketing problems of trying to forecast what sales would be in the future, and as we went through that the word got out that this kind of information was available and the people came looking for it, and that's when I got involved with the manufacturing manager who was newly appointed to the job and very anxious to find out what my information was going to say and what he should be doing about it; and the second half of the summer was almost exclusively spent in the area of facilities planning . . . . how to determine what kind of facilities and what kind of organization we'd like to have in the future.

PROFESSOR: This planning . . . was it all going on sort of informally . . . . and were you doing the major bulk of it and then shoving out your ideas to these people . . . ?

CRAIG: I was asking questions and then taking their answers and trying to work them into something that looked feasible.

PROFESSOR: Did you write a report on what looked feasible?

CRAIG: I didn't write a report but I produced a forecast for ten years
in terms of sales and broke it down into different areas. Then I produced
a . . . and these were a, you know, a table or a chart or something like
this . . . was usually what came out of it, and we also produced a report
trying to show how many hours of work would be required on each number
of machines in the different years involved. How much floor space we needed,
how many people, and we developed charts for all of these that were used
later in a presentation to top management in order to implement things,
the plan. But the planning itself . . . we didn't have a meeting and say:
"OK. We're going to have a planning meeting today." It came from moving
from one step to another, and I guess I was the one who produced the
format in terms of what steps should we go to next. And then I picked
it up and would go and talk to somebody and try to find out some answers.
He might not particularly know where I was going or why I was going
there, although I tried to let him know as much as I could about the background involved. But sometimes I didn't know myself until I got back and
looked over what I had and knew where I was going. It involved a lot
of duplication . . . If I sat down and thought very carefully just exactly
where I wanted to go I might have been able to go into one guy and ask
him a series of questions and come up with a series of answers, and then
go to the next guy and the next guy and never go back. But the way I
did it, I think, produced two results, or maybe three. First of all, I wasn't
tied to a procedure that, perhaps, could have locked me into an answer
that I didn't like, or not that I didn't like but an answer that wasn't the
best one as I saw it at the end. The second thing was, it got them interested
in what I was doing, got them some knowledge of what I was doing so
that the answers they gave me weren't just pat answers, they were interested
in doing this. They were interested in giving me answers that were worthwhile.
Several times they'd come back and say: "Gee, I've been thinking about
that . . . I think there's a better answer, or there's a better way to answer
it, and we should look at it this way or that way." And the other thing,
of course, was that I got almost all my ideas from them, by talking with
them and trying to find out how they thought the situation worked. Then
I'd go back and think about it and then I might come back to ask another
question or check to make sure, "Is this what you meant . . . Now,
does this, you know, this seems to imply that we don't have enough product?
Is that really what you meant? Did you really mean that we could do it
this way?" I can't think of a specific example right now. Well, I guess in
the government sales forecasting area the government marketing manager
had given me a forecast for two years and then for five years and ten years
. . . he had given me 1, 2, 5, and 10. And he had given me a forecast
one way for one and two and another way for five and ten. And when
I was trying to figure, when I was trying to develop the different categories
involved, I found that I had categories for one year here and then I didn't
have anything in that category for five and ten years, but I had other categories
for five and ten. So I thought about them and tried to relate them, tried
to relate the two categories and had to go back and say: "Is this really
what . . . if you meant this in this category, it seems as if you must have

meant it this way in another category." And I tried to get him to agree . . . all the way along the line I tried to do this, especially in the marketing area, to get them to agree that these are the numbers that they like the best. In fact, it got so that they were coming to me for these numbers because they had given them to me in one form and I'd spread them out into several forms and they knew this . . . they knew what the form was so they'd come back and say: "Hey, you've got that number . . . I've been looking for a number and I think you've got it somewhere in there." So the information we had was really getting used because people knew where it was and they knew what it was . . . and then, they went ahead.

PROFESSOR: I was just going to say, could you tell me what this finally jelled around . . . you mentioned a report to top management, and I'm getting sort of interested in its final, its impact as it begins to come into some form?

CRAIG: Sure, we had a . . . what we developed and a lot of people were pushing this . . . the factory was pushing it and the Harmonic Drive Division was pushing it, and we would . . . and when I say "we" now, I think I mean myself and the manufacturing manager at this point, because we were talking about a new facility. And we would each talk with the people, and some of the people that would have a hand in a decision on this matter and go in with our ideas and they'd ask questions and we'd come back out and we'd say: "Yeah, that's a good question . . . we should have thought of that before and we'd work that out." And finally we came up with a plan that both the factory and the Harmonic Drive Division was behind, and the general manager of the Harmonic Drive Division and the plant manager of the factory went to the . . . well, he doesn't really, he's the president of a company which is really a division of the holding, the major company, and made a presentation to him, using our charts and our numbers, asking that we get the money to make this plan work.

6 | *Sturbridge Electric Corporation*

Personnel of the Sturbridge Electric Corporation were entering the final stages of running acceptance tests on a computer they had contracted to supply to the armed services. One of the stipulations in the acceptance test of the computer was a demonstration by the contractor that it would function correctly and reliably under actual operating conditions with the special program prepared by Sturbridge Electric's chief programmer, Al Abrams.

Several days prior to the beginning of this test, Abrams submitted his program to his immediate superior, Bill Eden, who was computer project engineer (see Exhibit 1). Eden was to determine that the equation was in proper form so that when it had been run through the computer with predetermined inputs, the solution could be checked against hand-calculated values. It was not intended that Eden check the correctness of the translation from mathematical symbols to the computer "language," since the forthcoming operational tests would confirm that fact.

In the course of the check, Eden found that Abrams had taken some liberties in one of the terms of the equation. When asked about it, Abrams replied that he was aware of the discrepancy but that it would make no difference in the end result. Eden discussed the matter with Charlie Small, another computer engineer for Sturbridge, and they agreed that the program was not acceptable as presented. When Abrams learned of their decision, he became enraged and made some caustic remarks about their ability to pass judgment on his work. His closing comments were:

> I'm not going to have my work checked by everyone! I've been working on this program a long time, and I'm the only one that can

EXHIBIT 1
Partial Organization Chart—Missile Control Department

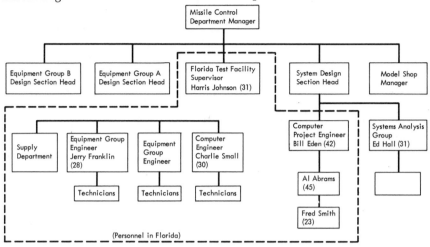

say whether or not it is OK. You guys have made my life miserable from the very start! You sneak around behind my back and pull all sorts of stunts. I deserve to know what's going on around here. Eden, you've driven me like a common laborer since you were assigned to this job. You've never given me any help—I've been all alone on this job. I don't know what to expect next! As far as I'm concerned this is the finish. I quit!

With that, he walked rapidly from the computer room. Harris Johnson, supervisor of the field test facility, who had heard the last part of the conversation, finally caught up with him at the door. Abrams tried to turn in his badge

HARRIS JOHNSON: I won't take your badge now. Take a minute to relax and calm down.

AL ABRAMS: Damn it! Take it!

JOHNSON: No! Go on home and cool down. If you still want to quit in the morning, I'll accept your badge then.

ABRAMS: I don't want to be mollified! I don't want to cool down! If you won't take my badge, I'll leave it with the guard at the gate!

Sturbridge Electric Corporation was a large manufacturer of electrical equipment for industry, the armed services, and the consumer. Its industrial electronics operations specialized in radar and all types of communications equipment. One of the subdivisions of this operation was engaged in the development of missile guidance equipment. The field test facility, at the special weapons test center in Florida, had been in operation for 14 months, its purpose being to conduct performance tests on the missile guidance system designed and built by the company. Although on a military base, the test facility operated as an independent entity insofar as the direction of its activities was concerned, and it relied on military personnel and supply for support only. For instance, though the buildings were within a classified area guarded by military police, the company retained responsibility for security of the project and could give or withhold permission for entrance to the area. When shipments had to be unloaded, it was done under the direction of company personnel but with the help of military personnel and equipment. (The military also supplied certain types of vehicles which were in turn driven by Sturbridge employees unless some specialized skill was required. In general, the relationship was such that the armed forces provided the needed services and facilities that might be common to Sturbridge and the various other contractors with test facilities on the base to preclude unnecessary duplication.)

Organizationally, the Sturbridge test facility supervisor reported directly to the manager of the missile control department at headquarters in Allentown, Pennsylvania. Johnson was placed in charge of the operation when it was first set up and took with him from Allentown several key people who would form the nucleus of the field organization. To these were added technicians and others from the local area in Florida. These personnel lived either in their own homes or in apartments nearby. The workday for the test facility staff, which numbered approximately 15, began at 7:00 A.M., with a coffee break at 8:00, when the post exchange coffee wagon made a stop at their building. The lunch period extended from 11:15 until 11:45; but because of the nature of their work, the personnel took the half hour when it was convenient rather than observing a strict schedule. The staff members were very congenial and enjoyed many outside activities together, such as beach parties, fishing trips, etc. The workday ended at 3:30 P.M., except when overtime was scheduled.

The bulk of the missile control equipment was built by the company in its Allentown plants. As it began to arrive in Florida, additional technical assistants were sent from Allentown on a temporary basis. These people reported to Johnson for administrative purposes while in Florida, although any technical direction specifically relating to their grouping of equipment was given by their respective supervisors at headquarters.

The large digital computer was the only major piece of equipment not designed and built by Sturbridge, though the company prepared the performance specifications for the machine. When it was delivered to Florida, there was still a great deal of work to be finished; hence, a large number of computer contractor personnel came also. To this group were added the several members of the Sturbridge computer group who had been dividing their time between Allentown and the contractor's plant in Concord, Massachusetts. The group, comprised of Eden, Abrams, and Fred Smith, although considered temporary personnel in Florida, stayed on indefinitely, while the visits of other temporary personnel rarely exceeded a week.

The group, with their families, occupied adjoining two-room motel apartments at a tourist court not far from the military base. Although their wives saw each other daily and their children played together, the families did not share many common social activities. Each apartment consisted of one bedroom, a large living room which made up into a bedroom, a combination kitchen and dining area which opened off the living room, and a bath. The motel was located on the ocean and, while reasonably comfortable, did not constitute luxurious accommodations by any means. Transportation to and from work was generally by company car, although all three families brought their own cars to Florida because of the extended period of time they would be there.

The fact that there were still many unresolved troubles in the computer when it was delivered made the workday rather hectic. The computer contractor's personnel had first priority, since they were vitally interested in completing their work as rapidly as possible. Headquarters' interest in completing the contract and the ever-mounting costs associated with the installation and check-out operation provided a sense of pressure on the daily work. Coupled with this was the necessity for Abrams to begin checking out portions of the computer program as soon as the machine was operational. It was necessary for Sturbridge to have a completed program before the computer could be put through its acceptance tests; yet, work on the program, by necessity, required machine time to complete. This made it mandatory to utilize any time when the contractor's employees were not performing work which interfered with machine operation for programming work. However, much of this time was lost due to Abrams's inability abruptly to interrupt his efforts on one phase of the program to place other parts of the program, which he might have mapped out several weeks ago, in the machine, to run it, and to evaluate the results.

Eden's purpose in Florida was to represent Sturbridge on installation questions with the contractor, make preparations for the acceptance tests of the machine, and generally to keep track of progress on the program. He did not have a great deal to keep him busy, since the workday soon settled down and became rather routine. A great deal of the time he merely stood by in the computer room observing the work being done by the contractor's personnel. He was always willing to take on special jobs suggested by Johnson from time to time and relished the opportunity to do something tangible.

Smith was kept busy running the many detailed computations on an electric calculator, since it was necessary to "prove" each part of the program as Abrams completed it. In this way the hand-calculated results could be checked against the computer results to indicate the validity of the computer program.

Abrams was 45 years old and had worked in three distinct fields: accounting, teaching, and engineering. His undergraduate college training had prepared him primarily for teaching, but his interest in mathematics led him into graduate work preparatory for a master's degree in that field. His quest for further knowledge carried him into electronics, and he completed in excess of 150 semester hours of undergraduate and graduate study in radio engineering.

Abrams began his business career in the tax department of New York State, but left it after two years to take a position as test planning engineer for Northern Electronics, Inc. While there, he also began teaching electronics for the Army Air Force. Following this, he ventured back to accounting and served for a year as agent in charge for a Bureau of Internal Revenue office, making examinations of the tax returns of individuals, corporations, estates, and trusts. During this period, he also began teaching freshman and sophomore engineering physics at a New York college and continued there for seven years. Concurrently, he operated his own business preparing financial statements and tax returns, which he continued until mid-1955. During an eight-month period, he also tried various positions with four different companies in which he reviewed tax reports, gave advice on items that might invite examination by the Bureau of Internal Revenue, audited books, and prepared financial statements. In late 1952, he accepted a position as a circuit and applications engineer with Erie Tube Corporation and remained with them until he came to work for Sturbridge in April 1954.

Upon coming to Sturbridge, Abrams was assigned to the missile control project, where he assisted in the preparation of the purchasing specification for the computer. During the time lag while the contractor was beginning production of the machine, he assisted the analysis group at headquarters on the solution of mathematical problems. Following this, he was sent to the computer contractor's plant in Concord, where he attended the school for programmers as well as filled a minor capacity in the coordination of the equipment manufacture. It was during this period that he also began work on programming the actual equations to be used in Florida. It was also during this period that the original Sturbridge computer project engineer, McAlpin, was promoted and Eden was assigned the technical responsibility for the computer

Abrams spent two months at the computer contractor's school for programmers. During this period, he learned the logic of the computer he was to work with, that is, the characteristics of the various sections of the machine, how they functioned in relation to one another, the forms in which data were placed in and taken from the machine, the speeds with which computations could be handled, and many other factors which provided him with the basic tools of programming. From there on, the work of translating a complex mathematical equation into electrical impulses that could be fed to and acted upon by the machine was up to the ingenuity of the programmer. This required a high degree of proficiency in mathematics and the type of mind that could, in an orderly, systematic fashion, juggle a vast number of factors, trying first one arrangement and then another until the desired result was obtained.

The programming process began with the breaking-down of the equation into its basic elements, that is, the solution for the sine of an angle, the taking of a cube root, or a multiplication, addition, or subtraction. Generally, provision had to be made to store various bits of information and the solution of some of the elements in either the electrostatic or the magnetic drum storage sections of the machine, since the value was to be used later in the solution of a subsequent step. Particular attention had to be given to the amount of time taken to perform each operation, since the problem was being solved in "real time," that is, the time required for the performance became an integral part of the problem and affected the final answer.

Because of the close interlocking relationship between computation time and sequence of operations, it was possible to have several days' programming work prove worthless because of an incongruity which suddenly appeared. When a particular element of the program was completed and proved, it was then pieced with a number of other elements to form a larger part of the entire sequence of computations and, in effect, pyramided the complications that could arise from incompatibility. Each element was, in effect, a building block, and it was not uncommon to find misfits, and hence many painful and time-consuming repeats became necessary. In absolute magnitude the job might have hundreds of separate and distinct operations that had to be considered and might require several man-years of work to complete. Abrams was the only member of the Sturbridge computer staff who had been through the entire programming school, although Eden and Smith had been exposed to portions of it.

One day, after lunch, Abrams walked into Johnson's office with a look of disgust on his face.

Abrams: I'm sorry, Harris, I just can't take it any longer. I've talked it over with my wife, and she agrees that my health is important. I want to resign, effective immediately. I've never had to take the kind of guff that I'm getting around here. (*Eden walked into the office, obviously disturbed.*) I don't know what this guy (*pointing to Eden*) expects of me. I've never taken the kind of treatment he's been giving me from anyone—even during the depression, when jobs were tough to find. He hounds me all day long. I just can't be driven, and I can't be paced by that machine!

BILL EDEN: Al, you know I do no such thing. I try to be as considerate of you as I possibly can. We've got a job to be done, and you've got to work on the machine when it's free.

ABRAMS: I don't work that way! When I get on a train of thought at my desk, I've got to follow it through. When you interrupt me, I lose the train, and it means I have to repeat the entire mental process that led up to it. I just can't stop in the middle of a programming sequence and run back to that damn computer just because it's free for a couple of minutes. I've been on a milk and crackers diet for the past two weeks because my ulcers are acting up again, and it's all because of this work. You're driving me crazy!

EDEN: That's not so, Al; you know damn well that I try not to aggravate you. You're so doggone touchy, it's pitiful!

JOHNSON: Hold on, now! It's not going to do either of you any good to get hot under the collar. Let's try to get at the root of the trouble without all the fuss.

ABRAMS: Just take today, for instance. You called me down to the machine this morning because it was going to be free for an hour. What happened? The damn thing wasn't working, and all my efforts were wasted. It took me two hours to retrace the steps up to the point at which you interrupted me.

EDEN: It wasn't the machine, Al; your program had a mistake in it. The machine was OK.

ABRAMS: That's not so! You know damn well the computer was consistently failing to meet the maintenance routine splatter test limits for the electrostatic storage. How in the hell do you expect me to test part of my program with an unreliable ESU?

EDEN: The program checks you were making didn't involve the ES.

ABRAMS: How the hell do you know what I was checking?

JOHNSON: All right, come on back to earth!

ABRAMS: This business had me so upset this morning that I called my wife and asked her to meet me at the PX right away so we could discuss it in private. I left here on the 11:00 A.M. bus. We decided that it just isn't worth it. My health is more important than this job. I know I'm not doing myself any good professionally by quitting, but it's the only answer. And that's not all; I got back here at 12:30; and the first crack out of the box, this guy says, "Where the hell have you been?" in a nasty tone of voice.

EDEN: I did not use a nasty tone of voice! You'd been gone for an hour and a half, and you didn't even have the courtesy to tell me when you left or where you were going!

ABRAMS: It was none of your damn business! I don't have to tell you every time I want to walk away from my desk. And for your information, I told Mary[1] when I left and when I'd be back.

JOHNSON: How about it, Bill? Did you check with Mary? You know, she keeps pretty good track of us.

---

[1] Office stenographer.

EDEN: No.

ABRAMS: Harris, I didn't have any trouble working in this group until Bill took over from McAlpin. Mac and I got along fine. And I don't want to put the company in an embarrassing spot by walking off before the program is complete. But I've got to think of myself.

The conversation continued along these lines for another half hour. Eden walked out after a while, and Johnson and Abrams discussed in detail some of the factors behind the blowup. It became evident that Abrams had been stewing over the interruptions to his work at the desk for several weeks. A previous incident that had occurred in Allentown was also rehashed. At that time, Abrams had mistakenly interpreted Eden's request for the name of one of the computer contractor's programmers as an indication that the company was trying to hire a replacement for him and that he was going to be discharged. Eden simply asked the question and gave no explanation. After Abrams thought about it for an hour or so, he became so incensed that he marched into the manager's office, broke up a meeting, and asked if they wanted him to quit. Johnson assured Abrams that the company did not operate in that fashion and that if they were ever dissatisfied with his work, the fact would be discussed completely with him. The conversation drew to a close with an agreement that Abrams would continue work on the program until it was finished. Johnson promised to try to arrange a transfer to another department as soon as it was complete and also to attempt to find a solution to his difficulties with Eden. With this, Johnson called Eden back into the office.

JOHNSON: Bill, Al has agreed to finish up on the main program. I hope you two will try to keep in mind the other fellow's feelings and try to be a little more tolerant and considerate. You know, Al is doing the sort of work that involves uninterrupted concentration, so make sure that the free machine time is really worth breaking in for. And Al, you know that Bill's chief concern is the schedule and that he is afraid we won't meet it. Understand that when he becomes apprehensive over your progress he is not being critical, but just wants to know where we stand. One thing more; I want it understood that neither of you has prejudiced your position by what has been said here today. You have honest differences, and we'll try to resolve them; but we'll need the cooperation of each of you. (*With this, Abrams left, but Eden stayed behind*).

EDEN: You know, Harris, I bend over backwards with that guy. I'm just as nice as I can possibly be. I never go near him unless it's absolutely necessary. I leave him completely free for the program and screen out all of the little detail matters. But he's so damn suspicious of everything you do. Why, one day the boss asked me to check on the name of a programmer. The Concord crowd owed us some instruction time under the terms of the contract; and since the fellow in question was familiar with our machine, the boss felt we might collect the time by sending some work up there.

All I did was to ask Al for his name, nothing more, and darned if he didn't think we were going behind his back and trying to hire someone to take his place. After he blew up and learned the whole story, he changed his tune to the effect that he wasn't being consulted on such matters, as he should be.

Eden, aged 42, graduated from college following World War II, during which he served as a first-class petty officer in the United States Navy. He was fortunate in not being required to take the "labs" associated with his major field, electrical engineering, at a large Midwestern university because his full-time, 40-hour-per-week job, which he maintained in addition to class preparation and attendance, was in the university's research laboratory.

In spite of the tremendous work load, he managed to complete the requirements for a bachelor's degree in three years. His wife, whom he met and married while they were both in the Navy, also obtained her degree. Following graduation, Eden continued as an engineer in the research laboratory, working on basic development work for the defense effort. A year later, he accepted a position with a large West Coast aircraft manufacturer, where he was placed in charge of a group preparing technical manuals. He left their employ in 1953 to accept a position with Sturbridge Electric Corporation as project engineer in the systems section. Eden had been dissatisfied with the prior job in part because of a golfing friendship that had developed between one of his subordinates and his boss. The subordinate's professional loyalty appeared to be open to question, and Eden felt that he used the golf course to further his own cause.

With Sturbridge, Eden did an excellent job of coordinating the many system functions assigned to him. Prior to his coming the entire design department had grown very rapidly. This, coupled with the new personnel's lack of familiarity with system concepts and requirements, the steady progress in design of the many hardware components of the system, and the pressure of early design and dates, had created impetus for assigning the detailed coordinating responsibility to one person who could work with all of the design sections and gather, sort, analyze, and evaluate data and design considerations. With the help of two assistant engineers, Eden accomplished the desired results. He continued in this capacity until the promotion of the former computer project engineer created the vacancy into which he moved.

When Johnson had occasion to leave the office for several days, he made it a practice to designate one member of the permanent staff as being responsible for the operation of the activity. On one such occasion, Jerry Franklin, who generally filled this spot, was playing bridge with several other members of the staff, as was the lunch-time custom. As the group was completing the final hand, Eden walked over to the group, who were sitting around a desk which served as their card table, and observed for a minute or two. He cleared his throat a couple of times and finally said: "Don't you fellows think it is about time that you all got back to work?" When the group did break up, he followed Abrams over to his desk.

EDEN: Say, Al, I'd like to get a progress report from you. Would you let me have the parts of the program you have completed?

Abrams's reply was to the effect that none of the work was in such a form that it would mean anything to Eden. He maintained that he had a series of notes in his file which contained the rough outline of the sequence in which the various computations were to be performed, and also had some finalized operations. He stressed that in their present form, they would be valueless to Eden and were more than likely subject to change in any event. Eden was nevertheless insistent, and the level of their voices rose. After several heated exchanges, in which charges and countercharges were hurled, Eden stalked off. When Johnson returned the following day, Eden stopped in to see him.

EDEN: If you've got a minute, there's something I'd like to discuss with you.

JOHNSON: Sure thing. Pull up a chair.

EDEN: Well, I had another run-in with Al the other day; and frankly, I'm worried. He just will not give me anything concrete in the way of a progress report. He maintains that he is making satisfactory progress and will tell me if he feels he is getting behind. You will recall that when he made his original estimate of how long it would take him to do the job, I made a point of letting everyone know I didn't agree that he had allowed sufficient time. Now, with his reluctance to let me see what he has done, I'm more convinced than ever that we will not finish on time and that he is hiding the fact. Every time I try to find out where we stand, he gets temperamental; and if there's anything I can't stand, it's a prima donna! When he finds that time has run out, he'll probably up and quit on us.

JOHNSON: Ouch! That's all we'd need! I hope you are misjudging Al.

EDEN: I hope so, too, but the fact remains that I have no means of measuring his progress and have only his word for assurance that we are on schedule. You know, the blood will be on my hands if we miss our dates, and I'm plenty worried.

JOHNSON: Well, for peace of mind, if nothing more, we have to determine the program status. After all, our schedule for the entire test facility is based to a large extent on Al's end date. If you had his file on the program, could you do a sufficiently comprehensive analysis of the contents to establish our position?

EDEN: Possibly, but I doubt it. Ed Hall up in Allentown would be in a much better position to do it, since he has had a great deal of general programming experience. But I know if you call in Hall for that purpose, it'll make Al mad.

JOHNSON: You're certainly right about that! However, if Hall would come down for a visit on a related matter, the progress report might be obtained as a by-product. With his work on system simulations, there should be plenty of common ground on which the two of them can get together.

EDEN: That's a thought.

JOHNSON: Suppose I discuss the matter with the boss and see what we can cook up.

A visit for Ed Hall was arranged. As a result of some rescheduling at headquarters, it was convenient to shift some programming work associated with the test phase of the Florida activity. It had originally been planned for Abrams to do this after completion of the main program. The stated purpose of Hall's visit was to coordinate this shift. After it had been arranged, Johnson called Abrams into his office and informed him of the plan and the reasons. Abrams thought it was a good idea and promised to help in any way possible. After the visit, Hall assured everyone that Abrams appeared to be making satisfactory progress and that for the present, at least, he had every chance of meeting the schedule.

On a Friday, several weeks following the scheduling controversy, Abrams stopped Johnson in the laboratory.

ABRAMS: Say, Harris, Bill wants Smith and me to work tomorrow, and I don't see the need for it. I'm keeping up with the schedule I've set for myself; and until I get behind, I see no reason for putting in overtime. Besides, I'd like to spend some time with my family.

JOHNSON: Can't say I blame you for that. Why does Bill feel that it is necessary?

ABRAMS: He just said that we should make use of every available minute now as a cushion against missing our schedule. I'm being very careful to maintain a progress rate consistent with our dates, and I feel that overtime now is a needless imposition. If I find myself falling behind in any week, I'll certainly tell you and request overtime.

JOHNSON: From what you've told me, I've got to agree with you. Suppose I talk it over with Bill and see what he has in mind.

ABRAMS: OK.

On his way back to the office, Johnson stopped at Eden's desk and asked him about the overtime situation.

EDEN: The two fellows from Concord who are experts on the electrostatic storage section are leaving for home on Sunday. So far this week, we haven't gotten in more than two hours of actual operating time on the machine; and I figured that if we worked Saturday, we could get in a solid eight hours with these boys standing by in case of trouble. In fact, they suggested that we do it so that they could be sure that the reliability of that section of the computer was up to par. Besides, it won't do any harm to get in all of the time we can now. I know Al is sore about it because he had planned to take off for Miami with his family tonight to spend the weekend with relatives.

Johnson agreed that they should work Saturday under the circumstances and walked back to the computer room to find Abrams. When Johnson related Eden's full story, Abrams quickly agreed to work. His closing remark was: "If Bill had only said something about the fellows leaving for Concord, there wouldn't have been any argument in the first place."

Two months later, just prior to the beginning of acceptance tests, Abrams blew up over the questioning of his modification to the equation, and Johnson was again faced with the problem of how to handle an administrative situation over which he had no direct line responsibility. Abrams and Eden worked for the systems section head; and although Johnson had kept him informed on all developments in Florida, the geographical separation seemed to Johnson to make him the one who had to cope with the problem on the spot. There was always a question as to what lengths he could go in handling the matter because of his inability to make any commitments which would be binding on the section head.

Readings

1 | Understanding and Managing Intergroup Conflict

Eric H. Neilsen

One of the important advantages of large complex organizations is that they are capable of coordinating the labors of many different groups of men, working simultaneously on different tasks and in different places, in the service of some superordinate goal. A by-product of this condition, however, is that the groups involved, though subunits of the same organization, enjoy contrasting experiences which lead their members to view the world in different ways. Such differences can often lead to intergroup conflict at the social interfaces where the work of the different groups is coordinated, and they always represent the potential for conflict.

Whether one views intergroup conflict as good or bad, desirable in some cases or at best a necessary evil, the fact remains that it is ubiquitous in large organizations and thus comprises a salient phenomenon with which managers must deal. This article avoids the issue of the value of intergroup conflict and attempts instead to present a way of thinking about this phenomenon and some of the methods available for coping with it which will enable the manager to predict the consequences of his actions more accurately and to choose those tactics which are best suited to his particular objectives in a given situation, objectives which he deems appropriate based on his own experience. In doing so, the author does not suggest that his own way of thinking about intergroup conflict is value free, but rather that he values a contextual analysis where as many as possible of the relevant issues and their interdependencies are taken into account before action is taken.

SOURCES OF INTERGROUP CONFLICT

There are four basic ways in which membership in different groups can create conflict; each involves a different aspect of the social structure and norms of a group. Membership in different groups may mean that individuals will (1) identify different personal characteristics as inherently attractive or unattractive; (2) see as legitimate different equations for determining how much reward—either in terms of status or goods—a person should have; (3) feel that different kinds of procedures and different interpretations of the same data make the most sense in performing a given task; and (4) feel that other persons' or groups' control over certain resources will be detrimental to their own group's interests. Of these issues only the latter seems always to promote a conflictual situation. The others may or may not, depending upon whether the relations between the groups involved make them salient. This is most likely to occur whenever agreement on one or more of these issues is necessary for effective cooperation. For this requires that members of at least one group change their definitions of issues, something they are not likely to want to do for fear of betraying their own long-term interests. Conformity to a given set of viewpoints is the payment men make for the emotional and material rewards their groups give them.

In the following sections we will elaborate on each of these factors and give some examples of how conflict is most likely to erupt because of them.

Differences in Reference Groups

The members of any group tend to hold in common a series of definitions of what they ideally would most and least like their group and themselves as its members to be like. Such definitions may involve any combination of attributes, skills, and objects, real or fictitious, that the mind is capable of imagining. The organizational units with which these definitions or images are associated in members' minds are commonly called reference groups, because by evaluating their current group in terms of them, members are able to place their progress toward their ideal and away from its opposite. In the terminology of psychoanalytic theory, conceptions of reference groups comprise an important part of members' superegos. Feelings of progress toward the group ideal are inherently positive, those away from it inherently negative.

Progress toward the group ideal involves conformity to group norms and the development of goals consistent with group values. It also involves attempts to associate with other live groups whose characteristics are seen by group members as more like those of their group ideal than their own group's characteristics presently are. Likewise, it involves attempts to dissociate from other groups and individuals whose characteristics are more antithetical to the group ideal than members believe the characteristics of their own group to be.

These attempts at selective association and disassociation form probably the most basic source of conflict in society. When the members of one group see those of another as possessing traits antithetical to their ideal, there is little way to create true cooperation between them other than through some process of resocialization. The basic paradigm encompasses all forms of prejudice, from racism to competitive social climbing. The intensity of feelings may vary, but they all have one thing in common. They are rooted in unconscious predispositions which individuals are not very capable of changing quickly, or of recognizing the need to change in the first place.

Distributive Justice

Numerous writers on organizational behavior, especially those who have studied workers at the blue-collar and clerical levels, have observed that work group status hierarchies are based on notions of distributive justice, that is, that each man's status is allocated according to his past and present performance along a number of criteria commonly valued by group members.[1] In some groups age, seniority, and ethnic background are especially important. In others education and skill are. Any set of criteria is possible. This phenomenon can be a second major source of intergroup conflict when those appointed to coordinate or control the activities of two or more groups are identified by the members of at least one of them as not worthy of such status in terms of their group's equation for granting it. Typically, a new coordinator will meet the criteria laid down by one group, the one from which he came, but not those adhered to by others.

The author has observed a good example of conflict stemming from this source at the management level in a small firm undergoing reorganization.[2] The firm in question had been operating in a highly stable industry and had relied for many years on field representatives to sell its products. Product development decisions had been in the hands of the engineering and production departments throughout the firm's history. Following a decision by top management to broaden the firm's market and seek new uses for its technology, a five-man marketing team was recruited and some of its members were given complete control

---

[1] See, for instance: George C. Homans, "Status among Clerical Workers," *Human Organization*, vol. 12 (1953); and A. Zaleznik, C. R. Christensen, and F. J. Roethlisberger, *The Motivation, Satisfaction, and Productivity of Workers: A Prediction Study* (Boston: Division of Research, Harvard Business School, 1958).

[2] Eric H. Neilsen, "Contingency Theory Applied to Small Business Organizations" (Ph.D. dissertation, Department of Social Relations, Harvard University, 1970).

over product development decisions heretofore held by the production and engineering groups. The marketing personnel given these powers had previously worked in firms where they controlled similar decisions and felt that their years of experience in the area and their educational backgrounds made them highly qualified for their jobs. The chief executives of the firm as well as the other marketing men expressed similar opinons.

The engineering and production personnel, on the other hand, felt that their control had been unduly usurped. As they saw it, long years of experience with their firm's particular products and ways of doing things were important criteria for possessing such control. Conflict between themselves and the newly appointed marketing personnel continued throughout the author's research.

Differences in Task Orientation and Experience

Men who spend many years performing a given kind of task tend to become accustomed to organizing their work, to orienting themselves to time deadlines, to basic personal goals, and to each other as individuals, in ways that help them perform that task in an effective manner. But current research suggests that different kinds of tasks, involving the management of different levels of certainty, require different work orientations and norms.[3] Tasks that are highly certain, for example, production tasks, can be done best through the use of steep, multileveled control hierarchies, directive supervision, and planning in terms of short-term deadlines. Tasks that are highly uncertain, for example, research tasks, can be done best with flat, one- or two-level hiearchies, participative supervision, and planning in terms of long-term deadlines. When men who have become accustomed to working on tasks with different levels of certainty start to work together on some joint project, conflict can arise due to these internalized differences in their work orientations. The way the other fellow does it may simply not make sense. In fact, it may seem highly detrimental to the success of the joint task.

For example, men used to working on highly certain tasks tend to check with their superiors on most of the task decisions they make. This is useful in these settings because superiors here tend to have access to more of the relevant information than their subordinates, and single decisions are likely to affect the chances for the whole unit's success. On the other hand, men used to working on highly uncertain tasks often do not check with their superiors before making task decisions. In these settings, so much information can be relevant to the task of the unit as a whole that superiors are incapable of assimilating

---

[3] Paul R. Lawrence and Jay W. Lorsch, *Organization and Environment: Managing Differentiation and Integration* (Homewood, Ill.: Richard D. Irwin, Inc., 1967).

all of the data and must rely on the subordinates who are closest to a given problem to make a decision related to it. Moreover, many single decisions are less crucial for the success of the unit as a whole. Thus, in cases such as these, it makes sense for subordinates to make decisions on their own.

When performers of certain and uncertain tasks get together, and men used to checking with their superiors deal with those who see no reason to do so, each side looks to the other as if it's doing things the wrong way. Differences in time horizons in the planning process create very similar effects.

Besides these kinds of orientations, which have developed over long periods of time, one can classify disagreements due to the possession of different information and its interpretation in different ways under this heading. The two go hand in hand. Men working on different tasks tend to seek out different kinds of data and to attach different levels of importance to the same events. A change in a delivery schedule may require little effort from a marketing manager, perhaps a little extra paper work. In the eyes of a production superintendent, however, such a change might mean a great deal of work—rearranging work assignments, overtime schedules, machine use priorities. While one man is tempted to treat the phenomenon cavalierly and use it as a small favor in his dealings with customers, the other sees it as a major problem to be avoided when at all possible.

Competition for Scarce Resources

A fourth major source of conflict involves competition between two or more groups for what their members identify as a finite set of scarce resources. The resources may be rewards the individual members desire or the materials they think they need for performing their tasks. They may be tangible—money, facilities—or nontangible—prestige, popularity, influence. Whatever they are they contribute to conflict when the men involved feel, realistically or unrealistically, that their availability is limited and that any gain in control over them by other groups represents a loss for their own.[4] (See Figure 1.)

Conflict over scarce resources has been studied extensively in laboratory settings. Subjects have been given games to play in which options are open for both helping and hindering each other, and the proportion of hindering moves has been shown to vary directly with the extent to which a win-lose orientation has been built into the reward structure. Still other experiments have been run in which the reward structure

---

[4] Louis R. Pondy's article, "Budgeting and Intergroup Conflict in Organizations," *Pittsburgh Business Review*, April 1964, deals specifically with this source of conflict as it relates to the creation and use of budgets.

FIGURE 1

Strategies for Resolving Intergroup Conflict

Behavioral Solution

                                        Attitudinal Change
                                             Solution
        1   2   3   4   5   6   7

1. Separate the groups physically, reducing conflict by reducing the opportunity to interact.
2. Allow interaction on issues where superordinate goals prevail and decision-making rules have been agreed to beforehand.
3. Keep groups separated but use as integrators individuals who are seen by both groups as justifying high status for the job, possessing personal attributes consistent with both groups' ideals, and having the expertise necessary for understanding each group's problems.
4. Hold direct negotiations between representatives from each group on all conflictual issues, in the presence of individuals who are seen as neutral to the conflict and who have personal attributes and expertise valued by both groups.
5. Hold direct negotiations between representatives from each group without third-party consultants present.
6. Exchange some group personnel for varying periods of time, so that contrasting perceptions and the rationales for them are clarified through day-to-day interaction and increased familiarity with the other group's activities, and then attempt direct negotiations after returning members have reported to their groups.
7. Require intense interacton between the conflicting groups under conditions where each group's failure to cooperate is more costly to itself than continuing to fight, regardless of how the other group behaves.

itself depends upon the extent to which the participants are willing to cooperate with or hinder one another, and the proportion of hindering moves here has been shown to vary with initial levels of trust, opportunities for communication, psychological predispositions toward agression and affection, and other relevant variables.[5]

METHODS OF CONFLICT RESOLUTION

Thus far we have identified what appear to be the four major sources of conflict, based on the available research literature. Let us now consider some of the tactics which can be used for coping with conflict.[6] There are literally an infinite number of ways in which one might go about stopping or reducing a particular pattern of intergroup conflict, but they all probably can be placed at some point along a continuum which

[5] Philip S. Gallo, Jr. and Charles G. McClintock, "Cooperative and Competitive Behavior in Mixed-Motive Games," *Journal of Conflict Resolution*, vol. 11, no. 1 (1967).

[6] Richard E. Walton, "Purposive Behavior in the Confrontation of Differences," Harvard Business School course note adapted from material reported by the same author in *Interpersonal Peacemaking: Confrontation and Third Party Consultation* (Reading, Mass.: Addison-Wesley Publishing Co., Inc., 1969). Reprinted by permission.

represents different combinations of two basic approaches—halting the conflictual behavior itself without regard to changes in attitude, on the one hand, and changing the attitudes of the protagonists so that they no longer see anything to fight about, on the other. (See Figure 1.)

Physical Separation

Physically separating the conflicting groups has the distinct advantages of preventing more damage from being done and of preventing the creation of further rationales for fighting based on what happens in combat itself. If the intervening party is sufficiently strong, it is something which can be done quickly. The tactic may be especially helpful where the groups in conflict are not highly interdependent or where the intervening party does not rely on their active cooperation with each other in order to secure some desired output. One of the tactic's disadvantages is that it may require continuous surveillance to keep the parties separate, especially if tempers are hot and energy levels high. Also, the tactic does not encourage the members of the conflicting groups to change their attitudes toward one another. On the contrary, lack of new objective information about an opponent encourages a group's members to reinforce their negative attitudes through unchecked fantasy building. Most important, the tactic is of little use to those who rely on the active cooperation between the conflicting groups for getting some job done. For them it is at best a stopgap measure, a way of preventing further damage until some other tactic can be devised.

Limited Interaction

Reducing interaction to issues where superordinate goals exist and where decision-making rules have been agreed to offers the advantage of getting some joint work done, but its utility depends upon whether the areas in which the protagonists are willing to cooperate, if any, are of any use to those in a position to impose this solution. Continued surveillance is also likely to be necessary, since the protagonists might easily make use of the available opportunities for communication for further attacks. The tactic may be of considerable use in situations where the interdependence between the two groups is clearly defined and stable over time, and where the joint decisions involved are generally routine. The tactic is least advantageous where the groups need to cooperate on a variety of issues or where areas requiring cooperation shift frequently as new decision-making procedures must continuously be established. Like the first tactic discussed, this one does little to encourage attitudinal change either, so that the basic motivation to fight may remain indefinitely or be redirected in a more damaging direction.

Using Integrators

Using as integrators individuals who are seen by both groups as possessing high legitimate status, high expertise, and a constellation of personal attributes consistent with group ideals creates the advantage of allowing the conflicting parties to coordinate each other's activities on a variety of issues while making it unnecessary for them to interact with each other directly. Thus it can be used in conjunction with a policy of physical separation, or with a policy where some interaction is permitted on routine issues. Lawrence and Lorsch have shown that this tactic is typically used by firms which need to maintain high levels of coordination among functional groups with clearly different work orientations.[7] For instance, in some segments of the plastics industry, the production task is highly certain, the research task highly uncertain. As discussed earlier, this kind of situation promotes intergroup conflict. These authors found that in organizations where the men who were assigned the task of coordinating the research and production units were rated high by both in terms of expertise and legitimate power, the quality of relations between these groups was better and their firms on the whole economically more effective than in those firms where the integrators did not have these characteristics. Some research done by this author indicates that the possession by integrators of commonly valued personal attributes—education, business background, personal style—can play a similarly important role.[8] While studying relations among departments in two small firms, he found that coordination between pairs of departments was considerably better where the integrators possessed personal attributes valued by both groups, even in cases where ratings of power and expertise would have indicated no differences in their quality of integration.

One major difficulty in executing this tactic is finding the golden men who fit all the requirements. Many firms simply may not have the resources or the sophistication to do so. Also, as with the previous two tactics discussed, this approach does not encourage attitudinal change. In some cases—where job demands require differences in orientation —this may be an important advantage. Where this is not the case, though, the tactic is obviously less desirable.

Third-Party Consultants

One tactic which represents something of a balance between attempts at attitudinal change on the one hand and the direct stopping of conflict

---

[7] Lawrence and Lorsch, *Organization and Environment.*

[8] Neilsen, *Contingency Theory.*

behavior on the other involves the use of direct negotiations between representatives of the warring parties in the presence of a third-party consultant whose advice and actions are valued by both groups.

The negotiating activity itself encourages the clarification of assumptions and the exploration of each party's motives—in essence a clear confrontation of differences. Thus, it sets the stage for new learning to take place. The presence of the third party, if the latter's opinions and counsel are sufficiently valued, inhibits lapses into name calling or other emotional outbursts and, in general, acts as a deterrent against further overt conflict behavior. If the third party is sufficiently skilled, he can also guide the negotiations in ways that tend to create the best results, for example, by sequencing differentiation and integration phases, keeping tensions at a moderate level, lending his status to a weaker party so that a balance of power is obtained and issues of ultimate influence do not get in the way of the confrontation process.[9]

Negotiations without Consultants

Bringing representatives together for negotiations without a third party present involves greater risk of further conflict. There is no one there to keep tempers under control. But one can argue that if the need to resolve differences is sufficiently important to both parties, the agreements under this condition might involve even more attitudinal change and acceptance. The participants are doing all the work themselves, and thus the experience is more intense. The key to making this tactic work, of course, is one of making the motivation to resolve the conflict so strong that the negotiators are willing to work their way through the issues in spite of the mistakes they are likely to make without a third party present. One method for creating such motivation is to make the need to cooperate crucial for each negotiator, regardless of what the other party does. For instance, if each negotiator's failure to cooperate is likely to result in losses either to himself or his group that are nearly equal or slightly greater than anything the other party can do to him, cooperation in and of itself becomes important and he is likely to be more flexible in his demands. An example of this would be a situation in which both groups were in danger of being dispersed or reorganized by a powerful third party, for example, top management, if their fighting continued, and thereby of suffering the same fate either one would if it were to lose control over its activities to the other. The relative strengths of the need to cooperate on the one hand and the need to meet group demands on the other must not be too disparate; otherwise agreements might be made simply for the sake of survival

---

[9] For a more thorough analysis of this approach, see Walton, "Purposive Behavior."

and no real differences aired. But if this disparity can be prevented, the tension created by attempting to serve two needs simultaneously can result in considerable attitudinal change.

Exchanging Members

One problem with negotiations of the sort where only representatives of the protagonists are involved is that agreements made at the bargaining table may be interpreted as a betrayal by those group members who have not taken part in the negotiations and who therefore have not been subjected directly to the strains of having to come to an agreement. Even where notions of betrayal do not arise, members may interpret a new agreement as a behavioral requisite only, caused by prevailing circumstances, and not encouraging them to change their minds about anything. One way of setting the stage for more pervasive attitudinal change is to have the warring groups exchange some of their members for sufficient lengths of time to let them become familiar with how the other group operates, what kinds of problems it faces on a day-to-day basis, and how its rank and file explain their own ideals, statuses, norms, and the like.

The exchanged individuals then return to their own groups and, as accepted members who have not been working under the strain of negotiations, are possibly in a better position to communicate these data to their cohorts than would potentially suspect representatives. These data can then be used both during and following negotiations to evaluate the agreements made and encourage greater acceptance of them.

The tactic has some noteworthy disadvantages. It takes time, perhaps more than an intervening party thinks he can afford. It takes sophistication, since an astute social analysis is a prerequisite. It requires the voluntary cooperation of both parties. Each group must be willing to give up some of its members. The exchanged members must be encouraged to gather their data objectively. Temporary outsiders must be responded to positively and provided with honest discussions of how one's group works and what its members actually believe. A visiting individual who is isolated or given poor data will probably hinder successful negotiations at a later date. Finally, the data visitors gain, even if honest and accurate, may possibly serve to convince one or more of the groups that they really do want to fight with the other or that agreements made later do not represent a change in attitude. Thus, a major risk is involved.

On the positive side, exchange of this sort can clear up important misconceptions, indicate to each party where the most fruitful negotiations might take place, and ultimately result in permanent attitude change so that the sources of conflict cease to exist. If the latter occurs, the intervening party or anyone relying on cooperation between the two groups no longer has to worry about the possibility of conflict or continue to invest his energies in preventing its occurrence.

Because of its disadvantages, this tactic is rarely used, if ever, in connection with major institutional disputes, such as those between labor and management. But it is used by firms to prevent or reduce conflict between members of different functional departments. For instance, numerous firms in industries that require close coordination between production and applied research departments require newcomers in each department to work for a time in the other to gain a greater familiarity with the problems the members of the latter face.

Multilevel Interaction

At the other end of the continuum from the reduction of conflict through physical separation is the encouragement of intense interaction among many or all of the members of opposing groups. Like the previous two tactics, an essential ingredient in its use is the development of a set of conditions under which the failure of each group to cooperate will result in major costs to itself, regardless of what the other group does. This situation, if an intervening party can create it, ideally forces an open confrontation of differences followed by basic attitudinal change. Besides the fact that, like all negotiations, it takes time, the main disadvantage of this tactic is that the requisite conditions may be hard to create and to maintain for the period it takes for the issues to be resolved. Whole groups are involved and not just a few negotiators whose behavior and status can be closely surveyed. Members of opposing forces are likely to start out by making peace in terms of norms of action while maintaining their negative attitudes. In some cases, only time and shared experience can open up the way for the development of positive emotional bonds. If the intervening party is unable to maintain the reward structure as described above on a continuous basis, even if the lapse in these conditions is only momentary, one or both of the protagonists might seize the opportunity to attack and set the process back several steps. The possibility also exists that if differences are strong enough, some of the protagonists may choose to incur the cost of refusing to cooperate and resolve the situation by leaving the group or being forced to leave. The intervening party has to accept this possibility and take into account his manpower needs and resources in the process.

THE MANAGER'S VALUES

Whether a manager uses a given tactic to resolve intergroup conflict should depend on at least four factors: (1) his ability to execute the tactic, (2) the costs he might incur in using it in comparison to those he might incur in using another, (3) the tactic's appropriateness for creating the degree of attitudinal and/or behavioral change he desires, and (4) his own personal values. The importance of the first three of these factors should be evident from the foregoing analysis. We have said little so far, however, about a manager's personal values in the conflict resolution process. We would argue that the more deeply rooted a conflict is in the personalities and life styles of the protagonists, the more carefully must a manager evaluate his actions in light of his own values, especially if he chooses to try to resolve the conflict through attitudinal change. The four sources of conflict we discussed earlier appear to fall along their own continuum in this respect.

Conflict due to differences in reference groups appears to be the most deeply rooted in group members' personalities. A reference group is part of a man's superego. His conceptions of an ideal group and its opposite are molded by the totality of his life's experience. While he may be able to identify some aspects of these images in terms of his conscious desire to attain particular goals, he may not be able to do so with regard to other aspects whose attractiveness or repulsiveness are rooted in forgotten experiences and not open to rational evaluation. On a conscious level the member simply wants his group to be a certain way by fiat.

When differences in reference groups are causing conflict, especially when members of conflicting groups identify cooperation with each other as antithetical to their ideals, tactics involving attempts at attitudinal change may provide the only long-run hope for resolution. The issue is not likely to resolve itself through the experiences of the opposing groups under conditions of physical separation. But attempting to change someone's reference groups involves the manager in what is clearly a moral issue. Such changes, if indeed they can be created, are likely to affect a man's behavior off the job as well as on it. One who attempts to create such changes must feel secure not only in the belief that he has a right to do so but also in the conviction that if he is successful, the effects he creates will benefit the individual as an independent entity as well as the organizational unit for which he works.

It is also important to consider the possibility that changes in reference groups can have an unintended snowball effect. Groups which start out hating each other, through joint experience under conditions where cooperation is necessary for survival, may not only learn to get along with one another but also come to like each other. As a result, they might become more concerned with each other's welfare than with the joint activity the instigator of the change was most concerned with. For instance, if two ethnic groups at the blue-collar level in a factory go from enemies to allies, their newfound friendships might create more headaches for management in terms of strikes, slowdowns, resistance to incentive systems, and so on than the results of their former hostilities did. Attempting to change reference groups is indeed a complex matter. In many cases a manager might be better off trying to stop conflictual behavior through physical separation in some degree, living with the costs of surveillance and the potential for more conflict involved. His own values and knowledge of what is likely to happen may be put to a major test if he chooses the attitudinal change approach.

Conflict which derives from differences in groups' perceptions of a just distribution of rewards appears to be somewhat less rooted in protagonists' personalities, and its resolution through attitudinal change may have a less pervasive effect on personal and firm life. The mere contention that another group should be attacked because it is getting more than it deserves involves a logical argument with a logical solution—reduce the group's rewards to what it deserves. In this respect, the unconscious desires of the individuals involved are less salient. However, belief in a given equation for reward may be deeply rooted in the superego and is likely to be hard to change without positive experience under a new system. Change in perceptions of a just equation for reward may affect family life. A man who gradually comes to believe that performance is a more important requisite for reward than seniority may find himself taking fewer days off, evaluating his friends in a different way, raising his children differently. For these reasons, attempting to change conceptions of distributive justice involves many of the same risks and moral dilemmas that attempting to change reference groups does.

Perhaps one way in which attitudinal change of this kind is less problematic is that the acceptance of a common equation for reward in and of itself is not likely to encourage stronger primary ties between two groups. Therefore, the threat of overreaction against the intervening party is less evident.

Conflict resulting from differences in work norms appears to be even less a part of the combatants' personalities, and reducing such antagonism through attitudinal change tactics is likely to have less pervasive effects on participants' personal lives. This is not to say that different work orientations themselves are not ingrained in the protagonists' superegos. They very well may be. The point, rather, is that the conflict which derives from such differences can be resolved in ways that require personalities to be changed relatively little. A man may prefer a given task orientation, but this does not mean that he is incapable of understanding when his own preferences do not meet task demands. The task of the intervening party here is not to change a conflictee's work orientation but to change his reasoning about the apparently illogical behavior of the people he disagrees with. As in the case of changing attitudes about distributive justice, the resolution of differences in work norms through attitudinal change is also less likely to encourage the development of strong primary ties between former enemies. One can easily understand and accept the rationale for doing things in different ways under different conditions without becoming enamored of persons who perform tasks that are different from one's own.

Finally, conflict stemming from competition for scarce resources appears to be the least rooted of all the sources in the personalities involved, and attempts at its resolution through attitudinal change are likely to involve the fewest moral dilemmas. Definitions of what scarce resources are, or how they should be used, do not have to be changed; only the attitude that one group will gain access to resources at the expense of another. This may involve a change in the notion of who should use the resources under different conditions, but such a change should have little effect on the basic desire to benefit from the resources on the job or on how one might use them at home where the situation can be defined as clearly different. Likewise, on the job, a clearer understanding of the logic of resource distribution should benefit the intervening manager, since members of the conflicting groups can use it as a goal for making sure that resources are distributed to other groups according to this logic and thereby used to the maximum benefit for their own.

INDIVIDUAL DIFFERENCES WITHIN GROUPS

In this paper we have focused on sources of conflict which derive directly from a group's social structure and norms. It seems worthwhile mentioning in closing that differences in individual personalities and roles add another dimension of complexity to the conflict process. For no single group member is likely to perceive his group's ideals, equations for reward, work norms, and resource priorities in exactly the same way that any other member does. While there may be considerable consensus on these issues, individual differences are bound to exist. Likewise, particular members are likely to feel different levels of allegiance to viewpoints held by most of their cohorts, to be attracted in different degrees to alternatives offered by other groups and individuals, and to be willing to stop conflict or to change their minds under different conditions.

This is especially important to note where attempts at conflict resolution involve negotiations between group representatives. The personality of each representative may be just as important as the social structure and norms of his group in determining how successful the negotiations will be. A representative might find one solution agreeable which the majority of his group's membership would reject. He might forego other solutions which his constituents would prefer.

Not only is the personality but also the status of a representative within his group worth noting. As a leader he might be in a position to change group opinion. Were he simply a member in good standing who did not hold a leadership position he would be less likely to do so. While members at the bottom of the status hierarchy would hardly qualify for the job of representative, for example, members who deviated a lot from group norms or those who had lost battles for controlling positions and were alienated from the group as a whole as a result, their behavior should also be considered for the negative roles they might play in the creation of conflict itself and in any attempt at resolving it. Such individuals might seek to misrepresent their groups or reveal internal tensions or negative feelings toward other groups as ways of getting back at the other members for their low status. They might do the same things simply out of their own misunderstanding of their groups' positions and policies.

In any case, any assessment of intergroup conflict should involve not only analysis of each group's shared perceptions and feelings but also of the perceptions, feelings, and statuses of the particular persons involved both in the conflict itself and in any attempts at conflict resolution which might be considered. The same tactics for handling intergroup conflict noted above can be applied to particular interpersonal relationships as well. The intervening manager should consider the use of a variety of tactics in conjunction with each other, some focusing on individuals, some on groups as whole units, in his attempts to cope with the intergroup conflicts that fall under his domain.

2 | The Two Faces of Power*

David C. McClelland

For over 20 years I have been studying a particular human mo-tive—the need to Achieve, the need to do something better than it has been done before. As my investigation advanced, it became clear that the need to Achieve, technically *n* Achievement, was one of the keys to economic growth, because men who are concerned with doing things better have become active entrepreneurs and have created the growing business firms which are the foundation stones of a developing economy.[1] Some of these heroic entrepreneurs might be regarded as leaders in the restricted sense that their activities established the eco-nomic base for the rise of a new type of civilization, but they were seldom leaders of men. The reason for this is simple: *n* Achievement is a one-man game which need never involve other people. Boys who are high in *n* Achievement like to build things or to make things with their hands, presumably because they can tell easily and directly whether they have done a good job. A boy who is trying to build as tall a tower as possible out of blocks can measure very precisely how well he has done. He is in no way dependent on someone else to tell him how good his performance is. So in the pure case, the man with high

* This essay is a revision of a paper originally presented at Albion College, Albion, Michigan. It is intended as a commentary on the lack of leadership in contemporary America noted by John Gardner in his paper *The Anti-Leadershp Vaccine* (1965 Annual Report, The Carnegie Corporation of New York).

Copyright by Columbia University. Permission to reprint from the *Journal of International Affairs*, vol. 24, no. 1 (1970), pp. 29–47, is gratefully acknowledged to the editors of the *Journal*.

[1] David C. McClelland, *The Achieving Society* (Princeton, N.J.: D. Van Nostrand Co., 1961).

n Achievement is not dependent on the judgment of others; he is concerned with improving his own performance. As an ideal type, he is most easily conceived of as a salesman or an owner-manager of a small business, in a position to watch carefully whether or not his performance is improving.

While studying such men and their role in economic development, I ran head on into problems of leadership, power, and social influence which *n* Achievement clearly did not prepare a man to cope with. As a one-man firm grows larger, it obviously requires some division of function and some organizational structure. Organizational structure involves relationships among people, and sooner or later someone in the organization, if it is to survive, must pay attention to getting people to work together, or to dividing up the tasks to be performed, or to supervising the work of others. Yet it is fairly clear that a high need to Achieve does not equip a man to deal effectively with managing human relationships. For instance, a salesman with high *n* Achievement does not necessarily make a good sales manager. As a manager, his task is not to sell, but to inspire others to sell, which involves a different set of personal goals and different strategies for reaching them. I shall not forget the moment when I learned that the president of one of the most successful *achievement*-oriented firms we had been studying scored exactly zero in *n* Achievement! Up to that point I had fallen into the easy assumption that a man with a high need to Achieve does better work, gets promoted faster, and ultimately ends up as president of a company. How then was it possible for a man to be head of an obviously achieving company and yet score so low in *n* Achievement? At the time I was tempted to dismiss the finding as a statistical error, but there is now little doubt that it was a dramatic way of calling attention to the fact that stimulating achievement motivation in others requires a different motive and a different set of skills than wanting achievement satisfaction for oneself. For some time now, research on achievement motivation has shifted in focus from the individual with high *n* Achievement to the climate which encourages him and rewards him for doing well.[2] For no matter how high a person's need to Achieve may be, he cannot succeed if he has no opportunities, if the organization keeps him from taking initiative, or does not reward him if he does. As a simple illustration of this point, we found in our research in India that it did no good to raise achievement motivation through training if the trained individual was not in charge of his business.[3] That is to say, even though he might be "all fired up" and prepared to be more active and entrepreneurial, he could not

[2] George H. Litwin and Robert A. Stringer, *Motivation and Orangizational Climate* (Boston: Division of Research, Harvard Business School, 1966).

[3] David C. McClelland and D. G. Winter, *Motivating Economic Achievement* (New York: The Free Press, 1969).

in fact do much if he was working for someone else, someone who had the final say as to whether any of the things he wanted to do would in fact be attempted. In short, the man with high n Achievement seldom can act alone, even though he might like to. He is caught up in an organizational context in which he is managed, controlled, or directed by others. And thus to understand better what happens to him, we must shift our attention to those who are managing him, to those who are concerned about organizational relationships—to the leaders of men.

Since managers are primarily concerned with influencing others, it seems obvious that they should be characterized by a high need for Power, and that by studying the power motive we can learn something about the way effective managerial leaders work. If A gets B to do something, A is at one and the same time a leader (i.e., he is leading B), and a power-wielder (i.e., he is exercising some kind of influence or power over B). Thus, leadership and power appear as two closely related concepts, and if we want to understand better effective leadership, we may begin by studying the power motive in thought and action. What arouses thoughts of being powerful? What kinds of strategies does the man employ who thinks constantly about gaining power? Are some of these strategies more effective than others in influencing people? In pursuing such a line of inquiry in this area, we are adopting an approach which worked well in another. Studying the achievement motive led to a better understanding of business entrepreneurship. Analogously, studying the power motive may help us understand managerial, societal, or even political leadership better.

There is one striking difference between the two motivation systems which is apparent from the outset. In general, in American society at least, individuals are proud of having a high need to Achieve, but dislike being told they have a high need for Power. It is a fine thing to be concerned about doing things well (n Achievement) or making friends (n Affiliation), but it is reprehensible to be concerned about having influence over others (n Power). The vocabulary behavioral scientists use to describe power relations is strongly negative in tone. If one opens *The Authoritarian Personality*,[4] one of the major works dealing with people who are concerned with power, one finds these people depicted as harsh, sadistic, fascist, Machiavellian, prejudiced, and neurotic. Ultimately, many claim, the concern for power leads to Nazi-type dictatorships, to the slaughter of innocent Jews, to political terror, police states, brainwashing, and the exploitation of helpless masses who have lost their freedom. Even less political terms for power than these have a distinctively negative flavor—dominance-submission, competition, zero

---

[4] Theodor W. Adorno, E. Frenkel-Brunswick, D. J. Levinson, and R. N. Sanford, *The Authoritarian Personality* (New York: Harper & Row, Publishers, 1950).

sum game (if I win, you lose). It is small wonder that people do not particularly like being told they have a high need for Power.

The negative reactions to the exercise of power became vividly apparent to me in the course of our recent research efforts to develop achievement motivation.[5] Out of our extensive research on the achievement motive, we conceived of possible ways to increase it through short intensive courses. At first people were interested and curious. It seemed like an excellent idea to develop a fine motive like *n* Achievement, particularly among under-achievers in school or relatively inactive businessmen in underdeveloped countries. But most people were also skeptical. Could it be done? It turned out that many remained interested only as long as they were really skeptical about our ability to change motivation. As soon as it became apparent that we could indeed change people in a relatively short period of time, many observers began to worry. Was it ethical to change people's personalities? Were we not brainwashing them? What magical power were we employing to change an underlying personality disposition presumably established in childhood and laboriously stabilized over the years? Once these questions were raised, we became aware of the fundamental dilemma confronting anyone who becomes involved in any branch of the "influence game." He may think that he is exercising leadership—i.e., influencing people for their own good—but if he succeeds, he is likely to be accused of manipulating people. We thought that our influence attempts were benign. In fact, we were a little proud of ourselves. After all, we were giving people a chance to be more "successful" in business and at school. Yet we soon found ourselves attacked as potentially dangerous "brainwashers."

To some extent, ordinary psychotherapy avoids these accusations because the power of the therapist seems to be relatively weak. Therapy does not work very well or very quickly, and when it does, the therapist can say that the patient did most of the work himself.

But consider the following anecdote. Johnny was a bright but lazy sixth-grade student in math. His parents were concerned because he was not motivated to work harder, preferring to spend his evenings watching television, and they were delighted when psychologists explained that they had some new techniques for developing motivation to which they would like to expose Johnny. Soon after the motivation training regime began, they noticed a dramatic change in Johnny's behavior. He never watched television, but spent all of his time studying, and was soon way ahead of his class in advanced mathematics. At this point, his parents began to worry. What had the psychologists done to produce such a dramatic change in their son's behavior? They had wanted him changed, but not *that* much. They reacted very negatively to the power that the psychologists seemed to have exercised over him.

---

[5] McClelland and Winter, *Motivating*.

This experience was enough to make us yearn for the position of the detached scientist or consulting expert so vividly described by John Gardner in *The Anti-Leadership Vaccine*[6] as the preferred role for more and more young people today. For the "scientist" ordinarily does not directly intervene—does not exercise power—in human or social affairs. He observes the interventions of others, reports, analyzes and advises, but never takes responsibility himself. Our research had led us to intervene actively in Johnny's life, and even that small, relatively benign exercise of influence had led to some pretty negative responses from the "public." My own view is that young people avoid sociopolitical leadership roles not so much because their professors brainwash them into believing that it is better to be a professional, but because in our society in our time, and perhaps in all societies at all times, the exercise of power is viewed very negatively. People are suspicious of a man who wants power, even if he does so for sincere and altruistic reasons. He is often socially conditioned to be suspicious of himself. He does not want to be in a position where he might be thought to be seeking power and influence in order to exploit others, and as a result he shuns public responsibility.

Yet surely this negative face of power is only part of the story. Power must have a positive face, too. After all, people cannot help influencing one another. Organizations cannot function without some kind of authority relationships. Surely it is necessary and desirable for some people to concern themselves with management, with working out influence relationships that make it possible to achieve the goals of the group. A man who is consciously concerned with the development of proper channels of influence is surely better able to contribute to group goals than a man who neglects or represses power problems and lets the working relationships of men grow up unsupervised by men. Our problem, then, is to try to discern and understand two faces of power. When is power bad and when is it good? Why is it often perceived as dangerous? Which aspects of power are viewed favorably, and which unfavorably? When is it proper, and when improper, to exercise influence? And finally, are there different kinds of power motivation?

It will not be possible to answer all of these questions definitively, but the findings of recent research on the power motive as it functions in human beings will help us understand the two faces of power somewhat better. Let us begin with the curious fact that turned up in the course of what are technically "arousal" studies. When an experimenter becomes interested in a new motive, he ordinarily begins to study it by trying to arouse it in a variety of ways in order to see how it influences what a person thinks about. Then these alterations in thought content

---

[6] John W. Gardner, *The Anti-Leadership Vaccine* (1965 Annual Report, Carnegie Corporation of New York).

are worked into a code or a scoring system which captures the extent to which the thinking of the subject is concerned about achievement or power or whatever motive state has been aroused. For instance, Veroff,[7] when he began his study of the power motive, asked student candidates for office to write imaginative stories while they were waiting for the election returns to be counted. He contrasted these stories with those written by other students who were not candidates for office. That is, he assumed that the students waiting to hear if they had been elected were in a state of aroused power motivation and that their stories would reflect this fact in contrast to the stories of students not in such a state. From the differences in story content he derived a coding system for *n* Power (need for Power) based on the greater concern for having influence over others revealed in the stories of student candidates for election. Later arousal studies by Uleman[8] and Winter[9] further defined the essence of *n* Power as a concern for having a *strong impact on others.* That is, when power motivation was aroused in a variety of ways, students thought more often about people having strong impact on others. This was true not only for student candidates for office awaiting election returns, but also for student experimenters who were about to demonstrate their power over subjects by employing a winning strategy in a competitive game that they had been taught beforehand.[10]

What surprised us greatly was the discovery that drinking alcohol also stimulated similar power thoughts in men. This discovery was one of those happy accidents which sometimes occurs in scientific laboratories when two studies thought to be unrelated are proceeding side by side. When we began studying the effects of social drinking on fantasy, we had no idea that alcohol would increase power fantasies. Yet we immediately found that it increased sex and aggression fantasies, and one day it occurred to us that certain types of exploitative sex and certainly aggression were instances of "having impact" on others and therefore could be considered part of an *n* Power scoring definition. We later found that drinking alcohol in small amounts increased the frequency of *socialized* power thoughts while in larger amounts it promoted thinking in terms of *personalized* power. We began to notice that these two types of power concern had different consequences in action. For instance, Winter found that some college students with high *n* Power scores tended to drink more heavily while others held more offices in

---

[7] Joseph Veroff, "Development and Validation of a Projective Measure of Power Motivation," *Journal of Abnormal and Social Psychology*, no. 54 (1957), pp. 1–8.

[8] J. Uleman, "A New TAT Measure of the Need for Power" (Ph.D. dissertation, Harvard University, 1965).

[9] D. G. Winter, "Power Motivation in Thought and Action" (Ph.D. dissertation, Harvard University, 1967).

[10] Uleman, "New TAT Measure."

student organizations. These were not, however, the same people. That is, a student with high *n* Power either drank more heavily or he was a club officer, though he was usually not both, possibly because heavy drinking would prevent him from being elected to a responsible office. In other words, Winter identified alternative manifestations of the power drive—either heavy drinking or holding office. Later we found that the orientation of the power thoughts of these two types of people was quite different. Men whose power thoughts centered on having impact for the sake of others tended to hold office, whereas those whose thoughts centered on personal dominance tended to drink heavily, or to "act out" in college by attempting more sexual conquests or driving powerful cars fast, for example.

Other studies have further illuminated this picture, and while it is still not altogether clear, its main outlines can be readily sketched.[11] There are two faces of power. One is turned toward seeking to win out over active adversaries. Life tends to be seen as a "zero-sum game" in which "if I win, you lose" or "I lose, if you win." The imagery is that of the "law of the jungle" in which the strongest survive by destroying their adversaries. The thoughts of this face of power are aroused by drinking alcohol or, more socially, by putting a person in a personal dominance situation in which he is threatened. At the level of action, a personal power concern is associated with heavy drinking, gambling, having more aggressive impulses, and collecting "prestige supplies" like a convertible or a Playboy Club Key. People with this personalized power concern are more apt to speed, have accidents, and get into physical fights. If these primitive and personalized power-seeking characteristics were possessed by political officeholders, especially in the sphere of international relations, the consequences would be ominous.

The other face of the power motive is more socialized. It is aroused by the possibility of winning an election. At the fantasy level it expresses itself in thoughts of exercising power for the benefit of others and by feelings of greater ambivalence about holding power—doubts of personal strength, the realization that most victories must be carefully planned in advance, and that every victory means a loss for someone. In terms of activities, people concerned with the more socialized aspect of power join more organizations and are more apt to become officers in them. They also are more apt to join in organized informal sports, even as adults.

We have made some progress in distinguishing two aspects of the power motive, but what exactly is the difference between the way the two are exercised? Again a clue came from a very unexpected source.

---

[11] David C. McClelland et al., *Alcohol, Power and Inhibition* (Princeton, N.J.: D. Van Nostrand Co., 1969).

It is traditional in the literature of social psychology and political science to describe a leader as someone who is able to evoke feelings of obedience or loyal submission in his followers. A leader is sometimes said to have charisma if, when he makes a speech, for example, the members of his audience are swept off their feet and feel that they must submit to his overwhelming authority and power. In the extreme case they are like iron filings that have been polarized by a powerful magnet. The leader is recognized as supernatural or superhuman; his followers feel submissive, loyal, devoted, and obedient to his will. Certainly this is the most common description of what happened at mass meetings addressed by Hitler or Lenin. As great demagogues they established their power over the masses which followed loyally and obediently.

Winter wished to find out exactly, by experiment, what kinds of thoughts the members of an audience had when exposed to a charismatic leader.[12] He wanted to find out if the common analysis of what was going on in the minds of the audience was in fact accurate. So he exposed groups of business school students to a film of John F. Kennedy's Inaugural Address as President of the United States sometime after he had been assassinated. There was no doubt that this film was a highly moving and effective presentation of a charismatic leader for such an audience at that time. After the film was over he asked them to write imaginative stories as usual, and contrasted the themes of their stories with those written by a comparable group of students after they had seen a film explaining some aspects of modern architecture. Contrary to expectation, he did not find that the students exposed to the Kennedy film thought more afterwards about submission, following obedience, or loyalty. Instead the frequency of power themes in their stories increased. They were apparently strengthened and uplifted by the experience. They felt more powerful, rather than less powerful and submissive. This suggests that the traditional way of explaining the influence which a leader has on his followers has not been entirely correct. He does not force them to submit and follow him by the sheer overwhelming magic of his personality and persuasive powers. This is in fact to interpret effective leadership in terms of the kind of personalized power syndrome described above, and leadership has been discredited in this country precisely because social scientists have often used this personal power image to explain how the leader gets his effects. In fact, he is influential by strengthening and inspiriting his audience. Max Weber, the source of much of the sociological treatment of charisma, recognized that charismatic leaders obtained their effects through *begeisterung*, a word which means "inspiritation" rather than its usual translation as "enthusiasm."[13]

---

[12] Winter, "Power Motivation."

[13] For a fuller discussion of what Weber and other social scientists have meant by charisma, see Samuel N. Eisenstadt, *Charisma, Institute Building, and Social*

The leader arouses confidence in his followers. The followers feel better able to accomplish whatever goals he and they share. There has been much discussion of whether the leader's ideas about what will inspire his followers come from God, from himself, or from some intuitive sense of what the people need and want. But whatever the source of the leader's ideas, he cannot inspire his people unless he expresses vivid goals and aims which in some sense they want. Of course, the more he is meeting their needs, the less "persuasive" he has to be, but in no case does it make much sense to speak as if his role is to force submission. Rather it is to strengthen and uplift, to make people feel like origins, not pawns of the socio-political system.[14] His message is not so much: "Do as I say because I am strong and know best. You are children with no wills of your own and must follow me because I know better," but rather "Here are the goals which are true and right and which we share. Here is how we can reach them. You are strong and capable. You can accomplish these goals." His role is to clarify which goals the group should achieve and then to create confidence in its members that they can achieve them. John Gardner described these two aspects of the socialized leadership role very well when he said that leaders "can conceive and articulate goals that lift people out of their petty preoccupations, carry them above the conflicts that tear a society apart, and unite them in the pursuit of objectives worthy of their best efforts."[15]

Clearly the more socialized type of power motivation cannot and does not express itself through leadership which is characterized by the primitive methods of trying to win out over adversaries or exert personal dominance. In their thinking about the power motive social scientists have been too impressed by the dominance hierarchies established by brute force among lower animals. Lasswell and other political scientists have described all concern with power as a defense, an attempt to compensate for a feeling of weakness. At best this describes the personalized face of the power motive, not its socialized face—and even at that, we can only say that the personalized power drive *perceives* the world in defensive terms, not that it originates as a defense. Personal dominance may be effective in very small groups, but if a human leader wants to be effective in influencing large groups, he must rely on much more subtle and socialized forms of influence. He necessarily gets more interested in formulating the goals toward which groups of people can move. And if he is to move the group toward achieving them, he must

---

Transformation: Max Weber and Modern Sociology (Chicago: University of Chicago Press, 1968) (and also Robert C. Tucker, "The Theory of Charismatic Leadership," *Daedalus,* no. 97 (1968), pp. 731–56.

[14] Richard deCharms, *Personal Causation* (New York: Academic Press, 1968).

[15] Gardner, *The Anti-Leadership Vaccine.*

help define the goals clearly and persuasively, and then be able to strengthen the will of the individual members of the group to work for those goals.[16]

Some further light on the two faces of power was shed by our experience in trying to exert social leadership by offering achievement motivation development courses for business leaders in small cities in India. As noted above, when we began to succeed in these efforts, some observers began to wonder whether we were coarsely interfering in people's lives, perhaps spreading some new brand of American imperialism by foisting achievement values on a people that had gotten along very well without them. Their reaction was not unlike the one just described in which an outsider seeing a leader sway an audience concludes that he must have some mysterious magical power over the audience. Did we have a similar kind of *power over* the Indian businessmen who came for motivation training? Were we psychological Machiavellians?

Certainly we never thought we were. Nor, we are certain, did the businessmen perceive us as very powerful agents. How then did we manage to influence them? The course of events was very much like the process of social leadership described by John Gardner. First, we set before the participants certain goals which we felt would be desired by them—namely, to be better businessmen, to improve economic welfare in their community, to make a contribution in this way to the development of their country as a whole, to provide a pilot project that the rest of the underdeveloped world might copy, and to advance the cause of science. These goals ranged all the way from the specific and personal—improving one's business—to improving the community, the nation, and the world. While a selfish appeal to personal power generally has not been as effective as an appeal which demonstrates that increased personal power leads to important social goals, the goals which we presented certainly were objectives that interested the businessmen we contacted. Second, we provide them with the means of achieving these goals, namely, the courses in achievement motivation development which we explained were designed to make them personally better able to move quickly and efficiently towards these objectives. We offered new types of training in goal setting, planning, and risk taking which research had shown would help men become more effective entrepreneurs. No one was pressured to undergo this training or pursue these goals. If there was any pressure exerted, it was clearly in the eyes of the outside observer noting the effects of our "intervention";

---

[16] To be sure, if he is a gang leader, he may display actions like physical aggression which are characteristic of the personalized power drive. But to the extent that he is the leader of a large group, he is effective because he is presenting, by personal example, objectives for the gang which they find attractive, rather than because he can keep many people in line by threatening them.

it was not in the minds of the participants at the time. Third, the major goal of all of our educational exercises was to make the participants feel strong, like origins rather than pawns. Thus we insisted that the initial decision to take part in the training sessions must be their own, and that they not come out of a sense of obligation or a desire to conform. In fact, we depicted the training as a difficult process, so that a high degree of personal involvement would be necessary to complete it. During the training, we never set goals for the participants, but let them set their own. We made no psychological analyses of their test behavior which we either kept for our private diagnosis or presented to them as evidence of our superior psychological knowledge. Rather we taught them to analyze their own test records and to make their own decisions as to what a test score meant. After the course they set up their own association to work together for common community goals. We did not provide them with technical information about various types of new businesses they might enter, but let them search for it themselves. We had no fixed order of presenting course materials, but constantly asked the participants to criticise the material as it was presented and to direct the staff as to what new types of presentations were desired. Thus, in our ceaseless efforts to make the participants feel strong, competent, and effective, we behaved throughout the entire experiment like effective socialized leaders. We expressed in many ways our faith in their ability to act as origins and solve their own problems. In the end many of them justified our faith. They became more active, as we expected them to, and once again validated the ubiquitous psychological findings that what you expect other people to do they will in fact tend to do.[17] Furthermore, we have good evidence that we succeeded only with those businessmen whose sense of personal efficacy was increased. This demonstrated the ultimate paradox of social leadership and social power: to be an effective leader, one must turn all of his so-called followers into leaders. There is little wonder that the situation is a little confusing not only to the would-be leader, but also to the social scientist observing the leadership phenomenon.

Now let us put together these bits and pieces of evidence about the nature of power, and see what kind of a picture they make. The negative or personal face of power is characterized by the dominance-submission mode: if I win, you lose. It is *primitive* in the sense that the strategies employed are adopted early in life, before the child is sufficiently socialized to learn more subtle techniques of influence. In fantasy it expresses itself in thoughts of conquering opponents. In real life it leads to fairly simple direct means of feeling powerful—drinking heavily, acquiring

---

[17] Robert Rosenthal and Lenore Jacobson, *Pygmalion in the Classroom* (New York: Holt, Rinehart and Winston, Inc., 1968).

"prestige supplies," and being aggressive. It does not lead to effective social leadership for the simple reason that a person whose power drive is fixated at this level tends to treat other people as pawns rather than as origins. And people who feel that they are pawns tend to be passive and useless to the leader who is getting his childish satisfaction from dominating them. Slaves are the poorest, most inefficient form of labor ever devised by man. If a leader wants to have far-reaching influence, he must make his followers feel powerful and able to accomplish things on their own.

The positive or socialized face of power is characterized by a concern for group goals, for finding those goals that will move men, for helping the group to formulate them, for taking some initiative in providing members of the group with the means of achieving such goals, and for giving group members the feeling of strength and competence they need to work hard for such goals. In fantasy it leads to a concern with exercising influence *for* others, with planning, and with the ambivalent bittersweet meaning of many so-called "victories." In real life, it leads to an interest in informal sports, politics, and holding office. It functions in a way that makes members of a group feel like origins rather than pawns. Even the most dictatorial leader has not succeeded if he has not instilled in at least some of his followers a sense of power and the strength to pursue the goals he has set. This is often hard for outside observers to believe, because they do not experience the situation as it is experienced by the group members. One of the characteristics of the outsider, who notices only the success or failure of an influence attempt, is that he tends to convert what is a positive face of power into its negative version. He believes that the leaders must have "dominated" because he was so effective, whereas in fact direct domination could never have produced so large an effect.[18]

There is, however, a certain realistic basis for the frequent misperception of the nature of leadership. In real life the actual leader balances on a knife edge between expressing personal dominance and exercising the more socialized type of leadership. He may show first one face of power, then the other. The reason for this lies in the simple fact that even if he is a socialized leader, he must take initiative in helping the group he leads to form its goals. How much initiative he should

---

[18] Why is a successful influence attempt so often perceived as an instance of personal domination by the leader? One answer lies in the simplifying nature of social perception. The observer notices that a big change in the behavior of a group of people has occurred. He also can single out one or two people as leaders in some way involved in the change. He does not know how the leaders operated to bring about the change since he was not that intimately involved in the process. As a result, he tends to perceive the process as an instance of the application of personal power, as founded on a simple dominance-submission relationship. The more effective the leader is, the more personal power tends to be attributed to him, regardless of how he has actually achieved his effects.

take, how persuasive he should attempt to be, and at what point his clear enthusiasm for certain goals becomes personal authoritarian insistence that those goals are the right ones whatever the members of the group may think, are all questions calculated to frustrate the well-intentioned leader. If he takes no initiative, he is no leader. If he takes too much, he becomes a dictator, particularly if he tries to curtail the process by which members of the group participate in shaping group goals. There is a particular danger for the man who has demonstrated his competence in shaping group goals and in inspiring group members to pursue them. In time both he and they may assume that he knows best, and he may almost imperceptibly change from a democratic to an authoritarian leader. There are, of course, safeguards against slipping from the more socialized to the less socialized expressions of power. One is psychological: the leader must thoroughly learn the lesson that his role is not to dominate and treat people like pawns, but to give strength to others and to make them feel like origins of ideas and of the courses of their lives. If they are to be truely strong, he must continually consult them and be aware of their wishes and desires. *A firm faith in people as origins prevents the development of the kind of cynicism that so often characterizes authoritarian leaders.* A second safeguard is social: democracy provides a system whereby the group can expel the leader from office if it feels that he is no longer properly representing its interests.

Despite these safeguards, Americans remain unusually suspicious of the leadership role for fear that it will become a vehicle of the personal use and abuse of power. Students do not aspire to leadership roles because they are sensitive to the negative face of power and suspicious of their own motives. Furthermore, they know that if they are in a position of leadership, they will be under constant surveillance by all sorts of groups which are ready to accuse them of the personal abuse of power. Americans probably have less respect for authority than any other people in the world. The reasons are not hard to find. Many Americans originally came here to avoid tyranny in other countries. We have come to hate and fear authority in many of its forms because of its excesses elsewhere. As a nation, we are strongly committed to an ideology of personal freedom and noninterference by government. We cherish our free press as the guardian of our freedom because it can ferret out tendencies toward the misuse or abuse of personal power before they become dangerous to the public. In government, as in other organizations, we have developed elaborate systems of checks and balances of divisions of power which make it difficult for any one person or group to abuse power. In government, power is divided three ways —among the executive, the legislative, and the judicial branches. In business it is divided among management, labor, and owners, and in the university, among trustees, administration, and students. Many of these organizations also have a system for rotating leadership to make sure that no one acquires enough power over time to be able to misuse it. A Martian observer might conclude that as a nation we are excessively, almost obsessively, worried about the abuse of power.

It is incredible that any leadership at all can be exercised under such conditions. Consider the situation from the point of view of a would-be leader. He knows that if he takes too much initiative, or perhaps even if he does not, he is very likely to be severely attacked by some subgroup as a malicious, power hungry status-seeker. If he is in any way a public figure, he may be viciously attacked for any misstep or chancy episode in his past life. Even though the majority of the people are satisfied with his leadership, a small vociferous minority can make his life unpleasant and at times unbearable. Furthermore, he knows that he will not be the only leader trying to formulate group goals. If he is a congressman, he has to work not only with his fellow congressmen, but also with representatives of independent sources of power in the executive branch and the governmental bureaucracy. If he is a college president, he has to cope with the relatively independent power of his trustees, the faculty and the student body. If he is a business manager, he must share power with labor leaders. In addition, he knows that his tenure of office is likely to be short. Since it is doubtful that he will ever be able to exert true leadership, there seems little purpose in preparing for it. Logically, then, he should spend his time preparing for what he will do before and after his short tenure in office.

Under these conditions why would any promising young man aspire to be a leader? He begins by doubting his motives and ends by concluding that even if he believes his motives to be altruistic, the game is scarcely worth the candle. In other words, the anti-leadership vaccine, which John Gardner speaks of, is partly supplied by the negative face that power wears in our society and the extraordinary lengths to which we have gone to protect ourselves against misused power. It is much safer to pursue a career as a professional adviser, assured some continuity of service and some freedom from public attack—because, after all, one is not responsible for decisions—and some certainty that one's motives are *good*, and that power conflicts have to be settled by someone else.

How can immunity against the anti-leadership vaccine be strengthened? Some immunity surely needs to be built up if our society is not to flounder because of a lack of socialized leadership. Personally, I would not concoct a remedy which is one part changes in the system, one part rehabilitation of the positive face of power, and one part adult education. Let me explain each ingredient in turn. I feel least confident in speaking about the first one, because I am neither a political scientist, a management expert, nor a revolutionary. Yet as a psychologist, I do feel that America's concern about the possible misuse of power verges at times on a neurotic obsession. To control the abuses of power, is it really necessary to divide authority so extensively and to give such free license to anyone to attack a leader in any way he likes? Doesn't this make the leadership role so difficult and unrewarding that it ends up appealing only to cynics? Who in his right mind would want the job of college president under most operating conditions today? A president has great responsibility—for raising money, for setting goals of the institution that faculty, students, and trustees can share, for student discipline, and for appointment of a distinguished faculty. Yet often he has only a very shaky authority with which to execute these responsibilities. The authority which he has he must share with the faculty (many of whom he cannot remove no matter how violently they disagree with the goals set for the university), with the trustees, and with students who speak with one voice one year and quite a different one two years later. I am not now trying to defend an ineffective college president. I am simply trying to point out that our social system makes his role an extraordinarily difficult one. Other democratic nations, Britain for example, have not found it necessary to go to such extremes to protect their liberty against possible encroachment by power-hungry leaders. Some structural reform of the American system definitely seems called for. It is beyond the scope of this paper to say what it might be. The possibilities range all the way from a less structured system in which all organizations are conceived as temporary,[19] to a system in which leaders are given more authority or offered greater protection from irresponsible attack. Surely the problem deserves serious attention. If we want better leaders, we will have to find ways of making the conditions under which they work less frustrating.

The second ingredient in my remedy for the anti-leadership vaccine is rehabilitation of the positive face of power. This paper has been an effort in that direction. Its major thesis is that many people, including both social scientists and potential leaders, have consistently misunderstood or misperceived the way in which effective social leadership takes place. They have confused it regularly, we have pointed out, with the more primitive exercise of personal power. The error is perpetuated by people who speak of leaders as "making decisions." Such a statement only serves to obscure the true process by which decisions should be taken. It suggests that the leader is making a decision arbitrarily without consulting anyone, exercising his power or authority for his own ends.

---

[19] Warren G. Bennis and Philip E. Slater, *The Temporary Society* (New York: Harper & Row, Publishers, 1968).

It is really more proper to think of an effective leader as an educator. The relationship between leading and educating is much more obvious in Latin than it is in English. In fact the word *educate* comes from the Latin *educare* meaning to *lead out*. An effective leader is an educator. One leads people by helping to set their goals, by communicating them widely throughout the group, by taking initiative in formulating means of achieving the goals, and finally, by inspiring the members of the group to feel strong enough to work hard for those goals. Such an image of the exercise of power and influence in a leadership role should not frighten anybody and should convince more people that power exercised in this way is not only not dangerous, but is of the greatest possible use to society.

My experience in training businessmen in India has led me to propose the third ingredient in my formula for producing better ideas—namely, psychological education for adults. What impressed me greatly was the apparent ease with which adults can be changed by the methods we used. The dominant view in American psychology today is still that basic personality structure is laid down very early in life and is very hard to change later on. Whether the psychologist is a Freudian or a learning theorist, he believes that early experiences are critical and shape everything a person can learn, feel, and want throughout his entire life span. As a consequence, many educators have come to be rather pessimistic about what can be done for the poor, the black, or the dispossessed who have undergone damaging experiences early in life. Such traumatized individuals, they argue, have developed non-adaptive personality structures that are difficult, if not impossible, to change later in life. Yet our experience with the effectiveness of short term training courses in achievement motivation for adult businessmen in India and elsewhere does not support this view. I have seen men change, many of them quite dramatically, after only a five-day exposure to our specialized techniques of psychological instruction. They changed the way they thought, the way they talked, and the way they spent their time. The message is clear: adults can be changed, often with a relatively short exposure to specialized techniques of psychological education. The implication for the present discussion is obvious. If it is true, as John Gardner argues, that many young men have learned from their professors that the professional role is preferable to the leadership role, then psychological education offers society a method of changing their views and self-conceptions when they are faced with leadership opportunities. The type of psychological education needed will of course differ somewhat from the more simple emphasis on achievement motivation. More emphasis will have to be given to the means of managing motivation in others. More explanations will have to be given of the positive face of leadership as an educational enterprise, and will have to provide participants with a better idea of how to be effective leaders. These alterations are quite feasible; in fact they have been tried.

Repeatedly we have discovered that leaders are not so much born as made. We have worked in places where most people feel there is not much leadership potential—specifically, among the poor and dispossessed. Yet we have found over and over again that even among people who have never thought of themselves as leaders or attempted to have influence in any way, real leadership performance can be elicited by specialized techniques of psychological education. We need not be as pessimistic as is usual about possibilities for change in adults. *Real leaders* have been developed in such disadvantaged locations as the Dehnarva peninsula of the United States, the black business community of Washington, D.C., and the relatively stagnant small cities of India. Thus I can end on an optimistic note. Even if the leadership role today is becoming more and more difficult, and even if people are tending to avoid it for a variety of reasons, advances in scientific psychological techniques have come at least partly to the rescue by providing society with new techniques for developing the socialized and effective leaders that will be needed for the prosperity and peace of the world of tomorrow.

Section V

Organizational Design

Cases

1 | Higgins Equipment Company (B)

In early 1960, the president of the Higgins Equipment Company, John Howard, confided to researchers that he was distressed by company personality problems and by their effects on his organization. Of major recent concern had been the director of engineering's behavior and its effect on relations between the two sections of the engineering department and between both of them and sales and production. The only solution to this problem, the president explained, was to ask Haverstick, the engineering director, to leave, a resolution made all the more difficult by virtue of the man's having been with Higgins for only a year. President Howard said:

> Personalities of Haverstick's type, this conflict type, bother one personally. I dislike strife, and I'm always trying to smooth it out. Now Stephen Spencer, the man we have chosen as Haverstick's successor, is peace loving. He's the opposite to what Haverstick was. I'm sure output could be increased by 5 to 10 percent with better cooperation. Haverstick was arrogant and too young. He was trying to tell people in other departments how to run their affairs without having a clean house himself. I find so far that I can turn to Steve who is very cooperative and very able. I think we'll be able to give him a bonus this year.

About a year later, just as the researchers were concluding their study, Steve Spencer was also discharged. Steve, it was said, "lacked qualifications." Sales and production had been upset by what they saw as a "lack of direction" in engineering. R&D, a subdivision of engineering, felt it was not getting proper technical assistance. New product developments continued to fall behind schedule, while development and expected product costs proved unpredictable.

COMPANY HISTORY

The Higgins Equipment Company manufactured a line of electrical testing and radio equipment for industrial and scientific customers. While the vast majority of dollar sales were composed of standard, assembly-line products, an increasing number of orders called for unique specifications, from a particular color of paint to an entirely untried basic design. Historically, the company had passed through three growth stages. Between 1917 and 1927 occurred the "production phase" in which the founder successfully constructed his own prototypes, personally supervised production, and arranged for sale of his products. The period 1927 to 1947 saw an accelerating emphasis on sales. Finally, 1947 to 1960 was an era of explosive growth. R&D became the spearhead of expansion. It was shortly before this last period that Howard became president.

DEPARTMENT HEADS

The organization chart (see Exhibit 1) shows Stephen Spencer to be both head of the entire engineering department and of the staff section, engineering services. Engineering services was the result of the growth of auxiliary services which accompanied the enlargement of R&D

EXHIBIT 1
Organization Chart—1960

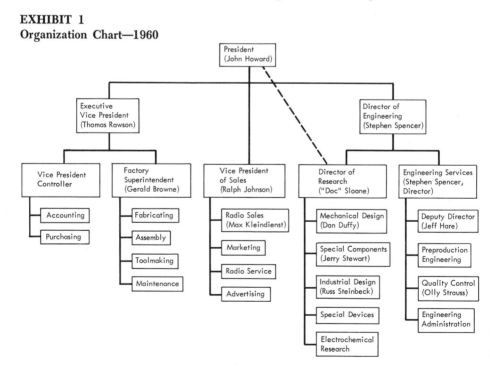

staff and activities. Originally all of these services had been performed by R&D men or by their personal assistants. In effect, there had never been a decision to establish an engineering services section. It had simply emerged as R&D men freed themselves of what they considered to be details.

The sales department was headed by Ralph Johnson, a vice president and heir apparent to the presidency of the company upon Howard's retirement which was scheduled for 1963. Sales administration problems had been greatly compounded by the addition of the radio line, which required new demands of distribution, sales personnel with entirely new technical and sales skills and, thus, actual sales organization. Growth of the department had never quite caught up with the rapidity of expansion which entry into the radio field brought about.

The production department was headed by Gerald Browne, who had the title of factory superintendent. While sales and engineering both reported directly to the president, the production and control departments reported to the executive vice president, Thomas Rawson. Because Rawson was relatively inexperienced in both of these areas and because of the dynamic personality of Howard, the production and control departments were not as forcefully represented in top-management deliberations as were sales and engineering. The production department was particularly sensitive about this imbalance, despite its deep affection for Rawson.

See Exhibit 2 for personal background data on the central figures in this case.

ROGER SLOANE (DOC)

In spite of occasional and sometimes frequent friction between department and subdepartment heads, there was one man who never became involved in these disputes. "Doc" Sloane, head of R&D, enjoyed universal admiration among Higgins's employees and officers. "Of course, everyone loves Doc," explained the president. "If you took a vote, I know he'd be the most popular man in the company." The president's interest in Doc's work had personal overtones. He explained, "I started out in-development work before devoting myself to sales. I like to think I can still contribute in both arenas. (The researchers noticed that the president's name plate hung on a cubicle door in the R&D department.) "I have always taken pride in the immaculate housing of our equipment and in its high quality, but why is there so much friction in getting our designs into production? A designer I trust asked me this the other day. 'Why should we work so hard when they deliberately foul things up?' We've got good men in R&D but something happens between their efforts and the end product to create problems for us."

EXHIBIT 2

Jeff Hare—deputy director of engineering services, 34 years old, bachelor's degree in engineering, brought to Higgins in 1960 by Stephen Spencer as his assistant. The deputy's job, as such, had not previously existed, although Hare took on some duties previously performed by a newly retired member of the department. Previously worked as engineering assistant in an engineering graduate school. Then had 11 years experience with Spencer's previous employer as junior and senior development engineer.

Preproduction engineer, 39 years old, technical high school graduate, joined Higgins in 1951. Experienced senior mechanical draftsman—designer and technician. Assumed the newly created post of preproduction engineer in 1954, supervising two engineering school trainees and working closely with the drafting department in fitting into a metal package the separate electronic and mechanical units of Higgins's products.

Olly Strauss—quality control, 38 years old, high school graduate, joined Higgins in 1949 and worked for eight years on final assembly and testing of equipment before taking over the newly integrated quality control operation. Previous work as a technician in a large engineering school.

Engineering administrator, 34 years old, undergraduate degree in business administration, joined Higgins in 1955. Experience in engineering scheduling and budgets. First man to fill the office of engineering administrator. With two clerks and a secretary he assembled the data necessary to develop time schedules and cost estimates for development projects. Administered these aspects of projects in progress.

Drafting foreman, 44 years old, technical high school graduate, in charge of fifteen draftsmen, many capable of mechanical design and electronic detail drafting. Many years experience as senior designer and section manager in drafting department of a large electronics firm.

Technician pool foreman, 36 years old, with Higgins for 17 years, 10 as assembler and assistant foreman in production, 7 as technician and pool manager in engineering. Administered affairs of and participated in working supervision of 50 technicians working as R&D assistants, pilot-run assemblers, and special devices production force (the latter section run by R&D engineers for the production of nonstandard orders).

Document section manager, 43 years old, high school graduate, long experience as production and engineering clerk and section supervisor. Joined Higgins in 1956 as engineering change-order clerk. Promoted in 1958 to manage a ten-man group responsible for collecting data for and publishing parts list, blueprints, change orders, and the other large volumes of paper which passed between R&D and production.

Technical writing supervisor, 40 years old, liberal arts graduate, many years experience as technical writer and supervisor. Came to Higgins in 1954 as supervisor of 12 men and women who wrote and illustrated instructional and promotional material for Higgins's products.

Librarian, 50 years old with a great deal of experience in public and school libraries, more recently in industrial libraries. Within a budget, he subscribed to technical journals, purchased books, and collected public data upon the request of R&D personnel.

Doc always appeared unhurried, contemplative, and candid in his approach to people and problems. His manner of dress and appearance gave the impression of a janitor rather than the most highly educated and renowned electronic designer at Higgins. He described his feelings about his job as follows: "We are a long way from being a research group in the usual sense of the word. There is no kidding ourselves we are anything but a bunch of Rube Goldbergs. But that is where the biggest kick comes from—solving development problems, dreaming up new ways to do things. That's why I so look forward to the special contracts we get involved in. We accept them not for the revenue they represent but for the subsidized basic development work for standard products which they let us do. I like administration the least. The most important thing in the relationships between people is mutual respect, not organizational procedures. Anyway, administrative work takes away from development time." Doc felt that production was resistant. "There are power interests in production which resist change. But you know I'm not a fighting guy. I suppose if I were I might go in there and push my weight around a little. In my view the company's future rests squarely on development engineering. Either we've got it there or we haven't. This is John Howard's conception, too."

It was Doc's suggestion in 1954 that the company reenter the radio field, which it had briefly been in during World War II, as well as maintain its position in the test equipment market. This proved a highly profitable venture, both in terms of sales and in terms of technical challenge. "Although," Doc said ruefully, "it took me further from my own bench."

R&D UNDER DOC SLOANE

The researchers found evidence to indicate that R&D had high morale and the capacity to accomplish among its interdependent subunits tasks free from the overlay of personal resentment and political intrigue. There seemed to be a close complementarity between the goals of this department and overall company goals. Central values expressed by members included personal learning, development, and independence. They also felt proud of personal contacts with technically oriented customers, which became increasingly necessary as Higgins's products became more technically specialized and sophisticated. Doc, himself, worked as a part-time sales engineer, consulting with customers.

Sociometric data[1] indicated that the R&D section consisted of three major social groups. These groupings correlated well with measures of individual competence and to some extent with education, experience, and age. The researchers called these three groups the "scientists," the "would-be scientists," and the "youngsters." Below is a schematic presentation of what the researchers interpreted from their observations and interviews each group was giving to and receiving from each of the others.

---

[1] Elicited by questions concerning friendship choices and through observations of work and nonwork interactions.

ENGINEERING SERVICES UNDER STEVE SPENCER

The other section of the engineering department, engineering services, was supposed to provide ancillary services to R&D and to conduct liaison between R&D and other Higgins departments. Top management described the functions of engineering services as, "establishing and maintaining cooperation with other departments, providing service to development engineers, and freeing more valuable men (R&D designers) from essential activities which are diversions from and beneath their

EXHIBIT 3

A. Prescribed Interaction-Influence Patterns*

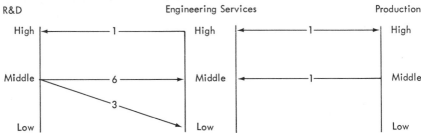

B. Observed Interaction-Influence Patterns†

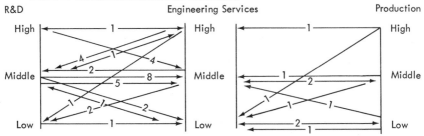

* As described by top management, in response to the question, "Who is supposed to communicate with whom and whose opinion, if either, should dominate?" The vertical lines represent an array of department members, broken into three groups according to job rank, as indicated by title, pay, and responsibilities. Arrows indicate interacting pairs of men. Numbers affixed to arrows represent the number of pairs in interaction. Double-ended arrows indicate a mutual influence, while single-ended arrows depict one-way influence between two men. The interaction recorded in this exhibit refers to personal contact rather than that which may also have occurred through the routine, nonpersonal, interdepartmental flow of paper.

† The researchers developed the chart of observed interaction influence by prolonged observation. Each interaction was recorded and a judgment made concerning the balance of influence between the individuals involved, on the basis of whose point of view tended to dominate most frequently. For example, far more often than not, when Browne was in discussion with Spencer concerning such matters as a production-originated engineering change order, Browne's opinion would carry the day. Or where Spencer and Sloane discussed such things as the budget for a new project, their ideas tended to merge and the decisions emanating from their deliberations tended to reflect the opinions of both men.

main competence." The background and experience of primary engineering services and other key personnel are shown in Exhibit 2.

Sociometric measures revealed that engineering services was not a cohesive group. Many of its members were located in other departments. Its quality control personnel were hardly noticeable in the midst of production's assembly operation. Its technicians, assigned to R&D's development engineers, worked primarily in R&D cubicles or the area devoted to production of special devices. Generally, the remaining engineering services offices were assigned to widespread leftover spaces between elements of R&D.

Among the main functions of engineering services were drafting and provision of technicians from a central pool. Other major functions included: engineering administration, which scheduled and expedited engineering projects; the document section, which compiled parts lists and published engineering orders; preproduction engineering, composed of several technicians who pulled together into mechanically compatible packages R&D's individual design components; and finally, quality control, which inspected incoming parts and materials, in-process subassemblies, and finished instruments against predetermined standards.

Researchers compared the interaction patterns *prescribed* (i.e., how people were supposed to behave) for engineering services personnel in their work relationship with R&D and production people with the *actual* patterns of interaction which they observed (see Exhibit 3).

Steve Spencer, when asked about his job, gave the following description:

> My role in the company has never really been defined for me. It is complicated by Doc's unique position. In a nebulous way, he works through me and I through him. But he is not the least bit interested in the routines of administration. My relationship with him and his people is somewhat ambiguous. He is highly regarded in this company, and I have a great deal of affection and respect for him myself. But I can't count on him for any responsibility in scheduling projects, checking budgets, or what have you. In some senses, I'm in charge of R&D and in others I'm not.
>
> My biggest problem is getting acceptance from the people I work with. I've moved slowly rather than risk antagonism. I saw what happened to Haverstick, and I want to avoid that. But although his precipitate action had won over a few of the younger R&D men, he certainly didn't have the department's backing. Of course, it was the resentment of other departments which eventually caused his discharge. People have been slow accepting me here. There's nothing really overt, but I get a negative reaction to my ideas.
>
> Browne [production head] is hard to get along with. Before I came and after Haverstick left, there were six months intervening when no

one was really doing any scheduling. No work loads were figured, and unrealistic promises were made about releases. This puts us in an awkward position. We've been scheduling way beyond our capacity to manufacture or engineer.

I wish I could be more involved in the technical side. That's been my training, and it's a lot of fun. But in our setup, the technical side is the least necessary for me to be involved in.

Steve went on to explain that:

Certain people within R&D, for instance Russ Steinbeck, head of the radio electronic design section, understand scheduling well and meet project deadlines, but this is not generally true of the rest of the R&D department, especially the mechanical engineers who won't commit themselves. Most of the complaints come from sales and production department heads because items are going to production before they are fully developed, under pressure from sales to get out the unit, and this snags the whole process. Somehow, engineering services should be able to interview and resolve these complaints, but I haven't made much headway so far.

Salespeople were often observed taking their problems directly to designers, while production frequently threw designs back at R&D, claiming they could not be produced and demanding the prompt attention of particular design engineers. The latter were frequently observed in conference with production supervisors on the assembly floor.

Steve was asked where he sought help:

I should be able to go to Howard, but he's too busy most of the time and he's only really interested in the electrical test equipment line. Howard sees himself as head of engineering but I have to take the initiative. Doc isn't interested in planning, and there are problems the front office just doesn't understand. Jeff Hare [Steve's deputy director] is a big help to me. He's here to help take the load off the development engineers [R&D], but they tend to feel they're losing something when one of us tries to help. They feel it's a reflection on them to have someone take over what they've been doing. They seem to want to carry a project right through the final stages, particularly the replacement boys. On the other hand, production people see themselves as methods and preproduction people and they want to get their hands on the product at an early stage. Consequently, engineering services people are used below their capacity to contribute, and our department is denied functions it should be performing. There's not as much use made of engineering services as there could be.

Steve Spencer's technician foreman added his comments:

Production picks out the engineer who'll be the "bum of the month." They pick on every little detail instead of using their heads and making the minor changes that have to be made. The 15- to 20-year men shouldn't have to prove their ability anymore, but they spend 4 hours defending themselves and 4 hours getting the job done. I have no one to go to when I need help. Steve Spencer is afraid. I'm trying to help him but he can't help me at this time. I'm responsible for 50 people and I've got to support them.

Jeff Hare, whom Steve had brought with him to the company as an assistant, gave another view of the situation:

> I try to get our people in preproduction to take responsibility, but they're not used to it, and people in other departments don't usually see them as best qualified to solve the problem.
> Production always says it is drafting that is making the errors. Well, that isn't fair because all engineering and R&D are involved, not just the last ones to handle the material. But I haven't made much headway in changing that point of view. There's a real barrier for a newcomer here. Gaining people's confidence is hard.

(Hare resigned from Higgins six months after coming to the company, stating, "There just isn't a job for me here.")

Another of Spencer's subordinates gave his view:

> If Doc gets a new product idea you can't argue. But he's too optimistic. He judges what others can do by what he does—but there's only one Doc Sloane. We've had 900 production change orders this year—they changed 2,500 drawings. If I were in Steve's shoes I'd put my foot down on all this new development. I'd look at the reworking we're doing and get production set up the way I wanted it. Haverstick was fired when he was doing a good job. He was getting some system in the company's operations. Of course, it hurt some people. But, there is no denying that Doc is the most important person in the company. What gets overlooked is that Howard is a close second, not just politically but in terms of what he contributes technically and in customer relations.

This subordinate explained that he sometimes went out into the production department but that Browne, the production head, resented this. Men in production said that Haverstick had failed to show respect for old-timers and was always meddling in other departments' business. This was why he had been fired, they contended.

Olly Strauss was in charge of quality control. He commented:

> I am now much more concerned with administration and less with work. It is one of the evils you get into. There is tremendous detail in this job. I listen to everyone's opinion. Everybody is important. There shouldn't be distinctions—distinctions between people. I'm not sure whether Steve has to be a fireball like Haverstick. I think the real question is whether Spencer is getting the job done. I know my job is essential. I want to supply service to the more talented men and give them information so they can do their jobs better.

R&D'S VIEWS OF ENGINEERING SERVICES

Said Dan Duffy of the mechanical design department:

> In olden days I really enjoyed the work—and the people I worked with. But now there's a lot of irritation. I get my satisfaction from a good design and from finding solutions to troublesome problems. But it's not as satisfying as it used to be. I don't like someone breathing down my neck. You can be hurried into jeopardizing the design.

Russ Steinbeck, head of the electronic design section, was another designer with definite views:

> Production engineering is almost nonexistent in this company. Very little is done by the preproduction section in engineering services. Steve Spencer has been trying to get preproduction into the picture, but he won't succeed because you can't start from such an ambiguous position. There have been three directors of engineering in six years. Steve can't hold his own against the others in the company. Haverstick was too aggressive. Perhaps no amount of tact would have succeeded.

Jerry Stewart was head of special components in the R&D department. Like the rest of the department he valued bench work. But he complained of engineering services:

> The services don't do things we want them to do. They tell us what they're going to do. I should probably go to Steve, but I don't get any decisions there. I know I should go through Steve, but this holds things up, so I often go direct.

VIEWS OF THE SALES DEPARTMENT

The researchers talked to representatives of the sales department—first its head, Ralph Johnson. Ralph explained that his reps made promises to customers, only to find the equipment months late in development. He was persistent in trying to get design engineers to conventions so that they could know the customer's point of view. "We shouldn't have to be after the engineers all the time. They should be able to see what problems they create for the company without our telling them." Ralph described himself as "a moderator—a man who settled disputes."

Max Kleindienst was head of radio sales under Johnson. He explained to the researchers that a great number of decisions concerning sales were made by top management. Sales was understaffed, he thought, and had never really been able to get on top of the job.

> We have grown farther and farther away from engineering. The director of engineering does not pass on the information that we give him. We need better relationships with R&D. It is very difficult for us to talk to customers without technical help. We need each other.

The whole of engineering is now too isolated from the outside world. The morale of engineering [services] is very low. They're in a bad spot—they're not well organized.

People don't take much to outsiders here. Much of this is because the expectation is built up by top management that jobs will be filled from the bottom. So it's really tough when an outsider like me comes in.

VIEWS OF THE PRODUCTION DEPARTMENT

The researchers paid a call on the production department and its head, Gerald Browne. Gerry said he believed in having a self-contained department. "There shouldn't be a lot of other people breathing down your neck." Gerry and his lieutenants universally expressed their preference for "getting new products into production, establishing procedures for getting standard products into the line and then spending our time doping out new methods and processes for getting our job done better."

One of Gerry's rules was that "I never talk to the underling of a department head. I always talk to the head himself. I always go down the line." He objected to final quality control (engineering services) being separated from his department. He felt it should be a continuation of assembly. "Olly Strauss's superiors don't understand Olly's problems. He'd rather work for me; he's told me that many times."

Purchasing should also have been under production, according to Gerry. Only a few days before he had thrown his storeroom master key on the boardroom table in front of the president. "Here, I don't want it any more. I've been accused of fouling up inventory control!"

Gerry later explained his feelings about engineering:

> The trouble with engineering is that they are tolerance crazy. They want everything to a millionth of an inch. I'm the only one in the company who's had any experience with actually machining things to a millionth of an inch. We make sure that the things that engineers say on their drawing actually have to be that way and whether they're obtainable from the kind of raw material we buy.

Engineering services "just didn't check drawings properly," Gerry explained. Gerry spent a considerable proportion of his time going over new product drawings, personally returning those which he found to be in error.

> So finally they have to listen to us. Changes have to be made because they didn't listen to us in the first place. Engineering services says we've got to keep our hands off quality control. But, then, something like this happens: Doc comes in here one day, with a sour look on his face, saying there was some burnt wire on the equipment sent to an electronic show. I said, "You just look here. We didn't make that equipment; your technicians did!"

Gerry recounted his pleasure in doings things which engineering had said were impossible. "But I never tell them how we did it. They ought to be as smart as we are out here in production. Of course, the thing that really gets them is that I don't even have a degree."

In the course of their work, the researchers learned that when the men presently in charge of production took control after World War II, they did so as the result of a management turnover occasioned by discovery of illegalities committed by previous production men during the war. Prior to that time, production had controlled purchasing, stock control, and final quality control (where final assembly of products in such cabinets was accomplished). Because of the wartime events, management decided on a check-and-balance system of organization and removed these three departments from production jurisdiction. The new production managers felt they had been unjustly penalized by this reorganization, particularly since they had uncovered the behavior which was detrimental to the company in the first place.

The researchers also talked to Tom Rawson, age 65, executive vice president of the company. Tom had direct responsibility for Higgins's production department.

> There shouldn't really be a dividing of departments among top management in the company. The president should be czar over all. The production boys ask me to do something for them, and I really can't do it. It creates bad feelings between engineering and production—this special attention that they [R&D] get from Howard. But then Howard likes to dabble in design. Browne feels that production is treated like a poor relation.

As the researchers were concluding their fieldwork at the Higgins Equipment Company, they found an opportunity to discuss the engineering department and its problems with the president, John Howard. He reflected on what he termed "the unhappy necessity of letting Steve Spencer go."

> I can't understand why we have such poor luck with engineering heads. The man in there before Haverstick was technically well qualified. He'd been a good designer for us before we promoted him to be the first head of engineering. But he took to drinking heavily, and we had to relieve him of the responsibility. Then Haverstick seemed so promising. They say he is doing well in his new job at the———company. But they operate much differently from the way we do. Then, Steve Spencer—he seemed to have all the qualifications we needed. And he certainly was a gentleman. But he never could get things done. Apparently he couldn't gain the respect of the design boys. So, here we are, looking for a new man. I'm beginning to wonder whether we'll ever find him.

2 | *International Metals Corporation**

In May 1961, Phillip Reisenger was wondering what action he should recommend to the president of International Metals Corporation in light of the internal problems the firm was facing. As part of his responsibilities as the company's personnel officer, Reisenger was in charge of organizational planning. He thought that most of the difficulties with which he was concerned could be traced to an organization change made in 1958 on the recommendation of his predecessor, Paul Wilson. Wilson had been the company's personnel officer until 1959 when he was promoted to the position of vice president of its ore refining operations which were carried on by several foreign subsidiaries.

International Metals Corporation was engaged in an extensive international trade in nonferrous metals, and in the ore concentrates and by-products related to the refining of these metals. Anthony Cola started in the trading business in 1923 on a partnership agreement. In 1925, when his partner sold his interest in the business, Cola incorporated the firm and became its first president. He ran the company almost single handedly during its early years.

It wasn't until the end of World War II that Cola felt able to relinquish some of his influence to a newly developing management team. In 1957 his nephew, Joseph Amante, was named to the presidency. As chairman of the board, however, Cola, who was 68 in 1961, remained active in the firm's day-to-day operations. Both he and his nephew, who was 23 years younger, maintained direct supervision over the company's trading division and also functioned as traders for copper and

* © 1961, by the Board of Trustees of the Leland Stanford Junior University.

zinc, an activity which accounted for about 30 percent of the company's sales in 1960.

Anthony Cola referred to copper and zinc as the most speculative items which the company traded. "Prices on these commodities and profitability," he said, "may vary widely from year to year. Last year, for example, we operated at a net loss on these two items, although in some years they have contributed the bulk of our profits."

A business associate who had known Anthony Cola for many years described him as follows:

> All the success of International Metals can be attributed to one man, Anthony Cola. He has certainly built himself an empire. Of course, now both he and his nephew share in running the company. But it was only after a long period of training as a trader that his nephew was given this responsibility.

Characteristic of companies engaged in international trade, the history of International Metals Corporation was one of wide variations and shifting emphasis. For example, during World War II, when imports of all offshore commodities were taken over by the government, the company cultivated new sources of supply for ore concentrates in Mexico and Canada.

It was the firm's stated policy to shift quickly when a given source of supply was cut off. The firm was constantly seeking new opportunities; when market conditions changed, the scope of its activities likewise changed. It was mainly by seeking out new, profitable commodities in which to trade that the company had shown a rising trend in earnings as well as in sales in its recent years. As Anthony Cola put it,

> As soon as a lot of companies start trading in the same commodity, there is no profit in it for anyone. It seems that competition is quicker than it used to be in moving in on you these days with our modern high speed methods of communication. The commodity that has contributed the bulk of our products over the past three years is a product we call "Crystallium." It is a rare earth whose market we were the first to pioneer. Already a number of competitors have started to move in.
>
> To make a profit in this business, a trader first of all has to have vision. He has to be able to find and recognize new opportunities. Then he also must have a quick mind and must be willing to take risks and speculate.

Cola also pointed out that the firm characteristically operated on narrow margins. "Despite our small margins," he said, "we are able to show substantial earnings relative to our net worth since, in comparison to a manufacturing concern, we are able to operate on a small amount of equity capital." Over its 35 years International Metals grew to where, including its subsidiaries, it employed 400 people and achieved more than $80 million in sales in 1960. Income statements for the years since 1955 are shown in Exhibit 1.

EXHIBIT 1
Income Statements for Years Ending December 31—in Thousands

	1960	1959	1958	1957	1956	1955
Sales	$82,048	$89,282	$62,759	$71,676	$79,981	$71,622
Expenses:						
Cost of sales	$76,310	$83,561	$58,343	$68,951	$77,102	$69,098
Storage & handling expenses	1,653	1,499	1,514	210	226	215
Selling & administrative expenses	2,218	2,194	1,679	1,447	1,450	1,379
Interest expense	689	532	438	434	508	473
	$80,870	$87,786	$61,974	$71,042	$79,286	$71,165
Net income before provision for income taxes	$ 1,178	$ 1,496	$ 785	$ 634	$ 695	$ 457
Provision for U.S. & foreign income taxes	558	741	396	223	345	173
Net income before deduction of minority interest	$ 620	$ 755	$ 389	$ 411	$ 350	$ 284
Minority interest in income of subsidiaries	24	93	80	8	7	6
Net income for year	$ 596	$ 662	$ 309	$ 403	$ 343	$ 278
Equity in income of affiliated companies	58	47				
Net income & increase in equity	$ 654	$ 709				

Source: Company financial statements.

OPERATIONS

By 1961, the company was represented by a branch office in San Francisco and by offices of subsidiary or affiliated trading companies located in Sydney, La Paz, London, Tokyo, and Osaka. The Sydney and La Paz offices were designated as buying offices. The San Francisco branch and the subsidiaries in England and Japan were manned by traders whose function it was to buy and sell for the parent company in the commodity market in their respective regions. Trading between each of these outlying offices was coordinated by the traders in the company's central headquarters in New York.

The two essential components of the company's business were its trading and traffic functions. Trading functions consisted of buying, selling, hedging, and negotiating contract terms. Traffic functions consisted of scheduling, booking space, chartering, and negotiating freight rates. Profits were realized by differentials existing between costs (purchasing, handling, storing, freighting, and financing) and market prices in the country to which a commodity was exported. These profits could be augmented by taking advantage of both fluctuating prices in the commodity markets and fluctuating prices in the shipping market. Therefore, the company occasionally speculated in the shipping market just as it did in the markets for the commodities it traded. Like his trading counterpart, a traffic man, for example, could "book" steamship space ahead of the firm's shipping requirements if he could thereby obtain a favorable rate. Often all the profits in a transaction were realized through the company's ability to obtain a favorable freight rate.

Each trade was composed of a purchase and a sale on the part of the trader. However, he did not necessarily have to make his purchase before his sale. If market conditions warranted it, he might sell first and then make his purchase. To buy, the trader kept in touch with the market conditions near his sources of supply, attempting to take advantage of cyclical variations so as to make his purchases at a favorable price. In selling his commodity, the trader would wire one or more of the firm's overseas sales offices stating the quantity he wanted to sell, the time at which he wanted to sell it and the sales price, including profit. Usually the overseas office was given some price leeway with which to negotiate with potential buyers. However, a price was stipulated below which he could not go. This minimum was based on the price which the trader had to pay for the commodity; the transportation charges; direct selling expenses, such as labor, documenting, and insurance; financing charges; and other general overhead expenses which would be applied to the sale.

Upon receipt of an offer to sell, the office receiving the offer had to return a reply reaching New York before the opening of business the following day. Otherwise the offer was automatically rescinded. Sometimes it took several exchanges of cablegrams before a sale was negotiated In cultivating a market for a new (to the firm) commodity, it took about one month to send samples, make a price offering, receive a counter offer, and negotiate final terms on a sale. On established commodities, however, negotiations were normally completed in two hours or less.

When the sale had been negotiated, the company's traffic personnel took over. Generally, one month ahead of the shipping dates, purchases were consolidated against sales since, in a given period, many individual purchases and sales were made. When shipping was tight, consolidation had to be accomplished as much as two months ahead of time. The consolidation completed, freight space was arranged for, or confirmed through a ship broker at the port. Ship brokers or steamship agents had a similar relationship to the steamship companies as manufacturers' representatives had to manufacturing concerns. They acted as independent sales agents for the steamship lines and were usually paid a commission of 1¼ percent of the freight by the steamship company to which they directed a given shipment. Finally, shipping instructions were sent to the suppliers instructing them on the quantities to ship and the date the commodity had to arrive at the port. A copy of the shipping instructions was also sent to a freight forwarder at the port of embarkation.

Generally, the company took physical possession of the commodity when the seller had loaded it on transportation destined for the port, the seller having paid the freight and insurance required for transit to the port. Upon arrival at the port, International Metals paid for all expenses incurred in storing and handling the commodity. The company's usual terms with a buyer were CIF, meaning that cost, insurance, and freight to the port of destination were included in the selling price. The buyer took physical possession of the commodity when it had been loaded on a vessel at the port of embarkation.

Representing the company's interests at the port of embarkation was a freight forwarder who was paid a commission by the company for each loading. His function was to prepare the bills of lading and the weight and quality certificates covering the shipment, and to see that the proper quantity of material was loaded on the vessel. The commission he was paid varied in accordance with the amount of work involved in a given loading. A freight forwarder depended on many shippers for his income. It was unusual for a firm the size of International Metals to have forwarders in its own employ since it shipped intermittently from many different ports.

The bills of lading, weight, and quality certificates were collected as soon as possible by International Metals' traffic personnel and were attached to sales invoices and drafts drawn on the buyer or his bank. These documents were then turned over to the treasury department for deposit or discount at the company's bank.

When the commodity reached its port of destination, the buyer or his agent checked the shipment. International Metals also paid a commission to a surveyor at this port to represent its interests when the shipment was checked. If the buyer had any claims against the company, they were first processed by traffic personnel to check for errors before being sent to the trader of the commodity involved for his approval or denial of the claim. If approved, the claim was sent to the comptroller's department for payment. If the trader denied the claim he would try to negotiate a settlement, failing which, the matter was taken to a court of arbitration as provided in the sales contract. In this case, the trader was responsible for drafting the arbitration briefs with the assistance of legal counsel. According to one of the company's traders, these claims arose quite frequently, but were usually settled out of court. Less than one in one hundred claims would go to arbitration.

INITIAL ORGANIZATION

Prior to the 1958 realignment in the company structure, the trading and traffic functions were organized under separate departments. Both of these departments were structured along roughly parallel lines according to commodity groupings. For example, the trader for titanium and magnesium had his counterpart in the traffic department who specialized in transporting these commodities. The two departments differed in one respect. There was an intermediary between the traffic personnel and the president, while each trader reported directly to the president and the chairman of the board. In addition to these two departments which were considered line elements, personnel, treasury, and control staff de-

EXHIBIT 2
Organization Chart, April 1958

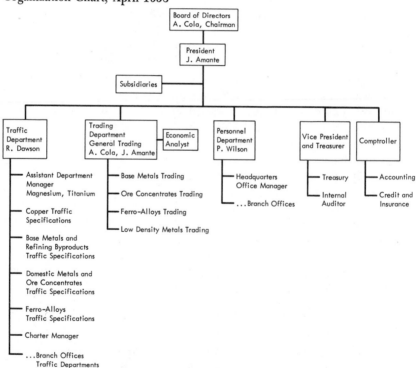

partments filled out the organization. Exhibit 2 shows the firm's organization chart immediately prior to the change.

The trading department had not always been organized by commodity groupings. This change had been made in 1954 at the suggestion of

Paul Wilson, the personnel officer, in anticipation of the change he was to propose in 1958. Previously the traffic department had been organized, as Wilson put it, "loosely," into two sections. The department manager headed a foreign traffic section while his assistant was in charge of a domestic traffic section. There was also a "loose" assignment of commodities to each traffic specialist. According to Wilson, the disadvantage he saw in this was that to complete a trading transaction, it was sometimes necessary for work and information to flow through each of the two traffic sections, thereby causing delays. In 1954 a more rigid assignment of commodities to each traffic specialist was made. In addition, most specialists were assigned the handling of both the foreign and the domestic aspects of transporting their respective commodities. Wilson said, however, that because of the different workloads involved for various commodities, it was impossible for the traffic department to parallel exactly the organization of the trading department.

CONSIDERATIONS LEADING TO A FURTHER CHANGE

In April, 1958, Wilson made the proposal that the company further realign its organization by breaking down the trading department into separate trading sections, each centered around commodity groupings, and each staffed by a trader, a traffic specialist, and the secretarial personnel required to handle the necessary paper work. Wilson cited four reasons for his proposal.

First, it was designed to give each trader direct control over the freighting of his goods. Both Wilson and the president recognized this control as being very important since many trading opportunities were dependent upon freight considerations. It was also designed to provide direct communications between the trader and the traffic man who specialized in arranging transportation of his commodities and to give the trader a better chance to insure that his transactions were executed as contemplated. Under the existing arrangement, when a trader needed information on shipping, he had to call or walk over to the traffic department. Because of the interruption and demand on the trader's time which this caused, he often relied upon his own familiarity with the transportation market rather than contacting the traffic specialist. In many cases, this resulted in errors in judgment on the trader's part in deciding the feasibility of a given trade. By improving communications, the change would also promote a better understanding and cooperation between trading and traffic personnel.

The second purpose behind the proposal was to shift administrative responsibility for trading and traffic detail to the trading section managers. This would provide a direct line of authority in the handling of all products, since it placed responsibility for all the operations necessary to complete a trade under each trader. With the trading and traffic operations divided into separate functional departments, it was difficult to pinpoint responsibility when problems arose. Moreover, there was a tendency for delays to creep into the system because only a few people in the traffic department were entrusted with making decisions of any importance. With many traffic personnel passing information upward for decision in their department, it was easy for bottlenecks to develop. Fast action in settling on the terms of a trade was of primary importance since, at the most, a trader had eight hours in which to reply to an offer or counteroffer. With a traffic specialist assigned to him, a trader could readily obtain the necessary traffic information. In addition, with his own department, each trader could organize and distribute his work in accordance with the requirement of the market in which he traded.

A third reason, correlative to the second, was to enable the company's traffic manager to devote more of his time to negotiating more favorable freight rates, setting traffic policy, investigating new ideas aimed at improvement of services or cutting of costs, analyzing and solving major traffic problems as they occur, and training all departments in better traffic methods. As a line manager, the pressure of day to day operations had left the traffic manager with little time for policy formulation and planning functions.

The fourth objective of the change was to give the company the opportunity to train its own traders. Typically it took 5 to 10 years to train a trader. The chairman of the board and the president believed that this period of apprenticeship was necessary in order to cultivate the "intuitive feel" for trading which they felt was an essential attribute of a successful trader. Since the company did not have productive positions which would also serve as training positions in its existing organization, it left an inordinate portion of the trading burden on the president and on the chairman of the board. With a traffic specialist or an assistant traffic specialist assigned to a trader, it would be possible to train a prospective trader by having him work in the traffic positions throughout the company. He would therefore obtain valuable contact with the various trading elements while he performed productive work in the traffic function. The traffic job typically was more clerical than a trading position, and hence it took a shorter period to train a man as a traffic specialist. In recruiting men to handle traffic jobs, the company looked for those having bachelor's degrees in transportation. Prospective traders, on the other hand, were recruited from men with bachelor's or master's degrees in either economics or international trade. However, background alone would not guarantee success in trading. In the experience of the company's two chief executives, it took a unique set of personal characteristics and a long period of training to develop the necessary "feel" for trading. Even after a trader had been with the company for more than 10 years, Joseph Amante and Anthony Cola kept close contact with his day to day trading decisions. They read all cablegrams sent from the company. Most of the traders also checked with them before making decisions which committed large amounts of funds or to which they felt the two chief executives might object for any reason. Each trader operated within credit lines and terms granted to his commodities by the president. To step outside of these limits required special permission from Joseph Amante.

EFFECTS OF THE CHANGE

After considering Wilson's proposal, Amante, with Cola's consent, decided to put the plan into effect in September 1958. Besides reassigning traffic specialists to the various traders, this involved a reapportionment of the main office building so that each trader had a section of the office which would accommodate the trader and the traffic specialists and clerks assigned to him. The change was first announced through a series of meetings with the traders and the traffic manager. After the physical move was made, a memorandum was circulated to all employees in which Wilson explained his reasons for the realignment and described the new reporting relationships and responsibilities of all employees who were affected by the change. Departmental responsibilities and job descriptions of the key people affected by the change as they appeared in this memorandum are shown in the Appendix. The firm's 1961 organization structure as it evolved after the change is shown in Exhibit 3.

In the series of personnel reassignments and promotions which followed the structural change in organization, Wilson was promoted to the new position of the company's director of manufacturing subsidiaries. He was subsequently given the title of vice president in this position. As director of manufacturing, he acted as the contact man in the parent company to whom the general manager of each of the company's foreign ore refining subsidiaries reported. Previously, they had reported directly to the president. This post was designed to relieve the already great burden on the president's time. Wilson also initiated studies concerning the possibility of adding new manufacturing concerns to the company.

Several of the company's traders said that Wilson's promotion had come as quite a surprise to them. "Until he was promoted," one said, "the only path of advancement to top level management was through trading. Then we found that there was more importance attached to our overseas manufacturing and to a man with an engineering degree." Wilson had received a degree in metallurgy from a well known midwestern college. He went on to receive a master's degree in business at the same school before joining International Metals.

EXHIBIT 3
Organization Chart, May 1961

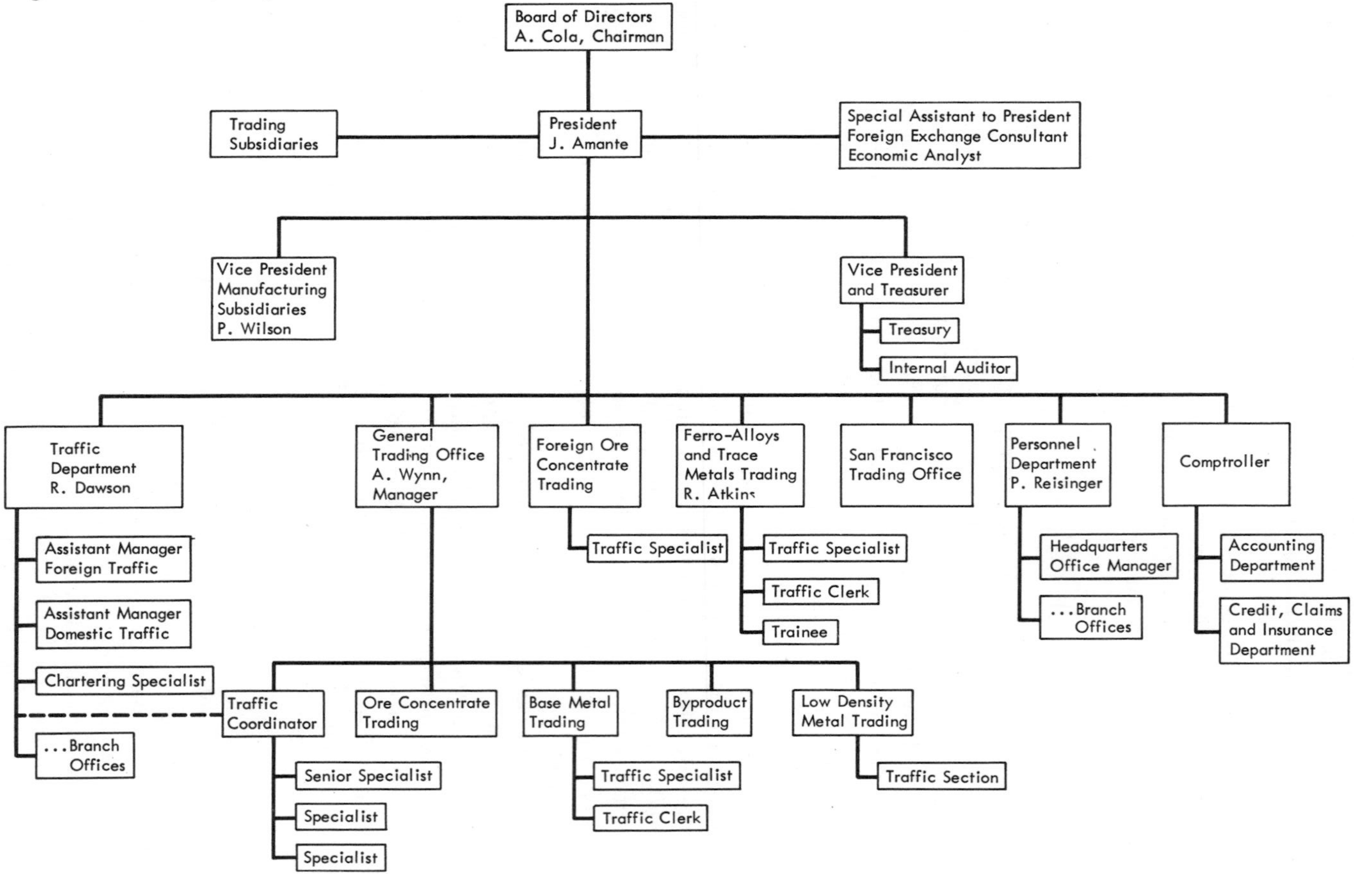

Succeeding Wilson as personnel manager was Phillip Reisenger. Reisenger had an educational background similar to Wilson's. While studying for his business degree, Reisenger also did some part time teaching in the areas of statistics and basic business organization. Toward the end of this program, Reisenger met Wilson, who interested him in International Metals and was instrumental in getting him a job with the company. Reisenger was hired in June 1957, as a management trainee, and thereupon was assigned several research projects under Wilson. Later he served for three months as a traffic trainee in one of the trading departments. In mid-1959 he was named as Wilson's assistant, and a year later took over the full responsibilities associated with the position of personnel officer.

When Reisenger took over his new job as personnel officer in 1959 there was still some confusion evident concerning the change. At the same time that the change had been put into effect, responsibility for billing domestic traffic was given to the traffic specialists. This, in effect, heaped more detail work on the traffic specialists and, according to Wilson, "May have caused some grievances on the part of the traffic specialists which were attributed to the change in organization rather than to the new assignment of duties."

It was not until a year later that Reisenger began to suspect that some of the problems with which he was concerned might be chronic, long term situations resulting from the change, rather than the transitory type which would be eliminated once people had become accustomed to the new arrangements.

The first problem arose when Ralph Dawson, the traffic manager, began to complain to Reisenger that his control over traffic operations had been considerably reduced as a result of the change. He maintained that it had become increasingly difficult for him to obtain up-to-date information on the traffic operations of the various trading departments. Even though he continued to review each shipping order made, he felt that he had lost contact with day to day traffic operations. Another weakness he pointed to was that he was no longer able to consolidate shipments of different commodities effectively. Under the old organizational arrangement, he said, he had been able to obtain significant freight savings by grouping shipments of various commodities so as to take up a more significant portion of a given ship's capacity.

After hearing Dawson voice his dissatisfaction with his new role in the company on several occasions, Reisenger decided to bring the matter to the attention of the president. When he did so, Amante asked, "Why doesn't Dawson come directly to me if he has a complaint? What has he done to try to correct the situation?" Reisenger concluded that Dawson had probably accepted the change as being irrefutable and something he had to live with in spite of his protests. During the conversation, Amante expressed the opinion that Dawson had lost nothing as a result of the change. As traffic manager he still had full responsibility for the company's traffic operations. The only thing that had changed was that each traffic specialist had been put in charge of all of the details necessary to complete the transportation phase of any trade in his assigned area. Since he reported to a man less familiar with the transportation function than he, this meant that each traffic specialist had to assume more responsibility than had been required under the previous organization structure. On the other hand, this meant that Dawson did not have to get involved in operating details but could devote more time toward planning and traffic policy formulation. It was Reisenger's opinion, however, that Dawson had continued to concern himself with following all the detailed phases of the traffic operation.

At one meeting in the president's office, the subject of Dawson's discontent with his role under the new arrangement came up when Wilson was present. Wilson made the suggestion that Dawson be moved over as head of all trading departments, thereby relieving the president from day to day trading responsibilities and allowing him to devote all of his time to "planning and controlling" the company's operations. Amante's reply to this suggestion was, "I don't think it will work. I don't think he is temperamentally suited to being a trader. He is far better qualified to supervise traffic work than trading. His weakness is in organizing his department, and he should be encouraged to spend less time on detail and more time on the broader aspect of his work, including organization."

Dawson, who was 53 in 1961, had joined the company in 1947 as traffic manager, with a background of long experience in the transportation field. His previous working experience had been in various jobs leading to his promotion to department manager for an east coast steamship company.

Another difficulty which Mr. Reisenger observed was that, in his opinion, even though the traders tended to be very independent people, most of them did not adequately fulfill their new role as department managers. This problem directly affected Reisenger's responsibilities as personnel manager, especially in the areas of personnel evaluation, development, and promotion. Some of the firm's traders, he observed, did not concern themselves with training their people or with how well they were doing. Under the previous organization, the traders were located in one room supported only by a secretarial pool. Therefore, they had no personnel responsibilities. Now with separate trading departments, each trader was required to make recommendations for promotion of their people and to pass out pay raises and promotions. Even though they were required to fill out a rating sheet on their people at least once a year, Reisenger felt that most traders did only a superficial job in supplying information which was called for on these forms.

Roger Atkins was in Reisenger's opinion the only trader, aside from the president, who adequately carried out his managerial responsibilities. But even he had indicated to Reisenger that personnel problems had now become a major concern, whereas previously he had only to concern himself with searching for trading opportunities. Atkins, who was 40, was considered by Reisenger to be the company's most enterprising trader. Vitally interested in his work, he often carried on trading in the evenings, initiating cablegrams from his home. He was constantly investigating new ideas on ways to operate his department, new methods of predicting trends in his markets, and new products in which to trade.

Some of Atkins' ideas took hold throughout the company. For example, on reading a *Fortune* article describing Consolidated Food Company's success with the profit center concept,[1] he proposed that International Metals try this out with its foreign subsidiaries. The company adopted this idea in late 1960 with its London subsidiary. He said that the change had a tremendous effect in boosting the morale of the traders in this subsidiary and improved his own working relationship with these traders. If the central office did not equal the best available terms, the subsidiary was authorized to trade outside the company. This also put the trader in the home office on his mettle in always trying to be able to offer the best terms.

Atkins' department had achieved the largest growth in sales volume of any department over the years since 1958. He said the president commented on this by saying, "OK, you've shown us that you can obtain sales volume, now see what you can do about profits." Atkins said that for 1961 he set for himself a goal of a profit of $200,000. This objective made him look critically at each of the commodities he was trading in terms of its contribution toward achieving it. He did this by comparing the gross margin of each potential trade with the direct expenses involved in making the trade, plus the general overhead which was allocated to his department. As a long standing company policy, general overhead was allocated on the basis of the dollar sales generated by each trader. Atkins had broken down all of his costs to a per pound basis so he could quickly determine the break-even point and profitability of any transaction. He was constantly searching for new profitable commodities in which to trade to replace those whose profit margins had eroded. Despite his concern with keeping his costs down, he had asked Reisenger several times in the past month to hire him an additional man. He already had the main office's only trader trainee in his department. A trainee from the London office was scheduled for training in

---

[1] C. Reiser, "Consolidated Foods: All over the Lot," *Fortune* (June 1960), p. 139.

his department starting in August 1961. Atkins said he had no difficulty in finding work for the people assigned to him.

At lunch one day, Reisenger questioned Atkins about his feelings about the change in organization. The following conversation ensued:

REISENGER: Roger, I'm trying to get an idea of how various people react to the new way we're organized. What do you think of our new set up?

ATKINS: You mean our profit center idea?

REISENGER: No, I meant the change to separate trading departments.

ATKINS: Didn't that happen about three years ago? I thought that was a dead issue. Don't tell me you're trying to instigate another shake up.

REISENGER: I'm trying to assess how well we're doing and see where we can make improvements.

ATKINS: Well, frankly Phil, I liked it better under the old set up. For one thing, there was closer association among the traders. We were located in one room, so when any of us got hold of any information which might be pertinent to someone else we could put him on to it right away. There is a strong interrelationship between all the commodities we trade. What happens in the market for one affects the markets for the others. So we could really help each other out under the old set up. Very little of this assistance takes place now. It's just too much trouble to get on the phone and get hold of another trader. For one thing, either he or his phone might be tied up. All of us are more tied up now looking after the administrative details in running our own departments. I think also that a sense of competition has crept in between trading departments. Even though we were judged on the basis of our sales before, just as we are now, there didn't seem to be much competition between traders. Now, about the only time the traders get together is to compare notes at the weekly trading meetings when we are given a rundown on the economic outlook for all our commodities. . . Of course, under the old arrangement, it was easier for full sessions to develop among the traders since we had so much in common. I don't feel that I have so much in common with any of the people in my own department. . . . I guess the present arrangement is more business-like. . . it's probably better for the company.

REISENGER: Do you feel you are getting better help in your traffic operations?

ATKINS: Yes, I can get the transportation end of a trade arranged much faster now. And I know that I can quickly get the answer to any traffic question without having to walk or call over to the traffic department.

REISENGER: How's Estes working out as a trainee?

ATKINS: O.K. But I wish you wouldn't tell our trainees what position they've been hired for. It would give us a lot more flexibility if the man wasn't told that he was being trained to be a trader. Why couldn't you tell trainees that the job they end up in depends on the aptitude they display during training?

REISENGER: It might be hard to hire people on this basis. But let me think about that one for awhile.

Reisenger asked William Morrow, whom he looked upon as a highly capable traffic man, for an opinion of the effects of the organization change. Morrow, the assistant traffic manager for foreign traffic, felt that the change served to give the traffic specialists more responsibilities and broader horizons to look forward to. Before the change, he said, they had been delegated pretty routine work.

In the course of the conversation, Morrow described how a Japanese trading company had been very successful with an organization composed of both traffic and trading line departments. Each of these departments was considered a profit center and was evaluated on the profits it contributed to the company. Morrow indicated that he thought a similar arrangement at International Metals would work better than the existing organization. When the International Metals Corporation had been composed of both traffic and trading line departments, the profit center concept had not been practiced. The accounting system was the same then as it was in 1961. That is, direct costs were applied to each commodity traded and overhead was based on dollar volume of sales and also applied to each commodity. Hence, under the previous organization, the only indications that corrective action was necessary in the traffic department were when incorrect paper work was spotted or when a trader complained that he was given erroneous information on freight rates and shipping schedules by the traffic department.

Reisenger next approached George Bell, the traffic specialist in Atkins' department, to get his reaction to the change. Bell said:

> At first I couldn't see what the company was driving at with the change. But now that I've seen how it works, I definitely think it is a change for the better. I think it gives each person in our trading department, even the secretaries, a feeling that they are part of a complete working unit. You get the feeling that you are a company within a company. By listening to the trader and the traffic specialist, everyone can see how a trade is put together and how the work they do fits in. Also, we can now wrap up a trade in minutes instead of hours. I think I am able to do my job better too. By getting to know the markets for the commodities we trade, I can plan my negotiations for freight space. I can also stand in for Atkins, and trade for him when he is away.
>
> As far as my relationship with the traffic department goes, I refer to them only on policy matters, like when we want to appeal to the Interstate Commerce Commission to have freight rates lowered in a new domestic marketing area we've opened up. I think it is pretty clear between what is a policy matter and what is an operating matter that I can handle myself. Of course, Bill Morrow, the assistant traffic manager, handles some of the traffic work on commodities we trade only occasionally. One of these items, though, really caught on, and

we started trading it regularly. Morrow has continued to handle the traffic for this product. I'm so busy with my other work that I couldn't relieve him of this job even if I wanted to.

Later Reisenger told Atkins of Bell's enthusiasm for the present arrangement. Atkins countered with:

> Maybe he has a point there. But I still think there is the disadvantage that I am called upon to make decisions which should be made by other people in my department. Making these decisions myself, or trying to get the people in my department to take the responsibility for making them on their own, cuts in on the time I have to analyze my markets or to look for new trading opportunities.

The only other issue that Reisenger perceived had been raised as a result of the change in organization was brought to his attention by Carl Mitchell, the traffic coordinator in the general trading office. This office was located in quarters separate from company headquarters in another part of New York City. It had its own trading and traffic elements, but relied on support from the staff elements in the headquarters office. The general trading office had been a subsidiary trading company which was consolidated within the parent organization in 1960. The two New York offices had not been consolidated into one location because of lack of space. By 1963, however, the company planned to move to new quarters which would make it possible to combine both offices.

Mitchell's complaint was that the general trading office was employing a needless amount of traffic personnel. He argued that if all the traffic people at this location were organized as a central traffic section reporting to him, the company could eliminate two traffic specialists from the general trading office. This, he said, would result in an annual savings to the company of the combined salaries of these two men, roughly $15,000, plus another 30 percent of this amount, $4,500, for fringe benefits. Based on the 1.5 percent before tax return on sales which the company earned in 1960, it would take well over a million dollars in sales to cover the total cost of retaining these two surplus positions.

In the general trading office were located two trading departments which had traffic personnel directly assigned to them. Two other departments, however, relied completely on a central traffic department organized under Mitchell to handle their traffic work (see Exhibit 3). One of the reasons for this exception to the general organization plan was that the general trading office had only recently been consolidated within the parent company. It had previously been operated with a centralized trading department. Following the consolidation, two trading departments with traffic personnel assigned to them were moved from the headquarters office to the general trading office. Reisenger cited another reason why he felt there had been no action taken to assign all traffic personnel in the general trading office to individual trading departments there. He said that this office was generally looked upon in the company as an advanced training area for traders. Therefore, a certain amount of flexibility was required in that office as responsibilities for trading more commodities were shifted to a new trader as he progressed in his training. Alfred Wynn, manager of the general trading office, had long experience as a trader. Aged 62, he was still active in trading certain commodities. As an adjunct to his trading duties he was valued as an excellent influence in helping develop traders who had advanced to the stage where they had been assigned a particular commodity to trade.

Reisenger was also familiar with still another alternative method of organizing a trading company. This was a method of dividing responsibility which was used by most European trading firms. There, the trader was responsible for buying, selling, and freighting his goods. A contract administration section in these firms was responsible for handling all documents, billings, claims, contract audits, and accounting. When a transaction had been initiated by a trader, contract administrators followed the transaction through to its completion and were familiar with every detail and cost involved.

Late in May, 1961, Reisenger was expressing some of his misgivings about the way the firm was organized in a meeting with the president. At one point in their conversation, after Reisenger had enumerated a number of the difficulties in the situation which led to his uncertainty as to what to recommend be done, Amante slammed his hand to the table with a loud report. "Damn it, Phil, we've dragged our feet long enough on this thing. At one time or another you've given me all the pros and cons involved in the way we're organized. Now it's your baby. Based on these pros and cons, what are your recommendations? How about giving me a report on this in three days?"

APPENDIX

Realignment of Duties of Traffic and Trading Personnel

The recent changes in the physical location of trading and traffic personnel in our New York office also signify some changes in responsibility, authority, and activity. More than ever before, it will be the responsibility of each trading department manager to keep the general traffic manager and his assistant managers fully informed of all facts concerning the movement of their commodities and to consult with them when any question concerning traffic policy or procedure is not clear. Accordingly, the following line-up of functions and responsibilities will take place as soon as practicable within each department.

Organization of the Traffic Department. The traffic department is responsible for the establishment of policies concerning the storage and movements of all products bought and sold by the International Metals Corporation and its subsidiaries, in both foreign and domestic transactions. This work includes:

1. Chartering ships and booking large parcel space for the various trading departments.
2. Negotiating rates and rate adjustments with transportation companies.
3. Obtaining transit differentials and maintaining transit records.
4. Establishing policies relating to proper shipping and documentation in conformance with shipping instructions and contract provisions.
5. Overseeing marine and war risk insurance placement.
6. Investigating and developing any traffic techniques.
7. Inspecting traffic operations in other locations.
8. Training and guidance of all personnel in proper traffic procedure.
9. Maintaining adequate records of contracts of sales and purchases.
10. Invoicing domestic transactions and dittoing contracts and shipping instructions.

Description of Jobs

General Traffic Manager—Ralph Dawson. The general traffic manager is responsible for the general supervision of all traffic and will coordinate all traffic work at New York, San Francisco, London, La Paz, Sydney, Tokyo, and Osaka.

Questions pertaining to general traffic policy and any problems in the coordination of traffic matters between the trading departments or other branch offices of the company are to be referred to him. He is responsible directly to the president, Joseph Amante. His major functions will be to establish and review general traffic policies, train and guide all personnel in proper traffic policy and procedure, anticipate trouble areas and help the departments concerned surmount them, and visit and inspect traffic operations in other locations.

Organization of Trading Divisions. The trading policy of the company is developed jointly by the chairman of the board and the president, assisted by the various traders and the economic analysis section. The chairman and the president trade in several commodities in their own right—assignment of these commodities to traders in the operating units will be secondary assignments.

Description of Jobs

Trading Department Manager. Within this framework, our trading department is divided into several commodity departments or operating units, each headed by a trading manager. Each manager is responsible to the president for general trading and administrative policy within his department, and shall keep him well advised of the market situation and of his own position in the market within the credit, price, and trading limits authorized by the president. Each manager will be directly responsible for the purchase, sale, and movement (under the traffic policies laid down by the traffic department) of the particular commodities assigned to him, and for the supervision of the traffic people charged with their movement. Traffic policy will be subordinate to trading policy and will be modified when outweighed by trading considerations. If disagreement arises between the trading and traffic departments, the matter shall be referred to the president.

In addition to the above, each trading manager shall be directly responsible for the following in regard to his purchases and sales:

1. Operating profitability within credit lines and terms granted his commodities and keeping the treasurer well advised of any sizeable, actual, or anticipated changes approved by the president.
2. Checking with the credit department prior to sale to or purchase from new accounts and keeping well posted on his accounts.
3. Preparation, signing, and following up of his contracts It shall be his responsibility to see that contracts are issued the day the trade is executed, amendments are issued promptly, contracts and confirmations are carefully checked, and that signed copies are returned to us promptly and forwarded to our central contract file.
4. Checking on traffic work, billings, commissions, insurance, expenses, and accounting work relating to his contracts and following up any late deliveries or shipments.
5. Checking actual costs against estimates; furnishing yearly budget information.
6. Working closely with the credit and claims department to effect prompt settlements of all disputes.
7. Following up monthly on all past due accounts.
8. Working with our advertising agency (when required) in preparation of copying.
9. Handling traffic matters in the absence of his traffic specialist.
10. Checking position reports in collaboration with assistant traffic manager, foreign or domestic, whichever applicable.

Traffic Specialist. Operating under the general traffic policy of the company, the traffic specialist under each trading department manager shall be responsible for all traffic functions relating to the commodities assigned to his commodity section. He shall be accountable directly to the trader and will be responsible for:

1. Obtaining of options and booking of freight space. This is done either through the assistant traffic managers in connection with large movements or directly in cases of small shipments as defined by the general traffic manager; in all cases, the traffic department must be kept fully informed of his actions.
2. Issuing ship orders and shipping instructions to suppliers except where jurisdiction of London office applies.
3. Requesting and executing shipping instructions from our buyers.
4. Assisting in the negotiations of rate adjustments.
5. Maintaining records of open purchases and sales, and regularly preparing position-reports, open purchase and sales contracts.
6. Checking all shipping and insurance documents for conformance with shipping instructions and contract provisions.
7. Placing adequate marine and war risk insurance, filing of claims.
8. Arranging for pumping, storage, sampling, analysis, and discharge of shipments.
9. Preparation (except final extension and distribution) and checking of domestic invoices and preparation of billing instructions on foreign sales.
10. Passing claims information to the credit and claims department.
11. Handling trading matters in the absence of his trading department manager.
12. Notifying trading manager of possible late deliveries or shipments so trading manager can follow up with broker.

3 | Aerospace Systems (D)

Dr. Roger Simon had just passed up an opportunity to teach at Yale, preferring instead to stay on at Aerospace and set up a new corporate research lab. Looking forward to his new role as director, he knew it would be a big job, one which would be not only profitable but challenging as well. In his short time at the Atomic Energy Division, Simon had convinced both his division president and the president of the corporation, Al Douglas, of the need for a central research facility staffed by topnotch scientists working at the frontiers of their disciplines. He now had to draw upon all his previous experience working at the Manhattan Project and in the Zeta Labs to build a research organization which would enable Aerospace to remain competitive in the future.

Aerospace had adapted successfully to previous changes in business strategy, but over the past 20 years most of the technical accomplishments were in the area of classical physics applied to large aircraft moving at low velocities. With the recent advances in quantum mechanics and relativity, the nature of the industry was changing dramatically; and to keep abreast of these changes Simon felt that Aerospace had little choice but to embark on this expensive undertaking. Only within a central research facility could a company as large and diverse as Aerospace attract and maintain a critical mass of fundamental scientists working at the forefront of their fields.

Simon had been recruited initially as a research scientist, but in less than a year he found himself planning for a \$3.5 million technical center with a projected annual budget of \$5 million. This represented a major commitment by the board to the role of basic research in its future business strategies, but money alone would not guarantee success. Simon had to confront the generic difficulty of establishing a research group working in areas of high uncertainty within a business environment where investments must be justified by performance.

AEROSPACE SYSTEMS: A COMPANY IN TRANSITION

In 1959, Aerospace was one of the largest companies in the industry, with contract sales to the U.S. government of well over a billion dollars per year. From its founding in 1933, Aerospace grew rapidly to become one of the largest producers of aircraft in the world until the close of World War II when, almost overnight, 90 percent of its contracts with the Defense Department were canceled. In adjusting to this, Aerospace adopted a policy of diversification with less emphasis upon production and more upon contracts for complex systems requiring greater technical competence. By the 1950s Aerospace was again one of the largest competitors in the field. With the change in business strategy, the older production-oriented structure in which the heads of the major functions all reported to the chief executive soon became unwieldy. To provide better support for its diversified activities, Aerospace decentralized its operations into eight separate divisions.[1] Each was given greater autonomy, being responsible to corporate headquarters solely on a profit basis. During the decade of the 1950s many divisions became the largest, or second largest, producer of their product or system in the world.

For a time decentralization proved to be an effective organizational solution to the problems of diversification and growth, but by the late 1950s there was a growing tendency within the divisions toward parochialism and interdivisional competition, leading to redundancy and concentration on short-run problems. Each division had its own research staff, but they tended to work on rather short-range projects. The one exception was in the Atomic Energy Division which employed the largest number of Ph.D. scientists; but the work here was done primarily for the Atomic Energy Commission, and this tended to limit both the scope of research activities and opportunities to draw upon this classified work in the other divisions. Several previous attempts had been made to establish a corporate research lab using AE scientists, but the resistance by other divisions stymied these efforts until the arrival of Dr. Roger Simon in July 1960.

Simon was well known in scientific circles as a theoretical chemist with numerous publications to his credit. An eminent scientist, he had nonetheless become increasingly interested in management. It was this that had caused Simon to leave Zeta Labs on two occasions for research

---

[1] These were the Radar, Aircraft, Space Systems, Rocket Engines, Electronic Systems, Atomic Energy, Information Systems, and Submarine Systems Divisions.

positions elsewhere. Speaking of his desire to become a manager, Dr. Simon said:

> I had been doing science for a good many years, and although I still had a certain amount of ambivalence, I felt that I ought to try my hand at a little bit of organization, to organize the world about me. The opportunity at Alfa Steel seemed interesting, something called an assistant director of research. But it turned out that, except for a small amount of fundamental work, they did not even do applied research; they put food in cans to see how long it would take for the cans to erode. I decided that this was simply not the place for me. I had the option of returning to Zeta with continuity of service, and I did.

> At Zeta, I spent my time totally involved with scientific matters, and I suppose nobody ever thought of me as a manager, although I did begin to express some of these views before I left. I thought—well, maybe I could knit together a chemical physics group for them. I was in fact the leader of that group without the title, simply because I was able to generate sufficient excitement of ideas—and most theoretical chemists are motivated by such ideas. To this day, the theoretical chemists at Zeta do not interact much with the rest of the lab, which is primarily physics oriented. They are a resource which is not fully utilized, and they can be tolerated because the laboratory is so successful anyway. My proposal was to make use of this resource for the company without destroying its scientific competence. They were willing to think about it, but they were not willing to do anything about it. I decided to leave again, since there was this interesting opportunity at AS.

> While I was at the Gordon conference,[2] a fellow from AE invited me to stop by and present a paper there. While I was there I was offered a job. I spoke to Howard Elliott, the director of research, and to the vice president of AE. What I noticed at AE was what I thought was a remarkable group of scientists. There were a lot of poor ones too—but nevertheless a remarkably high density of good scientists. But they were unconnected, they weren't interacting even among themselves, and they were unrecognized. I thought they were, as a group, as high quality as you could find at Zeta. Now there are a very few industries that have an opportunity like that. Some of these fellows were actually world authorities in their field, like Bruce Nelson and Carl Nadel.

> I told Howard Elliott, the director of research, that I would only be interested in coming if I had the chance to do some organization, particularly with these resources—it seemed like an exciting idea to bring them together somehow. I really had no firm idea how to do it. I had never thought of that sort of thing. I guess it was sort of rash to think I could do it. I finally joined AE as a research advisor, with the promise that I would become associate director of research after about six months. Howard Elliott was not interested in me as

---

[2] A series of yearly scientific conferences devoted to solid state physics and solid state chemistry.

a manager, he was interested in hiring me as a scientist—but he could only get me as a scientist by permitting me to do some organization.

At that time the research department was divided into four subdivisions: physics, chemistry, electron physics, and metallurgy. Each one was headed by a department head—all were competing for Howard Elliott's job. There was no coherence; they were all busy building up their empires by acquiring more contracts.

Supervisors and group leaders also spent much of their time doing paper work and had little time to do science. That is the main reason why some of the better scientists didn't want to be bothered with becoming group supervisors.

The average scientist behaved as if he were working for one of the national laboratories; he did research essentially for the AEC and was responsible for getting out the data—that was all. Some of the research was good, some of it wasn't so good. Nobody thought they were working for AE, to say nothing of AS. Each man had a special relationship with some sponsor at the AEC. There was a great deal of brochuremanship, of time being wasted in getting contracts. Each scientist was an entrepreneur in his own right; he had control over consultants, travel, recruiting, and equipment. He was not called upon to think about the relation of his scientific problem to anything else. It was a more pure research attitude than you would find at a university.

An executive no longer with AE described the situation as follows:

> Howard Elliott was a great guy, but he had to evaluate everything from three angles before he could make a decision. He was very soft spoken and technically very good. At meetings he would criticize things technically and everybody loved him and respected him. Roger Simon, with his extremely dynamic approach to life, was getting in there, muddying up the waters like crazy, and stirring things around to find out where the mud was going to travel.

When Howard Elliott had a skiing accident and was sent to the hospital, Roger Simon became acting director of research. In the meantime, Howard Elliott had received several offers from various universities, and he confided to Roger Simon that he was thinking of leaving. Roger Simon recalls:

> That was a bit disconcerting to me, because I thought it was unfair of him to have recruited me a few months before and then to run out before my feet were wet. I told him that I preferred that he stay on, while I myself was thinking of going because this was such a mess. I had had a nice offer from Yale University at $24,000 a year.
>
> At this time Sinclair Reed [the division president] was attempting to get a million dollars of internal funds to replace a like amount withdrawn by the AEC. Howard Elliott was still director of research, and I told Sinclair that my decision as to whether I would go to Yale hinged upon whether or not they got that million dollars. Without it, I was not interested in staying because there was too much instability.

To me, Sinclair was the ultimate; if I put enough pressure on him, then he could settle the problem. What I did not realize then was that he was not the ultimate, that putting pressure on him just squeezed him. Howard Elliott felt crushed more than anyone else, and after some discussion with Sinclair Reed he finally quit, and I became acting director of research without any obligation to stay on.

With the issue of the million dollars still pending, Roger Simon proceeded to tackle what he considered his two main problems. The first was to "weed out the deadwood."

The lab was in considerable turmoil as a result of Roger Simon's promotion. The section heads were disgruntled because their chance for promotion seemed to have vanished, and the bench scientists were apprehensive about the future of their jobs. These anxieties were not relieved when Simon promoted Bruce Nelson and Carl Nadel to associate directorships. Nelson had never held an administrative position, although he had a worldwide reputation as a scientist; Nadel, who had been in and out of management positions at the group leader level, was also well known as a scientist.

The unrest and anxiety produced by these rapid changes were utilized by Simon to get rid of many people he thought incompetent or useless. Those people who, in concert with Nelson and Nadel, Simon thought were valuable, were privately reassured of their positions and future with the company. In several instances Simon promoted people to positions of group leader based primarily on the criterion of scientific accomplishment. In like fashion, Bob Nordson, an ex-physicist turned administrator who had been with the research department for only a few months as administrative liaison, was promoted to research administrator. Nelson, Nadel, and Nordson became, with Roger Simon, the management team for AE's research department.

The second problem facing Roger Simon was to get the better scientists to relate their activities to the corporation and interact with others:

> I had already begun to motivate some scientists to relate to the overall mainstream of effort at AE. For example, Bill Tresbon and his group were working quietly on the electronic properties of metals and conductivity. Tresbon told me that he had discovered a very interesting high-field superconductor. I woke up one morning a few days after this and said to myself, "Why the devil don't they make a magnet?"
>
> Of course this was unheard of as far as they were concerned. They were not interested in this. They were going on to something else. So I went down to see one of the men in Tresbon's group [Tresbon was away] and said, "Look, why don't you try to make a magnet? But first we'll have to draw a wire," and he said, "Tresbon won't like that . . . it's such an applied thing," and I said, "Well, you know you might learn something from this."
>
> "Besides," he said, "you haven't got any money."

"How much will it take?"

"About $50,000."

"You start making that magnet and I'll get you the $50,000."

Very reluctantly he began, and we had the first superconductive wire of this type in the country. I said to Sinclair, "I'm going to make you very happy," and I told him about the discovery. "You do make me happy," he said; and I said, "Well, if you're so happy, get me $50,000 so that these fellows can go ahead." And he did.

When Tresbon came back, he was ready to go through the ceiling, but the day after the first sample of wire came in, it was interesting to see the reaction. It carried 10 to 15 times as much current as the original slab and it went to much higher fields. The point is—by having taken the first technological step, they added to their store of scientific knowledge. Then they became very interested and got into the magnet race. And these two guys, all by themselves, successfully competed with much larger efforts at Ipsylon, Zeta, and Gamma Labs.

There were several instances like this, and apparently Sinclair Reed developed confidence in me as a manager. Reed came to the conclusion that this was the time to ask Douglas not only for the million dollars but to establish some sort of central research effort, and he asked me to write a report telling Douglas what he would have to do to establish a research facility of this kind.

Roger Simon had two weeks to prepare his proposal. He achieved this by working together with Nelson, Nadel, and Nordson. The four men would discuss the issues, then Simon dictated his ideas which were subsequently edited by Nadel and Nordson. The brochure (Appendix) suggested a research laboratory geographically separate from AE, although organizationally part of AE, reporting to Reed.

Though the line of argument and the tone that the brochure would take had been discussed by Simon with Reed before publication, Reed did not read the final document until the day before it was to be presented to Mr. Douglas. Reed was in agreement with the general content and took the lead in presenting the idea of a geographically separate, corporate-oriented research center.

During the course of the meeting, Mr. Douglas's primary concern appeared to be how one might obtain the necessary interdivisional acceptance and utilization of the research effort if this corporate-oriented effort was to be a part of a single division. Reed responded with the key suggestion that the central research function be removed from his jurisdiction and placed under that of the general office. Although Reed's extemporaneous offer was well received by Douglas, no conclusions were reached at the meeting. In recalling the next few days, Mr. Simon said:

> Things went on for a couple of weeks; there was no comment from Douglas and no report as to what his decision was. I asked Sinclair how things were going and he said, "I haven't heard anything, so it looks pretty grim," so I said, "Well, Sinclair, summer is coming along

and I think I'm going to have to accept the job at Yale University." Sinclair said, "Let's go down and see Douglas before you make up your mind." So we went down to see Douglas and talked with him. This is the longest talk I ever had with Douglas. And then I detected after some minutes that there was a rapport between Douglas and me and right then and there I decided, "Well, this is a big company and they are good scientists. It will not only be challenging, but profitable, to establish a lab in an organization like this."

Alan Douglas recalled the meeting with Dr. Simon and events that led up to it:

> There were two thoughts in my mind. The first and foremost was the need to upgrade the technical excellence of the corporation and the fact that I did not possess the requisite technical background to accomplish this without a staff. Second, there was the intrinsic value of a science effort in the corporation during this period.
>
> Then I started hearing about Roger Simon. Sinclair Reed talked to me about Simon quite often, mentioning his intellectual capabilities and his abilities to form a lab, and I began to get interested. I began to talk to Roger Simon, and because his background was so different from mine, we had to go through an adjustment period before we could understand each other. In fact, he gave me a series of lectures that gave me some feeling about what the science that he had in mind was about. It developed at this point that he was also a good administrator, since he was running that lab at AE.
>
> The mental cycle that I went through was something like this: Here was this group working under contract for the AEC, working on their own problems, because you can't get a first-rate scientist to work on anything unless it is a problem he is interested in. But the restraining interest of government was considerable, and I started to give some thought to funding this research out of internal funds. The question was how to set up the lab. The idea of taking any of our research and development funds and putting them into this kind of an organization was not very popular with the divisional people who are product and development oriented.

Dr. Simon recalled his relationship with Mr. Douglas in this period as follows:

> In view of the urgency connected with the upgrading of science in the corporation, and because of the variety of unbalanced pressures to which I thought Douglas would be subjected, what I had to do was to learn to motivate him. I thought, "How can I motivate Douglas? I can't really motivate him because of my management experience, because I have none. I may have some brash ideas, but I can't really represent myself as a distinguished manager." The only thing I had to go on was my hopefully distinguished reputation as a scientist—a reputation that very few people at AS had the equivalent of; the only other people might be a few in the research department at AE—Nelson, Nadel, and Tresbon. So I made no effort; in fact, I told him point

blank I was no manager, but that I was a good scientist. I told him I was fed up with the way science was being managed at AS and for that reason I was going to Yale University. At this point he said, "Well, I want you to think about it a little longer."

I thought about it a little longer and went back a couple of days later, and he said, "We have been trying to establish a central research activity for a long time, but we have not had the man whom we could count on to do it. Now we think we have." I sat there very quietly. Then I warned him again that I had no experience as a manager, that he was gambling, that he would have to give me the authority to do this thing the way I wanted to do it, not to make me a shunt to him or anybody else. And he agreed! It was a startling thing, he agreed!

By July the Aerospace System's board of directors had approved the establishment of a corporate research center as outlined in Dr. Simon's proposal and recommended by Al Douglas. The research center was to become a separate division in October 1962 and in the interim period remain dependent on the Atomic Energy Division for facilities and administrative support. Prior to the board meeting Simon was spending most of his time in the day-to-day operations of the AE lab, but with this go-ahead decision things began to move fast.

In preparation for the early discussions with architects, Simon and his associate directors had to spend many late nights discussing what the laboratory would look like in terms of size and disciplines so they could pin down an appropriate physical layout. Building upon his initial proposal, Simon wanted to construct a lab based upon key scientific disciplines, for only in this way did he feel he could combine both specialization and flexibility in a single research unit. Each researcher would be eminent in his field, but the fields, being basic, could combine in numerous ways depending upon the interests generated. To support this each senior staff member would have his own lab, but in a facility which was compact to facilitate interaction. As the lab evolved in these meetings other factors such as the size and location of offices, the library, and even the cafeteria were all designed to maintain a stimulating collegial atmosphere.

Beyond these architectural considerations, many other issues were raised, but not fully resolved. The whole problem of financial support was only one of these. Based on their experience in AE they knew of the dangers associated with government contracts, and they were still not certain what the actual mix of outside to inside support should be. Related to this was the issue of whether divisions should be encouraged to pay for work in the laboratory on a "contract" basis, or whether all research should be corporately funded. This in turn raised the question of how the interface between the lab and the divisions could be arranged to promote autonomy of the lab while still having it in touch with the divisions.

Another problem they talked about dealt with the administrative components of the lab. To what extent should the day-to-day operation and liaison responsibilities be centralized and kept from the scientists? Since they were planning to spend in the order of $100,000 a man in each of 15 key scientific areas and they hoped to recruit top persons in each field, they wanted to avoid bureaucratic red tape and too many levels of management, which would constrain this talent. One possibility was for Simon, Nelson, and Nordson to have the key scientists report directly to them as a group. However, they felt that key personnel might end up spending too much of their time in meetings rather than in their labs. Simon and his group talked often about this problem in an effort to get a balance between autonomy for the individual scientists and some unity of purpose in the lab.

In addition to these questions on financing and direction, Simon and his team also were beginning to grapple with several related issues. Where would they recruit these scientists? Would they try to attract researchers from the other divisions as well as go outside? What type of compensation scheme would they offer to attract and motivate these people? And how would this be tied into performance evaluations?

APPENDIX

A Master Research Plan for Aerospace Systems

DEFINITION

It is best to begin with the definition of terms. By "research" I shall mean something distinct from "development," though the separation can never be complete. With this in mind, I classify under the heading of "research" those activities which are devoted to the creation of new understanding of both phenomena and materials.

NEED FOR A RESEARCH PROGRAM

Aerospace Systems, in consort with the rest of the industry, has as yet not demonstrated outstanding capacity in research in the sense in which I have defined it. It is important to note that research is a different activity in the sense that it is involved with the creation of new knowledge, and very often this is offered in terms of the molecular and sub-molecular mechanisms which underlie materials and phenomena. The developments at AS cited above have, with minor exception, all been based on the sound application of scientific principles which were thoroughly established at the time the developments were initiated. One might say that the science of yesterday is the engineering development of today. The converse is obvious. The engineering which we will do tomorrow will be the direct descendant of the research we do today.

Why is it that we can no longer rely solely on engineering applications? Even more important, the need for research stems from the fact that today's accelerated pace has drastically reduced the delay time between the moment when new science is created and the instant when it is utilized as a tool of development. It has become customary for the same organization to create the science and to exploit the development.

FUNCTIONS OF A PROFITABLE RESEARCH LABORATORY

If it is granted that the corporation must, literally, pursue research, there must next follow an understanding as to how a group of individuals, synthesized into a "laboratory," can come up with the necessary knowledge that the corporation seeks to exploit.

Maintaining Lines of Communication with the External Scientific Community. It is vital to become aware of new and exciting developments in the world of science as soon as they happen. In today's highly competitive atmosphere, time—even a little time—is a valuable commodity, and only early cognizance of important developments can provide the necessary time. There is no better way to establish broad lines of communication with the world of science than through the natural personal relationships which occur among scientists who are peers. If the laboratory has gained the respect of the scientific community and its scientists are similarly respected, then they will be welcomed within the most elite professional circles. The normal give-and-take of information which occurs within these groups will provide for the early transmission of news.

Many modern developments are so specialized that they can only be interpreted by a man who has a working familiarity in a new field. Thus it may sometimes be of value to support a specialist and his small research effort in order to keep an eye on the new field.

Stimulating Other Laboratories. An important function of a research laboratory is that of stimulating the community of science to work on problems which are of interest to the parent firm. This can, perhaps, best be indicated by the example of Bell Telephone Laboratories and the transistor. When the transistor effect was first discovered by Brattain and Bardeen, it was realized immediately that the effect could be converted into a useful device which Bell could use to replace costly, short-lived, and less reliable vacuum tubes which were found by the millions in the Bell System. On the other hand, there were grave materials problems of a fundamental nature, and even Bell's large staff could not be expected to solve them within a reasonable period of time. By inducing some of their most outstanding people to work and publish in this area, they succeeded in stimulating the entire world to concentrate on the field of solid state physics. So popular did the subject become that the solid state sessions at the Physical Society meetings permitted standing room only. The scientific community published the results of its work and the literature was available to Bell. In a sense, Bell achieved immense amplification of its own effort, and in fact they were able to actually use transistors in the Bell systems within a very few years. That other firms manufactured and sold transistors was of secondary importance. Bell only wanted to use them.

It is clear that this sort of strategy cannot be pursued with a second-rate staff. To nucleate interest, it is not enough to publish work in the field. The work must be imaginative, exciting, and clearly indicative of the possibilities for further inquiry.

Advising and Consulting with Development Groups. This is a fairly obvious function of a research laboratory. Sometimes a development man's problem can be solved as soon as he contacts the appropriate research man. The latter may have sufficient knowledge concerning the recent literature in the field so that the solution involves little more than the location of a specific reference. Alternatively, the knowledge may be available but not published and yet the research man may know of it. Sometimes the development man may be able to enlist the collaborative effort of the research man in the development problem itself.

THE RESEARCH MAN

When the need for research is accepted there must be a simultaneous acceptance of the fact that the research scientist is a different species from the engineer. Because of this, a whole new host of problems arises for which the solutions developed to fit the engineer are inappropriate. These problems are discussed here, but first a few words are in order concerning the motivation and attitudes of the truly outstanding and creative research scientist. Analyses of the scientist have appeared in many reports and are well documented. These remarks combine our own experiences with those of other well-known and well-established research organizations. *AS has been attempting to deal with the research scientist with methods applied previously to engineers.* An immediate result is that AS is not regarded by scientists as an especially desirable place to work.

It must be accepted from the very beginning that most scientists are profession oriented and not company oriented. It is not very far from the truth that scientists regard the company partly as a means to an end, that is, a means to advance scientific research. But the company wishes to use science as a means to its end, that is, to earn profits. Therefore, it is necessary that a compromise be made. The company must make peace with the world of science in order to extract information from it and to secure maximum allegiance from its workers.

To attract these top-notch research men, the company must display an enthusiasm for good science as an end in itself. It is generally true that the degree of company-oriented enthusiasm shown by the scientist is directly proportional to the degree of science-oriented enthusiasm displayed by the company. The surest way to alienate a talented research worker is to tolerate good science passively while exhibiting enthusiasm actively for the technical activities which are clearly directed toward a commercial goal. The enthusiasm must be felt; it cannot be produced by edict. But if senior management cannot honestly display enthusiasm for science, then it is probably fair to say that only among a few members of senior management does enthusiasm for science per se exist.

The research man considers himself a professional person. There is a large complex of small indignities in existence at AS which militates against providing the scientist with the dignity and atmosphere he seeks. Each one of these items considered by itself seems so trivial as to be of no consequence, but the entire complex of annoyances makes for a complaint of some significance. It is also true that some of the individual annoyances are not annoyances at all but are merely regarded so by the research workers.

In this instance we have an example of the importance of recognizing the personal characteristics of research workers as distinct from those of engineers.

In his personal nonscientific behavior the scientific worker is no more a logical individual than is any other person. For example, capable scientists are often completely unimpressed by an appeal for economy from management. This, in spite of the irrefutable argument that all funding, no matter how generous, is limited. One might say that this is an aspect of the real world which is not real to scientists.

If a company means to establish a research laboratory, it must be prepared to put up with all the seemingly illogical intangibles that go along with it.

MANAGERIAL AUTHORITY REQUIRED BY A RESEARCH LABORATORY

An atmosphere in which creative ideas will flourish can only be attained with certain managerial authorities granted to the laboratory by the corporation's senior management. Two such areas are the control and direction of the research program. One cannot employ a creative individual with a national reputation and then tell him what to do; his creative talent is often intimately bound to an independent nature. The principal elements of control available to the research director are: (1) the careful selection of personnel at the time of employment, and (2) those influence methods associated with the personal rather than business relationship with the scientist. For example, it is only reasonable to select as employees, workers whose natural interests are in those fields upon which it is felt that the company should concentrate. One also attempts to employ responsible individuals who will understand the nature of their obligation to the company. But once employed, the scientist must be allowed to work on that task to which his enthusiasm drives him. That extra spark that is needed to inspire a new idea will only come from the drive for understanding that the scientist finds within himself.

Another attribute of the better scientist helps channel the laboratory's energies into the desired fields. This is the fact that very few scientists enjoy working in isolation. Ordinarily they like to discuss their problems with colleagues whose interests are similar. Thus, if some central theme of scientific interest pervades the laboratory, the new employee will tend to gravitate towards it.

The important thing is to make everyone desirous of being a member of the team. The personality of the director may be used as a control element by appropriate use of enthusiasm or by development of interest through the active collaboration of the director himself in a new field.

If under this system workers occasionally pursue lines of inquiry which are not of immediate use to the company, then this is the price which must be paid in order to establish an atmosphere in which creative thinking will flourish, and to which outstanding personnel will be attracted.

The company must also make it clear that they will not be perpetually anxious about how their funds are being applied to research. They must be confident in the judgments of the research management. Constant detailed accounting of the manner in which funds are utilized should not be necessary.

Those limitations which the corporate management wishes placed on its research effort should be clearly and publicly delineated. Outside of these, research management should be given a free hand to create the most fertile environment that its ingenuity can provide.

It is clear that the principal emphasis must be placed on the acquisition of outstanding personnel. The success of the entire venture will stand or fall on the company's ability to recruit men of talent. The more creative scientist (measured by some suitable standard) may be 100 times as creative as the average. On this basis it is well worthwhile for the company to spend two or three times the average in support of such a man; the return per dollar is 30–50 times greater.

MANAGEMENT'S ATTITUDE TO THE RESEARCH PROGRAM

I have noted previously that one of the essential requirements for a productive research laboratory is a display of enthusiasm for good science on the part of the senior corporate and divisional managements. Displaying enthusiasm for science is an expensive thing, in connection with which more often than not direct financial return cannot be visualized. For example, it may be necessary at times to sponsor research projects having no direct bearing on current company interests. It will be necessary to have scholarly academic visitors whose consultant fees are high and who do little more than raise the morale of the organization. It may be necessary to provide scientists with paid sabbaticals during which they can visit other research institutes or universities. At times it will be necessary to sponsor topical scientific conferences, even to the extent of publishing the proceedings. It may even be necessary to employ scientists on a fulltime basis who spend only a part of their time in the company laboratory; for example, some of their time may be devoted to teaching.

THE RETURNS OF RESEARCH

Nobody can guarantee in advance just what return, if any, will be realized on the very appreciable sum of money which must be invested to establish an adequate research program. It, therefore, requires faith on the part of the investor that given first-class personnel surrounded by an atmosphere within which creative activity can flourish, the chances for profit are excellent. Faith is in a large measure familiarity. That the value of such a very unconventional mode of business function as has been described should be real can only become clear with sufficient familiarity.

Many businessmen, although highly intelligent and extremely sensitive to reasonable arguments, find it difficult to bring themselves to risk funds in a research effort because they have not acquired the necessary intimate familiarity with the details of the research process.

Another bitter pill must be swallowed. This is the fact that once having mounted the best possible kind of effort, no major advantage over competitors who have mounted similar efforts can be assured. The best that can be hoped for is the ability to remain abreast of the leaders, not to outdistance them. The aspects here are negative rather than positive in the sense that the firm without a first-class research effort will almost surely fall far behind.

Probably the best that can be done in the way of assuring a profitable research effort is to employ an outstanding research director and to place one's faith in him. The chances are, if he is competent and it is possible to provide an atmosphere in which he can recruit outstanding scientists, the effort will be profitable given enough time. This is at once the very most and very least that one can do.

I have deliberately emphasized the scientific rather than the applications aspects of some activities at AE. This is not to belittle the importance of an effective applied research effort. The scientific advances which AE scientists are apparently capable of making would have little significance for the company if there did not exist an effective product development department to which the research effort could be eventually coupled. I emphasize these specific activities in the realm of pure science because this is an exceedingly valuable effort currently owned by the company which has attracted too little attention.

The research discussed is of a caliber and significance equal to that found at the best universities or at an outstanding research institute. The fact that such work can be done indicates that AS has a nucleus of talent in these fields. In spite of the outstanding work which I have just described, this nucleus has not fulfilled its potential and in fact is in danger of dissolution. If we lose this group of scientists, it is questionable whether the company will ever mount a similar research effort in the future. In today's competitive market it will be almost impossible to recruit such talent again.

THE NEED FOR CENTRALIZATION

What is the trouble? Why has not the group fulfilled its potential? The answer is many-faceted. In the first place, the whole of a laboratory should be greater than the sum of its parts. There should be an integration of effort. Scientists should interact spontaneously with one another. There should be a feeling of teamness. The laboratory should reach a kindling temperature. Interaction is instrumental in achieving this kindling temperature, and it is also necessary for the research effort to attain a critical mass.

At AE there has not been much spontaneous interaction, and I suspect the same is true of the other divisions of AS. Certain things catalyze interaction. Instead of the things necessary for such catalysis, it seems as if just those which act to quench interaction have been present. For example, most of AE's research is supported by external sponsors. The resulting project system has compartmentalized the scientist's time and equipment. If he is stimulated by a colleague to investigate a problem outside the scope of his immediate project, how will he charge his time? More important, where will he find the equipment to pursue his interest?

In the end his mind also becomes compartmentalized and he is no longer susceptible to stimulation. There are several individuals who exemplify this effect at AE.

To achieve an integrated effort, there must be a centralized research effort within AS. This will have to come to pass before the kind of research I have been discussing can be realized. As it stands, there are not only costly redundancies within the company, but there is obvious interference between divisions. It seems unreasonable in the light of the scarcity of topflight research personnel that AS should further scatter its talents among its own several parts. Unfortunately there is an unsymmetrical distribution of both profitability and research talent among the various subdivisions of AS. For example, Rocket Engines and Electronic Systems are capable of large earnings, but there is little question that the largest concentration of research talent, as opposed to development talent, is lodged at AE. Therefore, AE would have to play a major role in the process of centralization. Of course, opposition to this concept may arise, but this has little bearing on the fact that it is required on the grounds of logic.

Consider the case of the high field superconducting program. It was a real stroke of luck that we, with our very small effort (supported entirely by AEC funds), were able to effect a breakthrough which our large and capable competition had not achieved. Because AS had not supported this research, our proprietary position was somewhat compromised, but worse yet, we had neither equipment, nor funds, nor personnel to capitalize on this breakthrough and to fully exploit the time advantage which had been given us.

Any research laboratory, in order to be successful, ought to have one or at the most only a few themes at a time. The development of high field superconductors seemed to provide excellent opportunity to bring the integration of purpose which can be initiated by so powerful a central theme, but very little of this plan could be effected as there are no uncommitted funds for the support of a diversified program of this sort. In this instance, time is a critical element, since there are very large research efforts functioning in the hands of our competitors. Worse yet, the capital equipment is not available.

I have quoted at length the high field superconductor to emphasize how ineffective our system is from the point of view of sponsoring a mobile and highly competitive research program. There is so much inertia associated with the ponderous mechanism for making up our collective mind that whatever advantage in time our research effort may have given us erodes until no advantage remains. I would say that all of this stems from the lack of a master plan for research, a commitment in advance to do certain things, and a placing of confidence in the person of some trusted and highly competent research director. The establishment of a corporate research center would undoubtedly provide some of the basis for the elimination of such difficulties. It would at least give us a master plan to which we could refer all decisions which have to be made in a hurry.

A master plan would have some further advantages. Where AEC or DOD sponsorship ceases for a project of scientific excellence before such work can be completed and published, the company should see to it that such work is completed. This is a part of the principle that the company should make peace with the world of science to establish an atmosphere and reputation which will attract the more outstanding personnel.

THE OPPORTUNITY EXISTS

In spite of the above criticisms, AS is situated at a point in time and space (circumstance and geography) which is especially opportune for the establishment of the best industrial research laboratory on the West Coast.

West Coast industrial laboratories are all of the same type, heavily involved with government contracts and committed to cost-plus research. There is little project security—even job security is uncertain—and in fact, a large class of what might be called migrant scientific workers exists who follow the contracts from company to company. Each laboratory has a few competent people, but no one is able to acquire the critical mass necessary to mount a really outstanding research effort.

Most of the personnel engaged by these laboratories continue on their jobs because, among other reasons, they prefer to live on the West Coast. If any one company would give the clear sign that it meant to conduct its affairs in a manner similar to the outstanding East Coast laboratories (Bell, GE, IBM), it would very rapidly accumulate the best personnel now scattered among the many similar mediocre firms. For AS to give this sign, it will have to give public demonstration to the acceptance of those precepts mentioned above. The establishment of this laboratory will require considerable initial expense. AS will have to let it be known publicly that such expense has not been spared and that the research is being heavily financed by company funds. Furthermore, it would have to be made clear that it was research, not development, which would be sponsored, and that the company was willing to be quite patient in connection with the time schedule for results, perhaps looking five to ten years into the future.

A MASTER RESEARCH PLAN

Development of a Research Theme. A master plan for research at AS requires, first, the statement of a theme or themes. An industrial research laboratory ought to be concerned with but a few all-consuming central research themes at any time.

To be appropriate to AS, a research theme should fulfill two criteria. First, it should be on the frontier of science. Second, it should evolve naturally from the corporation's fields of interest.

By tradition, AS has been a physics-based organization. It is, therefore, doubly appropriate that AS should concentrate primarily on physical research.

Fields of Research. It is appropriate that the phase of the master plan which indicates the areas of research of interest to the corporation be indicated in terms of those scientific disciplines for which we desire coverage. It will be the job of research management to integrate these diverse interests into a unified effort, now supporting one theme, and later, perhaps, another. In examining the list of disciplines it must not be assumed that the people assigned to one discipline will be limited to that particular field. People of the proper caliber will be able to work in a number of the areas contained within the list. One attribute of a good man is interest in allied disciplines. Through such cross-fertilization progress is made.

Many of the subjects can overlap; many of the people who are working at one time in one area might very easily work at another time in another area. It is only through juxtaposing people with such overlapping interests that it is possible to achieve the interaction and integration of purpose which is required to advance a currently important research theme. What is important is to have all of these people on board all of the time. It may seem expensive if at times we are not using all of them in connection with fields which are of primary interest to the company, but we cannot tolerate the lag which is involved in acquiring them only when we need them.

Personnel for the Central Research Laboratory. Since the research center is to be representative of the entire corporation, it ought to draw upon personnel from all divisions as required. The staff, however, should not come exclusively from the present divisions, and a large fraction of the required staff will have to be recruited from universities and other laboratories. The contribution of manpower from each of the divisions of AS to the initial staffing of the research center should depend on the qualifications of the scientists themselves, and no requirements should be imposed regarding proportionality to a division's size, solvency, or seniority. Any conflict based on this issue is liable to immobilize the plan at the outset. Any compromise to questions of personality is liable to do the same. If a large sum of money is to be invested, we ought to be sure that it is put to the best possible use. The corporate director of research should report directly to the general offices and be charged with the responsibility of showing no special bias towards any of the operating divisions.

We will need to recruit for the several disciplines not now adequately covered. Such recruiting must place very strong emphasis on the acquisition of creative people. Recruiting will be slow because of the lack of availability of adequate personnel. It should be reiterated that such personnel will be attracted to the corporate research center only if the proper image can be created. Everything must be done to produce and maintain this image. Once we acquire outstanding personnel and are provided with proper funding and adequate working conditions, the rest will almost take care of itself.

Size of the Central Research Laboratory. The corporate research center should have a minimum size in order to achieve the critical mass necessary for effective functioning. It has to be large enough to cover the wide variety of disciplines listed. It must have breadth in order to be cognizant of the latest developments in these fields. It must have depth in order to make it possible for AS to deploy its forces in the most efficient manner to meet the demands of the moment. It must be large enough to provide the community of science with a purposeful and respected image. It must provide a sufficient variety of fields to attract and interest a man of stature. It must promise a top-notch potential staff member an association with colleagues sufficiently learned and versatile to supply him with all desired support information.

How large is large enough? My best estimate gleaned from actual working experience is about 100 scientists of Ph.D. caliber. Each of these must have support to the extent of about one technician per scientist so that the entire research organization should involve about 200 direct people.

Physics:

Theoretical physics	8
Metal physics	5
Nonmetallic solids	7
Plasma physics	5
Geophysics	2
Nuclear physics	5
Field physics	5
Space physics	4
Surface physics	1
Biophysics	1
High temperature materials	6
Device physics	4
	53

Physical metallurgy:

Mechanical properties	6
Structure	4
	10

Chemistry:

Electrochemistry	4
Chemical kinetics	3
Radiation	2
Chemical thermodynamics	1
Theoretical chemistry	2
Combustion chemistry	2
Polymer chemistry	2
Surface chemistry	2
Biochemistry	1
Analytical chemistry	2
	21

Mathematics:

Statistics	1
Information theory	2
Operational analysis	3
Logic	1
Numerical analysis	2
	9

The number of people enumerated in the above list represents senior people, all of whom have the Ph.D. degree or equivalent. The total of the above is 93. To allow for imperfect estimates we propose to round the figure off at 100. In addition to these and the 100 supporting technicians there will be need for a staff of service and clerical personnel concerned with administrative service duties, a library, and a shop.

FACILITY NEEDS

In the previous section of this discussion, examples of impendences have been given, and it has been argued that a certain degree of managerial autonomy and stability of funding is necessary. For these reasons and others previously noted, a research center separate from the present AS divisions appears desirable and necessary. It would require approximately 120,000 square feet of laboratory and office space to house the number of people previously noted. This figure is, of course, only approximate and is presented here merely as a guide for further study.

4 | Lewis Equipment Company

When William Conrad, a casewriter from the Harvard Business School, approached Samuel Coates, the plant manager at Lewis Equipment, about case possibilities, he found that Coates did have a number of concerns that sounded like good case leads. Coates explained that even though he had been promoted to his present assignment several months earlier, he did not feel that he had as yet made nearly as many improvements in the plant's operations as he believed were possible. In particular, Coates expressed concern about his general foremen (see Exhibit 1 for a partial organization chart of the company).

Sam went on to explain that he personally was under considerable pressure from his superiors to improve factory performance. He did not believe these demands were entirely reasonable, but he believed he could make progress in meeting these demands if only he could find a way to get better coordination between his foremen. Sam also wanted his foremen to spend more of their time and interest on helping their own people overcome the daily problems on the factory floor. He believed his foremen were often too distracted to attend to the practical issues of training and encouraging their employees in getting their work done properly and on time. He wanted his foremen to feel responsible for all aspects of their unit and to fight for the things they felt were necessary to make their unit effective. Sam reported that he was having difficulty in getting his foremen thinking and working along these lines. Starting with this lead, William Conrad decided to spend some time with two of the foremen involved to learn more about the situation.

EXHIBIT 1
Partial Organization Chart

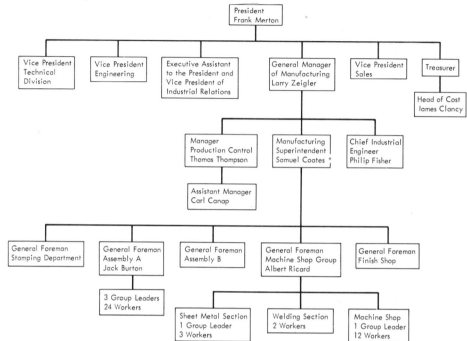

* Mr. Coates had left his former position as general foreman of the stamping department about a year earlier.

COMPANY BACKGROUND

The Lewis Equipment Company had been started some 15 years earlier as a science-based company producing an increasing line of equipment and instruments that were used primarily in the oil industry. After a period of early financial success and rapid growth, the company had, in recent years, experienced severe competition and had been operating at a loss for about two years. At this time the company employed approximately 900 people, of whom a considerable number were engineers and scientists. The factory operated on a job order basis, and most of the products were produced to customer specifications.

ASSEMBLY DEPARTMENT A

The first department that Conrad chose to study was assembly department A under the general foremanship of Jack Burton. During their first conversation Jack explained about the nature of his work and his problems:

BURTON: I have one main final assembly line that makes up 12 different types of equipment that are each produced 2 to 6 times a year. There are ten people in this production line along with a group leader. I also have a subassembly line that makes small quantities of a variety of components and also finishes some assemblies that are produced only once or twice a year. Then I have the wire and harness line—these are the harnesses and cables used in the finished assemblies.

We're having a lot of trouble with the specifications. The trouble is that we are not given enough time to work out the problems in specifications when they come to us. I have to accept what the engineers give me as the bible, even though there are plenty of errors from the engineers. All the control around here is really in the engineering department. The final test is also done by the engineers, but there is a logic in this because we could develop our own slipshod technique if we did not have the engineers for final tests.

I get a monthly schedule in rough draft form from production control that tells me what to do and when to do it. It keeps the material flowing. I usually get the report on the first of each month, which I don't like, because if I knew in advance what the work would be like for the ensuing months I could go around to the paint foreman, etc., and put pressure on him to get the specific materials that I need for a crash program, so I would be better off.

I get a weekly direct labor utilization report made out by accounting. The accounting department makes up this report from the timecards and tells me what percentage of productivity resulted from our past weekly efforts. My yearly percentage of productivity to date is 62 percent, officially, but this note on the side of the sheet shows that actually I should be at 64 percent productivity. Only a small number of the jobs are actually timed. The standards on about 90 percent of the jobs are estimated. Management is interested in improving the percent of productivity over last year's productivity. For instance, we are now at 62 percent while last year this department was at a 45 percent productivity. But that improvement isn't much help, because the selling price and the budget are based on the standard times so that no matter how high the productivity is, if it is anything lower than 100 percent, they always complain.

We would show an even better productivity percentage figure if the rework hours were counted in the proper place. For example, last January we had 21 percent rework. On rework we have to eat it. If a late engineering spec change causes rework, we have to eat it, as far as the productivity figures go.

I think they are hiding their heads in the sand. They don't want to know the true cost picture. If they cross-charged rework costs to the department that caused the trouble it would be waving a red flag in their faces and showing where the real problem lies.

THE DIRECT LABOR UTILIZATION REPORT

Burton's frequent references to the direct labor utilization report prompted Conrad to look into this subject. He learned that this particular control system had been initiated by Mr. Merton, the company president, shortly after he had arrived at the company some three years previously. This system, designed to alert management to possible problem areas and to assist in product and inventory control, encompassed all of the company's manufacturing and assembly activities and a somewhat smaller proportion of the remaining hourly paid labor force. Mr. Merton had made every attempt to have all of the manufacturing jobs and assembly operations rated, but with frequent design modifications requested by customers and the frequent introduction of new products, this goal had never quite been achieved. Currently, some 70 percent of the direct labor force in the manufacturing division were working on rated jobs.

Generally the control system was not unlike progressive cost accounting procedures found in other medium-sized firms working on a job order basis. It was primarily aimed at controlling manufacturing labor costs by comparing the total actual time expended in manufacturing work to the accumulated standard times for each part or assembly produced. These standard times for manufacturing the necessary individual parts and for their assembly were determined by industrial engineering.

The cost accounting department distributed weekly on Friday afternoon a direct labor utilization report for each department covered by the system along with a summary for the total factory organization and the total company. (See Exhibit 2 for a guide to the method of calculation of the various items.) The two most significant measures upon which subordinate organizations were evaluated were known as the productivity and efficiency ratings. Of these two ratings, the productivity figure was the more frequently quoted and discussed rating. Conrad asked James Clancy, the head of cost accounting, what the significance was of these weekly reports. The latter commented as follows:

CLANCY: The reports are of some significance since the president looks at the figures every week. He usually gets the productivity and efficiency for total company and total manufacturing and plots them on a big chart in his office, which goes back several years. Sometimes he asks for reports on individual departments, but he never looks at them for more than ten minutes. I would say Mr. Zeigler[1] better be interested in them, since he knows Merton is going to talk to him every week manufacturing's performance doesn't look good. . . . A lot of the managers say that the system is a bunch of rubbish—Mr. Zeigler always says that he doesn't believe in the system. But I know they're concerned because Merton believes in it. You watch them on Friday pacing up and down, waiting to see what the results are. Their actions show that they are interested in it.

The total factory productivity and efficiency percentages were currently averaging approximately 69 percent and 79 percent respectively, which were slight increases over the previous two years. Exhibit 3 charts the productivity and efficiency percentages for the factory by months for the two preceding years. The company percentages followed closely

---

[1] Mr. Zeigler was the general manager of manufacturing.

EXHIBIT 2
Sample Direct Labor Utilization Report with Guide to Method of Calculation

1. Total hours available = the total hours recorded on the timecards of the employees in the department concerned during the reporting period.

2. Hours used on indirect labor = % of group leader's × 8 hrs. × number of working time spent on supr. day days in reporting plus inspector's and period. clerical help's time

3. Hours available for direct labor = #1 minus #2.

4. Hours direct labor on nonrated jobs = total hours expended on jobs that industrial engineering hasn't rated and/or on special jobs requested by other departments.

5. Hours variance = hours expended due to "acts of God" (e.g., machine breakdowns, power failures, snow storms) plus total rework hours.*

6. Hours direct labor on rated jobs = #3 minus (#4 plus #5).

7. Standard hours produced = standard hours allowed for × jobs completed in reeach job porting period.

8. % efficiency on rated jobs = #7 divided by #6.

9. % total productivity = #7 plus #4 divided by #1.

10. Rework*
    a. Responsible
    b. Not responsible

---

* Work hours expended on rework were broken down into two classifications:
a. The unacceptable workmanship of the particular organization being measured.
b. The rework occasioned by subsequent faulty work in other departments or by revisions in product design made by engineering, necessitating a rework of the job. Mention was usually made at the bottom of the utilization report of the absolute amounts of rework completed during the reporting period.

EXHIBIT 3
Total Factory Labor "Efficiency" and "Productivity"

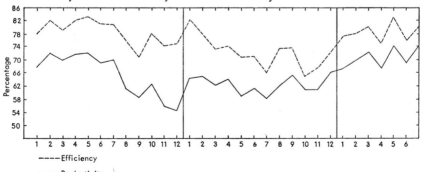

- - - - Efficiency
———— Productivity

EXHIBIT 4
Direct Labor Utilization Report
Total Machine Shop Group
(including the sheet metal and welding shops)

		Week Ending–				Total Month Ending 7/2
	6/4	6/11	6/12	6/25	7/2	
1. Total hours available.	565	892	946	800	812	4,015
2. Hours used on indirect labor	59	86	85	90	89	409
3. Hours available for direct labor	506	806	861	710	723	3,606
4. Hours direct labor on nonrated jobs . . .	8	26	37	44	17	132
5. Hours variance	18	19	13	16	5	71
6. Hours direct labor on rated jobs	480	761	811	650	701	3,403
7. Standard hours produced	303	388	508	484	266	1,949
8. Percent efficiency on rated jobs (std. hrs. produced/hrs. on rated jobs, 7/6).	63	51	63	74	38	57
9. Percent total productivity (std. hrs. + non std. hrs./hrs. available 7+4/1)	55	46	58	66	35	52
Rework						
a. Responsible	0	0	0	0	0	0
b. Not responsible	18	19	13	16	5	71

the total factory figures, owing to the fact that of the total company hours available, 75 percent were made up of hours contributed by the factory. Exhibit 4 is a sample of the actual reports that were distributed on a weekly basis to the managers and foremen concerned.

Conrad also secured direct evidence of Mr. Zeigler's concern with the productivity records. At the end of the first quarter of the current year, when labor utilization percentages were dropping in successive weeks, Mr. Zeigler sent the following note to his subordinates:

> Please write up your suggestions on how we are to salvage this situation. Remember, last month's productivity was only 69 percent. By Tuesday I will expect concrete courses of action from each of you, if you are to meet or beat budget.

Conrad learned that Mr. Zeigler had sent similar notes on other occasions.

Fortified with this information, Conrad went back to observing activities in assembly department A.

THE PUMP EPISODE

On one of his early trips to the assembly department Jack Burton started telling Conrad of a problem he was having:

BURTON: A little while ago my group leader of the subassembly group brought to my attention a problem concerning this pump unit. He was asking me how we could put them together and be sure they would pass final test. I noticed that there might be a chance of having some brass filings get in the critical parts if we were not careful. My group leader dug up the assembly specs which the engineers had drawn up in order to put this critical subassembly together. It called for cleaning the parts twice so that there would be positive assurance of a positive test. Then the group leader saw that the industrial engineers had not allowed enough time for the double cleaning. My group leader actually timed how long it took him to make the double cleaning, and it was considerably over the allotted time. I had the group leader figure the correct amount it would take so that we could resubmit it and get the actual time that we were spending on this cleaning operation put down.

Later in the afternoon when the casewriter was talking to Burton, Phil Fisher, the head of the industrial engineering department, came up and raised the topic of the standard allowed time on the cleaning operation.

FISHER: What's wrong on this pump assembly operation?

BURTON: Come over here and look at this. Our cleaning operation on the pump assembly is taking more time than you people have allowed. (*Hands him the engineering assembly sheet which describes the dual cleaning operation.*)

FISHER: (*after reading the sheet*):   I can't understand why they have duplicate cleaning operations on this. I don't think it's needed. Look, they've got 16 operations for this part. Look, the three sections to this assembly procedure show that parts A and C are almost the same thing. They're exactly alike.

BURTON: I've got to have those chips out of there to get these pumps past final assembly test. We go by the engineering specifications. Look, this is the engineering assembly S. O. P.[2] It says that we should have two cleaning operations.

FISHER: There's not such a thing as an engineering S. O. P. concerning assembly. I'm going up and see about this. I'm going to see if we can't get one of the duplicate operations for cleaning taken out of the specifications. We've got an ultrasonic cleaner that will do this job perfectly and eliminate one of these operations. That's what we've got the cleaner for anyway, to do jobs like this. This is ridiculous having so many operations. We'll be spending more time cleaning it than it takes to make it. How are we going to make any money doing this? (*Fisher leaves the room.*)

BURTON   (*to casewriter*):   He's worried about the cost of this—claiming that we will never be able to make a profit on the product if we have to have so many operations. Look at him worried about something like this. That's the chief engineer's job. The chief engineer is the one to worry about whether or not we can make a profit using so many operations with such

---

[2] Standard Operating Procedure.

designs. It's up to the chief engineer to determine whether we can sell a product and make a profit. It's not up to Phil Fisher.

Jack Burton leaves the room, and the casewriter talks to Phil Fisher, who is coming into Burton's office as the latter leaves.

FISHER: Boy, I just can't understand it. If I were to have seen that specification sheet with that many operations on it, I would have blown my top. Some engineer started on this, and because he didn't know what he was doing, he just kept applying more operations on operations. I know that if I were a foreman, I wouldn't allow that specification to come into my department without saying anything about it. How is the company going to make any money anyway? (*Jack Burton comes back into his office*).

FISHER: I want to try and clean a couple of pumps, using just one operation. I've got an idea how we can cut this down.

BURTON: Oh no you're not. I want to first check and see what final test has to say about the ones we've already done using two cleaning operations. I'm not going to have you trying to clean them with only one operation when maybe they aren't getting a positive test with two. (*Burton goes out and talks to the final test engineer and returns.*)

BURTON (*to Fisher*):   The test engineer said that the one we cleaned using the double operation didn't test positively. I'm not going to have you try to make a single operation out of it when we can't even get it with a double. I'm way behind on rework anyway and I can't afford the time messing around with it.

A little later on in the afternoon the casewriter had a chance to talk to Jack Burton further about the pump-cleaning incident.

BURTON: You know what Phil Fisher tried to do? He got my group leader behind my back and asked him to make up two complete units so he could try to test them, using only one cleaning operation. My group leader said definitely no. I'd already warned the group leader of what Phil might do and I told him not to play his game. It's this kind of thing that he does behind my back that really makes me mad. This is no isolated incident. This happens everyday around here with him. He's always going off on a different set of directions. He tells me every once in a while that I'm not cooperating with him. I don't know why I have to keep shuffling my people around to try out his ideas when I am so far behind on my work. If they want to test some parts and make a better operation, they can do it themselves. They can set it up. I'm not going to have them disrupting my operation.

A little while later Fisher approached Burton.

FISHER: Hey, Jack. Come on in the test room. I want to show you what we're doing. (*The group moves to the test room.*) Look, we have a valve on the pump in the ultrasonic cleaner. Using this device, we could eliminate the operation "C" (*pointing to the engineering specifications*).

BURTON: I don't care what you do. I just want a final result!

FISHER: I just wanted to show you what we were doing to keep you up to date. This way we can be sure that the top isn't scarred when we put it in the tester.

BURTON (*caustically*): I don't care if there's any scars on the top!

FISHER: I thought you said it had to pass final test with a good visual inspection?

BURTON: It's the fingerprints and the filings inside the pump that cause the trouble. I'm not interested in the outward appearance. It goes in a shield anyway.

FISHER: Oh. It goes in a shield? I didn't know that.

In a later interview with the casewriter, Fisher had a chance to explain some of his motives and methods in running the industrial engineering department.

FISHER: This pump-cleaning operation is the type of thing that Jack Burton should be doing and working on. That's the foreman's job. Jack's a good man but he doesn't have enough work to do. When Burton and I get together, it's rather rough between us. He's firm in his opinion, and I'm firm in mine.

I guess some people consider me the most hated man in the firm, but I'm rather proud of that position if we can get out of our present rut. I just don't have enough men in the industrial engineering department to do any real big work, so I have to rely on the foremen doing the job. What I have to do is create a big stink or something so that we get some reaction from these people. We raise the commotion in the department and let the foremen take over and do the improvements from there. I think we're on the verge of a breakthrough here if we can get these foremen up using a stop watch and watching these people and seeing if they're using the correct procedures. Why, on this pump-cleaning operation—sure, we're spending. We've got two of our men spending two hours of their time this afternoon in order that we can save a half hour when we finally go to assembly. But if this works out we'll save the company a lot of money. You've got to spend a dollar in order to make three.

Later, Jack Burton told the casewriter some of his views on Philip Fisher.

BURTON: Phil Fisher isn't held in very high esteem, because when he came into the company a little less than a year ago he had too much initiative and tried to do too many things. He got so many projects going that he hasn't had time to finish them up.

I really don't know what the industrial engineers do. It's all I can do to compose myself when I have to talk about them. I get so mad when I think about all their activities. Fisher has them doing so many projects that they don't have time to do the things that they're really supposed to be doing. Take, for instance, the harness board that I showed you earlier this morning. They're supposed to be making those up for us. The boards take about four hours to make up so that we can begin assembly. We're having to make up our own boards, eight hours of nonproductive time that we get charged with. The last run-through, we had to clear the boards that we already made several weeks before. It took one hour to clear them and then four hours of nonproductive time to build new ones. This is the type of job that they should be doing. They should be working on giving us better standards, too. The standards are way off because they are based on methods that haven't been worked out yet. That makes the productivity report an unfair basis for measuring our work. That's my big gripe with industrial engineering.

FINAL ASSEMBLY SHUTDOWN

When William Conrad arrived at the plant on the following day, he found that the main final assembly line had been temporarily shut down. This was necessary because production scheduling was unable to supply some front plates that were essential. The required plates had just been started into the paint shop that morning.

Burton commented:

> This shutdown is not unusual because we always have this. It's typical. Tom Thompson[3] works his production schedule from a predicted percentage of productivity figure that Zeigler gives him. I don't know where they get the figure. I know that recently they were talking about an 85 percent productivity. I don't know where they got that. I think it was something about fixing up the line so it would be more efficient, but it certainly has never reached that level of productivity. That 85 percent figure means purchasing has to hurry up and buy some more parts and materials. Then someone gets blamed for high inventories and it swings way over the other way.

THE MACHINE SHOP

Knowing that Sam Coates was also particularly concerned about the machine shop, Conrad decided to spend a few days observing this department and its foreman, Albert Ricardi.

In one of their early conversations Ricardi explained,

> When I took over this shop last year it was rapidly moving backwards. I took over and started instituting some changes. We've made some real progress, but it doesn't show in the figures. Accounting has been cutting us into bits. The standards being used are not real standards. They're guesses—pulled out of the air. Then we get hit with the productivity report and we're bums. All they're interested in is making us look bad. I have to spend about 97 percent of my time just coddling all the people who come down here from other departments.

---

[3] Production control manager.

The casewriter came in early the following Monday morning and was present when Tom Thompson, the production control supervisor for the manufacturing division, came into Ricardi's office.

THOMPSON: Al, we really need this job. There's only one operation left on it, and it has to be done. Al, I know you're in a bind, but we need this by today. Is there anything you can do?

RICARDI: We're really shorthanded today. Well, I could see what we could do about putting it in the process.

THOMPSON: I've talked to Brown over in the model shop, and he said he could do it for me, that is, if it's all right with you.

RICARDI: No. We don't get any credit on it that way. We've started the job, and I want to finish it.

THOMPSON: Well, Al, I understand how you feel about it and I know it will disrupt your operation.

RICARDI: Well, we'll see what we can do about it, but I'm not guaranteeing anything. Maybe we can get it out this afternoon. (*Thompson leaves.*)

CONRAD: Well, Al, how do you feel on this blue Monday?

RICARDI: Not so good. All my good workers and good machinists are out and I don't know what I'm going to do. My inspector is out and I'm really going to be running around like a chicken with his head cut off. I guess when your luck runs out, it really goes all at once. Saturday we were running around and found that the drill press operator had drilled the counterbore shallow on those plates we were doing. We had to run 84 of those pieces over again. You don't have to be a machinist to see that the men around here leave a lot to be desired. And then there's Tom Thompson coming down here. If they would leave us alone we would get ahead and get something running and we wouldn't have all these rush jobs. Every time they send in and ask us to do something of a rush nature, that cuts out our general efficiency and we just can't get ahead. That's why I ignored Thompson. When the men quit a job in the middle of it, they get confused or forget and make mistakes. It takes them time to get started again. Here's Thompson asking me to do a rush job. I just can't afford to do it.

SCHEDULING PROBLEMS

Several days later Conrad was walking through the shop with Ricardi when he commented on a pile of finished parts.

CONRAD: These castings really look nice, Al. I think Archie did a pretty good job on them.

RICARDI: Yes, they look nice all right, there is no doubt about that. But we have another lot of 50 more coming along right now. I just got the order in today.

CONRAD: What? I thought Archie just finished up this lot.

RICARDI: Yes, I know. They should all have been done at the same time. If we had had the order of 50 that we got today, it would have been a complete gift. As it is, now we will have to set up the machines again and run the whole batch through. They really don't know how much it is costing them. That's what's wrong with this company. They are afraid to ask how much something costs. When someone asks them or they try to price a product they use the standard hours, but the standards hours aren't near what we actually spend on making the product. They don't allow us any time for setups or making fixtures or for any unforeseen events. Those are the main times that are involved. I asked the accounting department one day how much it really cost to make a product and they gave me the computations from the standard hours; I told them that they were no good. They were left without any answer.

MACHINE SHOP AND PRODUCTION CONTROL

In the course of a number of conversations with Sam Coates, Conrad learned that Coates was well aware of the same signs of trouble in the assembly department and the machine shop that Conrad had seen. For instance, Coates told Conrad of a recent talk he had had with Ricardi.

COATES: Just today I happened to mention the production control group to Ricardi and he about exploded. He started pacing up and down. He said that Carl Canap, the assistant production control manager, was personally out for him. I was shocked by the vehemence. When he calmed down I asked him, "Al, what have I been saying to you!" He stopped. "You are running the shop, not Sam Coates or Larry Zeigler or production control. Now why do you feel threatened? Don't you realize that you have forgotten more machine shop operations and the scheduling of machine shop work than Carl Canap will ever learn?" I told him that he had to assert himself in a positive way. I told him that he was running the shop and no one else.

Mr. Coates told the casewriter that since this conversation he was attempting to remedy the conflict between Ricardi and Carl Canap by having the latter's boss, Tom Thompson, temporarily work with Ricardi instead of Mr. Canap. Sam continued, "If Tom can charm Al so that they work well together, then, later, when Al deals with Canap, he'll let all the little things that have been bothering him go by. Just for Al to be with Thompson will help out a lot in smoothing over the relationship between Al and Carl."

In the morning of the day following the Ricardi-Coates conversation, Conrad observed Tom Thompson talking to Ricardi about scheduling problems and procedures. Carl Canap had not made an appearance. Later in the day Coates and Ricardi were sitting in the former's office when Ricardi's assistant came in and stated that Carl Canap had just requested that the machine shop stop production of an item that was only partially completed and substitute a "rush job" which used the same machine. Ricardi immediately commented to Coates.

RICARDI: See, Sam, this is the type of thing that I have been talking about. We lose all our efficiency by breaking down in the middle of an operation.

COATES: Al, what have I been telling you for the last week and a half? You don't stop an order in the middle of production. You clear out the job before you start another.

RICARDI (*after a long pause*): What do I do?

COATES: Al, you're the foreman, not Carl Canap. You're the foreman of this shop, not anyone else.

RICARDI (*turning to face the assistant*): Don't do anything.

Approximately 15 minutes later Coates and Ricardi were interrupted in their conversation by Carl Canap, who burst through the doorway and with an angered tone of voice questioned Mr. Coates.

CANAP: Sam, I understand you and Al won't allow that rush job to be substituted. Is that true?

COATES: Don't look at me, Carl. Al is the foreman of this outfit, you talk to him.

CANAP: What about that, Al?

RICARDI (*pause*): That's right.

CANAP: Do you realize you are hurting the company, losing sales, losing money? What is this company coming to if we can't rearrange the schedule a little just because somebody wants to get a little extra credit on the weekly report. Do you realize what this means?

COATES (*angrily*): Listen here, Carl, Al is right. We're not going to switch, and henceforth you'll not be stopping production in the middle of any operation. This is my decision, and I want you to stick by it.

CANAP (*walking out of the office*): If that's the way you want it, that's the way it will be.

SAM COATES' VIEWS

Some few days later Sam Coates was talking to the casewriter about the general situation:

COATES: Higher management has become so concerned with the figures that they forget about what we're actually producing, what's finished, and what's good quality. The figures get divorced from what they stand for. But if you're going to have the system, you have to play along with it. I'm sure there are a lot of details about the figures that my foremen and particularly Al are overlooking. In fact, I think he's making himself look poor. His desk is in such a disarray and things come so fast that he just gives up and says, "Oh, to hell with it!" Al has got to learn that he can't work on a bunch of long and hard jobs at the same time and expect to get a good productivity rating. He's got to get his work finished up by Saturday so he can get credit for it. He's not making the most of what he's got down there.

5 | Empire Glass Company (B)

In the fall of 1963 a Harvard Business School case researcher visited the glass container plant of Empire Glass Company in French City, Canada. He was interested in studying the way a control system is perceived and used by plant personnel in a multiplant company and how it related to the other parts of the plant conceived as a sociotechnical system. Empire Glass Company had developed, in the years following World War II, a control system for use by its plants which was considered by some accountants to be quite sophisticated. Within its division of Empire, the French City plant was a preferred site for production management trainees because, according to a division training executive:

> The French City chaps look at the controls as tools. They show trainees that they really work. The French-Canadian atmosphere is good, too. In a French-Canadian family everything is open and aboveboard. There are no secrets. The trainees can ask anyone anything, and the friendliness and company parties give him a feel for good employee relations.

Empire Glass Company, in 1963, operated a number of plants in Canada. The principal products of the French City plant were glass jars and bottles.

The French City plant to some extent shipped its products throughout Canada, although transportation costs limited its market primarily to Eastern Canada. While some of the customers were large and bought in huge quantities, many were relatively small.

THE PLANT ORGANIZATION

Plant Manager, James Hunt

James Hunt had been manager of the French City plant since January 1961. Prior to that he had been assistant plant manager. He had risen from hourly worker through foreman up to plant manufacturing engineer in the maintenance end of the business. He presented to the researcher the appearance of self-assurance and intimate, firsthand knowledge of operations and events within the plant. He was seldom without a cigar clutched in his teeth, commonly at a rakish upward tilt.

As plant manager, Hunt had no responsibility for sales or research and development activities. In fact, both Hunt and the district sales manager in his area had separate executives to whom they reported in the division headquarters, and it was in the superior of these executives that responsibility for both sales and production first came together.

At the case researcher's first meeting with Hunt, he welcomed him to the plant with the comment: "Everything here is open to you. We think we have a pretty good plant here, but we want you to see for yourself."

In response to the researcher's indication of interest in the interrelationships of the people in plant management, Hunt went to a cabinet in his office, and from a number of manuals prepared by corporate staff in British City he pulled out a large loose-leaf volume labeled "Position Analysis Manual" and handed it to the researcher. There, for each person from assistant foreman to plant manager, he found six to ten pages reproduced from typewritten sheets which described the individuals' responsibilities and duties. Hunt said:

> You will see that frequently two managers with different job titles are assigned responsibility for the same task. [He implied that it was up to them to work out their own pattern of mutual support and cooperation.] However, I don't have to adhere strictly to the description. I may end up asking a lot more of the man at certain times and under certain conditions than is ever put down on paper.
>
> In effect, the staff[1] runs the plant. We delegate to the various staff department heads the authority to implement decisions within the framework of our budget planning. This method of handling responsibility means that staff members have to be prepared to substantiate their decisions. At the same time, it gives them a greater sense of participation in and responsibility for plant income. We endeavor to carry this principle into the operating and service departments. The foreman is given

---

[1] The personnel reporting directly to Hunt. The organization chart (Exhibit 1), which included a photograph of each individual, was widely distributed. An enlarged version, under glass, was mounted on a wall of the lobby at the main entrance where it could be seen by all plant personnel and visitors.

EXHIBIT 1
French City Plant
(March 1, 1963)

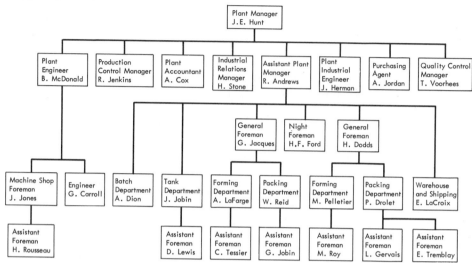

responsibility and encouraged to act as though he were operating a business of his own. He is held responsible for all results generated in his department and is fully aware of how any decisions of his affect plant income.

As our division personnel counsel and assist the plant staff, so do the plant staff counsel and assist the department foreman. Regular visits are made to the plant by our division manager and members of his staff. The principal contact is through the division manager of manufacturing and his staff, the manager of industrial engineering, the manager of production engineering, and the manager of quality control. [There was no division staff officer in production control.]

However, the onus is on the plant to request help or assistance of any kind. We can contact the many resources of Empire Glass Company, usually on an informal basis. That is, we deal with other plant managers directly for information when manufacturing problems exist without going through the division office.

Each member of the staff understands that we, as a plant, have committed ourselves through the budget to provide a stated amount of income, and regardless of conditions which develop, this income figure must be maintained. If sales are off and a continuing trend is anticipated, we will reduce expenses wherever possible to retain income. Conversely, if we have to gain in sales volume we look for the complete conversion of the extra sales at the profit margin rate. However, this is not always possible, especially if the increase in sales comes at a peak time when facilities are already strained.

Assistant Plant Manager, Robert Andrews

Andrews was something of a contrast to Hunt. He was tall and slender, while Hunt was relatively short with a tendency toward overweight. Andrews talked intently but with a reserve which contrasted with Hunt's ebullience. However Andrews, too, had a ready smile. He thought and moved quickly but without giving off as much visible nervous energy as Hunt. He had been promoted from quality control manager to his present position in January 1961. In talking about his job, Andrews said:

> I am responsible for all manufacturing operations within the plant. The operating group reports directly to me, and I also stay in constant contact with the staff departments to assume good communication and expedient handling of some items. During the summer months, which is our busiest period, the plant employs about 500 hourly persons. Approximately 250 work on the day shift, 150 on second, and 100 on the third shift. They are supervised by 15 salaried members of the supervisory staff plus a number of working supervisors who are appointed as activity increases. They usually supervise second- and third-shift operations.
>
> Our foremen have full responsibility for running their departments: quality, conditions of equipment, employee relations, production according to schedule, control of inventory through accurate reporting of spoilage and production, and cost control. They are just as accountable for these in their departments as the plant manager is for the entire plant.
>
> We have given the supervisory personnel status. Such things as "the white shirt,"[2] a personal parking spot, an office—these all assist in main-

---

[2] Andrews was referring to a norm that the researcher had already observed while circulating in the plant. The plant manager, the management staff, the foreman, the clerks in the office departments, all wore white shirts with ties but no coat. The union president, who worked at his production job except while handling union affairs, also wore a white shirt but without a tie. The vice president and other production workers wore colored shirts, usually sport shirts.

The force of this practice was observed by the researcher in an exchange between Ray Jenkins, production control manager, and Tom Voorhees, quality control manager, which took place in the main office area of the plant.

JENKINS: Hey Tom, where are you going? Knocking off for the day? Why are you so dressed up? [Voorhees had on a suit, white shirt, and tie.]

VOORHEES: No, I've just been in the office all morning. I usually don't stay there so long, but my assistant is kind of a fat fellow and likes the window open so I put my coat on because it was cool. I just kept it on when I ran down here.

JENKINS: Well, we'll let it pass this time.

RESEARCHER: I take it this is a coats-off organization?

JENKINS: Oh, very definitely. I would never think, for example, of wearing my coat out on the floor of the factory. That would be absolutely out of bounds.

RESEARCHER: Is it just accidental that everyone wears a white shirt, too?

JENKINS: Oh, no, it's a French City plant practice. You wouldn't last five minutes in here with that shirt (*pointing to researcher's striped shirt*) if you worked for

taining his position of authority in the eyes of his employees. He is
no longer the best man with the wrench—he is the man with the
best overall supervisory qualifications.

Production Control Manager, Ray Jenkins

Ray Jenkins was slight of build, moved fast, and talked fast. Like
James Hunt, he was practically a chain smoker, only he smoked cigarettes and a pipe instead of cigars. Jenkins described his job as follows:

> The production control manager is basically responsible to plan and
> control plant inventories and production schedules to meet sales require-
> ments consistent with effective and efficient utilization of facilities, mate-
> rials, and manpower. Our aim is to attain maximum length of run without
> affecting service and exceeding inventory budgets.
>
> I have a scheduler for each of the major operating departments,
> plus clerks to service the schedulers and a schedule coordinator reporting
> directly to me. The scheduler works very closely with his department
> foreman. Although their desks are just outside my office, the schedulers
> spend a good deal of time in the plant. They are also in frequent
> telephone contact with the sales offices at least once a week.
>
> Our high-volume food and beverage lines are, generally speaking,
> manufactured to estimate. We make a monthly manufacturing program
> which then is converted to a daily schedule. The lower volume lines
> are scheduled formally on a weekly basis with job priority listing made
> several times a week by the foreman and the scheduler.

Plant Accountant, Andrew Cox

This man appeared to be the oldest of the management staff, and
rather more serene. Cox talked of his job:

> I am responsible directly to the plant manager, but functionally to
> the division controller. My basic function is to develop and supervise
> an organization for the maintenance of accounting records and the prep-
> aration of reports therefrom in accordance with company policies and
> procedures. My organization is divided into three groups—general ac-
> counting, cost accounting, and office services. A few years ago we devel-
> oped a stenographic pool in office services, and now only the plant
> manager has a private secretary. Because of the diversity of products,
> many thousands of individual product costs must be developed and
> applied by the cost section. The annual proposed sales and income
> budget, because of its essentially financial nature, is coordinated by
> the plant controller. However, complete responsibilities for the develop-

---

Empire. You'd probably get a comment before you even got to your desk in the
morning.

RESEARCHER: Is this requirement written down somewhere?

JENKINS: No, it's just sort of in the air. A new man comes to work here and
he gets the message right away—no coat but a white shirt.

ment of departmental budgets are assigned by the plant manager to the responsible operating and staff groups concerned.

We are the auditors who see that every other department is obeying rules and procedures. It is our responsibility to know all that is in the instruction manuals. There are 12 volumes of general instructions and lots of special manuals.

Plant Industrial Engineer, Joe Herman

The researcher was impressed with the mobility of Herman's face and the high level of activity which he, as well as most of the other members of the management staff, exhibited. Herman stated:

> Industrial engineering in Empire Glass Company is active in the fields of time study, budgetary control, job evaluation, and methods improvement. Our company is on a standard cost system—that is, all our product costs are based on engineered standards, accurately measuring all labor, direct and indirect, and material that is expended in the manufacture of each and every item we make in our plants. All the jobs in the French City plant, up to and including the foreman, have been measured and standards set. Actually, there are company-wide benchmarks for most jobs, including the foreman's. For foremen the standard is used as a guide in increasing or reducing the supervisory force. If measurement shows that the quantity of supervisory work is less than 75 percent of standard, a foreman is taken off. If the work load is heavy and we find 75 percent of a supervisory job is there, we add a supervisor.
>
> Most of the machinery is just like that in other Empire Glass Company plants. Standards are established wherever the equipment is first used— which may be in the development engineering department in British City. We, of course, may make adjustment for local conditions. However, all our standards are forwarded to division which checks them against standards in use at other plants.
>
> Industrial engineering spearheads the cost reduction program within the organization. In fact, we should spend three quarters of our time on cost reduction. We have recently made an arrangement with the cost accounting group which is going to eliminate a lot of time this department has been spending in checking to see which standards applied to particular products being manufactured. Now cost accounting will do this work, which is essentially clerical and took time we could otherwise spend on cost reduction work. The budgeted savings this year from methods improvement is in six figures, and we now expect to exceed that by a substantial amount.

Industrial Relations Manager, Harold Stone

Stone was a large, slow-speaking man who wore a small mustache. He had been with Empire Glass Company a long time and had been assistant plant manager of one of its smaller plants before coming to French City. He was proud of the fact that the French City plant had never experienced a strike and that formal written grievances were almost unheard of.

In discussing company training programs which he conducted at the plant, Stone said that all management personnel, including foremen and assistant foremen, had taken the four-day "Communications Course," designed by the Empire corporate staff but conducted at the plant level, often with personnel from other Empire plants participating. The emphasis was on learning how to listen more effectively to unblock the flow of information up and down in the organization. A four-day course, "Conference Leadership," had been given to some of the management people and others were scheduled for its next repetition. Emphasis in this course was on role playing as a conference participant as well as conference leader.

Stone then commented on some of his other responsibilities. Several of them were represented by an impressive display in the manufacturing area near the main entrance, occupying a space about 50 by 20 feet. During the time the researcher was in the plant, the backdrop contained several panels about 12 or 14 feet high on safety, a housekeeping contest then underway, and on job security and industrial competition. All slogans and other comments were in both French and English. In the open area in front of the backdrop there were smaller displays, including a five-foot chart on an easel which showed the manufacturing efficiency rating (actual production cost versus standard cost) of the previous month for each of the Empire Glass Company plants, and their standings within their divisions.

Contests between departments were conducted frequently. Prior to the 13-week housekeeping contest, there had been a safety contest. Stone declared that in two of the last five years there had been only one lost time accident. Absenteeism was so low that statistics were no longer kept on it. Turnover was exceptionally low, which he attributed in part to the high wages and fringe benefits of the plant.

Turning to another aspect of Empire's personnel policy, Stone stated:

> We believe that it is important that the supervisor and the employee understand each other, that they know what the other person thinks about business, profit, importance of satisfying the customer, and any other aspect of business. While a great deal can be and is done within the regular business framework, we also believe that rapport between the supervisor and the employee can be improved in the social contacts which exist or can be organized. For this reason we sponsor dances, bowling leagues, golf days, fishing derbies, picnics, baseball leagues, supervision parties, management weekends, and many unofficial get-togethers. Over many years we have been convinced that these activities

really improve management-labor relations. They also provide a means for union and management to work closely together in organizing and planning these events. These opportunities help provide a mutual respect for the other fellow's point of view.

Some of these events were held in the plant cafeteria, which was another of Stone's responsibilities. The researcher was able to see the elaborate decorations prepared for an employees' children's Christmas party and for a supervisors' party. In addition, all employees, including the plant management, ate their lunches in the plant cafeteria, which was plain and functional except when decorated for a party.

It was Stone's responsibility to maintain the confidential file in connection with Empire's performance appraisal program for salaried employees. Procedures for handling the program were spelled out in one of the corporate manuals. Two forms were completed annually. One called for a rating of the employee by his supervisor, first on his performance of each of his responsibilities outlined in the Position Analysis Manual and then on each of 12 general characteristics such as cooperation, initiative, job knowledge, and delegation. In another section the supervisor and the appraised employee were jointly required to indicate what experience, training, or self-development would improve performance or prepare for advancement by the employee prior to the next appraisal. The appraisal was to be discussed between the supervisor and the employee; the latter was required to sign the form, and space was given for any comments he might want to make. The second form was not shown to the employee. It called for a rating on overall performance, an indication of promotability, and a listing of potential replacements. It was used for manpower planning; and after comments by the supervisor or the appraiser, it was forwarded to the division office.

MANAGERIAL PRACTICES AND RELATIONSHIPS

After becoming acquainted with most of the key executives at the French City plant and with their major responsibilities, the researcher turned his attention to some of their activities and how they related to each other in performing their duties.

He observed that Hunt and the four staff managers whose offices were closest to his[3] seldom worked alone at their desks. They were either in the manufacturing area or in each other's offices having impromptu meetings of twos, threes, or fours much of the time. Often a production supervisor or an office staff person would be in the group. The offices of Andrews, Jenkins, Herman, and Cox were identical to each other and similar to Hunt's except they lacked the carpet, drapes,

---

[3] See Exhibit 2.

EXHIBIT 2
Information about Certain Personnel

Name	Position	Approx. Age	Approx. Length of Service French City	EGC	College Education
James Hunt	Plant manager	40–45	8	18	None
Robert Andrews	Assistant plant manager	35	3	8	Agricultural Engineering
Andrew Cox	Plant accountant	50	15	23	None
Ray Jenkins	Production control supervisor	45	18	18	None
Harold Stone	Personnel supervisor	45–50	5	29	None
Joe Herman	Plant industrial engineer	30–35	1	10	Engineering
Tom Voorhees	Quality control supervisor	30	5	5	Engineering in Netherlands
G. E. Jacques	General foreman	45–50	25	25	None
Henry Dodds	General foreman	50	18	18	None
L. G. Adams	District sales, gr.	45–50	18	18	None

and polished wood furniture he was provided, and the upper part of their partitions were entirely of glass. They all contained a conference table and extra chairs. (See Exhibit 3 for a diagram of office areas.)

In addition to these frequent informal meetings there were a number of regular meetings involving plant management personnel. Most of these were held in a large, well-appointed conference room with a highly polished wooden table seating 20 or more people. The plant manager met monthly with the management staff and also with the production supervisors to discuss performance against the budget. The plant manager, assistant plant manager, and the industrial relations manager also held a monthly meeting with key union representatives. This was informal and the discussion centered on problems of one of the parties or mutual problems which were not current grievances.

The production control manager chaired a meeting held every Tuesday and Friday morning attended by the assistant plant manager and both general foremen. Each department foreman and his scheduler appeared briefly to discuss scheduling problems. A plant cost reduction committee was chaired by the plant industrial engineer; the plant manager, assistant manager, the plant engineer, the production control manager, and the general foremen were members. There were other committees involving fewer different interests or meeting less frequently.

Later interviews added to the researcher's understanding not only of the management practices, but also of the attitudes of the key executives toward their jobs and the requirements of the organization.

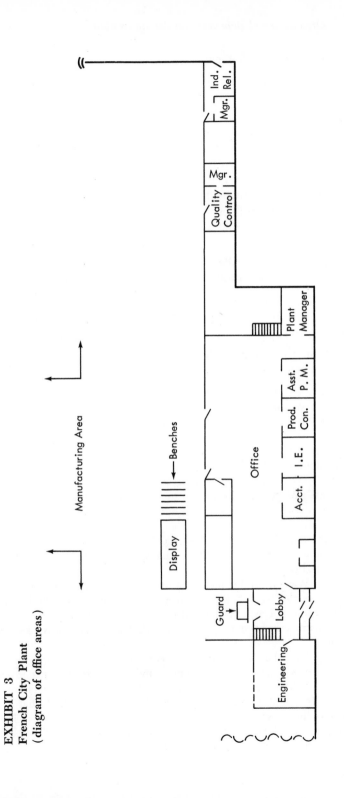

EXHIBIT 3
French City Plant
(diagram of office areas)

James Hunt, Plant Manager

During a discussion of the budget Hunt told the researcher that plant income was the actual sales realization, not a transfer price. Therefore income was adversely affected when either sales failed to come up to the forecast on which the budget was based or sales prices were reduced to meet competition. Hunt also informed the researcher that sales managers too have their incentives based on making or exceeding the budget and that their forecasts had tended to be quite accurate. Overoptimism of one group of products had usually been offset by underestimation of sales on other products. However, because no adjustment was permitted in budgeted profit when sales income was below forecast, the fact that sales were running 3 percent below the level budgeted for 1963 was forcing the plant to reduce expenses substantially in order to equal or exceed the profit budgeted for the year.

RESEARCHER: The budget rather puts you in a straitjacket then.

HUNT: No, the budget is a guide—a kind of signpost—not a straitjacket.

The researcher then suggested to Hunt that there were probably some accounts in the budget which left some slack for reducing expenses if sales fell below forecast.

HUNT: No, we never put anything in the budget that is unknown or guessed at. We have to be able to back up every single figure in the budget. We have to budget our costs at standard assuming that we can operate at standard. We know we won't all the time. There will be errors and failures, but we are never allowed to budget for them.

RESEARCHER: It seems to me that there must be some give somewhere.

HUNT: Well, I suppose there are some contentious accounts like overtime and outside storage. We do have arguments with division on those. For example, I might ask for $140,000 in the budget for overtime. The division manager will probably say $130,000—so we compromise at $130,000.

RESEARCHER: How about cost reduction? You budget a certain amount there, I understand. Do you have the specific projects planned when you prepare the budget?

HUNT: We budget for more than the savings expected from specific projects. We might have $100,000 in specific projects and budget $150,000.

RESEARCHER: I would think this is one place where you might really push for extra cost savings in order to offset an income loss like you've had this year.

HUNT: Yes, this is one of the areas we're pushing hard this year.

RESEARCHER: Can you delay repairs and overhauls to reduce expenses?

HUNT: At the time we make the budget we prepare an overhaul schedule in detail. It establishes the amount of labor and material that we expect to go into the overhaul as well as setting the time—which is cleared with production control so it will be the least inconvenient. Then any change from this schedule must be approved at the division level.

RESEARCHER: I understand you have an incentive for managers based on performance of the plant compared to budget.

HUNT: The bonus is paid on the year's results. It is paid as a percentage of salary to all who are eligible—they are the ones on the organization chart I gave you. There are three parts to it—one part is based on plant income, one on standards improvement or cost cutting, and the third on operating performance. We can make up to 20 percent by beating our plant income target and 25 percent on cost reduction and operating efficiency together. But we have to make 90 percent of our budgeted income figure to participate in any bonus at all.

I think we have the 25 percent on efficiency and cost reduction pretty well sewn up this year. If we go over our budgeted income, we can get almost 35 percent bonus.

RESEARCHER: Has the French City plant made a bonus in recent years?

HUNT: We have always made a certain amount—about 10 percent. In the past the bonus was based more on efficiency than anything else. We're one of the larger plants, and it made it harder for us. The larger plants just don't have the control. We don't know as well what the individual men are doing as in the smaller plants.

While Hunt and the researcher were at lunch early in December the conversation drifted back to the maintenance operation.

HUNT: We have been holding off work on molds [for shaping the jars and bottles] until next year. Jones [machine shop foreman] had been planning to wait until the new year to fix up the molds. They were laid aside after the production runs in which they were used ended. The only trouble is he started his program too early. Now we are going to have to run some more of some of those bottles this year and he'll have to repair the molds.

I told Jones he knew what had to be done, that I expected him to keep the savings he planned and I didn't want to hear about his troubles. However, I know I will have to go along if he can back up his reasons why he can't save all the money he projected for December.

At another time Hunt discussed with the researcher some of his practices as plant manager:

HUNT: I never look for answers to problems in these (*pointing to manuals in a cabinet in his office*). If I get a memo that refers specifically to an instruction in a manual, then I look it up. Otherwise I never touch them. I count on my accountant to keep me straight on rules and procedures. He has several shelves full of manuals and he's supposed to know what is in them. I don't look at this [loose-leaf book containing accounting reports] either. I don't look backward, I look forward. When I get information, I act on it right away. Once it goes in the book, I don't look at it except when I'm trying to spread a new budget over the year. Then I use past history.

Nor do I write many memos. When I have something to say I go tell the person or persons right away. I think people read into letters what they want. I guess you could say I follow the head-on approach. Unfortunately, I use the same approach with my superiors and once in a while I get called down for it.

RESEARCHER: I am interested in knowing which of the things you do you believe could not be delegated to someone else.

HUNT: For one thing, I can't delegate relations with sales. Production control handles individual scheduling problems with salespeople, but the manager has to look at the overall relationship. There are a lot of things production control can't do. The manager has to make the final decisions. Then there is capital budgeting. Third, the manager must be close to the people. For example, one of our foremen was having some trouble with his men. I suggested that he take them out and I allotted him some money to do it. He took them bowling and bought them some drinks. He got closer to them and his relationship with them improved a lot. He still has a lot of parties. At the foreman level I believe you can't get too close to your men. I think maybe a manager can get too close.[4]

Robert Andrews, Assistant Plant Manager

ANDREWS: Well, a budget system like this certainly doesn't leave much for the imagination. Your job is pretty well laid out for you. I suppose we could run a plant this size if this were the whole company without such an elaborate system. But with a big company, if you don't have a budget system that is pretty explicit, you can lose an awful lot of ground.

RESEARCHER: How important to you are the sales estimates?

ANDREWS: They affect everybody in the operation. Salespeople can put a lot of blue sky into their estimates because they can't afford to send a pessimistic estimate up to division. But it ends up hurting us. It simply causes inefficiency around here when things don't turn out the way sales predicted. I think we'd almost rather they would hand in pessimistic reports so we could be a little bit more sure where we stand on the production line.

RESEARCHER: When you talk of your duties, I don't hear you say anything about increasing production volume.

ANDREWS: We have standards. So long as we are meeting the standards we are meeting our costs and we do not worry about increasing production. We don't tell the foreman that he needs to get more goods out the door. We tell him to get rid of the red in his budget. I'm content with a 100 percent performance. I'd like 105 percent, but if we want more production it is up to IE to develop methods change.

RESEARCHER: What then are the principal skills you expect of a foreman?

ANDREWS: Communications and use of available control procedures. The foreman is expected to communicate effectively with all plant personnel, including staff heads. He must be able to convince his employees of the importance of certain aspects of their job, discipline or praise them when it is deserved. In all cases he must get his point across as "boss" and yet maintain the spirit of cooperation and teamwork that has marked our operation. Our

---

[4] Hunt took a daily tour of the plant and was observed by the researcher to call by name and speak in a folksy manner with many production workers and foremen.

control procedures are easy to apply. In each department there is an engineered standard for each operation covering labor, materials, and spoilage. Without waiting for a formal statement from accounting, a foreman can analyze his performance in any area and take corrective action if necessary. Then he receives reports from accounting to assist him in maintaining tight cost control. One is a daily report which records labor and spoilage performance against standard. The monthly report provides a more detailed breakdown of labor costs, materials and supplies used, and spoilage. It also establishes the efficiency figure for the month. This report is discussed at a monthly meeting of all of my supervisors. Generally the plant industrial engineer and a member of the accounting staff are present. Each foreman explains his variances from standard and submits a forecast of his next month's performance.

RESEARCHER: You mentioned communication between the foreman and staff managers. Does the foreman go directly to a staff manager with a problem or through you?

ANDREWS: A foreman may go directly to a staff manager, or more usually one of his assistants, or he may go to his general foreman or myself. And a staff manager may go direct to a foreman. I'm usually brought in on the more important ones.

RESEARCHER: How does the foreman know which ones to bring to you?

ANDREWS: I really don't know how, but they seem to know.

RESEARCHER: Do they keep you sufficiently informed, or do they bring too much to you?

ANDREWS: Oh, they do pretty well, on the whole. I don't think I ever get too much information, but I do have to get after a foreman occasionally for failing to tell me something he should have.

Production Control

The biweekly production control meetings observed by the researcher lasted about an hour. Jenkins and Andrews sat at the head of the conference table. The two general foremen were also present throughout the meeting while Hunt frequently dropped in for a time. Each production foreman and the production control scheduler working for his department came into the meeting at a prearranged time and when their turn came they reported on what products they were currently running and any problems they were having or which they anticipated. Most of the questions as well as instructions given in the meeting came from Andrews. It was also he who usually dismissed one foreman-scheduler pair and called on the next. Questions from Andrews or Jenkins were seldom clearly addressed to either the foreman or scheduler. They were answered more frequently by the scheduler than the foreman and often a scheduler would supplement comments made by the foreman. Generally the schedulers were younger but spoke with more self-assurance than the foremen.

There were frequent references to specific customers, their needs, complaints, and present attitude toward Empire Glass. Both Jenkins and Andrews tended to put instructions and decisions in terms of what was required to satisfy some particular customer or French City plant customers in general.

The researcher was especially interested in a part of a Tuesday production control meeting involving a foreman, "Mo" Pelletier, and the scheduler for his department, Dan Brown. While Dan was making the status report, the researcher observed that Mo was shaking his head in disagreement with Dan, but without saying anything. Dan was telling of his plan to discontinue on Friday the order being processed on a certain line, to shift to another order on Friday and then return on Tuesday to the product currently being produced.

ANDREWS: I don't think your plan makes much sense. You go off on Friday and then on again Tuesday.

Mo (*to Dan*): Is this all required before the end of the year? (*This was asked with obvious negative emotional feeling and then followed by comments by both Andrews and Jenkins.*)

DAN: Mind you, I could call sales again.

JENKINS: I can see the point, Dan. It is sort of nonsensical to change back after so short a run.

Mo: This would mean our production would be reduced all week to around 300 instead of 350. You know it takes four hours to make the changeover.

DAN: But the order has been backed up.

ANDREWS: It is backed up only because their [sales] demands are unreasonable.

DAN: They only asked us to do the best we can.

ANDREWS: They always do this. We should never have put this order on in the first place.

Mo: If you want to we could. . . . (*Makes a suggestion about how to handle the problem.*)

ANDREWS: Production-wise, this is the best deal. (*Agreeing with Mo's plan.*)

DAN: Let me look at it again.

ANDREWS: Production-wise, this is best; make the changeover on the weekend.

JENKINS (*summarizes; then to Dan*): The whole argument is the lost production you would have.

Mo: It'll mean backing up the order only one day.

ANDREWS (*after another matter in Mo's department has been discussed and there is apparently nothing further, Andrews turns to Dan and smiles*): It's been a pleasure, Dan.

Dan then returned the smile weakly and got up to go somewhat nervously. As Jenkins and the researcher were leaving the conference room after the meeting Jenkins commented to the researcher

Danny got clobbered, as you could see. I used to stand up for him but he just doesn't come up here prepared. He should have the plans worked out with his foreman before they come up.

After another one of the production control meetings, Jenkins again discussed an incident which had occurred in the meeting.

We in production control are the buffer between sales and operating people. That discussion about the Smith bottle you heard is an example. Andrews is basically concerned with efficiency. He doesn't want to make anything that can't be made to standard. Now those little cracks we're getting means that if we continue running, our spoilage rate will sky-rocket—maybe double or triple what it normally would be. Andrews hates this because it drives his efficiency down. But what he didn't know upstairs was that Jim Hunt had made a personal commitment to the customer to get those 50,000 bottles out today and he was going to do it come hell or high water. Andrews just never had a chance when he started making noises about shutting the line down. So I won and Bob lost this time, but he's able to be big about it and see the real issue. Where it really gets tough for him, though, is that by the end of the month this particular problem will have become lost in the figures. People will have forgotten that today, November 8, a decision went against Bob Andrews. All they will notice is that according to the accounting reports, Andrews had bad efficiency for the month of November. To avoid looking bad he has to find another operation where there is some slack and produce more efficiently. That's the only way he can protect himself, but it puts a lot of pressure on him. Bob and I are usually able to work these things out fairly well. We know that the problem is more or less built into our jobs.

In discussing his job Jenkins frequently commented on how he thought a decision or problem would affect someone else in the plant.

If all you had to do was manage the nuts and bolts of production scheduling and not worry about the customer or how people were going to react, this would be the easiest job in the whole plant. You could just sit down with a paper and pencil and lay it out the best way. But because the customer is so important and because you've got to look ahead to how people are going to react to a given kind of schedule, it makes the whole job tremendously complicated. It isn't easy!

Andrew Cox, Plant Accountant

Cox: We want the budget to be realistic; but we also want it to be something of a target for our management and operating personnel. At the French City plant our goal over the years has been to present budgets which reflect improvement in the percent return of gross plant income to gross plant sales as well as return on employed capital. We have been reasonably successful in this despite constantly rising labor and material costs.

The budget is a plan to insure the success of the company. We put a lot of stress on competition within the company and against other companies in our field. We here at French City want to do as well as any other plant in Empire Glass. . . . The essence of the present control system was developed 15 years ago. There were a lot of gripes and criticism when it was introduced. The big difference between then and now is that now the people on the floor use the reports as a tool. . . . We've done a lot of training since then. It took maybe ten years to get the job done.

RESEARCHER: Have there been changes in the bonus plan over the years?

COX: Yes, at one time the bonus plan was based on departmental results or department efficiency. Under this there was a tendency for the departments to work at cross purposes, to compete rather than cooperate with each other. For the last seven or eight years, the emphasis has been on the plant, not the department. The latest plan is geared not only to the attainment of budgeted cost goals, but also to the attainment of budgeted income. This is consistent with the attention we are placing on sales. I think the company was disturbed by what they sensed was a belief that those at the plant level can't do much about sales. Now we are trying to get the idea across that if we make better cans and give better service, we will sell more.

RESEARCHER: I assume there must be some accounts in the budget where you leave yourself some room to maneuver.

COX: Well, in this company there is very little opportunity to play footsy with the figures.

Guillaume Jacques, General Foreman

Jacques was completely bilingual, and he felt his French background was an advantage in dealing with the workers, an estimated 90 percent of whom were French-Canadians. In describing his job he stated that he worked closely with both the assistant plant manager and the production control manager, but more with the latter. He said the job of general foreman was to regulate the troubles of the department and compared it to the relationship of a father and his children.

RESEARCHER: Are the standards and the budget important in your work?

JACQUES: Yes, very important. Most of the time they ask you not only to meet your budget but to do better, saving such and such amount of money. The assistant foreman has to check constantly, each production line each hour, to be sure they are close to standard.

RESEARCHER: Can you keep the employee satisfied as well as meet the budget requirements?

JACQUES: Yes, you've got to make the worker understand the importance of keeping the budget. I get them in the office and explain that if we don't meet the budget we'll have to cut down somewhere else. It is mathematical. I explain all this to them, they have given me a budget to meet, I need them for this, they need me to give them work. We work like a team. I try to understand them.

RESEARCHER: Do you feel under tension in your work?

JACQUES: Sure I work under tension, but don't all supervisors? You try to go along with the temperament of the men as much as possible. Myself, I ask the men to go out to have a beer with me, to go to a party. It relaxes them from our preoccupations. Right now, for example, there is this party with the foremen coming up. At these gatherings it is strictly against the rules to talk about work. These things are necessary.

Jacques commented on the advances in technology and the reduction in the number of employees needed. He said that he felt management had done a good job with the union in persuading the workers that cost cutting, although it meant reducing the number of people on the floor, actually increases job security in the long run.

Henry Dodds, General Foreman

RESEARCHER: Do you and the foremen participate in establishing the budget?

DODDS: I'm responsible for preparing the budgets for my department, and the foreman participates in my area because I ask him for his thoughts. We have to make budget for each production department.

RESEARCHER: Does the foreman get a copy of the budget?

DODDS: Yes, they have a copy of the budget for their department. It's prepared by the industrial engineers and the accounting department from our work sheets.

RESEARCHER: Does the production worker see the budget?

DODDS: He doesn't see the budget. He has the machine operating standard; if he meets this he is doing his share. The standard is set so that if he works the machine at full capacity he achieves 110 percent of standard.

RESEARCHER: Since you don't have wage incentives, is there any problem in getting the employees to produce up to standard?

DODDS: Well, there is usually some needling when a man is down below standard. He's told, "Why don't you get to be part of the crew?" It doesn't hurt anything. . . . You only get a good day's work out of people if they are happy. We strive to keep our people happy so they'll produce the standard and make the budget. We try to familiarize them with what is expected of them. We have targets set for us. The budget is reasonable, but it is not simple to attain. By explaining our problems to the workers we find it easier to reach the budget.

Dodds emphasized that an understanding of plant problems and objectives on the part of the foremen was also important. He told of a current program to try to fill the need for a certain type of cutting machine in one plant area by releasing several similar machines from another area for conversion to accomplish the new purpose.

DODDS: Because the foremen understood the program they will cooperate to clear the machines of work and make them available.

RESEARCHER: Do you have situations where a foreman thinks a standard is too high and the worker cannot make it?

DODDS: We haven't run into an instance of that in eight years. The industrial engineer goes over the standard with the foreman and he has an opportunity to question it before it is approved by management. Usually they explain the standard to the operator, and they always tell the operator what the individual engineer is doing.

Foremen and Production Workers

Foremen and production workers who were interviewed were all very much aware of the budget, and workers often explained behavior of foremen in terms of the requirements of the budget. Most of the foremen and many of the workers accepted the necessity of keying their activities to the work standards and the budget. One notable exception was a foreman of many years' service who said:

> We have a meeting once a month upstairs. They talk to us about budgets, quality, etc. That's all on the surface; that's b——s——. It looks good. It has to look good but it is all bull. For example, the other day [a foreman] had a meeting with the workers to talk about quality. After that an employee brought to his attention a defect in some products. He answered, "Send it out anyway." And they had just finished talking to us about quality.

Although they accepted the necessity of standards and budgets, many foremen and workers expressed feelings of pressure from superiors and from the control system. In contrast were the comments of one of the younger and more ambitious foremen—a French-Canadian.

> What I like about this department is that I am in charge. I can do anything I like as long as I meet up with the budget. I can have that machine moved—send it over there—as long as I have good reasons to justify it. The department, that's me. I do all the planning and I'm responsible for results. I'm perfectly free in the use of my time (*gives examples of his different arrival times during the past week and the fact that he came in twice on Saturday and once on Sunday for short periods*). . . . One thing I like here is that we don't get swelled heads about the positions we hold. Each man here—foreman, manager, etc.—is an employee of the company. We each have a job to do. You can talk freely with any of the staff heads.

Most of the foremen were bilingual French-Canadians. Some expressed dislike of the troublesome problems they felt were inherent in a job directing the work of others. One declared he would not want the manager's job for this reason, "although he is well paid for it."

No negative statements by foremen about the plant manager or the management staff were heard by the researcher. However, one expressed a desire to return to hourly work. Another felt that the foremen needed a union.

Foremen tended to view the production worker as irresponsible and interested, insofar as his job was concerned, only in his paycheck and quitting time. One foreman expressed himself as follows: "We do all the work; they do nothing." Even an officer of the union commented:

> They don't give a damn about the standards. They work nonchalantly and they are very happy when their work slows up. If the foreman is obliged to stop the line for two minutes every one goes to the toilet. There are some workers who do their work conscientiously, but this is not the case with the majority.

When speaking of their work, several of the production workers expressed feelings of pressure, although others declared they were accustomed to their work and it did not bother them. One said:

> Everyone is obsessed with meeting the standards—the machine adjuster, the foreman, the assistant foreman. They all get on my nerves.

One old-timer clearly differentiated the company, which he considered benevolent, from his foreman:

> I'm not talking about the company. I'm talking about the foreman. I can understand that these men are under tension as well as we are. They have meetings every week. I don't know what they talk about up there. . . . The foremen have their standards to live up to. They're nervous. They don't even have a union like us. So if things go bad, well, that's all. . . . They make us nervous with all this. But there's a way with people. We don't say to a man, "Do this, do that." If we said, "Would you do this?" it is not the same thing. You know a guy like myself who has been here for 35 years knows a few tricks. If I am mad at the foreman I could do a few little things to the machine to prevent it from keeping up with the standards and no one would know.

Another said:

> I'd prefer working for a dollar an hour less and have a job that is less tiring. It is not really hard but you have to work fast. . . . Our nerves are on edge here. . . . The worst ones aren't the foremen but the schedulers. It is never the fault of the machines but always the operator. . . . They are always on us. But they are good people here just the same. They replace us when we are tired or want to go to the toilet. The foremen could be much worse.

Those who complained about their foremen, however, tended to contrast the manager and the management staff, as did one worker, who said, "They're people—polite people. They speak to you properly."

Although a number of workers expressed sentiments similar to those quoted above, most workers conveyed to the researcher a feeling of overall satisfaction with their jobs. Typical was the comment of the worker who said, "Truly, it is a good company, and it pays well." In a recent Harvard research study of a number of jobs in 12 plants in several different industries in the United States and Canada, the French City plant workers who were included ranked highest of the 12 plants in job satisfaction.

IN PURSUIT OF BUDGETED GOALS

The researcher was particularly interested in a series of events he observed which related to a special meeting of the entire French City plant management held in November. On his first visit to the plant, James Hunt and several of the staff managers had mentioned to him the fact that sales for the year had fallen below expectations and that their bonus was in jeopardy as a result.

One day in early November the researcher noticed an unusual amount of activity in the accounting section. Hunt came into the area frequently, and he and Cox from time to time would huddle with one of the accoun-tants over some figures. In the afternoon the researcher observed several management staff members saunter by the plant accountant's office, one of them two or three times, without the purposeful air they usually had when walking in the office. The researcher learned from Cox that the extra activity was due to the fact that the report on the October results was to be issued that day.

At one point in the afternoon, while the researcher was in Cox's office for a prearranged interview, Hunt walked in and sat down but said nothing. After a few minutes he started out the door.

Cox: Jim, did you want to see me about something?
Hunt: I'm waiting for your story (*referring to the report of October results*).

Hunt then strolled about the accounting area for a time and then left.

A week later Hunt scheduled a joint meeting of the management staff and the line organization to go over the October results. This was a departure from the usual practice of having the groups in separate meetings. Prior to the meeting Hunt discussed with the researcher what he hoped to accomplish in the meeting:

The meeting this afternoon is simply to get things straightened out. Those figures we got last week showed that some of the accounts did what they were expected to do, some did more, and some did a good deal less. The thing we have to do now is kick those accounts in the plants that are not making the savings they planned to make. What we've been doing is raising the expected savings as the time gets shorter. It may be easy to save 10 percent on your budget when you've got six months; but with only six weeks, it is an entirely different matter. The thing to do now is to get everybody together and excited about the possibility of doing it. We know how it can be done. Those decisions have already been made. It's not unattainable even though I realize we are asking an awful lot from these men. You see, we are in a position now where just a few thousand dollars one way or the other can make as much as 10 percent difference in the amount of bonus the men get. There is some real money on the line. It can come either from a sales increase or an expense decrease, but the big chunk has to come out of an expense decrease.

RESEARCHER: Do you expect some wrangles this afternoon about who is right and who is wrong?

HUNT: No, we never fight about the budget. It is simply a tool. All we want to know is what is going on. Then we can get to work and fix it. There are never any disagreements about the budget itself. Our purpose this afternoon is to pinpoint those areas where savings can be made, where there is a little bit of slack, and then get to work and pick up the slack.

RESEARCHER: Am I right that any time there is a departure from budgeted expense or budgeted sales, you and the other managers immediately begin to look for other plant accounts where the losses can be made up?

HUNT: Yes, that is an automatic decision, or else we'll give the department that has been losing money a certain period of time to make it up. Also, any time anybody has a gain, I tell them I expect them to maintain that gain.

The researcher also talked to Bob Andrews concerning the methods used to pick up the projected savings.

ANDREWS: When you have lost money in one sector you have to look around for something else that you can "milk" to make up the difference.

RESEARCHER: Do you ever ask for volunteers?

ANDREWS: No, we do the "milking." Those guys just have to do what we say. How much we can save pretty much depends on how hard the man in the corner office wants to push on the thing. I mean if we really wanted to save money we probably could do it, but it would take a tremendous effort on everybody's part and Jim would really have to crack the whip.

Special Line and Staff Meeting

The meeting was held in the conference room at 4:00 P.M. To accommodate everyone, two extra tables were brought in from the cafeteria and placed at the end of the polished table toward the door. Hunt and Cox sat at the far end of the table, facing the door, with an easel bearing a flip chart near them. The chart listed the projected savings in budgeted expense for November and December, account by account. The group of about 30 arranged themselves at the table so that, with only a couple of exceptions, the management staff personnel and general foremen sat closest to Hunt and Cox and the foremen and assistant foremen sat toward the foot of the table.

Hunt opened the meeting one or two minutes after four and declared that performance against budget for October would first be reviewed, followed by discussion of the November and December projections. He stated rather emphatically that he was "disappointed" in the October performance. Although money had been saved, it represented good performance in some areas but rather poor performance in others. The gains made in the areas where performance had been good must be maintained and the weak areas brought up, Hunt declared.

He then turned the meeting over to Cox, who reviewed the October results, reading from the report which everyone had in front of him. Where performance was not good, he called on the individual responsible for that area to explain. The essence of the typical explanation was that the original budgeted figure was unrealistic and that the actual amount expended was as low as it could possibly be under the circumstances. Hunt frequently broke into the explanation with a comment like, "Well, that is not good enough," or "Can you possibly do better for the rest of the year?" or "I hope we have that straightened out now." When he sat down, the person giving the explanation was invariably thanked by Cox.

Following this part of the meeting, Cox, followed by Jenkins, commented on the sales outlook for the remainder of the year. They indicated that for the two months as a whole sales were expected to be about on budget. After asking for questions and getting one from a foreman. Hunt said:

> Well now, are there any more questions? Ask them now if you have them. Everybody sees where we stand on the bonus, I assume. Right?

Hunt then referred to the chart on plant expense savings and began to discuss it, saying:

> The problem now is time. We keep compressing the time and raising the gain [the projected savings for the year had been raised $32,000 above what had been projected in October]. You can only do that so long. Time is running out, fellows. We've got to get on the stick.

Several times Hunt demanded better upward communication on problems as they came up. He gave an example from the previous month and declared:

> This sort of thing is absolutely inexcusable. We simply cannot have such a thing happen again. We've got to know ahead of time when these mix-ups are going to occur so that we can allow for and correct them.

As Cox was covering projections for November, account by account, the following exchange took place when he came to manufacturing efficiency:

Cox: Now we have come to you, Bob. I see you're getting a little bit more optimistic on what you think you can do.

ANDREW: Yes, the boss keeps telling me I'm just an old pessimist and I don't have any faith in my people. I'm still a pessimist, but we are doing tremendously. I think it's terrific, fellows (*pointing to a line graph*); I don't know whether we can get off the top of this chart or not, but at the rate this actual performance line is climbing, we might make it. All I can say is, keep up the good work. . . . I guess I'm an optimistic pessimist.

The following comments were made during the discussion of projected savings for December in the equipment maintenance account.

Cox: Where in the world are you fellows going to save $8,000 more than you originally said you would save?

McDONALD: (*A noncommittal response.*)

JONES: I'd just like to say at this point to the group that it would be a big help if you guys would take it easy on your machines. That's where we are going to save an extra $8,000—simply by only coming down to fix the stuff that won't run. You're really going to have to make it go as best you can. That's the only way we can possibly save the kind of money we have to save. You have been going along pretty well, but all I've got to say is I hope you can keep it up and not push those machines too hard.

Although Jones spoke with sincerity, the researcher noted that a number of sly smiles and pokes in the ribs were exchanged by foremen at the end of the table nearest the door.

Hunt concluded the meeting at about 5:30, still chewing on his cigar.

> There are just a couple of things I want to say before we break up. First, we've got to stop making stupid errors in shipping. Joe [foreman of shipping], you've absolutely *got* to get after those people to straighten them out. Second, I think it should be clear, fellows, that we can't break any more promises. Sales are our bread and butter. If we don't get those orders out in time we'll have no one but ourselves to blame for missing our budget. So I just hope it is clear that production control is running the show for the rest of the year. Third, the big push is on *now!* We sit around here expecting these problems to solve themselves, but they don't! It ought to be clear to all of you that no problem gets solved until it's spotted. Damn it, I just don't want any more dewy-eyed estimates about performance for the rest of the year. If something is going sour we want to hear about it. And there's no reason for not hearing about it! (*Pounds the table, then voice falls and a smile begins to form.*) It can mean a nice penny in your pocket if you can keep up the good work.
>
> That's all I've got to say. Thank you very much.

Interview with Ray Jenkins

The room cleared immediately, but the researcher engaged Ray Jenkins in further conversation in his office:

RESEARCHER: You got a nice little boost there at the end of the meeting.

JENKINS: No, I'm afraid that little bit of advice there at the end won't make a great deal of difference in the way things work out. I mean that; not that I don't appreciate that sort of thing. It's just that it won't make any difference. As I was telling you before, you have to play off sales against production. It's built into the job. When I attend a meeting like that one upstairs and I see all those production people with their assistants and see the other staff managers with their assistants, and I hear fellows refer to corporate policy that dictates and supports their action at the plant level, I suddenly realize that I'm all alone up there. I can't sit down and fire off a letter to my boss at the division level like the rest of these guys can do. I haven't got any authority at all. It is all based strictly on my own guts and strength. Now Bob is a wonderful guy, I like him and I have a lot of respect for him, but it just so happens that 80 percent of the time he and I disagree. He knows it and I know it; I mean it's nothing we run away from, we just find ourselves on opposite sides of the question and I'm dependent upon his tact and good judgment to keep from starting a war.

Boy, it can get you down, it really can after awhile, and I've been at it for—God—20 years. But in production control you've just got to accept it—you're an outcast. They tell you you're cold, that you're inhuman, that you're a bastard, that you don't care about anything except your schedule. And what are you going to say? You're just going to have to swallow it because basically you haven't got the authority to back up the things you know need to be done. Four nights out of five I am like this at the end of the day—just completely drained out—and it comes from having to fight my way through to try to get the plant running as smoothly as I can.

And Andrews up there in that meeting. He stands up with his chart and he compliments everybody about how well they are doing on efficiency. You know, he says, "Keep up the good work," and all that sort of stuff. I just sat there, shaking my head. I was so dazed you know, I mean I kept saying to myself, "What's he doing? What's he saying? What's so great about this?" You know, if I could have, I'd have stood up and I'd have said, "Somebody go down to my files in production control and pick out any five customer orders at random—and letters—and bring them back up here and read them—at random, pick any five." You know what they would show? Do you know how many broken promises and how many missed delivery dates and how many slightly off-standard items we've been pushing out the door here? I mean, what is an efficient operation? Why the stress on operating efficiency? That's why I just couldn't figure out why in the world Andrews was getting as much mileage out of his efficiency performance as he was. Look at all the things we sacrifice to get that efficiency. But what could I do?

Interview with District Sales Manager

Having heard how Jenkins felt about the pressures of the budget on sales, the researcher visited the district sales manager, L. G. Adams, and discussed the impact of the plant budget on the sales department with him.

ADAMS: That's probably my biggest problem on this job, getting the boys here to see that if they really want to serve the customer, they can't hold their own budget up as a shining standard all the time. The budget comes to dominate people's thinking and influence all their actions. I'm afraid even my salesmen have swallowed the production line whole. They can understand the budget so well they can't understand their customers. And the French City plant boys are getting more and more local in their thinking with this budget. They're not thinking about what the customer needs today or may need tomorrow, they just think about their goddamned budget.

If the customer will not take account of your shortcomings, and if you can't take account of the customer's shortcomings, the two of you will eventually end up at each other's throats. That's what this budget system has built into it. Suppose, for example, you want to give a customer a break. Say he has originally planned for a two-week delivery date, but he phones you and says he really has problems and if you possibly could he would like about four days knocked off that delivery date. So I go trotting over to the plant, and I say, "Can we get it four days sooner?" Those guys go out of their minds, and they start hollering about the budget and how everything is planned just right and how I'm stirring them up.

RESEARCHER: It is probably hard to do this very frequently.

ADAMS: That's for sure! You can't go running to them all the time, but only when you really need something in the worst way. You can't let those plant guys see your strategy, you know. I want to tell you, it is taking an awful lot out of a guy's life around here when he has to do everything by the numbers.

The researcher learned after the first of the year that the report being sent by Hunt to division would show, despite the fact that sales had fallen about 3 percent below budget, that profits for 1963 had exceeded the amount budgeted and that operating efficiency and cost reduction had both exceeded the budget by a comfortable margin. This enabled the managers and supervisors at the French City plant to obtain the salary bonuses for which they had been striving.

6 | *Alcon Laboratories, Inc. (Condensed)*

In the summer of 1966, Mr. George Leone, national sales manager of Alcon Laboratories, initiated an appraisal of the organization and morale of his 70-man sales force. Mr. Leone expressed particular concern over the high turnover in the sales force (28 percent in the fiscal year 1965–66). He had considered a number of changes which might reduce the turnover but was unsure as to just what action he should take. While he was willing to make any changes that might improve the situation, he felt that it would be better to do nothing than to attempt changes that were inappropriate to the needs of his organization.

THE COMPANY HISTORY

In 1947 in Fort Worth, Texas, two pharmacists founded Alcon Laboratories upon the principle that more accurate, sterile, stable pharmaceutical compounds could be manufactured by Alcon on a large-scale basis than was possible in retail drugstores, where most prescribed drugs were being compounded at that time.

In early years Alcon management decided to achieve growth by concentrating their marketing efforts in specialty fields. The field in which Alcon first specialized was ophthalmological drugs (drugs used in the treatment of defects and diseases of the eye). In 1947, 85 percent of all eye-care drugs were being compounded in drugstores.

As doctors became familiar with the company's products and their quality, they prescribed them more and more, and Alcon prospered.

By 1957 a sales force of 30 men was promoting the company's eye-care products nationally, and sales had grown to nearly $1 million.

Alcon Laboratories continued to grow both domestically and internationally. In fiscal 1966, total domestic and international sales of Alcon Laboratories were $9.1 million. The consolidated income statement is as follows:

	Year Ended *April 30, 1966* *(000)*
Net sales	$9,114
Costs and expenses:	
Cost of goods sold	$3,129
Selling, general, and administrative expenses*.	4,411
Total costs and expenses.	$7,540
Income before provision for federal taxes	$1,574
Provision for federal income taxes	753
Net Income	$ 821

    * Research and development represented a significant portion of general and administrative expenses.

Exhibit 1 shows selected historical operating and financial information for the period 1958 to 1966. Exhibit 2 shows the consolidated balance sheet for 1966.

Domestically, a 70-man sales force was promoting 33 eye-care products, and annual sales of these products had grown to $6 million by 1966. In addition, by purchasing another small specialized pharmaceutical firm, Alcon had entered a second specialty field. Furthermore, Alcon had achieved some backward integration by purchasing a manufacturer of plastic containers for pharmaceutical products.

Internationally, Alcon manufactured and sold its product line through foreign subsidiaries and joint agreements.

ALCON'S EYE-CARE PRODUCTS: THEIR USE AND DISTRIBUTION

Pharmaceuticals used and prescribed by ophthalmologists (medical doctors specializing in the treatment of eye diseases and defects) were generally classified into seven categories, depending on their use. These were:

1. Glaucoma products—for aid in the treatment of glaucoma, a disease where fluid pressure in the eye causes hardness of the eyeball and impairment or loss of vision.
2. Steroid products—for elimination of irritation and inflammation of the eye.

EXHIBIT 1
Highlights of Operating and Financial Data

	1966	1965	1964	1963	1962	1961	1960	1959	1958
Net sales	$9,114,329	$8,749,438	$8,696,600	$7,718,310	$6,392,141	$3,057,399	$3,094,197	$2,034,758	$1,347,283
Net income	821,129	663,039	749,647	534,164	403,761	267,710	214,892	162,985	69,277
Earnings per share.	1.30	1.05	1.20	0.86	0.66	0.50	0.40	0.31	0.13
Net working capital. . . .	3,261,854	2,447,996	1,845,882	1,064,999	734,241	185,737	531,879	380,518	169,478
Current ratio	3.24	3.06	2.39	1.96	1.87	1.31	2.25	2.03	2.02
Total assets	7,015,740	6,006,671	5,426,280	4,413,063	3,648,339	2,606,424	1,809,876	1,478,230	544,686

3. Antibiotic products—for anti-infective uses on the eye.
4. Surgical products—for use during eye surgery such as cataract operations.
5. Diagnostics/anesthetics—for use in identifying eye damage and anesthetizing for treatment.
6. Mydriadics/cycloplegics—for use when refraction or immobilization of the eye is needed.
7. Lubricants and astringents—for use in cleaning and lubricating the eye.

Alcon manufactured products in all seven of the above categories.

EXHIBIT 2

ALCON LABORATORIES, INC.
Consolidated Balance Sheets
As of End of Fiscal Year
($000)

	May 1, 1966
Assets	
Current Assets:	
Cash	$ 343
Marketable securities	1,856
Accounts receivable (less allowance–doubtful accounts)	1,578
Inventories	940
Total Current Assets	$4,717
Investment in unconsolidated subsidiaries	$ 237
Other assets	102
Property, plant, and equipment	$4,172
Less: Accumulated depreciation	2,213
Net fixed assets	$1,959
Total Assets	$7,015
Liabilities	
Current Liabilities:	
Current maturities of long-term debt	$ 18
Accounts payable	335
Accrued federal income taxes	585
Other accrued liabilities	517
Total Current Liabilities	$1,455
Long-term debt:	
First mortgage bond	$ 91
Total Long-Term Debt	$ 91
Capital stock and surplus:	
Common stock (50¢ par value)	$ 315
Capital surplus	1,006
Earned surplus	4,148
Net capital stock and surplus	$5,469
Total Liabilities	$7,015

Although some of these products could be purchased over the counter (i.e., without a prescription), 90 percent of Alcon's total sales of ophthalmological drugs were prescription products. Most prescriptions were written by the 6,000 ophthalmologists and 2,000 eye-ear-nose-throat doctors who practiced in the United States and who were called on regularly by Alcon salesmen.

Alcon products were available either directly or through wholesalers both to hospitals and to retail drugstores.

THE MARKET AND COMPETITION

In 1965, total retail sales of ophthalmological drugs in the United States were $30 million. Seventy-five percent of these sales were manufacturer-compounded products, and 25 percent were compounded from basic ingredients by pharmacists in drugstores.

Alcon Laboratories' share of the total domestic ophthalmological drug market was nearly 30 percent. Their competition came primarily from retail druggists, and from both small and large pharmaceutical firms. Retail druggists, when given a choice in how to fill a prescription, might prefer to compound the drug themselves and earn a gross margin of 80 percent to 90 percent instead of dispensing a precompounded, brand name drug which typically offered a margin of only 40 percent to 50 percent. Other small, specialized manufacturers like Alcon, which attempted to find a niche in the total market by catering specifically to the ophthalmic market competed directly with Alcon. Finally, Alcon competed with large, diversified drug manufacturers for whom certain segments of the ophthalmic market were large and lucrative enough to warrant attention. Alcon management stated that in 1966 two large drug manufacturing firms controlled about 30 percent of the domestic ophthalmic market.

The active chemical compounds used in various ophthalmological preparations were essentially the same, regardless of manufacturer. Competing products were differentiated primarily on the basis of their form[1] and vehicle.[2] Competing manufacturers were constantly looking for new preparations which would have performance superior to existing ones. While Alcon was interested in developing new compounds of active ingredients, the major thrust of their research was to improve the performance of existing compounds by developing better or new forms and vehicles.

---

[1] Form referred to whether the compounds came in solution, ointment, cream, pill, and so forth.

[2] The vehicle was comprised of the inactive ingredients which were important in determining such product qualities as the stability of the product, how well the product stayed in the eyes (instead of "sweating out"), the irritation and/or side effects of the product, etc.

Doctors were not unaware of the prices of various prescriptions, but industry sources thought that they did not typically consider price to be an important factor in deciding what to prescribe unless there was a large price difference among similar products. The average price of an ophthalmic prescription in 1965 was $2.34.

Alcon management believed that the company had been highly successful in filling a specialized need in the market, but that changing environmental factors might make success more difficult to achieve in the future. Threatening changes came from competing firms and government.

If large diversified pharmaceutical manufacturers became more interested in specialty areas and increased their activities in the ophthalmic market, they would be able to devote resources to product development and promotion which the smaller, specialized firms could not hope to match.

Within the government, the Food and Drug Administration had promulgated more stringent requirements for the testing and acceptance of drugs. Under these conditions, large and diversified companies had another advantage over small, specialized firms, because small firms were unable to spread the increased costs of development and testing over many end uses of the drug in question. For example, when a diversified drug company developed a new antibiotic it would be promoted not only in drugs for the treatment of eye diseases and defects but also in drugs for treating diseases affecting all parts of the body. In its different forms the drug would be prescribed by virtually all kinds of doctors.

Also, political pressure was rising to encourage doctors to use generic names rather than brand names in writing prescriptions. A generic name specified only the active chemical compound in a drug preparation, but not necessarily the form or vehicle. Prescriptions written by generic name gave the druggist the choice of filling the prescription either by compounding the drug himself or by using one of several manufacturers' products which contained the prescribed chemical compound. The advocates of generically written prescriptions maintained that if given a choice among several products, the retail druggist would be able to fill a prescription more cheaply than if he were limited to one product by a brand name prescription.

THE MARKETING DEPARTMENT

Organization

The marketing department of Alcon Laboratories was under the direction of the marketing director, who was also a vice president of Alcon and a member of the company's executive management group. Ed Scholl-maier who currently held this position was 32 years old and had risen rapidly at Alcon. After receiving his MBA at the Harvard Business School in 1958, he had started as a salesman with Alcon and in a short time he had been promoted to district sales manager. After less than two years with Alcon he had been called into the home office to assist in directing the sales effort. In 1963 he had been appointed director of marketing.

The men under Mr. Schollmaier were grouped into three functional areas:

1. Sales: The sales group was comprised of the field sales force and the supervisor group which directed it.
2. Product management: The product management group was comprised of product managers, each of whom had total marketing responsibility (other than direct sales) for a particular group of products.
3. Market research: The director of market research was responsible for gathering and making available to others information on the ophthalmic drug market and on the competitive activities of other firms. In the summer of 1966 the duties of the director of market research were being performed by one of the product managers.

Shown below is an organization chart of the marketing department:

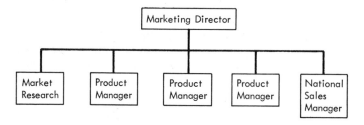

Activity

The primary responsibility of the marketing department was to assure the success of the sales effort. The home office was responsible for the design of the sales program, while the field sales organization was responsible for the program's execution. Great time and effort were typically expended in both areas. According to a 1965 study, drug and pharmaceutical firms' selling costs were twice those of U.S. industry as a whole. The survey showed that in 1964 the cost of selling pharmaceuticals amounted to 30.5 percent of gross sales revenue. The study presented the following breakdown of total selling costs:[3]

	Drug Industry	Average (all industries)
Salesmen's compensation	37.3%	45.2%
Salesmen's travel and other expenses	13.6	12.8
Sales management costs	14.0	16.2
Advertising, merchandising, and promotion	29.9	14.2
Servicing	3.0	7.4
All other costs	2.2	4.2
Total	100.0%	100.0%

Between 1961 and 1966, Alcon's total annual expenses for advertising, merchandising, and promotion increased from $90,000 to $750,000.

At Alcon the central activity was the planning of promotion programs, a joint responsibility of the product managers and the national sales manager. Prior to the beginning of each fiscal year, the product managers would meet with Mr. Leone, the national sales manager. On the basis of the size of the total promotion budget, the length of time since a product had been actively promoted, Mr. Leone's estimate of market potential, the current share of market held by the products involved, and competitive activity, this group would draw up a list of the particular products to be promoted in the coming year. Products on the list were then assigned specific dates for promotion. This promotion schedule was then approved by the marketing director.

In designing a promotional campaign, the product managers consulted with the national sales manager to obtain his ideas on what might go well in the market and his impressions on how the campaign would be received and handled by the sales force. Each product manager would design the entire promotional campaign for those of his products which were on the schedule. With the aid of an advertising agency, the product manager developed the direct mail literature, journal advertising, or visual aid material that was to be used. He would also write any technical, informational brochures that might be needed to reac-

---

[3] This study included as selling costs such items as seminars held for doctors to acquaint them with new drugs, and samples sent out as part of a product's introductory stage. Other industries did not have such expenses to the degree that the drug industry had, and some companies included similar costs in research and development for accounting purposes. Another factor to consider in comparing drug industry costs with those of other industries was that most consumer goods manufacturers shared costs of advertising with retailers; drug companies, on the other hand, bore most of these costs alone. In addition, allowances for returned merchandise were higher in the drug industry, since companies regularly took back unopened stock that was out of date.

quaint the sales force with aspects of the product. If the sales force was scheduled to promote an item to a customer on several individual calls, the product manager might even suggest which selling points should be made on the first and subsequent calls.

After the promotional campaign had been designed, it was turned over to the national sales manager who, with the help of his immediate subordinates, would teach the sales force how to carry out the promotion. Frequently, the product managers would attend meetings of the field sales organization to help present to the salesman the plans for the upcoming promotion.

A typical three-month promotional campaign for one product cost about $300,000 including salesmen's costs as well as advertising, direct mail, and other promotional materials. These costs were charged to the budget of the product manager responsible for that product. Each product manager was evaluated annually on the basis of the performance of his product(s) with respect to the achievement of sales goals and budgeted promotional spending.

To provide salesmen with the information that was desired by doctors, the marketing department needed the aid of the medical department and the research department.

The medical department was responsible for professional contact with members of the medical profession. Through a "Clinical Liaison Group" the medical department engaged physicians doing clinical research to conduct studies to test the uses or find new uses for Alcon's products. The findings were frequently used, in the form of professional articles or in technical bulletins, in promotional campaigns. It was not uncommon for a member of the marketing department to ask the medical department to help in developing some technical data to support particular claims for a product.

Alcon's R&D department was also important to the marketing effort. The development of new chemical compounds, new uses of existing compounds, and improvements in existing compounds, were all considered to be of prime importance. Introducing new and improved drug preparations was considered to be one of the most effective ways to increase sales and enhance the company's reputation in the medical community. Sales of various ophthalmological preparations tended to be more stable than the sales of pharmaceutical preparations in general, which were characterized by extreme volatility due to the frequent introduction of new chemical compounds which made existing compounds, in all types of forms and vehicles, obsolete. Alcon management stated, however, that "the impact of new products (i.e., new formulations of existing ophthalmological compounds) since 1960 accounted for more than half of Alcon's growth, and half of that growth was attributable to innovations in the steroid product category in particular."

The mutual interests of the marketing, medical, and R&D departments were coordinated through meetings of the product committee whose members included Mr. Ed Schollmaier, marketing vice president; Dr. Earl Maxwell, medical director and director of R&D; Mr. Frank Buhler, director of international operations; and Mr. William Conner, who was chairman of the board and president. For example, through the product committee the time and resources of the R&D department might be allocated to fill gaps in the product line, as determined by sales management and product managers. The need for and provision of technical data by the medical department was also coordinated through the product committee.

The National Sales Manager

Mr. George Leone headed the 70-man sales force in 1966. He had been with Alcon since 1950, when there were only six salesmen in the company. After doing an outstanding job as a salesman he was made a district sales manager in 1955, a regional sales manager in 1961, and national sales manager in 1963.

As national sales manager, Mr. Leone was responsible for the overall administration and performance of the sales force and for coordinating the activities of the sales force with other groups in the marketing department. In his administrative capacity, Mr. Leone was primarily concerned with the establishment of company programs in the areas of

EXHIBIT 3
Organization Chart of the Sales Group

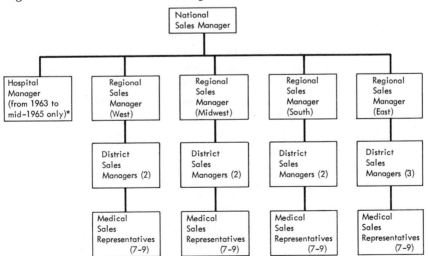

* Dropped in 1965 because of the overlap between calls on doctors when they were at the hospital and when they were at their private office.

recruitment and selection, training the development, supervision, standards of performance appraisal, and compensation and benefits. He was also responsible for identifying and developing field sales managers.

Mr. Leone directed three groups of men: regional sales managers, district sales managers, and medical sales representatives. The latter were more commonly known within the industry as salesmen, and were frequently identified by physicians as "detail men."

Exhibit 3 is an organization chart of the sales organization.

The Regional Sales Managers

Alcon divided the United States into four large sales regions, each supervised by a regional sales manager. The job description in the company's supervisory reference manual listed five major functions for the regional sales manager (RSM):

1. Recruiting and selecting candidates for field sales work (medical service representatives) with special emphasis on applicants with management potential.
2. Training and developing the district managers.
3. Supervising, directing, and controlling the activities of the district sales managers.
4. Maintaining communication with the home office through weekly reports and with the sales force through quarterly regional sales meetings.
5. Planning and organizing to help set the objectives for the region and to help the district sales managers set their goals.

The job description stated that the RSM should spend a minimum of 35 percent of his time in personal field visits with his district sales managers. He had no direct customer responsibilities.

Three of the four regional sales managers worked in the home office and spent a good deal of their time working with Mr. Leone in planning the national sales effort. They were involved in sales promotion, planning meetings, and in developing company policies and procedures for recruiting, selecting, training, and supervising the sales force. The fourth RSM was in the process of moving from Chicago to the home office.

The District Sales Managers

Reporting to each of the four regional sales managers were two to three district sales managers (DSM's). An Alcon district was a subdivision of a region (for example, the New England states comprised one district of Alcon's eastern region). The district sales managers' job description listed five major duties.

1. Recruiting, selecting, and, with approval from the RSM, hiring salesmen to become medical sales representatives.
2. Training and developing the field sales force.
3. Supervising, directing, and controlling the activities of the field sales force.
4. Maintaining communications with home office and with RSM, and conducting quarterly district sales meetings.
5. Planning and organizing operation of districts through setting objectives for field salesmen.

The job description further stated that the DSM should allocate his time as follows:

> A minimum of 75 percent of his time in personal field visits with the medical sales representatives, and the remainder (25 percent) at medical meetings, sales meetings, and visits with regional sales manager.

The DSM's, like the RSM's, had no direct customer responsibilities.

The Salesmen

Reporting to each of the nine district sales managers were seven to nine medical sales representatives (MSR's), or salesmen. These 70 salesmen were responsible for Alcon's direct customer contacts. Each MSR covered one Alcon "territory." The medical sales representatives' job description listed six major duties:

1. Call on each of the following:
   a. All eye physicians within his territory.
   b. All pharmacies on his drug call list.
   c. All hospitals on his call list.
   d. All wholesalers on his call list.
2. Follow the sales program including using all sales tools outlined by the program.
3. All MSR's must fulfill their performance standards and objectives each month in the following areas:
   a. Doctor call standards (item *a* above).
   b. Retail call standards (item *b* above).
   c. Wholesale call standards (item *d* above).
   d. Increase sales objectives (the DSM and MSR together set a specific objective as to how much sales will increase in the current year over the previous year).
   e. Ratio of increase sales to sales cost. For example:

	1965		*1966*	
$\dfrac{\text{Total territory sales}}{\text{Total territory costs}}$	$\dfrac{\$100,000}{\$12,000}$	$=\dfrac{8}{1}$	$\dfrac{\$120,000}{\$20,000}$	$=\dfrac{6}{1}$

f. Featured product (the one being promoted or detailed) objective.
g. Turnover order[4] objective.
4. Planning and organizing territory coverage by maintaining territory coverage plan and territory records.
5. Maintaining communications with supervisor and the home office by submitting the required daily, weekly, and monthly reports.
6. Meeting standards of self-development by attaining an adequate product knowledge, and knowing and complying with company policies on appearance, conduct, and maintaining company property.

Top management described the salesmen's activities as falling into two distinct categories: *creating demand* (when the MSR is in the doctor's office, trying to get him to prescribe Alcon's products), and *distribution* (supporting demand by getting the product to the wholesaler and retailer).

THE SALESMEN'S JOB

Salesmen in the drug industry as a whole made an average of 48 calls per week. Industry statistics indicated that the cost of making a sales call in the pharmaceutical field averaged $9, and ranged from $1.50 to $20. The average drug sale was $192. Alcon's medical sales representatives made three major types of calls: doctor calls, retailer calls, and wholesaler calls.

Each Alcon salesman used his home as the base of operations and traveled by car to see clients within his territory. The size of Alcon's territories typically required salesmen to spend three to four days each month in overnight travel. Each salesman carried at all times a case full of drug samples and other promotional materials.

The casewriter accompanied several salesmen on their daily rounds of calls. On one day he accompanied a salesman who called on nine doctors, one drug wholesaler, and three drug retailers. The casewriter believed, on the basis of the salesman's statements and from his own observations of other salesmen's activities, that this was a typical day.

The salesman began his day by driving 50 miles from his home to the city where he had planned calls for that day. Once in the designated city, the salesman spent a considerable part of his day simply getting from one client to another. Once in a client's office, he had to wait until he could be seen. One doctor kept him waiting as long as 30 minutes. While waiting to see the doctor, the salesman talked with the receptionist and gave away such small favors as notepads and other secretarial aids. (A kindly disposed receptionist could substantially aid a salesman in gaining prompt access or access at all to a doctor.)

---

[4] Turnover orders were those which the drug salesman wrote for the drug retailer and hand carried or mailed to the drug wholesaler to be filled.

The salesman the casewriter accompanied was able to see only five of the nine doctors he called on. With each of these five doctors he spent approximately five minutes. One doctor saw the salesman while having a sandwich between patients' appointments.

With the drug wholesaler and with each drug retailer, the salesman spent about 15 minutes.

At the end of the day the salesman returned the 50 miles to his home.

An Alcon salesman typically saw his DSM only once a month but maintained contact with him weekly by telephone. Alcon salesmen generally saw each other only at their bimonthly sales meetings. Although he had infrequent contact with other Alcon salesmen, the typical MSR had opportunity to have more frequent contact with other companies' salesmen who were detailing the same area as himself.

The Doctor Call

Alcon, as well as other drug companies, considered that "detailing" the doctor was one of the best ways to create demand for both new and existing products. It was for this reason that Alcon salesmen concentrated their attention on calls on eye doctors.

Large, diversified drug firms did not detail eye specialists as much as they detailed general practitioners, obstetricians, and pediatricians, because eye specialists did not use as wide a range of drugs. Most drug companies that detailed eye doctors called only once every three to six months, while they called on less specialized doctors every month. Alcon, however, as well as two other companies which specialized in ophthalmological drugs, called on eye doctors once a month.

Most eye doctors were ophthalmologists, typically located in large and medium-sized cities. A few older eye-ear-nose-and-throat doctors were still practicing in smaller communities, but their number was dwindling.

On a typical visit to an eye specialist, the Alcon salesman was expected to detail one primary product, one secondary product, and one "door-handle" product (one which was just mentioned on the way out). Any one product was usually detailed for three consecutive months. Some were detailed for only one month, while others were detailed as long as seven consecutive months.

While visiting the doctor the MSR was expected by management to show the doctor a "detail piece" (a visual aid that showed when to use the product and the advantages of Alcon's product). In addition he often left a journal reprint discussing the product, or a pamphlet (printed in a professional manner) along with some samples of the product. The MSR was supposed to discuss with the doctor whether he used the product being detailed and, if possible, to get a commitment that he would use it if he was not doing so already.

It was necessary for the salesmen to do this in a very brief period, however, as most doctors were extremely busy. One doctor commented to the casewriter that "[the detail men] have to see you at your office. I am very busy there so it is hard to find time to see them. I can only give them five to ten minutes and that is time away from seeing my patients." It was hoped that the salesman's brief presentation would make a lasting impression on the doctor. Journal advertising and direct-mail promotions from Alcon were timed to support the saleman's message to the doctor.

The Retailer Call

The Alcon salesman also called on the retail druggist. There were 55,000 drugstores in the United States, but, according to Alcon management, the Alcon sales force called only on the 10 percent which did the most business in ophthalmological drugs.

In the course of his call on the retail druggist the salesman would make it known which product(s) were being detailed in the area and thus which drug(s) doctors would probably be prescribing. It was antici-pated that the retail druggist would consequently increase his stock of the product(s) in question. If Alcon had any promotional deals on over-the-counter items (usually an offer of free goods with each pur-chase, for example, one free item with each 12 purchased), the MSR would bring these to the druggist's attention. During the call, the MSR checked the druggist's stock of Alcon products and indicated those areas which the druggist should replenish. The MSR attempted to pursuade the druggist to stock at least one bottle of all Alcon products and several bottles of the fast-moving items. The MSR would write up the order and mail it or take it to the wholesaler of the druggist's choosing.

The Wholesaler Call

To obtain adequate distribution of a product it was also important to call on drug wholesalers. The average Alcon territory contained six drug wholesalers who served as intermediaries between drug manufac-turers and drug retailers. Wholesalers maintained sales staffs of their own by which they contacted many more retail druggists than Alcon was able to do. A wholesaler's salesman would call on each retail drug-gist once a week, and would have daily contact with each druggist by telephone. Thus wholesalers, once sold on Alcon products, could shoulder a considerable part of the sales effort.

In 1964, U.S. drug wholesalers had annual sales of $3.7 billion. Two types of wholesale houses controlled this business: the full-line, full-service wholesalers, and the short-line or specialty houses.

The average sized full-line house typically carried 20,000 to 25,000 different items (each size of each brand of a product being considered a separate item) which had been purchased from some 1,200 to 1,500 manufacturers. Full-line houses sold about 90 percent of their dollar volume to retail drug outlets, and the remainder to hospitals, nursing homes, and clinics. The full-line houses' 1964 dollar volume of $1.76 billion represented almost 48 percent of total wholesale drug sales.

Short-line or specialty houses carried from 900 to 2,500 of the highest margin, fastest moving items, and typically sold these items to drug retailers at lower prices than those of full-line houses. The short-line houses competed by offering little more than selected items at low prices, but the full-line houses depended on their ability to offer the retailer several services as well as a wide product line. These services included assistance in finding and evaluating sites for new stores, store layout, and fixturing assistance, instore merchandising techniques, and anything else which might help the druggist in retailing efforts.

When a new product was being introduced, or when an existing product was being promoted, the Alcon salesman was expected to call on each wholesaler to gain his support of the product(s) in question. He was instructed to contact the wholesaler's sales manager initially and try to sell him on the product. The purpose of this effort was to persuade the sales manager to use his sales force to give special attention to Alcon's product. The Alcon salesman was supposed to show the sales manager the detail piece on the product, along with any literature he had.

After making this presentation to the sales manager and finding out how much support the product would get, the Alcon salesman would then go to the wholesaler's buyer. The salesman tried to persuade the buyer to order a large enough supply of the product (six to eight weeks' supply) to avoid the danger of running out.

During the months when Alcon did not introduce a new product or begin a new promotion on existing products, the MSR would simply call on the buyer and ask to go over the inventory record. If, on the basis of current or expected rates of movement, the wholesaler did not have the six to eight weeks of supply, the MSR would attempt to sell enough additional units of the product to raise the supply to the desired level.

It appeared to the casewriter, after observing several wholesale calls and talking to several salesmen, that most of the wholesale calls made by Alcon salesmen, whether or not there was a promotion involved, were of the latter, simpler type. The buyer and the sales manager of the wholesaler were likely to be pressed for time in which to listen to the presentation of the salesman in as much as they saw about 100 drug salesmen per week.

The Call Mix

Alcon's management explained that one salesman called on the doctor, the retailer, and the wholesaler because the calls were highly related and needed careful coordination. For instance, since no order was written in the doctor's office, the salesman would not know if the doctor would actually prescribe the detailed product or not. One of the best ways to find out was to call on the pharmacist a few days after detailing the doctor and inquire whether Dr. X was writing the product in question. If the salesman had established a good relationship with the pharmacist, the pharmacist would, in all likelihood, tell him. In fact the pharmacist often went so far as to let the salesmen check through the pharmacy's prescription file to see what all of the doctors were prescribing. With this type of information, the salesman knew which products were selling well and which products he should discuss with a doctor on his next visit.

In addition, Alcon managers emphasized that distribution and demand creation had to be closely coordinated. By handling all three types of calls, the salesman could assure the doctor that the pharmacist had in stock the drug he prescribed, and he could assure the pharmacist that the doctor would prescribe the drugs he stocked.

Alcon managers observed that the retailer calls and the wholesaler calls were directly related. First, they were both distribution calls. Secondly, the turnover order took the salesman back to the wholesaler with a definite order from the retailer, thus giving the salesman an opportunity to urge further purchases of Alcon's products.

While Alcon's management had agreed that one salesman should handle both demand creation (doctor calls) and distribution (wholesaler and retailer calls), in the past there had been a difference of opinion in the marketing department as to which of the two areas should receive the greatest emphasis. As a result emphasis had shifted from time to time.

In the past, when a new product was introduced, Alcon management had emphasized demand creation. Historically, this had resulted in a sales increase which was consistent with top management's commitment to rapid growth. As sales began to level off, however, an easy way to boost sales was to emphasize distribution by loading up the wholesaler and retailer with inventory. The distribution campaigns had included deals, the use of promotion money to the wholesaler's salesmen, and sales contests for Alcon's salesmen. In addition, "automatic" shipments (i.e., shipments of goods which Alcon estimated could be sold, but which had not been ordered by the wholesaler) would often be made to wholesalers during these periods.

There had been a number of "distribution campaigns" during periods of slow sales growth. The most recent one had been in May 1964, when a six-month distribution campaign was launched and a sales contest was initiated, in which the winner from each of the four regions won a trip to Mexico. When the contest was over, however, some wholesalers shipped goods back to Alcon (all of Alcon's sales were guaranteed, i.e., Alcon agreed to take back products which were unsold after a specific time). In one winner's territory, returns exceeded sales for a month or two. During the nine months following the contest, three of the four winners left Alcon.

Such distribution campaigns caused wide fluctuations in sales and strained relations with wholesalers and retailers. Management recognized the undesirable consequences of such actions and concluded that enduring sales growth came only from demand creation. In October 1964, with this in mind, Mr. Leone shifted the emphasis of the sales effort to demand creation. He instructed salesmen to spend 75 percent of their time calling on doctors (compared to 40 percent during the distribution campaign). The salesmen told the casewriter they welcomed this shift in their call mix because they preferred doctor calls to distribution calls. Management believed that men who preferred distribution calls, such as the four contest winners, left the company when the shift in emphasis took place.

Alcon maintained this emphasis on demand creation and managers stated that they did not intend to return to the practice of using distribution campaigns to boost sales in periods of slow growth.

ADMINISTRATION OF SALESMEN

Alcon, like the rest of the industry, had found that it was difficult to find and keep a man who could perform all of the required functions of the medical sales representative. In the past six years the annual turnover of Alcon's sales force had averaged approximately 33 percent.

Recruitment and Selection

The district sales manager was responsible for recruiting and selecting salesmen for his own territory. He had an instruction manual to help him. One page was entitled "The Man You Want" and listed the following characteristics:

25 to 35 years of age
preferably married—stable domestic life
college degree
scientific and business courses
above-average grades in school
good work history, preferably in sales/marketing
good grooming and physical appearance
good health, past and present
sound financial position
good diction and use of grammar—articulate
able to understand and project emotions and ideas
has self-confidence and poise
self-started
doesn't object to travel
enjoys working with people
ambitious with maturity
honesty and integrity
enthusiasm and capacity for work

The district managers used several techniques to find men with these qualifications. When a vacancy occurred in an area, the district manager typically first contacted schools if the opening occurred around commencement time.

Mr. Leone said that Alcon recruited at business schools in particular because Alcon liked to hire MBA's. He felt that the training and ambition of MBA's made them compatible with Alcon's objectives and organization.[5] A brochure in the Harvard Business School Placement Office contained the following statement:

> The company is small by usual standards, but it offers the opportunity
> for easy recognition of contribution and rapid promotion to greater

---

[5] Mr. Leone believed that Alcon had hired approximately 20 MBA's within the last ten years. Four to eight had left the company. Mr. Leone identified those still with Alcon as listed below. He believed that there were two others whom he had not included on the list.

Salesman	School Where Received MBA and Date	Present Position
A	HBS '57	Financial vice president
B*	HBS '58	Marketing vice president
C	HBS '60	Comptroller's department
D	HBS '59	Product manager
E*	HBS '62	Product manager
F*	HBS '64	Assistant product manager
G	Chicago	International comptroller
H*	N. Texas	Salesman
I*	Northwestern	District manager
J	Wharton '65	—

* Began by working as an MSR.

management responsibilities. Initial assignments are in field sales. MBA's are expected to reach district manager level within 18–24 months.

If qualified applicants were unavailable at schools, the district sales manager next contacted an employment agency, where he would typically interview about 40 people. After the first round of interviews he would narrow his interests to 10 to 12 applicants, with whom he would have second interviews.

If he was unable to fill vacant positions on his sales force using these sources, a district sales manager would then use a classified advertisement to recruit applicants. One district sales manager had used the following ad several times under such circumstances:

CAREERS IN SALES

Leading to sales management for qualified men based on performance. Young dynamic pharmaceutical company, growth rate of 47 percent per year. Leader in its field has openings local and away. Creative ambitious men with drive and determination, college degree. Science background helpful. Unusual remuneration and incentive plan tops in the industry. Excellent training program, liberal benefits, insurance, pension, stock options, profit sharing. Rare opportunity for growth for self-motivators. Men with an outstanding record of success in selling considered. Call OL 3-4818, Sunday, 1:00 to 5:00 P.M.

Résumés to
Box X
[City, State]

This sales manager reported to the casewriter that the ad had brought him an average of 75 résumés each time he had used it in a large, East Coast city. Forty to forty-five of these résumés he could discard immediately on the basis of age or educational background. After a telephone interview with the remaining 30 to 35 applicants, the sales manager would discard 10 to 15 more. He would then personally interview the remaining 10 to 15 applicants.

One district manager was quoted as saying, "My selection is generally made during the second interview as to my first, second, and third choices for a man to fill a vacancy. Then I have two or three more interviews with these men and their wives. The average interview time for a man who is hired is a total of approximately ten hours. By the time he is hired we really know one another and what we expect from one another. In rare instances, where there is competition for manpower from other industries in a given area, I may make a tentative offer on the spot during the first interview. In a case like this the first interview would run 1½ to 2 hours.

Selection was based primarily on the characteristics listed previously under "The Man You Want." The extent to which applicants fulfilled these characteristics was determined on the basis of information gathered through interviews, on application forms, and testing.

The district sales manager was required to spend a good deal of his time recruiting because of the high turnover in the sales force. In 1965–66 the region with the highest turnover had 6 men leave out of 19. It had the equivalent of four sales territories vacant for the year.

Training

After a new salesman was hired he entered a four-week training program. The program was under the direction of the DSM and took place in the field. In the first week the DSM worked with the new salesman and showed him how to call on the doctor, the wholesaler, and the retailer. In the evening the new MSR was expected to learn company policies and procedures, and to gain an adequate product knowledge, including (*a*) basic anatomy, physiology, and pathology of the eye; (*b*) basic ocular therapy and medical concepts; (*c*) basic pharmacology; (*d*) Alcon product advantages; and (*e*) competitive products.

During the second and third weeks the new MSR went into the territory of a senior salesman in the district and made as many field calls with the senior salesmen as possible, to perfect the first week's training. In addition he was expected to spend his evenings expanding his product knowledge.

In the fourth week the new MSR was to work in his own area under the supervision of the DSM. At this point the MSR was to be making most of the calls while the DSM was observing. The DSM made sure that the new MSR was prepared to handle his own territory

This concluded the formal training of the new MSR. After this initial training the DSM worked with the salesman only periodically to give him any additional training that was necessary. The new salesmen reported to the casewriter that while an effort was made to do this, the DSM was often too busy to carry out the training as planned.

In order to develop field sales managers, Alcon introduced at the end of 1964, a program for training managers called the Advanced Development Program (ADP). Outstanding salesmen who were interested in advancement were included in this program (there were nine ADP's in the summer of 1966). The program consisted of each ADP doing a number of individual projects which were usually activities performed by field managers; for example, the ADP would recruit and train new salesmen. Mr. Leone said, "Four of our best field managers today came from this program."

Control and Evaluation

In order to keep track of what each salesman was doing, Alcon required that two reports be submitted by each salesman to the DSM and the home office, including the following:

1. A daily report of all calls made, by type of call, and the number and amount of turnover orders. This report is cumulative on a monthly basis.
2. An expense voucher to be filled in daily and mailed to Fort Worth on Saturday morning.

In addition the MSR was required to keep territory records including a doctor call book with information such as the doctor's day off, the best time to see him, his specialty, etc.

Once a year the district sales manager conducted a performance appraisal of the MSR. The DSM then made a recommendation for a salary increase for the salesman, based upon this performance appraisal and the MSR's commission for the past year. Management maintained that the introduction of regular performance appraisals greatly improved the compensation of the sales force at Alcon, making it more equitable by relating salary increases more closely to performance. In addition the company made it a practice to terminate salesmen who did not meet the high standards set for salesmen.

Compensation

Compensation for salesmen was in the form of salary plus commission. Alcon's starting salaries ranged from $400 to $700 per month, depending on the training and experience of the new man. In 1966, Alcon's salesmen's salaries ranged from $500 to $916 per month, and averaged $580 per month. Each salesman was eligible for a salary increase each year, and the annual increase could be up to one half of the commission he received the preceding year. Exhibit 4 presents salesmen's salaries from 1962 to 1966.

EXHIBIT 4
Salesmen's Salaries at Alcon, Inc.*

Year Ending	Average Annual Salary of All Salesmen
April 30, 1962	$5,760
April 30, 1963	6,168
April 30, 1964	6,744
April 30, 1965	6,900
April 30, 1966	6,960

* Excludes commission.

Management expressed the opinion that although Alcon had been behind the industry in compensation a few years before, their significant salary increase in the past three years had made Alcon quite competitive with the drug industry. Exhibit 5 presents data on the drug industry's compensation of salesmen in 1964.

EXHIBIT 5

Data for the Pharmaceutical Industry's Salesmen's Total Compensation (salary and commission, 1964)

100th percentile.	$25,000
75th percentile.	9,000
50th percentile.	8,000
25th percentile.	7,000
1st percentile.	5,000

A group of 28 companies manufacturing drugs, chemicals, and cosmetics reported the following data concerning the compensation (salary and commission) of their salesmen:

Compensation for	*Highest Man*		*Top Half of Sales Force*	
	Midpoint	*Range*	*Midpoint*	*Range*
	$12,000	$8,000–$25,000	$9,000	$8,000–$10,000
Compensation for	*Lowest Man*		*Lower Half of Sales Force*	
	Midpoint	*Range*	*Midpoint*	*Range*
	$6,000	$5,000–$7,000	$7,000	$6,000–$8,000

Source: *Sales Management,* January 21, 1966.

Commissions were handled in the following manner: A new salesman was placed on commission after three months of employment with Alcon and following a performance review and approval by all levels of field supervision. Commissions were paid twice each fiscal year and were based on 10 percent of increased sales after total MSR expenses (including car expenses, motel, telephone, meals) had been deducted. The following is an illustration of the commission plan:

MSR's sales:	
1965	$75,000
1964	50,000
Sales increase	$25,000
Salesman's expenses	−12,000
	$13,000
	10%
Commission	$ 1,300

The current commission plan had been introduced in 1960 when the company was having trouble controlling salesmen's expenses. Recently some Alcon managers had expressed the feeling that the current plan was not equitable because it penalized the salesmen with a large territory requiring overnight travel. Total commissions paid to the 50 salesmen in 1965–66 were $26,000, ranging from $0 to $1,500 individually, but Mr. Leone observed that 80 percent of the commission payments went to 20 percent of the salesmen.

Profile of Current Salesmen

A profile of salesmen who had been hired since January 1964, and who were still with the company in June 1966 is shown in Exhibit 6.

MANAGEMENT, SALESMAN, AND CUSTOMER ATTITUDES

In the course of gathering material for the case, the casewriter interviewed individuals at different organizational levels within Alcon. In addition he interviewed a number of eye doctors, drug retailers, and drug wholesalers concerning their attitudes toward drug salesmen.

The two DSM's interviewed by the casewriter reported that other activities prevented them from spending 75 percent of their time with the MSR as their job description required. With a high turnover in the sales force it was necessary for them to spend a great deal of time on recruiting and selection of new salesmen. One DSM had three vacancies to fill in a four-month period, and it was necessary for him to spend nearly all his time trying to fill those vacancies during that period.

The other DSM interviewed said that it took a lot of time to do the paper work required of him by the company. In addition, the MSR's liked him to give them comparative figures on their sales in the current month compared to those of the previous month and other similar kinds of information. As a result, a lot of this DSM's time was occupied in sales analysis and filling out reports. The DSM also reported that "the job has changed a lot in the past two to three years. Before, I just worked with the men, but now I am running an organization. I hire, fire, train, and evaluate men. I also run a good bit of the sales meetings. We have one about every two months."

The Medical Sales Representatives' View

The following interview with Don Wade, who had been with Alcon over eight years, indicates what the casewriter believes to be a fairly typical attitude of Alcon's older salesmen toward customers.

Wade: The most important thing is to sell the doctor and create demand for your product. If you just get it into the retailer and then the doctor doesn't write it you have problems because the retailer will send it back. I provide information to the doctor. The doctors ask me about drugs, ours

EXHIBIT 6

Profile of Alcon Salesmen Hired and Retained since January 1964

Sales-man	Age	Marital Status	College Degree	Grade Average	Sales Experience	Other Experience
1	34	Married	B.S.–pharmacy	Upper ½	2*–drugs	2*–manager of drugstore
2	?	Married	B.S.–pharmacy	C	None	4–technician, pharmacy
3	?	Married	Business admin.	C	2	2–office merchandise
4	?	Married	Sociology	C+	None	–social worker
5	?	Married	Lib. arts, bus., and soc. sci.	B	2–office equip., clothing	2–acct. clerk, cashier
6	29	Single	Lib. arts, bus. admin.	C+	2–encyclopedia, medical equip.	3–truck checker, freight handler, adjuster
7	?	Married	B.A.–psychology	C+	1–sales & service	2–clerk, admin. asst.
8	?	Married	Pre-optometry	Top 5%	None	4–asst. research, pub. rel., clerk
9	?	Married	B.A.–pol. sci.	C	1–Am. Credit Bureau	1–tax search
10	?	Married	Marketing	–	None	3–stock clerk, timekeeper, assembly
11	25	Single	B.S.–zoology	Upper ½	None	–camera assistant
12	28	Married	B.S.–math ed.	B	1–food	–math teacher
13	40	Married	Pre-med –3 yrs.	C	1–drugs	1–police officer
14	27	Married	Gen. ed., bus. admin.	C		1–lifeguard
15	26	Single	No degree–law	B+	–shoes, elec.	1–teacher
16	26	Married	B.S.–P.E. & pol. sci.	C	None	2–examiner, janitor
17	25	Single	Pol. science	Top 25%	1–shoes	1–administrative
18	33	Married	B.A.–eng. & psy.	Upper 10%	2	2–clerk, claims, supervisor
19	32	Single	B.A.–bus. admin.	Upper 40%	1–retail & wholesale	1–international trading corp.
20	25	Married	Spec. ed.	Upper 50%	–	5–teacher
21	28	Single	B.A.–gen. bus., marketing	1.50	2–drugs, printing	3–repairman, drugstore, mailman
22	30	Married	No degree–eco. and marketing	–	2	8–insurance
23	29	Married	B.S.–finance	C	2–insurance, drugs	—
24	26	Married	B.S.–pub. admin.	B	None	—
25	28	Married	No degree–marketing	C+	1–shoes	–pub. rel., Gen Motors

* Years.

EXHIBIT 6 (*Continued*)

Salesman	Age	Marital Status	College Degree	Grade Average	Sales Experience	Other Experience
26	26	Single	Economics	80–85	None	—
27	24	Married	B.S.–bio., bus.	Top ⅓	None	—
28	36	Single	B.S.–biology	Middle	None	2*–chemist
29	27	Married	Sci.–chiropr.	80's	2*–medical equip.	—
30	32	Married	Marketing and sales	C	1 –	–cashier, foods mgr.
31	32	Engaged	Police science	C	2 –	–post office
32	29	Married	Industrial tech.	C+	None	2 –insurance inspector
33	28	Married	Education and psy.	B	None	–school guidance councilor
34	24	Married	History	B	None	–drugstore, book store, and service station
35	26	Single	History	C+	2 –	–Gimbel's toy mgr.
36	25	Married	Marketing	2.6	None	–teacher
37	26	Married	B.S.–biology	78	1 –	–lab technician
38	28	Married	B.A.–philosophy	2.4 (A)	None	–U.S.A.F. recruiting

* Years.

and our competition; they ask me what they are and what they do, etc. If I don't know about a product I don't try to bluff it so they trust me. If a competitor's product is good I tell the doctor it is. I've been with Alcon a long time so I know the doctors and they write my products. When I come around with a new drug the doctors trust me so they'll start right in and use it.

The doctor call is indirect selling; you don't write up an order and you don't know if you have sold him. That's what makes it such a challenge. I enjoy trying to match wits with the doctor, and I can tell about 80 percent of the time whether I have sold him or not. But you have to know what he is saying. A doctor will promise you anything. They want to be nice to you like they are to their patients, so they will say they will use your drug and then they won't follow up and do it.

You have to use finesse with the doctor—it's a soft sell. You have to know where he went to school, his likes and dislikes. The more you can get him to talk the better you can sell him. The doctor is more professional and more ethical.

A distribution call, on the other hand, is direct selling. The pharmacist is more interested in money so you have to show how your product will make him a profit. The pharmacist trusts me so I just check his inventory, decide what he needs, and write up the turnover order. Usually he doesn't even see it. I just send it to the wholesaler. It's the same way with the wholesalers. I have a good relationship with them, and they just let me write up the orders.

An interview with John Cook revealed the attitude of the younger, more ambitious salesmen. Cook had been with Alcon just one year, and was described by the DSM as a good management prospect.

COOK: It's a hard sell with the doctor. You're in there as a salesman to sell your product. You really have to know your doctors because you can really pin some of them down and get a commitment to write your product, but with others you can't do much. So you have to know which one to push. You have to get to know the receptionist, too, because she guards the doctor and can prevent you from seeing him.

CASEWRITER: Do you prefer to make a doctor call or a distribution call?

COOK: I would rather call on the doctor because he treats me like a professional man. It's just a chore to make retail calls. I spend 85 percent of my time calling on doctors because I'd rather call on them. Some of our wholesalers are upset because they say Alcon is high pressure as a result of the distribution campaign two years ago.

Bob Jensen, another salesman the casewriter interviewed, had been with Alcon for three years.

CASEWRITER: Why did you take this job?

JENSEN: I studied pre-med in college but I didn't have good enough grades to get into medical school. However, I still wanted some dealings with the medical profession so after I got some sales experience I came with Alcon. The eye doctors know that Alcon only calls on eye doctors so they like to see the Alcon man. So I am accepted more by doctors than the detail men from other companies are.

I enjoy calling on the doctor because he is more professional-ethical. The only problem is that you don't know when you've sold the doctor. You get better feedback from the pharmacist because you write up an order there.

Ninety-nine percent of the doctors accept me very well; about 50 percent of them call me by my first name, but it's taken two years to get on a first-name basis. The doctor would rather discuss products with a friend so if you have been calling on him a while and he knows you, he'll listen.

Jack Green had only been with Alcon for four months, but he had these comments about the customers:

> It used to bother me to call on the doctor because he has all the degrees. But I soon realized that he puts his pants on one leg at a time just like the rest of us, so why worry? Now I enjoy calling on the doctor because he appreciates what I do for him. The doctor treats me okay; his opening statement is "What's new?"—he's glad to see me. The pharmacist is just a businessman, and I can come and go and he doesn't appreciate what I do for him.

Doctors' Views of the Salesmen

Doctor Jones was about 45, had a large practice, and also did some work with a well-respected eye clinic in the large eastern city where he practiced. The casewriter believed that his views were typical of the busy, successful, ophthalmologist.

JONES: The detail man keeps the doctor informed. He makes the information available before it comes out in the journals [the journals are always months behind], and you can ask questions of him directly.

CASEWRITER: What kind of detail man do you like or dislike?

JONES: I like one that is pleasant and sincere, and one who has a knowledge of his product or at least is honest enough to let you know when he doesn't. Also I prefer one that makes no demands. Some of them will say, "I'll be back in ten days to see how you've gotten along with my product," and it puts you on the spot.

CASEWRITER: Which companies are doing the best job of promoting their products?

JONES: The question really should be which ones see you most frequently. The answer is Alcon, Smith Miller Patch, and Upjohn, I guess.

CASEWRITER: In what way do they do a better job?

JONES: Frequency of call. I tend to write more of their products when they call frequently and I have more knowledge of their products. I depend on the detail man to get information on things like products, sizes, availability, etc. They keep me up to date on new developments.

Dr. Barron was about 50 years old. He did not seem to be as busy as some of the other eye doctors, and he spent 20 minutes with the casewriter while the others would only spend 5 to 10 minutes.

BARRON: I am influenced by the detail man. I have an emotional affinity for him, and he leaves a lot of samples. I feel an obligation to him, and I'll write his drugs.

CASEWRITER: What kind of detail man do you like or dislike?

BARRON: I don't like the overpowering salesman. I like a neat, well-dressed, polite man who just gives me information. I think all detail men are frustrated doctors—you wouldn't really want to be a detail man. Generally the salesmen are very nice people and very cooperative. They all say that if there is ever anything that they can do, I shouldn't hesitate to call them. I could call them at three o'clock in the morning if I needed a drug and the pharmacy was closed. They are selling me good will. Let me give you an example. I like neat, polite guys but I didn't like one who called on me. He was an Italian. Now, I've got nothing against Italians, but he didn't speak correct English and his fingernails were dirty. I had an emotional antipathy to this fellow. A doctor has two degrees and he likes to meet and talk to intelligent people who are somewhat on his level.

Pharmacist's View of the Salesman

The attitude of the pharmacist toward the salesman was evident in this interview:

CASEWRITER: What is the job of the ethical drug salesman?

PHARMACIST: He tells us about new products, price changes, and what's being detailed, because that's what sells. He comes in and writes up the order. Then we check it over and cut back if he's put in too much of any product.

CASEWRITER: Which companies do the best job in calling on you?

PHARMACIST: All the major companies do a good job. Upjohn, Merck, etc. But the small companies have high turnover. They'll have a new man in here about every month. We sometimes have problems with them.

CASEWRITER: What does the salesman expect you to do for him?

PHARMACIST: He expects us to keep his products in stock; he sells the products to the doctor. He also asks for information on what the doctors are writing. We have a prescription file and he's welcome to look through it.

In making calls with Alcon salesmen the casewriter noted that Alcon seemed to have an excellent reputation with the pharmacist. In the eye section of the pharmacist's drugs Alcon usually had by far the most shelf space, and the Alcon drugs were usually the most accessible to the pharmacist.

Wholesaler's View of the Salesmen

The following interview with a buyer at a busy wholesaler's gives an indication of his attitude toward salesmen:

CASEWRITER: What kind of salesmen do you like or dislike?

BUYER: I like one that takes care of the details on his products, such as price changes, returns, checking inventory, and giving us information on new items.

Also, I don't like pressure. We are trying to sell merchandise, and in order to sell we have to buy. We don't need anyone to pressure us. It's just the new man or the fly-by-night guy who gets this pitch from the home office and tries to shove it down our throat. But by and large they tend to be quite professional in their approach.

CASEWRITER: We're currently writing a case on Alcon. Do they do a good job?

BUYER: Yes and no . . . they're a little pushy, a little bang-bang.

CASEWRITER: Is this more so now than in the past?

BUYER: No, if anything it's less so now than in the past. They tended to put up these deals at the home office and then put them off on us.

Sales Force's View of the Marketing Effort

A number of managers and salesmen pointed out that the quality of the promotion developed by the product managers could greatly influence a salesman's success. With a high-quality program and the support of direct-mail and journal advertising a salesman could significantly increase sales of featured products. The salesmen appeared to agree that the work of the product managers had improved a great deal in the past two to three years, and that they were doing an excellent job.

Many of the salesmen expressed concern, however, about the infrequency with which Alcon had introduced new products. One salesman said that in the past six years Alcon had introduced only "two big new products," and that it was only in those periods that the company had experienced rapid sales growth. One manager pointed out that Alcon had significantly expanded its R&D effort in the past two years and that "we now have in R&D more Ph.D.'s per sales dollar than anyone else in the industry, and we are currently spending 10 percent of sales for that purpose."

Salesmen's Views of the Company, Compensation, and Opportunity for Advancement

The following is another part of the interview with Don Wade who has been with Alcon over eight years:

WADE: You can't make big money in the drug business, and if you compare Alcon with the others in the industry their salary is not the best, but they hit a happy medium. I've been offered more money by other drug companies, but Alcon has a great future and they have a good relationship with the doctors.

CASEWRITER: How does Alcon compare on opportunities for advancement?

WADE: Alcon has the best opportunity for advancement in the industry, if you're looking for that. I'm not. I just want to be a salesman. The DSM has to travel too much, and I don't want to be away from my family any more than I am now.

CASEWRITER: How does Alcon's first line supervision compare with other companies?

WADE: Our company has been weak in supervision compared with other drug companies. At least we've been weak in the past. But now they're doing a better job of training a man before they make him a DSM. Nobody can learn the drug business in two years so our managers just haven't had enough field experience.

CASEWRITER: Why have so many salesmen left Alcon?

WADE: Alcon promises you the sky in terms of advancement and then they just don't come through. So, when the boys have been here a while and they don't get a promotion as soon as they were told they would, they leave.

Nearly everyone the casewriter interviewed said that they believed that there were excellent opportunities for advancement with Alcon. Management indicated, however, that there were no plans to expand the sales force or the number of field managers in the immediate future. When the casewriter presented this apparent contradiction to Dave Colton, a salesman who had been with Alcon for five months, Colton had replied that he expected to advance with Alcon because he believed that there would be an opportunity for him to be promoted into a management position in one of the companies that had been acquired or that would be acquired by Alcon.

SUMMARY

Management was aware that turnover was high among sales personnel throughout the drug industry (12.1 percent in 1964), but Alcon turnover was a great deal higher than other drug companies. In fact, it had been as high as 42 percent in 1964. (Exhibit 7 shows the turnover in Alcon's sales force from 1961 to 1966, and the length of service of the men leaving.)

Management was concerned about the high turnover for several reasons. First of all, it was costly. Although Alcon's figures were not available, one survey reported, "The cost of selecting, training, and supervising a new drug salesman averages $7,612 excluding salary." Just as important as cost was the fact that it took one to two years for a salesman to establish a satisfactory relationship with the doctor, the wholesaler, and the retailer. Most of the men who left had been with Alcon less than two and one-half years. These salesmen just barely got to know the customers before leaving.

EXHIBIT 7

Turnover of Alcon's Sales Force

Year Ending April 30	Percent Turnover
1961	35
1962	27
1963	35
1964	42
1965	34
1966	28

Length of Service of Salesmen Terminating

Number of Months Employment	Number of Personnel		Cumulative Number of Personnel	
6 months or less	4	13.8%	4	13.8%
12 months or less	8	27.6	12	41.4
18 months or less	4	13.8	16	55.0
24 months or less	2	6.9	18	62.0
30 months or less	5	17.2	23	79.5
36 months or less	1	3.5	24	82.7
42 months or less	1	3.5	25	86.6
48 months or less	1	3.5	26	89.6
60 months or less	3	10.3	29	100.0

Mr. Leone was uncertain about why so many men had left Alcon. He indicated that almost all of them said they were leaving because they were not earning enough money, but he was not sure that was the whole reason. Alcon had raised salaries considerably in the past three years, but men were still leaving. Mr. Leone felt that part of the problem may have been the shift in emphasis from "demand" to "distribution" and then back to "demand." Mr. Leone noted that Alcon's higher turnover had occurred in the years when they had distribution campaigns.

7 | Baines Electronics Corporation

Paul Jefferson, project manager on Baines's air defense missile contract with the U.S. Air Force, returned from a corporate level meeting late one afternoon in November 1961. The meeting had concerned the corporation's newly announced policy governing salary increases for all employees for the forthcoming year. After reviewing some notes and collecting his thoughts on what had transpired in the meeting, which had been chaired by the president of Baines, Jefferson called his secretary over the intercom and asked her to assemble the project's key leaders for a 4:00 P.M. meeting. The purpose of the meeting was to pass on details of the president's message.

GENERAL COMPANY BACKGROUND

Baines Electronics Corporation, a medium-sized company with annual sales of about $80 million, had its principal plants in a small town located 40 miles outside of Boston. A majority of Baines's 13,000 employees worked at that location. Founded in the late 1930s by Carlton Baines and several other talented engineers from National Electronics, Baines Electronics grew rapidly in the early days of World War II due to heavy involvement in the production of aircraft instruments. The company successfully weathered the postwar transition period, and by the late 1950s Baines had rapidly rising sales and prospects for continued good growth.

An important element of the Baines corporate policy was the fair treatment of employees. The company had pioneered in granting real and fringe benefits and had a record of stable employment second to none in the industry. Carlton Baines, up until his death in 1957, had always maintained an "open-door" policy for all his employees. Anyone could enter the president's office and "talk to the boss." Baines had also encouraged the formation of numerous company-sponsored activities, such as bowling and softball, and the founder's overall regard for the workers was an important factor in keeping the company nonunionized. When asked why they worked at Baines, many employees would remark that it was an enjoyable place to work, where friendliness and unanimity of purpose were main motivating factors.

All of Carlton Baines's policies were continued when a new president was selected from within the company to carry on after his death.

THE NEW PLAN

About ten people sat around Jefferson's conference table later that day. None of the men wore suit jackets, and it was apparent from the informal conversation that the missile project was a tightly knit organization, with relatively high morale. Most of the engineers on Jefferson's project and in other engineering groups at Baines had a B.S. or M.S. degree; about 5 percent of the engineers had a Ph.D. Jefferson had always prided himself on the fact that the men in his groups felt free to talk to him about both technical and personal problems. When all were present he began.

He explained that there had been a growing tendency, according to the president, for salary increases to be handed out annually without appropriate emphasis on the meaning behind the raise. Lately, or as it seemed to upper management, there was not much awareness on the part of either superior or subordinate that such raises were granted because of the specific contribution of the employee and because of a generally favorable overall corporate outlook. It was felt that the merit plan had acquired certain superficial aspects of a cost-of-living increase. Many employees, therefore, expected yearly increases, whether or not their work for the past period truly warranted special recognition and whether or not the company profit picture was favorable.

At this point Jefferson stopped and asked for comments, and in the ensuing discussion it was agreed by all those present that the situation had been accurately described by the president. Some changes certainly seemed in order. Jefferson returned to his notes.

In order to correct the problem and restore proper balance to the merit raise program, the president had requested that several measures be adopted immediately for the next year:

1. Over and above any plans now in progress, an immediate review was to be made of the salary status of all employees.
2. Those men who "really put out" were to be given raises in January or as soon thereafter as practicable.

3. Whenever a raise was granted, the supervisor was to make a special point—almost an ostentatious gesture of commendation—to highlight the relationship between an employee's salary increases and outstanding performance.
4. All raises intended for the next year were to be awarded before August (rather than spread throughout the entire year) with the general expectation that the better the man the earlier he was to receive his raise.

To further enhance the plan, the president announced that the dollar package set aside for raises for 1962 was to be nearly double the amount allotted in previous years. The president had ended his talk by reemphasizing that it was important to let people know where they stood so that they might be encouraged to improve both themselves and their value to the company.

As he summarized the president's remarks, Jefferson added his personal emphasis to the points listed above. He then requested that all his leaders forward their individual raise recommendations to him within one week.

THE OLD MERIT INCREASE SYSTEM

Although certain areas within the plants used special practices, all engineering groups used the basic system which is shown in Figure 1. This curve plots salary against years of experience and was intended to show that for any given number of years of experience a man's salary range was between points A and B. These points were the outer limits

FIGURE 1

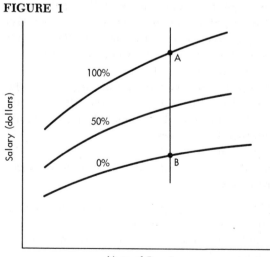

Years of Experience

of a band of possible salaries shown as "100 percent and 0 percent" lines. Everyone fell somewhere between these extremes, the idea being that everyone had a hypothetical evaluation factor between 100 percent and 0 percent. If one were a 90 percent man it meant that in the company's estimation only 10 percent of the people with similar experience were rated ahead of him. Similarly, if one were a 25 percent man, 75 percent of the men with identical experience were rated superior. The rating factor was accomplished in somewhat subjective terms at the project level and reviewed three times before final corporate approval.

A key point was that the individual ratings and the salary curves (the 100 percent and 0 percent limits) were known only to the evaluator (the immediate superior) and the salary administration group. These facts were not available to the individual employee, and no one had any knowledge of his own or his fellow employees' standing, particularly since good and average raises were awarded at random times throughout the year. An engineer who was to be awarded a raise was asked to come to his superior's office for a discussion, and at this meeting he was informed of his increase in salary.

This system had been used for nearly 20 years and had produced little or no griping at any level. Jefferson could recall few instances when he had received complaints about salaries.

WORKING OUT THE NEW PLAN

Jefferson spent many hours working over the recommendations of his subordinates and trying to fit these into a workable time-phased series of raises to be granted in 1962. When he finally submitted his project plan in December, both he and his project leaders were enthusiastic about the prospects for the coming year. More money was to be given out, and he felt that that facet of the plan certainly ought to be appreciated, since even the low-rated people would receive a bigger raise than usual.

8 | *Texana Petroleum Corporation*

During the summer of 1966, George Prentice, the newly designated executive vice president for domestic operations of the Texana Petroleum Corporation, was devoting much of his time to thinking about improving the combined performance of the five product divisions reporting to him (see Exhibit 1). His principal concern was that corporate profits were not reflecting the full potential contribution which could result from the close technological interdependence of the raw materials utilized and produced by these divisions. The principal difficulty, as Prentice saw it, was that the division general managers reporting to him were not working well together: "As far as I see it, the issue is where do we make the money for the corporation? Not how do we beat the other guy. Nobody is communicating with anybody else at the general manager level. In fact they are telling a bunch of secrets around here."

RECENT CORPORATE HISTORY

The Texana Petroleum Corporation was one of the early major producers and marketers of petroleum products in the southwest United States. Up until the early 1950s, Texana had been almost exclusively in the business of processing and refining crude oil and in selling petroleum products through a chain of company-operated service stations in the southwestern United States and in Central and South America. By 1950 company sales had risen to approximately $500 million with accompanying growth in profits. About 1950, however, Texana faced increasingly stiff competition at the retail service station level from sev-

EXHIBIT 1
Partial Organization Chart, 1966

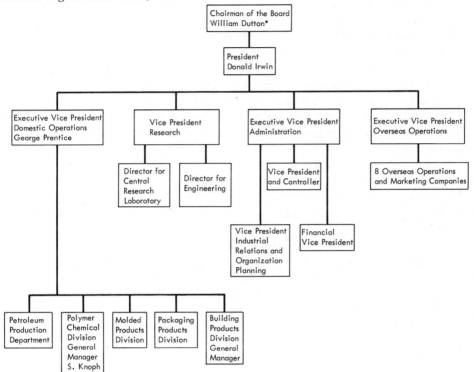

* Names included for persons mentioned in the case.

eral larger national petroleum companies. As a result sales volume declined sharply during the early 1950s, and by 1955 sales had fallen
to only $300 million and the company was operating at just above the
break-even point.

At this time, because of his age, Roger Holmes, who had been a
dominant force in the company since its founding, retired as president
and chief executive officer. He was replaced by Donald Irwin, 49, who
had been a senior executive with a major chemical company. William
Dutton, 55, was appointed chairman of the board to replace the retiring
board chairman. Dutton had spent his entire career with Texana. Prior
to his appointment as chairman he had been senior vice president for
Petroleum Products, reporting to Holmes.

Irwin and Dutton, along with other senior executives, moved quickly
to solve the problems facing Texana. They gradually divested the company's retail outlets and abandoned the domestic consumer petroleum

markets. Through both internal development and acquisition they expanded and rapidly increased the company's involvement in the business of processing petroleum for chemical and plastics products. In moving in this direction they were rapidly expanding on initial moves made by Texana in 1949, when the company built its first chemical processing plant and began marketing these products. To speed the company's growth in these areas, Irwin and Dutton selected aggressive general managers for each division and gave them a wide degree of freedom in decision making. Top management's major requirement was that each division general manager create a growing division with a satisfactory return on investment capital. By 1966 top management had reshaped the company so that in both the domestic and foreign market it was an integrated producer of chemicals and plastic materials. In foreign operations the company continued to operate service stations in Latin America and in Europe. This change in direction was successful; and by 1966 company sales had risen to $750 million, with a healthy rise in profit.

In spite of this success, management believed that there was a need for an increase in return on invested capital. The financial and trade press, which had been generous in its praise of the company's recovery, was still critical of the present return on investment; and top management shared this concern. Dutton, Irwin, and Prentice were in agreement that one important method of increasing profits was to take further advantage of the potential cost savings which could come from increased coordination between the domestic operating divisions, as they developed new products, processes, and markets.

DOMESTIC ORGANIZATION 1966

The product division's reports to Mr. Prentice represented a continuum of producing and marketing activities from production and refining of crude oil to the marketing of several types of plastics products to industrial consumers. Each division was headed by a general manager. While there was some variation in the internal organizational structure of the several divisions, they were generally set up along functional lines (manufacturing, sales, research and development). Each division also had its own controller and engineering activities, although these were supported and augmented by the corporate staff. While divisions had their own research effort, there was also a central research laboratory at the corporate level, which carried on longer range research of a more fundamental nature and was outside the scope of the activities of any of the product divisions.

The *Petroleum Products Division* was the remaining nucleus of the company's original producing and refining activities. It supplied raw materials to the Polymer and Chemicals Division and also sold refining products under long-term contracts to other petroleum companies. In the early and mid 1950s this division's management had generated much of the company's revenue and profits through its skill of negotiating these agreements. In 1966, top corporate management felt that this division's management had accepted its role as a supplier to the rest of the corporation, and felt that there were harmonious relations between it and its sister divisions.

The *Polymer and Chemicals Division* was developed internally during the late 1940s and early 50s as management saw its share of the consumer petroleum market declining. Under the leadership of Seymour Knoph (who had been general manager for several years) and his predecessor (who was in 1966 executive vice president—administration), the division had rapidly developed a line of chemical and polymer compounds derived from petroleum raw materials. Most of the products of this division were manufactured under licensing agreement or were materials the formulation of which was well understood. Nevertheless, technical personnel in the division had developed an industry-wide reputation for their ability to develop new and improved processes. Top management of the division took particular pride in this ability. From the beginning, the decisions of what products to manufacture were based to a large extent upon the requirements of the Molded Products Division and Packaging Products Division. However, Polymer and Chemicals Division executives had always attempted to market these same products to external customers, and had been highly successful. These external sales were extremely important to Texana since they assured a large enough volume of operation to process a broad product line of polymer chemicals profitably. As the other divisions had grown, they had required a larger proportion of the division's capacity, which meant that Polymer and Chemical Division managers had to reduce their commitment to external customers.

The *Molded Products Division* was also an internally developed division, which had been formed in 1951. Its products were a variety of molded plastic products ranging from toys and household items to automotive and electronic parts. This division's major strengths were its knowledge of molding technology and particularly its marketing ability. While it depended upon the Polymer and Chemicals Division for its raw materials, its operations were largely independent of those of the Packaging Products Division and Building Products Division.

The *Packaging Products Division* was acquired in 1952. Its products were plastic packaging materials, including films, cartons, bottles, etc. All of these products were marketed to industrial customers. Like the

Molded Products Division, the Packaging Division depended on the Polymer and Chemical Division as a source of raw materials but was largely independent of other end-product divisions.

The *Building Products Division* was acquired in 1963 to give Texana a position in the construction materials market. The division produced and marketed a variety of insulation roofing materials and similar products to the building trade. It was a particularly attractive acquisition for Texana, because prior to the acquisition it had achieved some success with plastic products for insulation and roofing materials. Although the plastic products accounted for less than 20 percent of the total division sales in 1965, plans called for these products to account for over 50 percent of division sales in the next five years. Its affiliation with Texana gave this division a stronger position in plastic raw materials through the Polymer and Chemicals Division.

Selection and Recruitment of Management Personnel

The rapid expansion of the corporation into these new areas had created the need for much additional management talent; and top management had not hesitated to bring new men in from outside the corporation, as well as advancing promising younger men inside Texana. In both the internally developed and acquired divisions most managers had spent their career inside the division, although some top division managers were moved between divisions or into corporate positions.

In speaking about the type of men he had sought for management positions, Donald Irwin described his criterion in a financial publication: "We don't want people around who are afraid to move. The attraction of Texana is that it gives the individual responsibilities which aren't diluted. It attracts the fellow who wants a challenge."

Another corporate executive described Texana managers: "It's a group of very tough-minded but considerate gentlemen with an enormous drive to get things done."

Another manager, who had been with Texana for his entire career, and who considered himself to be different from most Texana managers, described the typical Texana manager as follows:

> Texana attracts a particular type of person. Most of these characteristics are personal characteristics rather than professional ones. I would use terms such as cold, unfeeling, aggressive, and extremely competitive, but not particularly loyal to the organization. He is loyal to dollars, his own personal dollars. I think this is part of the communication problem. I think this is done on purpose. The selection procedures lead in this direction. I think this is so because of contrast with the way the company operated ten years ago. Of course I was at the plant level at that time. But today the attitude I have described is also in

the plants. Ten years ago the organization was composed of people who worked together for the good of the organization, because they wanted to. I don't think this is so today.

Location of Division Facilities

The Petroleum Products Division, Chemical and Polymer Division, and the Packaging Products Division had their executive offices on separate floors of the Texana headquarters building in the Chicago "loop." The plants and research and development facilities of these divisions were spread out across Oklahoma, Texas, and Louisiana. The Molded Products Division had its headquarters, research and development facilities, and a major plant in an industrial suburb of Chicago. This division's other plants were at several locations in the Middle West and East Coast. The Building Products Division's headquarters and major production and technical facilities were located in Forth Worth, Texas. All four divisions shared sales offices in major cities from coast to coast.

Evaluation and Control of Division Performance

The principal method of controlling and evaluating the operations of these divisions was the semiannual review of division plans and the approval of major capital expenditures by the executive committee.[1] In reviewing performance against plans, members of the executive committee placed almost sole emphasis on the division's actual return on investment against budget. Corporate executives felt that this practice together with the technological interdependence of the divisions created many disputes about transfer pricing.

In addition to these regular reviews corporate executives had frequent discussions with division executives about their strategies, plans, and operations. It had been difficult for corporate management to strike the proper balance in guiding the operations for the divisions. This problem was particularly acute with regard to the Polymer and Chemicals Division, because of its central place in the corporation's product line. One corporate staff member explained his view of the problem:

> This whole matter of communications between the corporate staff and the Polymer and Chemical Division has been a fairly difficult problem. Corporate management used to contribute immensely to this by trying to get into the nuts and bolts area within the Chemical and Polymer organization, and this created serious criticisms; however, I think they have backed off in this manner.

---

[1] The executive committee consisted of Messrs. Dutton, Irwin, and Prentice, as well as the vice president of research, the executive vice president of administration, and the executive vice president of foreign operations.

A second corporate executive, in discussing this matter for a trade publication report, put the problem this way: "We're trying to find the middle ground. We don't want to be a holding company, and with our diversity we can't be a highly centralized corporation."

Executive Vice President—Domestic Operations

In an effort to find this middle ground, the position of executive vice president, domestic operations, was created in early 1966; and George Prentice was its first occupant. Prior to this change, there had been two senior domestic vice presidents, one in charge of the Petroleum Products Division and Polymer and Chemicals Division and the other in charge of the end-use divisions. Mr. Prentice had been senior vice president in charge of the end-use divisions before the new position was created. He had held that position for only two years, having come to it from a highly successful marketing career with a competitor.

At the time of his appointment one press account described Mr. Prentice as "hard-driving, aggressive, and ambitious—an archetype of the self-actuated dynamo Irwin has sought out."

Shortly after taking his new position Prentice described the task before him:

> I think the corporation wants to integrate its parts better and I am here because I reflect this feeling. We can't be a bunch of entrepreneurs around here. We have got to balance discipline with entrepreneurial motivation. This is what we were in the past, just a bunch of entrepreneurs, and if they came in with ideas we would get the money; but now our dollars are limited, and especially the Polymer and Chemical boys haven't been able to discipline themselves to select from within ten good projects. They just don't seem to be able to do this, and so they come running in here with all ten good projects which they say we have to buy, and they get upset when we can't buy them all.
>
> This was the tone of my predecessors (senior vice presidents). All of them were very strong on being entrepreneurs. I am going to run it different. I am going to take a marketing and capital orientation. As far as I can see, there is a time to compete and a time to collaborate, and I think right now there has been a lack of recognition in the Polymer and Chemicals executive suite that this thing has changed.

Other Views of Domestic Interdivisional Relations

Executives within the Polymer and Chemicals Division in the end-use divisions, and at the corporate level, shared Prentice's view that the major breakdown in interdivisional relations was between the Polymer and Chemicals Division and the end-use divisions. Executives in the end-use divisions made these typical comments about the problem:

> I think the thing we have got to realize is that we are wedded to the Polymer and Chemicals Division whether we like it or not. We are really tied up with them. And just as we would with any outside supplier or with any of our customers, we will do things to maintain their business. But because they feel they have our business wrapped up they do not reciprocate in turn. Now let us emphasize that they have not arbitrarily refused to do the things that we are requiring, but there is a pressure on them for investment projects and we are low man on the pole. And I think this could heavily jeopardize our chances for growth.

> I would say our relationships are sticky, and I think this is primarily because we think our reason for being is to make money, so we try to keep Polymer and Chemicals as an arm's length supplier. For example, I cannot see, just because it is a Polymer and Chemicals product, accepting millions of pounds of very questionable material. It takes dollars out of our pocket, and we are very profit centered.

> The big frustration, I guess, and one of our major problems, is that you can't get help from them [Polymer and Chemicals]. You feel they are not interested in what you are doing, particularly if it doesn't have a large return for them. But as far as I am concerned this has to become a joint venture relationship, and this is getting to be real sweat with us. We are the guys down below yelling for help. And they have got to give us some relief.

> My experience with the Polymer and Chemicals Division is that you cannot trust what they say at all, and even when they put it in writing you can't be absolutely sure that they are going to live up to it.

Managers within the Polymer and Chemicals Division expressed similar sentiments:

> Personally, right now I have the feeling that the divisions' interests are growing further apart. It seems that the divisions are going their own way. For example, we are a polymer producer but the molding division wants to be in a special area, so that means they are going to be less of a customer to us; and there is a whole family of plastics being left out that nobody's touching, and this is bearing on our program. . . . We don't mess with the Building Products Division at all, either. They deal in small volumes. Those that we are already making we sell to them, those that we don't make we can't justify making because of the kinds of things we are working with. What I am saying

is that I don't think the corporation is integrating, but I think we ought to be, and this is one of the problems of delegated divisions. What happens is that an executive heads this up and goes for the place that makes the most money for the division, *but* this is not necessarily the best place from a corporate standpoint.

We don't have as much contact with sister divisions as I think we should. I have been trying to get a liaison with guys in my function, but it has been a complete flop. One of the problems is that I don't know who to call on in these other divisions. There is no table of organization, nor is there any encouragement to try and get anything going. My experience has been that all of these operating divisions are very closed organizations. I know guys up the line will say that I am nuts about this. They say to just call over and I will get an answer. But this always has to be a big deal, and it doesn't happen automatically, and hurts us.

The comments of corporate staff members describe these relationships and the factors they saw contributing to the problem:

Right now I would say there is an iron curtain between the Polymer and Chemicals Division and the rest of the corporation. You know, we tell our divisions they are responsible, autonomous groups, and the Polymer and Chemicals Division took it very seriously. However, when you are a three-quarter-billion-dollar company, you've got to be coordinated, or the whole thing is going to fall apart—it can be no other way. The domestic executive vice president thing has been a big step forward to improve this, but I would say it hasn't worked out yet.

The big thing that is really bothering the Polymer and Chemicals Division is that they think they have to go develop all new markets on their own. They are going to do it alone, independently, and this is the problem they are faced with. They have got this big thing, that they want to prove that they are a company all by themselves and not rely upon packaging or anybody else.

Polymer and Chemicals Division executives talked about the effect of this drive for independence of the divisional operating heads on their own planning efforts:

The Polymer and Chemicals Division doesn't like to communicate with the corporate staff. This seems hard for us, and I think their recent major proposal was a classic example of this. That plan, as it was whipped up by the Polymer and Chemicals Division, had massive implications for the corporation both in expertise and in capital. In fact, I think we did this to be a competitive one-up on the rest of our sister divisions. We wanted to be the best-looking division in the system, but we carried it to an extreme. In this effort, we wanted

to show that we had developed this concept completely on our own.
. . . Now I think a lot of our problems with it stemmed from this
intense desire we have to be the best in this organization.

Boy, a big doldrum around here was shortly after Christmas (1965)
when they dropped out a new plant, right out of our central plan,
without any appreciation of the importance of this plant to the whole
Polymer and Chemicals Division's growth. . . . Now we have a windfall
and we are back in business on this new plant. But for a while things
were very black and everything we had planned and everything we
had built our patterns on were out. In fact, when we put this plan
together, it never really occurred to us that we were going to get it
turned down, and I'll bet we didn't even put the plans together in
such a way as to really reflect the importance of this plant to the
rest of the corporation.

A number of executives in the end-use divisions attributed the interdivisional problems to different management practices and assumptions
within the Polymer and Chemicals Division. An executive in the packaging division made this point:

We make decisions quickly and at the lowest possible level, and
this is tremendously different from the rest of Texana. I don't know
another division like this in the rest of the corporation.

Look at what Sy Knoph has superfluous to his operation compared
to ours. These are the reasons for our success. You've got to turn your
guys loose and not breathe down their necks all the time. We don't
slow our people down with staff. Sure, you may work with a staff,
the wheels may grind, but they sure grind slow.

Also, we don't work on detail like the other divisions do. Our management doesn't feel they need the detail stuff. Therefore, they're [Polymer
and Chemical] always asking us for detail which we can't supply, our
process doesn't generate it and their process requires it, and this always
creates problems with the Polymer and Chemicals Division. But I'll
be damned if I am going to have a group of people running between
me and the plant, and I'll be goddamned if I am going to clutter
up my organization with all the people that Knoph has got working
for him. I don't want this staff, but they are sure pushing it on me.

This comment from a molding division manager is typical of many
about the technical concerns of the Polymer and Chemicals Division
management:

Historically, even up to the not too distant past, the Polymer and
Chemicals Division was considered a snake pit as far as the corporate
people were concerned. This was because the corporate people were
market oriented and Polymer and Chemicals Division was technically
run and very much a manufacturing effort. These two factors created
a communication barrier; and to really understand the Polymer and

Chemicals Division problems, they felt that you have to have a basic appreciation of the technology and all the interrelationships.

Building on this strong belief, the Polymer and Chemicals Division executives in the past have tried to communicate in technical terms, and this just further hurt the relationship, and it just did not work. Now they are coming up with a little bit more business or commercial orientation, and they are beginning to appreciate that they have got to justify the things they want to do in a business or commercial orientation, and they are beginning to appreciate that they have got to justify the things they want to do in a business sense rather than just a technical sense. This also helps the problem of maintaining their relationships with the corporation, as most of the staff is nontechnical; however, this has changed a little bit in that more and more technical people have been coming on and this has helped from the other side.

They work on the assumption in the Polymer and Chemicals Division that you have to know the territory before you can be an effective manager. You have got to be an operating guy to contribute meaningfully to their problems. However, their biggest problem is this concentration on technical solutions to their problems. This is a thing that has boxed them in the most trouble with corporation and the other sister divisions.

These and other executives also pointed to another source of conflict between the Polymer and Chemicals Division and other divisions. This was the question of whether the Polymer and Chemicals Division should develop into a more independent marketer, or whether it should rely more heavily on the end-use divisions to "push" its products to the market.

Typical views of this conflict are the following comments by end-use division executives:

The big question I have about Polymer and Chemicals is what is their strategy going to be? I can understand them completely from a technical standpoint, this is no problem. I wonder what is the role of this company? How is it going to fit into what we and others are doing? Right now, judging from the behavior I've seen, Polymer and Chemicals could care less about what we are doing in terms of integration of our markets or a joint approach to them.

I think it is debatable whether the Polymer and Chemicals Division should be a new product company or not. Right now we have an almost inexhaustible appetite for what they do and do well. As I see it, the present charter is fine. However, that group is very impatient, aggressive, and they want to grow, but you have got to grow within guidelines. Possibly the Polymer and Chemicals Division is just going to have to learn to hang on the coattails of the other divisions and do just what they are doing now, only better.

I think the future roles of the Polymer and Chemicals Division is going to be, at any one point in time for the corporation, that if it looks like a product is needed, they will make it. . . . They are going to be suppliers because I will guarantee you that if the moment comes and we can't buy it elsewhere, for example, then I darn well know they are going to make it for us regardless for what their other commitments are. They are just going to have to supply us. If you were to put the Polymer and Chemicals Division off from the corporation, I don't think they would last a year. Without their huge captive requirements, they would not be able to compete economically in the commercial areas they are in.

A number of other executives indicated that the primary emphasis within the corporation on return on investment by divisions tended to induce, among other things, a narrow, competitive concern on the part of the various divisional managements. The comment of this division executive was typical:

As far as I can see it, we [his division and Polymer and Chemicals] are 180 degrees off on our respective charters. Therefore, when Sy Knoph talks about this big project we listen nicely and then we say, "God bless you, lots of luck," but I am sure we are not going to get involved in it. I don't see any money in it for us. I may be a gold mine for Sy but it is not for our company; and as long as we are held to the high profit standards we are, we just cannot afford to get involved. I can certainly see it might make good corporate sense for us to get it, but it doesn't make any sense in terms of our particular company. We have got to be able to show the returns in order to get continuing capital and I just can't on that kind of project. I guess what I am saying is that under the right conditions we could certainly go in but not under the present framework; we would just be dead in terms of dealing with the corporate financial structure. We just cannot get the kinds of returns on our capital that the corporation has set to get new capital. In terms of the long run, I'd like very much to see what the corporation has envisioned in terms of a hookup between us, but right now I don't see any sense in going on. You know my career is at stake here too.

Another divisional executive made this point more succinctly:

Personally, I think that a lot more could be done from a corporate point of view, and this is frustrating. Right now all these various divisions seem to be viewed strictly as an investment by the corporate people. They only look at us as a banker might look at us. This hurts us in terms of evolving some of these programs because we have relationships which are beyond financial relationships.

The remarks of a corporate executive seemed to support this concern:

One of things I worry about is where the end of the rope is on this interdivisional thing. I'm wondering if action really has to come from just the division. You know, in this organization when you decide to do something new it always has been a divisional proposal—they were coming to us for review and approval. The executive committee ends up a review board—not us, working downward. With this kind of pattern the talent of the corporate people is pretty well seduced into asking questions and determining whether a thing needs guidelines. But I think we ought to be the idea people as well, thinking about where we are going in the future; and if we think we ought to be getting into some new area, then we tell the divisions to do it. The stream has got to work both ways. Now it does not.

Readings

1 | Managing the Psychological Contract

Roosevelt Thomas

Our purpose in this note is to consider the relationship between individual employees and the organization and its implications for the manager of a functional unit (e.g., a sales force, manufacturing plant, controller's department).

Since most business organizations are built on functional units, managers at this level are usually centrally involved in managing the interface between the work of the organization and the skills of the employee. They are responsible for not only ensuring that the technical resources for performing tasks are available (e.g., the necessary equipment, raw materials), but they must also manage the motivation of their employees. That is, they must create a relationship between employees and the firm so that their subordinates are willing to expend energy on organizational tasks.

THE RELATIONSHIP

The Notion of Reciprocation

In the relationship between the individual employee and the organization, each party participates *only* because of what it expects to receive in exchange for participation.[1] An individual, like an organization, is

---

[1] This discussion of the psychological contract is based primarily on: Harry Levinson et al., *Men, Management, and Mental Health* (Cambridge, Mass.: Harvard University Press, 1966), pp. 22–38; and David J. Lawless, *Effective Management: Social Psychological Approach* (Englewood Cliffs, N.J.: Prentice-Hall, Inc., 1972), pp. 144–64.

a system with its own particular needs. These two systems enter into a joint cooperative relationship only when it offers opportunities for the fulfillment of their respective needs. In other words, the organization employs the individual because his services are essential for the achievement of its goals; similarly, the individual contributes his services only when it leads to the fulfillment of his personal needs.

The Psychological Contract

The basis of this reciprocal relationship is the psychological contract, which may be defined as the mutual expectations of the individual and the organization as articulated by its managers.[2] Both parties bring to the relationship a set of expectations of what each will give and receive. (Figure 1 provides examples of areas in which the organization and the individual are likely to have expectations.)

FIGURE 1
Examples of Expectations

What the individual may expect to receive and the organization may expect to give:	What the individual may expect to give and the organization may expect to receive:
a. Salary	*a.* An honest day's work
b. Personal development opportunities	*b.* Loyalty to organization
c. Recognition and approval for good work	*c.* Initiative
d. Security through fringe benefits	*d.* Conformity to organizational norms
e. Friendly, supportive environment	*e.* Job effectiveness
f. Fair treatment	*f.* Flexibility and a willingness to learn and
g. Meaningful or purposeful job	to develop

Source: Adapted from John Paul Kotter, "The Psychological Contract: Managing the Joining-Up Process," *California Management Review* (Spring 1973), p. 93.

When each party enters into the relationship, it tacitly accepts the expectations of the other. The set of both the individual's and the organization's expectations becomes the basis of the psychological contract.

The individual-organization contract is termed "psychological" because much of it is often unwritten and unverbalized. There are several reasons why this may be so.

First, both parties may not be entirely clear about their expectations and how they wish them fulfilled. They may wish to avoid defining the contract until they have a better feel for what they want. This may be one explanation of the tendency of management recruiters and applicants to define their expectations in very general terms. Frequently the recruiter sees himself "buying brains" that will adapt to some as

---

[2] Levinson et al., *Men, Management, and Mental Health*, p. 36; Lawless, *Effective Management*, p. 147.

yet undefined job, while the applicant wants to maintain as much latitude as he can in specifying the type of job which interests him.

Second, employees and the organization's representative may not be aware of some of their expectations. For example, organizations frequently are not explicitly aware of how much loyalty they demand of their employees. Similarly, employees are not aware of the extent to which social contact on the job is important to them. The fact that the parties are unaware of these needs does not make them any less real; for if they are not fulfilled, both parties will quickly become aware of their reality.

Third, some expectations may be perceived as so natural and basic that they are taken for granted and left unstated. Two examples would be the expectations of "no stealing" and "an honest day's work for a day's pay."

Fourth, and connected to the above, cultural norms may inhibit verbalization. Wanting to be perceived in the "Horatio Alger tradition of self-starters" may prevent an employee from probing too deeply into what is expected of him; similarly, norms against the violation of individual privacy may make an organization's management cautious about expressing its expectation of loyalty on and off the job.

Though the psychological contract is largely unstated and unsupported by legal sanctions, it has a commanding quality. It represents each party's expectations for the continued existence of the relationship. At any given time, there will be some relatively fulfilled and some unfulfilled expectations; however, each party has a minimum acceptable level of fulfillment. If either party concludes that the fulfillment of its needs is below this minimum level, it will view the contract as having been violated.

Three options are open to the dissatisfied party. He may attempt to renegotiate the contract, he may continue the relationship in an alienated frame of mind, and/or he may sever the relationship. Once one of the parties becomes dissatisfied, he will send a signal to the other expressing a desire that the contract be renegotiated. Such signals may vary from a verbal complaint to a violent wildcat strike or acts of sabotage. Often, a complaining individual will attempt to enlist others in his cause. Such efforts may lead to collective bargaining arrangements or even to the creation of social movements. The California lettuce workers provide an example. Unable to prevail on their own, they have sought the support of society. Similarly, the federal government, the civil rights movement, and the women's liberation movement have acted to renegotiate psychological contracts between minorities and organizations. This phenomenon works both ways. Corporations may join together to form a single bargaining unit; also, they may appeal for public support as contracts (both psychological and legal) come up for renegotiation. In sum, both parties may seek help as they adjust to changing relationships.

If renegotiation fails or does not take place, either discontented party may become alienated, yet continue the relationship, but at the minimum acceptable level. Alienation of employees may be seen in the restriction of output and sabotage attributed to "blue-collar" workers.[3] Alienation on the part of the employer may be seen in the way top managers in some companies respond to an employee who fails to accept a "promotion" requiring a move. Such corporations have a series of "experience jobs" designed to foster the development of upwardly mobile employees. Occasionally, an individual on the way up will develop a strong liking for an "experience job" and refuse to accept a "promotion." When this happens, the developmental program is "blocked." This can cause serious problems for his superiors, for they will have to find a replacement for that slot in the program and are left with uncertainty about the employee's commitment to the company. A consequence of the individual's refusal to move is usually a decrease in his opportunities for promotion or significant salary increase.

A state of alienation may persist for years if neither party is moved to change the offending conditions. (An apocryphal quotation describes the situation: "We have too many people here who are no longer with us.") If renegotiation fails or when alienation becomes too uncomfortable, the relationship may be severed. But in our society most people are reluctant to fire individuals; instead many organizations prefer to "ease people out" or "move them into a corner." If these alternatives are not available either because the individual refuses to cooperate or because the organization lacks convenient "corners," then the corporation will have to face its situation. It may do this by changing the standards of what it will accept from the employee or by firing him.

On the other hand, the individual's willingness to sever the relationship is a function of his available alternatives—they must offer rewards at least equal to those provided by his present employer. If the individual concludes that his situation is "par for the course" and that alternatives do not offer significant advantages, he will be reluctant to quit. Clearly, if the alternatives are viewed as less rewarding, his willingness to endure alienation and dissatisfaction will be increased. The implication here is that the capacity of the organization and the individual to endure an unsatisfactory relationship may be considerable, and may depend heavily on factors in the environment. An economic downturn, for example, brings pressure to clear out the "deadwood" from corporate corners at the same time it reduces the number of alternatives available to the individual.

The psychological contract is dynamic and changes as the needs of

---

[3] See "Sabotage at Lordstown?" *Time*, February 7, 1972, p. 76.

the two parties change. For example, a company's needs may change as it moves from a small dynamic firm to a large mature one. Similarly, the individual's needs change as he or she moves from swinging bachelorhood through childrearing toward retirement.

Also, changes in the psychological contract may be caused by dramatic shifts in the environment. Public concern and legislation about occupational safety and health have caused many firms and their employees to rethink these aspects of their psychological contract. And public acceptance of the women's liberation movement has caused more and more women to demand more meaningful and challenging positions. In response to these demands and expectations, one large corporation has instituted a "Project Mobility" program designed to facilitate the upward mobility of its women clerical workers. Again the net effect is an alteration in the psychological contract.

The Nature of the Individual's Needs

What type of psychological contract an individual is likely to find attractive depends on the needs imbedded in his or her personality. For decades, management has assumed that fulfillment of their important needs will motivate employees to work. However, during this period several successive views of man have been popular with managers. (The discussion that follows is based primarily on Edgar Schein's "Organizational Man and the Process of Management" in *Organizational Psychology.*[4])

The *rational-economic* view of the individual, popular since the turn of the century, assumed that man's basic motivation was economic. Man, operating on a rational basis, would do whatever resulted in the greatest economic gain. However, man had feelings (emotions) which were largely irrational and which had to be neutralized. The implied managerial strategy was one of reward and control. The worker was rewarded with economic gains and controlled so that he would not fall victim to his irrational feelings.

In the 40s and 50s the *social man* model was advocated. Here the individual was motivated primarily by his desire for social contact at work, and he performed at work according to how well these needs were met. The employee was viewed as being more responsive to social forces than to management's incentives and controls. An effective manager had to meet the social needs of his employees.

In the *self-actualization model*, which was the next to come into vogue, the individual was seen as having a hierarchy of needs: "(1) survival needs, (2) social needs, (3) self-esteem needs, (4) need for autonomy and (5) need for self-actualization in the sense of maximum

---

[4] Edgar Schein, *Organizational Psychology* (Englewood Cliffs, N.J.: Prentice-Hall, Inc., 1970), pp. 50–79.

use of all his resources."[5] Man was considered to be self-motivated and self-controlled, and voluntarity meshed his goals with those of the organization. Here, the role of the manager was to make the work challenging and interesting; the manager's job was to define the task so that a person who desired challenge, autonomy, and the right to discipline himself would find the task attractive. In exchange for good performance, the organization was to provide opportunities for self-actualizing.

Each of the above schools of thought attempted to set forth a universal model of man. The *complex-man* model, which seems to better capture the nature of human personality, suggests that universal approaches to the individual are much too simple and that man is much more complex than is implied in any of the above perspectives. The complex-man model recognizes that the individual may have a variety of needs (e.g., self-esteem, identity, competence, achievement, affiliation, power) with a variety of strengths. This is because each individual has a history of different developmental experiences and genetic configurations.

To use this model a manager must have a diagnostic perspective and must be sensitive to the differences among his employees. However, the complexity is reduced because of the tendency of individuals with similar need patterns to be attracted to a given organizational unit. This is probably a result of both the organization's selection process and career choices by the individual. Nevertheless, it is still possible to have a mixture of significantly different individual need patterns in one multiunit organization. An example is the university. The employees of a university may be divided into four groups: physical plant staff, clerical staff, administrators, and faculty. In a recent research effort the writer found that each of these groups had uniform but unique sets of needs and expectations, centered around the nature of their jobs, pay, fringe benefits, and relationships with peers.

For the physical plant workers the most important aspect of work was the fringe benefits. The nature of their task was very much secondary. The clerical staff were much more concerned with the intrinsic nature of their tasks, although fringe benefits were still significant to this group. The faculty, on the other hand, was primarily interested in maintaining the autonomy and support necessary for effective teaching and research. Administrators expressed a need for more professionalism. The relative weights assigned to individual expectations thus varied significantly from group to group.

The Role of the Functional Unit Manager

As was indicated at the outset, because most organizations are built around functional units, the manager of such units is frequently the

---

[5] Ibid., p. 66.

person most responsible for implementing the psychological contract. His is the task of fulfilling the organization's end of the contract and reminding the individual of his contractual obligations. This requires that the functional manager provide an organizational design that will facilitate the performance of organizational tasks and that will ensure that employees have opportunities to realize their expectations at work.

Recent research suggests that maintaining a psychological contract which accomplishes these ends in a functional unit involves achieving a fit among the nature of the unit's task, the personalities of its members, and the unit's organizational design.[6] When such a fit exists, the unit gains effective results and the individual members gain feelings of competence which lead to a continuing motivation to perform their jobs well.

For example, in manufacturing plants it was found that management and professional employees had a relatively low tolerance for ambiguity, preferred to work more closely with colleagues and preferred stronger direction from their superiors. The tasks upon which they were working were short term, relatively repetitive and predictable, and highly independent. However, only in the effective plants (lower costs, more on time deliveries, higher quality, etc.) did the design of the organization fit both the personalities of members and the nature of their work. In these plants there was an organizational design which provided relatively tight control and coordination, established routines for how to conduct the work, and measured short-term results.

Similarly, in research laboratories, scientists and managers had a higher tolerance for ambiguity, preferred to work more alone, and without close supervision. Here the task was highly uncertain with little interdependence required, and results were achieved only over a long time span. Again, only in effective laboratories (more innovations contributing to company products and processes) was there an organizational design which matched these factors. In these laboratories the organization allowed a great deal of autonomy and influence for individual scientists and placed emphasis on measuring results over the long term.[7]

As Figure 2 suggests, such a contingency among organizational, task, and human variables seems to lead to a psychological transaction which is beneficial to both the organization and the individual. This diagram also emphasizes the often neglected point that the very act of performing the job well (belonging to a winning team) can also be an important motivational force.

From this perspective, the functional manager concerned with main-

---

[6] Jay Lorsch and John Morse, *Organizations and Their Members: A Contingency Approach* (New York: Harper & Row, Publishers, 1974).

[7] Lorsch and Morse, *Organizations and Their Members.*

FIGURE 2

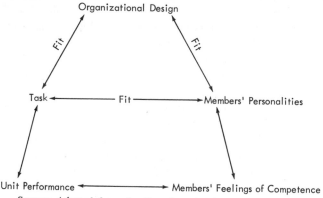

Source: Adapted from Jay Lorsch and John Morse, *Organizations and Their Members: A Contingency Approach* (New York: Harper & Row, Publishers, 1974), p. 115.

taining a viable psychological contract with his subordinates must arrange the organizational design variables available to him to fit the task and individual factors in his unit. We now turn to a review of four of the principal design tools available to functional managers as they work toward a "good fit" and fulfillment of the psychological contract: measurement practices, rewards, job design, and personnel selection criteria.

Measurement Practices

Measurement systems are multipurpose. For example, they provide data which is useful for decision making and future planning. However, the use we shall focus on here is their role as the basis for evaluating an individual's performance, for it is in this respect they have the most direct impact on the psychological contract.

The unit of measurement used to evaluate performance may be any of a variety of indices. In a sales unit possibilities are volume, size of volume increase, number or sales returns, number of visits to customers, number of new contracts, or the size of individual orders. Similarly, in a manufacturing unit, quality of output, quantity of output, timing of output, and the size of backorders are possible units of measurement. Regardless of the measurement used, it must be congruent with task requirements and the individual's expectations and predispositions; otherwise, unit effectiveness and individual motivation will suffer. The examples below illustrate what may take place when an inappropriate measurement scheme is used.

A research laboratory in a large corporation had as its primary mission "basic" or "pure" research, as opposed to "applied" research. The primary unit of measurement for the lab was the "completed project." Performance was evaluated informally on a quarterly basis and formally on an annual basis. At each evaluation, the emphasis was on the number of "completed projects." The rationale for this measurement system was that while the corporation was interested in basic research, it wanted ideas brought to fruition as soon as possible. The measurement system was an attempt to get around the "academic" inclination of scientists to "drag projects out." As a result of this practice, many scientists became quite unhappy, while others designed narrowly focused projects that could be more readily completed. Both behaviors were undesirable from the corporation's perspective. The dissatisfaction led to a decrease in the unit's productivity; also, the narrowly focused projects were usually "applied" research. Several of the top scientists have left, and others are threatening to do so in search of a place "where they understand research."

A reputable eastern liberal arts college had a faculty that had done relatively little research or writing. Though the president often stressed the importance of research, research output was not used as a criterion in promotion or salary decisions. Instead, teaching effectiveness and length of service were much more crucial. The college's president was puzzled as to why the faculty was not publishing more. However, using the concept of fit, the nature of the problem is quite obvious. The use of teaching and length of service as measurements of performance signaled that research was relatively unimportant despite the president's rhetoric. If research was truly a part of the psychological contract, or if the president wished that it be included, then it should have been reflected in the measurement system.

In hopes of minimizing the frequency of such "misfits," many companies have turned to management by objective (MBO) as a performance appraisal device. In theory, a properly functioning MBO system should result in measurements congruent with the task requirements and the employees' personalities.

Alva Kindall has suggested that ideally there should be five steps in the MBO process.[8] First, the employee develops a position description and outlines his areas of responsibilities and accountability. This is done in discussions with his immediate superior. Once agreement has been reached between the superior and subordinate on the employee's position and the results for which he is responsible and accountable, the process may proceed to step two. Here, the individual prepares a list of goals that he believes represents acceptable performance in his areas of respon-

---

[8] Alva F. Kindall, *Personnel Administration: Principles and Cases* (Homewood, Ill.: Richard D. Irwin, Inc., 1969), pp. 411–15.

sibility. This list should be prepared in the context of the organization's objectives and should include the person's plans for self-development. In step three, the subordinate seeks agreement from his superior on his list of goals. Here, the superior is to act as a "questioner, advisor, counselor, trainer, developer, and even 'warner'"; however, in no case is he to act as "God or judge." In step four, the individual and his manager jointly determine which standards (measurements or checkpoints) will be used in evaluating the subordinate's success in attaining his objectives. Step five is a review of the individual's results.

Depending on the objectives of the manager, MBO may be used for a variety of purposes. For example, Levinson has suggested that MBO may be used to:

—measure and judge performance
—relate individual performance to organizational goals
—clarify both the job to be done and the expectations of accomplishment
—foster the increasing competence and growth of the subordinate
—enhance communications between superior and subordinate
—stimulate the subordinate's motivation
—serve as a device for organizational control and integration[9]

In sum, MBO may be described as a means of establishing measurements congruent with the functional unit's objectives and the individual's own expectations. Though, as Levinson points out, there have been problems in effecting MBO programs, our comments will be based on the assuption that the concept can be implemented if the conditions spelled out below are met.[10]

MBO attempts simultaneously to signal to the individual what is desired behavior and to make provisions for the realization of individual expectations. It may be described as an effort to verbalize parts of the psychological contract and to establish measurements for evaluating the quality of its implementation. As such, however, it will only be useful when the MBO process "fits" the task requirements and the individual employee's personality. MBO is no panacea. It works best where the task is inherently rewarding, allows employee discretion and judgment, and where the employees and their superiors are predisposed to utilize such a consultative and participative process. In tasks where minimum discretion is allowed and the work is repetitive and routine, the objectives are often predetermined and little is gained by asking an employee to list the obvious. Further, some employees are not comfortable with their role in an MBO program. They do not feel they should take the lead in identifying their areas of accountability and responsibility; in-

---

[9] Harry Levinson, *The Great Jackass Fallacy* (Boston: Division of Research, Harvard Business School, 1973).

[10] Ibid.

stead, they prefer being told what to do by their superiors. Where employees hold this view, implementation would be difficult. Similarly, there are some managers who do not feel comfortable allowing their subordinates to set goals. For this group also MBO will not be a suitable tool. On the other hand, where the task calls for individual judgment and discretion, and where subordinate autonomy is welcomed by subordinates and superiors, the concept of MBO is more appropriate.

Rewards

The rewards which managers have available as design tools can be divided into those which are intrinsic to the job itself and those which are extrinsic. The intrinsic rewards, which stem from doing the job itself, we shall consider below when we deal with issues of job design. Extrinsic rewards, which we shall discuss first, include pay, promotional opportunities, fringe benefits, distribution of office space, and similar manifestations of status and prestige. Of these we shall focus here on two—pay and promotional opportunities.

Pay is frequently the first thing managers turn to in considering rewards. Yet until very recently there have been very few even general guidelines for thinking about rewards. Porter and Lawler have provided one such set of criteria for thinking about rewards in general and compensation in particular.[11] They suggest that management should ensure that:

1. Rewards provided should be those most desired by the employee in return for performing the job well. (This means that the pay system must be designed and administered in a manner that will allow the individual to realize his expectations. Other provisions should be made for expectations that cannot be realized through the pay system. For example, employees' expectations of friendly interaction with peers cannot be met through the pay system; instead, spatial arrangements are a more relevant means for fulfilling this expectation. Similarly, the employees' expectations of advancement as a reward for good past performance can only be met through rewarding and meaningful career paths. A critical job for managers, therefore, is focusing accurately on employees' expectations. An abundance of rewards that are not those most desired by employees can result in employee dissatisfaction. The classic example of this was the reaction of paternalistic companies to unionization attempts. Having provided the employees with an abundance of material needs (company houses, good pay, fringe benefits, etc.), the top manage-

---

[11] Lyman W. Porter and Edward E. Lawler III, "What Job Attitudes Tell about Motivation," *Harvard Business Review* (January–February 1968), pp. 118–26.

ments of these companies were puzzled when their employees began to press for unionization; however, they had failed to recognize the individuals' expectations of being treated like adults, not children.

2. Superior performers should be given more extrinsic rewards and should be provided with more opportunities to gain intrinsic rewards . . . than inferior performers. (The implication is that pay must differentiate between high and low performers and between desirable and undesirable behavior. Failure to do this will result in the communication of incorrect signals to employees. Here, a prerequisite is a measurement system capable of differentiating between high and low performers and between desirable and undesirable behavior.)

3. Reward practices should lead individuals in the organization to *see* and *believe* that good performance leads to both extrinsic and intrinsic rewards. The pay system must be understood and believed by the employees. In sum, the pay system's credibility must be maintained.

Within such broad guidelines for the design of a pay system, specific aspects will be dictated by how the manager plans to use financial compensation. For example, the manager may desire to use pay to meet only the employee's economic needs. The managerial problem would then be to set pay at a level compatible with the employees' economic expectations; also, pay differentials would be comparatively small and only marginally related to performance. However, in these circumstances, the managers must ensure that the individuals' other expectations are addressed in other ways. An example of this approach may be found in the higher grades of the civil service. In a recent *Business Week* article, the government's small differentials for these civil servants were criticized as not offering enough monetary incentive and rewards; however, another explanation would be that the government does not view the pay system as the major reward device at the super grade level.[12] Perhaps the designers of the system felt that at this level the major rewards were inherent in the performance of the work itself and the opportunity for public service. On the other hand, a manager may wish to use pay as a means of fulfilling the competence needs of his workers and as a signal of what is desired behavior. Here, pay differentials would be larger between different job levels and between high and low performers. Also the relationship between pay and performance would be emphasized. In essence, the extent to which compensation is tied to performance and to which the differentials are established between jobs must "fit" the nature of the task and employees' expectations.

---

[12] Arch Patton, "Government's Pay Disincentive," *Business Week*, January 19, 1974, pp. 12–13.

The manager in administering and designing the pay system must also be cognizant of what leads to satisfaction with pay on the part of his employees. Lawler's Model of the Determinants of Pay Satisfaction suggest that there are several relevant variables.[13] Such satisfaction is a function of the gap between the individual's perception of what he *should* get and his perception of the amount of pay received. The employees' perception of what they should receive is based on their personal attributes (skill, experience, training, effort, age, seniority, company loyalty, past and present performance), their perception of what their peers are doing and receiving, their perception of their job's characteristics (level, difficulty, time span, amount of responsibility), their perception of nonmonetary rewards that will also be forthcoming, and their own wage history. Similarly, the employees' perception of their actual pay is determined by their wage history, their perception of the pay of their reference group, and the actual pay rate. If the employees' perception of what they should receive is equal to their perception of what they actually receive, they will be satisfied. When pay falls short of their perception of what they should receive, they will be dissatisfied. Finally, when actual pay exceeds perception of what should be received, the employee will experience feelings of guilt and inequity. The implications of Lawler's work for the design of pay schemes are straightforward. The amount of pay provided must be consistent with these perceptions of employees or the consequences are likely to be dissatisfaction on the one hand or guilt on the other.

A second source of extrinsic reward to the individual employee is a meaningful career path. Here the expectation is that promotions will offer developmental opportunities and also greater opportunity to experience job intrinsic satisfaction as well as more money. Again, our message is the same: Career paths must "fit" the task requirements and the individuals' expectations. While career paths should offer meaningful promotional opportunities for the individual, they must also provide for organizational stability; that is, career paths should not interfere with the unit's ability to perform its tasks.

An example where career paths do not fit task requirements was found in a consumer products company. MBAs were lured to the company's marketing department with promises of rapid promotion through the product management ranks. The company kept its commitment moving new employees up the ladder at one- and two-year intervals. The result was great challenge for the individual, but a great deal of confusion within the marketing function and the company. Employees moved so quickly that they did not have a chance to execute marketing plans they had developed. Consequently, it was difficult to hold any individual

---

[13] Edward E. Lawler III, *Pay and Organizational Effectiveness: A Psychological View* (New York: McGraw-Hill Book Co., 1971), pp. 205–30.

responsible for results. Further, as a result of so much rapid movement, the marketing department's relations with other functions deteriorated. Managers in research, manufacturing, and sales complained that the frequent job changes made it impossible to know who to contact in marketing about mutual problems, so they quit trying.

Job Design

Functional managers became concerned with the content of individual jobs when they became interested in increasing employee motivation by increasing the intrinsic satisfaction inherent in the performance of a task. There have been two concepts recently associated with the design of job content: job enlargement and job enrichment.

Job enlargement is the "broadening of job duties and responsibilities," and its purpose has been to reduce the negative effects of repetitive work.[14] Frequently, job enlargement means the combining of several operations in hopes of reducing the amount of repetitiveness. However, many times this has resulted in the combining of several repetitive functions which did not contribute to the reduction of repetitiveness. Job enrichment, which grew out of these problems with job enlargement, is an attempt to enhance employee responsibility and autonomy through the broadening of job definitions to emphasize the opportunity for individual achievement and creativity.[15] The reasoning was that job enrichment would lead to improved employee morale which in turn would lead to greater motivation.

The conclusions of recent discussions of job enrichment are in line with our theme: To be effective, the design tool (job enrichment) must "fit" the task and the individuals' predispositions. Morse has reported on his recent research efforts with Lorsch. The implications of their research for job enrichment is that it is most likely to result in improved job performance when it fits both "(1) personalities of the individuals whose jobs are being designed, and (2) the technology or the task."[16] Morse suggests that the improved performance is not due to increases in employee morale but to increases in employee motivation. Where job enrichment works, it facilitates task performance and results in greater effectiveness. This increase in effectiveness meets the individual's expectation of feeling competent. The realization of this expectation increases the employee's willingness to expend energy on the task and thus further contributes to greater effectiveness.

Morse also points out that there are some jobs where repetitiveness and monotony are impossible to avoid; examples are those industries

---

[14] John J. Morse, "A Contingency Look at Job Design," *California Management Review* (Fall 1973), p. 68.

[15] Ibid., p. 68.

[16] Ibid., p. 69.

with large capital investments in assembly lines and similar processes. Further, some individuals do not desire autonomy and variety and are more comfortable on repetitive tasks with clear direction. In these situations, Morse suggests that job enrichment may be less appropriate. Where individuals value autonomy and variety, and the task and its technology are not so constraining and allow employee discretion, judgment, and autonomy, job enrichment can facilitate task performance and the employees' development of a sense of competence.

The Selection Process

The process used for selecting employees is the final design tool available to managers of functional units that we shall discuss. In the context of the concepts of "fit" and the psychological contract, the selection process is really a matching process between the employee and the organization. In any ongoing functional unit, there is an existing psychological contract. The selection process must bring to the functional unit individuals who will be comfortable with the existing arrangement. In order for the selection process to function properly, the manager and the candidate must accurately communicate their expectations at the employment interview. This means that the manager must be skilled in articulating his expectations and in understanding the individual's expectations and predispositions. Let us be clear here. The manager does not have to do a psychological interpretation of the applicant's personality; instead, he must take into consideration the manifestations (his expectations) of his need structure and personality. The manager must make a judgment as to whether an applicant would be able to accept the existing psychological contract in his unit. He must make a judgment on the match between the organization's expectations and those of the individual. Poor judgment here may be detrimental to the functional unit's effectiveness. Kotter found that job satisfaction, productivity, and turnover varied with the quality of the "match" between the expectations of new employees and the organization—the higher the number of matches, the greater the job satisfaction.[17]

In this discussion of design tools, we have viewed them as a means of implementing the tacitly accepted psychological contract. We have suggested that the tools may be used to implement the psychological contract. It also has been repeatedly stressed that the effectiveness of the design tools as implementation aids depends on their "fit" with the organization's task and the employees predispositions and expectations. No one tool is a panacea for all situations. We should also stress that the ideas presented here suggest only a broad framework for thinking about these issues. The functional manager still must use discretion and judgment in selecting and using these design tools.

---

[17] Kotter, "The Psychological Contract," p. 93.

Implementation of Change

There is one other respect in which the notion of the psychological contract is useful. Not only can it provide a useful way for thinking about issues of organization design, but it also provides important insights into the issues of implementing changes in organization design variables with the minimum disruption and discontent. Any such change represents a threat to the existing psychological contract in a unit. Thus, employee resistance to change may be viewed as evidence of the individual's concern that the existing contract is threatened. The individual will resist change until a new and acceptable contract is arranged. Thus, if the manager wishes to understand and deal with resistance to change, he or she must always ask: What effect will a proposed change have on the existing psychological contract?

After the manager has identified the possible effects and the likely areas of resistance, he or she has at least three options. One, steps may be taken to ensure that the employees' expectations can be realized under the new arrangement. He or she must then communicate to employees that their expectations can be fulfilled under the changed conditions. Two, a new contract can be arranged with employees. Frequently, an environmental development will dictate a change that must be made if the organization is to survive. Under these circumstances, resistance to change is likely to disappear once the employees understand the threat. One may hypothesize that as a result of the "energy crisis" the airlines and the automobile companies may have to make drastic changes and renegotiate psychological contracts with their employees. Because of the severity of the crisis, employee resistance to change will probably be much less than under "normal" conditions. Three, the manager may ignore the resistance. This option is usually exercised when the manager wishes to force the resignation of those resisting, or when he or she thinks the resistance will eventually subside. This option is frequently exercised by managers who view the individual as being "naturally" opposed to change.

Using the "psychological contract" as a way of thinking about change offers the manager a better chance to understand and manage resistance to change. The alternate view often expressed by managers is that resistance to change is almost always an automatic employee response. While some resistance to change may very well be natural and inevitable, by understanding the psychological contract, managers should recognize that most of it may be quite legitimate from the employees' point of view. As a result they should be more likely to plan change tactics which can deal with it effectively.

2 | *Organization Design*

John P. Kotter

Every design problem begins with an effort to achieve
fitness between two entities: the form in question and its
context. The form is the solution to the problem; the
context defines the problem. In other words, when we
speak of design, the real object of the discussion is not
the form alone, but the ensemble comprising the form
and its context. Good fit is a desired property of the
ensemble which relates to some particular division of the
ensemble into form and context.

—*Notes on the Synthesis of Form*
CHRISTOPHER ALEXANDER

Anyone who has had broad experience in managing firms or their
parts will realize that there is no such thing as one "best" way to organize.[1] Research units, sales units, and production units in successful
firms are usually organized differently. Large and small firms in the
same industry, successful firms with different product-market strategies,
and firms in different industries all tend to have different organizational
designs.

It is not unusual, however, for a businessman or government administrator who has not had experience in a variety of organizations to assume
that there is a single "correct" way to organize. That "correct" way
is usually the one form of organization which he has seen work successfully. Often such a person is not even consciously aware of his assumptions about organization. More than one manager has moved to a very
different firm or agency and then failed because he reorganized it in
an inappropriate way.

This insight, that an appropriate organization is contingent upon a
number of situational factors, is by itself, however, not very useful.

---

[1] Some of the best literature on this subject can be found in F. E. Kast and
J. E. Rosenzweig, *Contingency Views of Management and Organization* (Chicago:
Science Research Associates, Inc., 1973).

One needs also to know what those factors are, and what the nature of their relationship to organizational form is. A successful manager with broad enough experience will ultimately develop a "gut feeling" for these factors and relationships. One of the purposes of a course in organizational behavior is to help you develop some of this "feeling" rather quickly through the condensed process of discussing cases. To facilitate this learning process, a "map" or set of concepts that relates to organization is needed. In this reading we will present such a map along with its connection to the concrete tools which are available to managers.

AN INFORMATION PROCESSING CONCEPTUALIZATION

There are many ways that one can think about organizations in the abstract. Perhaps the most useful conceptualization developed in the past decade describes firms as information processing units.[2] That is, the key activities which go on in a firm are information gathering, information transmittal, and decision making. The purpose of these activities is to help the firm engage in exchanges with its environment which are advantageous for the firm and which collectively meet its goals.

A typical corporation exchanges its products for money; its money and other rewards for people's services; its scientific expertise and human effort for product innovation; its money for supplies; its supplies, machinery, and effort for finished goods; its interest payments for the loan of money, and so on. In a large company many such complex exchanges go on continuously. Traditionally at least, the primary goal of profit-making corporations has been to maximize in the long run the dollar surplus from these exchanges.

The key to a net favorable exchange for such a corporation is to have information which can be used to its advantage about those entities or environments with which it is exchanging things. It is to the company's benefit, for example, to learn its customers' preferences and to transport that information to wherever product design decisions are made; it is to its advantage to learn where it can get a better lending rate, and to get the information to wherever financial decisions are made; it is to its advantage to learn what means, less costly than those now used, can motivate its employees; to find out where it can obtain better supplies for less cost; to learn how it can satisfy a regulatory agency; and so on.

Communicating and then utilizing information once obtained is often as great a challenge as getting that information in the first place. Al-

---

[2] Jay Galbraith has been particularly important in this development. See his *Designing Complex Organizations* (Reading, Mass.: Addison-Wesley Publishing Co., Inc., 1973).

though a sales manager might have some crucial information about customer attitudes toward a certain type of product, that information might never get to the design engineer who is working on such a product. Even if it does, the designer might ignore the sales manager's information because he doesn't think it relevant, or because he doesn't trust salesmen.

The more competent an organization is at gathering, communicating, and then utilizing information about those environments which are relevant to its strategy, the more successful it will be in its exchanges with those environments and therefore in achieving its goals. To understand what makes for information processing competence, one needs to examine the nature of the tasks organizations face and the nature of their resources (especially employees).

Even a small firm engages in many types of information processing tasks. Some of these involve bringing information into the firm, while others involve internal transmission and decision making. The nature of these tasks varies considerably depending upon the type of information involved and its sources.[3] In some information processing tasks, the information is terribly complex and voluminous, while in others it is rather simple and terse. The information involved can sometimes be treated analytically, other times it can not. Sometimes the source of information wants to give it up, sometimes the source doesn't, and sometimes one doesn't know where to find the source.

Gathering, communicating, and utilizing information about the effects of gamma rays on a celluoid membrane in one's product is obviously different from gathering and utilizing information about a customer's order at a restaurant. Moreover, both are very different from information processing at a bargaining session with a hostile opponent. Gathering information from salesmen, merchandising managers, and designers to decide what colors to use in next year's sweater line is again quite different. Getting information on probable sales volume from 500 salesmen, on labor availability from 20 foremen, on raw material and in process and finished inventories from 6 production managers, all in a half an hour to establish today's production schedule, is different again.

Competent information processing results when behavior patterns (organization) are consistent with the demands of the different types of information processing tasks. Therefore, we would expect to find firms with different sets of tasks to be organized differently. Of course, this is precisely what we do find.

The exact set of tasks that a particular firm will face is a function of its strategy and its environments. A firm's strategy, by specifying products, services, markets, etc., outlines which environments are relevant to a firm. The goals inherent in the strategy specify the types

---

[3] See Charles Perrow, *Organizational Analysis: A Sociological View* (Belmont, Calif.: Wadsworth Publishing Co., Inc., 1970).

of exchanges the firm wants to have with those environments and therefore what types of information it needs for them. The environments themselves have unique characteristics which directly influence how one can get information from them.

Although machines (i.e., computers) are taking on a more and more substantial role today, the predominant information processing and decision-making resources in firms are still people. Factory workers, computer programmers, sales executives, comptrollers, and others, all to some degree gather information, make decisions, and transmit information.

In one sense, the employees of a firm represent a scarce resource: at any time a firm can obtain (or afford) only so many. Individuals have certain relatively stable characteristics insofar as what they can or cannot do; and an appropriate organizational form must be contingent upon these realities also. A hypothetical set of behavior patterns might, at least on paper, fit perfectly with a set of tasks to produce extremely effective information processing. However, if the firm's employees are unable or unwilling to assume those behavior patterns, then obviously the hypothetical organization is not very useful.

At the beginning of this reading we suggested that the appropriate organization in any particular situation was one that was contingent upon a number of factors. We now can see what those factors are (Figure 1).

The exact nature of the contingencies shown in Figure 1 are quite complex. No simple formula can relate strategy, resources, and environ-

FIGURE 1
Factors upon Which an Appropriate Organization Is Contingent

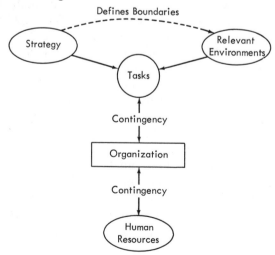

ments to organization. To help you gain an understanding of these complex relationships, we need to introduce two more concepts.

Differentiation and Integration

The term differentiation refers to the process of developing specialized differences in something. Integration denotes the process of making something whole or complete by adding or bringing together its parts. Historically, natural scientists (such as biologists and ecologists) have found these concepts useful. Recently, organization theorists have also found that these terms can help them to better describe the nature of the fit between an effective organization and its context.

Using these two concepts in a study of six organizations in three different industries, Lawrence and Lorsch found that the more successful organizations in each industry were differentiated in a way that fit their situation, while they also attained a high level of integration. The less successful firms were not differentiated appropriately and had difficulty with integration.[4]

Research suggests that when a firm is differentiated appropriately in light of its tasks and its resources, it will effectively identify and gather relevant information about its various environments. When it achieves a high level of integration, it will effectively process and utilize this information to help it in its exchange relationships.

The Organization—Task Linkage

Lawrence and Lorsch identified a number of key dimensions that describe the diversity in a firm's tasks and a number of dimensions that describe the differentiation in its organization. In effective firms (see Figure 2) they found a direct relationship between these two sets of characteristics.

Any task will have a set of key variables that are associated with it that most accurately reflect how well the task is being performed. (For example, the sales task, as it is usually defined, has sales volume and number of customer complaints as two of its key variables.) Insofar as the managers working on a task orient themselves to the key variables as important goals, they will tend to process accurate data about their success on the task. If they don't focus on those variables, they will tend to be ineffective at task performance. Thus, for example, if a quality

---

[4] Paul Lawrence and Jay Lorsch, *Organization and Environment* (Boston: Division of Research, Harvard Business School, 1967). For their research purposes, they defined differentiation as "the difference in cognitive and emotional orientation among managers in different functional departments" and integration as "the quality of the state of collaboration that exists among departments that are required to achieve unity of effort by the demands of environment."

FIGURE 2

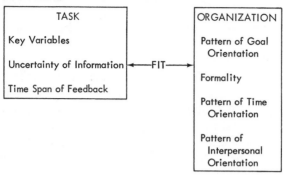

control manager who is promoted to plant manager doesn't change his goal orientation, he might tend to ignore some information about costs which is crucial to the performance of his new job.

The uncertainty of the information associated with a task seems to be directly related to the degree of formality of the organization which can best deal with that task. If the task is absolutely certain and predictable, then one can predetermine what type of behavior can lead to effective information processing. An appropriate organization does just that, and as a result is quite "formal." At the other extreme, if a task is very uncertain, then it is impossible to specify in advance what type of behavior pattern is needed. An appropriate organization should reflect this by being less formal.[5]

All tasks have a certain time span associated with them. In some tasks one can get meaningful feedback on changes in key variables almost immediately after he takes some action. In other tasks, feedback on major decisions may take years. If the managers dealing with a task have a time orientation which is inappropriate in terms of the task's time span, they will tend to look for and process misleading information. The scientific manager who almost daily asks his subordinates about their progress, despite the long time span associated with the research task, will tend to make premature judgments based on inadequate data.

A number of studies besides Lawrence and Lorsch's have found that as the situation facing a manager goes from very favorable to very unfavorable, an effective leadership style varies from task oriented to people oriented back to task oriented.[6] For various reasons, in very

---

[5] Numerous studies have found this relationship. See, for example, Harold J. Leavitt, *Managerial Psychology* (Chicago: University of Chicago Press, 1972), chap. 18.

[6] See Fred Fiedler, *A Theory of Leadership Effectiveness* (New York: McGraw-Hill Book Co., 1967). Fiedler defines "very favorable" as a situation in which the task is very structured, the leader has considerable position based authority, and the leader

favorable and very unfavorable situations, a task-oriented interpersonal orientation works best. In between, a more social interpersonal orientation seems to work best. This finding certainly fits with most people's stereotype of the task-oriented production manager, the people-oriented sales manager, and the task-oriented research manager.

Figure 3 displays how all of these dimensions fit together for a suc-

FIGURE 3

		TASKS		
		Production Task	Sales Task	Scientific Task
Dimensions Describing Diversity in the Firm's Tasks	Key Variables	Costs, Quality, Etc.	Sales, Volume, Number of Complaints, Etc.	Quality and Volume of New Ideas, Utilization of Technical Talent, Etc.
	Uncertainty of Information	Low	Moderate	High
	Time Span of Feedback	Short	Medium	Long

FIT

		ORGANIZATION OF MANAGERS DEALING WITH		
		Production	Sales	Research
Dimensions of Differentiation in the Organization	Pattern of Goal Orientation	Focused on Costs, Quality, Etc.	Focused on Sales, Customer Service, Etc.	Focused on Discovery of New Knowledge, Utilizing Talent, Etc.
	Formality	High	Moderate	Low
	Pattern of Time Orientation	Short	Medium	Long
	Pattern of Interpersonal Organization	Task	Social	Task

Source: Adapted from Lawrence and Lorsch, *Organization and Environment.*

cessful firm in the plastics industry. Lawrence and Lorsch also identified a second set of dimensions which describe a firm's tasks as they relate to integration (see Figure 4).

As opposed to less successful firms, successful ones seem to achieve a high level of integration, especially among key task interdependencies. In the container firms that Lawrence and Lorsch studied, for example, success was very much dependent upon the company's ability to respond to customers' needs. Consequently, the interdependence between sales

---

is liked by his subordinates. Likewise, at the opposite extreme, he defines very unfavorable as a situation with an unstructured task, little position based authority, and poor leader-subordinate relations.

FIGURE 4

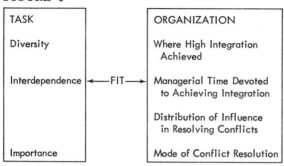

and production was indispensable, and the successful firm achieved a much higher integration here than the less successful one.

The amount of managerial time and effort required to achieve this high level of integration seems to be dependent upon two factors: diversity and interdependence. The more diverse the tasks of the firm's main units, the more differentiated those units will be in an effective firm. Differentiation, by creating different points of view, generates conflict. Thus, the greater the differentiation, the larger the potential conflict and the more effort it takes a manager to resolve these conflicts in a way that benefits the entire firm. Furthermore, the more interdependent the tasks of the firm's main subunits are, the more information processing is required between them, and thus the more effort is required for effective integration. For example, a public relations department and an engineering department might be able to work on their tasks without much consideration of each other because of their relative independence. If so, little effort is required for integrating them. On the other hand, the tasks of a production department and a plant engineering department might require actions whose consequences have a mutual and immediate impact. As a result of their interdependence, more effort at integration is required.

The effective container firm in Lawrence and Lorsch's study had both low diversity and low interdependence among the tasks of its main subunits. Thus, the amount of managerial time it devoted to integration was low. By contrast, the effective plastics firm had high diversity, high interdependence, and a large amount of managerial time devoted to integration.

Lawrence and Lorsch found one behavior pattern related to integration which was common in all the successful firms and did not seem to be contingent upon the firm's tasks. Conflicts among the firm's subunits tended to be resolved primarily by *confronting* the issues at hand and looking for the best solution, as opposed to avoiding the issues, smoothing over them, forcing one party's solution on the other, or bargaining for a resolution. The firms that replied primarily on patterns of conflict avoidance, smoothing, forcing, or bargaining tended to have great difficulty achieving integration simply because those patterns inhibit internal information processing.

At the same time, however, the three types of successful firms which were studied differed with respect to their patterns of influence in resolving these conflict-confronting episodes. In the container firms, with their relatively low task diversity and low task interdependence, influence was distributed in an almost pyramidal fashion, with the few people on top dominating. Low task diversity allowed those few people to process information from all the firm's environments and make good decisions. Because of the low interdependence, not much information needed to be processed internally, so those people on top could handle the job without becoming overloaded with work. In the plastics industry, on the other hand, the high task diversity and interdependence made it impossible for a few top people to handle the internal information processing since they didn't have the time or the expertise. As a result, influence was distributed more evenly throughout the successful firm.

In all three industries, some tasks were simply more important than others, and success or failure at those tasks could be crucial to the firm's success or failure. In the more successful firms, the subunits which worked on critical tasks tended to be more influential in resolving conflict than the other units. In the food industry firms studied by Lawrence and Lorsch, the sales and research tasks were central to success. When conflict among those units and production arose in the effective firm, production was less influential in the ensuing discussions. This particular pattern of influence seems to assure that crucial information gets sufficient attention in the firm's decision making.

The exact set of relationships (reported by Lawrence and Lorsch) between the tasks of the successful firm in three industries and the firm's integration is shown in Figure 5. This figure, like Figure 3, is important and deserves careful attention.

The dimensions Lawrence and Lorsch have identified are not the only ones which relate tasks to appropriate organization, but they are important ones. In describing important differences in tasks, other researchers have focused on differences in the technologies used,[7] the differences in the analyzability and complexity of the information involved,[8] and differences in the kind of task interdependence.[9] The common

---

[7] Joan Woodward, *Industrial Organization: Theory and Practice* (London: Oxford University Press, 1965).

[8] Charles Perrow, *Organizational Analysis: A Sociological View* (Belmont, Calif.: Wadsworth Publishing Co., Inc., 1970).

[9] James Thompson, *Organizations in Action* (New York: McGraw-Hill Book Co., 1967).

FIGURE 5

		CONTAINER FIRMS	FOODS FIRMS	PLASTICS FIRMS
Dimensions Describing the the Firm's Main Subunits	Diversity	Low	Moderate	High
	Amount of Interdependence	Low	Moderate	High
	Key Interdependencies	Sales–Promotion	Sales–Research Research–Production	Sales–Research Research–Production
	Key Subtask to Achieving Goals	Sales	Sales–Research	Integrating Unit's Task
FIT				
Dimensions of Integration in the Organization	Unit where High Integration Achieved	Everywhere, Especially Sales Production	Everywhere, Especially Sales–Research and Research to Production	Everywhere, Especially between the Integrating Unit and All Others
	Managerial Time Devoted to Achieving Integration	Low	Moderate	High
	Pattern of Influence in Resolving Conflicts	Pyramidal, with Sales Having More Say than Other Departments	Fairly Evenly Distributed with Sales and Research Having More Say	Fairly Evenly Distributed with Special Integrating Unit Having More Say
	Predominant Mode of Conflict Resolution	Confrontation	Confrontation	Confrontation

ground of these and other researchers is their search for ways to describe how information and information processing vary among tasks and how this affects organizational form.

THE ORGANIZATION—PEOPLE LINKAGE

There are a number of important aspects of the relationship between an appropriate organization and the human resources a firm commands (or can obtain). As in the case of the organization-task linkage, these relationships are complex.

First of all, some states of differentiation and integration require more resources than others. For a firm to increase its differentiation while maintaining a high level of integration requires more human resources. For example, Lawrence and Lorsch found that an effective firm in the container industry had no employees outside the management hierarchy whose full-time job was to aid the integration effort. Yet the more differentiated, effective food industry firm had 18 percent of its managers working full time on integration. The effective plastics firm, which was differentiated even more, had 22 percent of its managers performing integration full time.

Regardless of the number of resources a firm has, an organization which demands behavior from its members which they are incapable of supplying is obviously unworkable. Human beings have limited information processing capabilities.[10] They can identify, remember, and communicate just so much; and some are obviously more capable than others. Because of their particular backgrounds, education, and genes, people also tend to have different information processing capabilities. Clearly for example, an M.D. is capable of processing information about a person's biological disorders much more competently than a non-M.D. At the same time, however, a doctor might be totally incompetent at processing information concerning automobile disorders. Indeed, all highly trained specialists are capable of processing certain types of information much more competently than the average person. But lengthy specialized training is not the only reason why people differ in information processing capabilities.

In the past half century psychologists have created a number of labels to describe various relatively enduring cognitive and affective characteristics of people. These characteristics often develop during our early years and change in our adult lives only slowly and in small increments. A number of these characteristics, such as integrative complexity, tolerance for ambiguity, attitudes toward authority, and attitudes toward individualism,[11] clearly either help or hinder one in processing specific types of information.

A person who is very shy and introverted will find it difficult to behave in a people-oriented manner; and if that's what the organization (such as a sales organization) calls for, he is not the person for that role. A person who has a low tolerance for ambiguity will generally find himself somewhat immobilized in a highly informal and unstructured organization (like a basic research group). A person who consciously or unconsciously doesn't like "authority figures" will generally not work out well in an organization where a boss constantly gives him orders.

Any forms of differentiation and integration which demand cognitive or affective orientations and behaviors which the firm's members, or others it could hire, don't have, are of course unattainable. Among other things, this means that firms are very much dependent on the institutions in their society that shape people. If those institutions, especially the family and the school, do not produce people whose orientations fit a certain type of organization's needs, a society will simply have to

---

[10] For an interesting discussion of this issue, see James March and Herbert Simon, *Organizations* (New York: John Wiley & Sons, Inc., 1958), chap. 6.

[11] These four characteristics are used in a study by Jay Lorsch and John Morse, described in *Organizations and Their Members: A Contingency Approach* (New York: Harper & Row, Publishers, Inc., 1974).

live without that type of organization or with a relatively inefficient form of it.[12] Even in a society like our own, feasible organizational forms are very dependent upon the types of professionals our educational institutions develop.

Finally, an organization is appropriate only if it demands from its human resources what they are willing to supply. The organizational-individual relationship is a reciprocal one. People participate in an organization because they believe that given other opportunities, what they are getting is fair considering what they are giving.[13] If an organization demands behavior which people are unwilling to supply unless rewarded more than the firm can afford, then that organization is not appropriate.

ORGANIZATIONAL PROBLEMS

To summarize briefly, whenever a firm's organization does not fit its strategy, environments, and resources, the firm's performance will suffer. If the firm's strategy, environments, and resources never changed, one would only once have to find an appropriate organization and then never face organizational problems again. In the real world, all three of these elements change continuously, and as a result organizational problems are common.

Problems of incorrect differentiation are found especially among firms whose strategy, environments, or resources have changed considerably in the recent past. Firms which decide to add a second product line or begin a rapid expansion program sometimes don't recognize the organizational implications of these strategic changes until some obvious problems develop. It is not uncommon for a firm to operate for years in a fairly stable, calm, and certain set of environments and not even recognize when they begin to change in fundamental ways. Even when the firm's performance begins to fall lower and lower, it often has difficulty grasping the organizational problems involved. Because organizational changes are difficult and energy consuming, growing firms often cling to the "organizational form which has served us well for years" until the problems either force a change in differentiation or destroy the firm. In general, whenever a firm is differentiated in a way which doesn't fit its tasks, it loses relevant information and will not be able to maximize its advantage in its exchange relationships.

---

[12] If a society's institutions produce people whose orientations are suitable for farming but not for factory work, that society will discover (as many have) that the plant form of industrial development will grow very slowly there. If, on the other hand, its institutions produce people who are ideal for factories and bureaucracies, then those types of organizations will flourish (e.g., Japan and Germany).

[13] For an elaboration of these issues, see "Managing the Psychological Contract," pp. 465–80.

A firm can overdifferentiate, given the resources it commands. When this happens, it will either fail miserably at achieving the high integration necessary for success, or it will achieve integration by using more resources than it can afford. In the first case, the firm will make poor decisions about its exchanges; in the second, it will run the risk of an unnecessary drain on its financial resources.

Integration problems are also common in organizations. A sales manager, two design engineers, a production engineer, and a division manager argue for two days straight over a new product's specifications before giving up without having made a decision. A salesman promises his biggest client a large order delivered in one week, only to learn that current inventory is at zero and other orders are backlogged for one month. A department within a research unit successfully finishes a two-year development at a cost of $1 million only to find out that marketing feels that the resulting product can't be sold at a satisfactory price or in sufficient volume.

A firm faces problems of again establishing a high level of integration whenever it increases its differentiation. In addition, shifts in the firm's environments, strategy, and resources can create integration problems. If these changes prevent the firm from achieving a high level of integration, it will "waste" information and make poor decisions affecting its exchange processes.

While a firm can't really create too high a level of integration, it can create more integrative patterns than it needs and thus waste scarce resources. The feeling that most people at some time have had that they feel they are wasting their lives in useless meetings is a concrete example of this problem.

There is yet another type of common organizational problem. Sometimes a firm will recognize that it needs a different form of organization, even realize exactly what it needs, and yet not be able to create that form. A manager will take a corrective action only to discover that either nothing changes or that the change is not the type he desired. In these cases, the problem is probably related to the manager's inability to select and introduce the tools available to create the organization he wants.

ORGANIZATIONAL DESIGN TOOLS

A variety of formal tools are available to the manager who is engaged in organizational problem solving (see Figure 6). Almost all of them can be used to contribute to differentiation *or* integration, although some tend to be primarily differentiation devices and some primarily integration devices. The structural tools are probably the most important, and we will discuss them first.

FIGURE 6
Organizational Design Tools
Structure:
  Division of labor
  Special integrating roles and units
  Teams and task forces
  Hierarchy
  Rules and procedures
  Plans and goals
Measurement systems:
  Performance appraisal practices
  Control systems
  Information systems
Reward systems:
  Compensation schemes
  Promotion schemes
  Job and assignment practices
Hiring and development systems:
  Recruiting and selection practices
  Training and development practices

Structure

A number of important design tools are components of what is generally referred to as structure. Together these elements help communicate
to the organization's members what behavior is expected of them, what
tasks to work on, what not to do, what goals to work toward, whom
to work with, whom to obey, whom to direct, and so on. In an organization which is "highly structured," these tools communicate expectations
which cover almost all aspects of behavior, leaving little room for individual discretion. In a "loosely structured" organization, these tools cover
few areas of behavior, leaving the individual with considerable discretion
in defining his own role.

The formal division of labor is that device which specifies distinct
and separate organizational units, from divisions down to individual
jobs, and gives each a different task. For any given firm, there is probably
an infinite number of ways to divide the tasks and people into subunits.
There are, however, three common "macro" alternatives which firms
consider (see Figure 7). The first is the functional structure, in which
each specialized function is made into a different subunit. The second
is the divisional structure, in which all tasks associated with each product
(or technology or geographic region) are grouped together. The third
is the matrix structure, in which all people and tasks are put into two
groups—one associated with their function, the other associated with
their product (or customers, or geographic area, or technology).

Each of these three basic structures has advantages and disadvantages. The functional and matrix structures can achieve greater func-

FIGURE 7

Basic Functional Structure

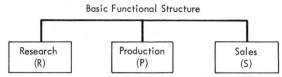

Basic Product Structure (one form of divisional structure) [a]

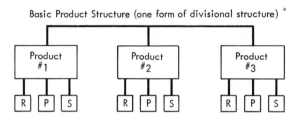

Basic Matrix Structure

	P	P	P
	Production Unit		
	R	R	R
	O	O	O
	D	D	D
	U	U	U
	Sales Unit		
	C	C	C
	T	T	T
	Research Unit		
	#	#	#
	1	2	3

tional differentiation than the product structure can. By putting different specialists to work on different tasks in the same unit, they tend to lose some of their specialized orientations as they interact with each other. Both the product and matrix structures can achieve better integration among functional specialists than can the functional structure (because they group these people together). The matrix structure, while combining some of the best points of the other two, requires more resources than either of them and creates special problems. Since everyone is in two units with two bosses, administrative overhead is high and the chain of command is ambiguous.

All firms also seem to rely on a second structural design tool—the formal hierarchy of authority. Along with the basic division of labor, this is what is displayed in the classical "organization charts." Hierarchies can contain either few (flat) or many (tall) levels from the top to the bottom. They can distribute authority fairly evenly throughout, or they can concentrate nearly all of it at the top.

Hierarchies usually provide some differentiation in the organization, although not of the lateral type (like the division of labor). That is, as one goes up the hierarchy, one finds jobs not just with more formal authority or with more people reporting to them, one finds jobs that are different in fundamental ways. At the extremes of foreman and president, this is obvious. Different orientations and behavior tend to be required at the lower (operational control), middle (the managerial control), and upper (the strategic control) levels in an organization because the tasks are different.[14] A tall hierarchy can facilitate this differentiation more than a flat one by simply putting a greater "distance" between the different levels.

Even more important, however, the hierarchy is designed and used to aid integration. It provides for information channels that connect all the organization's units. If units A and B need to be coordinated, or if they have some conflict, relevant information is sent up the hierarchy to whichever person has both units within his responsibility. That person then coordinates the units, resolves their conflicts, and so on. If the sales and production managers in the electronics division cannot agree on how much integrated circuit inventory to have on hand in April, the information is passed to their boss, the division manager, who then decides.

Historically, the hierarchy has probably been by far the most important integration device in firms. It works well as long as it does not have to process a great deal of information. If it does, because of high interdependence between the organization's units, for example, it quickly becomes overloaded and breaks down. Executives find themselves spending 14 hours a day settling disputes while a backlog of needed decisions begins to grow.

Sometimes, to facilitate integration, organizational designers create special full-time integrating roles like the product manager, or even special integrating units such as a project office. A product manager, for example, could be in charge of helping to integrate all the activities that are associated with one or more of the firm's products.[15] Since he will be dealing with different types of people with different orientations (goal, time, interpersonal), his effectiveness will depend partly upon his ability to have an orientation midway between the orientations

---

[14] See Robert Anthony, *Planning and Control Systems: A Framework for Analysis* (Boston: Division of Research, Harvard Business School, 1965).

[15] In a sense, an organization with a functional division of labor and product managers is halfway between a functional structure and a matrix structure.

of those people he needs to integrate.[16] Likewise, integrating units, whose task it is to integrate the activities of other units, seem to work best if their organization is not identical to those other units but is at a midpoint between them on most dimensions.

Managers also sometimes create task forces and teams of people to facilitate integration. These can be short-term, temporary measures to deal with some specific issue, or they can be a permanent part of the team member's job description. To help integrate sales and production, for example, the production scheduler, the head foreman, the manager of sales, and the assistant controller might meet regularly to identify and resolve integration problems between the two groups, or perhaps they would meet only sporadically to identify specific problems. Teams, like special roles and units, can be very useful in dealing with difficult integration problems. At the same time, however, they are an expensive resource drain.

Rules and procedures represent another important design tool which is used for both differentiation and integration. Managers can help create appropriate differentiation by designing different sets of rules and procedures for different units and jobs. If they want tightly regulated behavior, they can create many comprehensive rules. If they want more flexible behavior, they can create few rules.

Rules can sometimes be used to ensure that the output of two departments or units "adds up" in favor of the total firm. Production and sales often have integration problems because a product is passed from one to the other. If production gets behind, the company can lose sales. If sales gets behind, the company can incur a large cost in inventory storage. One way to integrate these units is with a series of rules for each. "All sales orders should be sent immediately to the production scheduler." "The production schedules should not allow for a backlog of more than $10,000 in orders before ordering overtime production." And so on.

As long as the firm's situation (strategy, environment, resources) doesn't change very often, rules can be a remarkably inexpensive and useful tool compared to others. In a situation with much change, constantly updating the rules can be very expensive.

One final structural tool which managers use is goals and plans. Sometimes units which require integration can agree on goals and plans at the outset, and then go their separate ways knowing that their activities, when completed, will be integrated. In the sales-production case, the sales unit might use historical data and market surveys to establish weekly sales goals which are then given to the production scheduler who can use them to plan in advance.

---

[16] Paul Lawrence and Jay Lorsch, "New Management Job: The Integrator," *Harvard Business Review*, November–December 1967.

In selecting appropriate structural design tools and determining their use, a manager needs to ask himself three questions: First, what combination of tools will achieve the differentiation and integration I want? Second, what is the long-run cost of these devices? Third, what is the short-term cost?

Not only do different organizations use the same tools in different ways but organizations use different tools. Lawrence and Lorsch found that successful firms in the three industries they studied relied on different combinations of structural tools for integration (see Figure 8). The

FIGURE 8

Industry	Container	Foods	Plastics
Integration Needs	Low	Moderate	High
Integration Devices Used	Hierarchy, Procedures, Some Plans	Roles, Plans, Hierarchy, and Procedures	Teams, Roles, Departments, Hierarchy, Plans and Procedures

container firm required less internal information processing because of the low interdependence and small amount of diversity among the tasks of its main subunits. As a result, just three structural integration tools (the hierarchy, rules, and plans) were necessary to meet its needs. At the other extreme, the plastics firm required considerable internal information processing and achieved it by using six structural tools for integration (teams, roles, departments, hierarchy, plans, and procedures).

Some of these devices are more expensive than others. For routine issues, rules are cheap compared to full-time integrators. The manager's goal, obviously, is to use the cheapest devices which will get the job accomplished. However, if introducing a large number of rules causes the union to go out on a three-month strike, then its short-run cost is obviously rather large. Shifting the distribution of influence in the hierarchy often leads to costly turnover on the part of upset people. Change costs money, and it must be taken into account in design decisions.

There is no magic formula which can direct a manager in selecting these tools. The process may seem imprecise, and to a degree it is.

Measurement Systems

The variety of ways firms measure performance is almost endless. In some organizations measurement systems are simple and inexpensive, in some they are complex and costly.

Measurement systems can facilitate differentiation or integration (or neither if they are poorly designed) by gathering, transmitting, and highlighting information on certain variables. Measurement systems tend to orient people toward those variables both because of their visibility and because performance on those variables is usually linked to the organization's reward system.

Most organizations have two types of measurement systems, one that measures the performance of a unit and another that measures the performance of individuals. There are a number of typical unit measurement systems: revenue center, cost center, profit center, and investment center.[17] Each focuses attention on a different key variable. There are even more types of individual measurement systems. In a sense, they tend to vary on one continuum from very objective, precise, and clear to very subjective and ambiguous.

If the unit measurement and individual measurement systems implicitly demand different and contradictory behavior, they will obviously not serve the organization well. If either or both are not backed by a set of consistent operating procedures, they may have little or no impact on behavior. When the measurement system shows that something is wrong in plant X, whether this information will be heeded is a function of many things: the plant manager's faith in the system, what corporate management does, how "right" and "wrong" were originally defined, etc

There are no simple rules of thumb that one can use in selecting measurement systems for a particular firm. Since the same system under different circumstances can have a very different effect on behavior, the organizational designer must be particularly sensitive to the context in which he is working. Under certain circumstances, an "odd-looking" system can be the appropriate one.[18]

Reward Systems

There are many types of rewards which organizations offer their members for adequate or better performance. Some are intrinsic to the job itself, such as meaningful, interesting, and challenging work, while others are extrinsic, such as pay, promotional opportunities, and office space.[19]

Insofar as a reward given to an organizational member is not perceived by that member to be reasonable, it will not necessarily aid

---

[17] For a further discussion of these issues, see Richard F. Vancil, "What Kind of Management Control Do You Need?" *Harvard Business Review*, March–April 1973.

[18] For example, Vancil describes a case in which it is appropriate for a company to use a "profit center" system for its manufacturing unit and another "profit center" system for its marketing unit.

[19] See "Managing the Psychological Contract" pp. 465–80 for more discussion on reward systems.

differentiation or integration. If it is seen as fair, legitimate, desired, and large enough, then it will tend to reinforce whatever behavior the member perceives as having led to the reward. If that behavior was performance in a job as a functional specialist, the reward will tend to reinforce differentiation. If that behavior was collaboration with other functional specialists, then the reward will tend to reinforce integration.

In designing a reward system, a manager needs to consider (among other things) the following: (1) Does the system need to reinforce differentiation, integration, or both? (2) What are the needs of the people involved? (3) What package of rewards can satisfy the first two criteria but at the least cost?

Hiring and Development Systems

Formal hiring and development systems, like measurement and reward systems, can be simple, elaborate, or even nonexistent. Typically, until a firm reaches a certain size, all recruiting, selection, training, and development will be handled informally.

Hiring policies can facilitate differentiation enormously by correctly identifying and selecting people whose orientations are appropriate for the firm's tasks. If a task calls for a particular information processing skill, the hiring policy attempts to translate that as much as possible into specific recruiting and selection procedures. The more complex the task and the information processing skills involved, the more difficult this translation becomes.[20] Hiring policies can also facilitate integration by bringing in people who seem to have a capacity to relate to and work with organization members in more than one specialty.

Training and development systems can aid differentiation by providing experiences which help develop certain perspectives and certain information processing skills. These experiences can be of the classroom variety, or they can be oriented toward on-the-job training.

Development experiences can facilitate integration by helping organization members gain the skills and awareness necessary to collaborate effectively with persons different from themselves. In the past 15 years, applied behavioral scientists have developed a whole technology, often called organizational development (O.D.), aimed at facilitating integration in this way.[21]

---

[20] For an interesting discussion of recruitment, testing, and selection, see Edgar Schein, *Organizational Psychology* (Englewood Cliffs, N.J.: Prentice-Hall, Inc., 1965).

[21] See Dick Beckhand, *Organizational Development: Strategies and Models;* Warren Bennis, *Organizational Development: Its Nature, Origins, and Prospects;* and Blake and Mouton, *Building a Dynamic Corporation through Grid Organizational Development.* All three are published by Addison-Wesley Publishing Co., Inc., Reading, Mass., 1969.

Development systems can also facilitate integration by moving people from their specialty and exposing them to other perspectives. Corporations, realizing that one of top management's key roles is in facilitating integration, often make sure that people on the way up are moved through as many as four different functional departments.

Formal training systems, in particular, can be quite expensive. To some degree there is a tradeoff between spending money in the hiring system versus spending it in the development system. At one extreme, a firm could spend little money for hiring and simply take minimally qualified applicants whom they would have to train extensively. At the other extreme, a firm could spend a fortune identifying and inducing well-qualified applicants to join the firm, and spend no money on training and development.

DESIGNING SUCCESSFUL ORGANIZATIONS

To improve operations, a manager engaged in organizational design or organizational problem solving needs a thorough understanding of the three factors upon which an appropriate organization is contingent: (1) his firm's or unit's strategy, (2) the nature of its relevant environments, and (3) the human resources which are available to him. It is essential to know how these have changed recently, if at all. The designer needs to derive from the current strategy and environments a list of the firm's primary tasks, including a detailed description of how the tasks are different and how they are interdependent from an information processing point of view. The designer also needs a thorough understanding of his current organization in terms of differentiation and integration, the nature of the design tools which are used to maintain it, and any symptoms of problems.

With this background information, he can diagnose and change his situation by searching for answers to these complex questions:

1. Is my current organization significantly under, over, or incorrectly differentiated?
2. Is my current organization significantly under, over, or incorrectly integrated?
3. What configuration of design tools can support an appropriate differentiation and integration, at the lowest cost?
4. How can I introduce these changes?

Organizational problems represent a significant challenge to managers. Answering the above questions requires judgment and is often difficult. Nevertheless, the process of organizational design is one that can be mastered.

3 | *"Classical" Organization Theory**

Louis B. Barnes

1. SCIENTIFIC MANAGEMENT

Taylor saw the primary organizational problem to be that of analyzing the relation between human characteristics and the purposive aspects of organizations. "The goal was to use the rather inefficient human organism—by specifying a detailed program of behavior—that would transform a general-purpose mechanism, such as a person, into a more efficient special purpose mechanism."

The data relevant to solving the problem thus posed were largely restricted to the physiological; and Taylor's group quite naturally, therefore, focused on that relatively narrow range of tasks found on the production floor or in clerical departments. These tasks were highly repetitive, did not require complex problem-solving activity, and were susceptible to direct observation, simple description, and straightforward categorization and measurement. In this milieu worked the time-study man, whose aim was "to define the task as to restrict considerably the behavioral alternatives with which the worker is faced." Job method choices were restricted both by the detail of the description and by the time standard set for performance.

---

* This historical survey of the traditional conceptions of organizational behavior is based on the second chapter of *Organizations* by James G. March and Herbert A. Simon (New York: John Wiley & Sons, Inc., 1958).

The authors distinguish two facets of the tradition: Taylor's "scientific management" and Urwick's and others' theories of departmentalization. See F. W. Taylor, *Scientific Management* (New York: Harper & Row, Publishers, Inc., 1947), or *The Principles of Scientific Management* (New York: Harper & Row, Publishers, Inc., 1911); and L. Urwick, *The Elements of Administration* (New York: Harper & Row, Publishers, Inc., 1944).

Scientific management theorists, then, were concerned with the development and optimum operation of "man-machine systems." The dimensions along which their theory and procedures developed were the capacity, speed, durability, and cost of the composite mechanism. The inherent limits within which the mechanism must work, according to the theory, were the subject of considerable investigation. Speed was a primary focus of research toward which the Gilbreths and many others devoted their efforts. The attempts in this respect to develop standard-unit (therblig, etc.) systems are undoubtedly known to the reader.

Fatigue, a prime component of the durability dimension, was the basis for considerable study during the 1920s by Elton Mayo and others. Their findings led to the development of conceptual structures whose dimensions were sufficiently different from those of the scientific management group as to create an entirely new school of thought.[1]

The units of the cost dimension were money and time. Wage rates were stipulated to be competitive and sufficient to motivate the worker to produce at an optimum rate. March and Simon point to three areas of question which cast doubt on the simple relationship of monetary reward and productivity posited by scientific management theory: "(a) that wage payments represent only one (but perhaps the major single one) of a number of rewards in the system; (b) that the utilities associated with wages may be discontinuous—reflecting some notion of satisfactory wages—and hence may not be at all linearly (or even monotonically) related to wage payments; (c) that these utilities change through time and with shifts in aspirations, so that the impact of wage incentives is not stable."[2]

The propositions of physiological organization theory can be summarized as follows: Find the best way of performing a job, provide the worker with an incentive to use the best way at a good pace, and use specialized experts to set the conditions within which the worker is to perform.

2. THEORIES OF DEPARTMENTALIZATION

Under this heading, March and Simon discuss a second, overlapping development which they call "administrative management theory." It shares with scientific management "a preoccupation with the simpler neurophysical properties of humans and the simpler kinds of tasks that are handled in organizations." They point out, however, that this second

---

[1] Elton Mayo, *The Human Problems of an Industrial Civilization* (New York: Macmillan Co., 1933; Boston: Division of Research, Harvard Business School, 1946); F. J. Roethlisberger and W. J. Dickson, *Management and the Worker* (Cambridge, Mass.: Harvard University Press, 1939).

[2] March and Simon, *Organizations*, p. 19.

group of theorists carries their analysis well beyond the limits set by Taylor and his followers.

The general problem addressed is how, given a statement of organization purpose, the unit tasks necessary to achieve that purpose can be identified. Once identified, how can these unit tasks be grouped into jobs, jobs into administrative units, and administrative units into top management departments at minimum cost? The basis for understanding this theory, the authors point out, is "to recognize that the total set of tasks is regarded as given in advance."

The departmentalists have attempted so to assign activities that a minimum number of task groups are formed consistent with man-days available. The difficulty of optimizing this efficiency lies in the fact that departmentalization along the lines of purpose may conflict with ideal task groupings based on process specialization. For example, the rationale behind the formation of a marketing department may constrain against the efficient use of stenographers across department boundaries.

Finally, March and Simon note the tendency in administrative management theory to view an organization member as an inert instrument performing an assigned task. Personal characteristics are, furthermore, seen as "givens" rather than variables. "[The] grand theories of organizational structure have largely ignored factors associated with individual behavior and particularly its motivational bases."

3. CONSEQUENCES OF THESE THEORIES

In order to highlight the consequences of these models of organization (called by these authors and others the "machine model"), March and Simon, in the third chapter of their book, describe how three sociologists view the machine model in operation; one of these will be described briefly here.

> *Robert K. Merton.*[3]   Merton proposed that the top hierarchy imposes a demand for control on the organization in the form of increased emphasis on the reliability of behavior, i.e., representing a need for accountability and predictability of behavior. Control is sought by institution of standard operating procedures and by ensuring that procedures are followed.
>
> The consequences, as Merton sees them, are a reduction in personalized relationships (organization members are viewed not as individuals but as possessors of positions), an increase in the internalization of rules (procedures take on the positive values initially accruing to the goals they were designed to achieve), and a narrowing of the range

---

[3] See, among other writings of Merton, *Social Theory and Social Structure*, 2d ed. (Glencoe, Ill.: Free Press, 1957). In these writings, Merton draws heavily on the work of Max Weber, which was concerned primarily with government bureaucracies.

within which decisions are made (categories for thinking through a problem are decreased). In turn and as a result, behavior becomes more rigid, an intense *esprit de corps* develops, and a propensity to defend organization members from outside attack is increased.

The net result within the organization is a high degree of reliability, maximized defensibility of behavior, and a reduced effectiveness in dealing with extraorganization individuals and groups (e.g., customers). Since part of the system is maintained by these techniques, there is a continuing pressure to reinforce the same techniques. Even customer dissatisfaction and resultant complaints serve to redouble efforts to maintain control. The system is circular. March and Simon reproduce the diagram shown in Exhibit 1 as a summary of this system.

EXHIBIT 1

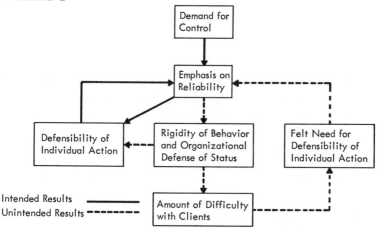

4 | The Human Side of Enterprise[*]

Douglas Murray McGregor

It has become trite to say that industry has the fundamental know-how to utilize physical science and technology for the material benefit of mankind, and that we must now learn how to utilize the social sciences to make our human organizations truly effective.

To a degree, the social sciences today are in a position like that of the physical sciences with respect to atomic energy in the thirties. We know that past conceptions of the nature of man are inadequate and, in many ways, incorrect. We are becoming quite certain that, under proper conditions, unimagined resources of creative human energy could become available within the organizational setting.

We cannot tell industrial management how to apply this new knowledge in simple, economic ways. We know it will require years of exploration, much costly development research, and a substantial amount of creative imagination on the part of management to discover how to apply this growing knowledge to the organization of human effort in industry.

MANAGEMENT'S TASK: THE CONVENTIONAL VIEW

The conventional conception of management's task in harnessing human energy to organizational requirements can be stated broadly in terms of three propositions. In order to avoid the complications introduced by a label, let us call this set of propositions *Theory X*:

[*] *Adventures in Thought and Action: Proceedings of the Fifth Anniversary Convocation of the School of Industrial Management*, M.I.T., Cambridge, Mass., April 9, 1957 (Cambridge, Mass.: Technology Press, 1957), reprinted by permission.

1. Management is responsible for organizing the elements of productive enterprise—money, materials, equipment, people—in the interest of economic ends.
2. With respect to people, this is a process of directing their efforts, motivating them, controlling their actions, modifying their behavior to fit the needs of the organization.
3. Without this active intervention by management, people would be passive, even resistant, to organizational needs. They must therefore be persuaded, rewarded, punished, controlled—their activities must be directed. This is management's task. We often sum it up by saying that management consists of getting things done through other people.

Behind this conventional theory there are several additional beliefs—less explicit, but widespread:

4. The average man is by nature indolent—he works as little as possible.
5. He lacks ambition, dislikes responsibility, prefers to be led.
6. He is inherently self-centered and indifferent to organizational needs.
7. He is by nature resistant to change.
8. He is gullible, not very bright, the ready dupe of the charlatan and the demagogue.

The human side of economic enterprise today is fashioned from propositions and beliefs such as these. Conventional organization structures and managerial policies, practices, and programs reflect these assumptions. In accomplishing its task, with these assumptions as guides, management has conceived of a range of possibilities.

At one extreme, management can be "hard" or "strong." The methods for directing behavior involve coercion and threat (usually disguised), close supervision, tight controls over behavior. At the other extreme, management can be "soft" or "weak." The methods for directing behavior involve being permissive, satisfying people's demands, achieving harmony. Then they will be tractable, accept direction.

This range has been fairly completely explored during the past half century, and management has learned some things from the exploration. There are difficulties in the "hard" approach. Force breeds counter forces: restriction of output, antagonism, militant unionism, subtle but effective sabotage of management objectives. This "hard" approach is especially difficult during times of full employment.

There are also difficulties in the "soft" approach. It leads frequently to the abdication of management—to harmony, perhaps, but to indifferent performance. People take advantage of the soft approach. They continually expect more, but they give less and less.

Currently, the popular theme is "firm but fair." This is an attempt to gain the advantages of both the hard and the soft approaches. It is reminiscent of Teddy Roosevelt's "speak softly and carry a big stick."

IS THE CONVENTIONAL VIEW CORRECT?

The findings which are beginning to emerge from the social sciences challenge this whole set of beliefs about man and human nature and about the task of management. The evidence is far from conclusive, certainly, but it is suggestive. It comes from the laboratory, the clinic, the schoolroom, the home, and even to a limited extent from industry itself.

The social scientist does not deny that human behavior in industrial organization today is approximately what management perceives it to be. He has, in fact, observed it and studied it fairly extensively. But he is pretty sure that this behavior is *not* a consequence of man's inherent nature. It is a consequence rather of the nature of industrial organizations, of management philosophy, policy, and practice. The conventional approach of Theory X is based on mistaken notions of what is cause and what is effect.

Perhaps the best way to indicate why the conventional approach of management is inadequate is to consider the subject of motivation.

Physiological Needs

Man is a wanting animal; as soon as one of his needs is satisfied, another appears in its place. This process is unending. It continues from birth to death.

Man's needs are organized in a series of levels—a hierarchy of importance. At the lowest level, but preeminent in importance when they are thwarted, are his *physiological needs*. Man lives for bread alone when there is no bread. Unless the circumstances are unusual, his needs for love, for status, for recognition are inoperative when his stomach has been empty for a while. But when he eats regularly and adequately, hunger ceases to be an important motivation. The same is true of the other physiological needs of man—rest, exercise, shelter, protection from the elements.

A satisfied need is not a motivator of behavior! This is a fact of profound significance that is regularly ignored in the conventional approach to the management of people. Consider your own need for air: Except as you are deprived of it, it has no appreciable motivating effect upon your behavior.

Safety Needs

When the physiological needs are reasonably satisfied, needs at the next higher level begin to dominate man's behavior—to motivate him. These are called *safety needs*. They are needs for protection against danger, threat, deprivation. Some people mistakenly refer to these as needs for security. However, unless man is in a dependent relationship where he fears arbitrary deprivation, he does not demand security. The need is for the "fairest possible break." When he is confident of this, he° is more than willing to take risks. But when he feels threatened or dependent, his greatest need is for guarantees, for protection, for security.

This fact needs little emphasis that, since every industrial employee is in a dependent relationship, safety needs may assume considerable importance. Arbitrary management actions, behavior which arouses uncertainty with respect to continued employment or which reflects favoritism or discrimination, unpredictable administration of policy—these can be powerful motivators of the safety needs in the employment relationship *at every level,* from worker to vice president.

Social Needs

When man's physiological needs are satisfied and he is no longer fearful about his physical welfare, his *social needs* become important motivators of his behavior—needs for belonging, for association, for acceptance by his fellows, for giving and receiving friendship and love.

Management knows today of the existence of these needs, but it often assumes quite wrongly that they represent a threat to the organization. Many studies have demonstrated that the tightly knit, cohesive work group may, under proper conditions, be far more effective than an equal number of separate individuals in achieving organizational goals.

Yet management, fearing group hostility to its own objectives, often goes to considerable lengths to control and direct human efforts in ways that are inimical to the natural "groupiness" of human beings. When man's social needs—and perhaps his safety needs, too—are thus thwarted, he behaves in ways which tend to defeat organizational objectives. He becomes resistant, antagonistic, uncooperative. But this behavior is a consequence, not a cause.

Ego Needs

Above the social needs, in the sense that they do not become motivators until lower needs are reasonably satisfied, are the needs of greatest significance to management and to man himself. They are the *egoistic needs,* and they are of two kinds:

1. Those needs that relate to one's self-esteem—needs for self-confidence, for independence, for achievement, for competence, for knowledge.
2. Those needs that relate to one's reputation—needs for status, for recognition, for appreciation, for the deserved respect of one's fellows.

Unlike the lower needs, these are rarely satisfied; man seeks indefinitely for more satisfaction of these needs once they have become important to him. But they do not appear in any significant way until physiological, safety, and social needs are all reasonably satisfied.

The typical industrial organization offers few opportunities for the satisfaction of these egoistic needs to people at lower levels in the hierarchy. The conventional methods of organizing work, particularly in mass production industries, give little heed to these aspects of human motivation. If the practices of scientific management were deliberately calculated to thwart these needs, they could hardly accomplish this purpose better than they do.

Self-Fulfillment Needs

Finally—a capstone, as it were, on the hierarchy of man's needs—there are what we may call the *needs for self-fulfillment.* These are the needs for realizing one's own potentialities, for continued self-development, for being creative in the broadest sense of that term.

It is clear that the conditions of modern life give only limited opportunity for these relatively weak needs to obtain expression. The deprivation most people experience with respect to other lower-level needs diverts their energies into the struggle to satisfy *those* needs, and the needs for self-fulfillment remain dormant.

MANAGEMENT AND MOTIVATION

We recognize readily enough that a man suffering from a severe dietary deficiency is sick. The deprivation of physiological needs has behavioral consequences. The same is true—although less well recognized—of deprivation of higher-level needs. The man whose needs for safety, association, independence, or status are thwarted is sick just as surely as the man who has rickets. And his sickness will have behavioral consequences. We will be mistaken if we attribute his resultant passivity, his hostility, his refusal to accept responsibility to his inherent "human nature." These forms of behavior are *symptoms* of illness—of deprivation of his social and egoistic needs.

The man whose lower-level needs are satisfied is not motivated to satisfy those needs any longer. For practical purposes they exist no longer. Management often asks, "Why aren't people more productive? We pay good wages, provide good working conditions, have excellent fringe benefits and steady employment. Yet people do not seem to be willing to put forth more than minimum effort."

The fact that management has provided for these physiological and safety needs has shifted the motivational emphasis to the social and perhaps to the egoistic needs. Unless there are opportunities *at work* to satisfy these higher-level needs, people will be deprived, and their behavior will reflect this deprivation. Under such conditions, if management continues to focus its attention on physiological needs, its efforts are bound to be ineffective.

People *will* make insistent demands for more money under these conditions. It becomes more important than ever to buy the material goods and services which can provide limited satisfaction of the thwarted needs. Although money has only limited value in satisfying many higher-level needs, it can become the focus of interest if it is the *only* means available.

The Carrot-and-Stick Approach

The carrot-and-stick theory of motivation (like Newtonian physical theory) works reasonably well under certain circumstances. The *means* for satisfying man's physiological and (within limits) his safety needs can be provided or withheld by management. Employment itself is such a means, and so are wages, working conditions, and benefits. By these means the individual can be controlled so long as he is struggling for subsistence.

But the carrot-and-stick theory does not work at all once man has reached an adequate subsistence level and is motivated primarily by higher needs. Management cannot provide a man with self-respect, or with the respect of his fellows, or with the satisfaction of needs for self-fulfillment. It can create such conditions that he is encouraged and enabled to seek such satisfactions *for himself,* or it can thwart him by failing to create those conditions.

But this creation of conditions is not "control." It is not a good device for directing behavior. And so management finds itself in an odd position. The high standard of living created by our modern technological knowhow provides quite adequately for the satisfaction of physiological and safety needs. The only significant exception is where management practices have not created confidence in a "fair break"—and thus where safety needs are thwarted. But by making possible the satisfaction of low-level needs, management has deprived itself of the ability to use as motivators the devices on which conventional theory has taught it to rely—rewards, promises, incentives, or threats and other coercive devices.

The philosophy of management by direction and control—*regardless of whether it is hard or soft*—is inadequate to motivate because the human needs on which this approach relies are today unimportant motivators of behavior. Direction and control are essentially useless in motivating people whose important needs are social and egoistic. Both the hard and the soft approach fail today because they are simply irrelevant to the situation.

People, deprived of opportunities to satisfy at work the needs which are now important to them, behave exactly as we might predict—with indolence, passivity, resistance to change, lack of responsibility, willingness to follow the demagogue, unreasonable demands for economic benefits. It would seem that we are caught in a web of our own weaving.

A NEW THEORY OF MANAGEMENT

For these and many other reasons, we require a different theory of the task of managing people based on more adequate assumptions about human nature and human motivation. I am going to be so bold as to suggest the broad dimensions of such a theory. Call it *Theory Y*, if you will.

1. Management is responsible for organizing the elements of productive enterprise—money, materials, equipment, people—in the interest of economic ends.
2. People are *not* by nature passive or resistant to organizational needs. They have become so as a result of experience in organizations.
3. The motivation, the potential for development, the capacity for assuming responsibility, the readiness to direct behavior toward organizational goals are all present in people. Management does not put them there. It is a responsibility of management to make it possible for people to recognize and develop these human characteristics for themselves.
4. The essential task of management is to arrange organizational conditions and methods of operation so that people can achieve their own goals *best* by directing *their own* efforts toward organizational objectives.

This is a process primarily of creating opportunities, releasing potential, removing obstacles, encouraging growth, providing guidance. It is what Peter Drucker has called "management by objectives" in contrast to "management by control." It does *not* involve the abdication of management, the absence of leadership, the lowering of standards, or the other characteristics usually associated with the "soft" approach under Theory X.

Some Difficulties

It is no more possible to create an organization today which will be a full, effective application of this theory than it was to build an atomic power plant in 1945. There are many formidable obstacles to overcome.

The conditions imposed by conventional organization theory and by the approach of scientific management for the past half century have tied men to limited jobs which do not utilize their capabilities, have discouraged the acceptance of responsibility, have encouraged passivity, have eliminated meaning from work. Man's habits, attitudes, expectations—his whole conception of membership in an industrial organization—have been conditioned by his experience under these circumstances.

People today are accustomed to being directed, manipulated, controlled in industrial organizations and to finding satisfaction for their social, egoistic, and self-fulfillment needs away from the job. This is true of much of management as well as of workers. Genuine "industrial citizenship" (to borrow again a term from Drucker) is a remote and unrealistic idea, the meaning of which has not even been considered by most members of industrial organizations.

Another way of saying this is that Theory X places exclusive reliance upon external control of human behavior, while Theory Y relies heavily on self-control and self-direction. It is worth noting that this difference is the difference between treating people as children and treating them as mature adults. After generations of the former, we cannot expect to shift to the latter overnight.

Steps in the Right Direction

Before we are overwhelmed by the obstacles, let us remember that the application of theory is always slow. Progress is usually achieved in small steps. Some innovative ideas which are entirely consistent with Theory Y are today being applied with some success.

Decentralization and Delegation. These are ways of freeing people from the too-close control of conventional organization, giving them a degree of freedom to direct their own activities, to assume responsibility, and, importantly, to satisfy egoistic needs. In this connection, the flat organization of Sears, Roebuck and Company provides an interesting example. It forces "management by objectives," since it enlarges the number of people reporting to a manager until he cannot direct and control them in the conventional manner.

Job Enlargement. This concept, pioneered by IBM and Detroit Edison, is quite consistent with Theory Y. It encourages the acceptance of responsibility at the bottom of the organization; it provides opportunities for satisfying social and egoistic needs. In fact, the reorganization of work at the factory level offers one of the more challenging opportunities for innovation consistent with Theory Y.

Participation and Consultative Management. Under proper conditions, participation and consultative management provide encouragement to people to direct their creative energies toward organizational objectives, give them some voice in decisions that affect them, provide significant opportunities for the satisfaction of social and egoistic needs. The Scanlon Plan is the outstanding embodiment of these ideas in practice.

Performance Appraisal. Even a cursory examination of conventional programs of performance appraisal within the ranks of management will reveal how completely consistent they are with Theory X. In fact, most such programs tend to treat the individual as though he were a product under inspection on the assembly line.

A few companies—among them General Mills, Ansul Chemical, and General Electric—have been experimenting with approaches which involve the individual in setting "targets" or objectives *for himself* and in a *self*-evaluation of performance semiannually or annually. Of course, the superior plays an important leadership role in this process—one, in fact, which demands substantially more competence than the conventional approach. The role is, however, considerably more congenial to many managers than the role of "judge" or "inspector" which is usually forced upon them. Above all, the individual is encouraged to take a greater responsibility for planning and appraising his own contribution to organizational objectives; and the accompanying effects on egoistic and self-fulfillment needs are substantial.

Applying the Ideas

The not infrequent failure of such ideas as these to work as well as expected is often attributable to the fact that a management has "bought the idea" but applied it within the framework of Theory X and its assumptions.

Delegation is not an effective way of exercising management by control. Participation becomes a farce when it is applied as a sales gimmick or a device for kidding people into thinking they are important. Only the management that has confidence in human capacities and is itself directed toward organizational objectives rather than toward the preservation of personal power can grasp the implications of this emerging theory. Such management will find and apply successfully other innovative ideas as we move slowly toward the full implementation of a theory like Y.

THE HUMAN SIDE OF ENTERPRISE

It is quite possible for us to realize substantial improvements in the effectiveness of industrial organizations during the next decade or two. The social sciences can contribute much to such developments; we are only beginning to grasp the implications of the growing body of knowledge in these fields. But if this conviction is to become a reality instead of a pious hope, we will need to view the process much as we view the process of releasing the energy of the atom for constructive human ends—as a slow, costly, sometimes discouraging approach toward a goal which would seem to many to be quite unrealistic.

The ingenuity and the perseverance of industrial management in the pursuit of economic ends have changed many scientific and technological dreams into commonplace realities. It is now becoming clear that the application of these same talents to the human side of enterprise will not only enhance substantially these materialistic achievements, but will bring us one step closer to "the good society."

5 | Beyond Theory Y*

John J. Morse and
Jay W. Lorsch

During the past 30 years, managers have been bombarded with two competing approaches to the problems of human administration and organization. The first, usually called the classical school of organization, emphasizes the need for well-established lines of authority, clearly defined jobs, and authority equal to responsibility. The second, often called the participative approach, focuses on the desirability of involving organization members in decision making so that they will be more highly motivated.

Douglas McGregor, through his well-known "Theory X and Theory Y," drew a distinction between the assumptions about human motivation which underlie these two approaches, to this effect:

1. Theory X assumes that people dislike work and must be coerced, controlled, and directed toward organizational goals. Furthermore, most people prefer to be treated this way, so they can avoid responsibility.

2. Theory Y—the integration of goals—emphasizes the average person's intrinsic interest in his work, his desire to be self-directing and to seek responsibility, and his capacity to be creative in solving business problems.

It is McGregor's conclusion, of course, that the latter approach to organization is the more desirable one for managers to follow.[1]

McGregor's position causes confusion for the managers who try to

---

* Reprinted by permission from *Harvard Business Review* (May–June 1970), pp. 61–68.

[1] Douglas McGregor, *The Human Side of Enterprise* (New York: McGraw-Hill Book Co., 1960), pp. 34–35 and 47–48.

choose between these two conflicting approaches. The classical organizational approach that McGregor associated with Theory X does work well in some situations, although, as McGregor himself pointed out, there are also some situations where it does not work effectively. At the same time, the approach based on Theory Y, while it has produced good results in some situations, does not always do so. That is, each approach is effective in some cases but not in others. Why is this? How can managers resolve the confusion?

A NEW APPROACH

Recent work by a number of students of management and organization may help to answer such questions.[2] These studies indicate that there is not one best organizational approach; rather, the best approach depends on the nature of the work to be done. Enterprises with highly predictable tasks perform better with organizations characterized by the highly formalized procedures and management hierarchies of the classical approach. With highly uncertain tasks that require more extensive problem solving, on the other hand, organizations that are less formalized and emphasize self-control and member participation in decision making are more effective. In essence, according to these newer studies, managers must design and develop organizations so that the organizational characteristics *fit* the nature of the task to be done.

While the conclusions of this newer approach will make sense to most experienced managers and can alleviate much of the confusion about which approach to choose, there are still two important questions unanswered:

1. How does the more formalized and controlling organization affect the motivation of organization members? (McGregor's most telling criticism of the classical approach was that it did not unleash the potential in an enterprise's human resources.)
2. Equally important, does a less formalized organization always provide a high level of motivation for its members? (This is the implication many managers have drawn from McGregor's work.)

We have recently been involved in a study that provides surprising answers to these questions and, when taken together with other recent work, suggests a new set of basic assumptions which move beyond Theory Y into what we call "Contingency Theory: the fit between task,

---

[2] See, for example, Paul R. Lawrence and Jay W. Lorsch, *Organization and Environment* (Boston: Division of Research, Harvard Business School, 1967); Joan Woodward, *Industrial Organization: Theory & Practice* (London: Oxford University Press, Inc., 1965); Tom Burns and G. M. Stalker, *The Management of Innovation* (London: Tavistock Publications, 1961); Harold J. Leavitt, "Unhuman Organizations," *Harvard Business Review* (July–August 1962), p. 90.

organization, and people." These theoretical assumptions emphasize that the appropriate pattern of organization is *contingent* on the nature of the work to be done and on the particular needs of the people involved. We should emphasize that we have labeled these assumptions as a step beyond Theory Y because of McGregor's own recognition that the Theory Y assumptions would probably be supplanted by new knowledge within a short time.[3]

THE STUDY DESIGN

Our study was conducted in four organizational units. Two of these performed the relatively certain task of manufacturing standardized containers on high-speed, automated production lines. The other two performed the relatively uncertain work of research and development in communications technology. Each pair of units performing the same kind of task were in the same large company, and each pair had previously been evaluated by that company's management as containing one highly effective unit and a less effective one. The study design is summarized in Exhibit 1.

EXHIBIT 1
Study Design in "Fit" of Organizational Characteristics

Characteristics	Company I (predictable manufacturing task)	Company II (unpredictable R&D task)
Effective performer	Akron containers plant	Stockton research lab
Less effective performer	Hartford containers plant	Carmel research lab

The objective was to explore more fully how the fit between organization and task was related to successful performance. That is, does a good fit between organizational characteristics and task requirements increase the motivation of individuals and hence produce more effective individual and organizational performance?

An especially useful approach to answering this question is to recognize that an individual has a strong need to master the world around him, including the task that he faces as a member of a work organization.[4] The accumulated feelings of satisfaction that come from successfully mastering one's environment can be called a "sense of competence." We saw this sense of competence in performing a particular task as helpful in understanding how a fit between task and organizational characteristics could motivate people toward successful performance.

---

[3] McGregor, *Human Side of Enterprise*, p. 245.

[4] See Robert W. White, "Ego and Reality in Psychoanalytic Theory," *Psychological Issues*, vol. 3, no. 3 (New York: International Universities Press, 1963).

Organizational Dimensions

Because the four study sites had already been evaluated by the respective corporate managers as high and low performers of tasks, we expected that such differences in performance would be a preliminary clue to differences in the "fit" of the organizational characteristics to the job to be done. But, first, we had to define what kinds of organizational characteristics would determine how appropriate the organization was to the particular task.

We grouped these organizational characteristics into two sets of factors:

1. Formal characteristics, which could be used to judge the fit between the kind of task being worked on and the formal practices of the organization.
2. Climate characteristics, or the subjective perceptions and orientations that had developed among the individuals about their organizational setting. (These too must fit the task to be performed if the organization is to be effective.)

We measured these attributes through questionnaires and interviews with about 40 managers in each unit to determine the appropriateness of the organization to the kind of task being performed. We also measured the feelings of competence of the people in the organizations so that we could link the appropriateness of the organizational attributes with a sense of competence.

MAJOR FINDINGS

The principal findings of the survey are best highlighted by contrasting the highly successful Akron plant and the high-performing Stockton laboratory. Because each performed very different tasks (the former a relatively certain manufacturing task and the latter a relatively uncertain research task), we expected, as brought out earlier, that there would have to be major differences between them in organizational characteristics if they were to perform effectively. And this is what we did find. But we also found that each of these effective units had a better fit with its particular task than did its less effective counterpart.

While our major purpose in this article is to explore how the fit between task and organizational characteristics is related to motivation, we first want to explore more fully the organizational characteristics of these units, so the reader will better understand what we mean by a fit between task and organization and how it can lead to more effective behavior. To do this, we shall place the major emphasis on the contrast between the high-performing units (the Akron plant and Stockton laboratory), but we shall also compare each of these with its less effective mate (the Hartford plant and Carmel laboratory respectively).

Formal Characteristics

Beginning with differences in formal characteristics, we found that both the Akron and Stockton organizations fit their respective tasks much better than did their less successful counterparts. In the predictable manufacturing task environment, Akron had a pattern of formal relationships and duties that was highly structured and precisely defined. Stockton, with its unpredictable research task, had a low degree of structure and much less precision of definition (see Exhibit 2).

EXHIBIT 2
Differences in Formal Characteristics in High-Performing Organizations

Characteristics	Akron	Stockton
1. Pattern of formal relationships and duties as signified by organization charts and job manuals	Highly structured, precisely defined	Low degree of structure, less well defined
2. Pattern of formal rules, procedures, control, and measurement systems	Pervasive, specific, uniform, comprehensive	Minimal, loose, flexible
3. Time dimensions incorporated in formal practices	Short-term	Long-term
4. Goal dimensions incorporated in formal practices	Manufacturing	Scientific

Akron's pattern of formal rules, procedures, and control systems was so specific and comprehensive that it prompted one manager to remark: "We've got rules here for everything from how much powder to use in cleaning the toilet bowls to how to cart a dead body out of the plant."

In contrast, Stockton's formal rules were so minimal, loose, and flexible that one scientist, when asked whether he felt the rules ought to be tightened, said:

"If a man puts a nut on a screw all day long, you may need more rules and a job definition for him. But we're not novices here. We're professionals and not the kind who need close supervision. People around here *do* produce, and produce under relaxed conditions. Why tamper with success?"

These differences in formal organizational characteristics were well suited to the differences in tasks of the two organizations. Thus:

1. Akron's highly structured formal practices fit its predictable task because behavior had to be rigidly defined and controlled around the

automated, high-speed production line. There was really only one way to accomplish the plant's very routine and programmable job; managers defined it precisely and insisted (through the plant's formal practices) that each man do what was expected of him.

On the other hand, Stockton's highly unstructured formal practices made just as much sense because the required activities in the laboratory simply could not be rigidly defined in advance. With such an unpredictable, fast-changing task as communications technology research, there were numerous approaches to getting the job done well. As a consequence, Stockton managers used a less structured pattern of formal practices that left the scientists in the lab free to respond to the changing task situation.

2. Akron's formal practices were very much geared to *short-term* and *manufacturing* concerns as its task demanded. For example, formal production reports and operating review sessions were daily occurrences, consistent with the fact that the through-put time for their products was typically only a few hours.

By contrast, Stockton's formal practices were geared to *long-term* and *scientific* concerns, as its task demanded. Formal reports and reviews were made only quarterly, reflecting the fact that research often does not come to fruition for three to five years.

At the two less effective sites (i.e., the Hartford plant and the Carmel laboratory), the formal organizational characteristics did not fit their respective tasks nearly as well. For example, Hartford's formal practices were much less structured and controlling than were Akron's, while Carmel's were more restraining and restricting than were Stockton's. A scientist in Carmel commented:

"There's something here that keeps you from being scientific. It's hard to put your finger on, but I guess I'd call it 'Mickey Mouse.' There are rules and things here that get in your way regarding doing your job as a researcher."

Climate Characteristics

As with formal practices, the climate in both high-performing Akron and Stockton suited the respective tasks much better than did the climates at the less successful Hartford and Carmel sites.

Perception of Structure. The people in the Akron plant perceived a great deal of structure, with their behavior tightly controlled and defined. One manager in the plant said:

"We can't let the lines run unattended. We lose money whenever they do. So we make sure each man knows his job, knows when he can take a break, knows how to handle a change in shifts, etc. It's all spelled out clearly for him the day he comes to work here."

In contrast, the scientists in the Stockton laboratory perceived very little structure, with their behavior only minimally controlled. Such perceptions encouraged the individualistic and creative behavior that the uncertain, rapidly changing research task needed. Scientists in the less successful Carmel laboratory perceived much more structure in their organization and voiced the feeling that this was "getting in their way" and making it difficult to do effective research.

Distribution of Influence. The Akron plant and the Stockton laboratory also differed substantially in how influence was distributed and on the character of superior-subordinate and colleague relations. Akron personnel felt that they had much less influence over decisions in their plant than Stockton's scientists did in their laboratory. The task at Akron had already been clearly defined and that definition had, in a sense, been incorporated into the automated production flow itself. Therefore, there was less need for individuals to have a say in decisions concerning the work process.

Moreover, in Akron, influence was perceived to be concentrated in the upper levels of the formal structure (a hierarchical or "top-heavy" distribution), while in Stockton influence was perceived to be more evenly spread out among more levels of the formal structure (an egalitarian distribution).

Akron's members perceived themselves to have a low degree of freedom vis-à-vis superiors both in choosing the jobs they work on and in handling these jobs on their own. They also described the type of supervision in the plant as being relatively directive. Stockton's scientists, on the other hand, felt that they had a great deal of freedom vis-à-vis their superiors both in choosing the tasks and projects, and in handling them in the way that they wanted to. They described supervision in the laboratory as being very participatory.

It is interesting to note that the less successful Carmel laboratory had more of its decisions made at the top. Because of this, there was a definite feeling by the scientists that their particular expertise was not being effectively used in choosing projects.

Relations with Others. The people at Akron perceived a great deal of similarity among themselves in background, prior work experiences, and approaches for tackling job-related problems. They also perceived the degree of coordination of effort among colleagues to be very high. Because Akron's task was so precisely defined and the behavior of its members so rigidly controlled around the automated lines, it is easy to see that this pattern also made sense.

By contrast, Stockton's scientists perceived not only a great many differences among themselves, especially in education and background, but also that the coordination of effort among colleagues was relatively low. This was appropriate for a laboratory in which a great variety of disciplines and skills were present and individual projects were important to solve technological problems.

Time Orientation. As we would expect, Akron's individuals were highly oriented toward a relatively short time span and manufacturing goals. They responded to quick feedback concerning the quality and service that the plant was providing. This was essential, given the nature of their task.

Stockton's researchers were highly oriented toward a longer time span and scientific goals. These orientations meant that they were willing to wait for long-term feedback from a research project that might take years to complete. A scientist in Stockton said:

"We're not the kind of people here who need a pat on the back every day. We can wait for months if necessary before we get feedback from colleagues and the profession. I've been working on one project now for three months and I'm still not sure where it's going to take me. I can live with that, though."

This is precisely the kind of behavior and attitude that spells success on this kind of task.

Managerial Style. Finally, the individuals in both Akron and Stockton perceived their chief executive to have a "managerial style" that expressed more of a concern for the task than for people or relationships, but this seemed to fit both tasks.

In Akron, the technology of the task was so dominant that top mana-

EXHIBIT 3
Differences in "Climate" Characteristics in High-Performing Organizations

Characteristics	Akron	Stockton
1. Structural orientation	Perceptions of tightly controlled behavior and a high degree of structure	Perceptions of a low degree of structure
2. Distribution of influence	Perceptions of low total influence, concentrated at upper levels in the organization	Perceptions of high total influence, more evenly spread out among all levels
3. Character of superior-subordinate relations	Low freedom vis-à-vis superiors to choose and handle jobs, directive type of supervision	High freedom vis-à-vis superiors to choose and handle projects, participatory type of supervision
4. Character of colleague relations	Perceptions of many similarities among colleagues, high degree of coordination of colleague effort	Perceptions of many differences among colleagues, relatively low degree of coordination of colleague effort
5. Time orientation	Short-term	Long-term
6. Goal orientation	Manufacturing	Scientific
7. Top executive's "managerial style"	More concerned with task than people	More concerned with task than people

gerial behavior which was not focused primarily on the task might have reduced the effectiveness of performance. On the other hand, although Stockton's research task called for more individualistic problem-solving behavior, that sort of behavior could have become segmented and unco-ordinated, unless the top executive in the lab focused the group's atten-tion on the overall research task. Given the individualistic bent of the scientists, this was an important force in achieving unity of effort.

All these differences in climate characteristics in the two high per-formers are summarized in Exhibit 3.

As with formal attributes, the less effective Hartford and Carmel sites had organization climates that showed a perceptibly lower degree of fit with their respective tasks. For example, the Hartford plant had an egalitarian distribution of influence, perceptions of a low degree of structure, and a more participatory type of supervision. The Carmel laboratory had a somewhat top-heavy distribution of influence, percep-tions of high structure, and a more directive type of supervision.

COMPETENCE MOTIVATION

Because of the difference in organizational characteristics at Akron and Stockton, the two sites were strikingly different places in which to work. But these organizations had two very important things in com-mon. First, each organization fit very well the requirements of its task. Second, although the behavior in the two organizations was different, the result in both cases was effective task performance.

Since, as we indicated earlier, our primary concern in this study was to link the fit between organization and task with individual motivation to perform effectively, we devised a two-part test to measure the sense of competence motivation of the individuals at both sites. Thus:

The *first* part asked a participant to write creative and imaginative stories in response to six ambiguous pictures.

The *second* asked him to write a creative and imaginative story about what he would be doing, thinking, and feeling "tomorrow" on his job. This is called a "projective" test because it is assumed that the respon-dent projects into his stories his own attitudes, thoughts, feelings, needs, and wants, all of which can be measured from the stories.[5]

The results indicated that the individuals in Akron and Stockton showed significantly more feelings of competence than did their counterparts

---

[5] For a more detailed description of this survey, see John J. Morse, "Internal Organizational Patterning and Sense of Competence Motivation" (Boston: Harvard Business School, Ph.D. diss., 1969).

in the lower-fit Hartford and Carmel organizations.[6] We found that the organization-task fit is simultaneously linked to and interdependent with both individual motivation and effective unit performance. (This interdependency is illustrated in Exhibit 4.)

EXHIBIT 4
Basic Contingent Relationships

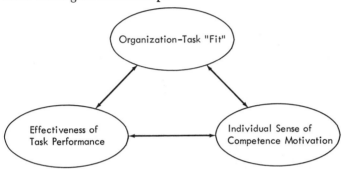

Putting the conclusions in this form raises the question of cause and effect. Does effective unit performance result from the task-organization fit or from higher motivation, or perhaps from both? Does higher sense of competence motivation result from effective unit performance or from fit?

Our answer to these questions is that we do not think there are any single cause-and-effect relationships, but that these factors are mutually interrelated. This has important implications for management theory and practice.

CONTINGENCY THEORY

Returning to McGregor's Theory X and Theory Y assumptions, we can now question the validity of some of his conclusions. While Theory Y might help to explain the findings in the two laboratories, we clearly need something other than Theory X or Y assumptions to explain the findings in the plants.

For example, the managers at Akron worked in a formalized organization setting with relatively little participation in decision making, and yet they were highly motivated. According to Theory X, people would work hard in such a setting only because they were coerced to do so.

---

[6] Differences between the two container plants are significant at .001 and between the research laboratories at .01 (one-tailed probability).

According to Theory Y, they should have been involved in decision making and been self-directed to feel so motivated. Nothing in our data indicates that either set of assumptions was valid at Akron.

Conversely, the managers at Hartford, the low-performing plant, were in a less formalized organization with more participation in decision making, and yet they were not as highly motivated as the Akron managers. The Theory Y assumptions would suggest that they should have been more motivated.

A way out of such paradoxes is to state a new set of assumptions, the Contingency Theory, that seems to explain the findings at all four sites:

1. Human beings bring varying patterns of needs and motives into the work organization, but one central need is to achieve a sense of competence.
2. The sense of competence motive, while it exists in all human beings, may be fulfilled in different ways by different people depending on how this need interacts with the strengths of the individuals' other needs—such as those for power, independence, structure, achievement, and affiliation.
3. Competence motivation is most likely to be fulfilled when there is a fit between task and organization.
4. Sense of competence continues to motivate even when a competence goal is achieved; once one goal is reached, a new, higher one is set.

While the central thrust of these points is clear from the preceding discussion of the study, some elaboration can be made. First, the idea that different people have different needs is well understood by psychologists. However, all too often, managers assume that all people have similar needs. Lest we be accused of the same error, we are saying only that all people have a need to feel competent; in this *one* way they are similar. But in many other dimensions of personality, individuals differ, and these differences will determine how a particular person achieves a sense of competence.

Thus, for example, the people in the Akron plant seemed to be very different from those in the Stockton laboratory in their underlying attitudes toward uncertainty, authority, and relationships with their peers. And because they had different need patterns along these dimensions, both groups were highly motivated by achieving competence from quite different activities and settings.

While there is a need to further investigate how people who work in different settings differ in their psychological makeup, one important implication of the Contingency Theory is that we must not only seek a fit between organization and task, but also between task and people and between people and organization.

A further point which requires elaboration is that one's sense of competence never really comes to rest. Rather, the real satisfaction of this need is in the successful performance itself, with no diminishing of the motivation as one goal is reached. Since feelings of competence are thus reinforced by successful performance, they can be a more consistent and reliable motivator than salary and benefits.

Implications for Managers

The major managerial implication of the Contingency Theory seems to rest in the task-organization-people fit. Although this interrelationship is complex, the best possibility for managerial action probably is in tailoring the organizaton to fit the task and the people. If such a fit is achieved, both effective unit performance and a higher sense of competence motivation seem to result.

Managers can start this process by considering how certain the task is, how frequently feedback about task performance is available, and what goals are implicit in the task. The answers to these questions will guide their decisions about the design of the management hierarchy, the specificity of job assignments, and the utilization of rewards and control procedures. Selective use of training programs and a general emphasis on appropriate management styles will move them toward a task-organization fit.

The problem of achieving a fit among task, organization, and people is something we know less about. As we have already suggested, we need further investigation of what personality characteristics fit various tasks and organizations. Even with our limited knowledge, however, there are indications that people will gradually gravitate into organizations that fit their particular personalities. Managers can help this process by becoming more aware of what psychological needs seem to best fit the tasks available and the organizational setting, and by trying to shape personnel selection criteria to take account of these needs.

In arguing for an approach which emphasizes the fit among task, organization, and people, we are putting to rest the question of which organizational approach—the classical or the participative—is best. In its place we are raising a new question: What organizational approach is most appropriate given the task and the people involved?

For many enterprises, given the new needs of younger employees for more autonomy, and the rapid rates of social and technological change, it may well be that the more participative approach is the most appropriate. But there will still be many situations in which the more controlled and formalized organization is desirable. Such an organization need not be coercive or punitive. If it makes sense to the individuals involved, given their needs and their jobs, they will find it rewarding and motivating.

CONCLUDING NOTE

The reader will recognize that the complexity we have described is not of our own making. The basic deficiency with earlier approaches is that they did not recognize the variability in tasks and people which produces this complexity. The strength of the contingency approach we have outlined is that it begins to provide a way of thinking about this complexity, rather than ignoring it. While our knowledge in this area is still growing, we are certain that any adequate theory of motivation and organization will have to take account of the contingent relationship between task, organization, and people.

Section VI

Organizational Change

Cases

1 | Denver Transportation Company*

Bill Hall had just entered his office when the telephone buzzed, and he picked up the receiver:

> Bill, this is George Willis, Mountain Air Lines; you boys have fouled up again. The crew on 326 this morning were kept waiting an hour for a car to take them to their hotel, and the captain's mad as hell. If you can't prevent this we're going to have to make other arrangements.
>
> I'm awfully sorry, George—I'll look into it right away. We'll give you good service. We're working on improvements in airport dispatching right now.

The conversation ended shortly afterwards.

Complaints such as this were of great concern to Hall. One year ago he had been brought in as operations manager for Denver Transportation Company with instructions to improve its service, and he was not at all satisfied with his progress. He had done everything within his knowledge to improve operational procedures and planning, to train and increase supervision, to firm up supervisory responsibilities, and to better communication facilities (see Exhibit 1). Further, he had secured sufficient additional drivers and equipment to handle the rapidly increasing airport and tourist business. For the most part Hall's activities were well received by drivers, supervisors, and dispatchers. Still complaints came in. They were items such as "the buses were late"; "they were overcrowded"; "the wrong type of limousine was sent." They were being caused by errors in judgment and planning on the part of supervisors and dispatchers, and Hall did not know what to do about it.

---

* All names have been disguised.

EXHIBIT 1

Major Steps Taken to Improve Supervisory and Dispatching Effectiveness, 1955–56

---

1. Worked personally with each supervisor and dispatcher, firming up his authority, responsibilities, and functions.
2. Had weekly meetings attended by supervisors, dispatchers, and the sales manager to iron out problems and to plan ahead.
3. Discussed complaints with the dispatcher and/or supervisor involved, trying to get at the cause and to help the man prevent making the error again.
4. Added one man to the dispatcher force and increased airport supervision by one. Warner added to dispatching; Smith and Goodhue to airport supervision; Smith to replace Bemis, who retired, and Goodhue as additional help.
5. Assisted in the training of the new supervisors.
6. Established an automatic telephone exchange for D.T.C. which enabled dispatchers and supervisors to contact drivers at taxi stands, terminals, hotels, the airport, etc., by dialing a local rather than going through the old D.T.C. switchboard. The same dial service allowed the driver to contact his supervisor or dispatcher directly as well.
7. Had constructed a magnetic dispatch board for the purpose of spotting the location of each D.T.C. vehicle and pointing up which were busy and which were available for hire. This replaced a clumsy peg board used for the same purpose.
8. Improved the forms used in the operations department. A major improvement was the establishment of one form with carbons to transmit orders from sales to supervisors to dispatchers to drivers. This replaced several separate forms and the chance of errors in time, date, place, etc., in transcribing.
9. Developed a chart allowing the airport supervisor and dispatchers to keep track of all arrivals and departures on one master sheet, rather than separate sheets for each airline.

Denver Transportation Company, known as D.T.C., was founded in 1926 to provide transportation for airline passengers and crews to and from the Denver airport. It had grown by adding sightseeing buses, chauffeur driven limousines, taxis, and U-drive cars as well as airport buses as the airport and tourist business expanded. After World War II there was a mushrooming of tourist trade and considerable growth in general business and federal government operations in this city, and D.T.C.'s business expanded vigorously. Their 1940 fleet of 16 buses, 45 taxis, 11 chauffeur driven Cadillacs and crew cars, and 41 U-drive cars had increased threefold by 1956, and the passenger miles operated[1] had increased even more.

D.T.C.'s business came from three sources:

1. From individuals who decide on their own to take a D.T.C. bus, taxi, or limousine.
2. From various agencies that sell tickets for airport to hotel transporta-

---

[1] Number of passengers carried times miles traveled.

tion and for sightseeing; this would include travel agents, hotel desks, and airline tour departments.

3. From organizations that contract with D.T.C. for transportation services; this includes transporting airline crews to and from the airport in special cars and many charter bus assignments ordered by airlines and others.

Management considered the latter two sources to be the most important. These organizations demanded top service from a ground transportation firm because their customers blamed them, not D.T.C., for poor ground transportation.

In airport and sightseeing activities D.T.C. had the bulk of the Denver business prior to World War II. With the great expansion in the area after the war, competition moved in. D.T.C. was not only unable to develop fast enough to hold all of the new business but in addition its service had deteriorated to the point where in recent years some customers were being held mostly by promises and personal friendships of D.T.C. management.

The owners of D.T.C. were intent on maintaining leadership control of the Denver transportation activities in which they were engaged. They had recently secured capital for additional equipment, and it was up to Bill Hall, the operations manager, to obtain drivers, to put the new equipment to optimum use, and to give the kind of service that would satisfy the airlines, hotels, and travel agents. The airport, taxi, and sightseeing departments were all receiving complaints, and Hall realized that something would have to be done to correct the poor judgment and planning exhibited by the supervisors and dispatchers involved. Exhibit 2 shows the 1956 organization chart of the operations departments. Exhibit 3 represents a page from the company's operations manual, indicating the duties of various supervisors and dispatchers. Exhibit 4 lists the 1956 supervisory and dispatching employees and their backgrounds.

Management had always believed in seniority and in promoting men up through the ranks for dispatching and supervisory jobs; the position of operations manager was the only exception to this policy. New men were started as taxi drivers, moved up to airport drivers, then to sightseeing bus or limousine drivers, and finally to dispatching or supervisory jobs. The drivers and dispatchers were members of the teamsters union, and management's seniority and promotion policies were spelled out in the contract:

> Section 5. *Seniority.* In the event of any layoff of employees, employees with the least amount of seniority shall be laid off first. In the event of any rehiring of employees, the employee with the most seniority shall be rehired first.

In making promotions, if there is no material difference between qualifications of applicants, the one having the greater length of continuous service will be selected. If there is a material difference between the qualifications of the applicants, the best qualified applicant will be selected; however, he shall be on a probationary period for six (6) months.

In 1940, D.T.C. had been able to secure plenty of young men who were willing to start out as taxi drivers. Furthermore, dispatching and supervisory jobs were simpler then, and so management's promotion policy worked well. In 1956, Hall was having considerable difficulty in employing taxi drivers who had the ability to progress in the company. There were in fact plenty of taxi drivers available, but they were not men who possessed the characteristics that would enable them to be good sightseeing drivers, dispatchers, or supervisors.

Taxi drivers received a guaranteed salary of $225 per month or 40 percent of gross revenue produced, whichever was greater. Since anyone who owned an automobile could start a taxi firm by paying a small business license fee and firms were unrestricted as to the number of cabs that they might license, competition was keen. For several years

EXHIBIT 2
Organization Chart, 1956

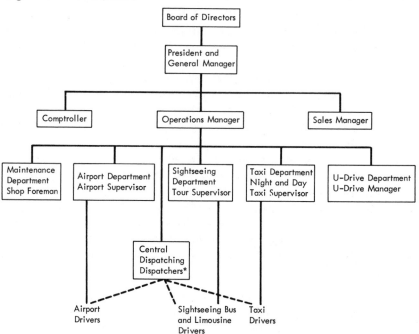

EXHIBIT 3
Functions of Supervisors and Dispatchers, 1956

Airport Supervisors
1. Direct movements of airline passengers and crews to and from the airport by bus, taxi, or crew car.
2. Keep in close touch with airlines as to passenger load, times of arrival and departure, special flights, and related information.
3. Inform central dispatching as to flight times and the number and types of vehicles needed.
4. Answer questions of passengers, assist in the loading of buses, and record the passengers per bus for control purposes.
5. Train airport drivers.

Tour Supervisors
1. Schedule sightseeing buses and limousines according to presold tickets and anticipated cash business.
2. Coordinate large movements and clear them with the police department, hotel doormen, and other interested parties.
3. Inform central dispatching as to the times of tours and the types of vehicles needed.
4. Train sightseeing bus and limousine drivers.

Taxi Supervisors
1. Schedule maximum taxi coverage for peak hours and for special downtown events.
2. Inform central dispatching of such schedules.
3. Spot check D.T.C. taxis on the road.
4. Train taxi drivers.

Dispatchers
1. Supply vehicles at the times ordered by supervisors.
2. Take telephone orders for taxis and dispatch them.
3. Take telephone orders for buses and limousines and supply them after clearing with the supervisor involved.
4. Handle all customer calls at night when the sales office is closed. If people call about sightseeing tours, try to sell them on going by D.T.C.

---

the D.T.C. taxi department had represented little more than a break-even operation for Denver Transportation Company. Taxi competition held down the number of trips available to a D.T.C. driver, and as a result his salary and tips were low. This, coupled with the lack of prestige involved in "operating a hack" and the availability of good jobs in the community, did not serve to encourage able young men to become taxi drivers. Recently Hall had suggested to the president that the taxi department be eliminated, for it caused a good deal of the dispatching load and was relatively unprofitable. The president, however, felt strongly that a taxi department was necessary to give 24-hour service to the hotels and airports, for the many independent taxi operators only worked during the peak hours, and the airlines, hotels, and others relied on D.T.C. for service at odd hours.

EXHIBIT 4
Operations Personnel, 1956

Name	Position	Age	Years of Service	Previous Employment	Education
Abbott	U-drive mgr.	42	10	Mechanic	11 grade
Candis	Dispatcher	28	8	Miner	12 grade
Goodhue.	Ass't. airport sup.	35	5	Accountant	College
Hall.	Operations mgr.	45	1	Traffic mgr.	College
Hayman	Tour sup.	49	·16	Bus driver	7 grade
Jacobs	Ass't. airport sup.	40	11	Farm hand	10 grade
Johnson	Night taxi sup.	56	20	Truck driver	6 grade
Kelly	Airport sup.	51	18	Carpenter	9 grade
Matola	Dispatcher	36	6	Taxi driver	10 grade
Pollock.	Dispatcher	30	6	Clerk	12 grade
Roscoe	Ass't. airport sup.	38	12	Miner	7 grade
Smith.	Ass't. airport sup.	44	5	Mechanic	9 grade
Sontag	Day taxi sup.	55	23	Taxi driver	5 grade
Trigger	Dispatcher	33	4	Clerk	11 grade
Warner, T.	Dispatcher	27	6	U.S. Army	12 grade
Warner, R.	Dispatcher	34	10	Truck driver	11 grade

Hall could find plenty of men who would like to drive a sightseeing bus or limousine. Here the pay was good, the tips were high, and there was a certain amount of prestige. These jobs required men with good appearance, manners, and personality. On the sightseeing buses the driver had to speak well over a microphone, know his tour thoroughly, be able to handle a group of people skillfully, and be entertaining. Some of the tours lasted for six to eight hours. To keep 30 people interested for this length of time required a personable driver-conductor.

Though to a lesser degree, Hall would also be able to find good men to start out in airport bus work. The pay was good, and the job was only one step removed from a sightseeing assignment. In fact, since airport buses were used for sightseeing work on occasions when the airport was not very active and the sightseeing load was heavy, it was necessary for the day shift airport drivers to be able to handle the shorter sightseeing tours. With the company policy of promoting airport drivers to sightseeing jobs, a good percentage of the men reaching the airport-driver level should have the characteristics necessary to make good sightseeing drivers. The turnover rate among taxi drivers was 38 percent a year; among airport drivers, 15 percent a year; and among sightseeing bus and limousine drivers, 6 percent a year.

As D.T.C.'s operations expanded, the job of dispatcher or supervisor became increasingly more complex. Airport supervisors who used to keep the schedules of plane arrivals, D.T.C. equipment available, and other such information in their heads now had to resort to scheduling on paper and long-range planning. Better coordination had to be maintained with central dispatchers. Dispatchers who in the past were able to get by when sending a sightseeing bus a little late to a hotel to pick up a load of people now found these errors were compounded when two or three buses were called for, and a hundred or more people were kept waiting. Sometimes, when the dispatching loads would get heavy, the dispatchers would neglect to give taxi and bus drivers sufficient information about a particular assignment. Bill Hall knew that in following up the Mountain Airlines complaint at the beginning of the case he would get an answer such as this from the airport supervisor:

> I was really busy then—three planes had just arrived, and the buses were filling up. Central dispatch told me the crew car was on its way, and I thought it would be right along.

Then Hall would say to himself:

> This man should have found out when the crew car left downtown and exactly when the dispatcher thought it would arrive at the airport. He has instructions to send the crew in taxicabs at our expense if a crew car isn't available. He just doesn't use his head. The rest of the supervisors aren't any better—except Tom.[2] He's certainly improved the scheduling on the late airport shift, but the men don't seem to like him yet.

Bill Hall had studied the drivers carefully and felt that the current supervisors and dispatchers were the best available among the work force. Some of the sightseeing drivers were more intelligent than their supervisors and dispatchers, but they lacked any desire to assume supervisory responsibility. They were extroverts and thoroughly enjoyed guiding tourists. Several of them had been supervisors or dispatchers at one time or another and had been transferred back to driving because they did poorly or because they disliked the job and requested the transfer. Many of the sightseeing and airport drivers felt fully qualified to be supervisors and even though some did not want supervisory jobs, Hall thought they seemed resentful when Tom Goodhue, a D.T.C. accountant, was given the position of assistant airport supervisor.

In Hall's judgment, D.T.C. drivers, especially the old-timers, were very loyal to the company and high morale was evident. For many years the company had maintained benefits such as one week's paid vacation, life and hospitalization insurance on a joint, employee-employer contribution basis, and a no-interest loan policy. When bus drivers became too old to handle a big bus, they were given limousine assignments or work on one of the company's several commercial parking lots. Company parties for drivers and their wives or girl friends were held several times a year and

---

[2] Tom Goodhue was an accountant who had been transferred to operations two months ago because of developing eye trouble.

were thoroughly enjoyed by the workers. The small executive force of the company knew all the drivers by their first names and maintained a genuine "open-door policy."

On their own the sightseeing drivers had formed a small cowboy band which played at company parties. When big tourist groups were going on eight-hour sightseeing tours, they were supplied with box lunches and the cowboy band played for them during the lunch period. This made a big hit with the tourists and was a strong selling point for D.T.C. with travel agents. The band had made up a vocal number entitled "Sightsee with D.T.C." which they played often at gatherings. The company planned to use this song for promotional purposes.

The teamsters union had moved in seven years ago through the organizing help of several D.T.C. taxi drivers. Management believed that the union was voted in at the N.L.R.B. election only because of the large number of relatively new taxi drivers in the total driving force. Quite a few of the old-timers came to management and asked them whether they should join the union. Management had encouraged them to join on the grounds that they wanted men on their side within the union rank and file. Unionizing had improved the relations between D.T.C. drivers and the employees of many of D.T.C.'s customers such as the hotels (doormen), railroads, and airlines. Furthermore, when D.T.C. was asked to handle conventions (which were very profitable), they chartered buses from the local transit system and trucks to carry luggage from a moving company. Since all of these firms were teamster organized, their drivers used to resist working with D.T.C. (since it was nonunion), and many difficulties resulted.

In the seven years in which the teamsters union had been bargaining agents for D.T.C. workers, they had been unsuccessful at increasing wages except to partially cover cost-of-living rises—and these small increases were offered by management independently. No changes had been made in worker fringe benefits, and management felt that the D.T.C. old-timers were responsible for the lack of union aggressiveness. Hall realized that any activities on the part of management that reduced the driver morale could very well increase the union's strength with D.T.C. drivers. Furthermore, as the work force grew larger and, as a result, less familiar with management, Hall was afraid of a corresponding increase in union power. He feared this especially because large wage and/or fringe benefit increases would work a real hardship on D.T.C. A service firm such as this has wages as its main item of expense, and its rates were pretty well set by what the customer considered "fair." Any increase in rates could very well discourage people from sightseeing and/or increase competition.

There were several reasons why management established the policy of promoting men through the ranks; those most often cited were:

1. Management felt that able and senior workers should be rewarded.
2. Management felt that a man who had had experience in all of the operations would make a better supervisor or dispatcher.

In regard to the second reason the president felt that a supervisor could better understand the drivers and their problems, having been a driver himself. He felt that it would be difficult to absorb the many details of a supervisory job without having had driving experience. The same applied to dispatching, for drivers and customers would ask a dispatcher a multitude of questions involving train and flight departures, street and building locations, rates for trips between two points by taxi, sightseeing tour information and rates, and airport bus schedules and rates. Further, it was felt that a supervisor or dispatcher employed from the outside would have difficulty getting the cooperation of the drivers. On the other hand, Hall pointed out that in two months Tom Goodhue had learned the airport job and was already out-performing the old supervisors in duties such as planning and scheduling. Hall realized, however, that Goodhue had not as yet gotten the full cooperation of the drivers and that it would not be wise to put him in full charge of an airport shift until he did.

2 | *Supra Oil Company*

John Nichols, a university research worker, had a talk with Mr. Bennett[1] about the headquarters sales organization of the Supra Oil Company, one of the larger integrated oil companies in the country. Excerpts from the conversation follow:

NICHOLS: You mentioned that you're planning to make some organizational changes here at headquarters. I wonder if you could tell me something about that.

BENNETT: Well, sure I will. I don't want to take too much credit for this thing, but it sort of got started because in the last couple of years I've been doing some beefing around here about the fact that I was being kept terribly busy with a lot of the operating details of the sales organization. You can see what I mean by looking at the organization chart we have been working under. (*Mr. Bennett produced a chart from his desk drawer and indicated all the people that were currently reporting to him.*) [See Exhibit 1 for a copy of this chart.]

You can see that with all these people looking to me for leadership I am not in a position to give them the right kind of guidance that I think they should have on their jobs. I just couldn't take the time. It didn't work too badly some time ago, but since I've been made a member of the board of directors, those activities have taken more of my time. What with being on additional committees and things of that kind, I just couldn't give 17 headquarters' division managers the amount of help and attention that they really need. I think one of the things that they miss is that they're not in close enough touch with me or anybody else higher up the line so that we can be in a good position to appraise their work. We hear about it from some of the field people when they are doing a lousy job, but we

---
[1] Mr. Bennett was assistant general manager of sales.

EXHIBIT 1
Partial Organization Chart of the Sales Department

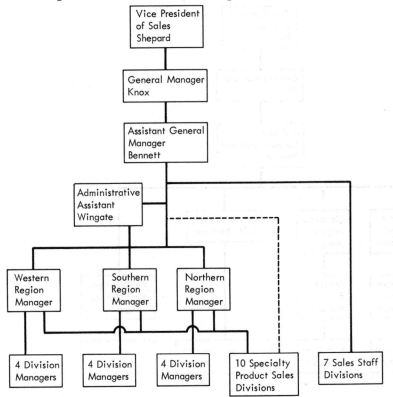

don't hear much about it if they're doing a good job. Occasionally a field man will report that he is getting a lot of help from some staff outfit here, but that's rather rare. So we don't have a very good basis for appraising the good things that they do. So we started talking about what might be done to straighten this out.

Our plans are taking pretty definite shape now. Let me show you what we have in mind. (*Mr. Bennett sketched on a pad of paper a diagram to indicate the planned organizational changes.*) [See Exhibit 2.] You see, we will have two regional managers instead of three. We'll be making one of the present regional managers the manager of the headquarters sales divisions. Those are the divisions that specialize in promoting and selling our different specialty products. Then we'll set up a new job for Wingate, who has been acting as an administrative assistant here at headquarters. He'll take charge of a good number of headquarters sales staff divisions that were reporting directly to me. Those are staff divisions like price analysis and advertising. We will also give each of the two remaining regional managers an assistant manager. Those will be new positions too.

EXHIBIT 2
Proposed Organization Chart of the Sales Department

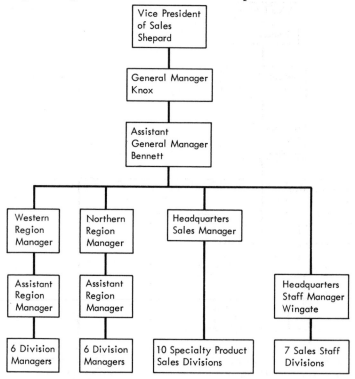

NICHOLS: How did you get these plans started?

BENNETT: I raised it with Shepard [vice president of sales] quite a while back.

NICHOLS: Would you say that was maybe six months ago?

BENNETT: I think it probably was six months ago. Shepard's first reaction was unfavorable. You see, I expected him to feel that way because he was the one that had the most to do with setting up our current organizational plan. But I approached him on it two or three times and complained a little bit and kept raising the question, and finally he said, "Well, I'm going to be leaving here pretty soon. You people have got to live with the organization. If you think it would work better some other way, I certainly won't object to your changing it." Well, that sort of thing gave me the green light, so then I went ahead and raised the question with Mr. Weld [president]. That is, Mr. Knox [general sales manager] and I did. The first time we went to him we talked about it just verbally in general terms. He said he thought it sounded like a pretty good idea and asked that we come back with two or three alternative ways of doing the thing in very specific terms. We talked to him once since then and, as a matter of fact, I'm going to see him this afternoon to see if he'll give us a final OK to go ahead with these plans.

NICHOLS: If you get his approval, what would you predict—that it might be another month before the change actually takes place?

BENNETT: Well, I would say so. I think if we've got this thing going in a month that we will be doing pretty well. I'm going to want to talk to my regional managers and then the headquarters divisional managers about this, but they should buy it all right. I think it will be a fairly simple job to sell it to them. You see, they will in effect be getting more chance to have access to their boss. I think it will work out much better, and they will see the point to it.

NICHOLS: You say that you are making one less region and making the third regional manager the head of—I guess you are calling him the headquarters sales manager. Are all three of those jobs going to continue to be on an equal level?

BENNETT: Yes, they will, but actually this job of headquarters sales manager will be sort of a training position for somebody to step into my job here as assistant general sales manager. That's what we have in mind. I think it will be a good assignment for training for my job. Then too, we're going to be able to open up a couple of new positions here, the assistant regional managers. I think that is going to be very useful from a management development standpoint. You see, one of our problems is that a number of the top executives here are all about the same age. You see, Knox and myself and the three regional managers are all about the same age, and then the heads of a lot of our headquarters divisions here are men of about our age who—well, they won't retire immediately, but they don't have a terribly long time to go. So we can't look to too many of those people to be our successors here at headquarters. We want to bring in some people from the field who will step in here as assistant regional managers in training for the job of regional managers.

NICHOLS: I take it then that you will be picking the people for those jobs from your field division men on the basis of talent and ability rather than on the basis of seniority.

BENNETT: Yes, that's right, we're going to pay very little attention to seniority in picking them. As a matter of fact, the two people we have in mind are two of our newest division managers, but they are both very able people. We think this will give us a chance to give them a good training for future development here.

This change that we are proposing, however, will not drastically change anybody's status here at headquarters, and I don't think it is going to cause us much trouble to put it in. You see, nobody will be jumped over the head of anybody else ahead of them in the management line. We think it's going to help a lot to have an assistant regional manager in here because that means that both he and the regional manager will be able to spend more time out with the field organization. One will be able to cover matters here at headquarters while the other is gone.

NICHOLS: Does that mean that your field people will be getting more top-level supervision as a result of this change?

BENNETT: Well, in a sense that's true of course, but it won't be taking any authority or responsibility from the field people. We just feel that they will be in closer personal contact with the people here at headquarters. We think it is very necessary that we do more of that. You see, if our regional managers and assistant managers can get out in the field and meet with the people, they will have a better basis for appraising different people that come along, and they can make sure we get the best people in the jobs that open up. Sometimes it's pretty hard to tell here at headquarters just who some of the best people are out in the field. You see, some division may have a job open up, and they will have a candidate for that job whom they will recommend highly for the promotion. That may be all well and good, but we want to know whether or not there may be a better man in some other division whom we aren't hearing about who might be shifted over for that promotion. You can't blame the division people for that sort of thing because they will have their favorite candidate and will of course be recommending him. We've made a few mistakes along the way because of this sort of thing, and if we have more personal contact we will be able to do a better job of it.

NICHOLS: Will this mean that you will be able to spend more time in the field?

BENNETT: Yes, I do hope that it will mean that. I want to do that very much. I think I ought to get out in the field more to keep in touch with what's going on in the market. It's really pretty hard to keep in touch with things while you are spending your time here at headquarters. You know, I want to get out and talk to people and see what they are talking about and see what kind of problems they are up against.

NICHOLS: I've heard several comments on this business of getting a feel for the market by getting out in the field. I take it that is quite a different process from keeping in touch with the market on what you might call a statistical basis?

BENNETT: Well, yes, it is. You see, I can look at the reports here in the office, and I may see that some district or some division is not doing too well at all on the basis of the figures in comparison with the competition. But I don't know just what the story is behind those figures. On a personal basis I could probably begin to get some answers to it. It could be any one of a number of things. I might go out there and find that it's a temporary situation because the competition is in effect going out and buying the business away from us, or I might find out that our people are not being very smart or aggressive about promoting our products, or I might find out that they do not know some of the facilities that we have available that would help them compete for the business. You see, one way we can compete for the business is the fact that this company has available some pretty good capital resources; and if we don't have good outlets in a given district, we're often in a position to offer to put up some capital to get some better outlets. That way we can do a better job of competing for the business, and sometimes the local people don't know that those possibilities exist, or perhaps they're a little reticent about putting up proposals. Or even if they do put up proposals, if we haven't been out in the field to see for ourselves what's going on, we probably don't do as good a job of appraising the proposals they do put up.

NICHOLS: In other words, the figures tell you that maybe something ought to be checked into, but you've got to go out and talk to people to find out what is really going on?

BENNETT: Yes, that's right. You have to take a personal look. You can find out a lot faster than you can by correspondence just what is going on and what can be done about it.

NICHOLS: Won't this reorganization mean that some of the people both here and in the field will have new bosses now?

BENNETT: Yes, that's right, but it's not too drastic a change. You see, we used to have only two regional managers some time ago. I guess we shifted off that system some four or five years ago. When I was out in the field as manager of a division, I was reporting in to the northern regional manager, who was Mr. Shepard at that time. Then I was brought in here as his assistant for the whole region. It was about that time that we set up this business of having three regions and I was named one of the regional managers, and at that time Mr. Shepard became general manager.

NICHOLS: Well, it sounds as if that previous move might have been motivated somewhat by a desire to develop people and perhaps give you a chance to take over a regional managership before you might otherwise have had a chance to.

BENNETT: Yes, I think that's right. At that time, that move was the way we could open things up for further management development, and now we are sort of doing it the other way around. Everybody knows that the arrangement we are now proposing may well be changed again in a few more years.

We like to change the organization around a little bit like this from time to time just to let people know that we are not going to be static about things. Of course, we want to do it in a way so that some of our senior people do not get bypassed or jumped over by some of the younger ones, because that not only bothers the individual but it also hurts morale further down in the organization. You see, when some of the people further down see some of that sort of thing happening, they are apt to conclude that it might happen to them some day, and it's pretty discouraging to them. The way we are doing it now we can bring up some younger people without jumping over anybody's head who is senior.

I think an organization change of this kind is also useful in that it indicates to some of our younger people that they need not feel discouraged if they are in a position where someone is above them in line who shows no signs of being promoted on up. This situation might make a person feel that he is being blocked from future promotion by his boss. But he is encouraged when he sees an occasional organizational shift of this kind because it makes him realize that things can happen in the future that might shift the organization around to a point where he can be sprung loose for a move on up even though his boss may not be promotable.

NICHOLS: Then I take it that one of the predominant thoughts in this whole reorganization was one of management development?

BENNETT: Oh, that's certainly true. That was one of the prime reasons we're proposing this, because we think it will help us develop our managers and this gives us a way of doing it without upsetting the organization too much.

That afternoon Mr. Bennett kept the appointment with Mr. Weld that was mentioned in the conversation above. Upon entering Mr. Weld's office, Mr. Bennett handed Mr. Weld a copy of the revised sales organization chart.

BENNETT: Here's a final version of our reorganizational plans. Do you think it is all right to go ahead on this?

3 | Dan Weber

In November 1963, Mr. Dan Weber, assistant chief of operations research in the research and development department of the Aircraft Propulsion Division, was concerned about the positions of himself and his operations research group in the departmental organization. Divisional management had just made an announcement that a complete reorganization of the R&D department would occur at the end of the calendar year. No details of the change were made available at the time of the announcement.

In the seven years since coming into the R&D department, Mr. Weber had already been involved in two major reorganizations. In this same period he had advanced from the usual starting position of engineering draftsman to his current assignment as assistant chief of the OR group. Mr. Weber took pride in the fact that while he had been in the OR group it had expanded from a two-man group to its current staff of 15 engineers.

Yet this accomplishment had not left Mr. Weber without concerns for his own career advancement and for the OR group's future role in the R&D department. One of these concerns, he told the casewriter, was that the upper echelons of departmental management did not yet comprehend the full significance and potential usefulness of OR techniques for the programming and planning of departmental activities. At the same time, he expressed concern about his own career strategy. Should he stay with OR work and the satisfactions it provided, in view of the fact that the traditional internal routes to top positions in departmental management and higher were through project management and design engineering? On the other hand, he believed that the OR operations had potential utility for the Aircraft Propulsion Division which if recognized and realized could also bring him significant promotions. In the context of the upcoming reorganization, Mr. Weber was giving serious consideration to the resolution of these concerns.

BACKGROUND

The Aircraft Propulsion Division, a division of a large, widely diversified corporation, had experienced severe cutbacks in its government contracts for both production and R&D business following the end of the Korean conflict. Lagging somewhat behind other jet engine producers, the top management of the Aircraft Propulsion Division had taken two steps to reorient its R&D department: In 1957, a four-year program for increasing research facilities had been undertaken with a budget of $40 million; and early in the same year, the R&D department had been completely reorganized. The pure projects system had been discarded in the reorganization in favor of a systems engineering approach. Management explained the change as follows:

> In the emerging aerospace age, the wide variety of devices and components that must be coordinated into the development of advanced, high-performance weapons systems requires a new R&D approach, a new vision. The "systems approach" is an answer to this need; it provides the technical viewpoint to integrate the many and diverse components into a smoothly functioning whole.

Under the systems approach the unit of management changed from specific R&D projects to the more specialized systems areas wherein similar component systems for several projects could be grouped. Before the change a project manager had direct responsibility for everyone working on a given project, such as the development work for a lightweight gas turbine suitable for powering helicopters and subsonic air-breathing missiles. Under the new structure the project manager was eliminated and the direct responsibility for the engineers was divided among systems managers according to the particular type of system on which each engineer was working. Continuing the above example, the development of the lightweight gas turbine would be staffed by some engineers reporting to the chief of the design group, some to the chief of the metallurgy group, some to the chief of the thermodynamics group, and so on.

These early actions in the Aircraft Propulsion Division were specific cases of a more widespread industry response to the changing nature of airpower as a component of national defense. Overshadowed by the expediency of the production effort for the Korean conflict, the rapidly increasing technology of electronics, rocketry, nuclear power, and space travel opened possibilities of radically different propulsion systems for aerospace weapons and reconnaisance vehicles. These developments plus the likelihood of jet-propelled commercial airliners before the end of the 1950s commenced a reorientation in the aircraft engine industry toward the probable future requirements for survival in the emerging aerospace industry. Exhibit 1 indicates the magnitude and swiftness

EXHIBIT 1
National Expenditures for Air Defense and Sales, 1951 through 1962
(in millions of dollars)

Year	National Expenditures (Year Ended 6–30)				Percent of Total			Aircraft Propulsion Division (1942–1949 = 100)
	Aircraft	Missles	Space	Total	Aircraft	Missles	Space	
1962	$6,449	$3,523	$1,300	$11,272	55%	32%	13%	$221
1961	5,898	2,972	744	9,614	61	31	8	229
1960	6,670	3,500	401	10,571	63	33	4	194
1959	7,658	3,339	145	11,132	69	30	1	179
1958	8,448	2,737	89	11,274	75	24	1	197
1957	7,978	2,095	76	10,149	78	21	1	312
1956	7,146	1,168	71	8,385	85	14	1	493
1955	8,037	718	74	8,829	91	8	1	243
1954	8,335	504	–	8,839	94	6	–	291
1953	7,417	295	–	7,712	96	4	–	370
1952	4,888	169	–	5,057	97	3	–	368
1951	2,412	21	–	2,433	99	1	–	113

Source: *Statistical Abstract of the United States.*

of the change in government spending from conventional aircraft to missiles and space vehicles.

For the Aircraft Propulsion Division the task of shifting emphasis to the aerospace orientation was formidable. For 15 years, the division had been one of the leading developers and producers of jet engines for military fighters and bombers. One of the first to begin volume production of jet engines, the division had achieved an industry-wide reputation for development of improved designs enabling more favorable thrust-weight ratios. Post-World War II and the Korean conflict were periods of volume production for the division's highly successful engines. In 1956, the division had received approval for production of a high-thrust jet engine to power a new advanced supersonic all-weather fighter.

Despite the assurance of a minimum five-year production run on this latest power plant and subsequently modified versions, management had realized that the future of jet engines for the defense market would be limited. The demonstrated advances in rocketry and the possibilities of nuclear power for aircraft propulsion were signaling an inevitable revolution in propulsion for military airpower. Rocket-powered missiles and space vehicles would shortly present feasible alternatives to the interception, bombing, and surveillance functions of conventional military aircraft.

The significance of the impending change was that the new engines were not an evolution of the gas turbine but were based on radically different design principles. Whereas before, the power plant was a separate and interchangeable component within the total aircraft system, in the new era, aerospace vehicles basically would be "nonair-breathing" rocket engines upon which would be mounted a nose cone containing a war head and/or electronic guidance and surveillance devices. The change promised to be considerably more complex for the industry than had been the change from piston engines to jet engines.

But the Aircraft Propulsion Division had more direct evidence of change than the above. The 1956 cancellation of a development contract in the division for a new design gas turbine engine capable of extremely high altitude performance sharpened the realization of the alternatives presented by rocket power. As part of a development package for an advanced high-altitude reconnaisance plane, the entire project had been canceled when an analysis of comparable lead times indicated that an alternative missile system would make the aircraft obsolete shortly after planned production would have begun. The division had spent over $65 million on this project and had strongly anticipated eventual production. Only about two thirds of this expenditure had been covered by government contract. The 1957 reorganization followed shortly thereafter.

1957 REORGANIZATION

Mr. Weber had been working on a development project for a lightweight gas turbine engine about three months prior to the reorganization of 1957. During this time he was an engineering draftsman in the design area of the project. Working with him under the supervision of Mr. Frank Mintz were seven other engineering draftsmen. In the reorganization Mr. Mintz was assigned to take over and restaff the operations research group. Two years earlier the OR group had been initiated when two mathematicians had been hired by the department for that purpose. These men were unfamiliar with the problems endemic to the R&D department, and the applications of OR had been few. Both of the men had resigned shortly before the reorganization was effected. Mr. Mintz chose Mr. Weber to join him in the OR group and decided that initially the two of them would comprise the group. Neither of the men had any background in OR, although both were familiar with some of the recent developments in the field. The two of them formulated the initial activities of the group by reading books and visiting an OR operation at a nearby aircraft company. Mr. Mintz had been with the division for ten years and was familiar with both the methods of operation and the problems of coordination of the R&D department. Mr. Weber had majored in aeronautical engineering as an undergraduate and obtained a masters in mathematics before coming to the division directly out of college.

At the departmental management level, several major changes were made in the organization (see Exhibits 2 and 3). Mr. Edward Lovio,

EXHIBIT 2
R&D Department (partial)
(prior to 1957)

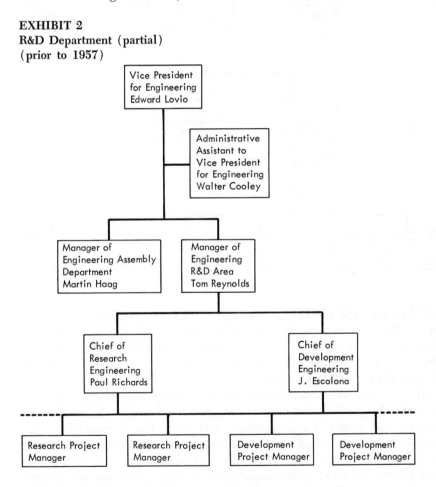

previously in command of the entire department as vice president for engineering, became vice president for research and development. The number of engineers under his command was reduced from 2,500 to 150. Mr. Lovio had come to the company during World War II and

EXHIBIT 3
R&D Department (partial)
(1957–59)

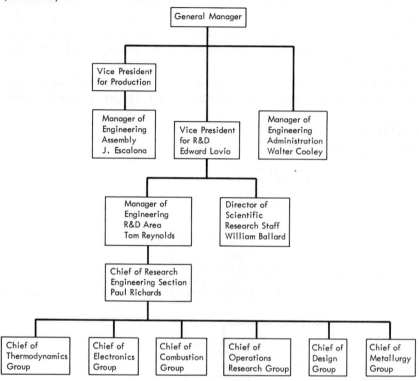

had become well recognized throughout the gas turbine industry as an outstanding designer. He was given credit for the successful engines developed at the close of World War II and during the Korean conflict, and he was generally considered to be the chief engine designer in the Aircraft Propulsion Division.

Mr. J. Escalona, formerly chief of the development group, was promoted to the position of manager of engineering assembly. In the reorganization the production department took over the responsibility for engineering assembly and Mr. Escalona reported to the vice president for production after the change. Mr. Escalona had been primarily concerned with the development of the high-thrust jet engine that was just beginning production. Engineering assembly was charged with the responsibility of providing all engineering services needed in connection with actual engine production and had employed 2,000 of the R&D department's 2,500 professional personnel. Mr. Escalona replaced Mr. Martin Haag who was retiring from the company at this time. Mr. Haag had advanced to his former position in a manner similar to Escalona's move. In 1949, when a highly modified version of the principal jet engine then in production was phased from development into production, Mr. Haag, who had had chief responsibility for its development, was promoted to head engineering assembly.

Under Mr. Lovio the R&D function was divided into two sections. A small scientific research staff was established under the leadership of William Ballard. Staffed with ten engineers and scientists, the staff was to work on any problems which the vice president for R&D, Mr. Lovio, deemed important. The second subdivision was the R&D area. Mr. Tom Reynolds remained as manager, and reporting to him as chief of the research engineering section was Mr. Paul Richards.

With the phasing of the high-thrust engine out of development and into production, and with the cancellation of the high-altitude jet engine development contract, the R&D department was left without any sponsored development contracts. Approximately 400 of the previous 500 engineers employed in the R&D area were in development projects, the remaining 100 in research. Fifty of those development engineers were transferred to engineering assembly pending the start-up of volume production on the high-thrust engine. Another 50 were transferred to the research engineering section, and the remaining 300 were laid off. The 150 engineers in the research engineering section were reorganized into systems groups as follows: thermodynamics, electronics, combustion, design, metallurgy, and OR (see Exhibit 3).

Mr. Weber interpreted the 1957 reorganization and subsequent events as follows:

> If you wanted to come up with the first big blow—this was really a big blow to Ed Lovio. The major amount of manpower was taken away from him. He is one of the original engineers of the division and very well respected in the industry. He considers the past successes of the division as his successes, as his engines. I would say there is a major portion of truth to this; but whenever you have a large organization, there are many, many people who have actually contributed to the design. It becomes a fine line of distinction as to whose design it really is at that point. Probably back in World War II our first production jet engine was his design. The modified versions produced during the Korean conflict are a little more hazy; and the current production engine becomes even more hazy. My impression is that he would have liked to go out in a blaze of glory with some basically new engine design. He has stayed on waiting for the division to get a new major contract of this type. I've been with the division for about seven years, and the R&D department still hasn't come up with such a contract. You could almost see the pressure building up, getting near retirement, he wanted this one last success.
>
> The scientific research staff was sort of a window dressing. It had ten people or so to start with. The major effort of this whole R&D department went down through a chain of three people: Lovio, Reynolds,

and Richards. There were many conflicts between these three men in that each was trying to run the entire 150-man section independently of the others. Each of them prior to this reorganization had several major areas of responsibility. Then, they were left with only 150 engineers between them, and the getting of new business was looming all the more important. If you were at the bottom as I was, you got a lot of conflicting directions. One day one would come in and say to do this; later another would come in and say to do that; and so back and forth, each one trying to somehow get the project moving in a good direction.

After a while more business started to come in, and they resolved the problem after a fashion. The chief of research engineering, Mr. Richards, was interested in missiles, so he worried about a project to develop cases for the rocket engine of a surface-to-surface guided missile. Dr. Reynolds was interested in getting into the guidance area, so he worried about a nose-cone development contract we had obtained. And Mr. Lovio worried after the few jet engine projects in a vague sort of way.

As business picked up in 1957, the problems of coordination between various systems groups became of concern to Mr. Richards; he assigned a group of technical writers to the OR group to improve communications and coordination in the development of research proposals for government contracts. Mr. Weber described this phase in the development of the OR group in the following way:

> After the reorganization there were no formal project managers or anything like this in the new organization. It turned out that OR was doing a lot of the lower level coordination unofficially. We were assigned a number of technical writers who prepared proposals for contracts. There are a lot of sections that have to be prepared: aerodynamics, structures, electronic systems, etc. Many different pieces of information came into this proposal from group chiefs responsible for the specific areas, and often you would find a lot of inconsistencies. For example, someone would say that the design was this and someone else would say it was that; and in the end we were actually resolving the technical differences that had not shown up until the proposal had got to the point at which each section had to put it down on paper and submit it as part of the whole proposal.
>
> We are actually doing a lot of the in-between coordination and getting the project divisions clarified. At first all the groups were relatively small, and we were in a one-room type of thing. The whole outfit was about 150 engineers; so we all knew each other.

CHANGES IN R&D RESOURCES

The Aircraft Propulsion Division in 1958 revised upward its planned expansion of R&D facilities. Under the revision $56 million would be expended by 1963 with an increased emphasis on electronic and metallurgical research. The core of this latter expenditure was to be the construction of an $18 million research center for basic studies in aerospace and materials science.

Adjustments in personnel during this same time period also reflected the reorientation. Both additions and reductions were made to the R&D staff between 1957 and 1959. The shrinkage was concentrated among those engineers with backgrounds principally in gas turbine design. At the same time, the department was hiring for the new research facilities which were under construction. This recruitment focused on engineers and scientists trained in the basic sciences or the developing space technology.

1959 REORGANIZATION

By the middle of 1959, the R&D department had grown to 250 engineers and scientists. Several projects were underway, and poor coordination increasingly delayed completions of projects beyond scheduled dates. It was in this context that the general manager of the Aircraft Propulsion Division announced another reorganization of the R&D department (see Exhibit 4) that also involved some higher management shifts (see Exhibit 5). The 1959 reorganization involved five important steps as follows:

1. The functions of R&D and engineering administration were centralized under the position of a vice president for engineering. To fill this position the division hired a retired air force general who had spent 25 years in logistics work. This man, Mr. Raymond Montgomery, was unfamiliar with aeronautical engineering, and Mr. Richards was placed as assistant to the vice president for engineering.

2. Mr. Lovio remained as vice president for R&D but was given the additional position of research advisor to the general manager of the division.

3. At this time an additional section was formed reporting to Mr. Lovio, the supersonic transport project, directed by Mr. Fred Rinehart. Mr. Rinehart had been recently hired from an aircraft firm. This section was to bring together the various R&D activities that had been going on toward the development of an advanced turbojet engine to power a supersonic transport which might be produced by the late 1960s. Rinehart's project was to have high priority since it appeared by late 1958 that the division was not going to obtain a significant share of the jet engine market for commercial airliners as the airlines changed from piston engines to gas turbines in the immediate future.

4. The R&D department under Mr. Reynolds was reorganized to include a section of project chiefs to coordinate the various engineering

EXHIBIT 4
R&D Department (partial)
(1959–63)

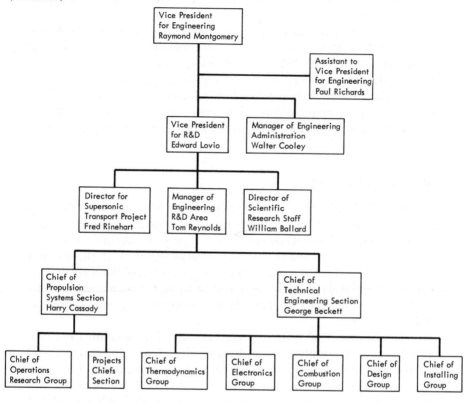

activities needed on particular contracts. These project chiefs along with the OR group now reported to the manager of propulsion systems, Mr. Harry Cassady. The other systems groups reported to the manager of technical engineering, Mr. George Beckett. Both Mr. Cassady and Mr. Beckett were formerly group chiefs.

5. A systems planning committee was organized within the R&D department. This committee was to meet weekly with the primary tasks of: (1) recommending to the executive committee of the division those projects which should be undertaken by the R&D department, (2) determining the levels of effort to be expended on each of these proposals, and (3) selecting those projects upon which the R&D department should enter bid proposals to government agents. The vice president for engineering was committee chairman, and his assistant, Mr. Richards, was secretary. The regular membership also consisted of the vice president for R&D, the manager of R&D, the manager of engineering assembly,

EXHIBIT 5
"Division-Level" Management (partial)
(1959–63)

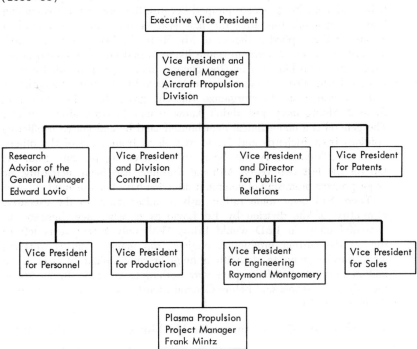

and two members from the sales department. Other members of the R&D department, the production department and the sales department could attend upon invitation of a regular member.

Mr. Weber had the following comments to make about the 1959 reorganization:

> There was some interesting running around during the 1959 reorganization. Paul Richards ran out from under Mr. Lovio and Dr. Reynolds and started working directly with the new vice president for engineering. Mr. Richards pretty much initiated it himself. He and Mr. Lovio had often gotten into arguments in departmental meetings—so much so that it got to be an open antagonism. Richards felt that Lovio was old-fashioned in his approach and often told him so in project review meetings. So Richards pretty much ran out from under Lovio. Yet it was sort of a mutual type of thing. General Montgomery had very little, if any, engineering background. He was brought in as a manager rather than as an engineer; and initially he didn't understand the R&D department. Being where he was in a new organization, he was trying to figure out what was going on; and he needed someone to lean on.

Following the reorganization, Paul Richards was a pretty high-status individual. He had a lot to say about the R&D activities. Many of the communications that came from the general went through Richards. If he said something, people jumped because they figured it was coming from the general. But after the first year or so, there was a gradual erosion of the implied authority of Mr. Richards. Just now he has little influence or status. People are more likely to find out if communications have come from him or from the general before going ahead. Richards is a good administrator and engineer. He gave Frank Mintz the authority and encouragement to reorganize the OR group back in 1957. But, General Montgomery just didn't know whom to trust after a while. The general is a nontechnical man himself, and he had gotten conflicting opinions from Richards and Lovio as well as from some of the others. Then, too, Montgomery has been under increasing pressure from the top for the last two years. Although business had been increasing, no major projects promising of volume production have been secured.

There had been some rather rash promises made to the executive committee of the division by Ed Lovio as to what new business an increased effort in R&D would bring. With only a few years left to run on the current production engines, top management is worrying what they're going to do with a huge assembly plant of over three million square feet of floor space with nothing to assemble. In one sense, this whole thing was sold before General Montgomery ever arrived. He is the innocent victim.

Shortly after the 1959 reorganization, Mr. Mintz was given the responsibility of being a project chief in addition to his duties as chief of the OR group. Unlike the typical project chief assignment, Mintz's project reported directly to the general manager of the division. Mintz was to coordinate not only engineering but also sales and production planning activities related to his particular project. With the increased responsibilities of his promotion, Mintz devoted less attention to the OR group. In late 1963, Mr. Weber expressed the following:

> About 80 to 90 percent of the time Mintz is over in his project job. Actually, for about the last three years, I have been running the OR group or really doing his job, although he's had the title. I've had pretty much of a free hand in operating and running the area, and working directly with the project chiefs and group chiefs. With Mintz being in the job by title but not having direct contact with the work, we lose a certain amount of "ear" at the management level. He's not up on everything that's going on in the OR group; he couldn't be when he's doing another full-time job. Being one level lower, I don't have a direct line to the management level when certain problems come up where we should be represented. He may be at some of the meetings, but he's not cognizant of some of the work we've done. And in one sense management will say the area is being represented and they want it represented; but he's not really capable of representing

it at this time. This really presents a problem. I think that the use of OR would have progressed a little faster if the situation weren't as hazy as it has been for these three years.

ACTIVITIES IN THE OR GROUP

Following the 1959 reorganization, the separation of coordinating activities from OR and the promotion of Mintz to his additional duties allowed Mr. Weber to redirect the activities of the OR group. He described the post-1959 activities as follows:

> We've primarily worked on the analysis of propulsion systems. Our OR activities have involved systems analysis rather than business analysis. We have helped in the definition phase of a project—the directions it should go and things like that. In the main this is a type of analysis they need in order to develop new weapon systems. We can analyze a given propulsion system and determine the various capacities and limitations that are inherent in the integrated system. Mr. Cassady, manager of propulsion systems, has been the principal user and has shown the principal interest. His interest is confined mainly to turbojet systems. Another area that has shown an interest has been the sales department. Several people, particularly the director of advanced engine sales, have worked closely with us in that a lot of the studies that we do are sales oriented, such as an attempt to show one of our power plants as superior to someone else's under a range of probable conditions.
>
> In addition to the system analysis function, another area for OR is in showing that the concepts that R&D are coming up with are good ones for the long-run development of the entire division as against an alternative approach to R&D. Essentially this involves problems flowing from the other direction—from top management. We've got several pressing problems of this type in the R&D department. One is the choice of projects and then the allocation of the resources of the division to the chosen projects. These two are related, of course, and I think we can be of some help on these. But the attitude here toward resource allocation and advanced planning using OR techniques has been less than favorable. I still envision this as an R&D department problem and as an R&D department task. Primarily it's R&D work and the systems planning committee's primary task is essentially this. An example of this kind of application would be when there are a lot of proposals or requests for proposals from the various military services or NASA and there has to be an evaluation and decision as to which should be bid. It's done on a hit-and-miss basis now; we could develop some logical criteria for selection, assign relative values to each proposal, and analyze various combinations of potential projects as alternative programs for the department.
>
> Finally, I see a third function for a continuing OR group. This would be the generation and improvement of OR techniques themselves within the group. We stumble across both the needs and potential of new

techniques as we make applications in various areas. Unfortunately we haven't gotten to this point with our group yet.

One thing we've always found—when we get a request for work, it is not usually a clearly defined request. We spend a lot of time trying to decide just what the problem is. Definition has always been one of our major concerns. In terms of the final approach to the problem, we generally determine this and seldom are refused by the manager requesting the work. This definition phase also gives us an "in" to generate additional applications. I would say that 50 percent of the work that we do is generated within our group. We see a need and tell the chief what we can do; he agrees and off we'll go and do it.

For the most part we have not been too much involved in coordination of the type we did with the publications responsibility when we had the technical writers. However, on occasion, because of our way of thinking of problems from the broad systems viewpoint, we end up working for a project chief. Like the project chiefs we had to work with the various group chiefs to get our work done. Cooperation has to be there. I've worked with most of the fellows long enough and know them well enough, and they know what we're doing well enough that cooperation hasn't been a major problem. We've worked most closely with the growing electronics guidance area. Lovio's suspicion of OR has caused some friction in our work with the design group, but my having worked with them when I first came to Western allows me to have a pretty good relationship with most of the people in that area. Of course, you can't be pushy with them; I've done many jobs for them and helped them out so that when I need something we usually work it out together.

When you consider the three functions that OR can fill in the Division—systems analysis, planning and project selection, and development of OR techniques—I guess the question is where within the organization we can most effectively perform the task. One possible place that OR could be located would be as a staff operation to the vice president for engineering, like the position that Paul Richards has as assistant. We have worked on some problems with General Montgomery which have filtered down to us through Mr. Richards. On the other hand, there are advantages of doing the systems analysis type of work—being down in the R&D organization gives us close working relationships with a direct line to the technical groups on whom we depend for information and mutual problems. If we tried to split off part of the group to go as a staff operation with the rest staying where we are now, we probably would lose the balance of talents that we now have.

We have many different kinds of people working in the OR group, ranging from mathematicians to economists. I don't want to divide the men into a substructure, because each one's particular talent may be needed on any given problem. Most of them have worked with me now for several years and identify me as their section head. It's been small enough that they know that I am aware of what they are doing.

I perform two functions—one is arbitration among the fellows, the other is to assign the men to the specific problems. On certain jobs where the scope is broad or unusual, I'll call a general meeting to discuss that job and in essence to get the benefit of the various talents in the group. Considering the value of these talents, it just doesn't seem feasible to split the group into separate operations.

On the other hand, as the group gets larger, more and more of my time goes to administration. There are a million administrative problems in this kind of operation. This is one thing that I don't like about the job—I'm getting farther away from the technical side. I really don't have time to get into an OR problem. In one sense I do stay involved—most of the fellows like to use me as a sounding board for their approach to various problems, and the blackboard in my office sees a lot of use. I try to provide time for them, but it's getting to be a problem of keeping track of each activity. In addition to this I have to make visits to various government agencies to explain our analyses and to make presentations at the various meetings here. Then I have the meetings of the Operations Research Society to attend several times each year.

THE SYSTEMS PLANNING COMMITTEE MEETING

In October 1963 Mr. Weber was asked to attend a regular meeting of the systems planning committee. He later described this experience as follows:

> We had a meeting of the systems planning committee where General Montgomery, Mr. Lovio, Harry Cassady, myself, and about three representatives of the sales department were present. We were discussing whether to start up a new project on a particular type of power plant, and if we did, what procedure we would use. I had some ideas which I expressed on how to go about it. I got shot at by Mr. Lovio in a general sort of way—not on the ideas but on the area of OR in general. He had used it as a scapegoat in many cases, always as an excuse for the government not letting more development contracts. "Too much studying being done and not enough doing," he would say. We have had a few discussions on this privately and also some openly before. He took this meeting as one of the times he was going to shoot me down. Well, it ended up with everyone talking at once. I happened to be sitting next to General Montgomery, so I started telling him my ideas on what should be done. He was sitting and listening while the others were talking in small groups.
>
> I was more than a little annoyed at the actions in this meeting. Being the junior man of the whole group by several levels, I was upset that none of my superiors had even attempted in any way or shape to defend the area of OR. I felt that if they call you into a meeting for something like this they want your opinion—that's what you are there for. You're not there just to sit around and listen. Otherwise they wouldn't want you in the meeting. At least one of them could have

defended the general area of OR. I don't think they necessarily had to agree with my specific approach to the problem, but I think they shoudn't have let me get shot at in the general area of OR.

I addressed this feeling to Mr. Mintz and Mr. Cassady after the meeting. We were in Mr. Mintz's office, and I told them that the support for me should have come from Dr. Reynolds in that he was at a high enough level to mean something and I was in the meeting because of him. About the time I was telling this to Mintz and Cassady, in walked Dr. Reynolds. Mr. Cassady said something like, "Dan felt like he didn't get any support today and that you're not in favor of OR!" Dr. Reynolds replied, "Oh yes, I am. Yes, I am; you know it, Dan! I felt like asking, "When?"

Apparently Reynolds later talked with Mr. Lovio because a day or two later he came by and apologized to me, saying that there was nothing personal in what he had said at the time. I had not taken it personally as much as a matter of needing support for the area and not having any reasonable success in getting it. There in an open meeting with General Montgomery and especially an outside influence, the sales department, we were having an inside fight. Maybe that's why I didn't get any support—no one wanted to have an inside fight at that time.

ANTICIPATED 1963 REORGANIZATION

The events surrounding the meeting described above were still on Mr. Weber's mind when he was informed of the impending reorganization. He commented to the casewriter at the time:

All this poses an interesting question for me. Should I shoot for top management or not? Where does one want to go? I think I could be happy staying in the OR type of work. I like the work; I like the challenge; and the headaches are relatively few compared with departmental management. The difference in compensation is not that great. It's probably more than double what I am getting now; but if I were chief, my potential salary wouldn't be far under that of departmental management. Of course, there is a great difference between what a departmental manager makes and what the divisional general manager is paid. Then you're talking over $100,000 a year, and I wouldn't be adverse to that position or salary.

I would like to see the area of OR move up. Sometime in the future I think it could become a division-level activity. Although this would not be top management or top salary, it would certainly be considered an advancement in terms of prestige or status. The status of the OR operation depends on the stature of the person running it. If he is valuable to the operation and they know it, the man and OR will get divisional-level rather than departmental-level position. The corporation will be forced to do this in order to hold on to the fellow. This is how I look at it from a practical viewpoint.

I go to meetings of the OR Society, and invariably the discussion

gets around to "how to sell OR." I have always been convinced that
you do not really have to sell OR; if you do a good job, it will sell
itself. We follow the idea that if people are not feeding us problems,
we ask ourselves: "What are the significant problems the department
is facing?" Then we attack them and put out what we've done. Once
that someone sees that an OR approach can be useful to them, they're
going to ask for more. I don't mean to sound like we can solve all
of the division's problems with OR, but I do definitely think we have
a valuable contribution to make.

EXHIBIT 6
R&D Department Ages and Seniority of
Management
(partial listing)

	*Age**	*Seniority**
Edward Lovio	65	20
Martin Haag	63†	14†
Raymond Montgomery.	61	4
Walter Cooley	58	20
William Ballard	52	16
Tom Reynolds.	48	18
Paul Richards	45	16
George Beckett	43	16
Harry Cassady	43	13
J. Escalona.	41	14
Frank Mintz	39	16
Fred Rinehart	38	4
Dan Weber	34	7

* As of 1963.
† At time of his retirement in 1956.

4 | *Randley Stores, Inc. (C)* *

In 1957, Randley Stores, Inc., operated over 100 supermarkets located in and around a large metropolitan area. Although a few small, "neighborhood" stores remained in the chain, most stores were large, modern supermarkets consisting of complete grocery, meat, and produce departments and offering up to 5,000 different items to the shopper. Since the early 1950s the company had added six to ten stores a year, many of them in new suburban shopping centers. See Exhibits 1 and 2 for recent sales and earnings data.

The food distribution industry had witnessed a number of changes in the post-World War II period These included a trend away from neighborhood ("mom and pop") stores and toward modern supermarkets, increasing population migration to the suburbs, a trend from service to self-service stores, and rapid growth in the number of different items handled by supermarkets. Merchandising methods had also undergone considerable revision with the advent of prepackaged meat and produce; increasing use of promotion premiums, stamp plans, and give-aways; and growing emphasis on both newspaper advertising and point-of-sale merchandising. During this same period, the industry had experienced a continued trend toward lower operating margins which reflected both severe competition and the need for increasing emphasis on cost reduction and effective control of payroll expenses.

---

* This case is a revision of Randley Stores, Inc. (A) and (B), supplemented by data from Paul R. Lawrence, *The Changing of Organizational Behavior Patterns* (Boston: Division of Research, Harvard Business School, 1958).

EXHIBIT 1
Selected Operating Data
(thousands)

Year	Sales	Net Income	Wages	Shareholders' Equity
1948	$ 45,879.1	$ 645.0	$ 4,502.8	$ 5,554.6
1949	50,227.2	758.0	5,278.2	6,137.1
1950	50,039.3	874.0	5,469.9	6,777.4
1951	56,453.8	780.0	5,642.6	7,316.0
1952	62,576.8	749.0	6,630.6	7,912.4
1953	66,791.9	827.0	7,482.5	8,439.5
1954	79,651.0	802.0	9,158.9	8,908.2
1955	82,430.3	1,003.0	9,710.0	9,561.7
1956	98,189.3	1,374.4	10,718.1	10,537.4
1957	123,106.2	1,757.8	12,980.9	11,846.6

EXHIBIT 2

RANDLEY STORES, INC.
Consolidated Income Statements
(thousands)

	Fiscal Year Ended 6/29/57	Fiscal Year Ended 6/30/56
Sales (at retail)	$123,106.2	$98,189.3
Less: Cost of sales and operations	119,643.8	95,345.6
	$ 3,462.4	$ 2,843.7
Add other income:		
Cash discounts on purchases, interest income, etc.	810.9	682.2
Gain on sale of capital assets, etc.	100.4	83.4
Income before depreciation, interest, and federal income taxes	$ 4,373.7	$ 3,609.3
Deduct:		
Depreciation of buildings, equipment, trucks, and automobiles	$ 1,039.2	$ 841.4
Interest on unsecured loans, etc.	203.1	127.7
Total.	$ 1,242.3	$ 969.1
Income before federal income taxes	$ 3,131.4	$ 2,640.1
Less: Federal income taxes	1,373.6	1,265.7
Net Income	$ 1,757.8	$ 1,374.4

THE 1954 ORGANIZATION

Exhibit 3 shows the 1954 management organization of Randley Stores. A central merchandising function negotiated purchases, set prices, and developed company-wide merchandising programs. The typical Randley supermarket, along with its parking lot, covered nearly half a city block

EXHIBIT 3
Partial Organization Chart, 1954

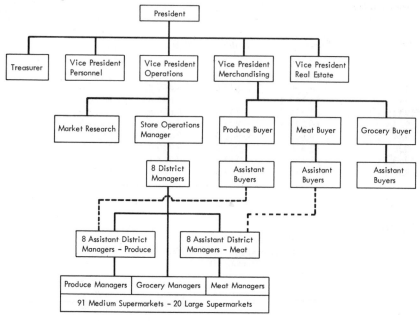

and employed upwards of 50 people (counting both full- and part-time workers). Each store had three separate departmental managers (for grocery, meat, and produce) each of whom was given direct and detailed supervision by a district manager or by his two assistant district managers (one for meat and one for produce). Final decisions as to new equipment, merchandise displays, employee promotions and demotions, work assignments, and much of the merchandise ordering were made almost entirely by one or more of the members of these district supervision teams. Each district manager and his assistant managers supervised 10 to 12 stores.

TOP MANAGEMENT'S REAPPRAISAL

By 1954 Randley's top management was becoming increasingly concerned with the pressures that both growth and changing industry conditions were placing on its current organizational arrangements. While considerable "centralization" had been useful during Randley's earlier years, new stores were now being built further and further away from the headquarters to handle an increasingly wide variety of merchandise, and for minimum volumes of $2 million a year. Management was also concerned with its competitive posture vis-à-vis modern supermarket chains, particularly those run by strong, local independents. One executive noted,

> Our toughest competition is from local independents. Chains don't bother us too much, but when a fellow is right there on the spot and can battle with local conditions, he's got an edge on us if we can't move quickly enough. What we've got to do is to be sure that we're always in a good competitive position relative to the other people in this business. We think the important thing in doing this for the next few years is to be a little more flexible and a little more aggressive in our stores, and in order to do that we have to have a clear-cut organization behind those stores. We want the advantages of the independent in being able to take quick, appropriate action on the local scene combined with the advantages of big business—merchandising specialists, high-volume purchasing, areawide advertising, well-known names, and that sort of thing.

On the basis of these concerns, a group of five high-ranking executives set out to study organizational approaches of other supermarket chains, to conduct extensive interviews with Randley personnel at all organizational levels, and to devise an improved organization for the company.

1955 REORGANIZATION PLAN

Based on the recommendations of its management study team, Randley instituted a set of major organizational changes in 1955. The objectives of this reorganization plan, which included altering the company's basic structure and developing new control and communication procedures, were cited as "decentralization" and "systematic mangement procedures."

Changes in Structure and Personnel

The first step in the reorganization plan was to make certain structural and personnel changes at the top-management level. The management study team had been particularly concerned that a split command at the top had frequently led to lack of consistent follow-up on programs as well as conflicting signals to department managers in the stores. To help remedy this problem the jobs of vice president of operations and vice president of merchandising were combined into the single job of vice president of sales (see Exhibit 4). The former vice president of merchandising was transferred to a different post in the company. The former store operations manager left the company and was replaced by one of the members of the management study group, and the newly created job of merchandising manager was filled by another member

EXHIBIT 4
Partial Organization Chart, 1955

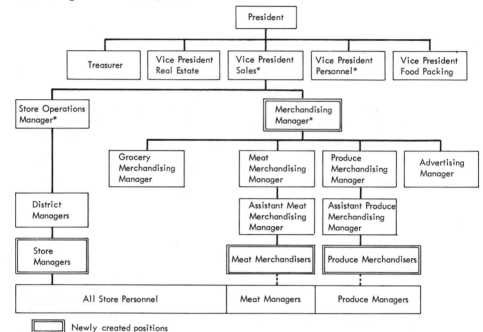

Newly created positions

* Men with major roles in planning organization.

of the group. These moves at the top level put the executives who initiated the reorganization plan in a position to exercise the formal authority to implement the plan.

These executives believed that the most important part of the reorganization plan was the development of a new position, the store manager, who would be responsible for all departments in his store. These jobs were to be staffed by people chosen from among the ranks and given a two months' training program in which they would spend time in each of the three departments in a variety of stores. Initially, these store managers would be assigned to newly opened stores; however, the ultimate goal was to have all stores headed by such managers.

Management hoped to gradually build a cadre of "strong" store managers who would play a key role in Randley's strategy of combining the advantages of a large business with those of a strong, local chain. More specifically, management believed that effective store managers could ultimately:

Provide their stores with unified administrative leadership,
Improve communications between the stores and the headquarters,

Develop more creative local merchandising methods,
Formulate the work toward systematic, planned objectives,
Deploy store personnel more effectively, and
Keep payroll costs in line.

One executive summarized these goals by noting, "We want someday to have real administrators running our stores—not just errand boys."

Closely related to the idea of developing strong store managers were certain changes in the supervisory link between the home office and the stores. Assistant district managers were shifted from the line function of directly supervising the perishables departments in each store to the staff job of acting as field merchandisers (see Exhibit 4). Where these men had been reporting to the district managers, they were now to report directly to their respective merchandising managers (formerly called buyers). The objective of this change was to build a single, unified chain of command from the store operations manager through the district managers directly to the new store managers, while still providing the perishables departments with staff merchandising help through the new merchandisers.

New Control Procedures

In addition to changes in structure, Randley began budgeting sales volume and payroll expenses in each of the stores. Prior to the start of each three-month period, each district manager was expected to work out with his store managers or department managers a target for sales volume and payroll. In turn, the store operations manager worked out his own targets for each of the stores. Then two sets of targets, which had been independently developed, were reconciled through discussions between the store operations manager and the district managers. Once these targets were agreed upon, they were used as a comparison against actual operating results, which were reported to the stores by four-week and again by three-month periods. The new merchandising manager simultaneously worked out sales targets by product classification (grocery, meat, and produce) with his different managers.

Management was also working on a more systematic way of evaluating field personnel. They looked to the new budgeting procedures as one source of information, but they were also adopting systematic forms for the periodic review of performance of each person in the organization. A program was also underway to write up more complete and accurate job descriptions for all positions. Management felt that the discussions which would have to precede an agreement on the new job descriptions would help the people in the organization to clarify in their own minds just what was expected of them. Also, the resulting descriptions would be useful in training people who were new to Randley or moving into new assignments. Management was particularly concerned that the descriptions arise out of meetings that were to be held at different levels so that greater agreement would be reached on the content and nature of different jobs.

A final program initiated by management was a new system for ordering merchandise in the stores. This procedure centered around a mathematical formula which used the previous week's sales for each item in a store as a basis for determining the next week's order for that item. The system was designed to keep each store's inventory at a minimum while also providing safeguards against its stocking out of any item. As part of this system, procedures were also developed for allocating shelf space for many of the items carried.

New Communication Procedures

As a final part of its reorganization plan, management developed several new communication routing procedures. Every other week all district managers were called to a meeting at the headquarters which consisted of two parts. The first part was a session with the merchandising manager and his key people to discuss future merchandising plans. The second part was conducted by the store operations manager to discuss with his district manager group some of their current problems. On alternate weeks it was planned to call all the store managers into a meeting at headquarters to have discussions of their common problems with the store operations manager. The new merchandising manager also conducted weekly meetings at headquarters with each of his major merchandising groups.

In addition to this schedule of meetings, top management developed systematic approaches for keeping in touch on an individual basis with people in the field. For instance, the store operations manager scheduled three days of every week to travel with his district managers as they made their supervisor tours of the stores. The other top people also scheduled a considerable number of days to travel with the district managers.

THE REORGANIZATION IN ACTION: DISTRICT MANAGERS AND STORE MANAGERS

Some six months after the reorganization plan was announced, a researcher from the Harvard Business School asked to observe some of the store situations in which organizational changes were occurring. The researcher talked with and observed several district managers over a period of several weeks and in a variety of contexts. The following data on district managers 1 and 2 are representative of the range of responses of this group to the reorganization plan.

District Manager 1

Beliefs about Himself as a District Manager. "One thing I've done lately is stop worrying about being fired. It happened mostly last summer when I was sick. I had a lot of time to think. I decided that it wasn't worthwhile worrying about things like that, and that I might as well go ahead and do what I was going to do and stop worrying about it. I also decided I was going to speak up more when I disagreed about something. So, I go ahead and say what I want to say, and I'm perfectly willing to take what follows. I don't think I'm going to get fired because actually I think I'm doing a pretty good job as a district manager."

"I'm the sort of person who is pretty critical of himself; and so when I think I'm doing reasonably well, that must mean that my bosses think that I'm doing pretty well."

"I don't think any of us should be too proud to use the good ideas that somebody else has."

"The important thing is to teach yourself the new tricks first, and then you might have a chance to teach someone else."

"I've always been known as a maverick in this organization."

Attitudes toward Subordinates. "My notion of a good supervisor is one who doesn't talk any more than his subordinates do. Of course, you've got to do some of the talking to explain to him the kinds of things he ought to know about what the company wants him to do, but you have also got to give him plenty of chance to talk about his problems and the things he has on his mind or you are not going to get very far."

"I'm interested in my store managers' opinions and, of course, I want them to know what mine are."

"I won't do the same thing every time I go into a store; if I did I would blow my brains out after a while because this job would be so dull. Of course, I don't do things the way I used to a few years ago. Even in the stores without store managers I've been letting the department managers handle more matters, like working out displays, than I used to, more than I imagine some of the other district managers do. Besides how the hell am I going to develop my men if I don't let them do things like that?"

"I believe that if a store manager can come up with his own answer to a problem, it is going to be the best answer in almost every case.

I may not agree exactly with the way he would do it; but unless he is really wrong, you ought to go ahead and let him do it in his own way and he'll be better off. That is the only way you can teach them to take the initiative on these matters."

"You know you can't expect perfection out of people, and different people work differently. They can't all be as fast as some."

"As far as I'm concerned, the number one part of a store manager's job is that he has got to have administrative ability. He's got to get people to do the job—that is the best definition of administration I know of."

"I let the store manager know where he stands. At regular times I sit down with the fellow and we work out a written report evaluating and improving his performance. It is done with the man right there because it isn't going to do him any good if we just file a report in the head office. Sometimes these sessions are pretty frank and a little tough on the fellow, but as far as I am concerned he has to know his shortcomings and straighten them out."

Attitudes towards Superiors. "The people who run this business make some mistakes but they are really decent people. I don't hesitate to disagree with [the vice president of sales] on something or other, and you can really discuss things with him. He's hardworking, too. Of course, after we have discussed things he has to decide what he is going to do; and if he says we are going to do something, I'll do the best I can to make it work."

"A couple of things came up recently that I think the district managers should have been consulted on by top managers. On one item I was so upset I got hold of my boss on the spot. It was a matter that affected the people in our stores, and the district managers should have been consulted before the decision was made. We are closer to the situation; and I think, actually, most of the top men would be glad to get our opinion."

"This is a very friendly company, and I don't know anyone in the company who is afraid to speak up to anybody else. It has always been like that since I can remember, and I think it stems largely from the top."

Attitudes toward Reorganization. "This store manager program is still pretty new . . . but I think it is already showing that it is paying for itself. We can add the store manager's salary to our store payroll and still have a better overall performance in that store. He can give us a lot of valuable supervision in there."

"I have to keep watching myself in working consistently through the store manager. Every once in a while I slip back into the habit of speaking to whomever happens to be handy when I see something I don't like, but you really lose the effectiveness of what you are trying to do if you do that. Sometimes I have to remind other people too that come into the store to deal with the store manager."

District Manager 2

Beliefs about Himself as a District Manager. "I think the first thing you are in here for is to make some money for the company. In order to do that you have got to go out and get a volume of business. You've got to be selling things and selling them in a way that doesn't run your costs up too much. To do that you have got to keep your shelves filled up with good merchandise properly presented. These are the fundamentals. If you do those things right, it will show up in the figures."

"I'm getting paid to have good merchandising ideas. Anybody who is a district manager has got to be interested in merchandise and selling merchandise, and in doing this you have to work with people to get them to understand this stuff so they can do it themselves."

Attitudes toward Subordinates. "You really have to train store managers to look after those details, and I have to follow up to make sure it is done. You see I've written out complete notes about everything I talked to this store manager about today so there is no excuse for his not doing something about them. Then I'll check these notes with him when I come back. You have to spend a lot of time with some of these fellows explaining these things to them."

"I find in my own experience that I can work much better with the people under me who've learned to accept my criticisms, even welcome them, instead of those who seem to be fighting them."

(*To store department heads*) "I want each of you fellows to know that the store manager is constantly getting demands from above on how to do things. When he comes to you with something it is not just personal, he is getting orders from the district people to do things, and he has to follow through on them."

"You saw that I had to go down and go all over with that store manager again what I want done on that drug counter down there. Now I've done all that before, and I've gone into all those details before. He told me once before it couldn't work out there and I showed him how to make it work, and then today we have to go right back through the whole thing all over again. Now that is not the way you should have to treat the manager. I shouldn't have to spell things out that way for him. If I had [store manager X] here I would just say to him, 'Put the drug counter up there' and that would have been the end of it. It would have been done. Now that is my idea of a good store manager."

Attitudes toward Superiors. "I may argue about something ahead of time, but once the decision is made, right or wrong, I will carry it out."

"This is the first time I've found out what this new system is all about. Can you imagine that! They ought to tell us about these things if people are going to come in and put them into our store."

"I used to be pretty outspoken and that was part of the thing that got me in trouble. I was known as the great dissenter but I've stopped all of that now."

"People at headquarters always accused me of not being patient enough to work out the problems that come along with new changes in the organization. I don't think they practice what they preach."

Attitudes toward Reorganization. "I'm one of the few people who doesn't like this new setup. I thought the old way was much better. I had a team with my two assistant district managers operating in my territory that you just couldn't beat."

"I'm one of the few guys in the business who thinks this whole inventory control theory simply won't work."

"I'm perfectly willing to live with the way things are. You sort of have to learn to do that, you know. I wasn't too happy when this country was being run by Democratic presidents but I lived through it, and there is something to be said for the things they did. It is the same way in this company. They have some reasons for doing what they are doing. I just don't happen to think it is right, but I'm perfectly willing to live with it."

INTERACTIONS BETWEEN DISTRICT MANAGERS AND STORE MANAGERS

The following are selections from interactions observed between the two district managers and their respective store managers.

District Manager 1

DM 1:   [SM], do you want to place an order for some new display steps with a formica top? Here is the story on them, and this is what it would cost you to order them.

SM: Let's see what that would figure out to be. It sounds like it would run to $400 or $500.

DM 1: Well, how many two- or three-tier displays do you have now?

SM: I've got three of the three-tier and two of the two-tier, so you see it would be a lot of money. I can't see spending that much.

DM 1: That is what I feel too, that is an awful lot of money. You've got to sell a lot of merchandise to make $500. Ok, so much for that. Have you figured out how much the wage rate changes are going to affect your weekly payroll?

SM: I don't think it is going to be very much.

DM 1: Well, I think you had better figure it out. I think you don't realize how much it is going to be. It turns out to be more in some of these stores than they think. It can easily be $100 a week.

SM: I don't think so. Last week we had a man out but we also had some overtime, and you see the figures didn't go up at all. I think it ought to go up at the most about $50.

DM 1: Well, maybe that's right. You may be that lucky, but I thought you might want to figure that out. Let's go on to something else.

On one occasion DM 1, SM, and the grocery department manager were having a discussion about the new inventory control methods.

DM 1: Well, I think you fellows have a point; but when our methods consultant sends in a report that we should mark merchandise when it goes on the selling floor and not in the basement, I've got to listen to him, even though that does require a whole new system, because I'm not a technician and I don't know about these things. My only point is—I say that let's not close our minds to this thing, because when a fellow like that comes up with a recommendation, I think we've got to consider it.

GROCERY MANAGER: What about the payroll in those stores? Is it the same?

DM 1: Yes, it is. It doesn't cost any more the other way; and as a matter of fact, it costs a little bit less and they cut down the inventory.

SM: Well, our problem here is that our shipment from the headquarters warehouse comes in on Thursday. Everybody in the store is on the selling floor, waiting on customers, and you can't concentrate on the storage area. You simply couldn't handle a demand marking system here, because our part-timers come in Thursday at three o'clock and they are here for three hours. Well, if those fellows had to mark merchandise, they simply wouldn't be able to get it on the shelves by six o'clock, they just couldn't do it.

DM 1: Well, I can certainly see that, and it is obvious that every store is not the same. But you fellows don't have the new shelf allocation system here, and when you do get that system you can go through a whole week on all but a very few items by just putting them up once. That is all part of the new inventory control system that is going in. Your shelves won't look as good—I know that, I won't argue that fact. The shelves and your display counters and tables may look very poor, and I don't like it. But it will cost you a lot less to put out merchandise on Monday, Tuesday, and Wednesday than on Thursday, Friday, and Saturday, when your whole selling area is packed with people. I think you are completely right, that when you don't have the shelf allocation system, you can't go to demand marking. You've certainly done a tremendous job here in this store, and I have no complaint at all about it.

GROCERY MANAGER: Well, yes, but it is all guesswork, though.

DM 1:   That is right. We've found, in the other stores that you can cut your labor way down if you're on the shelf allocation system, no matter how good guesses you have made in the past about the kind of stuff you need and when you need it.

SM: Well, when they put us over on that shelf system, I'll consider it.

DM 1:   Well, you're right. I think that is the time to consider it. You have certainly done a hell of a job here, and I think it is tremendous.

GROCERY MANAGER: Well, it's not just me, it's guys here like Bobbie. (*Points to a young fellow who is opening a carton.*)

District Manager 2

The researcher and DM 2 entered a store one day. DM 2 walked immediately up to the store manager and said:

DM 2:   Boy, it is hot in here, what's going on?

SM: Yeah, it sure is hot. I just went down and turned off the heating system.

DM 2:   Well, it is too hot. Just what are you doing about it?

SM: Well, this happened once before, and it got too hot. You see the thermostat is hooked up so it is tied in with the outside weather, and it works that way. There was something that didn't work right about it so I got the repair people out here to look it over, and they said they got it all fixed.

DM 2:   Well, what are you doing about it now?

SM: Well, I turned the heat off and I called the office.

DM 2:   Can you adjust the thermostat you've got?

SM: No, it is all locked up. You've got to get the maintenance people out here, and they are coming out.

DM 2:   Boy, it's just too hot in here, it's too hot.

SM: For Christ's sake, of course it is too hot. What do you think I've got my coat off for; even in my shirt it is too hot.

DM 2:   Well, what can I do for you on this thing? Can I give you any help until you get it squared away?

SM: No, I don't think there is anything you can do. We are doing what we can. I've got the heat turned off now, so it should cool off.

On one occasion the researcher observed the opening day of a new store. During the morning the only interactions between DM 2 and his new store manager were as follows:

DM 2:   [SM], you better keep an eye on the front entrance where they are passing out carriages and keep the flow in and out going steadily.

The store manager nodded and for the next four hours remained at that task almost continuously.

DM 2 told another store manager once to get some merchandise out of the employees' lunchroom, and when the store manager carried them out and set them in the hall, DM 2 then told him to take it down to the store office and put it there.

SM: Well, the trouble is the office is too full to put them in.

DM 2:   What have you got down there?

SM: Some cases of cash register tapes.

DM 2:   Well, that shouldn't be. The thing for you to do is to move that tape out there and then you can put this merchandise down here.

SM: OK.

After discussing some further points with this SM, DM 2 continued:

DM 2:   [SM], what I suggest for you to do is to get yourself a notebook just like this one I carry to keep these notes in that I'm telling you—to write down now. Then you will have them in one place and be able to keep track of them. It is sort of a little datebook. Well, I guess that's all I've got. Any questions?

SM: No.

Comments by Store Managers

The researcher talked to the various store managers who worked for DM 1 and DM 2. The following comments were typical.

SM: [who worked for DM 1]: Yes, I've really got a good deal here in this store because I've got good boys, and we work together pretty well. . . . There's a lot of little things that go together that make a good store. . . . The district manager has to be on your side. He can't be doing things that will keep you from moving in as boss, but there's a lot more to it besides that. You've got to have good personalities in the store on a department head level and on the store manager level, and if your district manager is going to criticize somebody or pay somebody a compliment, he should have you along and maybe he could mention it was the store manager's idea. So if you get all these things working together, and they are really all just little things, you're going to have a good store.

SM [who worked for DM 2]:   You know DM 2 really goes by the book on things like special displays and does things the way the company wants, and that's the way they have to be done here. He really sticks by the book and that's the way it should be, because, of course, if you go by the book, you're going to keep out of trouble. Now I know there's a lot of DMs who wink at stuff like that because they realize a fellow has got a few cases of junk that he wants to move, and island wings are usually a good way to do it. I know that Charlie has got a hell of a lot of stuff down there in the back room that he'd like to clean out; but, gee, if I ever let him start putting up carriages of merchandise around the store, he'd have those carriages all over the place. You know they don't stay in one place either. You put a carriage down there by that drug table that has a few items on it, and you come back in a half hour and some damned little kid has pushed it way over there to the coke machine. And you just can't have stuff like that. Of course it's the same sort of things in any job. You have to figure out what kind of a fellow your boss is and play the game his way. You figure out how your boss wants it done, and that's how you do it.

To secure a more systematic comparison of the behavior of DM 1 and DM 2, the researcher designed a simple method for recording interactions between these district managers and their various store managers.

EXHIBIT 5

DM–SM Interaction Analysis by Classification of Speech and Topics

Category	DM 1	SM	DM 2	SM
Average percent of talking time	58	42	75	25
Average percent of talking time asking questions	9	4	9	2
Average percent of talking time giving information	17	23	26	17
Average percent of talking time giving opinions	17	10	12	4
Average percent of talking time giving suggestions/directions	15	5	28	2
Average percent of new topics initiated	77	23	86	14
Average percent of total talking time of both DM and SM spent on people	48		11	
Average percent of total talking time of both DM and SM spent on merchandise	16		32	
Average percent of total talking time of both DM and SM record systems	22		47	
Average percent of total talking time of both DM and SM physical plant	7		10	
Average percent of total talking time of both DM and SM spent on small talk	7		0.5	

Notes:
1. Topics were classified as follows: Such questions as, "Is Joe doing a good job?" "What would you think of transferring Mary?" "Is Bill still asking for more money?" "Why did you assign that work to John?" were considered as "discussion of people." Under "merchandise" fell communications about the amount, kind, handling, and explaining of merchandise. Under "record systems" came all discussions of payroll records, procedures for scheduling people, sales figures, etc. Under "physical plants" were included discussions of store maintenance, housekeeping, new equipment, etc. "Small talk" was all joking, kidding, and talk not related to business.
2. The record of DM 1 covered 227 minutes of which 157 minutes occurred during early days of the week and 70 minutes late in the week. The number of separate comments were 1,115 recorded on nine separate store visits with three different store managers.

   The record of DM 2 covered 456 minutes, of which 293 were early, and 173 late in the week. The number of separate comments were 2,092 recorded on four separate store visits with three different store managers.

He recorded who talked; the length of each separate speech; the category of speech (i.e., asking a question, supplying information, giving an opinion, giving directions or suggestions); the type of topic involved (discussion of people, merchandise, record systems, physical plant, and small talk), and, finally, who initiated new topics. The results are shown in Exhibit 5.

THE REORGANIZATION IN ACTION:
PRODUCT MERCHANDISERS

Another important aspect of the Randley reorganization was redefining the roles of the former assistant district managers. This entailed their moving from a "line" job to a staff role as product merchandisers who advised and consulted with the perishable department managers in the stores while reporting to the merchandise managers of meat and produce at headquarters. This shift in job function, title, formal authority, and reporting relationships affected a group of 18 men.

Management was well aware that it would be difficult for these men to make an effective transition into their new organizational roles. Many of them were older, long-service employees. Furthermore, their new superiors, the merchandise managers, were senior company executives who would be accustomed to giving orders and pushing their subordinates to achieve a high sales volume and quick turnover on the perishable items. However, top management, and especially the vice president of sales (46, 24),[1] was convinced that this move was necessary to build up the proper role for the store manager without losing the merchandising know-how of the old ADMs. The store operations manager (38, 16) also stated that one of his big jobs with his district managers and store managers was in getting them to work together with the product-merchandisers in such a way as to develop the merchandising ability of the store managers as well as to insure good merchandising in the perishables departments.

Observations at Antioch

As part of his work the researcher spent a considerable amount of time in a new store at Antioch just before and after its opening. The following series of events center around the produce department in this store.

Around 12:30 P.M. on the day before the opening of the new store,

---

[1] Numbers indicate the age and years of service with Randley, respectively, of the individual involved.

the researcher saw the manager of the produce department standing in front of his empty display tables. The researcher asked him when his people were going to start putting up the produce and how long it took to set up a stand of this size.

PRODUCE MANAGER (46, 11): Well, we're waiting for the bosses to come out and tell us how to do it. You know the produce merchandise manager (55, 29) and his assistant (39, 20) have to set everything up on one of these openings, and we're just waiting until they get here, and then we'll all go to work. It'll be up, though.

Three weeks later around 8:00 in the morning, the researcher was talking with the store manager (48, 23) at Antioch:

STORE MANAGER: Gee, the produce merchandisers were in yesterday. You should have been here. They really raised hell. Of course, I really can't blame them too much because our men didn't use too good judgment over in the fruit department. You know, you are supposed to alternate the color of the green vegetables with the yellow ones, then the red ones, and so on, and then when they found out that they were backed up on lemons and limes—I guess they had about eight cases of lemons and three cases of limes—he really went through the roof. It's a funny thing about those guys though. They never ask, they just start raising hell.

Around 8:20 the researcher noticed the produce department manager putting up his produce. In the back room the "Number 2 man" and "Number 3 man" in the fruit department were busily wrapping produce. Since the researcher had never met these men, he explained to them that he was interested in seeing how this store got set up and some of the problems of running a supermarket.

No 3: Talk about business problems—you just stick around here a little while and you'll see plenty of problems (*laughs*).

No. 2: Yeah, we've got problems around here. You should have been around here yesterday if you wanted to see some real problems.

RESEARCHER: What was that?

No. 2: Oh, some of the bosses landed on me in here. They were really working me over. My head was bobbing back and forth so fast that I didn't know what was going on.

RESEARCHER: What was the trouble?

No. 2: Well, a lot of things. They thought we weren't doing the job right. Principally they were mad about the fact that we had some inventory piled up back here. I don't know what they think I'm supposed to do about this thing. They sent me in here to help out the produce manager, you know. He's an awful nice guy but he hasn't had much experience in these bigger stores. I'm supposed to be backing him up and helping him do this right. Well, what am I supposed to do? Do they expect me to squeal on my boss? I didn't fill out that order last week. About all I could do was take it.

RESEARCHER: Was this the assistant produce merchandise manager that was in here?

No. 2: Yeah, that's who it was. He and the produce merchandiser (44, 21) for the Antioch store. The assistant produce merchandise manager kept saying, "I'm not supposed to talk to you about these things, but . . ." and then he'd let me have another one. And he kept saying, "I've worked in a store, I know you can do this." Well, he may have worked in a store, but I'm sure he's forgotten how hard it is to estimate what your sales are going to be just two weeks after you've opened a new store in a new town. How do we know just what's going to sell? Why, for the first two weeks around here we couldn't get enough potatoes and onions to keep the shelves loaded up, they were selling so fast. So we ordered a good slug of them, and now we've got them backed up. This isn't a problem that is too serious. There is nothing in here that will spoil. We'll get it all unloaded by next Saturday. We just won't send in a big order this week, and we'll get it all out of the way. But they don't like that. They hate to see the inventory so they've got to jump on us for it. So you can see what we were up against. You stick around and you'll see some more today. I think the produce merchandiser is going to be back.

RESEARCHER: How do you figure that?

No. 2: Well, he must have been catching it yesterday. So he's got to dish it out to somebody. I think he'll come in today. I tipped off the produce manager as soon as we got in today to expect him around. It was the produce manager's day off yesterday, and I had to catch it all.

About 9:40 the researcher saw the No. 2 man out in front having a cup of coffee.

No. 2 (*in a whisper*): You should have been around a few minutes ago. Things are already happening.

RESEARCHER: What's the story?

The No. 2 man put his finger up to his lips and walked on into the store. The researcher followed him and saw the produce merchandiser at the produce tables rearranging the fruit and vegetables. The produce department manager was following behind him. There was no talking going on. The produce merchandiser was rearranging all the produce on the display table. A second later the produce department manager walked up and started rearranging the same boxes, trying to line them up perhaps even a little neater. The produce merchandiser said nothing during the next ten minutes except at one point when he said, "Tell your boys not to put these price tags on the baskets," and the produce department manager nodded.

The researcher walked up after a while and introduced himself to the produce merchandiser and told him a little bit about who he was.

RESEARCHER: Looks like you have some problems here?

PRODUCE MERCHANDISER: You leave this place alone for one day and everything goes to hell. (*He turned away after this comment.*)

Later, in a conversation with the store manager, the researcher learned that the store's district manager (DM 2) (55, 33) had been in the store on the previous day at the same time as the assistant produce merchandise manager.

RESEARCHER: What did DM 2 do when those head office guys were chewing out the fruit department?

STORE MANAGER: Oh, he agreed with them all along. I guess it did look pretty sloppy over there.

RESEARCHER: Well, then DM 2 joined in with them? I thought the merchandisers were supposed to come to you if they had any problems and not raise hell with the men in the stores.

STORE MANAGER: Well, it all depends on the guy. It's different under each one of them. Each DM is different, too. Actually, you know, this was a pretty drastic change for these old ADMs. They've had complete charge of their own departments for 20 years. This store manager program is a pretty big change, and I don't think they've gotten used to it yet. Also, I don't think they've gotten together with the DMs and ADMs and the store managers off in some hotel room someplace and really spelled out to everybody how this new program is supposed to work and particularly how these ADMs are supposed to behave in the store now that we have changed over to this program. It's a pretty big change for those guys to get used to, and it's not written down any place how we're all supposed to act under this new deal. I remember on the training program, when I was with a store manager, he went into his fruit department in the morning and asked to see some guy, one of the clerks, and the fellows told him he wasn't there any more. The store manager said, "What do you mean he isn't here any more?" And the fellow said the produce merchandiser transferred him last night. He was supposed to report to this other store in the morning. And the store manager said, "Temporarily?" And the other guy said, "No, permanently." We went back to the manager's office and he was really pretty upset about the thing because he figured, "My God, how's the store manager's program coming along if I don't even know what's going on in my own store?" And he said it made him look like a chump to everybody and tore down the whole store manager's program in the eyes of the fruit department.

But I don't know, those guys did have a point yesterday. Those watermelons looked pretty sloppy, and I certainly don't know how many watermelons are supposed to be cut at the beginning of the week. I figure the fruit man should know those things, or he wouldn't be a fruit man. All I can do is look at the department through the eyes of the customer like they told us on the training program, and if things look okay to me, okay, that's all I can do about it. But then these fruit guys come in here and tear everything apart.

RESEARCHER: Have you ever talked to them about it?

STORE MANAGER: No, I've never talked to them about it. Maybe it's good to have these outside guys prodding the fruit people now and again. After all, the guys in the fruit department see me every day and I don't know the details of this fruit business. But I couldn't go up to the produce

ADM and say, "Look here, you guys, if you've got any trouble bring it to me, I'm the store manager here." They'd go to DM 2 and he'd think I had a swelled head or something with my new title.

I don't know, it's not too bad though. As long as things run fairly smooth and we're making a profit that's all I can ask for. It'll just take time, I guess, and we'll have to sweat it out. But I know it's tough for those guys to change just like it was tough for me to change from being a grocery manager to being a store manager. After all, I had been in the grocery business 23 years as manager, and they must feel sort of the same way about it. I don't know what's in the company's mind, you never know. Maybe they'll do away someday with ADMs, you don't know.

DM 1 and Produce Merchandising

About the same time the researcher learned of another incident that involved conflict between the produce executives and the store executives—in this instance centering around the produce merchandise manager and another district manager, DM 1 (48, 22). This instance also gave the researcher a chance to observe the store operations manager (SOM) handling such a conflict between two important groups. DM 1 introduced the subject during a conversation with SOM in one of the stores.

DM 1:   I suppose you had a lot of fireworks in your merchandise meeting yesterday at headquarters?

SOM: No, not particularly.

DM 1:   I thought you would have heard a lot from the produce merchandise manager.

SOM: I heard a lot from the PMM afterward about some of the troubles you have been giving his stomach.

DM 1 (*with strong feeling*):   Well, that's nothing compared with what he's been doing to us. You know the produce merchandise manager dug into an issue here that for once I don't intend to give an inch on. I think I'm right on this and I don't intend to back down.

SOM (*to researcher*):   Maybe you'd like a little background on this issue. . . . We first got interested in prepackaging produce back, I think it was during the war. You see, the old practice in the produce business was to sell by the unit. You know, a dozen oranges, etc. But the best way of measuring most kinds of produce is by weight. More recently DM 1, in some of his stores, has been turning completely to the prepackaging of fresh produce and not using the scales at all on the selling floor. The current problem with PMM is partly this prepackaging thing with some other issues thrown in. As I got the impression from talking to him, he ran into a number of situations while he was out looking around at some stores of DM 1's on Wednesday that were an odd combination of circumstances. Partly they reflected matters of bad judgment on the part of some of our people in the stores, but, of course, the whole combination of events sparked PMM into blaming prepackging for the whole problem and he got very upset. This isn't the first time PMM has got upset, and he really gets upset. I'm sure it's true that he couldn't eat a thing for lunch Wednesday because what he saw bothered him so.

DM 1:   He wasn't the only one that was bothered.

SOM: Well, that's true, but you know PMM is sort of an artist about his work. He thinks almost constantly about trying to get the best possible kind of produce into the stores to be sold. He also has worked very closely with most of the men who are handling produce in our stores. He thinks of them as his boys, and he's trained a lot of them. When he sees something going on he doesn't think is right, he takes it as a personal reflection on him. I think he's got two or three comments in his whole barrage of statements that he had to say about what happened Wednesday—two or three things that have some logic to them. I think he mentioned one thing that is a potential problem in prepackaging. It's not a good argument for dropping the prepackaging, but it's an argument for something we've got to be careful about or we will get into trouble. He pointed to the fact that when you have to prepackage your produce this tempts the store to prepackage some of it the day before to have it ready to set out the first thing in the morning to get started fast when the store opens. He said if they start prepackaging too much of it the night before it's going to come out in worse shape than it would if they had put it up fresh on the day they were going to sell it. I think he's got something of a point here. Of coure, we have given our people instructions that they are to prepackage only a minimum amount the night before so that most of it will be freshly packed for the next day. If they are not rushed the night before, there is always a temptation to package too much and save the rush the next morning.

DM 1:   Well, that's all right, but it just wasn't true that that's what he ran into on Wednesday. I am willing to admit that the store he went into Wednesday morning wasn't in very good shape, but it was the day right after the holiday. He was dealing with a fruit man who likes to put all the stuff away when he closes down for holidays, so he didn't have everything in good shape when PMM went in there Wednesday morning. But he hadn't prepackaged a lot of that stuff before—it had just gone out that morning.

SOM: Well, in his mind there was too much prepackaging the night before.

DM 1:   But it really wasn't so.

SOM: Well, I think that's right, but you know PMM, he could have talked our produce man into agreeing with him.

DM 1:   Well, that's true. I know that department manager would probably say, "yeah, yeah" to PMM, just to get rid of him and save the argument.

RESEARCHER: When PMM sees something that bothers him, I take it he just starts talking to the nearest person.

SOM: Oh, he sure does. You ought to hear him, he really blows up. He goes at it full force (*he mimicked some of PMM's swear words*).

DM 1:   The worst part of this is that it was his own assistant merchandise manager who gave us the idea of going to complete prepackaging in the stores. It really saved us a lot of money. One thing PMM saw that he was upset about was that we were selling some junk peppers for the price of a higher quality pepper. He was right on that and that was a mistake, but the mistake was made in the warehouse when they sent us out junk peppers when we ordered high-quality peppers, and they charged us for the high-quality peppers, too. I'll admit that my produce men should have noticed that, but we didn't make the initial mistake.

At this point the produce merchandiser (PM 1) (39, 19) who covered most of DM 1's stores walked up and joined the conversation.

SOM: PM 1, we were just talking about the stores that PMM visited on Wednesday and got all upset about.

At this point DM 1 walked across the store to take care of some other business.

SOM (*to researcher*): PM 1 here is right in the middle of this whole problem.

PM 1: You're certainly right—I'm in the middle.

SOM: You see, he works for PMM's organization but he has to get along with all the people in the stores.

DM 1 (*coming across the floor*): Take a bite of this pear, PM 1.

PM 1: No, thanks.

DM 1: Isn't that an awful looking pear? We've got a whole bunch of these out in the back room.

PM 1: That's nothing, we've got an awful lot more down in the warehouse. We'll be spending a long time getting rid of those. We've been trying to do it in small baskets and then in individuals and then in big baskets, and we can't sell them any way.

DM 1: You were saying that PMM is an artist and really a terrific buyer. You know, I could make a few comments about his buying.

SOM: Just hold that, DM 1. That's not the issue here.

PM 1: You know, PMM got all upset because he didn't find things the way he wanted when he came into one of our stores, but he got there at 11 o'clock on the day after a holiday and was surprised that things weren't in good shape. He went out and came back at 1:30 and everything was all right by then. He just hit a store where our produce manager was really conscientious and put all his produce away for the holiday. That meant it took him longer to get it out on the shelves when he started out on a Wednesday.

DM 1: Well, I think we should have had one more man in that store that morning and that was my fault. But those mistakes happen once in a while, and PMM's got to expect that. Besides, if we let him have his own way, he'd have us having so many people in the produce department that it would run our payroll all out of control. Another thing is that he thinks that all the produce men ought to get up at 2 o'clock in the morning and start to work setting up their merchandise. He doesn't realize that these people are working on hours these days.

PM 1: You know that's absolutely right. During the Easter week I was out with him at 6:30 one morning lining up some plants to sell in our flower shops. He told me at 6:30 to call up the Highland Park store and speak to them about the plants. I started to go to the telephone to put in the call, and I suddenly realized that nobody would be at the stores at that time in the morning. I went back and told him that. He thought I ought to call anyway. He couldn't really get it through his head that people wouldn't be working at that hour of the day. He knows it but he just won't accept it. He had me going out placing phone calls to that store at quarter of seven, seven, seven-fifteen, seven-thirty, right on down to almost eight o'clock when we finally got somebody.

SOM: That's certainly true, he knows that we are on hours now but he does find it awfully hard to accept it. But I do think we have got a couple of things that we have to do now in order to smooth over this present problem that has come up with PMM. I picked up a couple of ideas from him out of all the rash of things that he is upset about that I think have a certain validity to them, and I think we ought to do something about them. As I get it, one thing I think we can do is to leave our scales out on the produce floor instead of taking them out of there and putting them in the back room. I think we could use them out there just for those few instances when we have to get started fast some morning on an emergency basis. Instead of stopping to prepackage some items then, we could just dump a few things out loose in the bin and sell them in bulk.

DM 1: Well, that makes a lot of sense. I can accept that all right. That's no problem; we can do that. As a matter of fact the only reason we took them into the back room is we thought we might use that space for something else. But that isn't important.

PM 1: Yeah, that's right. I think that's a good idea. We can bring those out and have them there for those special times.

DM 1: I want to make sure that everybody understands though, PM 1, that they'll just use them that way during an emergency period, and as fast as possible we're to get on a prepackage basis on all items so we can stop having a man look after the scales.

PM 1: That's right, we'll just use it for emergencies.

SOM: Another thing I think we could do is to lean over backwards to try to get our produce people to understand that they are not to prepackage any more than the bare minimum to get them started the next morning. That is, they're not to prepackage too much stuff the night before that will be a little bit less than fresh when they put it out to sell the next morning. They could get into some sloppy habits on that. I think PMM is right. It's something we can take care of though if we check up on them, give them close supervision, and train them right to do this job.

PM 1: That's all right, I will make that clear to them.

DM 1: Sure, that kind of thing could be abused. We'll have to watch that.

SOM: Well, I think if we really lean over backwards on this thing for the time being and try to make sure we don't get into those sloppy habits we'll be a lot better off, and of course that will help the situation with PMM.

DM 1:   Then you want no other changes?

SOM: No, aside from those things I think we ought to run just the same. And I want you to tell your men it's better not to take orders from anyone but you as the district manager, or, of course, the store manager.

DM 1:   Well, good. I'm glad to hear you say that.

SOM: There's no reason you can't have them say that very politely to anybody who starts trying to give them instructions.

DM 1:   Oh, that's right. I always tell them to be very polite about it but, nevertheless, to make it clear that they aren't in a position to take instructions from anyone but me or the store manager.

PM 1:   Well, that's fine. I think that's all right.

The District Managers' Meeting

A few days later SOM told the researcher that he was going to discuss the relationship between the produce merchandisers and the DMs at the next district manager's supervisory meeting. The researcher attended this meeting; and toward the end of the biweekly meeting, SOM raised the topic.

SOM: Now, I want to raise the general subject we're going to spend the rest of the morning on. That is the question of how it's working out with you district managers under the new setup for your special product merchandisers in meat and produce. DM 2, I think you're the one that asked that we have a discussion of this topic. Why don't you start in and tell us what you have in mind.

In the discussion that followed, DM 2 reported that he seemed to be getting somewhat slower action on the problems the product merchandisers should be solving. DM 1 reported that after working through some initial problems the new arrangement had been going very well. The rest of the district managers were either mildly positive or noncommittal about their experience.

At about this time the vice president of sales entered the meeting and sat quietly near one end of the table.[2] After a few minutes of general discussion, a district manager trainee who was attending the meeting spoke up.

DISTRICT MANAGER TRAINEE: One thing I've noticed while running around with some of these produce merchandisers is that it seems to me they're having a lot of trouble convincing some of the department heads in the stores to give them the space they want to handle the merchandise they want to sell. For instance, I was going around with a man trying to get space for this special on roses a week ago, and it was really pathetic to watch his struggles to get the space.

---

[2] The vice president of sales often came to these meetings late so that committee members would have "plenty of time to warm up" without his presence.

DM 1:   Now, hold on there. I don't think he had such a tough time.

VICE PRESIDENT OF SALES: Well, I'm glad to hear he did have a tough time. I'd much rather hear that people are fighting for space than apathetic about it. I like to see some of that fighting going on in the organization over who is going to have the space. It's only when that stops that I begin to worry about it.

DM 3:   I think it's a good thing, too. I think they're getting the space they need but I think it's a good thing that they have to argue with some of our store people in order to get it.

VICE PRESIDENT OF SALES: I think that's right. The final decision as to who should have the space should rest with you district managers and in turn the store people. The merchandise people have to convince you that they are going to be using the space to maximize your sales and profits.

DM 2:   Well, I'm glad this has come up because you know that's what really bothers me about this whole merchandiser thing. I was really bothered about that fellow canceling out our date to travel around with me simply because his merchandise manager happened to get the bright idea that he'd like to travel with him that day, and I was just wondering who really ought to have priority on that kind of thing.

DM 5:   The first man who made the appointment ought to govern.

VICE PRESIDENT OF SALES: Didn't your produce merchandiser tell his merchandise manager that he had a prior date with you?

DM 2:   No, that's what bothered me. He didn't even tell him. He just agreed to go with him and then called me back and told me he couldn't go with me.

VICE PRESIDENT OF SALES: That just isn't right. That's just plain discourtesy. There's no excuse for that. You really can't blame that on the merchandise manager. I think you ought to tell the merchandiser what you think of that, DM 2.

DM 1:   Well, let me mention something that happened to me. I'll have to bring personalities in on this thing but I think it's all just between us here in the room. I ran into PMM in one of my stores a while back and he was hopping mad because he discovered for the first time when he walked in that store that we were prepackaging some of our produce and preweighing it prior to putting it in the racks. He thought it was terrible and he told me he wanted it changed right there. I told him that the whole program had been cleared with his assistant and that I thought it made a lot of sense and was working out very well. Well, you know PMM can be pretty strong when he talks about these things. He wanted me to change it right on the spot. I didn't do it. I showed him what we were doing and talked about it, and I think probably a week from now he's going to be convinced that we've got the right answer to the thing. But he sort of acted as if he could tell us how to do that kind of thing in the store.

VICE PRESIDENT OF SALES: I want to make myself perfectly clear on this issue—and I can speak on this because I'm in an organizational position to make it stick. Those merchandise managers and the merchandisers under them are a service function to the district managers and to the store managers. The final decisions as to what goes on in the store are up to you men right here. If they start to dictate or think they can dictate what goes on in the store, it's up to you to resist their intrusion. Otherwise we're going to get all mixed up. And if there's any question about it, you know where I stand on this matter. And I intend to make it stick. I think 99 percent of the instances where there is an intrusion of this sort you people ought to be able to handle it yourself on an informal basis with the man involved. But you should feel perfectly free to force the issue on up if you have to get it settled.

SOM: I told the group earlier that on some of these instances where there's a problem on coverage, I could handle some of these things on an informal basis if they do get into trouble of this kind. (*To the men*) Sometimes if you let me know about it I can handle it without really causing a lot of trouble, and in other cases I think probably it would be better if you could handle it yourself through a direct contact with the merchandise manager concerned.

Vice president of sales: I can just imagine what happened to PMM on that thing. I bet he came back here and really bawled out his assistant for not telling him that he had OK'd that change in the store and to make sure that wouldn't happen again. What that thing with PMM amounted to was a slipup in communication between him and his own assistant. And if I know PMM that won't happen anymore; and as you say, DM 1, he'll probably be all for that plan as soon as he has time to think about it.

SOM: Well, I see it's after 12:00 and I think we've about squeezed this topic dry. Why don't we call it quits at this point?

Suggestion for a Meeting

About two months later SOM called on the vice president of sales with the suggestion that he hold a meeting with the product merchandisers to spell out clearly the merchandisers' position in the organization since the organizational change. SOM had received several reports from his district managers that the merchandisers were not happy with their present position as they saw it. Their old positions as ADMs had been recognized to be a stepping stone to the district manager's job, and now they feared they were in a dead-end assignment. Moreover, in the change some of the merchandisers had been given a number of the smaller stores to handle which, since they were older and not very profitable, were less desirable assignments than the large supermarkets.

In thinking over SOM's request for a meeting, the vice president of sales reviewed his own thinking on the purposes and goals of the organizational change as it related to the product merchandisers. It was his own conviction that the product merchandisers must assist the store managers, not only in helping them to run their stores but also in helping them develop merchandising ability. He thought to himself, "We are double-talkers as far as our stores are concerned. We tell the manager 'You've got to have a complete line,' and then the next day we come in and say, 'You're heavy on inventory.' We tell him he's got to give the customer good service, and then we come in and tell him to keep the payroll down. We tell him he's got to have a snappy looking fruit department, and then we come in and tell him that he's too heavy on perishable items."

The vice president of sales realized that this sounded contradictory, but he felt that there was a "razor's edge" in the middle that he had to achieve—a fine balance between good operation and successful merchandising. When the organizational change was initiated, he had realized there would be a potential conflict between the store manager who had overall responsibility for a given store and the produce merchandiser who was concerned with his limited area. He had predicted the conflict, and he also knew that it would be one of his big jobs during the year to deal with it satisfactorily.

The idea of a specific meeting with the produce merchandisers had not occurred to the vice president of sales; and he wondered whether or not such a meeting should be held, what it might accomplish, and what might go on at such a meeting.

5 | *Superior Slate Quarry*

PART 1

The Superior Slate Quarry in the 1920s was one of the largest and oldest in the Vermont—New York slate belt. It had always enjoyed a good reputation, not only for the product it turned out but also for its treatment of employees. It had recently been sold to Thomas North, who had formerly owned a minor interest in it. Although North had never directly operated slate quarries, his family had for two generations owned slate properties, and he was well regarded in the town of Gorham, a community of about 2,500 persons, where he lived. The population of Gorham was about one half Yankee, one fourth Irish, and one fourth Welsh.

Gorham's principal industry was slate quarrying and slate milling. The quarries where slate roofing was produced were located at the edges of the town. These slate quarries were open pits in which quarrymen drilled holes in the bedrock and blasted pieces of it loose. The large blocks were then hoisted on overhead cables from the quarry pit to the top and there lowered onto small cars on rails, which workers known as rockmen pushed to the nearby splitting shanties. The blocks were dumped off in front of the shanties, which were cheaply constructed wooden frame buildings about 10 by 10 feet in size. They were placed in rows along the track that ran from the quarry top.

Two slate splitters and one trimmer worked in each shanty; and at Superior Slate Quarry, there were eight such shanties. The splitters and trimmers were paid by the hour. The splitters worked on opposite sides of the shanty door while the trimmer at his foot-pedal trimming machine stood at the back. Although they were equipped with coal stoves, the shanties were usually cold in winter; and they were hot in summer. After a rockman had dumped his large block, which was always irregular in shape and size, the splitters marked it to guide them in breaking it up into sizes for the final splitting. This operation on the large block required a knowledge of the grain of the rock, for the block had to be broken along this grain. When the grain was determined, one splitter had to steady the block on its edge while the other splitter struck the block a blow with a large wooden mallet, called a "beetle." It usually required only one blow before the block fell apart along the grain line. When the block was reduced to three or four smaller blocks, the splitters carried them into the shanty.

Here, each took a block, turned it on its side, and proceeded with chisel and mallet to split it along the grain into thinner and thinner pieces. When the blocks were reduced to pieces about three sixteenths of an inch in thickness, the pieces were placed on a low table between the two splitters and in back of the trimmer. The trimmer took each piece from the table, placed it along the cutting bar of the trimming machine, and proceeded to make it into as large a rectangle as he could get out of the piece. After it was trimmed, an operation which usually took only four cuts of the trimming blade, he placed it in a pile according to size. The trimmer was also expected to keep the waste chips of slate cleared away from his machine. When the day's work was done, these piles of shingles were removed from the shanties and placed outside in long rows.

The slate mills were within the town, along the river from which they derived their power. In these mills, structural slate products such as flooring, tile, billiard table tops, and other articles were finished. Because of the scraping and cutting of the planers and saws, millwork was noisy and dusty. Millwork in general required less skill and experience than slate splitting. Pay for millwork was lower by about a third than for slate splitting.

Exhibit 1 provides a further description of the technology of slate splitting.

The splitters and trimmers employed at the Superior Slate Quarry were all Welsh, while the slate mill employees were primarily Irish. The Welsh were all born in Wales; in contrast, the Irish were mostly first generation, born in this country. The Welsh workmen were men past middle age, and few of their children were old enough to work at the quarries, and those who did were not skilled in slate splitting. Many of the Welsh became citizens; and although they could speak English, they preferred to use their native tongue. They were more thrifty than the Irish, and many owned their homes.

EXHIBIT 1°

. . . An intimate knowledge of the physical properties of slate is essential in properly breaking and splitting the blocks. A skilled slate worker will drive a wedge, or plug, into a plug hole until a strain is placed on the rock, and he then procures a straight break by striking a blow at a particular point on the rock with a wooden sledge. Thus he can within certain limits force a fracture where desired. The slate is split on the grain into masses about 14 to 24 inches wide, and these masses are then broken across into the desired sizes for splitting into roofing slates. Various methods are used to subdivide the slate masses across the grain. Where they do not break readily or where the surfaces are very uneven when broken, they may be placed on a saw bed and cut across with a circular saw. If this method is used the blocks as they come from the quarry are sawed across and are later scalloped in the grain. Sawed blocks present smooth, even ends that facilitate rapid splitting.

Some slates, however, break very readily and give a smooth, uniform surface. Under such conditions breaking by hand is considered more economical than sawing. At one quarry observed the block is notched on two corners with a chisel and a cut made in the bottom of each notch with a small saw. The block is then turned and the opposite edge is cut smooth with a chisel. It is then struck one or two heavy blows with a large wooden mallet at a point exactly opposite the notches, with the result that a smooth, even break is obtained. To cushion the blow and thus preserve the slate from damage, a thin flake of slate or a handful of fine slate rubbish is usually placed on the rock surface at the point where the mallet strikes. At one quarry where the rock breaks readily the corners are not notched but are cut with a small handsaw. The surface is then simply marked with a chisel which is struck repeated blows with a hand hammer. The slab is then turned over and sledged with a wooden mallet, or "beetle," on the opposite edge in the usual fashion.

. . . The trimmer takes the slabs from the splitter and cuts them to a rectangular shape. The most common trimming equipment in Pennsylvania is a straight blade about three feet in length run by a foot treadle. The outer end of the blade is attached to an overhead spring pole so that the blade strikes repeated blows when once set in motion with the treadle. The use of manpower machines undoubtedly diverts much of the energy that could be used in handling the slates, and obviously mechanical cutting blades would result in a considerably greater production of slate per man with a much smaller expenditure of human energy. The operators in the soft-vein slate belt of Pennsylvania are aware of the increased production that might result from the use of mechanical trimmers, but attempts to introduce them have been unsuccessful. This lack of success is said to be due to inability to increase on decrease the speed of the trimmer for different grades of slate. With the foot-treadle machine the trimmer runs the machine at a slower speed for the weaker slates. The mechanically driven machines, running at constant speed, so greatly increased the percentage of slate breakage that they were abandoned in favor of the foot-treadle machines.

° Excerpts from *The Technology of Slate*, by Oliver Bowles (Washington, D.C.: U.S. Government Printing Office, 1922), pp. 64–66.

PART 2

The Welsh kept to themselves socially and maintained their traditional clannish customs, habits, and beliefs. They mingled little with either

Irish or Yankee. It was generally recognized that the Welsh and the Irish did not get along well together.

The Welsh were without exception men who took great pride in the product of their hands; they had been accustomed for generations to working together in small groups. They looked down on work in mills as dusty, noisy, "unhealthy" places where "unskilled" Irishmen worked. They loved the rock and took great pride in working it by hand at every stage from quarry to yard. They often said: "Machines, no matter how well built, can never tell the grain. They leave marks which often mar the beauty of the finished stone."

The three men in a shanty helped each other with the work. Often, when the pieces to be trimmed were piling up, one of the splitters stopped his own work to clear away the waste chips which fell from the trimming machine. Likewise, when the trimmer was ahead of the splitters, he brought them fresh water from the spring or helped them carry their blocks. When the whistle blew for lunch, they all sat down together to share their food. Each night, as the men picked up their lunch boxes to leave, they viewed with pride the work of their hands. As they passed by their neighbors' shanties, they looked in at the neat piles and exclaimed at the number of squares others had finished. Then, talking in their native tongue, they moved on slowly toward their homes.

The superintendent at the Superior quarry was Mr. Williams, called "Jack" by the men. He was Welsh, and a leader among them in Gorham. His office was in a one-room building a short distance from the quarry. Here, he kept records on production, inventory, and hours of labor. He spent much of the day going from shanty to shanty talking in Welsh to the splitters. At other times, he visited the pit and checked with the quarry foreman on the rock.

PART 3

Four years after he purchased the Superior Slate Quarry, North was faced with the problem of deciding whether or not to invest a considerable amount of money to erect a large mill to house his slate splitters and trimmers. At this time the slate-roofing industry was receiving stiff competition from manufacturers of composition shingles. Although its competitors were able to benefit from technological improvements, the slate industry in Vermont, because of the nature of the rock, could use few new inventions. The slate rock still had to be split by hand, and the industry as a whole remained at the handicraft level. The Federal Bureau of Mines, however, had made an intense study of this problem and had sent materials on its findings to all slate quarry operators.[1]

---

[1] Examples of these materials can be found in Exhibit 1 and Exhibit 2.

EXHIBIT 2*

One of the most efficiently planned slate mills observed is that of the Auld & Conger Co., between Poultney, Vt., and Granville, N.Y. The plan of the mill is shown in [the figure below], which represents but three of the 10 units of the plant. The blocks are unloaded beside the track A, where they are reduced to proper size for the slate splitters. One skilled operator marks the position of drill holes on the blocks and supervises drilling and wedging, which may, therefore, be done by relatively unskilled men. The slabs when prepared for the splitters are piled on the arms of rotating racks, D, which occupy spaces in the wall of the closed shed. In cold weather cold-air currents through the spaces thus opened in the wall may be shut out by means of canvas flaps. The splitter working at E in the closed shed rotates the rack until the loaded arms are inside the shed within convenient reach. While he is occupied in splitting, a further supply of slabs is being prepared and loaded on the outer arms. The split slates are likewise placed on the arms of the rotating rack F, and by a half revolution they are brought within convenient reach of the trimmer at G. One great advantage of the rotating rack is that the trimmer is freed from the danger of accident to his fingers, a danger which is ever present where the splitter is throwing slates on the pile from which the trimmer is taking them. Belt conveyors H beneath the floor carry the waste from trimmers and splitters to dump carts on a depressed roadway at the side of the mill. Finished slates are piled on rack cars. In the morning the loaded cars are run out to the yards, and empty cars back to the trimmers for their day's work.

A roofing-slate unit may consist of two men, a trimmer and splitter, who prepare their own slabs from the larger blocks. At most plants the slabs are prepared for the splitters so that splitting and trimming are uninterrupted. Skilled slate workers having the slabs prepared for them may finish a maximum of a square an hour, though six to eight squares a day is an average accomplishment. A square is the amount of slate required to cover 100 square feet of roof.

PLAN OF AULD & CONGER CO. ROOFING SLATE MILL

A, Track for Bringing Blocks of Slate; B, Compressed-Air Line; C, Space for Block Makers; D, Rotating Racks for Slate Blocks; E, Splitters; F, Rotating Racks for Split Roofing; G, Trimmers; H, Belt Conveyor for Waste.

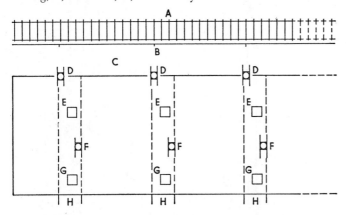

* Excerpts from *The Technology of Slate,* by Oliver Bowles (Washington, D.C.: U.S. Government Printing Office, 1922), pp. 66–68.

North, after looking over the government's suggestions for improving quarry methods, decided to draw up plans for a large mill to house the slate splitters and trimmers who worked at his quarry. He postponed the decision on whether or not to erect it until he had seen final plans, which he and Williams drew up together. (See Exhibit 3 for the plan of the new mill.) The new mill would eliminate many operations which the splitters customarily did. The blocks, as they came from the quarry, were to be brought into the mill by an overhead mechanical crane and lowered by electric lifts onto two saw beds, one at each end of the mill. Here, they were to be sawed up into correct sizes for splitting. The operation would not only relieve the splitters of breaking up the blocks but would also leave the blocks with one or more squared sides and would thus help the trimmers to eliminate waste.

Blocks would then be carried from the saw bed by an unskilled, low-paid worker to the splitters, whose only job would be to split the blocks. They would place the pieces which they split on a car, which was to be pushed over rails to another part of the mill where the trimmers would be lined up in a row at power-driven trimming machines. The trimmers were to be relieved of removing waste chips by another low-paid man. The finished shingles would be removed by motor trucks to the yard.

North designed the new mill to be more comfortable in winter than the shanties by installing a hot-water heating system. In summer the

EXHIBIT 3
Superior Slate Quarry, Plan of New Mill

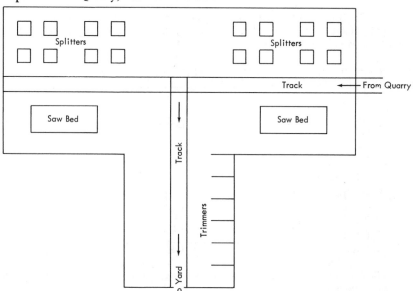

mill would be cooler than the shanties, since the ceiling would be high and the mill well ventilated. The saws, of course, would be noisy and would raise some dust; yet, it would not be harmful, nor would it compare with that in the mills in town.

By streamlining the flow of material, and by operating with the new machines and equipment, the superintendent and the owner expected production to improve substantially. The same number of splitters and trimmers were to be employed. The only new men to be hired would be the two sawyers, who were to be Welsh, and the two low-paid workers, who were to be Irish.

PART 4

When the plans of the new mill had been completed and North had made additional estimates of costs and production, he decided to erect the mill. When it was first completed and put into use, the men were enthusiastic about the change and expressed their satisfaction to Williams. After a month, however, they had less and less to say about the new setup. Some of the splitters even suggested that it was too dusty. They were not intent on their splitting work and often looked around as if to see what their neighbors, now more numerous than before, were doing. Some complained of the noise; and when the whistle blew at night, they wasted little time in leaving for home.

Fewer and fewer of the men passed "the time of day" with Williams when he came into the mill; and he, too, became less communicative. At first, he planned and carried out many changes which he thought would improve the efficiency of the operation. Later, he came less often to the mill and spent more time in his office going over figures in the production ledger. A typical series of figures for the months after the new mill opened was as follows: 1,248; 1,260; 1,250; and later, 1,175; 1,150.

After eight months of operation in the new mill, Williams advised North to raise pay rates 5 cents an hour. This increase brought the splitters' pay to 72 cents an hour and the trimmers' to 67 cents, higher rates than any paid in the slate district. Production did not increase.

6 | Continental Steel Company

In December of 1967 Mr. Grant Ambrose, assistant general manager for mills of Continental Steel Company's Lake Michigan Works, was considering the computerization of several proposed rolling mills. Continental Steel Company, seventh largest steel manufacturer in the United States, had pioneered the application of computer control to the rolling of steel with a computerized hot strip rolling mill in 1965. Ambrose was interested in seeing what Continental could learn from that experience as an aid to future planning of new mills and the implementation of computer control.

The Lake Michigan Works also had two manually controlled hot strip mills, as well as a number of cold strip, tin, shaping, and plate mills.[1] Mr. Ambrose was responsible for all of these mills, as shown in Exhibit 1. The Lake Michigan Works complex employed 22,000 people and was the third largest steel manufacturing site in the country. Over half of Continental Steel's production was located at this site.

Continental's computerized 80-Inch Hot Strip Rolling Mill was the first computer-controlled hot mill in the industry, and it had been the subject of widespread attention and numerous tours by industrial and educational groups. The 80,[2] as it was referred to by Continental personnel, incorporated many advancements in the state of the art as well as a computer controlled process, and differed in many respects from the company's older 76 and 44 hot mills. The 80's rolling mill was nearly a half a mile long, over twice as long as the 76, and was also three times as fast.

---

[1] Hot strip rolling mills rolled hot steel into strip and were called hot mills by steel makers.

[2] 80 refers to the width of the rolls on the mill.

EXHIBIT 1
Simplified Organization Chart–Lake Michigan Works

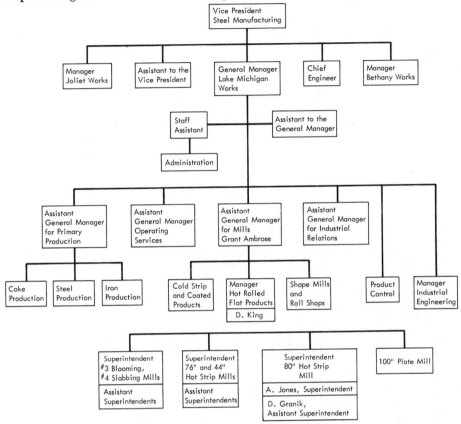

Six hundred and eighty employees worked in the 80's three-shift operation. Thirty men were directly involved in operating the process—10 on each shift's operating crew, as opposed to 20 per shift in the older 76. The remainder of the 680 employees were involved in supervisory maintenance, administrative, and supporting functions. All of the 80's employees had been transferred from the older hot mills and were experienced in steel manufacture.

ORGANIZATION OF THE 80-INCH HOT STRIP DEPARTMENT

The 80-inch hot mill was organized as shown in Exhibit 2. The mill's superintendent, Mr. Oscar Jones, reported to Mr. Dwight King, manager of hot rolled flat products, who in turn reported to Ambrose. The six general foremen reported to Don Granik, assistant superintendent.

EXHIBIT 2
Organization Chart—80-Inch Hot Strip Mill Department

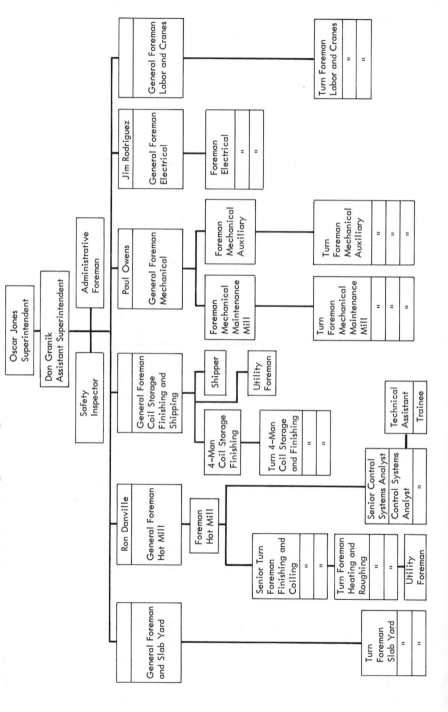

The mill's general foreman was responsible for the operation of the rolling process for all shifts, and as such was the most influential of the general foremen. The 80, unlike the other hot mills, had a foreman-hot mill, directly below the general mill foreman. It was felt that this additional level of supervision was needed to integrate the programming and the computer room activities with the mill's operational needs.

In actuality, both the mill general foreman and the foreman–hot mill were involved in both mill and computer room affairs, though the general mill foreman was more heavily involved in production activities and the foreman–hot mill in the computer room. In the realm of production, the general mill foreman concentrated on the more complex finishing end operations, and the foreman–hot mill on the preparatory and initial operations.

Since the mill operated on a three turns (shifts) per day basis, each turn had a senior turn foreman. The senior turn foremen and the senior control systems analyst reported to the general mill foreman through the foreman–hot mill. There were about 120 men working under the general mill foreman.

The 80's electrical and mechanical groups were organized differently than in other mills. Traditionally, the electrical and mechanical crews were matched to the various operating crews in a mill. In the 80, however, each group was organized into areas by equipment. For example, there were three electrical areas. The first included the least sophisticated equipment in the 80 such as cranes, furnaces, and the simpler equipment on the first part of the mill process. The second area included the 80's more sophisticated water treatment works and the roughing mills. The third area included the computer room and the very complex equipment in the finishing end of the mill. The mechanical function was divided into two areas, rolling equipment and all other equipment.

THE HOT STRIP ROLLING PROCESS

The hot strip rolling process was one of a series of processes in the making of strip steel. As shown in Exhibit 3, steel ingots were rolled into slabs by a slabbing mill before they entered the hot strip rolling mill. Hot strip mills were called hot mills because the slabs were reheated to about 2200° F in furnaces and then rolled into strip steel while still red hot. The coils of strip steel from the hot mills were then either sold directly to the customer or sent to the cold mills for further rolling and surface finishing.

The slabs which entered the hot mill were relatively large—averaging about 8 inches in thickness, 30 feet in length, and of varying widths (up to 74 inches). These slabs were reheated for two to three hours

EXHIBIT 3
Simplified Diagram–Steel Coil Manufacturing

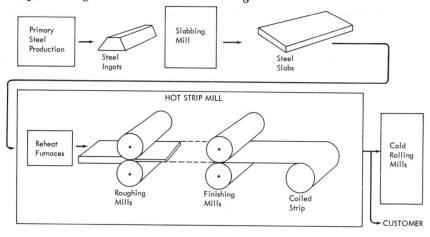

and then put through a series of roughing mills (each set of rolls was called a mill) for reduction in thickness and rolling to proper width.

The slabs moved along a long, conveyor-like mill table which passed through the roughing and finishing mills, and terminated at the coiler. After going through the roughing mills, the slabs were called bars. They continued along the mill table into the finishing mills where they were rolled to the required thickness. The bar would enter into one end of the finishing train (a series of finishing mills) and emerge from the other end as strip steel. The final process along the mill table was the winding of the strip into coil.

Continental Steel's 76 hot mill, built in 1932, was typical of manually controlled mills. Exhibit 4 shows its layout and the locations of members

EXHIBIT 4
Simplified Layout of the Manually Controlled, 76-Inch Hot Strip Mill

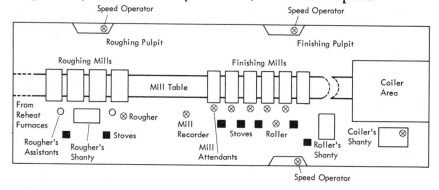

of the operating crew. To the uninitiated, such a hot mill was a noisy and dramatic place, with glowing hot slabs entering each of the rolling stands with a boom. The constant noise in the mill necessitated the use of hand signals for most communication on the mill floor. Normally a hot mill such as the 76 was housed in a large, unheated building which was hot in the summer and cold in the winter. Thus in the winter time, operators who were stationed along the mill table were alternately exposed to the intense heat of the bars going through the mill and the cold of the winter day. Often the area adjacent to the rolling stand was wet from sprays used in the process and from water which cooled the rolls. "Warming" stoves were placed along the mill table to alleviate these conditions in the winter.

Each slab which entered a rolling mill (whether computerized or not) was designated for a specific customer order, with specified finished coil dimensions for thickness, width, surface quality, and metallurgy. Continental Steel's central production planning department prepared a "rolling schedule" for each hot mill, giving the rolling sequence and dimensions of the slabs and the finished specifications on the orders to be rolled in a turn (shift). The rolling schedules were arranged in order of decreasing widths to obtain even wear on the rolls. Orders of similar widths and other dimensions were arranged together and called "sections."

TRADITIONAL MILL WORK ROLES

There were two key people in a manually controlled mill such as the 76: the roller, who as seen in Exhibit 4, operated the finishing mills, and the rougher, who operated the roughing mills.

The roller's job was the most critical to rolling good steel; and unlike the other members of the crew, he was salaried. His role was important because he determined the settings on each finishing mill for every bar processed. Since each bar and order was different, the roller had to call on his experience and judgment for setting up the mills. Often he was able to judge the settings for each of the finishing mills from "feel," while at other times he calculated them in the roller's shanty. Bad settings would result in unacceptable dimensions for the order, and, more importantly, incorrect settings could cause "cobbles" or "wrecks" in the mill.[3] A cobble spoiled the steel in the mill, but could also cause the scrapping of bars coming down the mill table behind it, if these bars cooled too much while the cobbled bar was being re-

---

[3] Cobbles occurred when the mills damaged the steel being processed so that it was unusable. A wreck was a cobble where not only the steel was ruined but the mill itself or the rolls were damaged.

moved from the mill table. Bars that were too cool to roll had to be removed and scrapped like cobbles. The decision whether to roll or scrap a cooling bar was made by the roller, since steel that was too cold to roll could cause a wreck in the mill, and wrecks meant the expense of damaged equipment (rolls cost about $20,000 a pair) and costly down time. Hence, the roller's judgment and his ability to make decisions quickly had a great effect on productivity and cost.

Most rollers had come up through the ranks and had a great deal of experience, the majority having worked 30 years or more in the steel mills. These men had "strong mill sense," which enabled them to determine how the steel would react under varying settings and conditions of pressure and temperature. The rollers often recorded unusual situations in little books which they carried with them.

The "art" still left in steel manufacture made the roller a valuable person, as reflected by the $20,000 to $25,000 a year in salary and incentive, which rollers of large hot mills normally received.

Each of the mills in the finishing train had a *finishing attendant*, except for the last mill. These men set up the mills for each slab according to the roller's hand signal instructions. The roller set the last and most critical mill himself. The speeds and accelerations of the finishing train were operated by the *finishing speed operator* who sat in the finishing pulpit, an enclosed room attached to the front wall about 30 feet above the mill floor with windows overlooking the finishing mills. The speed operator also received his instructions from the roller's hand signals. Because this job required considerable experience and skill, it was one of the highest paid jobs on the operating crew.

The *rougher* served much the same function for the roughing train as the roller did for the finishing train, although less skill was required to operate the slower and less complex roughing mills. This position was considered the top nonsalaried job in the mill. Roughers usually had worked in every job in the mill's operating crew and for the most part had over 30 years of experience.

The rougher had two *roughing assistants* who helped him set up his mills. There was also a *roughing mill operator* who worked in the roughing pulpit, similar to the finishing pulpit, overlooking the roughing mills. He set the rolling rate of the mill and observed the operation of the roughing mills and table.

The *coiler* and several *coiler's helpers* operated the coiling machines. Correct coiling had an effect on the finished coils' quality, and was, therefore, a critical part of the process.

With each new section (change in width or gauge), the *mill recorder* walked alongside the mill table ahead of the first slab of the new section and advised each operator of the change. The rougher and the roller then checked the change in section with their rolling schedules and calculated the necessary setups; each then walked along his train and informed his mill attendants and speed operators of the new setups by hand signals.

All of the operating crew were paid on a base rate plus incentive based on tonnage, and all but the roller were nonsalaried.

Each turn had a *mill turn foreman* who supervised the coil operations, the roughing train, and the furnace operations. Historically, these foremen had relied heavily on the rollers, who were theoretically under their direction for the technical aspects of setting the mills and rolling the steel. Foremen tended to concentrate on the maintenance and administrative aspects of the operating crew.

Considerable coordination was required along the mill table. The roller was dependent on the roughing mills for proper width and suitable dimensions of the bars, and both the roughing and finishing trains had to be coordinated for good pacing of production. Coordination was especially important when a cobble or wreck occurred, so that the cobble could be removed rapidly enough to minimize the loss of other steel. Once a bar or slab was in a mill it could not be stopped, and the ability of the mill personnel to act rapidly and correctly during a cobble was very important.

THE COMPUTERIZED WORK PROCESS
IN THE 80-INCH HOT MILL

The 80 had begun rolling steel manually in early 1965 and had first gone "on computer" in July of 1966. The computer was not the only difference between the 80 and the older 76 and 44. The 80's equipment was faster and larger, as evidenced by the 80's half-mile length, considerably larger than the 76's 920-feet length. The 80 was also capable of strip speeds of more than 3,800 feet per minute at the last finishing stand, which was over three times as fast as the 76. In addition, the mill included a large enclosed slab yard, as shown in Exhibit 5, and several adjacent support buildings.

Because of greater maintenance needs, the 80 averaged 25 percent down time, and the older mills averaged 20 percent down time.

The 80's production output averaged 3,000 tons per turn by December 1967, compared to 1,400 tons per turn of the 76. This greater output was achieved by the 80's 680 employees as compared to the 76's 900 employees. This increased productivity was due to the greater mechanization in the rolling and peripheral operations, as well as to the computer.

By late 1967, the computer calculated and set up almost all of the variables in the process, including all operations from the furnace to the coiling operation. The setup computations for all the mill stands were made by the computer, and the 80 had no rougher or roller. The computer also performed the section changes automatically, drastically

EXHIBIT 5
Simplified Layout of the Computer Controlled, 80-Inch Hot Strip Mill

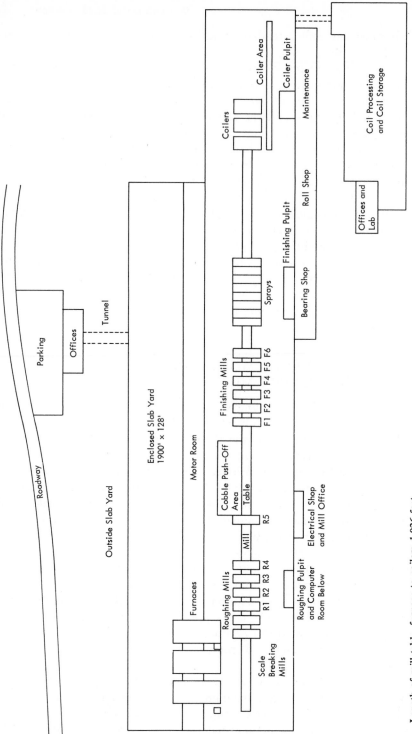

Length of mill table, furnace to coilers–1,926 feet.

changing the mill recorder's role. In the 80, the mill recorder worked in one of the pulpits, keeping records and announcing section changes over a public address system. His latter function was performed only as a safety precaution in case the computer failed to perform the change properly.

Each turn had a senior turn foreman who was responsible for the entire hot rolling process which included the furnaces, the roughing train, finishing train, and the coiler. Reporting to him was the heating and roughing foreman who supervised the furnaces, roughing train, and the 80's water treatment plant.

The rolling schedule for the 80 was prepared by the work's centralized production planning department, as were the rolling schedules for the 76 and 44. Production planning also prepared a punch card for each slab to be rolled by the 80, giving the slab's initial dimensions and the specifications of the finished coil to be rolled from the slab. These cards were then arranged according to the rolling schedule and fed to the computer in correct order.

The operating crew on the 80 included a roughing attendant and a utility man at the roughing pulpit (see Exhibit 5), a finishing attendant, an assistant finishing attendant, the mill recorder, and two utility men in the finishing pulpit. The coiling operation included a coiler and a utility man in the coiler's pulpit, and an inspector and several coiler utility men in the coiler area. The pulpits were attached to the front wall about 30 feet above the mill floor overlooking the process. All of the pulpits were heated and, unlike those in the older mills, air conditioned. Although the operating crew were housed in these pulpits, most of the area adjacent to the mill table was heated by large heaters.

As seen in Exhibit 5, these pulpits were approximately one-sixth mile . apart from each other. The roughing attendant monitored all of the setups which the computer calculated for each slab before it entered a roughing mill. These computer-calculated settings were displayed on a control panel in the roughing pulpit. The computer also displayed the actual settings of each of the six roughing mills. The roughing attendant intervened manually in the process any time the computer and actual settings did not match (a nonmatch caused the background of the incorrect setting to become red on the display panel). He also intervened whenever he felt that the computer's settings were incorrect on any of the 30 variables he monitored.

In the finishing pulpit, the finishing attendant operated the last three finishing mills and his assistant the first three. The speed and acceleration were usually set manually by these men, although the computer calculated and displayed speed and acceleration settings for each bar. They also monitored the displays for all other settings on the six finishing mills. As part of his responsibilities, the finishing attendant determined whether or not to roll steel that had cooled while a cobble was being removed. He often operated the mills manually for very wide widths of steel.

One of the utility men in the finishing pulpit operated a crop shear which cut off the tip of each bar before it entered the finishing train. The other utility man operated the sprays which were used to cool the strip to specified temperatures before it entered the coiler. Neither the crop shear nor the spray functions had been completely computerized.

All the employees in the 80 were paid on a base rate plus incentive based on production output. The operating crew shared in the same incentive, which was computed for each turn based on that eight-hour period's output. The electrical and mechanical support groups shared in another incentive based on each preceding two-week period's output. The furnace and slab yard crews shared an incentive based on a week's output. The other occupational crews, such as crane and general labor, coil handling, and shipping, also shared in incentives based on the output over the period of time influenced by their performance.

The operating crew, as in the older 76, included the personnel actually operating the rolling mills and the people in the coiler area. In late 1967, their pay, including incentive, ranged from $3.90 per hour for a utility man to $5.42 per hour for a finishing mill attendant. Incentive pay accounted for roughly 30 percent of the operating crew's total pay; the incentive pay earned by crews on different turns varied, with some crews making more than others. The crews worked eight hours per turn and ate when they could during the turn, since no formal lunch period was observed.

MILL MANAGEMENT'S PHILOSOPHY ON THE COMPUTER

As shown by the biographic data in Exhibit 6, the 80's management team had substantial steel-making experience. Oscar Jones had been superintendent of several mills before the 80; and assistant superintendent, Don Granik, was one of the few men who was a college graduate and a member of management to have been a roller on an important mill. Granik had rolled the 76 for over six years and was generally acknowledged to be a "top steel-maker with good practical knowledge of the business." The general mill foreman, Ron Danville, was mainly experienced in production also, although he had received considerable computer training and had presented a paper on the computer control of the 80 to a technical society.

Jones summarized the attitude prevalent among the 80's management by saying:

> Our philosophy is that the computer is a tool which helps us make better steel. The computer is on line about 95 percent of the running

time, and the operators are now glad to use it. But we want *them* to be responsible for the job. Our attitude has been not to be computer dependent. We want to be able to go off-computer and keep rolling steel if we have to. Some of the newer computerized mills in other companies are not like this. When the computer's down, the mill goes down.

EXHIBIT 6
Biographic Data–Key Management Personnel–80-Inch Hot Strip Mill

Oscar Jones, 44, superintendent, B.S. mechanical engineering. Began career in the electrical department.

Electrical general foreman	#3 & #4 slabbing mills
Electrical general foreman	#3 cold mill
Mill general foreman	76" hot strip mill
Mill general foreman (for pre start-up planning) 1 yr.	80" hot strip mill
Assistant superintendent, 6 mos. (for start-up operations)	80" hot strip
Superintendent, 1½ yrs.	76" and 44" hot strip
Superintendent, 9 mos.	#1, #2 cold mills
Superintendent, 3 mos.	80" hot strip

Donald Granik, 41, assistant superintendent, B.S. business administration. Began career as turn foreman in 76" hot strip.

Turn foreman ⎫	76" hot strip
Relief roller ⎬ 6 yrs.	76" hot strip
Roller ⎭	76" hot strip
Mill general foreman, 1 yr. 6 mos.	76" hot strip
Assistant superintendent, 2 yrs.	80" hot strip

Ronald Danville, 31, general mill foreman, B.S., M.S. engineering, Columbia University. Joined Continental Steel on its training program from college.

Turn foreman	76" hot strip
Turn foreman	80" hot strip
Senior turn foreman	80" hot strip
Foreman–hot mill (for phasing-in of on-line computer control)	80" hot strip
Mill general foreman	80" hot strip

Paul Owens, 29, general mechanical foreman, B.S. mechanical engineering. Joined Continental Steel after college. Considerable engineering and supervisory experience in mechanical area before being assigned to the 80.

James Rodriguez, 31, general electrical foreman, B.S. electrical engineering. Joined Continental Steel after college. Varied experience in engineering and supervisory positions. General electrical foreman in a mill before being assigned to 80.

Mr. Jones pointed out that one of the reasons that the computer room and the programmers reported to the general mill foreman was that Continental felt that those operations should be an integral part of the manufacturing operation.

Jones further commented:

> In my opinion it's not yet feasible to run the mill on computer 100 percent of the time because the computer doesn't have every possible situation programmed into it. We want the operator to intervene when he can handle a situation better than the computer. The reason for our attitude is that we have literally hundreds of analog signals which feed the computer information. They all come from input devices which sense the process. These input devices can deteriorate, and when they do, they give wrong signals. If the computer gets a bad signal it says tilt. When this happens you have to be able to keep rolling steel without the computer, because when you're working with hot metal you can't just stop, you've got to get it out of whatever part of the process it's in and quickly.

Mr. Granik elaborated on the fact that not all parts of the process were yet computer controlled:

> It hasn't been possible to put every single function on computer because some settings in the process are so variable and are affected by so many things that our program can only cover part of the normal situation. Our approach is to continue to refine these programs based on what we learn. When something can be done better manually than by the computer, we do it that way.

Ron Danville summarized his feelings simply by saying:

> I tell the men that the computer is a tool to use. They're still making the steel. When we can do something better with manual control, we do it that way until the program is improved.

BACKGROUND ON THE COMPUTER'S START-UP

The 80 began rolling steel in February of 1965 under manual control. The setups themselves were made manually but were calculated by the computer off-line. The computer was not put in on-line control of the process until July of 1966. During the year and a half period of manual control, the original programs were debugged and rewritten, based on the results of actual rolling experience. Mr. Jones amplified on this by saying:

> It's important to understand that we began rolling the 80 without a roller or an on-line computer. People used to ask, "How the hell is that mill rolling?" We rolled by using the computer's off-line calculations, trying them out, and improving on them. We kept a data log of these settings and their revisions, which we called the "butcher book." These improvements were fed back into the program. The off-line operaton allowed us to concentrate on the steel-making process before taking on all the problems of an on-line computer. We still use the "butcher book" whenever we go to manual control.

Mr. Danville described this period and his role in the following way:

> During this period we were finishing the wiring of the computer
> to the process, improving the program, and learning to roll the mill
> manually. I was a turn foreman and later a senior turn foreman through-
> out this time. I worked prettly closely with the computer room people
> on the debugging of the problem and also whenever we tried the com-
> puter on-line. On these occasions the systems analyst and I would go
> up to the pulpit and take the controls while the operators sat back
> and watched us. The operators didn't show any antagonism, but I think
> they were skeptical. They'd give us a lot of good-natured kidding.

Little conflict or direct interaction occurred between the operating
personnel and the computer room during this period except at Mr. Danville's level. There was, however, resentment on the part of some turn
foremen to claims made by one of the senior systems analysts that eventually the direction of mill practices would originate in the computer
room.

In preparation for putting the computer on-line, the mill went down
for four days. Concurrent with the transition, Mr. Danville was promoted
to foreman–hot mill and became responsible for both the mill operations
and the computer room, and the two senior systems analysts were promoted out of the computer room to other assignments. Mr. Danville
described the preparation for the transition to on-line computer control
in the following way:

> We brought in all the finishing and roughing attendants and the
> assistant finishing attendants and trained them in the pulpits using ghost
> slabs (slabs which the computer simulated). We tried to explain how
> their roles would change and we tried to give them an understanding
> of how the total system worked which included taking them down
> to the computer room.
>
> When we first went to the on-line operation, we had a lot of problems
> with the program as you'd expect. There were complaints that the com-
> puter had cut down production. I had to try and sell them on the
> short-term losses for long-term gains. The on-line wasn't hurting them
> in the pocket book, though, because the crew was on an interim incentive
> during the start-up which was a flat plan that paid some incentive
> from the first ton of output. This was because Continental didn't want
> to commit itself to an incentive rate until we knew what the true capacity
> of the mill was.

After the mill had gone on-line, the 80 became the subject of much
trade press attention because it was the first complete computerized
hot mill. Trade journals were more than generous in making claims
for the computer's capabilities, with the result that some personnel in
the mill felt that the part played by operating and support crews and
mill supervision was being overlooked.

In general, however, the acclimation to an on-line process went on without major hostility to the computer. Mr. Danville described the attitudes of the operating crews in the following way:

> We had problems, and the computer got blamed for a lot of things which it didn't cause. There were also some problems between the turn foreman and the computer room, especially when I wasn't around. But I don't think that there was ever any serious resistance to the computer. To begin with, we'd always been reliant on the computer for setups and calculations even when we were controlling the mill manually. The original setup calculations were good, better than most people felt they could have done themselves. So the initial performance was good enough to inspire confidence in the program.
>
> I don't think that the turn foremen resented the new role of the computer because the 80 is so much bigger and complex than the 76 or the 44 that coming here was a big step up in responsibility for the foremen. Their responsibility has increased as our tonnage has gone up and so has the foreman's esteem in the eyes of the people in the mill; so I don't feel they lost any prestige in the transition. Neither have the attendants, because they now control much more equipment than they did before.
>
> People became much more interested in the computer when we tried to operate it on-line and learn what could be done with it. Don Granik was a big influence in this because he took a close interest in the program and in seeing how it could be manipulated and improved. There are a lot of people who are interested in improving it now. Now that the system is more stable, the operating crews rely on it and can produce much more on-line than manually.

A number of supervisors in the 80 agreed that the greatest difficulty during the phasing in of the computer's on-line operation was in getting the operating personnel to understand the capabilities and limitations of the computer's program.

PROCESS OPERATION

The computer had been improved by late 1967 to perform the pacing of production coming down the mill; and since it had already performed most of the setup operations, there was much less need for interdependence between operators than in the old mills during normal operations. However, when a wreck or cobble occurred, part of the mill would go off computer, and the pacing function stopped. This required rapid coordination, especially between the coiler and the finishing attendant if the cobble occurred in the coil area, and between the finishing and roughing attendants if it occurred in the finishing train.

All of the pulpits were connected by a PA system which could be heard throughout the mill on loudspeakers. The PA was a key link during a cobble and also served as a means for informal bantering between pulpits, including some needling when production was being lost because of problems at one of the areas. "OK, you guys, why don't you get your hand out of my pocket," or, "It looks like you want to give all the tonnage to the next turn," were remarks characteristic of the kidding that went on. It was the mill's policy for operators to use their judgment in intervening with the computer. Often when an operator encountered a slab which was not behaving as expected, he would use the PA to warn the stations farther down the mill about it.

The PA was also used by the mill recorder to announce the next section coming down the mill as a backup net in case the computer failed to perform its integration function; this was a holdover procedure from the days when the computer was first put on-line. The mill recorder also posted the delay reports on down time and did other paper work.

The finishing pulpit was the busiest of the three, since the senior turn foreman had his desk there and a quality control man was also stationed there to record rolling information. Exhibit 7 shows a layout

EXHIBIT 7
Finishing Pulpits

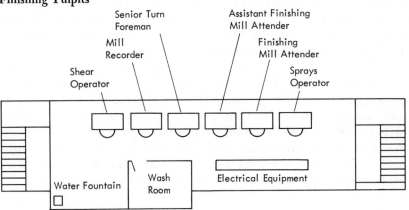

Personnel in or out of the finishing pulpit in an hour and a half period:
People shown in diagram above.
An assistant finishing mill attendant trainee.
A systems analyst.
Three electricians working on an item of equipment in the display panel.
Electrical turn foreman.
Roll shop foreman.

of the pulpit and lists the people who came into the pulpit in a typical 1½ hour period. A blackboard for posting turn information was located at the end of the pulpit. The blackboard was also used by the crew to spoof one another or management. As an example of this, the casewriter found a reference to a recent trade article about the mill's automatic roll changing equipment on the blackboard which read:

WELCOME TO FANTASYLAND

> Our role changes are completely automatic and they only take two minutes!

In contrast to the finishing pulpit, which a number of people entered over the course of a day, the roughing pulpit was often only occupied by the roughing attendant, joined occasionally by the utility man. The tone in all of the pulpits, however, was generally hushed except for the intermittent comments over the PA.

Compared to the older mills, there were relatively few people on the mill floor, except when an equipment problem occurred with one of the rolling stands, and in the words of one operator, "People seem to come out of the walls." When such problems occurred, the first person seeing the problem would call for mechanical or electrical personnel by sounding a horn which could be heard all over the mill or by using the mill's PA.

An example of the sense of immediacy in such a situation was observed by the casewriter during an early visit to the mill. Ron Danville, the mill general foreman, a utility man, the roughing operator, and some visitors were in the roughing pulpit when Danville noted that a bar was not entering a roughing stand properly. Danville and the utility man immediately ran to the roughing stand, while the operator pulled the bar out of the stand and called to stop more bars from coming. At the roughing stand, Danville determined that one of the rolls was not turning; and using hand signals, he communicated this up to the operator who sounded the horn for some mechanical assistance. While the repair was being made, the operator called for a crane to remove the cooled bar from the table. The necessary adjustment was made, and the mill was rolling again in less than five minutes' time.

THE COMPUTER ROOM

The computer room was directly below the roughing pulpit and housed the activities of the senior systems analyst, a control systems analyst, two programmers, a programming trainee, and four console operators—one for each turn. A large schematic display of the computerized process, arranged as a flow diagram showing the succession of operations, was built into one of the walls. This display had a light representing each location in the process where input devices tracked the slabs. The console operator monitored the complete process by watching the display. He also monitored the interventions made by the various operators and any "alarms." "Alarms" were print-outs by the computer indicating that something was wrong, such as an input sensor not operating, or that some parameter of the process was incorrect.

Whenever one of these situations occurred, the console operator would call the pulpit involved and warn them of the problem. Communications also initiated in the pulpit when an automatic adjustment failed to occur. The pulpit affected would call the computer room to inform them of the malfunction, in order to see if it was a program or computer problem. Any of the above situations would normally result in the affected part of the process going off computer control. Generally the communications between the computer room and the pulpits were not of a routine nature and occurred only around problems. Calls from the computer room were customarily made over a telephone line, rather than over the PA, although the computer room was connected to the PA.

OPERATOR'S REACTIONS TO THE COMPUTER

As suggested by the description above, the operator's roles in the 80 were considerably different from those in the older mills. Eli Smith, a finishing attendant, explained the differences:

> The biggest difference is that with a computerized process a man has a lot more responsibility than in the old mill, a lot more to worry about if he does this job the way it should be done. Maybe you do less physical work than before, but there are lots of things that you have to check on, be on top of. In the old mill there was a speed operator, and an attendant for each mill in the finishing end. And the roller told them all what to do. Each man was responsible for concentrating on one part of it except for the roller. Well now, me and the assistant attendant watch all of it. It's a strain; you always monitor the computer because you know it isn't right 100 percent of the time. A good operator catches it before there's a problem.
>
> With the computer on the process, any one of a hundred little things that isn't right, like a bad heat detector or a slipping motor someplace, affects the process. The program does the right thing only when everything is right. Most of the time the computer is OK. But you have to be watching for the one time that something goes wrong. That's the difference between the good operator and a guy who isn't so good.
>
> Now if a guy doesn't give a damn, and a lot of them don't, he doesn't feel the strain. The computer's great for him. He just sits back and doesn't worry about it until he has a wreck in the mill.
>
> Just the opposite thing happens if you get a man like Slovak (an assistant finishing attendant) who worries a lot. In a job like this he has real troubles because there are a lot of things to follow on the panel. He gets very anxious, so that when something does go wrong he panics and he makes a mess. He's all nerves. This morning we

were having troubles—all morning—and Slovak was so nervous I wouldn't let him touch a control. I had one of the trainees work the first three mills.

. . . We worry about a lot of the things the roller does in the old mill and we have to do the watching that the five mill attendants do in the other mill. I guess you could say that the finishing operators and the computer have replaced the roller.

But people haven't changed. You got a guy who is interested in making good steel, he was good in the old mill and he makes good steel here, too. He uses the computer to help him. The guys who were weak or didn't give a damn in the old mill are the same ones who have troubles here.

Tom Slovak, the assistant finishing mill attendant referred to above, described his feelings in the following way:

It gives you a different kind of fatigue. You're mentally tired; it's not physical. I get all strung up at the end of a day. In the other mill I could get along on five hours' sleep and once I got in the mill I was wide awake. But here, I can't do the job unless I've had eight hours' sleep because it's constant concern—watch everything and it moves quick—everything is faster than the old mill.

Another operator commented about the men's attitudes by saying:

Most of the men like the computer. But when things go haywire you'll hear them say it's because of the "goddamn computer." Things will be better when the programmers gain a little more experience. Every time something goes wrong and the mill goes off computer, the reasons go down to the computer room. Eventually all this information will make the programs better. We've got some good supervision here—guys who know the computer business and understand the steel end of things. That's what's going to make this baby work—bringing the computer know-how together with the experience of running the mill.

MANAGEMENT'S REACTION TO THE COMPUTER

The computer not only posed changes in the concerns of operators but, as implied above, in the concerns of the mill's management. Mr. Jones discussed some of the differences in managing a computerized mill by saying:

We have all the concerns they have in the older mills plus all the problems that are unique to a computer. The older mills have been shaken down but we're dealing with new problems. The decisions are not as clear-cut. You now have to determine whether the cause of a problem is internal to the computer, or because of our mill practice, or a combination. You constantly have to be asking if the computer is really helping you.

One thing it's done is make everything more interdependent. The computer requires that everything electrical and mechanical be in pretty top shape. Before, the roller could keep rolling with a mill limping along because he knew from experience how far he could go. The computer is much more sensitive and has narrower limits, and it won't work with bad equipment. Don Granik and the general foremen get together in a daily meeting to coordinate around mill problems and sort out what's causing what.

There are so many more interdependencies now that responsibilities are not so clear-cut. In the old mill I could pin the responsibility on someone. Here it's hazier. But I know I'm responsible for everything.

One of the problems in managing a computerized operation is that we have a tendency as a society to (*a*) oversell process computers and (*b*) feel that the computer will take care of everything. For example, people on the top don't understand the limitations. They tend to say, "How the hell can you be off gauge—you've got a computer!" The salesmen sell its capabilities to the customers, and this results in closer and closer manufacturing tolerances.

Don Granik further elaborated on the issue of people's expectations of a computerized process:

Sometimes people in higher management and in other parts of the company just don't have awareness of the limitations of a computerized mill or what it takes to make it run well. People expect such unrealistic things from the mill, that it's hard to get a sense of personal achievement especially if you pride yourself on being a steelmaker. You know what you're doing, but not too many people outside really appreciate what's involved.

One of the problems is that no one had a computerized hot mill before Continental. Our sales force developed a good story based on "a computerized process." Most of our competition reacted by also building computerized mills, some of which are now finished. The general result was that everyone's sales force attempts to oversell their capabilities to top the competition.

The whole industry has talked itself into severe restrictions. And everyone is forced to talk it up when in fact many are having a rough time. You don't hear this through official channels, but over a couple of beers from the guys who run the mills, after a conference or after a visit to their mill.

As implied in Mr. Jones's comments, the computerized process had resulted in a greater interdependence between the electrical, mechanical, and mill crews. Both the electrical and mechanical general foremen felt this had affected their jobs.

Mr. James Rodriguez, electrical general foreman of the 80, attempted to describe these differences in the following way:

> Electrical is much more important to the successful operation of the 80 than in a noncomputerized mill. It means that we have to understand the process of making strip from slab, because the electrical is now so interwoven with the process that the operating crew has to rely on us more. It also means that we may get blamed for quality which in other mills would be unheard of. You'd blame some operators for being off gauge. But here it could reasonably be our fault. We also have a greater effect on the pacing of tonnage because it's automated.
>
> The computer has also made us work closer with mechanical because the automatic control requires that machines be better mechanically than in the old mills. This makes the problems a little fuzzier and it's harder to determine the cause. It's not so clear whether it's a mechanical or an electrical problem, so we often have to work at it jointly.
>
> Owens (mechanical general foreman), Danville, and I get together with Granik every morning and go over the delays of the past 24 hours and decide who attacks what. It's natural for mechanical or electrical to try to minimize his effort and move it on the other, so that's where Don (Granik) comes in; he assures that the right decision is made.
>
> The electrician's life here is also different from the older mills. Our men have to deal with some pretty sophisticated equipment so they need to be highly trained. In fact, the Continental Apprenticeship Program[4] partially resulted from our need for better trained electricians. Most of the electricians have a strong interest in electrical things, and they like to study on the side. A lot of them transferred here because they wanted to work on the equipment. But we also have a few people just looking for a job.
>
> Some of them are still afraid of the monster and feel relieved when a foreman or an engineer arrives when they have a problem. A guy has to have a lot of confidence in himself not to feel afraid of it.

Paul Owens, mechanical general foreman, described the influence of the computerized process on his group:

> Automation affects us more than the computer aspect of it. To do something automatically, everything has to be mechanically right. And to do things automatically you need more mechanical equipment. This requires more inspection, preventive maintenance, and actual maintenance.
>
> In the old mills you could just go out on the floor to see what the problem is. Our problems show up in the read-out or feedback from the computer. It can be a gear that's wearing, and the slight

---

[4] This was a program whereby mechanical and electrical apprentices attended special session: taught at a large well-known midwestern university for Continental, which covered a number of basic sciences and advanced subjects. Completion of various portions of this program enabled these personnel to advance rapidly to senior skilled job levels.

wear has to be fixed or the computer won't react correctly. In an old mill the part could go until it broke down completely. This means you have to prethink and anticipate problems and the foreman has to then plan the shutdown turns in much more detail.[5]

In other mills, electrical have their problems and mechanical theirs, and they can work pretty independently. But here we can't. We meet every morning at 9:00 with Don Granik to decide whose problem is what.

For example, the computer calls for a section change and the side-guides don't move to the new position. The operator calls an electrician, and he sees it's not the electrical switches that are causing it. So they tell us and we investigate to see if it's the gears or some other mechanical problem. We can narrow it down pretty much by looking at it more closely. That will generally give us an area to look at on the down turn. We also get this kind of thing from the mill people. But in an older mill you'd never hear about it until it physically broke down because it wouldn't make any difference until then.

The demands on the mechanics are different also. The problems here are not obvious. When a finishing attendant calls for a mechanic, it's usually not a problem that he can see. The older mechanics are stumped about where to look. They're not used to figuring things out. He has to have the mental ability to put things together and figure things out. The Continental Apprenticeship guys can do this. The older guys aren't threatened because they're so secure, but they're probably a little bitter because it took them so long to make top grade, and the Continental Apprenticeship Program allows men to go up rapidly.

MANAGEMENT'S CONCERNS FOR THE FUTURE

The mill's management had a number of concerns about the future and related problems. Mr. Jones described the generally greater reliance on the computer by the operating crew as a mixed blessing:

Now that the programs are all running well enough so that we're on computer most of the time, we find that when we do have to go off computer we don't produce as much as we used to in the manual, off-line days. People are no longer used to coping with all the details they used to. Should we arrange it so that people perform some functions manually when we're on-line so that they can better handle these situations when they occur?

Another problem is building the men we need to run computerized mills. You have to have someone who can talk everybody's language at the general foreman, assistant superintendent, and superintendent's level. How do you build this kind of man? What kind of experience should he get?

---

[5] The down turn was a weekly eight-hour period when the mill was closed down for preventive maintenance and repairs.

Mr. Granik also had some concerns for the future:

> Most of the people in the 80 came with plenty of mill experience. A lot of them had good mill sense. But the next generation will be completely computer dependent and they will have very little mill sense. Can you give people mill sense in a computerized process? I think you can, but how do you do it?

Both Jones and Granik were aware that these questions had some bearing on the larger issue facing Mr. Ambrose and Continental's top management in assessing future computerized mills. They also wondered what could be learned from the 80's successes and difficulties which would be of assistance in planning new computerized operations.

Readings

1 | Organization Change and Development

Larry E. Greiner
Louis B. Barnes

The gap between designing a new organization on paper and bringing it into reality is the domain of organization change and development. Kurt Lewin, a famous social psychologist, once wrote that a social organism becomes understandable only after one attempts to change it. It often happens therefore that management's awareness for a new organization design emerges only after the start of an intensive change process. And even if it were possible for an omniscient manager to develop a master blueprint before introducing organization change, it is doubtful that other employees would readily accept the new design or have the required skills for making the design work. For these reasons, managers need to be as skillful at handling the question of *how* to introduce change as they are in diagnosing *what* needs to be changed.

The cases and readings in this section of the book focus on large-scale organization change, not on individual or small group change. The latter are obviously essential building blocks to organization change, but by themselves do not assure that a larger organizational unit will itself be transformed. Attention to additional variables beyond the individual and group is required in any organizational change, including such dimensions as multiple levels of authority, relationships between departments, environmental forces impinging on the organization, the climate of the organization, and the nature of the work flow that moves across departmental boundaries.

We shall first discuss some common objectives of organization change, then describe a few basic approaches to change, and finally identify some underlying concepts and issues that pertain to understanding and managing the overall process of organization change. The reader should be cognizant during this discussion that our knowledge about organization change is still in its infant stages; research has only begun to make some promising inroads. At present the collective experience of many organizations and managers remains the best source of knowledge. Several of these experiences have been reported in the cases in this section of the book. This reading presents some useful ideas and conceptual guidelines for interpreting what is happening in these cases.

OBJECTIVES OF ORGANIZATION CHANGE

If one were to "step back" after observing a number of organization changes, a variety of goals would seem to be present. These goals may be explicit and written down, or they may be implied by the actions of management. On the surface, the most common goals can be categorized under such labels as higher performance, acceptance of new techniques, greater motivation, more innovation, increased cooperation, reduced turnover, and so forth. Organizational changes are frequently directed at one or more of these general goals.

Underlying these more obvious goals are usually two overarching objectives: (1) changes in an organization's level of *adaptation* to its environment, and (2) changes in the internal *behavioral patterns* of employees. Organizations are continually struggling to adapt themselves better to their external environment. Because the management of an organization cannot completely control its environment, they are continually having to introduce internal organizational changes which allow them to cope more effectively with new challenges presented from outside by increased competition, advances in technology, new government legislation, and pressing social demands. Most frequently organizational changes are introduced in "reaction" to these environmental pressures. In some cases, however, changes are made in "anticipation" of future pressures. This latter course, while more difficult to pursue because employees do not recognize its immediate importance, is a standard that can often be applied to organizations that lead rather than follow their industries. Such "proactive" organizations can be said to engage in attempting to change their environments as well as themselves.

The second goal of organization change, to achieve modifications in behavior patterns, becomes obvious if one recognizes that an organization's level of adaptation is not improved unless many of its employees behave differently in relationship to each other and to their jobs. Organizations do not operate through computers but through people making decisions, and every organization has its unique patterns of decision-making behavior. These patterns stem from both formal and informal ground rules which specify how a "good" manager or employee should behave in relating to others and in making decisions. Thus, any organization change, whether it be introduced through a new structural design or a training program, is basically trying to get employees to adopt new patterns of behavior and ground rules for relating to each other and to their jobs. For organization-wide effects to be felt, these new behavior patterns must emerge not only within superior-subordinate relations but between and within work groups, and extend out to include larger subsystems (departments and divisions) of the total organization.

APPROACHES TO ORGANIZATION CHANGE

Organization change can be introduced through any number of approaches, used singly or in combination. Some of these approaches emphasize the content of what is to be changed, others stress the process of *how* change is to be accomplished.

A commonly used conception of the *what* approaches is presented in a later reading by Harold Leavitt, who delineates three approaches to organization change: "structure, technology, and people."[1] "Structural" approaches introduce change through new formal guidelines and procedures, such as the organization chart, budgeting methods, and rules and regulations "Technological" approaches emphasize rearrangements in work flow, as achieved through new physical layouts, work methods, job descriptions, and work standards. "People" approaches stress alterations in attitudes, motivation, and behavioral skills, which are accomplished through such techniques as new training programs, selection procedures, and performance appraisal schemes.

Other descriptions have focused more on the *how* approaches to organization change. Larry Greiner, in another paper based on a survey of previous studies of organization change, identifies seven approaches most frequently used by managers.[2] He categorizes these approaches under three alternative uses of power.

A. Unilateral Power:

1. *The Decree Approach.* A "one-way" announcement originating with a person with high formal authority and passed on to those in lower positions.
2. *The Replacement Approach.* Individuals in one or more key organizational positions are replaced by other individuals. The basic as-

---

[1] H. J. Leavitt, "Applied Organization Change in Industry: Structural, Technological, and Human Approaches," in *New Perspectives in Organization Research* (New York: John Wiley & Sons, Inc., 1964).

[2] L. E. Greiner, "Patterns of Organization Change," *Harvard Business Review,* May–June 1967.

sumption is that organizational changes are a function of a key man's ability.

3. *The Structural Approach.* Instead of decreeing or injecting new blood into work relationships, management changes the required relationships of subordinates working in the situation. By changing the structure of organizational relationships, organizational behavior is also presumably affected.

B. Shared Power:

4. *The Group Decision Approach.* Here we have participation by group members in selecting from several alternative solutions specified in advance by superiors This approach involves neither problem identification nor problem solving, but emphasizes the obtaining of group agreement to a particular course of action.

5. *The Group Problem Solving Approach.* Problem identification and problem solving through group discussion. Here the group has wide latitude, not only over choosing the problems to be discussed, but then in developing solutions to these problems.

C. Delegated Power:

6. *The Data Discussion Approach.* Presentation and feedback of relevant data to the client system either by a change catalyst or by change agents within the company. Organizational members are encouraged to develop their own analyses of the data, presented in the form of case materials, survey findings, or data reports.

7. *The Sensitivity Training Approach.* Managers are trained in small discussion groups to be more sensitive to the underlying processes of individual and group behavior. Changes in work patterns and relationships are assumed to follow from changes in interpersonal relationships. Sensitivity approaches focus upon interpersonal relationships first, then hope for, or work toward, improvements in work performance.

Although both Leavitt's and Greiner's conceptions are useful, they can be taken too simplistically. One can infer that "structural" approaches are rather formal, impersonal, and arbitrary, while "people"-oriented approaches are more humanistic and democratic. This quite obviously does not have to be the case. Alterations in organization structure can have a strong "people" focus in terms of trying to promote more collaboration or give more autonomy to managers. On the other hand, a "people" approach, such as one based on sensitivity training, can, if used inappropriately, turn out to be quite coercive and stifling to individual autonomy and creativity. In addition, more than one approach will likely have to be used in any organization change. For example, a "people" approach, implemented through the use of a training program to teach new behavioral skills, may fall flat if new structural arrangements are not found to encourage the application of these learned skills on the job.

Notwithstanding these qualifications, one can identify certain common denominators which cut across all approaches. Managers need to give recognition to these denominators because they imply important choices which have to be consciously considered rather than left to default.

a) Plan (from structured to unstructured)

The process of change can be carefully planned in advance with a particular strategy imposed on the situation. Or it can be allowed to emerge as various issues become clearer to the people involved. Some changes can be introduced through a series of detailed steps and time-tables, such as "Tomorrow morning the top team has to get together and decide such and such." Or it can be more open-ended, such as, "Let's send all our key managers off to a training program and let them apply whatever they learn in their own individual ways."

b) Power (from unilateral to delegated)

While the introduction of change through a new formal structure may at first glance seem like a very "directive" approach, many organizations have permitted plants or departments to design their own structures in place of having one imposed upon them. In contrast, an educational approach to change, while seemingly nondirective, can be imposed and administered in a very directive and mechanical fashion. At heart here is the issue of power—who is making the decisions and on what basis? Unilateral decisions tend to be based on the positional authority of top people, while delegated decisions depend more on the knowledge and skill of lower level managers.

c) Relationships (from impersonal to personal)

Every approach can take on very personal or impersonal overtones. An educational approach can directly confront managers on their personal leadership styles or it can impersonally acquaint them with new style alternatives through lectures and readings. A new structure can be implemented with much discussion and explanation of personal implications or it can be described in the impersonal tones of a formal document. Just how far one goes in terms of personal considerations is a difficult but important decision to be made in any change process.

d) Tempo (from revolutionary to evolutionary)

All approaches take on a particular tone in terms of just how far and how fast the change process should evolve. A structural change can begin with many far-reaching changes or it can start more modestly, on the assumption that wider changes will gradually evolve. Much testing will go on as a change takes its course to determine and clarify the limits of the change process. In some situations it may make sense for the process to happen in a piecemeal and gradualistic fashion, while in others it may require a more immediate and wide-ranging approach to provoke the changes required in the behavior of employees.

At the risk of sounding "middle-of-the-roadish," our own experience suggests that orthodox adherence to extremes on any one of these dimensions is not likely to be very effective. Rather, the intriguing challenge, we believe, is to find new and complementary combinations of these extremes—such as a structured plan that permits unstructured actions to emerge! For example, certain degrees of structure may be essential for bringing together appropriate people and focusing their attention on specific problems. Beckhard's article on "The Confrontation Meeting" illustrates how key managers can be required to attend a meeting and discuss change-related issues in a planned sequence.[3] At the same time, solutions to the problems identified by these managers are not planned in advance. Rather they design and "tailor-make" their own solutions as they interact within a structured problem-solving atmosphere.

MODELS OF ORGANIZATION CHANGE

Organization change is far more complex than the particular approach used to implement change. A variety of forces are usually at work before any approach is even decided upon. In addition, once a particular approach comes into contact with a complex organization, many unanticipated problems are likely to arise. Too often managers are quick to grab for a neatly packaged approach to change without knowing if it is appropriate to their situation. Their action-oriented concerns frequently take them into questions of what *should* happen before they are sufficiently clear on what is *actually* happening.

One way for a manager to get at what is actually happening is to have in mind a conceptual framework about the change process. This can help him avoid the pitfall of falling back on his own assumptions and intuitions about change, which frequently say more about the particular manager than about his situation. Recent research has made avail-

---

[3] Richard Beckhard, "The Confrontation Meeting," *Harvard Business Review*, March–April 1967.

able some useful conceptual ideas which may help managers to see their situations more clearly and objectively. These concepts also suggest certain actions which may be more appropriate at one point in the change process than at another.

The principal overarching concept is to think of organization change as an evolving *series of stages.* It is quite clear from research findings that organization change does not occur in one fell swoop. Rather there are obvious phases which set necessary conditions for moving into subsequent stages. Omission of one stage appears to make it exceptionally difficult for the change process to continue forward on an effective basis. When top management overlooks an early stage, they often find themselves frustrated and perplexed as resistance grows at lower levels. A common response at this point is to "push harder" instead of recognizing that numerous managers, including themselves, may have to learn to crawl before they walk.

Kurt Lewin was the earliest pioneer in identifying three phases of change: unfreezing, changing, and refreezing.[4] The unfreezing stage represents a necessary first step in stimulating people to feel and recognize the need for change. Here some provocative event is usually necessary to motivate a person to search for new ways of relieving his suddenly felt anxiety. Next, the changing stage involves the introduction and application of new methods and guidelines for change. Finally, the refreezing stage offers the necessary reinforcement to insure that new behavior patterns are adopted on a more permanent basis.

This basic model of Lewin's has served as a foundation for more intensive inquiry into not only the specific nature of various change phases but the relationships between them. Organizational researchers have pointed to two major processes of change which appear to underlie all stages of organization change. One is a "micro" process of *social and personal learning,* where managers gradually unlearn old patterns of behavior and adopt new ones. Historically, this learning process has been treated as one which usually does not require a preparatory and more formal educational experience. For example, organizations shifting to decentralized structures have often let managers learn on the job as they adjust their behavior to new and more autonomous role demands. Recent years, however, have seen more formal educational methods used in preparation for change, such as programs based on personal counseling, sensitivity training, or the Managerial Grid. These programs have developed out of a growing recognition that managers frequently need more explicit educational guidance and personal insight than they are able to obtain indirectly on the job.

---

[4] K. Lewin, "Group Decision and Social Change," in T. Newcomb and E. Hartley, eds., *Readings in Social Psychology* (New York: Holt, Rinehart & Winston, Inc., 1947).

An examination of the influence learning process is presented in a paper by Dalton.[5] His scheme, in Figure 1, highlights four broad phases and four specific subprocesses of learning. These stages and subprocesses were identified primarily from a survey of five studies of relatively "successful" organization changes. Dalton's model makes clear that the learning process for managers is far more complex than merely acquiring new cognitive or intellectual skills from a classroom lecture. Rather, in instances where individuals are successfully influenced to change their behavior, he found that the self-esteem of those being influenced had often been threatened, prior social ties were broken, new objectives were set with outside help, experimental solutions were attempted, and finally, increased self-confidence resulted from successful and rewarding applications of new behavior on the job.

A second and more "macro" process cutting across all stages of change involves the question of power and its distribution within the organization. Any change in decision-making patterns usually requires a change in allocation of power. Moreover, research evidence strongly indicates that large numbers of managers cannot learn and apply new forms of decision-making behavior unless top managers with more power are willing not only to give their encouragement to the adoption of new forms of behavior, but also to set consistent examples in their own behavior. An intriguing issue now being debated among students of organization change is that of "power equalization" versus "power expansion." Power equalization implies that power is a fixed quantity which requires that some managers must gain and some must lose power during an organization change. On the other hand, power expansion suggests that it is possible for *all* managers to increase their power over decisions. This occurs when managers A and B adopt a mutual problem-solving attitude where they can combine their ideas, influence each other, and, as a result, develop better solutions than if they were acting alone.[6]

Support for the power expansion theory is presented in Greiner's reading.[7] He surveyed a large number of organization change studies to find that successful changes evolved more from shared power than from unilateral or delegated approaches. For the shared approach to work, however, a particular sequence of phases appears necessary. Figure 2 reveals that initially key power figures become disturbed by external and internal pressure; then they seek help from an outsider; followed by their willingness to engage in "shared" problem-solving discussions

---

[5] See G. Dalton, "Influence and Organization Change," unpublished paper, Harvard Business School.

[6] A more thorough discussion of the power expansion versus equalization theories can be found in Arnold Tannenbaum, *Control in Organizations* (New York: McGraw-Hill Book Co., 1968).

[7] Greiner, "Patterns of Organization Change."

FIGURE 1
Dalton's Model of Induced Organization Change
(phases of change)

Processes of Change	Tension Experienced within the System	Intervention of a Prestigious Influencing Agent	Individuals Attempt to Implement the Proposed Changes	New Behavior and Attitudes Reinforced by Achievement, Social Ties, and Internalized Values—Accompanied by Decreasing Dependence on Influencing Agent
Setting objectives		Generalized objectives established	Growing specificity of objectives—establishment of subgoals	Achievement and resetting of specific objectives
Altering social ties	Tension within existing social ties	Prior social ties interrupted or attenuated	Formation of new alliances and relationships centering around new activities	New social ties reinforce altered behavior and attitudes
Building self-esteem	Lowered sense of self-esteem	Esteem-building begun on basis of agent's attention and assurance	Esteem-building based on task accomplishment	Heightened sense of self-esteem
Internalized motives for change		External motive for change (new scheme provided)	Improvisation and reality testing	Internalized motive for change

FIGURE 2

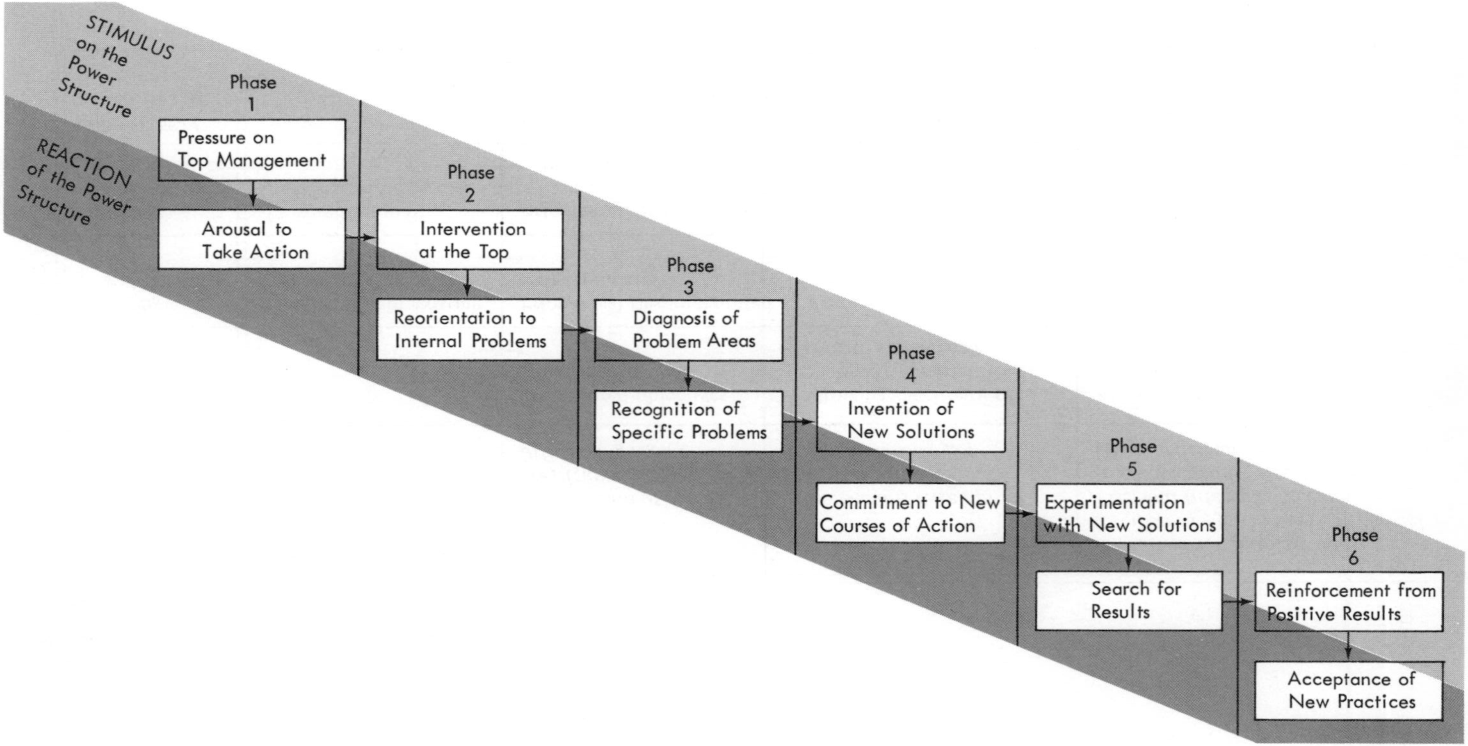

STIMULUS on the Power Structure

REACTION of the Power Structure

Phase 1
- Pressure on Top Management
- Arousal to Take Action

Phase 2
- Intervention at the Top
- Reorientation to Internal Problems

Phase 3
- Diagnosis of Problem Areas
- Recognition of Specific Problems

Phase 4
- Invention of New Solutions
- Commitment to New Courses of Action

Phase 5
- Experimentation with New Solutions
- Search for Results

Phase 6
- Reinforcement from Positive Results
- Acceptance of New Practices

with subordinates; then they support experimental attempts at change; and finally they reward and reinforce those managers who adopt new behavior patterns.

CONCRETE DECISIONS

The purpose of this introductory reading has been to give an overview of ideas and issues facing managers concerned with introducing, managing, and responding to organizational changes. With this broad picture in mind, we should not lose sight of the end result, which is for managers to think and act more skillfully in terms of how, when, where, what, and who must be involved and affected by the process of organization change. In this vein, we would like to suggest four areas of decision-making concern for the involved manager: (1) diagnosing organization problems, (2) planning for change, (3) launching change, and (4) following up on change.

As a word of caution, we should point out that all of these areas overlap to a considerable extent. Even though we emphasize the importance of making a thorough diagnosis prior to introducing change, this can be seriously misleading if considered too independently of the other steps. Much diagnosis will continue to take place after a change has been launched, especially as unanticipated problems arise and as new data become available. Also, the change process often gets underway early in the diagnostic stage, depending on who does the diagnosis and the methods chosen for diagnosis. For example, if a "confrontation meeting" is used to identify and analyze major problems, then action is already being taken to involve and affect the change expectations of key managers.

1. Diagnosing Organization Problems

This is essentially a job of drawing conclusions from an intensive diagnosis of the situation. If an analysis is to be more than an academic exercise, it must reach decisions about: (a) What are the specific problems to be corrected? (b) What are the determinants of these problems? and (c) What forces are likely to work for and against change? Answers to these questions are difficult to derive because managers are easily overinvolved or insulated from the sources of problems in their organizations. A variety of diagnostic techniques may have to be employed—such as the use of meetings, consultants, conferences, task forces, interviews, questionnaire surveys, informal conversations, and so forth. The central concern here is to gather reasonably *valid* information that is not skewed to fit only the biases of a few managers or a newly hired outside consultant. Because the impact of organization change can be so significant, we believe it pays to spend sufficient time in this stage to gather information from a wide range of sources and to accomplish this through a variety of data-gathering techniques.

2. Planning for Change

Even when much is known about the problems and their determinants, there is the next important stage of translating a thoughtful diagnosis into an appropriate action plan. There are three essential steps here: one is deciding about the overall goals for change, two is selecting the basic approach for reaching these goals, and three is planning a sequence of detailed steps for implementing the basic approach. Again we must emphasize that this overall plan should be tailor-made to fit the conclusions of the diagnosis. For instance, if the basic problem appears to be one of destructive conflict arising out of a simple and rigid pyramidal structure's being imposed upon complex jobs, it makes little sense to get a general goal of "increased upward communication." Nor would a sensitivity training program be relevant as the basic approach to change. Rather the general goal here should be one of reducing unnecessary conflict through introducing a more flexible organization structure. At the same time, immediate structural changes may be impossible because of resistant attitudes among certain key people. Step-by-step plans will therefore have to be laid for overcoming these negative attitudes.

3. Launching Organization Change

If any change is to get off the ground, it must come from the realm of a plan and be put into action. This is where a manager's interpersonal skill receives its fullest test. For the richness and variety of human response to change can seldom be fully anticipated in *a priori* plans. What specific behavior will influence one's superiors to recognize the need for change? What if an approach is resented by a vocal minority of senior managers? What if the person advocating change is suddenly told that "he too" is part of the problem and must also make changes in his own behavior? As mentioned earlier, change advocates must usually have considerable authority (of knowledge and position) if their proposals are to receive serious attention from those key people who must introduce a change. But even these credentials are seldom enough. Considerable research on organization change indicates that top managers are unwilling to introduce large-scale change unless they feel themselves under intense pressure. Yet this pressure is by no means an automatic stimulus for organization change. Managers can react defensively to blame their anxieties and inaction on circumstances outside their control. Consequently, the change advocate will, in the early stages of organization change, frequently have to exercise consummate skill in helping other managers to overcome their anxious feelings, to recognize the need for change, and to feel commitment for a particular plan of action.

4. Following Up on Organization Change

Once an organization change is underway, a fatal flaw can be for the manager to sit back and relax. Instead, the introducers of change must remain alert to such questions as: How can we find out if lower levels are only paying lip service to change? How can we determine if end targets are being reached? What additional help must be given to those who are struggling to see the implications of change for their particular jobs? Careful monitoring of any change is essential, especially in terms of getting accurate feedback on what is *really* taking place. Lower level managers can easily be tempted to pass on "good news" to those who want so much for "their" change program to succeed. Top management may therefore choose to conduct a systematic evaluation of their change efforts, going so far as to use outside evaluators and "control" organizations to compare themselves against. At least they should consider the use of frequent critique sessions where numerous managers can contribute their reactions and suggestions. An ear finely tuned to this feedback will allow the planners of change to correct deficiencies and to take added steps which had not been anticipated. Typically, they will find that many additional changes will be required if their initially planned change is to be reinforced and accepted as an ongoing part of organization life.

SUMMARY

This reading has described a variety of approaches to organization change, offered some conceptual notions for understanding the change process, and reminded the manager of a few questions to keep in mind as he weaves his way through the complex maze of organization change. It should be obvious by now that there is not one "best" approach to the solving of organizational problems. Rather the skillful manager must develop a change strategy which seeks a pragmatic "fit" between the elements of people, organization, and task for his particular organization. Not only do these elements take on a different configuration from one organization to the next, but they vary from one time period to another in the same organization. This is what turns the job of a manager into an exciting and frustrating series of paradoxes. He must be decisive and yet willing to change. He must be critical and yet supportive. He must be visionary and yet practical. He must lead and yet follow. Perhaps this is what organization change is all about—to develop managers and organizations that can tolerate and express these paradoxes more effectively.

2 | *How to Deal with Resistance to Change**

Paul R. Lawrence

One of the most baffling and recalcitrant of the problems which business executives face is employee resistance to change. Such resistance may take a number of forms—persistent reduction in output, increase in the number of "quits" and requests for transfer, chronic quarrels, sullen hostility, wildcat or slowdown strikes, and, of course, the expression of a lot of psychological reasons why the change will not work. Even the more petty forms of this resistance can be troublesome.

All too often when executives encounter resistance to change, they "explain" it by quoting the cliché that "people resist change" and never look further. Yet changes must continually occur in industry. This applies with particular force to the all-important "little" changes that constantly take place—changes in work methods, in routine office procedures, in the location of a machine or a desk, in personnel assignments and job titles.

No one of these changes makes the headlines, but in total they account for much of our increase in productivity. They are not the spectacular once-in-a-lifetime technological revolutions that involve mass layoffs or the obsolescence of traditional skills, but they are vital to business progress.

Does it follow, therefore, that business management is forever saddled with the onerous job of "forcing" change down the throats of resistant

---

* This article was first published in the May–June 1954 issue of the *Harvard Business Review*. It has been used and reused by businessmen ever since; requests for reprints, for instance, have continued steadily to this day—evidence that the author's analysis of the problems and of how to deal with them continues to be valid. The article was republished as an "HBR Classic" with a "Retrospective Commentary" in January–February 1969.

people? My answer is *no*. It is the thesis of this article that people do *not* resist technical change as such and that most of the resistance which does occur is unnecessary. I shall discuss these points, among others:

1. A solution which has become increasingly popular for dealing with resistance to change is to get the people involved to "participate" in making the change. But as a practical matter "participation" as a device is not a good way for management to think about the problem. In fact, it may lead to trouble.

2. The key to the problem is to understand the true nature of resistance. Actually, what employees resist is usually not technical change but social change—the change in their human relationships that generally accompanies technical change.

3. Resistance is usually created because of certain blind spots and attitudes which staff specialists have as a result of their preoccupation with the technical aspects of new ideas.

4. Management can take concrete steps to deal constructively with these staff attitudes. The steps include emphasizing new standards of performance for staff specialists and encouraging them to think in different ways, as well as making use of the fact that signs of resistance can serve as a practical warning signal in directing and timing technological changes.

5. Top executives can also make their own efforts more effective at meetings of staff and operating groups where change is being discussed. They can do this by shifting their attention from the facts of schedules, technical details, work assignments, and so forth, to what the discussion of these items indicates in regard to developing resistance and receptiveness to change.

Let us begin by taking a look at some research into the nature of resistance to change. There are two studies in particular that I should like to discuss. They highlight contrasting ways of interpreting resistance to change and of coping with it in day-to-day administration.

IS PARTICIPATION ENOUGH?

The first study was conducted by Lester Coch and John R. P. French, Jr. in a clothing factory.[1] It deserves special comment because, it seems to me, it is the most systematic study of the phenomenon of resistance to change that has been made in a factory setting. To describe it briefly:

The two researchers worked with four different groups of factory operators who were being paid on a modified piece-rate basis. For each

---

[1] See Lester Coch and John R. P. French, Jr., "Overcoming Resistance to Change," *Human Relations*, vol. 1, no. 4 (1948), p. 512.

of these four groups a minor change in the work procedure was installed by a different method, and the results were carefully recorded to see what, if any, symptoms of resistance occurred. The four experimental groups were roughly matched with respect to efficiency ratings and degree of cohesiveness; in each group the proposed change modified the established work procedure to about the same degree.

The work change was introduced to the first group by what the researchers called a "no-participation" method. This small group of operators was called into a room where some staff people told the members that there was a need for a minor methods change in their work procedures. The staff people then explained the change to the operators in detail and gave them the reasons for the change. The operators were then sent back to the job with instructions to work in accordance with the new method.

The second group of operators was introduced to the work change by a "participation-through-representation" method—a variation of the approach used with the third and fourth groups which turned out to be of little significance.

The third and fourth groups of operators were both introduced to the work change on a "total-participation" basis. All the operators in these groups met with the staff men concerned. The staff men dramatically demonstrated the need for cost reduction. A general agreement was reached that some savings could be effected. The groups then discussed how existing work methods could be improved and unnecessary operations eliminated. When the new work methods were agreed on, all the operators were trained in the new methods, and all were observed by the time-study men for purposes of establishing a new piece rate on the job.

Research Findings

The researchers reported a marked contrast between the results achieved by the different methods of introducing this change:

No-Participation Group. The most striking difference was between Group #1, the no-participation group, and Groups #3 and #4, the total-participation groups. The output of Group #1 dropped immediately to about two thirds of its previous output rate. The output rate stayed at about this level throughout the period of 30 days after the change was introduced. The researchers further reported:

> Resistance developed almost immediately after the change occurred. Marked expressions of aggression against management occurred, such as conflict with the methods engineer, . . . hostility toward the supervisor, deliberate restriction of production, and lack of cooperation with the supervisor. There were 17% quits in the first 40 days. Grievances were

filed about piece rates; but when the rate was checked, it was found to be a little 'loose.'

Total-Participation Groups. In contrast with this record, Groups #3 and #4 showed a smaller initial drop in output and a very rapid recovery not only to the previous production rate but to a rate that exceeded the previous rate. In these groups there were no signs of hostility toward the staff people or toward the supervisors, and there were no quits during the experimental period

Appraisal of Results

Without going into all the researchers' decisions based on these experiments, it can be fairly stated that they concluded that resistance to methods changes could be overcome by *getting the people involved in the change to participate in making it.*

This was a very useful study, but the results are likely to leave the manager of a factory still bothered by the question, "Where do we go from here?" The trouble centers around that word "participation." It is not a new word. It is seen often in management journals, heard often in management discussions. In fact, the idea that it is a good thing to get employee participation in making changes has become almost axiomatic in management circles.

But participation is not something that can be conjured up or created artificially. You obviously cannot buy it as you would buy a typewriter. You cannot hire industrial engineers and accountants and other staff people who have the ability "to get participation" built into them. It is doubtful how helpful it would be to call in a group of supervisors and staff men and exhort them, "Get in there and start participation."

Participation is a feeling on the part of people, not just the mechanical act of being called in to take part in discussions. Common sense would suggest that people are more likely to respond to the way they are customarily treated—say, as people whose opinions are respected because they themselves are respected for their own worth—rather than by the stratagem of being called to a meeting or being asked some carefully calculated questions. In fact, many supervisors and staff men have had some unhappy experiences with executives who have read about participation and have picked it up as a new psychological gimmick for getting other people to think they "want" to do as they are told—as a sure way to put the sugar coating on a bitter pill.

So there is still the problem of how to get this thing called participation. And, as a matter of fact, the question remains whether participation was the determining factor in the Coch and French experiment or whether there was something of deeper significance underlying it.

RESISTANCE TO WHAT?

Now let us take a look at a second series of research findings about resistance to change. While making some research observations in a factory manufacturing electronic products, a colleague and I had an opportunity to observe a number of incidents that for us threw new light on this matter of resistance to change.[2] One incident was particularly illuminating:

We were observing the work of one of the industrial engineers and a production operator who had been assigned to work with the engineer on assembling and testing an experimental product that the engineer was developing. The engineer and the operator were in almost constant daily contact in their work. It was a common occurrence for the engineer to suggest an idea for some modification in a part of the new product; he would then discuss his idea with the operator and ask her to try out the change to see how it worked. It was also a common occurrence for the operator to get an idea as she assembled parts and to pass this idea on to the engineer, who would then consider it and, on occasion, ask the operator to try out the idea and see if it proved useful.

A typical exchange between these two people might run somewhat as follows:

ENGINEER: I got to thinking last night about that difficulty we've been having on assembling the x part in the last few days. It occurred to me that we might get around that trouble if we washed the part in a cleaning solution just prior to assembling it.

OPERATOR: Well, that sounds to me like it's worth trying.

ENGINEER: I'll get you some of the right kind of cleaning solution, and why don't you try doing that with about 50 parts and keep track of what happens.

OPERATOR: Sure, I'll keep track of it and let you know how it works.

With this episode in mind, let us take a look at a second episode involving the same production operator. One day we noticed another engineer approaching the production operator. We knew that this particular engineer had had no previous contact with the production operator. He had been asked to take a look at one specific problem on the new product because of his special technical qualifications. He had decided to make a change in one of the parts of the product to eliminate the problem, and he had prepared some of these parts using his new method. Here is what happened:

He walked up to the production operator with the new parts in his hand and indicated to her by a gesture that he wanted her to try as-

---

[2] For a complete report of the study, see Harriet O. Ronken and Paul R. Lawrence, *Administering Changes: A Case Study of Human Relations in a Factory* (Boston: Division of Research, Harvard Business School, 1952).

sembling some units using his new part. The operator picked up one of the parts and proceeded to assemble it. We noticed that she did not handle the part with her usual care. After she had assembled the product, she tested it and it failed to pass inspection. She turned to the new engineer and, with a triumphant air, said, "It doesn't work."

The new engineer indicated that she should try another part. She did so, and again it did not work. She then proceeded to assemble units using all of the new parts that were available. She handled each of them in an unusually rough manner. None of them worked. Again she turned to the engineer and said that the new parts did not work.

The engineer left, and later the operator, with evident satisfaction, commented to the original industrial engineer that the new engineer's idea was just no good.

Social Change

What can we learn from these episodes? To begin, it will be useful for our purposes to think of change as having both a technical and a social aspect. The *technical* aspect of the change is the making of a measurable modification in the physical routines of the job. The *social* aspect of the change refers to the way those affected by it think it will alter their established relationships in the organization.

We can clarify this distinction by referring to the two foregoing episodes. In both of them, the technical aspects of the changes introduced were virtually identical: the operator was asked to use a slightly changed part in assembling the finished product. By contrast, the social aspects of the changes were quite different.

In the first episode, the interaction between the industrial engineer and the operator tended to sustain the give-and-take kind of relationship that these two people were accustomed to. The operator was used to being treated as a person with some valuable skills and knowledge and some sense of responsibility about her work; when the engineer approached her with his idea, she felt she was being dealt with in the usual way. But, in the second episode, the new engineer was introducing not only a technical change but also a change in the operator's customary way of relating herself to others in the organization. By his brusque manner and by his lack of any explanation, he led the operator to fear that her usual work relationships were being changed. And she just did not like the new way she was being treated.

The results of these two episodes were quite different also. In the first episode there were no symptoms of resistance to change, a very good chance that the experimental change would determine fairly whether a cleaning solution would improve product quality, and a willingness on the part of the operator to accept future changes when the industrial engineer suggested them. In the second episode, however, there were signs of resistance to change (the operator's careless handling of parts and her satisfaction in their failure to work), failure to prove whether the modified part was an improvement or not, and indications that the operator would resist any further changes by the engineer. We might summarize the two contrasting patterns of human behavior in the two episodes in graphic form; see Exhibit 1.

EXHIBIT 1
Two Contrasting Patterns of Human Behavior

	Change		Results
	Technical Aspect	*Social Aspect*	*Results*
Episode 1	Clean part prior to assembly	Sustaining the customary work relationship of operator	1. No resistance 2. Useful technical result 3. Readiness for more change
Episode 2	Use new part in assembly	Threatening the customary work relationship of operator	1. Signs of resistance 2. No useful technical result 3. Lack of readiness for more change

It is apparent from these two patterns that the variable which determines the result is the *social* aspect of the change. In other words, the operator did not resist the technical change as such but rather the accompanying change in her human relationships.

Confirmation

This conclusion is based on more than one case. Many other cases in our research project substantiate it. Furthermore, we can find confirmation in the research experience of Coch and French, even though they came out with a different interpretation.

Coch and French tell us in their report that the procedure used with Group #1, i.e., the no-participation group, was the usual one in the factory for introducing work changes. And yet they also tell us something about the customary treatment of the operators in their work life. For example, the company's labor relations policies are progressive, the company and the supervisors place a high value on fair and open dealings with the employees, and the employees are encouraged to take up their problems and grievances with management. Also, the operators are accustomed to measuring the success and failure of themselves as operators against the company's standard output figures.

Now compare these *customary* work relationships with the way the Group #1 operators were treated when they were introduced to this particular work change. There is quite a difference. When the management called them into the room for indoctrination, they were treated as if they had no useful knowledge of their own jobs. In effect, they were told that they were not the skilled and efficient operators they had thought they were, that they were doing the job inefficiently, and that some "outsider" (the staff expert) would now tell them how to do it right. How could they construe this experience *except* as a threatening change in their usual working relationship? It is the story of the second episode in our research case all over again. The results were also the same, with signs of resistance, persistently low output, and so on.

Now consider experimental Groups #3 and #4, i.e., the total-participation groups. Coch and French referred to management's approach in their case as a "new" method of introducing change; but, from the point of view of the *operators* it must not have seemed new at all. It was simply a continuation of the way they were ordinarily dealt with in the course of their regular work. And what happened? The results—reception to change, technical improvement, better performance—were much like those reported in the first episode between the operator and the industrial engineer.

So the research data of Coch and French tend to confirm the conclusion that the nature and size of the technical aspect of the change does not determine the presence or absence of resistance nearly so much as does the social aspect of the change.

ROOTS OF TROUBLE

The significance of these research findings, from management's point of view, is that executives and staff experts need not expertness in using the devices of participation but a real understanding, in depth and detail, of the specific social arrangements that will be sustained or threatened by the change or by the way in which it is introduced.

These observations check with everyday management experience in industry. When we stop to think about it, we know that many changes occur in our factories without a bit of resistance. We know that people who are working closely with one another continually swap ideas about short cuts and minor changes in procedure that are adopted so easily and naturally that we seldom notice them or even think of them as change. The point is that because these people work so closely with one another, they intuitively understand and take account of the existing social arrangements for work and so feel no threat to themselves in such everyday changes.

By contrast, management actions leading to what we commonly label "change" are usually initiated outside the small work group by staff people. These are the changes that we notice and the ones that most frequently bring on symptoms of resistance. By the very nature of their work, most of our staff specialists in industry do not have the intimate contact with operating groups that allows them to acquire an intuitive understanding of the complex social arrangements which their ideas may affect. Neither do our staff specialists always have the day-to-day dealings with operating people that lead them to develop a natural respect for the knowledge and skill of these people. As a result, all too often the men behave in a way that threatens and disrupts the established social relationships. And the tragedy is that so many of these upsets are inadvertent and unnecessary.

Yet industry must have its specialists—not only many kinds of engineering specialists (product, process, maintenance, quality, and safety engineers) but also cost accountants, production schedulers, purchasing agents, and personnel men. Must top management therefore reconcile itself to continual resistance to change, or can it take constructive action to meet the problem?

I believe that our research in various factory situations indicates why resistance to change occurs and what management can do about it. Let us take the "why" factors first.

Self-Preoccupation

All too frequently we see staff specialists who bring to their work certain blind spots that get them into trouble when they initiate change with operating people. One such blind spot is "self-preoccupation." The staff man gets so engrossed in the technology of the change he is interested in promoting that he becomes wholly oblivious to different kinds of things that may be bothering people. Here are two examples:

In one situation the staff people introduced, with the best of intentions, a technological change which inadvertently deprived a number of skilled operators of much of the satisfaction that they were finding in their work. Among other things, the change meant that, whereas formerly the output of each operator had been placed beside his work position where it could be viewed and appreciated by him and by others, it was now being carried away immediately from the work position. The workmen did not like this.

The sad part of it was that there was no compelling cost or technical reason why the output could not be placed beside the work position as it had been formerly. But the staff people who had introduced the change were so literal-minded about their ideas that when they heard complaints on the changes from the operators, they could not comprehend what the trouble was. Instead, they began repeating all the logical arguments why the change made sense from a cost standpoint. The final result here was a chronic restriction of output and persistent hostility on the part of the operators.

An industrial engineer undertook to introduce some methods changes in one department with the notion firmly in mind that this assignment presented him with an opportunity to "prove" to higher management the value of his function. He became so preoccupied with his personal desire to make a name for his particular techniques that he failed to pay any attention to some fairly obvious and practical considerations which the operating people were calling to his attention but which did not show up in his time-study techniques. As could be expected, resistance quickly developed to all his ideas, and the only "name" that he finally won for his techniques was a bad one.

Obviously, in both of these situations the staff specialists involved did not take into account the social aspects of the change they were introducing. For different reasons they got so preoccupied with the technical aspects of the change that they literally could not see or understand what all the fuss was about.

We may sometimes wish that the validity of the technical aspect of the change were the sole determinant of its acceptability. But the fact remains that the social aspect is what determines the presence or absence of resistance. Just as ignoring this fact is the sure way to trouble, so taking advantage of it can lead to positive results. We must not forget that these same social arrangements which at times seem so bothersome are essential for the performance of work. Without a network of established social relationships, a factory would be populated with a collection of people who had no idea of how to work with one another in an organized fashion. By working *with* this network instead of *against* it, management's staff representatives can give new technological ideas a better chance of acceptance.

Know-How of Operators Overlooked

Another blind spot of many staff specialists is to the strengths as well as to the weaknesses of firsthand production experience. They do not recognize that the production foreman and the production operator are in their own way specialists themselves—specialists in actual experience with production problems. This point should be obvious, but it is amazing how many staff specialists fail to appreciate the fact that even though they themselves may have a superior knowledge of the technology of the production process involved, the foreman or the operators may have a more practical understanding of how to get daily production out of a group of men and machines.

The experience of the operating people frequently equips them to be of real help to staff specialists on at least two counts: (1) The operating people are often able to spot practical production difficulties in the ideas of the specialists—and iron out those difficulties before it is too late; (2) the operating people are often able to take advantage of their intimate acquaintance with the existing social arrangements for getting work done. If given a chance, they can use this kind of knowledge to help detect those parts of the change that will have undesirable social consequences. The staff experts can then go to work on ways to avoid the trouble area without materially affecting the technical worth of the change.

Further, some staff specialists have yet to learn the truth that, even after the plans for a change have been carefully made, it takes *time* to put the change successfully into production use. Time is necessary even though there may be no resistance to the change itself. The operators must develop the skill needed to use new methods and new equipment efficiently; there are always bugs to be taken out of a new method or piece of equipment even with the best of engineering. When a staff man begins to lose his patience with the amount of time that these steps take, the people he is working with will begin to feel that he is pushing them; *this* amounts to a change in their customary work relationships, and resistance will start building up where there was none before.

The situation is aggravated if the staff man mistakenly accuses the operators of resisting the idea of the change, for there are few things that irritate people more than to be blamed for resisting change when actually they are doing their best to learn a difficult new procedure.

MANAGEMENT ACTION

Many of the problems of resistance to change arise around certain kinds of *attitudes* that staff men are liable to develop about their jobs and their own ideas for introducing change. Fortunately, management can influence these attitudes and thus deal with the problems at their source.

Broadening Staff Interests

It is fairly common for a staff man to work so hard on one of his ideas for change that he comes to identify himself with it. This is fine for the organization when he is working on the idea by himself or with his immediate colleagues; the idea becomes "his baby," and the company benefits from his complete devotion to his work.

But when he goes to some group of operating people to introduce a change, his very identification with his ideas tends to make him unreceptive to any suggestions for modification. He just does not feel like letting anyone else tamper with his pet ideas. It is easy to see, of course, how this attitude is interpreted by the operating people as a lack of respect for their suggestions.

This problem of the staff man's extreme identification with his work is one which, to some extent, can only be cured by time. But here are four suggestions for speeding up the process:

1. The manager can often, with wise timing, encourage the staff man's interest in a different project that is just starting.

2. The manager can also, by his "coaching" as well as by example, prod the staff man to develop a healthier respect for the contributions he can receive from operating people; success in this area would, of course, virtually solve the problem.

3. It also helps if the staff man can be guided to recognize that the satisfaction he derives from being productive and creative is the same satisfaction he denies the operating people by his behavior toward them. Experience shows that staff people can sometimes be stimulated by the thought of finding satisfaction in sharing with others in the organization the pleasures of being creative.

4. Sometimes, too, the staff man can be led to see that winning acceptance of his ideas through better understanding and handling of human beings is just as challenging and rewarding as giving birth to an idea.

Using Understandable Terms

One of the problems that must be overcome arises from the fact that the typical staff man is likely to have the attitude that the reasons why he is recommending any given change may be so complicated and specialized that it is impossible to explain them to operating people. It may be true that the operating people would find it next to impossible to understand some of the staff man's analytical techniques, but this does not keep them from coming to the conclusion that the staff specialist is trying to razzle-dazzle them with tricky figures and formulas—insulting their intelligence—if he does not strive to his utmost to translate his ideas into terms understandable to them. The following case illustrates the importance of this point:

A staff specialist was temporarily successful in "selling" a change based on a complicated mathematical formula to a foreman who really did not understand it. The whole thing backfired, however, when the foreman tried to sell it to his operating people. They asked him a couple of sharp questions that he could not answer. His embarrassment about this led him to resent and resist the change so much that eventually the whole proposition fell through. This was unfortunate in terms not only of human relations but also of technological progress in the plant.

There are some very good reasons, both technical and social, why the staff man should be interested in working with the operating people until his recommendations make "sense." (This does not mean that the operating people need to understand the recommendations in quite the same way or in the same detail that the staff man does, but that they should be able to visualize the recommendations in terms of their job experiences.) Failure of the staff man to provide an adequate explanation is likely to mean that a job the operators had formerly performed with understanding and satisfaction will now be performed without understanding and with less satisfaction.

This loss of satisfaction not only concerns the individual involved but also is significant from the standpoint of the company which is trying to get maximum productivity from the operating people. A person who does not have a feeling of comprehension of what he is doing is denied the opportunity to exercise that uniquely human ability—the ability to use informed and intelligent judgment on what he does. If the staff man leaves the operating people with a sense of confusion, they will also be left unhappy and less productive.

Top line and staff executives responsible for the operation should make it a point, therefore, to know how the staff man goes about installing a change. They can do this by asking discerning questions when he reports to them, listening closely to reports of employee reaction, and, if they have the opportunity, actually watching the staff man at work. At times they may have to take such drastic action as insisting that the time of installation of a proposed change be postponed until the operators are ready for it. But, for the most part, straightforward discussions with the staff man in terms of what they think of his approach should help him, over a period of time, to learn what is expected of him in his relationships with operating personnel.

New Look at Resistance

Another attitude that gets staff men into trouble is the *expectation* that all the people involved will resist the change. It is curious but true that the staff man who goes into his job with the conviction that people are going to resist any idea he presents with blind stubbornness is likely to find them responding just the way he thinks they will. The process is clear: whenever he treats the people who are supposed to buy his ideas as if they were bullheaded, he changes the way they are used to being treated; and they *will* be bullheaded in resisting *that* change!

I think that the staff man—and management in general—will do better to look at it this way: When resistance *does* appear, it should not be thought of as something to be *overcome*. Instead, it can best be thought of as a useful red flag—a signal that something is going wrong. To use a rough analogy, signs of resistance in a social organization are useful in the same way that pain is useful to the body as a signal that some bodily functions are getting out of adjustment.

The resistance, like the pain, does not tell what is wrong but only that something *is* wrong. And it makes no more sense to try to overcome such resistance than it does to take a pain killer without diagnosing the bodily ailment. Therefore, when resistance appears, it is time to listen carefully to find out what the trouble is. What is needed is not a long harangue on the logics of the new recommendations but a careful exploration of the difficulty.

It may happen that the problem is some technical imperfection in the change that can be readily corrected. More than likely, it will turn out that the change is threatening and upsetting some of the established social arrangements for doing work. Whether the trouble is easy or difficult to correct, management will at least know what it is dealing with.

New Job Definition

Finally, some staff specialists get themselves in trouble because they assume they have the answer in the thought that people will accept a change when they have participated in making it. For example:

In one plant we visited, an engineer confided to us (obviously because we, as researchers on human relations, were interested in psychological gimmicks!) that he was going to put across a proposed production layout change of his by inserting in it a rather obvious error, which others could then suggest should be corrected. We attended the meeting where this stunt was performed, and superficially it worked. Somebody caught the error, proposed that it be corrected, and our engineer immediately "bought" the suggestion as a very worthwhile one and made the change. The group then seemed to "buy" his entire layout proposal.

It looked like an effective technique—oh, so easy—until later, when we became better acquainted with the people in the plant. Then we found out that many of the engineer's colleagues considered him a phony and did not trust him. The resistance they put up to his ideas was very subtle, yet even more real and difficult for management to deal with.

Participation will never work so long as it is treated as a device to get somebody else to do what you want him to. Real participation is based on respect. And respect is not acquired by just trying; it is acquired when the staff man faces the reality that he needs the contributions of the operating people.

If the staff man defines his job as not just generating ideas but also getting those ideas into practical operation, he will recognize his real dependence on the contributions of the operating people. He will ask them for ideas and suggestions, not in a backhanded way to get compliance, but in a straightforward way to get some good ideas and avoid some unnecessary mistakes. By this process he will be treating the operating people in such a way that his own behavior will not be perceived as a threat to their customary work relationships. It will be possible to discuss, and to accept or reject, the ideas on their own merit.

The staff specialist who looks at the process of introducing change and at resistance to change in the manner outlined in the preceding pages may not be hailed as a genius, but he can be counted on in installing a steady flow of technical changes that will cut costs and improve quality without upsetting the organization.

ROLE OF THE ADMINISTRATOR

Now what about the way the top executive goes about his *own* job as it involves the introduction of change and problems of resistance?

One of the most important things he can do, of course, is to deal with staff people in much the same way that he wants them to deal with the operators. He must realize that staff people resist social change, too. (This means, among other things, that he should not prescribe particular rules to them on the basis of this article!)

But most important, I think, is the way the administrator conceives of his job in coordinating the work of the different staff and line groups involved in a change. Does he think of his duties *primarily* as checking up, delegating and following through, applying pressure when performance fails to measure up? Or does he think of them *primarily* as facilitating communication and understanding between people with different points of view—for example, between a staff engineering group and a production group who do not see eye to eye on a change they are both involved in? An analysis of management's actual experience—or, at least, that part of it which has been covered by our research—points to the latter as the more effective concept of administration.

I do not mean that the executive should spend his time with the different people concerned discussing the human problems of change as such. He *should* discuss schedules, technical details, work assignments, and so forth. But he should also be watching closely for the messages that are passing back and forth as people discuss these topics. He will find that people—himself as well as others—are always implicitly asking and making answers to questions like: "How will he accept criticism?" "How much can I afford to tell him?" "Does he really get my point?" "Is he playing games?" The answers to such questions determine the degree of candor and the amount of understanding between the people involved.

When the administrator concerns himself with these problems and acts to facilitate understanding, there will be less logrolling and more sense of common purpose, fewer words and better understanding, less anxiety and more acceptance of criticism, less griping and more attention to specific problems—in short, better performance in putting new ideas for technological change into effect.

RETROSPECTIVE COMMENTARY

In the 15 years since this article was published, we have seen a great deal of change in industry, but the human aspects of the topic do not seem very different. The human problems associated with change remain much the same even though our understanding of them and our methods for dealing with them have advanced.

The first of the two major themes of the article is that resistance to change does not arise because of technical factors per se but because of social and human considerations. This statement still seems to be true. There is, however, an implication in the article that the social and human costs of change, if recognized, can largely be avoided by thoughtful management effort. Today I am less sanguine about this.

It is true that these costs can be greatly reduced by conscious attention. Managements that have tried have made much progress during the past 15 years. Here are some examples of what has been done:

Fewer people are now pushed out of the back doors of industry—embittered and "burned out" before their time.

Fewer major strikes are the result of head-on clashes over new technology and its effects on jobs.

Progress is being made in putting the needs of people into the design of new technological systems.

Relevant inputs of ideas and opinions of people from all ranks are being solicited and used *before* (not after) plans for change are frozen.

At the same time that well-established work groups are disrupted by technical imperatives, special efforts are made to help newly formed work groups evolve meaningful team relations quickly.

Time and care have been taken to counsel individuals whose careers have to some degree been disrupted by change.

All of these ways of reducing the human costs of change have worked for the companies that have seriously applied them. Still, I am more aware than in 1954 of the limits of such approaches. They do not always enable management to prevent situations from developing in which some individuals win while others lose. The values lost as skills become obsolete cannot always be replaced. The company's earnings may go up but the percentage payouts from even an enlarged "pie" have to be recalculated, and then the relative rewards shift. In these situations enlightened problem solving will not completely displace old-fashioned bargaining, and better communication will only clarify the hard-core realities.

The second theme of the article deals with ways of improving the relations between groups in an organization—particularly when a staff group is initiating change in the work of an operating or line group. The gap that exists in outlook and orientation between specialized groups in industry has increased in the past 15 years, even as the number of such groups has continued to escalate. These larger gaps have in turn created ever more difficult problems of securing effective communication and problem solving between groups. Coordinating the groups is probably the number one problem of our modern corporations. So this second theme is hardly out-of-date.

Today, however, there is both more knowledge available about the problem than there was in 1954 and more sophisticated skill and attention being given to it. And there is increasing understanding of and respect for the necessity for differences between groups. There is less striving for consistency for its own sake. More managerial effort is being applied, in person and through impersonal systems, to bridge the gaps in understanding. While the conflicts between specialized groups are probably as intense now as ever, they are more frequently seen as task-related—that is, natural outgrowths of different jobs, skills, and approaches—rather than as redundant and related only to personality differences.

The major criticism that has been brought to my attention about the article is that it has damaged the useful concept of participation. Perhaps this is true. But the view of participation as a technique for securing compliance with a predetermined change was a widespread and seductive one in 1954—and it is not dead yet. Subsequent research has not altered the general conclusion that participation, to be of value, must be based on a search for ideas that are seen as truly relevant to the change under consideration. The shallow notion of participation, therefore, still needs to be debunked.

As a final thought, I now realize that the article implied that workers resist change while managers foster and implement change. Many of the changes of the intervening period, such as the computer revolution, have exposed the inadequacy of this assumption. It is difficult to find any managers today who do not at times feel greatly distressed because of changes, with their own resistance level running fairly high. We are all, at times, resistors as well as instigators of change. We are all involved on both sides of the process of adjusting to change.

In light of this, let me reemphasize the point that resistance to change is by itself neither good nor bad. Resistance may be soundly based or not. It is always, however, an important signal calling for further inquiry by management.

3 | *Applied Organization Change in Industry: Structural, Technical, and Human Approaches**

Harold J. Leavitt

This is a mapping chapter. It is part of a search for perspective on complex organizations, in this instance, through consideration of several classes of efforts to change ongoing organizations. Approaches to change provide a kind of sharp caricature of underlying beliefs and prejudices about the important dimensions of organizations. Thereby, perhaps, they provide some insights into areas of real or apparent difference among perspectives on organization theory.

To classify several major approaches to change, I have found it useful, first, to view organizations as multivariate systems, in which at least four interacting variables loom especially large: the variables of task, structure, technology, and actors (usually people). (See Figure 1.)

FIGURE 1

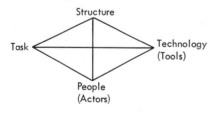

* Reproduced with permission from *New Perspectives in Organization Research,* (New York: John Wiley & Sons, Inc., 1964).

Roughly speaking, "task" refers to organizational *raisons d'etre*—manufacturing, servicing, etc., including the large numbers of different, but operationally meaningful, subtasks which may exist in complex organizations.

By "actors" I mean mostly people, but with the qualification that acts usually executed by people need not remain exclusively in the human domain.

By "technology" I mean technical tools—problem-solving inventions like work measurement, computers, or drill presses. Note that I include both machines and programs in this category, but with some uncertainty about the line between structure and technology.

Finally, by "structure" I mean systems of communication, systems of authority (or other roles), and systems of work flow.

These four are highly interdependent, so that change in any one will most probably result in compensatory (or retaliatory) change in others. In discussing organizational change, therefore, I shall assume that it is one or more of these variables that we seek to change. Sometimes we may aim to change one of these as an end in itself, sometimes as a mechanism for effecting some changes in one or more of the others.

Thus, for example, structural change toward, say, decentralization should change the performance of certain organizational tasks (indeed, even the selection of tasks); the technology that is brought to bear (e.g., changes in accounting procedures); and the nature, numbers, and/or motivation and attitudes of people in the organization. Any of these changes could presumably be consciously intended; or they could occur as unforeseen and often troublesome outcomes of efforts to change only one or two of the variables.

Similarly, the introduction of new technological tools—computers, for example—may effect changes in structure (e.g., in the communication system or decision map of the organization), changes in people (their numbers, skills, attitudes, and activities), and changes in task performance or even task definition, since some tasks may now become feasible of accomplishment for the first time.

Changes in the people and task variables could presumably branch out through the system to cause similar changes in other variables.

We can turn now to the central focus of this chapter, namely, a categorization and evaluation of several approaches to organizational change—approaches that differ markedly in their degree of emphasis and their ordering of these four variables.

Clearly most efforts to effect change, whether they take off from people, technology, structure, or task, soon must deal with the others. Human relators must invent technical devices for implementing their ideas, and they must evaluate alternative structures, classing some as consonant and some as dissonant with their views of the world. Structuralists must take stands on the kinds of human interaction that are supportive of their position, and the kinds that threaten to undermine it, etc.

Although I differentiate structural from technical from human approaches to organizational tasks, the differentiation is in points of origin, relative weightings, and underlying conceptions and values, not in the exclusion of all other variables.

This categorization must be further complicated by the fact that the objectives of the several approaches to organizational change are not uniform. All of them do share a considerable interest in improved solutions to tasks. But while some of the technical approaches focus almost exclusively on task solutions, that is, on the *quality* of decisions, some of the people approaches are at least as interested in performance of task subsequent to decisions. Although improved task solution serves as a common goal for all of these approaches, several carry other associated objectives that weigh almost as heavily in the eyes of their proponents. Thus some of the early structural approaches were almost as concerned with maintaining a power status quo as with improving task performance, and some of the current people approaches are at least as interested in providing organizations that fulfill human needs as they are in efficacious performance of tasks.

The several approaches are still further complicated by variations in the causal chains by which they are supposed to bring about their intended changes. Some of the structural approaches, for example, are not aimed directly at task but at people as mediating intervening variables. In these approaches, one changes structure to change people to improve task performance. Similarly, some of the people approaches seek to change people in order to change structure and tools, to change task performance, and also to make life more fulfilling for people. We can turn now to the several varieties of efforts themselves.

THE STRUCTURAL APPROACHES

Applied efforts to change organizations by changing structure seem to fall into four classes. First, structural change has been the major mechanism of the "classical" organization theorist. Out of the deductive, logical, largely military-based thinking of early nonempirical organization theory, there evolved the whole set of now familiar "principles" for optimizing organizational performance by optimizing structure. These are deductive approaches carrying out their analyses from task backwards to appropriate divisions of labor and appropriate systems of authority. These early structural approaches almost always mediated their activities through people to task. One improves task performance by clarifying and defining the jobs of people and setting up appropriate relationships among these jobs. Operationally one worried about modifying spans of control, defining nonoverlapping areas of responsibility and authority, and logically defining necessary functions.

In retrospect, most of us think of these early approaches as abstractions, formal and legalistic, and poorly anchored in empirical data. They were also almost incredibly naive in their assumptions about human behavior. In fact, almost the only assumptions that were made were legalistic and moralistic ones: the people, having contracted to work, would then carry out the terms of their contract; that people assigned responsibility would necessarily accept that responsibility; that people when informed of the organization's goals would strive wholeheartedly to achieve those goals.

The values underlying these early approaches were thus probably more authoritarian and puritanical than anything else. Order, discipline, system, and acceptance of authority seemed to be dominant values. The objective, of course, was optimal task performance, but within the constraints imposed by the hierarchy of authority.

In one variation or another, such structural approaches are still widely applied. It is still commonplace for consultants or organization planning departments to try to solve organizational problems by redefining areas of responsibility and authority, enforcing the chain of command, and so on.

A second widespread approach to structural change, allied to the first, somewhat more modern and sophisticated and somewhat narrower, too, is the idea of decentralization. The idea of changing organizations by decentralizing their structure was probably more an invention of the accounting profession than anyone else, though it has been widely endorsed by structuralists and by human relators too. Almost nobody is against it. Not too long ago, I heard the senior officer of one of the nation's largest consulting firms remind his large staff of young consultants that their firm was founded on the "bedrock principle of decentralization."

Decentralization affects the performance of tasks partially through its intervening effects on people. By creating profit centers, one presumably increases the motivation and goal-oriented behavior of local managers. One also adds flexibility so that variations in technology appropriate to the different tasks of different decentralized units now become more possible; so do subvariations in structure, and local variations in the use of people. Decentralization can be thought of as a mechanism for changing organizations at a meta level, providing local autonomy for further change. Thus, within limits, decentralized units may further change themselves through the use of any one of the many alternatives available, and perhaps for this reason no group has questioned it, at least until the last couple of years.

Recently, two other structural approaches have shown up, but they have not yet reached a widespread level of application. One of them is best represented by Chapple and Sayles. Theirs is a form of social engineering aimed at task, but via people. They seek to modify the behavior of people in order to improve task performance, but they do it by modifying structure, in this case, the flow of work. Out of the tradition of applied anthropology, they argue that planning of work flows and groupings of specialties will directly affect the morale, behavior, and output of employees. One of the failings of earlier structural models, in their view, is that the design of work was almost entirely determined by task and technical variables, and failed to take account of human social variables. They provide illustrative cases to show that appropriate redesigning of work, in a social engineering sense, affects both human attitudes and output.

I cannot overlook in this discussion of structure the implications of a second approach—the research on communication networks. I know of no *direct* applications of this laboratory research to the real world, though it has had some indirect influence on structural planning. In that research, variations in communication nets affect both routine and novel task performance rather significantly. The results suggest that appropriate communication structures might vary considerably within a complex organization, depending upon the type of task that any subunit of the organization undertakes. Thus for highly programmed repetitive tasks, highly centralized communication structures seem to operate most efficiently, but with some human costs. For more novel, ill-structured tasks, more wide-open communication nets with larger numbers of channels and less differentiation among members seem to work more effectively.

TECHNOLOGICAL APPROACHES TO ORGANIZATIONAL CHANGE

My first entry in this technological category is Taylor's *Scientific Management*. Its birth date was around 1910, its father, Frederick W. Taylor. Its tools were work measurement tools. It bore none of the abstract deductive flavor of the structural approaches. From the classic programming of the labors of Schmidt, the immigrant pig-iron handler at Bethlehem, on to the more sophisticated forms of work measurement and analysis of succeeding decades, Taylorism has constituted a significant force in influencing task performance in American organizations.

Scientific Management, almost from its inception, took a position outside of the task, not of it. Taylor created a new technical skill—industrial engineering—and a new class of specialized practitioners—the industrial engineers. Theirs was a staff skill, a planning skill. They were the organizers and designers of work. The Schmidts were the doers.

Like the early structural approaches, Scientific Management was thus to a great extent ahuman, perhaps even inhuman. For in creating the separate planning specialist, it removed planning from its old loca-tion—the head of the doer of work. Many observers, both contemporary and subsequent, saw this phase of scientific management as downright demeaning of mankind. Taylor put his foot deeply into his mouth by saying things like this: "Now one of the very first requirements for a man who is fit to handle pig iron . . . is that he shall be so stupid and so phlegmatic that he more nearly resembles . . . the ox than any other type. . . . He must consequently be trained by a man more intelli-gent than himself."

But despite the flurry of congressional investigations and active coun-terattack by Taylor's contemporaries, Scientific Management grew and prospered, and radically changed structure, people, and the ways jobs got done. Indeed, it spread and flourished until no self-respecting manu-facturing firm was without time-study men, methods engineers, work standards, piece rates, and job classification schemes.

The range of Scientific Management, however, was limited by its relatively simple tools largely to the programming of eye-hand and mus-cle jobs. Though Taylor and his fellows were ready to generalize their methods to almost any organizational problem, the methods themselves fell pretty short when applied to judgment and think-type jobs.

If one asks why Scientific Management flourished, several reasonable answers appear. The environment of the day, despite counterattacks by Upton Sinclair and others, was probably supportive. It was an envi-ronment of growth, expansiveness, and muscle flexing. Work in associ-ated disciplines was supportive, too. Psychology, for example, was physi-ologically oriented, concerned with individual differences and anxious to be treated as a science. Hence it, too, was measurement happy.[1] Finger dexterity tests meshed neatly with Taylor's motion study.

But most of all, Taylorism, like many other ideas, seemed to be carried by its own operational gimmicks—by its cheap, workable, easily taught techniques and methods.

Scientific Management receded into a relatively stable and undramatic background in the late 1930's and 1940's and has never made a real comeback in its original form. But the technological approaches were by no means dead. The development of operations research and the more or less contemporaneous invention and exploitation of computers have more than revived them.

---

[1] See for example Bendix's account of the early enthusiasm of industrial psycholo-gists. He quotes Hugo Munsterberg appraising the promise of industrial psychology in 1913: ". . . Still more important than the valued commercial profit on both sides is the cultural gain which will come to the total economic life of the nation, as soon as everyone can be brought to the place where his best energies may be unfolded and his greatest personal satisfaction secured. The economic experimental psychology offers no more inspiring idea than this adjustment of work and psyche by which mental dissatisfaction with the work, mental depression, and discouragement may be replaced in our social community by overflowing joy and perfect inner harmony."

I submit that operational operations research methods for changing organizational problem solving can be reasonably placed in the same category with Scientific Management. They have both developed a body of technical methods for solving work problems. They both are usually *external* in their approach, essentially separating the planning of problem-solving programs from the routine acting out of solutions. Operations research, too, is quickly developing, in its operational form, a new class of hot-shot staff specialists, in many ways analogous to the earlier staff efficiency man. What is *clearly* different, of course, is the nature of the techniques, although there may be larger differences that are not yet so clear.

The operations research and information processing techniques are turning out to be, if not more general, at least applicable to large classes of tasks that Scientific Management could not touch. Now, armed with linear programming methods, one can approach a task like media selection in an advertising agency, though it would have been nonsense to time study it.

But note the overall similarity: change the setting of the movie from Bethlehem, Pa., to Madison Avenue; the time from 1910 to 1962; the costuming from overalls to gray flannel suits; and the tasks from simple muscular labor to complex judgmental decisions. Turn worried laborer Schmidt into worried media executive Jones. Then replace Taylor with Charnes and Cooper and supplant the stopwatch with the computer. It is the same old theme either way—the conflict between technology and humanity.

A distinction needs to be drawn, of course, between operational operations research and other computer-based information-processing approaches, although they are often closely allied. "Management Science" hopefully will mean more than highly operational applications of specific techniques, and organizations are also being changed by simulation techniques and by heuristic problem-solving methods. Their impact has not yet been felt in anything like full force; but tasks, people, and structures are already being rather radically modified by them. In fact, one wonders if these task-directed efforts will not end up having at least as radical an impact on structure and on the role of humans as on task solutions themselves. For out of new information-processing methods we now begin to reconsider the bedrock issue of decentralization and to reconsider the permanency and primacy of human judgments for making certain classes of decisions. All the way round the organization, visible changes are being generated out of technical innovations.

Without delving further into the substance of these more recent technological approaches, it may be worth pointing up one other characteristic that they share with many of their predecessors—a kind of faith in the ultimate victory of *better* problem solutions over less good ones. This faith is often perceived by people-oriented practitioners of change as sheer naïveté about the nature of man. They ascribe it to a pre-Freudian fixation on rationality; to a failure to realize that human acceptance of ideas is the real carrier of change, and that emotional human resistance is the real roadblock. They can point, in evidence, to a monotonously long list of cases in which technological innovations, methods changes, or operations research techniques have fallen short because they ignored the human side of the enterprise. It is not the logically better solutions that get adopted, this argument runs, but the more humanly acceptable, more feasible ones. Unless the new technologist wises up, he may end up a miserable social isolate, like his predecessor, the unhappy industrial engineer.

Often this argument fits the facts. Operations research people can be incredibly naïve in their insensitivity to human feelings. But in another, more gracious sense, one can say that the technological approaches have simply taken a more macroscopic, longer view of the world than the people approaches. Better solutions do get accepted in the long run, because deeper forces in the economy press them upon the individual organization—competitive forces, mainly. Macroscopically these ahuman or people-last approaches may encounter bumps and grinds in the microcosms of the individual firm; but sooner or later, in the aggregate, human resistances will be allayed or displaced or overcome, and the steam drill must inevitably defeat John Henry.

The technological approaches assume some communication among firms, and between firms and the world; and they assume further that the demonstration of more economic solutions will eventually result in their adoption, though the road may be rough.

The technological approaches seem not only to predict the victory of cleaner, more logical, and more parsimonious solutions but also to *value* them. Failure of human beings to search for or use more efficient solutions is a sign, from this perspective, of human weakness and inadequacy. People must be teased or educated into greater logic, greater rationality. Resistance to better solutions is proof only of the poverty of our educational system; certainly it is not in any way an indication that "optimal" solutions are less than optimal.

THE PEOPLE APPROACHES

The people approaches try to change the organizational world by changing the behavior of actors in the organization. By changing people, it is argued, one can cause the creative invention of new tools, or one can cause modifications in structure (especially power structure). By one or another of these means, changing people will cause changes in solutions to tasks and performance of tasks as well as changes in human growth and fulfillment.

In surveying the people approaches, one is immediately struck by the fact that the literature dealing directly with organizational change is almost all people-oriented. Just in the last four or five years, for example, several volumes specifically concerned with organizational change have been published. All of them are people-type books. They include Lippitt, Watson, and Westley's *The Dynamics of Planned Change;* Lawrence's *The Changing of Organizational Behavior Patterns;* Ginsberg and Reilly's *Effecting Change in Large Organizations;* Bennis, Benne, and Chin's *The Planning of Change;* and Guest's *Organizational Change.*

This tendency to focus on the process of change itself constitutes one of the major distinguishing features of the people approaches. The technological and structural approaches tend to focus on problem-solving, sliding past the microprocesses by which new problem-solving techniques are generated and adopted.

Historically, the people approaches have moved through at least two phases. The first was essentially manipulative, responsive to the primitive and seductive question, "How can we get people to do what we want them to do?"

Although most of us identify such questions with borderline workers like Dale Carnegie, much of the early work (immediately post-World War II) by social scientists on "overcoming resistance to change" dealt with the same issues.

Carnegie's *How to Win Friends and Influence People* was first published in 1936, a few years ahead of most of what we now regard as psychological work in the same area. Like the social scientists that followed, Carnegie's model for change focused on the relationship between changer and changee, pointing out that changes in feelings and attitudes were prerequisites to voluntary changes in overt behavior. Carnegie proposes that one changes others first by developing a valuable (to the other person) relationship, and then using that relationship as a lever for bringing about the change one seeks. One does not attack with logic and criticism and advice. *A* offers *B* support, approval, a permissive atmosphere; and having thus established warm, affective bonds (invariably "sincere" bonds, too), *A* then requests of *B* that he change in the way *A* wishes, while *A* holds the relationship as collateral.

Though social scientists have tended to reject it out of hand, current research on influence processes suggests that the Carnegie model is not technically foolish at all, although we have disavowed it as manipulative, slick, and of questionable honesty.

The Carnegie model, moreover, has some current social scientific parallels. Thus Martin and Sims, for example, directly attack the issue of how to be a successful power politician in industrial organizations. They argue that dramatic skill, capacity to withhold certain kinds of information, the appearance of decisiveness, and a variety of other calculatedly strategic behaviors, appear to be effective in influencing behavior in organizational hierarchies.

In fact, Carnegie-like interest in face-to-face influence has finally become a respectable area of social scientific research. Several works of Hovland et al. on influence and persuasion provide experimental support for the efficacy of certain behavioral techniques of influence over others.

But if we move over into the traditionally more "legitimate" spheres of social science, we find that much of the work after World War II on "overcoming resistance to change" was still responsive to the same manipulative question. Consider, for example, the now classic work by Kurt Lewin and his associates on changing food habits, or the later industrial work by Coch and French. In both cases, *A* sets out to bring about a predetermined change in the behavior of *B*. Lewin sets out to cause housewives to purchase and consume more variety meats—a selling problem. Coch and French set out to gain acceptance of a preplanned methods change by hourly workers in a factory. In both cases the methodology included large elements of indirection, with less than full information available to the changes.

But whereas Dale Carnegie built warm personal relationships and then bargained with them, neither Lewin nor Coch and French are centrally concerned about intimate relationships between changer and changee. Their concern is much more with warming up the interrelationships among changes.

Thus 32 percent of Lewin's test housewives exposed to a group-decision method served new variety meats, as against only 3 percent of the women exposed to lectures. Lewin accounts for these results by calling upon two concepts: "involvement" and "group pressure." Lectures leave their audiences passive and unpressed by the group, whereas discussions are both active and pressing. Similarly, Coch and French, causing the girls in a pajama factory to accept a methods change, emphasize *group* methods, seeing resistance to change as partially a function of individual frustration, and partially of strong group-generated forces. Their methodology, therefore, is to provide opportunities for need satisfaction and quietly to corner the group forces and redirect them toward the desired change.

But it is this slight thread of stealth that was the soft spot (both ethically and methodologically) of these early people approaches to change, and this is the reason I classify them as manipulative. For surely no bright student has ever read the Coch and French piece without wondering a little bit about what *would* have happened if the change being urged by management just did not seem like a good idea to the "smaller, more intimate" work groups of Coch and French's "total participation" condition.

One might say that these early studies wrestled rather effectively with questions of affect and involvement, but ducked a key variable—power. Coch and French modified behavior by manipulating participation while trying to hold power constant. In so doing, the artistry of the "discussion leader" remained an important but only vaguely controlled variable, causing difficulties in replicating results and generating widespread discomfort among other social scientists.

Other contemporary and subsequent people approaches also avoided the power problem and encountered similar soft spots. The Western Electric counseling program that emerged out of the Hawthorne researches sought for change through catharsis, with a specific prohibition against any follow-up action by counselors—a "power-free" but eminently human approach. Later, users of morale and attitude surveys sought to effect change by feeding back anonymous aggregate data so that the power groups might then modify their own behavior. But the very anonymity of the process represented an acceptance of the power status quo.

It was to be expected, then, that the next moves in the development of people approaches would be toward working out the power variable. It was obvious, too, that the direction would be toward power equalization rather than toward power differentiation. The theoretical underpinnings, the prevalent values, and the initial research results all pointed that way.

But though this is what happened, it happened in a complicated and mostly implicit way. Most of the push has come from work on individuals and small groups, and has then been largely extrapolated to organizations. Client-centered therapy and applied group dynamics have been prime movers. In both of those cases, theory and technique explicitly aimed at allocating at least equal power to the changee(s), a fact of considerable importance in later development of dicta for organizational change.

Thus Carl Rogers describes his approach to counseling and therapy:

> This newer approach differs from the older one in that it has a genuinely different goal. It aims directly toward the greater independence and integration of the individual rather than hoping that such results will accrue if the counsellor assists in solving the problem. The individual and not the problem is the focus. The aim is not to solve one particular problem, but to assist the individul to grow.

At the group level, a comparable development was occurring, namely, the development of the T (for training) group (or sensitivity training or development group). The T group is the core tool of programs aimed at teaching people how to lead and change groups. It has also become a core tool for effecting organizational change. *T* group leaders try to bring about changes in their groups by taking extremely permissive, extremely nonauthoritarian, sometimes utterly nonparticipative roles, thus encouraging group members not only to solve their own problems but also to define them. The *T* group leader becomes, in the language of the profession, a "resource person," not consciously trying to cause a substantive set of changes but only changes in group processes, which would then, in turn, generate substantive changes.

Though the *T* group is a tool, a piece of technology, an invention, I include it in the people rather than the tool approaches, for it evolved out of those approaches as a mechanism specifically designed for effecting change in people.

In contrast to earlier group discussion tools, the *T* group deals with the power variable directly. Thus Bennis and Shepard comment:

> The core of the theory of group development is that the principle obstacles to the development of valid communication are to be found in the orientations toward authority and intimacy that members bring to the group. Rebelliousness, submissiveness or withdrawal as the characteristic responses to authority figures . . . prevent consensual validation of experience. The behaviors determined by these orientations are directed toward enslavement of the other in the service of the self, enslavement of the self in the service of the other, or disintegration of the situation. Hence, they prevent the setting, clarification of, and movement toward, group shared goals.

I offer these quotes to show the extent to which the moral and methodological soft spots of the early manipulative models were being dealt with directly in group training situations. These are not wishy-washy positions. They deal directly with the power variable. Their objective is to transfer more power to the client or the group.

But these are both nonorganizational situations. For the therapist, the relationship with the individual client bounds the world. For the *T* group trainer, the group is the world. They can both deal more easily with the power variable than change agents working in a time-constrained and work-flow-constrained organizational setting.

At the organizational level, things therefore are a little more vague. The direction is there, in the form of movement toward power equalization, but roadblocks are many and maps are somewhat sketchy and undetailed. McGregor's development of participative Theory *Y* to replace authoritarian Theory *X* is a case in point. McGregor's whole conception of Theory *Y* very clearly implies a shift from an all-powerful superior dealing with impotent subordinates to something much more like a balance of power:

People today are accustomed to being directed and manipulated and controlled in industrial organizations and to finding satisfaction for their social, egoistic and self-fulfillment needs away from the job. This is true of much of management as well as of workers. Genuine "industrial citizenship"—to borrow a term from Drucker—is a remote and unrealistic idea, the meaning of which has not even been considered by most members of industrial organizations.

Another way of saying this is that Theory "X" places exclusive reliance upon external control of human behavior, while Theory "Y" [the theory McGregor exposits] relies heavily on self-control and self-direction. It is worth noting that this difference is the difference between treating people as children and treating them as mature adults.

Bennis, Benne and Chin specifically set out power equalization (PE) as one of the distinguishing features of the deliberate collaborative process they define as planned change: "A power distribution in which the client and change agent have equal, or almost equal, opportunities to influence" is part of their definition.

In any case, power equalization has become a key idea in the prevalent people approaches, a first step in the theoretical causal chain leading toward organizational change. It has served as an initial subgoal, a necessary predecessor to creative change in structure, technology, task solving, and task implementation. Although the distances are not marked, there is no unclarity about direction—a more egalitarian power distribution is better.

It is worth pointing out that the techniques for causing redistribution of power in these models are themselves power-equalization techniques—techniques like counseling and T group training. Thus both Lippitt et al. and Bennis et al. lay great emphasis on the need for collaboration between changer and changee in order for change to take place. But it is understandable that neither those writers nor most other workers in power equalization seriously investigate the possibility that power may be redistributed unilaterally or authoritatively (e.g., by the creation of profit centers in a large business firm or by coercion).

If we examine some of the major variables of organizational behavior, we will see rather quickly that the power-equalization approaches yield outcomes that are very different from those produced by the structural or technological approaches.

Thus in the PE models, *communication* is something to be maximized. The more channels the better, the less filtering the better, the more feedback the better. All these because power will be more equally distributed, validity of information greater, and commitment to organizational goals more intense.

Contrast these views with the earlier structural models which argued for clear but limited communication lines, never to be circumvented, and which disallowed the transmission of affective and therefore task-irrelevant information. They stand in sharp contrast, too, to some current technical views which search for optimal information flows that may be far less than maximum flows.

The PE models also focus much of their attention on issues of *group pressure, cohesiveness,* and *conformity.* The more cohesiveness the better, for cohesiveness causes commitment. The broader the group standards, the better. The more supportive the group, the freer the individual to express his individuality.

These, of course, are issues of much current popular debate. But as factors in effecting change, they are almost entirely ignored by the technical and most of the structural models. In their faith that best solutions will be recognized and in their more macroscopic outlook, until very recently at least, the technical and structural models did not concern themselves with questions of human emotionality and irrationality. If these were treated at all, they were treated as petty sources of interference with the emergence of Truth.

Evidence on this last question—the question of whether or not truth is obscured or enhanced by group pressures—is not yet perfectly clear. On the one hand, Asch has shown in his classic experiments that group pressures may indeed cause individuals to deny their own sense data. On the other hand, Asch himself has warned against interpreting this denial as an entirely emotional noncognitive process. When 10 good men and true announce that line *A* is longer than line *B*, and when the 11th man, still seeking truth, but himself seeing *B* as longer than *A*, still goes along with the group, he may do so not because he is overwhelmed by emotional pressure but because "rationally" he decides that 10 other good sets of eyes are more likely to be right than his own.

Moreover, some data from some recent experiments being conducted at Carnegie Tech and elsewhere[2] suggest that in-fighting and debate will cease rather rapidly within a group when a solution that is prominently better than other alternatives is put forth. This is to say that people use their heads as well as their guts; though at times in our history we have vociferously denied either one or the other.

Consider next the *decision-making* variable. Decision making, from the perspective of power equalization, is viewed not from a cognitive perspective, nor substantively, but as a problem in achieving committed agreement. The much discussed issues are commitment and consensual validation, and means for lowering and spreading decision-making opportunities.

Contrast this with the technical emphasis on working out optimal

---

[2] As reported in a personal communication from T. C. Schelling, 1961.

decision rules, and with the structuralist's emphasis on locating precise decision points and assigning decision-making responsibility always to individuals.

SUMMARY

If we view organizations as systems of interaction among task, structural, technical, and human variables, several different classes of efforts to change organizational behavior can be grossly mapped.

Such a view provides several entry points for efforts to effect change. One can try to change aspects of task solution, task definition, or task performance by introducing new tools, new structures, or new or modified people or machines. On occasion we have tried to manipulate only one of these variables and discovered that all the others move in unforeseen and often costly directions.

We have more than once been caught short by this failing. The Scientific Management movement, for example, enamored of its measurement techniques, worked out efficient task solutions only to have many of them backfire because the same methods were also evoking human resistance and hostility. The human relations movement, I submit, is only now bumping into some of the unforeseen costs of building a theory of organization exclusively of human bricks, only to find that technological advances may obviate large chunks of human relations problems by obviating large chunks of humans or by reducing the need for "consensual validation" by programming areas formerly reserved to uncheckable human judgment.

Approaches with strong structural foci have also on occasion fallen into the one-track trap, changing structure to facilitate task solution only then to find that humans do not fit the cubbyholes or technology does not adapt to the new structure.

On the positive side, however, one can put up a strong argument that there is progress in the world; that by pushing structural or human or technical buttons to see what lights up, we are beginning gropingly to understand some of the interdependencies among the several variables.

What we still lack is a good yardstick for comparing the relative costs and advantages of one kind of effort or another. We need, as Likert has suggested, an economics of organizational change.

If we had one, we could more effectively evaluate the costs of movement in one direction or another. Likert urges an economics of change because he believes the presently unmeasured costs of human resistance, if measured, would demonstrate the economic utility of organizational designs based on PE models. But such an economics might also pinpoint some of the as yet unmeasured costs of PE-based models. For the present state of unaccountability provides a protective jungle that offers quick cover to the proponents of any current approach to organizational change.

If I may conclude with a speculation, I will bet long odds that, as we develop such an economics, as we learn to weigh costs and advantages, and to predict second and third order changes, we will not move uniformly toward one of these approaches or another, even within the firm. We will move instead toward a mélange, toward differentiated organizations in which the nature of changes becomes largely dependent on the nature of task. We have progressed, I submit; we have not just oscillated. We have learned about people, about structure, about technology; and we will learn to use what we know about all three to change the shape of future organizations.

4 | *Managing Change*

Jay W. Lorsch

The major focus of this section of the book has been on issues of organization design: What structure, measurement, and reward practices are appropriate to a given situation? However, another persistent theme in many of the cases has been the problem of introducing changes in organizational design without disrupting operations, adversely affecting the firm's performance, and/or damaging morale. If we use the analogy of taking a trip, the selection of destination is equivalent to the problem of organizational design. What are our goals? Where do we want to go? The issue of how one gets to the destination is analogous to the issue of organization change. How rapidly do we go? What methods do we use to get to our goals? In this reading we shall focus on such issues of organizational change. However, it should be emphasized that the ideas presented here are tentative and intended to stimulate your thinking as much as to provide any final answers about managing change. This is so because there have been relatively few empirical studies upon which to base generalizations about the process of managing change.

CHANGE AS A MANAGEMENT ISSUE

As the 20th century has approached the three-quarter mark, futurologists have widely predicted that change will be one of the hallmarks of the next several decades.[1] To the extent that events in the current business scene can be extrapolated into the future, there is little basis for arguing with such generalizations. The "energy crisis" is but the

[1] Alvin Toffler, *Future Shock* (New York: Random House, Inc., 1970).

most recent in a series of events which have confronted managers with the necessity of rethinking their firm's strategies as well as various organizational practices. Changes in technology, of which the computer is the most dramatic example, are another constant source of strategic and organizational design changes. Similarly, changing social currents such as the emphasis on minority employment and opportunities for women are yet another source from which the need for changes in internal practices emanate. Thus change is an important management issue because it is so pervasive. To be effective, managers must be able to introduce changes in strategy, technology, and/or organizational design which enable their firms to anticipate and/or adapt to changes in their external environment.

While it is easy to get carried away with the importance and pervasiveness of change, there is another reason that it is of such concern to managers. This is because it is often difficult to get members of an organization to accept change in organizational structures, procedures, strategy, etc. To understand why this is so, we need to be more precise about what we mean by change. While the term, as is so typical of most behavioral science jargon, is used in various ways, we have a definite meaning in mind. When we speak of change, we mean an alteration in organization design or strategy, or some other attempt to influence organization members *to behave differently*. Such an alteration may mean new ways of thinking in reaching decisions about the company's strategy; or it may mean working with a new group of colleagues; or it may require carrying out one's job in a different way; or it may require relating to one's superiors and/or subordinates with a different frequency and in a different manner. If we think about change in this way, it should be evident that shifting organization design variables is one way for management to signal to the organization that a new pattern of behavior is desired. Similarly, a conscious decision to issue a new strategy statement is a way of letting decision makers know that top management wants them to think about and reach decisions based upon a different set of assumptions. With this explanation of what we mean by change, management's concern about the difficulty of introducing it becomes more understandable. What managers are concerned about is why persons resist attempts to get them to adopt different behavior patterns.[2]

RESISTANCE TO CHANGE

Why do people resist attempts to get them to do things differently? Are they stubborn like a Missouri mule? or just basically conservative?

[2] Paul Lawrence, "How to Deal with Resistance to Change, " *Harvard Business Review,* May–June 1954.

If you stop to think for just a minute about change situations you have seen in cases, or ones you have lived through yourselves, you will probably conclude that the answer to both of these questions is no. Examples of resistance to change get much of the attention because they are the "bad news" that commentators on the business scene like to write about—for example, the workers at the Lordstown General Motors plant. However, the "good news" is that there are many other instances where organization members readily change their behavior.

The way persons respond to an attempt to change their behavior seems to depend on an implicit cost-benefit analysis which they make of the change. As we have seen, each organization member has developed a psychological contract with the organization. (See "Managing the Psychological Contract," pp. 465–80.) If the change he or she is asked to make violates that contract, the individual is apt to drag his or her feet in altering behavior. However, if the change does not damage this understanding, the individual is often quite willing to accept the change.

More specifically, for example, a change in organization structure may reduce the career opportunities for a group of managers by eliminating a position to which they had aspired. Or, structural change may reduce the power certain managers have over decisions. Similarly, a change in compensation practices may adversely affect a particular group of employees by seeming to require more effort for the same pay. Less obvious, but equally important, a change in work procedures or job assignments might require persons to learn a new way of handling their jobs or might cause them to break up a valued pattern of social relationships. In any of these examples if there were no offsetting gain to employees from the behavior change they are being asked to make, they will quite likely feel that the psychological contract has been broken. One way to handle this feeling, consciously or unconsciously, is to decide that the change is a poor idea and to accept it halfheartedly, or even to oppose it.

Persons may also resist changes because the new behavior violates the psychological contract by requiring them to act in ways beyond their personal capabilities. It may require a set of skills which they find it impossible to develop. Also, persons may find that the new behavior is inconsistent with their personalities and established ways of interacting with others.

Another reason why resistance to change is so frequent is that a request for change in behavior often creates increased uncertainty for the individual. New ways of performing a job or the need to relate to a new set of colleagues can be upsetting psychologically for some people just because it creates more uncertainty than they are comfortable with. Similarly, the anticipation of a forthcoming change can create uncertainty just because individuals are not clear what it will mean to them, and this makes some people uncomfortable. Obviously, there are other individuals who relish the uncertainty of new ways of acting, and these individuals probably are less apt to object to attempts to get them to act differently.

One of the side effects of the uncertainty which accompanies change efforts is rumors about the impact of the change. For example, in the reorganization of the sales force of a particular consumer products company, each of the five product divisions had had its own sales force. The goal of management was to reduce the existing five sales forces to four. However, the rumor circulating among field salesmen before the announcement of the change was that there would be a consolidation of all sales forces into one. Because of the anxiety about how the change would affect them and the uncertainty associated with the change, this rumor, though completely out of phase with the facts, gained credibility because it provided a semblance of certainty where there was too much uncertainty for many of the salesmen to accept. Just because such rumors do provide an anchor in the face of a great deal of uncertainty, they are a frequent accompaniment to change efforts, and they must be taken into account in planning the change process.

This view of the problem of managing the change process is consistent with how we have been thinking about organizations up to this point in the readings in this section. Basically we have argued that:

1. Organizations can be conceived of as information processing systems in which the job of members is to process information, reach decisions, and to act to implement those decisions. (See "Organization Design," pp. 481–501.)

2. Organization members have a psychological contract with the company which implicitly and explicitly defines the terms of the exchange they expect. (See "Managing the Psychological Contract," pp. 465–80.)

Introducing change becomes a problem when organization members receive information about the change which alters negatively, from their perspective, their psychological contract with the firm. Their cost-benefit analysis says the change will cost them more than they will get from it. Managers can get into such a situation for several reasons. First, the managers instituting the change may not have gone through the type of analysis that this discussion suggests. They might not be aware of the impact of the change (e.g., some of the ways just described), upon those who are being asked to change their behavior. Not having considered this, the initiator of change encounters resistance which is based upon an accurate evaluation by those being asked to change that "there isn't enough in it for me." One remedy to this situation is to more carefully assess the psychological contract and to develop changes which do not have such a negative impact upon those being asked to change.

A second reason initiators of change can encounter problems is that even though they have carried out a thorough analysis of the impact of a change on others and recognize the negative consequences, they believe the change is necessary to meet the goals of the firm. Basically, the initiators of change are saying the psychological contract must be altered to meet the firm's goals. In such a situation, the initiators of change must use whatever processes of communication and influence they have available to create understanding about the necessity for change.

Finally, initiators of change may encounter resistance because they have done a poor job of communicating about the changes, the reasons for them, and their impact. Quite obviously, again the available remedies focus on the areas of improved communication and influence. In sum, once a careful diagnosis has been made and design decisions reached, the success of the change is quite likely to rest upon the initiator's effectiveness in communication and influence with those who are required to behave differently.

CRISIS AND CHANGE

Studies of the change process suggest that one factor which often accompanies effective change programs is an awareness on the part of those affected by the change that there is a clear and critical need for a new mode of behavior.[3] One example of this is the decision by the steel industry and the United Steel Workers to submit all contract disputes to binding arbitration. In this situation top management of the steel companies and the union leadership both agreed to change their behavior in contract negotiations in a fundamental way. They apparently did so because they recognized that the threat from foreign competition was so great that to do otherwise would seriously jeopardize the profitable operations of the steel companies and the jobs of a large number of union members. The crisis in the industry was so visible that both parties clearly recognized the need for change.

Another example of the impact of a crisis is the case of the General Foods Company in 1972. Here a large write-off of assets in the company's Burger Chef operation created an awareness among top and middle managers that there was a need for change. The shock of this large write-off was a cause of concern to a management whose company

---

[3] Larry E. Greiner, "Patterns of Organizational Change," *Harvard Business Review,* May–June 1967.

had a long tradition of continued growth in earnings. The interesting aspect of this situation was that reverberations extended far beyond the Burger Chef operation into the company's main domestic grocery business. Though the Burger Chef operation was at the center of the quake, the shock waves were so great that they unlocked many of the assumptions top management had held and caused them to reassess their methods in their mainline grocery business. This led to a major restructuring, with accompanying behavior changes, of the grocery organization that had little direct relationship to the Burger Chef problem.

The common lesson from the steel industry and the General Foods experiences is that a visible crisis facing a company (or an industry) can be an important force for bringing about behavior change, even though such change may have important costs for those being asked to change. In essence, such a crisis has an unfreezing effect on members of the firm, causing them to question their established attitudes and behavior patterns. During such a period, the organization is in a fluid state and persons are more apt to accept new ways of thinking and acting. But such crises do not spring to the awareness of organization members full blown. One way they become aware of such crises is when the top manager personally communicates the need for change. At General Foods, for example, after the resignation of the president, the chairman of the board and the new president actively communicated the need for change.

Another way that top managers signal the need for change, either intentionally or unintentionally, is through the use of external consultants. The consultants may serve several purposes—they may identify the causes of the problem, propose solutions, and even help plan the change process. But whatever else consultants accomplish, they also create an awareness that a problem exists and thus they too can be an important force in causing organization members to recognize the need for change. Similarly, the need for change in a particular part of a company can be signaled by bringing in a new top manager.

Whether the vehicle for communicating the necessity for change is a top-management pronouncement, the entry of consultants, or the bringing in of new top management, the impetus for the change is at the top of the organization. Support for the view that this is the way most changes are initiated is also available in the organizational literature.[4] As Table 1 suggests, according to this view, the top echelons of the organization originate design changes. The middle levels elaborate and enact the changes, while the lower levels administer within the established organization design. Such a view means that managers at each level must have different sets of skills and knowledge. At the top there

[4] Daniel Katz and Robert Kahn, *The Social Psychology of Organizations* (New York: John Wiley & Sons, Inc., 1966), pp. 312–35.

TABLE 1

The Locus of Change and Various Organizational Levels

Change Role	Appropriate Organization Levels	Abilities and Skills
Initiation of change in modifying organization designs.	Top echelons	Organization-wide perspective; charisma
Interpolation: elaborating and enacting design changes.	Intermediate levels	Two-way orientation; communication skills
Use of existing design.	Lower levels	Technical knowledge and understanding of design; concern with equitable administration

Source: Adapted from Daniel Katz and Robert Kahn, *The Social Psychology of Organization* (New York: John Wiley & Sons, Inc., 1966).

is a need for an organization-wide perspective and for managers who have the personal charisma to attract and/or maintain the loyalty of a large number of subordinates. At the middle levels managers at each level must be more concerned with understanding the directions coming from above while simultaneously understanding the concerns of subordinate levels. They are truly men and women in the middle, and must have interpersonal skills which enable them to communicate effectively in both directions. Finally, according to this view, the lowest level of management needs to have technical knowledge of the work and an understanding of the rules of the game in the organization which enable them to equitably and effectively administer their units.

A quite different view of how change should be managed has been suggested by other writers on the topic.[5] This alternate approach calls for involving a wider segment of the organization in the process of establishing and diagnosing the need for change and in planning directions for change. Through small group meetings, subordinates are asked to identify the issues with which they are concerned and to think about what changes would resolve these issues.

Presented this way these two approaches to change appear like mutually exclusive alternatives, and much of the literature on the topic also treats them in this fashion. However, in reality the approaches which managers use can be either the top-down approach or the more participative method, or some fusion of the two. The problem facing the manager concerned with successfully introducing change is to find a way of thinking about the entire change process which not only helps to reach a decision about communicating a need for changes but also about how to implement them.

---

[5] See, for example, Greiner, "Patterns of Organizational Change."

PLANNING THE CHANGE PROCESS

The process of introducing change involves several steps:

1. Creating an awareness of the need for change.
2. Making a diagnosis of the situation which creates the need for change and determining the direction for change.
3. Communicating the change to those affected.
4. Monitoring the change and making adjustments as these seem appropriate.

While these steps are listed separately, there is considerable overlap and interconnection among them. For example, as one begins to talk about the need for change, one is likely to get feedback which indicates what others see as the causes of the problem, so that the diagnostic phase has started. Similarly, the very act of a systematic analysis of the causes of a problem can lead those involved to see the need for change in their own behavior and cause them to act differently.

As top managers think about these interconnected steps, they must deal with two underlying issues, First, how will they use their power to work through this process? Second, how much time are they willing to allow to elapse before the change is introduced? As we shall see, these two issues are not unrelated.

Power Holding versus Power Sharing

From the moment top managers become aware of the necessity of some change, they are implicitly making choices about how they wish to use their power to affect change. If they take the top-down approaches to signaling the need for change, they are implicitly saying that they hold the power to introduce change and that they will use it toward this end. In contrast if they seek the participation of a wider segment of the organization in evaluating the importance of change, they may be implicitly suggesting that they are ready to share their power with others in the organization to plan and manage the change process. As we have suggested, these two approaches are not mutually exclusive. But if we treat them as if they were for a few moments, it can help us to develop a way of thinking about the use of power throughout the change process.

There are several factors which seem to indicate which of these approaches can be most effective:[6]

---

[6] The importance of many of these factors has been confirmed by Victor Vroom and Philip Yetton in *Leadership and Decision Making* (Pittsburgh: University of Pittsburgh Press, 1973).

1. Who has the relevant data to determine the need for change, the direction of change, and the likely consequences? If such knowledge rests with top management, then they can be effective in planning and directing the change from above. However, if much of these data are held by a wider segment of the organization, the change process will be improved by gaining their more active involvement.

2. The existing norms about involvement of subordinates in decisions can also have an important impact. If the members of the organization expect that top management will make important decisions and communicate them to the organization, then the top-down approach to change will be highly consistent. If, on the other hand, the organizational norms emphasize wide participation in the decision-making process, then the power sharing approach to change will be expected. Using an approach to managing change which is inconsistent with existing norms about member involvement in decisions, is, in effect, initiating a change. That is, it suggests that top management wants a change in the decision-making process. If this is in fact an important element in the required change, then using power in a way which is inconsistent with existing organizational norms may be desirable. Otherwise, the change tactics management uses should be consistent with the organization's norms about the use of power.

3. Related to this, the approach selected must be consistent with the leadership style of the top managers in the firm. If they are comfortable and skillful in a power sharing process their subordinates will not only expect it, they will also see it as an opportunity for real participation. If, on the other hand, managers try a power sharing approach because they believe that other situational factors dictate this approach, but they are not comfortable with it or skillful at it, subordinates are likely to see the process as synthetic. In essence, whatever tactics top managers use must be congruent with their own leadership styles.

4. The size of the organization is a fourth factor which can affect management's thinking about how it uses power to introduce the change. Even in situations where other factors suggest a power sharing approach, the large size of an organization can make such an approach impractical. For example, a recent major structural change affecting a thousand upper and middle managers in several divisions of a large company ideally might have included the active involvement of these managers in the change process. They had knowledge to contribute to the discussions, and the change would have a deep impact on their jobs and relationships. Yet the sheer number of persons who would have to be involved made such an approach impractical. Instead, top management constituted several task forces

made up of a representative cross section of managers to work on various aspects of the change. Such an approach had the benefits of gaining the selected managers' ideas on the change and helped to build their commitment. But it did little to build the commitment of those managers not included in these working groups.

With these general guidelines a manager concerned with change has a way of thinking about what approach to the use of power will be most effective. In thinking about these factors, the manager is not really faced with a dichotomy between these two approaches. Rather, as the preceding example suggests, a blend of the two can be developed. What appears useful, however, in this way of thinking is that it provides a clear view of what some of the trade-offs are between the two approaches. As a manager thinks about the problem of introducing change, these factors should help him to think through the consequences of various alternatives.

Speed of Introduction

The second major issue underlying the selection of a change strategy is the rapidity with which top management wants to introduce the change. Traditional wisdom and some recent experience suggest that the top-down approach to power has implicit in it a more rapid introduction of change. Thus, the conditions mentioned above which favor a top-down approach are also those which lend themselves to a speedy introduction of change, and those which favor a power-sharing approach lend themselves to a more gradual approach. Where there is an expectation of a directive strategy, where resistance is apt to be low, and where top management has the knowledge necessary to plan the change, it can make sense to move with speed. When the opposite conditions are present, moving more deliberately allows time for the involvement of many others within the organization and gives them time to understand the problems, develop solutions to them, and accept proposed solutions.

While there appears to be this close connection between the use of power and the speed with which change is introduced, other considerations in determining the rate of speed are relatively independent of the way power is used. One such issue is how the speed with which the change is handled will affect the anxiety of those affected. One school of thought argues that rapid change, while it generates greater anxiety, contains that anxiety in a short time frame, whereas a gradual approach drags it out. For example, supporters of this view argue that it is best to move quickly so that if some individuals will have to change jobs, they find out and get it over. The counter view is that gradual change allows more time to handle such human dislocation .and thus assures a more humane resolution for the individuals affected.

A similar debate can also focus on what rate of progress will have the most disruptive effect on operations. Some experienced managers argue that moving rapidly limits the effect of the change to a relatively short time frame. Their argument is "let's take our lumps all at once and get it over with." Others argue that a slower approach will cause less disruption and therefore is to be preferred in any case.

It is not our intent to resolve these arguments here, because we know of no simple resolution or even general guidelines. Rather, the manager concerned with change needs to examine his specific situation and determine how the rate of speed will affect the operations of his organization and its impact on those dislocated by the change. He can then factor these considerations in with the factors summarized in Table 2 to think through the most appropriate change strategy.

TABLE 2
Factors Affecting Change Process*

Use of Power	*Speed*	*Locus of Data*	*Norms about Involvement*	*Top Management's Leadership Style*	*Clarity of Crisis*	*Likely Resistance*	*Size of Organization*
Top down	Rapid	With top management	None	Directive	Very visible	Little	Large
↕	↕	↕	↕	↕	↕	↕	↕
Power shared	Gradual	Spread through organization	Pervasive	Participant	Less visible	Great	Small

* Arrows represent a continuum.

THE BEHAVIORAL SCIENCES AND ORGANIZATIONAL CHANGE

Table 2 suggests that the more a manager is faced with conditions at the top of the diagram, the more he or she will find it effective to communicate the need for change by edict, define and plan the change unilaterally at the top, and move with speed. The more he or she faces the conditions at the bottom, the more appropriate it is to involve organization members actively in the change process to define the need for change and plan its direction. Such an approach must necessarily be more gradual. At this stage of our knowledge about the change process, it is not possible to be more specific than this. However, at least these ideas provide a way of thinking about the change process which recognizes that the most effective approach will depend upon the specifics of the situation. This is in contrast to many of the prevailing views on change put forth by behavioral scientists.

Over the past decade a variety of approaches and techniques have been developed for dealing with the change process. Most of these have been developed by academicians, consultants, and staff personnel in companies—groups who are interested in applying the behavioral sciences to management. The values and skills of these professionals have led them to emphasize the power-sharing approach to introducing change as the one best approach. Thus, tools often consist of permutations of laboratory training. Typical of these approaches are the techniques which put much emphasis on learning from face-to-face feedback in small group settings. To the extent that such techniques fit the people, tasks, and traditions of a particular situation, they can be effective.

The problem, however, has been that these tools and many of their proponents have become swept up in what is almost a religious movement, "organization development." The central value of this movement seems to be to create more power sharing, more openness, and more trust in relationships, etc., regardless of whether these directions fit the organization's situation. This, however, does not mean that the tools which have been developed should be themselves discredited. Rather, the central issue facing managers is to determine when this set of tools or any other is relevant to their change problems. This is why we have placed so much emphasis on diagnosis as an initial step to determining the direction for change. Throughout these readings our emphasis has been upon understanding what pattern of behavior will fit both the environmental realities facing the firm and the predispositions of its members. In essence we have been providing a set of tools for diagnosing organizational problems and determining the direction for change.

Our emphasis in thinking about how to signal the direction for change has been on organizational design variables in "Managing the Psychological Contract" and "Organization Design." Basically, we have emphasized that design variables are an important way to signal to organization members what changes in behavior are desirable. The large size of many business firms makes this position necessary. Further, the fact that design variables can create sustained intrinsic and extrinsic rewards for organization members makes them powerful tools for encouraging new patterns of behavior. In both these respects the reliance on small group methods to create change has shortcomings. Small group methods are difficult, expensive, and time-consuming to apply in large organizations. Furthermore, the changed behavior learned in these small group settings is difficult to sustain back on the job without corresponding changes in design variables. However, the emphasis on design variables is not meant to imply that these are the only tools necessary to produce behavioral change. The use of face-to-face groups to diagnose problems, plan change, and clarify expectations can be valuable tools at the various stages of the change process. For example, they can be used to plan design changes—when a power-sharing strategy seems appropriate or they can be used in a more top-down approach as a means for communicating the change and to give those affected a chance to work through their feelings and understand more fully how the change will affect them.

While these and the other aspects of the change process have been illustrated in many of the cases in this book, there are two aspects of the change process which are difficult to capture from the case discussions but which are important issues in the business world. First is the question of data collection. In class discussions you have been presented with a case which contains much of the data a manager would need to reach decisions about design and change issues. However, on the job one is unlikely to have such a neat summary of the situation. Managers must in effect write their own cases. Assuming that the manager needs more data than he has from his firsthand experience, how does he get it? We have already suggested several approaches. One is the use of outside consultants or an internal staff group to collect data through interviews, gathering quantitative data, etc. Another approach is to use group meetings or task forces of those affected to gather data and develop a diagnosis. A third method, which we have not discussed, but which is frequently employed, is the use of questionnaires or attitude surveys to determine how employees think and feel about a situation. Such an approach is very suitable in large organizations where it is impossible to meet face to face with all employees. The use of surveys of this sort can also be helpful in gathering data as the change is implemented so that managers can see how employees are responding and thus gain feedback about the need for adjustments in change activity.

A second issue which the case method does not address adequately is connected to this issue of monitoring the change process. This is the question of the duration of a change effort. Even in a situation where an attempt is made to move rapidly, the change program's progress is measured by months. In other situations where management moves more deliberately the process can involve years. What is required to be successful in such undertakings are simple, but elusive, personal qualities of patience, persistence, and flexibility. Patience and persistence are necessary to maintain the drive for change in the face of what are almost inevitable setbacks in misunderstanding and resistance. Flexibility is necessary to take in feedback about results and search for new solutions which will avoid road blocks and overcome resistance. No matter which approach to change seems appropriate, these qualities of mind and guts are necessary to sustain a manager through the challenge of managing change.

Indexes

Index to Cases

Index to Readings